PROJECTIVE TECHNIQUES

IN PERSONALITY ASSESSMENT

With Contributions by

Joel Allison
Samuel J. Beck
Sidney J. Blatt
Leonard P. Campos
Paul G. Daston
Emanuel F. Hammer
Mary R. Haworth
Wayne H. Holtzman
Jules D. Holzberg
Max L. Hutt
Betram P. Karon
Walter G. Klopfer
Leonard M. Lansky
David Levine
Charles Neuringer
A. I. Rabin
George C. Rosenwald
Jerome L. Singer

PROJECTIVE TECHNIQUES

IN PERSONALITY ASSESSMENT

A Modern Introduction

Edited by A. I. RABIN
Michigan State University

Weatherford, Oklahoma

SPRINGER PUBLISHING COMPANY, INC. • NEW YORK

Copyright © 1968

SPRINGER PUBLISHING COMPANY, INC.

200 Park Avenue South   New York, N.Y. 10003

Library of Congress Catalog Card Number: 67-27713

Type set at Topel Typographic Corporation, New York

Printed in U.S.A.

Preface

This volume was planned to meet the need for a new and comprehensive introductory text on projective techniques, a need that has been apparent for quite some time. Several such texts had been published shortly after World War II, but none has appeared since that time.

In the past two decades, projective techniques have been modified, revised, and refined, and these changes have been reported in numerous articles, manuals, symposia, and monographs; several anthologies of articles which had been previously published have also appeared. The recent concern has been with such aspects of projective techniques as their validity, the processes underlying the response to projective stimuli, and the theory of projection itself. The contributions that make up this book present a panoramic view of projective techniques and a critical evaluation of developments in this field.

The volume was planned so that each author would have a free hand in treating his or her assigned topic. Consequently, some chapters are written largely from a clinical viewpoint, championing the idiographic approach; others are more psychometric in orientation and nomothetic in nature. This diversity, we believe, is all to the good. The student in the areas of clinical psychology, personality, and personality assessment, as well as the practicing clinician and researcher in the field of personality, will find the book useful as a systematic coordination and juxtaposition of theories and applications.

The framework of the book also made it possible to strike a balance between general issues and specific techniques. Parts I and VII deal with the broader aspects of projective methods, history, theoretical interpretations, and clinical and research applications. Parts II through VI are devoted to methods that have stood the test of time or more recent ones that appear particularly useful and promising. The techniques are, for the most part, described in considerable detail and are critically evaluated; relevant research literature is summarized, too, in these Parts.

All of the chapters were especially written for this book. By making original contributions, the authors have made the book a timely and modern introduction. I am very grateful for their efforts and for their willingness to share their expertise.

Grateful acknowledgment is also made to those publishers who gave permission to quote or reproduce materials from their publications. Specific acknowledgments appear in the individual chapters.

It is hoped that this volume will not only prove of value as a summary of past work, but will also serve to stimulate creative developments in the field of personality assessment.

Okemos, Michigan   A. I. RABIN
November 1967

Contributors

Joel Allison. Assistant Professor of Psychology, Yale University School of Medicine; Senior Psychologist, Yale Psychiatric Institute.

Samuel J. Beck. Professorial Lecturer, Department of Psychiatry, and Lecturer, Department of Psychology, University of Chicago.

Sidney J. Blatt. Associate Professor of Psychology, and Chief, Clinical Psychology, Department of Psychiatry, Yale University.

Leonard P. Campos. Staff Psychologist, O.H. Close School for Boys, Stockton, California; Visiting Lecturer, Department of Psychology, University of the Pacific.

Paul Daston. Professor of Psychology, University of Maryland; Consultant: Veterans Administration, Frederick Chusid Company, Walter Reed Army Hospital, Social Security Administration.

Emanuel F. Hammer. Director of Psychology, Psychiatric Clinic, New York City Criminal Courts; faculty member at New York University School of Arts and Sciences clinical doctoral program, National Psychological Association for Psychoanalysis, and Metropolitan Institute for Psychoanalytic Studies; Chief Psychologist, Lincoln Institute of Psychotherapy.

Mary R. Haworth. Executive Secretary, Research Career Program, National Institute of Mental Health.

Wayne H. Holtzman. Professor of Psychology and Education; Dean, College of Education, University of Texas.

Jules D. Holzberg. Professor, Wesleyan University.

Max L. Hutt. Consultant in Clinical Psychology, Michigan Department of Mental Hygiene; Consultant, Ypsilanti Public Schools; psychotherapist.

Bertram P. Karon. Associate Professor of Psychology, Michigan State University.

Walter G. Klopfer. Professor of Psychology, Portland State College; Executive Editor, *Journal of Projective Techniques and Personality Assessment.*

Leonard M. Lansky. Professor of Psychology and Associate Director, Center for Research and Training in Higher Education, University of Cincinnati.

David Levine. Professor of Psychology, University of Nebraska.

Charles Neuringer. Associate Professor of Psychology, University of Kansas.

A. I. Rabin. Professor of Psychology, Michigan State University; Consultant, Veterans Administration and Michigan Department of Corrections.

George C. Rosenwald. Associate Professor of Psychology, and Assistant Chief, Psychological Clinic, University of Michigan.

Jerome L. Singer. Professor of Psychology and Director, Clinical Psychology Training Program, City College of the City University of New York.

CONTRIBUTORS

Contents

CONTENTS

INTRODUCTION

The primary purpose of this section is to present a general background for projective techniques. Following a brief historical chapter on the earlier antecedents of projective methods, the beginnings of their development and attempts at description and definition, there are three chapters which are concerned with the theoretical aspects of projective methods, relations to psychopathology and therapy, and problems of validation.

In their earliest stages, projective methods were primarily empirical techniques which were not clearly embedded in personality theory. Subsequently, a number of authors tried to establish some connections between the personality theories they espoused and the operations underlying projective methods. They proceeded beyond the general "projective hypothesis" to relatively detailed theoretical explanations of the processes involved in projective testing. In Chapter 2, Dr. Holzberg offers a panoramic view of a variety of theoretical orientations as they apply to projective techniques. The applications of learning theory, psychoanalytic theory, perception, cognitive, adaptation level, field and developmental theories to projective methods are treated in some detail. There is an attempt to close the "gap separating personality theory and techniques" and to integrate projective methods and psychology in the broader sense.

The third chapter in this section is, in a sense, both theoretical and clinical, or applied. Since it makes frequent reference to specific techniques the reader may do well to return to it, after a cursory reading, and after familiarization with the rest of the volume, for more thorough comprehension of the issues which the author presents. Essentially Hutt comes to grips with such important matters as the assessment of the personality process, especially in the pathological personality, and with the significant relationship between assessment and psychotherapy. The latter relationship has been woefully neglected in recent years by American clinical psychology and is in need of clarification and re-emphasis.

Finally, issues of the reliability of projective methods are considered in the last chapter of this section by Dr. Karon. The problem of whether the conventional methods of determining reliability, dictated by standard measurement theory, are applicable to projective techniques has been a bone of contention among various proponents of these techniques. These differences in approach are implicit in the different treatment of the issue by the several authors of the chapters that follow. In this chapter an attempt is made to grapple with the problem and introduce, perhaps, some rather unorthodox solutions.

1

Projective Methods:
An Historical Introduction

A. I. RABIN

Methods of personality assessment that were to become known as projective techniques developed gradually over a long period of time. It is even tempting to paraphrase Ebbinghaus' remark about psychology (Boring, 1929), that projective techniques have a "long past but a short history." The penchant of man for imposing his own ideas and interpretations upon unstructured stimuli was noted, and occasionally recorded, centuries ago. For example, Leonardo da Vinci reports in his *Introduction to the Painter* concerning the associative experiences possible as a result of viewing a blot made by a sponge upon the wall: ". . . various experiences can be seen in such a blot, provided one wants to find them in it—human heads, various animals, battles, cliffs, seas, clouds or forests and other things . . ." (quoted in Zubin, et al, 1965, p. 167). Also mentioned by Leonardo is the possibility of "hearing" words when a bell is ringing. The stimuli are, therefore, not restricted to any one sensory modality as to their potential to evoke the associative experiences.

Some centuries later, in 1857, Justinus Kerner published a volume entitled *Die Klecksographie*. In it the author reproduced a series of blots accompanied by rhymes expounding their meaning. Many of the blots were described "as scenes of Hades" (Tulchin, 1940; Zubin, et al., 1965).

These are instances from the pre-scientific or pre-experimental era which exemplify the potential of unstructured stimuli to induce a wide array of associations and responses once the subject gives himself free rein and permits his imagination to range untrammeled by reality considerations. Toward the end of the 19th century, and at the beginning of the 20th, psychologists attempted to exploit visual stimuli, inkblots and pictures, in a more systematic and experimental fashion. These efforts were briefly described by Tulchin (1940), early in the era of the projective techniques.

In 1895 Binet and Henri suggested the use of a series of inkblots in the investigation of visual imagination. About the same time, in 1897, Dearborn at Harvard proposed the use of inkblots in experimental psychology. "Content of consciousness," "memory," "qualitative and quantitative imagination," etc., were some of the areas to be investigated by means of the inkblots. In a paper the following year, he actually reports detailed findings accompanied by some interesting observations concerning the problem of inhibition in producing responses and the important effects of early experience upon the imaginative productions.

A number of other studies, using inkblots, followed during the subsequent two decades into the 20th century. Stella Sharp (in 1899) used inkblots as a test of imagination. She evolved a typology on the basis of the responses obtained. The "constructive or imaginative type" organized details into wholes, whereas the "matter-of-fact or scientific type" exhibited primarily analytic activity. Kirkpatrick (in 1900) noted age differences in the performance of children responding to inkblots. Pyle's (1913-1915) studies of several groups of children centered on the concept of association. He employed 20 inkblots which he felt tested the same kind of ability as the association test (which will be mentioned later in this section). He also reported differences due to age, sex, brightness and race. In 1917, Parsons studied the range of associations in boys and girls, classified the content of the associations to a standard series of inkblots and reported some detailed age and sex differences. The standard series of inkblots she employed was contained in Whipple's *Manual of Mental and Physical Tests,* published in 1914-15. Other early experimenters with inkblots were F. C. Bartlett in England, F. L. Wells in the United States, and Rybakow in Russia.

From the above we may note that considerable research interest was focused on the medium of inkblots, prior to the time when Hermann Rorschach first published his test results in the *Psychodiagnotik* (1921).

The early concern with imaginative productions, such as stories told to pictures, which heralded the arrival of what was to be called later the Thematic Apperception Test (TAT), was much more limited and circumscribed (Zubin, et al, 1965). In 1905 Binet and Simon used pictures to stimulate verbal responses from which intellectual development was assessed. In 1906 Brittain studied differences in stories told by boys and girls; he noted systematic differences in content and related them to the differences in the living conditions of the sexes at that time, especially to restrictions of the social environment. Libby studied, in 1908, the imagination of adolescents via their responses to a picture, dealing primarily with objectiveness and subjectiveness in the stories as a function of age. Schwartz (1932) used pictures as an aid in interviewing delinquent boys. This is, perhaps, the first "clinical" employment of pictures: they were used to gain rapport and facilitate the acquisition of more extensive information about the subjects. A possible additional precursor of the TAT is Van Lennep's Four Picture Test (1951) which is traced by its originator to the year 1930.

Another method which is frequently included among the projective techniques is the Word Association Test. This method has a distinguished experimental and clinical history—beginning with Galton, then in Wundt's laboratory, Kraepelin's clinic and Jung's consultation room. In this method, the stimulus is a word, not a picture or an inkblot. Moreover, the presentation is usually auditory, not visual. The subject is asked to respond with the first word that comes to his mind. Here the associative processes (and their inhibitions) are studied. This method is thought to have had considerable influence on the subsequent development and theoretical rationale of a number of projective methods.

It is not the purpose of this section to trace the earliest origins of *all* of the methods which have become known as projective, but to sample some of the trends, especially the ones that have anticipated the development of the two major techniques—the Rorschach and the TAT. We are now ready for an account of the development of some of the major projective methods proper—the dominant techniques of the present time, which are described in greater detail in other parts of the book and in the chapters that bear their names.

METHOD AND PERSONALITY THEORY

Hitherto, our brief overview of experiments with inkblots, pictures and words has indicated that the findings were limited in scope. They dealt with such concepts as mental content, imagination, individual differences, and so on. No attempts were made to describe *personality*. This is due, in part, to the status of personality as a concept and a theory during that period. No encompassing concept or psychological theory of personality was yet available. Personality was not part of the psychology of that period. It was at the advent of psychoanalysis and its crystalization as a full-fledged personality theory that the various methods found a conceptual home. The data obtained, and their interrelationships, assumed greater meaning and significance. It is in the beginning of this new era in psychology and psychiatry, in the 1920's, that we see the true roots of development in the field of projective techniques.

RORSCHACH'S INKBLOTS

The relationship of the earlier work with inkblots to Rorschach's test is not at all clear. It is actually not known whether Hermann Rorschach was at all acquainted with the work of his predecessors. After experimenting for some time with various geometrical forms of different colors, he was led to prefer the less structured inkblots and finally selected a series of ten. The results of his experiments are reported in his monograph *Psychodiagnostik* (1921), which is subtitled "Methodology and results of a perceptual-diagnostic experiment (interpretation of accidental forms)."

Whereas previous experiments with inkblots were primarily concerned with imagination and associational content, Rorschach stressed the formal characteristics and determinants of the responses, the modes of perception, and their relationship to personality and psychopathology. He was quite modest in presenting his findings, with normals and with several neuropsychiatric groups, as "provisional" and as an "experiment"; also, he introduced the work by pointing out its primarily empirical nature and its incomplete theoretical foundation. Yet, he points out the value of the method, both as a test and as a research tool.

It is not the purpose of this presentation to discuss the details of Rorschach's empirical hypotheses. This will be done elsewhere in this volume. Suffice it to say, however, that the influence of Freud in the interpretive process and the more direct reliance upon Jungian psychology are evident in the *Psychodiagnostik*. The psychoanalytic influence is even more clearly discerned in Rorschach's posthumous paper (1924) published by Oberholzer. In it the congruence between the personality description based on the test (blind analysis) and the one based on psychoanalytic material, obtained by Oberholzer, is illustrated in detail.

Interest in the Rorschach technique was far from immediate. During the first ten years following the publication of Rorschach's work, only 38 studies dealing with the method appeared in the professional literature. However, in the 1930's there was a marked increase of work with the method; by 1940 Rorschach publications numbered 251 (Krugman, 1940). The small trickle burst into a veritable flood. By 1945 there was a bibliography of 786 Rorschach items, and the years 1945-1955 produced nearly 1900 additional items (Klopfer, et al, 1956). This phenomenal escalation in research activity stimulated by Rorschach's test shows few signs of abatement (Rabin & Hurley, 1964). It may also be mentioned, parenthetically, that the bulk of the Rorschach publications appeared in the United States.

Dàvid M. Levy imported the Rorschach from Switzerland around 1925 and introduced it to Samuel J. Beck, whose lifelong career since his first publication on the method in 1930 has been intimately connected with it. Beck's primary efforts include the first Rorschach manual in English (Beck, 1937)—an *Introduction to the Rorschach Method*. Around the same period, in the early and middle 1930's, Marguerite Hertz, Bruno Klopfer, and others began to teach the Rorschach and write extensively concerning it. Under the leadership of Klopfer, a periodical devoted exclusively to Rorschach work, *The Rorschach Research Exchange,* was founded. The Research Exchange was eventually transformed into the *Journal of Projective Techniques and Personality Assessment* which is vigorously continuing publication as the organ of the Society for Projective Techniques and Personality Assessment—the heir of the Rorschach Institute—with a membership of over 800 at the of the Rorschach Institute—with a membership of over 800 at the time of this writing.

Thus, the Rorschach was not only the first major clinical and research instrument to be classified later as a projective technique, but it was also most important in spearheading the projective techniques movement. Since the Rorschach method was not readily acceptable to university psychology departments, most of the instruction in the administration and interpretation of the test proceeded in special workshops and institutes. This trend prompted the projective movement to be viewed as a movement of dissent, a deviant from psychology's "establishment." Hence, a separate and autonomous organization, concerned with the new methods, was established.

MURRAY'S TAT

In 1935 the Rorschach was joined by a native son—the Thematic Apperception Test (Morgan & Murray, 1935). This method, according to the authors, "is based upon the well-recognized fact that when a person interprets an ambiguous social situation he is apt to expose his own personality . . ." Unlike the Rorschach, the first publication was more modest in its dimensions, and the pictures themselves, portraying the "ambiguous social situations," were revised several times before the final series, as we know it today, was established.

In the context of the epoch-making *Explorations in Personality* (Murray, et al, 1938) the TAT, although only one of many methods described in the volume, gained its stature, significance and subsequent popularity. The "Explorations," which was the culmination of the efforts of a number of psychologists under the leadership of Henry Murray, set out to construct both a *theory* of personality as well as *techniques* for its assessment. Thus, the TAT, unlike the mainly empirical Rorschach, was from the start embedded in a theoretical framework which was markedly influenced by the dynamic principles of psychoanalysis. With the orientation that "personalities constitute the subject matter of psychology," Murray and his associates rejected the exclusive positivism, peripheralism and elementarism which dominated the psychology of that period. They advocated a more dynamic approach to personality; one that is concerned with "drives, urges, needs, or instincts." This revolt against the traditional, academic, and arid psychology of that period started a new era in American psychology. Of the numerous techniques pressed into the service of new theory construction expressing the disaffection with the extant psychology, the TAT became the main survivor and the most durable instrument.

The TAT did not remain exclusively wedded to the conceptual matrix from which it arose. The standard manual (Murray, 1943) served as a starting point. Furthermore, the instrument proved to be most flexible, and a host of scoring methods, representing different orientations, have been spawned (Murstein, 1963). Discussion of these developments would lead us far afield and is beyond the scope of the present introductory chapter.

The flexibility of the TAT did not only engender a variety of approaches to scoring and interpretation, but also facilitated its ready adaptation to the clinic as well as to the research laboratory. A tremendous research and clinical literature has accumulated in which the TAT is the prime instrument. Moreover, numerous derivative methods, based on the design of the TAT, have been created and fruitfully applied and investigated.

The Advent of "Projective Techniques"

As noted earlier, actual experimental application of various unstructured stimuli for the purposes of personality assessment by psychologists is traceable to the end of the 19th century. However, the term *projective techniques* or *methods* and the placement of a number of extant modes of personality diagnosis under one umbrella did not take place until the late 1930's and the early 1940's.

It was in the ground-breaking volume *Explorations in Personality* (1938) that Murray first introduced the term "Projection tests." He described these methods as follows: "In an attempt to discover the covert (inhibited) and unconscious (partially repressed) tendencies of normal persons, a number of procedures were devised. These procedures are simply different methods of stimulating imaginative processes and facilitating their expression in words or in action."

The section in the "Explorations" that deals with the projection tests, lists, in addition to the Thematic Apperception Test (TAT), which had been introduced three years earlier (Morgan & Murray, 1935), several other techniques, such as the Rorschach, a "musical reverie test" and a "Dramatic Production Test." It is also well to note that Murray concluded the volume by pointing out that "of all our technical procedures, the series that were termed projection tests, which were designed to evoke imagery and fantasy, brought to light the most significant data" (1938, p. 728).

During the same year—1938—when the "Explorations" was published, Lawrence Frank, in a "privately circulated memorandum," first used the term *projective methods*. The following year he published the first theoretical paper on "Projective methods for the study of personality"

(Frank, 1939), which was subsequently expanded into the well-known monograph entitled *Projective Methods* (Frank, 1948). In this monograph the author presents a detailed theoretical discussion of personality against the background of recent developments in science and philosophy of science. He also lists and describes a series of procedures which he terms *projective techniques*. Essentially Frank describes a projective technique as "a method of studying the personality by confronting the subject with a situation to which he will respond according to what the situation means to him and how he feels when so responding" (p. 46).

A more complete and up-to-date characterization of projective techniques and their distinctive features will appear in a later section of this chapter, following the discussion of the concept of projection which is basic to them.

Concerning projection

Before we attempt a complete definition of projective methods, it is imperative that we deal with the fundamental concept of projection.

Originally, the term "projection," introduced by Freud, involved only psychopathological connotations. It was considered the main mechanism underlying paranoia and paranoid disorders. The tendency on the part of the patient to externalize unacceptable inner drives and other undesirable internal proclivities to the outer world was described as projection. To date, projection is widely viewed as a defense mechanism, similar to many others, the purpose of which is to avoid the experience of guilt or anxiety.

This usage of the term in psychopathology is well established and undisputed. However, it is too limited an application. In later years, Freud and some of his followers extended the meaning of the term. The extended and broader meaning of projection is a most significant ingredient in the understanding and definition of projective methods.

Some time after the introduction of the term, Freud (1911) wrote concerning projection that ". . . it makes its appearance not only in paranoia but under other psychological conditions as well, in fact it has a regular share assigned to it in our attitude to the external world. For when we refer the causes of certain sensations to the external world, instead of looking for them (as we do in the case of others) inside ourselves this normal proceeding, too, deserves to be called projection" (p. 452).

Consonant with the broader definition of projection is Rapaport's (1952) statement covering ". . . a graduated continuum which becomes more general extending from the externalization of a specific type of tension in paranoid projections to that of any kind of tension in infantile projection, to that of a whole system of attitudes and tensions in transference phenomena, to where it imperceptibly shades into the externalization in the form of a 'private world' defined by the organizing principles of one's personality" (p. 270-271).

In their review of the concept of projection, Murstein and Pryer (1959) set aside the theoretical discussions and examined the research literature in which the term was employed. They evolved four categories of the concept of projection: *classical, attributive, autistic* and *rationalized*. The *classical* view of projection is the one originally suggested by Freud—that of attribution of one's characteristics to the outside world because of their unacceptability to ego and their anxiety-evoking nature. *Attributive projection* refers to the process of "ascribing one's own motivations, feelings and behavior to other persons." This usage is broader than the classical one; it contains it, and is consonant with Freud's later and more encompassing definition of projection referred to above. *Autistic projection* is most closely related to perception; it is the process by which the needs of the perceiver influence what he perceives. Finally, *rationalized projection* describes the process whereby the individual uses unconscious, classical projection but "attempts to justify it by inventing a rationale."

Projection, as used in projective techniques, is most consonant with the broad attributive definition as well as with the elements of autistic projection. This broader definition of the term is illustrated in an early statement by Freud in *Totem and Taboo* (1919):

> "But projection is not especially created for the purpose of defense, it also comes into being where there are no conflicts. The projection of inner perception to the outside is a primitive mechanism which, for instance, also influences our sense perceptions, so that it normally has the greatest share in shaping our outer world. Under conditions that have not yet been sufficiently determined even inner perceptions of ideational and emotional processes are projected outwardly, like sense perceptions, and are used to shape the outer world, whereas they ought to remain in the inner world" (p. 107-108).

Thus, as I have pointed out previously (Rabin, 1960), "perhaps the broader term 'externalization' is more appropriate in the case of projective techniques. It avoids the constricting misconception of projection as a mere defense mechanism . . ." (p. 4). This is the sense in which the originator of the term "projective techniques" and subsequent authors in the field have understood and employed the term "projection." Viewing it in the broader context made it possible for workers with these methods to ferret out trends of the whole range of defense mechanisms from projective test data, including the defense mechanism of projection itself.

Although the process of projection is a prerequisite for projective techniques, it is by no means sufficient for a definition of these methods. In the broader sense of projection a person is "projecting" all the time when he perceives and responds to the environment as an individual with personal needs, motivations, and unique tendencies. There are actually two basic aspects to any projective technique. First, the particular situation or stimulus with which the subject is confronted; and, second, the responses of the subject in terms of the meaning the particular stimulus or situation has for him. Thus, as Frank has pointed out, any situation may evoke the "idiomatic way" of responding in the individual which gives a basis for inference concerning his personality process. Frank (1948) further characterizes projective techniques as follows:

"The essential feature of a projective technique is that it evokes from the subject what is in various ways expressive of his private world and personality process" (p. 47).

The "private world" referred to by Frank is one which is created by the individual himself as a result of his special experiences under the influences of the geographical, cultural and social environments throughout his development. Personality, to which projective techniques are the key, is viewed as "a dynamic process, the conformal activity of the individual who is engaged in creating, maintaining and defending that 'private world' . . ." (Frank, 1948).

Earlier definitions of projective techniques have stressed the response and its interpretation, but not the stimulus or "situation." More recent attempts include an awareness of the nature and characteristics of the stimulus, its objective features which may evoke common responses, as well as its "unstructured" nature which allows for uniqueness and "private world" responsiveness.

More recently, after an analysis of several definitions of projective techniques and of the criteria on which they are based, Lindzey (1961) proposed the following definition: *"a projective technique is an instrument that is considered especially sensitive to covert or unconscious aspects of behavior, it permits or encourages a wide variety of subject responses, is highly multidimensional, and it evokes unusually rich and profuse response data with a minimum of subject awareness concerning the purpose of the test."* He adds further that *"the stimulus material presented by the projective test is ambiguous, interpreters of the test depend upon holistic analysis, the test evokes fantasy responses, and there are no correct or incorrect responses to the test"* (p. 45, Lindzey's italics).

Thus, the ingredients of any thoroughgoing and complete definition of projective techniques are threefold. In the first place, the nature of the stimulus is characterized mainly by its ambiguity or, more appropriately, by the freedom it allows the respondent, due to the fact that it is not overly limited to conventional form requiring conventional response. Secondly, the response, the task of the subject, involves quantity, variety and richness with little awareness of the purpose to which the material may be put, and the implications that may be drawn from it. Third, the task of the examiner-interpreter is complex, for his analysis is holistic-ideographic, and he attributes to the responses that he obtains a multi-dimensionality necessary for such analysis.

VARIETIES OF TECHNIQUES

Not only did Frank attempt to define and provide a rationale for the projective methods, but he also suggested a classification for the wide array of techniques which he felt are to be encompassed by the general term "projective" (Frank, 1948). The criterion for the categorization. centered upon "what they require or seek to evoke from the subject." His five-fold grouping of methods is as follows: *Constitutive* methods involve the imposition of structure upon relatively unstructured material. The Rorschach is the most obvious candidate for this category. *Constructive* methods require arrangement of materials into certain patterns, as in the mosaics test. *Interpretive* methods, such as the TAT, involve the subject in "an interpretation of some experience . . . in which he finds a personal meaning or affective significance." *Cathartic* methods, for example, doll play, are expressive—they stimulate emotional reaction —as in doll play. *Refractive* methods are those in which conventional modes of communication are altered idiosyncratically. Handwriting qualifies under this rubric.

After surveying a number of previous attempts to classify projective techniques, including Frank's, Lindzey (1961) proposed still another classification. He recognizes that different criteria adopted may dictate different classifications. The criteria he noted are: the attributes of the test material; origins of method, whether from theory or empirical findings; manner of test interpretation (formal vs. content analysis) ; the target or purpose of the test—whether directed to the assessment of motives, conflicts or some form of psychopathology; mode of administration of the test; and, finally, the kind of *response* the technique elicits from the subject. This last criterion is the one considered by Lindzey as most significant as a basis for the classification of projective techniques. The five-fold classification that emerges from this analysis is not too unlike the one offered by Frank 13 years earlier. Some important differences, however, may be discerned in the following list:

1. Association techniques (Word association, Rorschach, etc.)

2. Construction techniques (TAT, Blacky)

3. Completion techniques (Sentence completion, Picture-Frustration Study)

4. Choice or ordering techniques (Szondi, Picture Arrangement Test)

5. Expressive techniques (Psychodrama, painting)

The preceding, all-too-brief discussion not only illustrates the wide range of projective methods, but the complexity involved in finding the common elements that characterize them. Furthermore, the implications of these difficulties for "projective theory" should not escape us.

The Hospitable "Zeitgeist"

In the preceding few sections of the chapter we made a brief excursion of a theoretical nature, into the field of projection and projective techniques. We shall now pick up the historical thread at the point when the term projective techniques as well as the techniques themselves began to gain currency and much popularity. The late 1930's and the subsequent 15 years or so mark a period of hospitality and burgeoning development in this field.

The hospitable atmosphere for the projective techniques, in the 1940's and later, was due to certain fundamental changes in American psychology itself and to certain events and social forces in our society around the mid-century. Some of the causes of the new trend, the new "Zeitgeist" which provided the hospitality, will be discussed in the paragraphs that follow.

First we must consider the budding discipline of clinical psychology in the 1920's and '30's. Traditional academic psychology supplied it with few concepts and even fewer means by which it could attain the status of a full-fledged profession. Aside from being limited to the diagnostic function, the clinical psychologist had very few tools even for this circumscribed area of activity. He was a tester and had precious few tests at that. His kit contained the Stanford-Binet and some personality inventories of limited range. His diagnostic contribution was primarily in terms of numerical indices—IQ's, percentiles on introversion or dominance scales, and similar bits of nomothetic information. The new projective techniques, which he so avidly embraced, gave him a tremendous boost and an opportunity to communicate something meaningful to his professional colleagues about the personality structure, dynamics, and diagnosis of his patients. They also facilitated contribution to the planning of the therapeutic process.

Another facilitating circumstance in the adoption and popularity of projective techniques was the advances and dissemination of dynamic theories of personality. Psychoanalytic theories and methods have gained great influence in American psychiatry and, eventually, in psychology. The concepts of the unconscious, of repression, defenses, etc., have become central in the mental health field. As a result, they have also favored the development of special methods, such as projective techniques, which were by their very nature and definition suitable in the assessment of these dynamic processes.

Last, but not least, were the pressures and needs created by World War II for a variety of assessments—including personnel selection and screening as well as clinical assessment. The Binet and the Bernreuter were no longer sufficient. Projective techniques became a major part of the psychologist's armamentarium in the fulfillment of the service demands placed upon him. These experiences, and the post-war crystallization of a full-fledged profession of clinical psychology provided increasing receptiveness to the penetrating instruments for personality assessment and clinical diagnosis.

The popularity of projective methods among clinicians, and the involvement of the universities in the formal training of clinical psychologists immediately after the War, gained entrance for these methods to the curricula of the training programs in clinical psychology. It was during this period that several significant and influential books were published. Among these may be mentioned the report of the Menninger group on the Word Association Test, Rorschach, and TAT (Rapaport, 1946). In reporting the detailed test findings for a number of diagnostic groups with the three projective methods and by relating the empirical results to psychodynamic theory of pathology, Rapaport and his colleagues noticeably extended the horizons of clinicians and advanced the development of projective techniques in their *Diagnostic Psychological Testing.* Bell's *Projective Techniques* ("a dynamic approach to the study of personality") offered a useful survey of a wide range of methods (1948). The extended theoretical presentation of the methods by Frank (1948), mentioned earlier, and the publication of several introductory textbooks, such as *Projective Psychology* (Abt & Bellak, 1950) and *An Introduction to Projective Techniques* (Anderson & Anderson, 1951), supplied many a budding clinician in the university training programs with the fundamentals of the projective methods. In addition to the more general presentation of projective techniques, a number of specialized technical manuals for the application of specific methods also appeared during the '40's and '50's. The work of Beck, Klopfer, and Piotrowsky with the Rorschach; of Tomkins, Stein, and Henry with the TAT are some of the more prominent examples. Moreover, the inventiveness of clinicians and researchers extended to the creation of new methods. The new methods introduced by Blum, Sargent, Shneidman, and many others (to be described in subsequent chapters of this book) further exemplify the stimulation of projective techniques and of the "projective hypothesis" to American psychology and personology.

Finally, this period was also marked by burgeoning research activity. As we mentioned earlier, work with the Rorschach alone is represented by nearly 2000 titles during the decade following World War II. Much of the research dealt with the investigation of the projective techniques themselves. However, a great deal of work employed projective techniques as a method of investigation of personality processes, psychopathology, culture-personality relationships, and other theoretical issues as well as clinical and applied problems. Some of the methods were also "adopted" by less holistically oriented psychologists for the purpose of studying more isolated personality variables instead of "total" personalities.

THE PROLIFERATION OF METHODS

The sudden freedom from the shackles of the psychometric tradition that was experienced by some psychologists led to rather spurious trends in the field of projective techniques. Since projection and projective techniques were so broadly defined, any type of situation that was conducive to the elicitation of individual differences and "uniqueness" or idiosyncracy in response could be nominated to membership in the new assessment armamentarium. Many issues of journals published "still another projective technique," mainly on the basis of novel stimuli of different modalities and some differentiation between normals and some psychopathological classifications. Little attention was paid to the theoretical underpinnings of these new methods or to the conceptualization of the response patterns within some theoretical framework of personality theory. Many of them were mere suggestions, prematurely published, and lacking in sufficient data of a validating nature, especially construct validity. Some author likened this state of affairs to the opening of a Pandora's box.

In reaction to this "rampant empiricism" this author (Rabin, 1963) raised the question, "Do we need another projective technique?" The response to this question was conditional: "New projective techniques are needed, but the novelty is not to consist solely of new stimulus materials. The new methods should be genuinely new in conception, and should validly tap significant personality variables, buttressed by sound psychological theory" (p. 76) .

CURRENT STATUS

During the past decade there has developed a new "spirit" in American psychology and a more sober and balanced view of projective techniques. A number of factors have contributed to this trend.

First to be considered is the change that has taken place in clinical psychology as a profession. It is quite clear that the *practice* of clinical psychologists has been steadily shifting from assessment and diagnosis to psychotherapy and behavior modification. There are many reasons for this trend. At any rate, as Shakow (1965) pointed out, diagnosis has become "infra dig" and treatment is the clinician's activity of prestige.

Thus, along with other diagnostic devices, projective techniques no longer enjoy the status they once had. Shakow bemoans this state of affairs, for aside from the whole issue of "therapy without diagnosis," psychological workers miss the opportunity for the development and the sharpening of their assessment tools.

Another source of the change in the atmosphere may be found in the projective methods themselves. Numerous studies reporting negative or equivocal findings with the several methods have had a sobering effect upon the original unqualified enthusiasm of workers in the field. Psychometrically oriented psychologists who have been more interested in precision of measurement than in the substance and significance of what is measured have never accepted projective techniques, which they considered methodologically unmanageable and "sloppy." Psychologists who have been interested in the study of "persons" and their problems remain convinced of the significant contribution projective techniques can continue to make to the understanding of personality dynamics and in the study of human problems.

Finally, it must be pointed out that the recent trend is that of "re-entrenchment of the academe." Academic psychology has been moving back into its ivory tower, to study behavior of infrahumans or isolated and trivial behavior variables extirpated from the living and functioning person. This led Sanford to raise the very pertinent question: "Will psychologists study human problems?" (1965). Projective techniques remain an important method and an important source of information in the study of human problems. The criterion problem is still a most thorny issue in the validation of personality assessment methods. Continued research in assessment will proceed with constant research in personality and behavioral criteria, for their mutual benefit..

REFERENCES

Abt., L., & Bellak, L. (Eds.). *Projective Psychology*. New York: Knopf, 1950.

Anderson, H. H., & Anderson, Gladys L. (Eds.). *An Introduction to Projective Techniques*. New York: Prentice-Hall, 1951.

Beck, S. J. Introduction to the Rorschach method: A manual of personality study. *Amer. Orthopsychiat. Assn. Monogr.*, 1937, *1*.

Bell, J. E. *Projective Techniques*. New York: Longmans, Green, 1948.

Boring, E. G. *A History of Experimental Psychology*. New York: The Century Company, 1929.

Frank, L. K. Projective methods for the study of personality. *J. Psychol.*, 1939, *8*, 389-413.

Frank, L. K. *Projective Methods*. Springfield, Ill.: Charles C Thomas, 1948.

Frank, L. K. Toward a projective psychology. *J. proj. Tech.*, 1960, *24*, 246-253.

Freud, S. *Totem and Taboo*. New York: Moffatt, Yard & Co., 1919.

Freud, S. Psycho-analytic notes upon an autobiographical account of a case of paranoia (dementia paranoides). *Collected Papers*, Vol. III. London: The Hogarth Press, 1949. (originally published in 1911).

Klopfer, B., et al. *Developments in the Rorschach Technique*, Vol. II. Yonkers-on-Hudson, N.Y.: World Book Co., 1956.

Krugman, M. Out of the inkwell: the Rorschach method. *Character & Pers.*, 1940, *9*, 91-110.

Kutash, S. B. The impact of projective techniques on basic psychological science. *J. proj. Tech.*, 1954, *18*, 453-469.

Lennep, Van D. I. The four-picture test. In H. H. Anderson & Gladys L. Anderson (Eds.). *An Introduction to Projective Techniques*. New York: Prentice-Hall, 1951.

Lindzey, G. *Projective Techniques and Cross-cultural Research*. New York: Appleton-Century-Crofts, 1961.

Morgan, Christiana D., & Murray, H. A. A method for investigating fantasies. *Arch. Neurol. Psychiat.*, 1935, *34*, 289-306.

Murray, H. A., et al. *Explorations in Personality*. New York: Oxford University Press, 1938.

Murray, H. A. *Thematic Apperception Test Manual*. Cambridge, Mass.: Harvard University Press, 1943.

Murstein, B. I. *Theory and Research in Projective Techniques*. New York: Wiley, 1963.

Murstein, B. I., & Pryer, R. S. The concept of projection: a review. *Psychol. Bull.*, 1959, *56*, 353-374.

Rabin, A. I. Projective methods and projection in children. In A. I. Rabin & Mary R. Haworth (Eds.). *Projective Techniques with Children*. New York: Grune and Stratton, 1960.

Rabin, A. I. Do we need another projective technique? *Merrill-Palmer Quart.*, 1963, *9*, 73-77.

Rabin, A. I., & Hurley, J. R. Projective techniques. In Abt, L., & Reiss, E. (Eds.). *Progress in Clinical Psychology*, Vol. VI. New York: Grune and Stratton, 1964.

Rapaport, D. *Diagnostic Psychological Testing*, Vol. II. Chicago: Year Book Publishers, 1946.

Rapaport, D. Projective techniques and the theory of thinking. *J. proj. Tech.*, 1952, *16*, 269-275.

Rorschach, H. *Psychodiagnostik*. Bern and Leipzig: Ernst Bircher Verlag, 1921.

Rorschach, H., & Oberholser, E. The application of the interpretation of form to psychoanalysis. *J. nerv. ment. Dis.*, 1924, *60*, 225-379.

Sanford, N. Will psychologists study human problems? *Amer. Psychologist*, 1965, *20*, 192-202.

Schwartz, L. A. Social-situation pictures in the psychiatric interview. *Amer. J. Orthopsychiat.*, 1932, *2*, 124-133.

Shakow, D. Seventeen years later: clinical psychology in the light of the 1947 committee on training in clinical psychology report. *Amer. Psychologist*, 1965, *20*, 353-362.

Tulchin, S. H. The pre-Rorschach use of ink blot tests. *Rorch., Res. Exsch.*, 1940, *4*, 1-6.

Zubin, J., Eron, L. D., & Schumer, Florence. *An Experimental Approach to Projective Techniques*. New York: Wiley, 1965.

2

Psychological Theory and Projective Techniques

JULES D. HOLZBERG

There is a considerable gap separating personality theory and techniques used to measure personality variables even though theoretical considerations guide the use of projective techniques from the initial selection of the specific method to the final step of interpreting the data derived from it. Many of these theoretical conceptions are often the idiosyncratic products of the practicing clinical psychologist rather than formal psychological theory. This chapter is concerned with the latter—explicit attempts to formally relate psychological theory to projective techniques. It has been suggested (Abt & Bellak, 1950) that theory can serve to reduce two types of clinical errors, i.e., incautious generalizations and over-restricted interpretations. Holt (1954) stresses that understanding the psychological processes involved in projective testing would provide the clinician with greater flexibility in studying personality while it would check his tendency to engage in rank speculation. Rotter (1954) has expressed the opinion that only by explicating the theoretical assumptions underlying methods of personality study will psychologists be able to improve upon these methods and to develop newer and, hopefully, better methods. Furthermore, he feels that with theory the psychologist is better prepared to cope with the unusual client and with new clinical problems.

Where there is emphasis on techniques with theory minimized, there is the danger of developing diagnostic technicians rather than scientist-clinicians. The need to relate techniques and theory, in order to reduce the potentially destructive division between practice and theory, is particularly pressing (Holzberg, 1957). A considerable quantity of research has challenged the value of projective techniques, but Korner (1965) suggests that the failures here may be due less to these techniques than to the current state of theories guiding their use. Lindzey (1961) has indicated that if projective techniques can be related to psychological theory, this would in itself provide some measure of validation of these methods.

Three general attitudes among psychologists regarding the relation of projective techniques to psychological theory have been described (Holzberg, 1954). One attitude, shared by some experimental and academic psychologists, is that projective techniques are "foreign intrusions" without any roots in psychological theory. A second attitude, characteristic of some clinical psychologists, is that current psychological theory is adequate as a base for projective techniques and that the field of projective techniques must have, at one time, developed its own theoretical substructure. The third attitude, one with which this author is identified, is that projective techniques have their theoretical structure in contemporary psychological theory although no *single* theory yet developed is capable of providing the sole base. This position implies that a special set of psychological principles need not be invented for projective techniques since psychological phenomena and processes discovered in other situations can be functionally applied to projective testing.

This chapter is an overview of explicit attempts to relate psychological theory and projective methods. It makes no pretense of being complete since it reports only on those attempts which seem to the writer to be most germane to this problem.[1]

LEARNING THEORY

Since learning theory plays a dominant role in American psychology, it is appropriate that projective techniques be examined from this point of view. Auld (1954) made one of the first attempts to relate behavior theory, i.e., learning theory, to projective technique responses, with particular stress on the TAT. According to Auld, the problem of the tester is to determine the subject's habits in order to predict how he will behave under various conditions. Thus, one has to know both his habits and the situations he is likely to encounter. Auld conceives of "habit" as a potentiality or disposition that is presumed to be present even when its response is not occurring.

The habits manifested in the *test situation* were learned earlier in a training or *origin situation,* although the origin situation did not teach the overt responses that are observed in the testing situation. What was learned in the origin situation and generalized to the test situation were *emotional habits.* These emotional habits are also generalized to real-life situations in the present *criterion situations.* If the tester can determine what emotional habits the subject learned in the origin situation, he can make predictions about how the subject will respond in the criterion

---

[1] The only other serious attempt known to the author to review the relationship between projective techniques and psychological theories is that of Lindzey (1961). What follows is patterned after his outline but provides a more extensive coverage of the different theoretical orientations.

situation. Thus, the emotional habits provide the link between the three situations. *Generalization* represents the degree to which habits learned in the origin situation appear in the test and criterion situations. Tests, including projective techniques, become tools for determining what the subject has learned in the origin situation.

The tester need not know what the origin situation was, but he must be aware of the existence of an origin situation from which current responses are generalized. There is a need to know what stimulus in the origin situation evoked the response, and in what way current stimuli are similar to or different from that stimulus.

This reasoning leads to the five fundamental concepts needed to apply learning theory to testing: *habit, generalization, test situation, origin situation* and *criterion situation*. Two additional concepts that are needed are *habit strength* and *conflict*.

One needs to know not only whether the subject has a certain habit, but also its strength, if one is to make accurate statements regarding the generalization of a habit. If a habit is weak, it will lose out in competition with other habits. *Habit strength* can be judged 1) by the probability that a response will occur or by its frequency of occurrence; 2) by the vigor or magnitude of the response; 3) by the speed or latency of the response; and 4) by the closeness of the response to a goal in situations where the subject has tendencies both to approach a goal and to avoid it.

Probability or frequency is viewed as a measure of strength when the tester describes the subject as a more aggressive person because he tells more stories with aggressive themes than others do. Vigor or magnitude of the response is based upon such criteria as the subject's verbal description of the action (e.g., "he beat him to a pulp"), his tone of voice, etc. Speed or latency is judged, for instance, by how early in the story aggression takes place and how much provocation there is before it comes about. The closeness of a response to a goal is considered when the psychologist notes the kind of response made, e.g., killing represents a stronger habit than fighting, and fighting is stronger than verbal expression of hostility. The kind of stimulus to which the response is made is also important. Hitting a person represents a stronger habit than hitting an object. In general, the nearer the goal the response is, the stronger the habit is presumed to be.

Auld stresses the necessity of assessing avoidance or inhibitory tendencies as well as approach or positive tendencies, drawing upon the conflict theory of Miller (1944; 1951) and Dollard and Miller (1950). Whether the overt response will occur or not depends on the balance between approach and avoidance tendencies. If both the approach and avoidance tendencies can be measured, the tester can predict to what degree the subject will act on his tendencies to approach. Such measures of approach and avoidance should also determine which content areas are fraught with conflict. These would be the areas where strong tendencies to act are counterbalanced by equally strong opposing tendencies.

Thus, Auld suggests that certain concepts drawn from learning theory can be used to interpret data procured from projective techniques. However, while Auld identified certain congruencies between learning theory and projective methods, he has not promoted the systematic linking of these two areas (Lindzey, 1961).

A more systematic attempt to interpret projective test behavior in stimulus-response terms is that of Goss and Brownell (1957) and Brownell and Goss (1957).

Goss and Brownell first examine the nature of the stimulus in the projective test situation. They identify two main classes of *external environmental stimuli*, i.e., contextual events, and properties of the test stimuli themselves. Contextual events consist of features of the examination room and attributes of the examiner. The examiner serves as a stimulus in terms of his physical properties and of his actions and behavior (his instructions, his administration of test stimuli, other verbal and manipulative actions and questions). Test stimuli *per se* make up the remaining set of immediate external events.

Stimuli prior to the subject's introduction to the test situation and contextual and test stimuli of the test situation are presumed to evoke explicit and/or implicit verbal, locomotor-manipulative, and visceral responses. These responses during the testing are additional sources of stimuli with cue and drive properties. These are the *response-produced stimuli* which result from a response made by the subject.

Stimuli may be classified according to their persistence or recurrence during the testing. Thus, features of the room, physical characteristics of the examiner, stimuli due to deprivation, and occasionally, verbal response-produced stimuli are usually fairly constant or similar throughout the testing of a subject. Other stimuli, although not relatively continuous, will be repeated frequently in essentially the same form—among these are the examiner's actions and verbalizations in presenting each test stimulus and subsequent questions.

However, the items of the test stimuli, e.g., successive TAT pictures or the ten Rorschach blots, are relatively different or novel events within the context of sets of persisting or recurring stimuli. The novelty of the various test stimuli and the consequent variations in responses underlie the consideration of test stimuli as the most significant differential antecedents of responses to projective situations.

The authors next offer stimulus-response explanations for response occurrence. They advance a number of stimulus-response concepts which may be utilized to account for the occurrence of responses to projective test stimuli. *Receptor-orienting responses* determine which particular aspects or features of the test stimuli are isolated and experienced. Many responses elicited by the aspects of stimuli fixated upon by the subject can be attributed to *primary generalization and discrimination,* supplemented when necessary by principles of *response-mediated generalization and discrimination. Associative chaining* may explain the elaboration of responses into response sequences while *habit or stimulus summation* may contribute to such chaining. In addition, *associative strength* may interact with *drive.* Responses may be in *conflict* or in opposition to each other.

The details of projective test stimuli which function as actual stimuli when isolated and fixated are determined not only by such stimulus qualities as size, complexity, patterning, etc., but also by the strengths of different *receptor-orienting responses.* The receptor-orienting responses which occur will be influenced by pretest experiences, the specific instructions to look at or manipulate the materials, and the characteristics of both test and contextual stimuli.

Once a stimulus or some detail of it is attended to, previously reinforced responses that have been made to similar stimuli in the past can be expected to occur *(primary generalization).* Previously learned responses should be elicited with strengths which are direct functions of such similarity—the more similar the stimuli, the stronger the response. Thus, responses in the doll play situation occur because of generalization to doll play stimuli from various social situations, particularly those involving members of the immediate family (Sears et al, 1953). The complementary process of *discrimination* learning with respect to extra-test stimuli is also relevant. Thus, subjects who have learned different responses to similar stimuli in the past can be expected to respond to such similar stimuli differently from those who make the same response to those social stimuli.

Once responses have been elicited on the basis of primary stimulus generalization, these responses become stimuli which may function to increase or decrease the similarity of extra-test and test stimuli and hence influence the probabilities of occurrence of other responses *(response-mediated generalization* and *discrimination).* Thus, identification of a TAT figure as a "boy" would be expected to facilitate additional responses that had in the past been evoked by such labeling and to differentiate these responses from those elicited by the label "girl."

Demonstrations of explicit and implicit *associative chains* indicate that the evoking of one response may arouse one or more additional responses. Such chains, varying from individual to individual because of unique prior experiences, probably account for much of the elaboration which follows initial labeling of particular stimuli. Because of these chains, the subject offers a flow of responses following the initial labeling response. *Habit* or *stimulus summation* explains the fact that two stimuli with slight capacity to evoke a response may combine to increase the tendency to make the response.

Changes in the antecedent conditions of a subject may lead to changes in the *drive* state which can combine with factors discussed above to elicit responses.

The diagnostic value of projective tests, according to Goss and Brownell, lies in their relatively greater effectiveness in eliciting behavior which permits inferences about conflict and derivative phenomena, i.e., *inhibitory reactions, displacement, projection* and *reaction formation.* Utilizing Miller's (1948) model of conflict behavior, the authors assume the existence of approach and avoidance gradients and that the avoidance gradient is steeper than the approach gradient. The steeper gradient of avoidance implies that avoidance decreases more rapidly with distance from the original stimulus. Thus, a stimulus that resembles the original stimulus may elicit the inhibited response, but to a weaker degree than the original stimulus. A weaker approach response elicited by a similar stimulus is referred to as *stimulus displacement.* A response that is related to but not the same as an inhibited response is called *topographic displacement. Projection* is stimulus displacement of a response toward the self which is inhibited because of conflict and is expressed in connection with another person who is a similar but more remote object. *Reaction formation* is topographic displacement in which an inhibited response is replaced by a dissimilar or opposite response.

In a second paper (Brownell & Goss, 1957), these authors apply stimulus-response concepts and principles to the understanding of the antecedents of responses to projective test stimuli and to the prediction of responses to other test and extra-test stimuli.

They suggest that a *response with short latency* presumably does not occur to a stimulus when some incompatible response is aroused simultaneously. Thus a short latency presumes the absence of conflict. It can therefore be predicted that if the subject responds to stimuli that are more closely related than the original stimulus, latency of response will become even shorter and the probability of such a response's occurring will become even greater. If the stimuli are less similar than the original stimulus, however, longer latencies and lower probabilities can be expected.

A very *long latency of response* or no overt response to a particular projective test stimulus is more complex to interpret for this might be due to either low associative strength between stimulus and the response or the presence of conflict and resulting inhibition.

Any of the following aspects of test behavior might suggest inhibition due to conflict: 1) No response even though the subject's past history suggests the likelihood of such a response; 2) long latency of response when the response which does occur is the same or similar to the response frequently obtained with similar subjects but with significantly shorter latency; 3) long latency followed by an unusual or bizarre response; 4) speech disturbances such as vacillation, voice changes, etc.; 5) vasomotor changes such as sweating, blushing, signs of tension, etc. Long latency of response, in the absence of any of these signs, would suggest low associative strength rather than conflict.

Difficulties in the estimation of the latency and probability of responses resulting from conflict are confounded by the problem of specifying the separate strengths of conflicting approach and avoidance responses. The authors discuss some hypothetical ways of estimating the independent strengths of the approach and avoidance responses since different combinations of the strengths of approach and avoidance responses may result in equal net strength of the emitted response.

Lindzey (1961) has observed that these two papers serve a function in providing a detailed analysis of the stimulus properties of projective methods and of the test situation and in offering stimulus-response explanations for response occurrence, conflict, and understanding the antecedents of responses. In addition, their analysis indicates that certain kinds of additional data could be of use in interpretation, e.g., responses to extra-test stimuli which are related to projective stimuli. However, Lindzey offers the criticism that the theoretical model that is advanced fails to specify the criteria for stimulus similarity and response similarity, even though the model describes hypothetical relations that depend upon these dimensions of stimulus and response similarity. Furthermore, the theoretical analysis offers little with regard to the content of behavior. It is Lindzey's final criticism that these papers have more to say about learning theory than they do about the interpretation of projective data as witnessed by ". . . the relative wealth of theoretical statements and the paucity of clear translations into the language of projective testing" (p. 116).

Another attempt to relate projective techniques to learning theory is to be noted in the work and theorizing of McClelland and Atkinson (Atkinson, 1954; 1958; McClelland, 1955; McClelland et al, 1953). Focusing upon the TAT, they have been less concerned with a comprehensive bridging of these two domains and more interested in a theoretical rationale for assessing motive strength from projective methods, primarily from thematic content. Much of their concern has centered on the assessment of need for achievement, although other motives such as sex and affiliation have also been studied.

Atkinson has stressed that fantasy activity provides a measure of *motive strength*. As the strength of a motive increases, imaginative stories are dominated by thoughts describing such overt actions or problem-solving sequences as would be expected from a motivated person. Certain kinds of imaginative responses occur more frequently when a specific motive is experimentally aroused. Individual differences in the frequency of these responses reflect individual differences in motive strength, which in turn result from differences in antecedent learning experiences.

These authors also draw upon a kind of expectancy theory. Thus, the disposition to respond is not only a function of the strength of a learned motive but also of the *performance expectancy* aroused by cues. In other words, when the subject is both motivated and has the expectancy that his response will be instrumental in the attainment of the goal, then a response will eventuate. Thus, a motive is an anticipatory goal state that has been aroused by cues linked to past experiences.

There are three classes of *cues* in the projective test situation which may serve to arouse a motive and influence the frequency of imaginative responses: 1) Cues in the normal environment or in the thought processes of the individual; 2) cues introduced deliberately by the examiner; and 3) cues in the stimuli themselves, e.g., in TAT pictures. To assess individual differences in motives, all of these cues should be held constant and variations in the subjects' responses noted.

A motive is thus aroused by specifiable cues which are related to specific affective states (positive and negative) and this arousal activates a set of responses ("perceptual and instrumental response dispositions") that have been associated with these affective experiences in the past.

Individual differences in the frequency of motive-related imaginative responses to thematic pictures are seen as a justifiable basis for inferring that subjects' motivations in real-life situations would be similar to those portrayed in the pictures. Atkinson believes that an important part of the variance in response to a particular picture can be attributed to learning experiences which produced differences in the strength of the motive.

Atkinson assumes that picture cues can arouse motives and performance expectancies just as cues do in everyday situations. Furthermore, the capacity to be aroused by picture cues has derived from past experiences not unlike those involved in the usual learning of a motive. As a result, any differences in productions of imaginative content would reflect differences in motivation.

In general, Atkinson, McClelland et al stress that projective stimuli arouse motives that stimulate the subject to give imaginative responses that are related to past experiences involving these motives. This permits the assessment of motive strength. They also spell out a direct relationship between fantasy and overt behavior. Lindzey (1961) correctly points out that the strength of their orientation lies in the extensive research it has provoked. However, he feels they have contributed more to the understanding of motivation than to the understanding of projective methods.

One conclusion of Atkinson's has prompted a lively controversy with Lazarus (1961). Atkinson has indicated that motives are directly expressed in TAT story-telling and consequently the manifest content of imaginative responses will predict the kind of overt behavior to be expected from the subject who is similarly motivated under similar everyday conditions. Lazarus' position is that there may be an inverse relationship, i.e., that motives will appear in imaginative productions when they are not expressed overtly. He labels this the *substitutive* principle. Lazarus' outlook is not unlike that of Rotter (1960) who views goal-oriented behavior as being influenced by the individual's interpretation of the situation. Thus, the behavioral manifestations of a motive cannot be predicted without knowledge of certain cognitive processes such as the subject's interpretation of the test situation.

According to Lazarus, story-telling in the case of the TAT can be playful fantasy, problem solving, or varied combinations of the two. Lazarus feels that the position of Atkinson is that story-telling is problem solving—stories derived from aroused motives are efforts to find symbolically the *instrumental acts* necessary to satisfy the motive. Lazarus' position is that the particular combination of playful fantasy and problem solving, dependent upon how the subject defines the situation, will determine whether a motive is positively or negatively correlated to overt behavior.

Lazarus (1961) also refers to another process which will affect whether a motive will be directly expressed in fantasy. This is the process of defense to which Atkinson also refers to explicate a study by Clark (1952) dealing with sexual arousal in college students. The defensive principle is applicable to situations of conflict where the expression of a motive is inhibited because of externally based prohibitions or internalized personal values. The defensive process is another instance to account for motivation and story content not being positively related to overt behavior.

Lazarus thus offers another dimension to the problem of relating fantasy productions to overt behavior by stressing the importance of understanding the subject's definition of the test situation.

A recent paper (Epstein, 1966) has brought into question Miller's (1944, 1948, 1951, 1959) model of conflict in terms of approach and avoidance as applied to projective techniques. According to this view of Miller, approach-avoidance conflict would appear in a projective device as over-responding at the low goal-relevant end of a stimulus dimension while simultaneously under-responding at the high goal-relevant end of the same dimension (e.g., over-responding to a stimulus with minimal aggressive cues while under-responding to one with minimal aggressive cues). This should occur because the gradient of avoidance is steeper than that of approach, reflecting the fact that avoidance is a higher order response. Epstein's research on conflict has failed to support this hypothesis when conflict was defined in terms of Miller's *behavioral approach* and *behavioral avoidance*. However, Epstein's data has supported the hypothesis when conflict in the projective test was evaluated in terms of *verbal expression* and *verbal inhibition*. It is Epstein's thesis that *expres-*

sion and *inhibition* of words, as in repression, and not *approach* and *avoidance* in actions, are relevant for understanding conflict in the projective technique.

Thus, Epstein speaks of two distinctive kinds of conflict, approach-avoidance and expression-inhibition. Within this framework, it is possible for a person to verbally express what he behaviorally avoids and to verbally inhibit what he behaviorally approaches. The latter behavior would describe a person who is lacking in insight. The two sets of conflict can be consistent, which accounts for positive findings when the behavioral approach-avoidance model is applied to projective techniques. However, when the two sets of conflict are not consistent, the behavioral approach-avoidance conflict must be re-interpreted in terms of expression-inhibition conflict if correct predictions are to be made.

Epstein poses another issue in assessing conflict. A person may inhibit a conflicted motive in response to cues of high goal relevance while at the same time express the motive in response to cues of low goal relevance. This may be threatening to the subject since he may find himself producing drive-related responses to stimuli which do not strongly suggest the drive. The advantage that low drive-relevant stimuli may possess is that they permit expression of the drive in a *displaced* manner. If this is so, according to Epstein, it is important to select low drive-relevant stimuli which permit expression of the drive in a subtle and acceptable form.

Epstein also examines the case for stimulus ambiguity, i.e., the more ambiguous the stimulus, the greater the payoff in personality data. This is based on the premise that perception is a function of both stimulus and perceiver and where the stimulus influence is minimized, the influence of the perceiver is maximized.

Epstein argues that most drives and response dispositions are latent and require appropriate stimuli to be aroused. This is based upon the assumption that drives do not exist independent of cues, i.e., drive is a multiplicative function of a state of tension and drive-relevant cues. According to Epstein, a person is made hungry by the smell of food as well as by deprivation. When tension or drive-relevant cues are zero, drive is zero (Epstein, 1962).

It is his thesis that an ambiguous stimulus does not provide specific need-arousing cues (see Atkinson, 1954, 1958) and thus serves as a screen for those drives which have been aroused by uncontrolled and unrecognized stimuli. His argument is limited to content interpretation and does not apply to the formal aspects of a response such as Rorschach locations and determinants.

There are two possible effects of stimulus ambiguity in projective techniques and each may contradict the other. One effect has to do with the fact that the more a stimulus is ambiguous, the more likely the stimulus will penetrate defenses with the result that *all* drives will have the same access to expression. On the other hand, stimulus ambiguity is less capable of arousing specific drives.

Epstein also rejects the notion that ambiguous stimuli provide a more valid picture of response dispositions because the latter are uncontaminated by specific stimulus requirements. He argues that this fails to recognize that a stimulus, however ambiguous it may be, usually has stimulating characteristics of its own, often unknown to the examiner, and varying from subject to subject. For one person, it may constitute a fear that he will lose control of his functioning while for another it may provide a gratifying release to be permitted to respond to an unstructured stimulus.

Epstein does not reject the notion that ambiguous stimuli have a role to play in testing. Rather, he is concerned with specifying the implications of stimulus ambiguity and ascertaining whether different degrees of ambiguity can make different kinds of contributions. This leads him to state that the question of whether structured or unstructured stimuli are superior can only be answered within the context of the purpose for testing.

In assessing the values of structured stimuli, he indicates, first, that they activate specific drives. Second, they permit the tester to decide what he wants the subject to respond to. Third, the use of structured stimuli gives the examiner a reference for interpreting responses to a stimulus whose significance is known.

Structured stimuli also have limitations. Because the intent of the stimulus may be more obvious to the subject, greater defensiveness can result. However, even this limitation is not critical since one can infer drives from the defenses they arouse, or from physiological responses.

Epstein recognizes that stimuli of varying degrees of ambiguity can be used to arouse response dispositions to varying degrees. Persons with a strong latent need will require minimal cues to produce need-relevant responses while persons with a low need would require clearly structured stimuli to produce need-relevant responses. Therefore, the strength of needs of the subjects can determine the degree of stimulus ambiguity required. Another advantage of a properly composed stimulus is that the significant features of the stimulus, other than the one that is intentionally varied, can be held constant.

Epstein's discussion adds important conceptual meaning to two aspects of projective testing—the assessment of conflict within a model of verbal expression and inhibition rather than behavioral approach and avoidance, and the clarification of stimulus ambiguity, including the assets and limitations of such ambiguity.

Rotter has evolved a social learning theory (1954) which he has applied to the problem of personality measurement (1960). In brief, he has stipulated that the potentiality (*need potential*) of a given behavior's occurring is a function of two values: the expectancy that the given behavior will lead to reinforcements (*freedom of movement*) and the value of these reinforcements for the subject (*need value*).

Rotter's formulation derives from his objection to the notion that prediction of behavior is simply a function of need strength, a thesis advanced by some theoretical positions. According to the latter thesis, needs can be ordered in terms of strength and, in any given situation where multiple needs are operative, behavioral predictions can be made from the strongest need. It is Rotter's objection that one cannot successfully predict from the strongest need since people are known to often behave in ways which are consistent with less than the strongest need. Thus, certain of these theoretical positions will postulate "interaction of needs" to account for the discrepancy between a strong need and overt behavior.

Rotter introduces an *expectancy* construct in the prediction of goal-directed behavior. In social learning theory terms, behavioral prediction requires knowledge of the individual's expectancy, on the basis of previous experience, that the behavior in question will eventuate in a satisfying outcome (*positive reinforcement*) rather than punishment in terms of failure (*negative reinforcement*).

Rotter discusses the necessity to devise tests not to predict personality needs and behavior in the abstract but to predict to specified situations or classes of situations. In devising tests, what is necessary is that account be taken of the similarity between situations, e.g., similarity between the test situation and the criterion situation. In social learning theory, it is hypothesized that the situation provides cues for the subject which bear a relationship to his expectancies for reinforcement for different behaviors.

Rotter implicitly is suggesting that test procedures, including projective techniques, must be concerned with assessing the magnitude of expectancy for reinforcement of different behaviors and the importance and value of these reinforcements for the subject. In some ways, his formulation may be labeled more an expectancy theory than a pure learning theory.

Learning theory has provided a rich reservoir of ideas of varying relevance to projective techniques. Most pertinent to the practicing clinical psychologist is Auld's general discussion of interpretive principles based on a learning theory orientation and Epstein's reinterpretation of conflict and his analysis of the significance of stimulus ambiguity. Of conceptual significance is the emphasis of Epstein, Atkinson, McClelland, et al on the drive-arousing properties of stimuli and the assessment of motive strength; Lazarus and Atkinson on the relationship between fantasy and overt behavior; Rotter, Lazarus and Atkinson on the role of the subject's expectancies in affecting his responses. While each of these makes a contribution to some specific aspect of projective techniques, none attempts a systematic bridging of these methods and learning theory. This is attempted by Goss and Brownell in their two papers wherein they offer a detailed analysis of the stimuli operating in the projective test situation; of the role of antecedents in projective test responses; of the use of responses to extra-test stimuli to interpret responses to projective tests. However, as Lindzey (1961) correctly evaluates their analysis, they have illuminated learning theory more adequately than projective techniques.

PSYCHOANALYTIC THEORY

There is an extensive literature that has attempted to relate psychoanalytic theory to projective techniques. Rorschach himself refers to psychoanalytic theory in his original description of the technique identified with his name (1921). Rorschach and Oberholzer (1921) compare Rorschach data and therapeutic data on a patient Oberholzer psychoanalyzed and demonstrate some consistency between the two sets of data.

Rapaport (1942, 1945, 1950, 1952) was among the very first psychoanalytic theorists who attempted to conceptually bridge these two areas and who was keenly aware that such bridging is both complex and obscure. While he cautioned against precipitously and uncritically using psychoanalytic theory in understanding projective techniques, he nevertheless was firmly committed to the belief that this theoretical system had much to contribute to the understanding of these methods (Rapaport, 1952). In contrast of the attempts of others to relate psychoanalytic theory to projective methods, it was Rapaport's belief that the newer ego psychology rather than the "instinct" psychology of psychoanalysis held the greater promise. Rapaport had been involved in the development of a psychoanalytic theory of thinking which he felt would be an important theoretical tool in illuminating the nature of the intervening process between projective stimulus and the subject's response. Unfortunately, he died before he was able to carry his theoretical formulations to their conclusion, but what he has done is a monumental record of accomplishment in theory building which has not been fully recognized in American psychology, for he, like projective techniques, was caught up in the emotional response to psychoanalytic theory.

In his important work on diagnostic testing (Rapaport, Gill & Schafer, 1945; 1946), he states that one of the critical assumptions underlying the use of projective techniques is that the psychologist is attempting to procure information from the subject of which the subject is unaware. Thus, projective techniques rests upon the acceptance of *unconscious motives* which is a central pillar of psychoanalytic theory.

Rapaport (1952) felt that a theory of thinking would ultimately be the bridge between projective techniques and psychoanalytic theory. He examines the concept of "projection" and states that there are many varieties of projection of which "externalization" is most involved in projective techniques. However, externalization is not necessarily synonymous with projection as a defense mechanism. He therefore feels that further study of externalizing processes is necessary.

In interpreting projective tests, the examiner must recognize a hierarchy of motives since motives are not of equal significance in an individual personality. Some motives derive from other motives and such derived motives may eventually enjoy their own autonomy.

One of his significant contributions was his differentiation of two types of cognitive processes, i.e., the application of known concepts or *"fixed tools of thought"* and the formation of concepts or *"process of thought"* (1952). This led Rapaport to stress the importance of the structure of a test inasmuch as the more highly structured tests, e.g., Wechsler Intelligence Scale, were seen by him as yielding information on "fixed tools of thought" while the less structured tests, e.g., Rorschach, yielded information about the "process of thought." Understanding of the thinking process requires that the "fixed tools" and "process of thought" both be studied. The conceptual breadth of a person like Rapaport is seen in the extent to which he attempted to integrate structured and unstructured tests, rather than engaging in a polemic as to which type of technique was superior to the other. He even extended the application of the concept of projective techniques by indicating that stylistic characteristics of the subject, while unknown to the subject, can be reflected in well-structured tests such as intelligence tests.

Another contribution of Rapaport (1952) was his attempt to understand the meaning of the variations among subjects in their "conscious experience" of the perceptions that they describe on the Rorschach. He carefully describes what has been observed by every clinician—some subjects describe their percepts as if they are real objects; some offer an easy and popular response with the conviction that they are creating something that is unusual; still others report physiological phenomena that they experience in concurrence with their perceptions. Rapaport offered the conclusion that these differences in performance are intimately related to two psychoanalytic phenomena: *reality testing* and *constriction of inner experiences.*

In a brief report, Rapaport (1942) discusses the processes of *choice* and *organization,* particularly in relation to the TAT. In understanding the TAT response, one must recognize that choice is involved in deciding with whom to identify the figures in the picture and in the selection of behaviors from the total menu of behaviors appropriate for the picture. The choices must then be organized to create the sequence of events and outcome of the story.

One of Rapaport's significant conceptualizations (1946) was his attempt to understand the intervening process between stimulus presentation and the emitting of a response on the Rorschach. His breadth is no more clearly demonstrated than here—as a psychoanalyst drawing upon perception and association theory.

He observes that a familiar object seen under usual conditions is recognized very readily and without effort because secure memories are available to guide recognition. When an unusual object or a normally familiar object in a new context is seen, a more labored process of recognition, characterized by effort and conscious experiencing, results. This is so because secure memories are not as readily available and other memories are needed to establish similarities and differences between the new object and other known objects.

This leads Rapaport to consider that responding to the Rorschach involves a *perceptual organizing process* which has continuity with perception in everyday life. In addition to the active process of perception, Rapaport stresses the role played by the *association processes*. In responding to the Rorschach, the subject must draw upon concepts relevant to the stimulus from internal ideas and images. Thus, the stimuli trigger an association process.

It is his thesis that both perception and association are always involved and integrated in every Rorschach response. Percepts derive meaning from associations which they trigger and the associative process is dependent upon a perceptual process to adequately test reality. The latter provide reality anchor points and prevent the associations from being exclusively dictated by subjective needs. Thus percepts and associations are mutually integrated in the well-integrated personality.

Rapaport describes the process of responding to the Rorschach as beginning with vague perceptual impressions which trigger the associative processes. The association processes are triggered by some salient aspect of the vague perceptual impression of the inkblot and produce memories and images which have some congruence with the percept. As the associative process proceeds, changes in the original perception occur and move the percept beyond the first vague perceptual impression. Throughout this interactive process, perception binds the associations to reality. Where perception fails to perform this function (e.g., the association process does not use the cues in the perceptual raw material), responses will be autistic or very vague. The associative process terminates when an idea and its corresponding image is sufficiently congruous with the perceptual impression, although what is congruous for one subject may not be for another.

Rapaport thus approached the task of bridging psychoanalytic theory and projective techniques by developing a theory of thinking. Such a theory led him to distinguish "fixed tools of thought" and "process of thoughts"; to view projective test performance as an index of reality assessment; and to offer a rationale of Rorschach responses in terms of the "cogwheeling" of perception and association.

Schafer (1954a, 1954b) has probably made the most significant functional contribution in his attempt to relate psychoanalytic theory to projective techniques. His formulations have unquestionably had the greatest impact on the practicing clinician. Schafer begins by stressing the need to understand the interpersonal context in which test data are gathered, including both the rational and irrational aspects of what transpires and how this affects the subject's responses. One set of irrational aspects has to do with *transference* and *countertransference* in the projective technique situation. These two concepts emerged from observations in psychoanalytic therapy. Attitudes such as fears and expectancies on the part of the patient (transference) and the biases and needs of the tester (countertransference) influence perceptions of the other member of the dyad and affect behavior between them in the testing situation. Because the examiner is reacting to the subject, the attempt to obtain absolute examiner objectivity is difficult, if not impossible. Consequently, the tester must come to learn the nature of the circumstances under which his objectivity tends to be diminished in order that he may take into consideration how this affects the subject's test performance and the examiner's interpretations. It is of course true that while on the one hand the tester does not have available the patient's associations to the situation as he would in therapy, on the other hand, he must look upon transference and countertransference not as unwelcome intrusions, but as useful aids—as he would in therapy. While focusing on these irrational aspects, the examiner must not ignore the reality factors also influencing the relationship, since there is much more transpiring between subject and tester than that which results from irrational attitudes.

The examiner in his testing role brings into the test situation certain demands, anxieties, resentments, etc. that are a function of the particular role of the clinical psychologist in the setting in which he is operating as well as a function of the clinician's personality. With regard to the role of the clinical psychologist, Schafer emphasizes a problem of identity in that the clinical psychologist often has confusion concerning his professional role, confusion emerging out of a sense of inferiority to other professionals, particularly psychiatrists. The clinician also brings to testing his own personal problems, his set of ego defenses, his fearful impulses, and the gratifications he seeks through testing. Furthermore, partly as a function of his role, partly as a function of his personality, the tester enters into the test situation with a set of expectations about the subject, just as the subject enters the test situation with a set of expectations about the psychologist and the examination. The tester wants the subject to be cooperative, to give responses that are unambiguously scoreable and interpretable, etc.

Schafer has quite carefully and sensitively delineated certain role dimensions of the examiner which are present in all examiners. To the extent that the psychologist is an observer of the patient's conscious and unconscious processes, he is operating with a *voyeuristic* attitude. Inasmuch as the psychologist must control the testing situation in order for the testing to be accomplished, he must assume an *autocratic* role. Since the clinical psychologist uses his training and knowledge to draw significant psychological conclusions, he plays an *oracular* role. Last, but by no means least, since testing usually occurs in the context of a patient suffering or needing help, the psychologist functions in a *saintly* role. It is Schafer's thesis that these role demands influence the attitudes of the tester and his expectations from the patient. Where the patient's extent and manner of responding run counter to these expectations, the tester may unknowingly behave in ways that will distort the subject's responses and their interpretation.

While these role performances are seen by Schafer as implicit in the clinical testing situation and therefore as imposed on all clinical testers, although to varying degrees, he does identify certain idiosyncratic personality attributes of the tester that may operate to affect the responses of subjects to the test situation. He lists a number of relevant personality types among clinicians: the tester with a weak sense of personal identity; the inhibited or assertive tester; the dependent tester; the highly intellectualized and constricted tester; the sadistic tester; and the masochistic tester. He can be seductive, withdrawn, querulous, overconscientious, etc. These are but some of the qualities to be found among testers—as well as among therapists of all disciplines—and which influence the subject's perception of the testing situation and affect the rate, spontaneity, variety, and even content of responses. These qualities may also influence interpretations leading to an overemphasis on sexual conflict, dependency, normality, etc.

Schafer then lists aspects of the subject that play a role in determining his response to the test situation. Where projective tests, such as the Rorschach, are utilized, there is a threat to the subject's personal privacy; the patient, by professional definition, cannot control the interpersonal relationship in the testing situation; he may fear being confronted through the test with objectionable aspects of his own personality; he may be threatened by the encouragement to regress to more immature psychic levels in order to produce responses; he can be frightened by the freedom offered by projective test situation, as in the case of the Rorschach, where the patient is given almost complete freedom to respond in any way that he wishes.

Schafer further indicates that responses will reveal various kinds of defensive reactions as they are characteristic of the subject's personality since the testing and its attendant anxieties will elicit the subject's characteristic pattern of defenses. The patient's characteristic defenses will be revealed in the quality and structure of his responses, his manner of responding, his relationship to the examiner, and variations from test to test since each test poses a different type of stress situation. The most common defenses encountered in the Rorschach are projection, isolation, intellectualization, compulsive perfectionism, repression, denial, reaction formation, counterphobic defense, masochistic strategies, ingratiating maneuvers and rebellious operations. Schaefer indicates how the Rorschach can be analyzed so as to lead to understanding of the subject's characteristic defensive style. While the subject's defensive posture will influence his test performance and thus make more difficult the task of interpretation, this effect on test behavior provides a vehicle for assessing the defensive organization.

Another contribution of Schafer should be indicated. Drawing upon Freud's concepts of primary and secondary process, Schafer (1958) has developed a formulation that attempts to explain the response process occurring in the patient. The most primitive level of psychic organization, where there is no concern for the demands of reality, constitutes the *primary process*. *Secondary process* functioning occurs where the child in his development becomes not only aware of reality but attempts to constructively adapt to its demands. Schafer has attempted to illuminate the response process, particularly in the Rorschach, using these concepts. When the examiner introduces the subject to the testing situation, he deliberately encourages the patient, particularly with a technique like the Rorschach, to engage in free fantasy (primary process) but with a careful testing of reality (secondary process), i.e., the patient being able to justify his responses. To the extent that the subject operates principally under the influence of the pleasure principle without regard for the realistic nature of the stimulus, one might say that primary process is dominant. To the extent to which the subject responds with an objective and rational assessment of the stimulus, to this extent we may speak of the secondary process being dominant. It is Schafer's thesis that subjects show marked individual differences in the extent to which these two processes predominate, and that the same individual may vary from time to time in terms of the dominant process. If one conceptualizes primary process functioning as being more regressed than that of secondary process functioning, Schafer's formulation takes on significant meaning. Regression can occur either as a function of a weak ego or of a strong one. He has applied the concept of *regression in the service of the ego,* used by Kris (1952) in his study of creativity, to explain the capacity of an individual to retreat to a more regressed mode of functioning in order to serve the function of adaptation. Furthermore, Schafer sees the projective test situation as one that invites the subject to "regress in the service of the ego" and that individuals differ in terms of the degree to which they can engage in this process, the areas in which they can regress, their ability to recover from this process and their use of the products of regression. Some subjects can only function in the Rorschach test situation by simply describing the blots very concretely, implying there is some inability or unwillingness to regress. Others may engage in very imaginative activity, and permit themselves to play intrapsychically so as to produce spontaneous and creative responses which can be justified. This would represent adaptive "regression in the service of the ego." Others may regress very readily, but begin to produce content that is bizarre and reflective of deep unconscious conflicts, responses which may themselves be distressing to the subject. This would constitute an inability to control the regressive process and is likely to be present in an individual whose ego is significantly impaired.

Finally, Schafer discusses the analysis of *ego identity* (Erikson, 1950) and internalized social roles from projective test data by examination of the subject's private and often unconscious self-image. The examiner may assess the dominant approach to a Rorschach, e.g., whether it is artistic, pseudo-masculine, anti-aesthetic, intellectual, etc., which would be revealing of the self image. Figures on the Rorschach or TAT will be accepted while other figures are rejected; this can illuminate accepted identities as well as rejected ones. The latter may indicate what the subject dare not become. Such ego identity analysis must be assessed in the context of sex, age, cultural background, etc.

Schafer thus has emphasized the need to analyze the total testing situation in order to determine how it affects the subject's responses. This means understanding the expectations and anxieties that the subject brings to the testing situation as well as the motives, attitudes, and general theoretical orientation brought by the examiner. He has delineated different levels of psychological functioning and the importance of the individual's ability to adaptively regress in order to meet the demands of the projective test situation. He has indicated the typical modes of defense of the subject which can affect the way he responds to test stimuli. While this inevitably complicates the process of interpretation, it nevertheless provides an additional means for determining the kind of defensive structure brought to the testing situation by the subject. Finally, his emphasis on the phenomenon of identity and the roles imposed upon tester and subject are significant contributions. Central to all these is his concern with conscious and unconscious motivation operating in both subject and tester, and how operations similar to transference and countertransference operate in the test situation. It is his conclusion that these factors can either result in distortions of the subject's responses and their interpretation or, if used with clinical acumen, can lead to more sensitive understanding of the subject's personality.

Holt (1954) has also examined the relationship between psychoanalytic theory and the Rorschach, particularly as it pertains to the interpretation of content. His analysis in part parallels that of Schafer.

He indicates that the Rorschach is specially adapted to elicit both *primary process* content (more primitive mental content appropriate to the psychological world of dreams, infancy and psychosis) and *secondary process* content (mental content depicting the more logical and controlled psychological activity appropriate to the more mature adult). A highly novel suggestion regarding the Rorschach is his attempt to introduce the psychoanalytic concept of the *neutralization* of sexual and aggressive energy (Hartmann, 1950). Psychoanalytic theory indicates that the fixed energy of the organism is originally invested in the sexual and aggressive drives. To the extent that this energy can be neutralized of its sexual and aggressive content, it is more freely available to serve other personality functions. Holt indicates that the Rorschach provides data as to the availability of such neutral energy. To the extent that a drive has not been neutralized, the drive will control the content of thought. This concept bears a relationship to contemporary thinking in psychoanalysis having to do with the *conflict-free ego*. What Holt is saying is that neutralization of drive energies is characteristic of secondary process functioning whereas primary process is dominated by drive-connected energy.

Holt has developed a scoring system for the Rorschach assessment of the degree to which a subject's performance is dominated by primary as opposed to secondary processes (Holt & Havel, 1960). Primary process thinking can be identified not only by its linkage to drives but also by its formal characteristics, e.g., autistic logic, distortions of reality and loose associations. The mechanisms operative in dreams also characterize primary process: *condensation,* or the blending of several ideas; *displacement,* or shifting from one content or object to another; *symbolization,* or the substitution of an image for another. These qualities of primary process form the basis of Holt and Havel's scoring system.

Holt (1961), applying psychoanalytic theory, grapples with the relationship of fantasy and projective techniques, an issue needing clarification inasmuch as many projective devices require fantasy activity on the part of the subject. He examines the similarities and differences between daydreams and TAT stories. His listing of differences is of significant interest and includes the roles of motives and defenses, quality of consciousness, affective involvement, spontaneity, self-relevance, etc. It is evident that Holt feels that the relationship between fantasy and projective responses needs further elaboration. Holt (1954) also elaborates the thesis that the Rorschach provides information on the extent to which the subject is capable of identifying with others.

Holt's chief contribution lies in his operationalizing the constructs of primary and secondary processes in terms of a scoring scheme that can be applied to Rorschach responses. His extension of energy neutralization, formal thought processes and mechanisms of dream work to the assessment of primary and secondary process is a unique contribution.

Blum (1949, 1950) has developed a projective technique (Blacky

Test) which is distinguished by being one of the rare methods designed to assess variables specific to a particular theory, i.e., psychoanalytic theory. These variables are: oral eroticism, oral sadism, anal expulsiveness and retentiveness, oedipal intensity, masturbation guilt, castration anxiety, identification, sibling rivalry, generalized guilt feelings, ego ideal, and narcissistic or anaclitic love object. Blum (1956) has also extended the test to assess a subject's preferences for certain defense mechanisms such as reaction formation, regression, projection and avoidance. While Blum is not concerned with erecting a bridge between psychoanalytic theory and projective techniques, our discussion of this subject requires some mention of his test. As Lindzey (1961) has observed, ". . . if we alter our question from which theories are at present integrated with projective techniques to which tests are specifically *dependent* upon particular psychological theories, we would have to conclude that the fate of the Blacky Test is more closely linked to the fate of a single psychological theory than is any other projective technique" (p. 128).

Lindzey (1961), in reviewing the relationship between projective methods and psychoanalytic theory, finds many elements of congruity. A number of concepts drawn from psychoanalytic theory seem to have real relevance for these methods. However, he deplores the absence of a more precise specification of the relationship. "Although several interesting and encouraging attempts have been made to demonstrate the utility of some portion of psychoanalytic theory in understanding or interpreting some segment of projective-technique response, a rational and carefully specified bridge from psychoanalytic theory to projective techniques remains a hope for the future—it is definitely not an accomplishment of the past" (p. 128).

Psychoanalytic theory has provided significant and fruitful ideas that are congruent with projective techniques. The contributions of Rapaport and Schafer are indeed monumental in this regard. While Rapaport laid an important groundwork in linking psychoanalytic theory to projective techniques, it has been Schafer who has provided the most sensitive syntheses of these two areas. To be sure, as Lindzey (1961) indicates, this synthesis is far from systematic, but this should not blind us to Schafer's contribution in moving us closer along the way to that ultimate systematization. Rapaport saw the link in a theory of thinking and Schafer elaborated this in his search for those aspects that would affect the style and content of thinking—the situation itself, the role of different levels of psychological functioning, the subject's characteristic defensive postures and the role of ego identity. The centrality of psychoanalytic concepts can be noted in the writings of Schafer—unconscious motivation, psychosexual fixation, defense mechanisms and transference and countertransference. Rapaport's emphasis on the "rationale" of tests led to the important delineation of the roles of perception and association in Rorschach performance. The practical applications of psychoanalytic theory to projective techniques are to be noted in Blum's development of the Blacky Test and Holt's development of a scoring system for the assessment of primary and secondary process functioning.

PERCEPTION THEORY

Since the process of perception is involved in every response to a projective technique, there have been many attempts to link perceptual theory and projective methods. One of the earliest was that of Bruner (1948) whose paper attempted to relate perception and the Rorschach. Bruner observed that Rorschach described his monograph (Rorschach, 1942) as "A Diagnostic Test Based on Perception." Bruner was most emphatic in stressing that the Rorschach is "no separate species of perceptual stimulus" that requires a special theory of Rorschach perception. Rather, what is needed is a general theory of perception that will encompass the Rorschach as a special case.

In developing principles of perception, Bruner describes perception as serving two adaptational functions: *construction* of a world to which the individual can adjust and *defense* against external threats. Both processes serve to sensitize the individual to certain events while making him insensitive to others.

Any perceptual experience is the result of an interaction between the stimulus and the state of the perceiver. Bruner states that the less structured the stimulus is, the greater will be the role of the *mediating processes* in the perceiver in determining the perceptual organization. And the greater the strength of "directive factors," e.g., the subject's set, needs, expectancies, etc., the more these will affect the perceptual organization.

Bruner describes perception as being on a motivational continuum, with autistic wishes seeking *gratification* at one extreme and hypervigilance to ward off threat at the other. The former would describe perception in the psychotic, the latter in the acutely anxious individual. Both poles describe two types of "pathological" perception, with "normal" perception somewhat between—an appropriate mixture of gratification and vigilance.

Drawing upon tachistoscopic research on perceptual defense, Bruner defines several kinds of defensive operations which can be seen in the Rorschach and other projective techniques: 1) The subject is unable to interpret the stimulus, e.g., "it's a blot," usually because it represents a highly charged emotional area. This is "a tendency to blankness" and is a form of *"perceptual blockage."* 2) The subject gives a nonsensical or meaningless response. A poor form response on the Rorschach or a bizarre interpretation on the TAT might correspond to this type of perceptual defense. 3) The subject engages in "warding off by *contra-valuance*" (Postman, Bruner & McGinnies, 1948). In the tachistoscopic experiment, the subject, when presented with a word which symbolizes a value he derogates, will not see the word but rather a derogatory word, e.g., the antireligious subject responds with "sucked" to the word "sacred." According to Bruner, such responses provide a defense by raising the recognition threshold. An example from the Rorschach would be the response "witch" to a stimulus interpretable as a maternal figure by a subject who could thus avoid confrontation with his negative attitudes toward his own mother. Bruner suggests that the Rorschach be used to evaluate these varieties of defense.

Bruner discusses a limitation of the Rorschach as a method of studying perceptual defense. Because inkblots have no intrinsic meaning, they demand interpretation rather than perceptual recognition. Study of perceptual defense requires the use of structured, meaningful stimuli.

Bruner finally discusses *"perceptual vivification,"* the process by which certain perceptual events are selectively accentuated, made vivid and salient. Bruner sees this process of perceptual vivification as being a function of its relevance to the perceiver and feels that this process should be applied to the Rorschach by identifying percepts that are perceived with special vividness.

He concludes that Rorschach methodology and interpretation are linked to perception theory: "The future will perforce witness the coalescence of research on perception and research on diagnostics. The two belong together" (p. 167).

Bruner's paper thus highlights the relevance of perception theory for the Rorschach, and by indirection, for all projective techniques. He stresses the interaction of stimulus and the state of the perceiver in determining perception and recognizes the role of stimulus structure in the eventual perceptual response. He views the Rorschach as an effective instrument for the study of perceptual defense.

Abt (1950) has attempted a more systematic linking of perception theory and projective techniques, even though he denies that existing psychological theories can provide the basis for projective techniques and advances the notion that what is needed is a "projective psychology" derived from the clinical use of these methods. While his approach encompasses field theory and organismic theory, it is perception theory which is emphasized. His interest in perception theory stems from his belief that perception is the central process in projective methods and knowledge of the nature and function of perception should therefore be a prime objective.

Abt stresses the selectivity of the perceptual process, selectivity which is a function of certain *external* and *internal* factors. Traditional Gestalt psychology has investigated the external or *autochthonous factors* influencing perception, and has developed laws concerning stimulus structure. However, it is apparent that Abt considers these external factors of lesser significance in explaining projective techniques as perceptual response tools.

It is the internal factors that command Abt's attention and he approaches these internal factors through the examination of the "internal frame of reference," a construct developed by Rogers (1951) to understand how a person views himself. This "internal frame of reference" is consonant with the construct "self-concept" which would be viewed as a "learned perceptual system" that is subject to the same principles of perceptual organization as other objects of perception. The self-concept influences behavior, such that awareness of a changed self often results in changes in behavior. The external observer may note logical conflicts in a person's self-concept but these may not be experienced as conflicts for the person. Even negative aspects of the self may be defended if they are experienced as an integral part of the self-concept. The importance of this discussion for Abt lies in the fact that the self-concept, as the regulator of behavior, will determine how stimuli are perceived and whether they are remembered or forgotten. Thus, if the self-concept is altered, hitherto repressed material may be recalled. This description of the self-concept regards the internal or subjective factors in perception as crucial in affecting the behavior of the individual.

Abt observes that there is a relationship between the internal (needs of the individual) and the external factors (nature of the stimulus field) in perception. The more the stimulus field is structured, the more behavior is influenced by the external factors in perception. Conversely, the more vague and ambiguous the stimulus field, the more internal factors in perception operate. Even in a completely unstructured stimulus field, the behavior of the individual is to be regarded as lawful, but the lawfulness of such behavior arises from the needs within the individual which are the internal factors. It is the internal and external factors in perception in relation to the nature of the stimulus fields which are the basis upon which projective methods rest.

Past perceptual activity provides the individual with a sense of security in regard to the consequences of present perceptual experiences. Percepts that in the past have been validated by subsequent experience become *"perceptual response tendencies"* and lead to feelings of security. Percepts that have not enjoyed such subsequent validation lead to tension and are experienced with anxiety.

One of the prime functions of perception is defensive, i.e., to protect the individual from painful and threatening experiences. In doing so, perception plays a homeostatic role by permitting the individual to maintain that level of anxiety which he can comfortably tolerate. The perceptual process determines the use of defense mechanisms, such as projection. Thus, for Abt, projection is a perceptual process designed to protect against excessive anxiety.

While recognizing that stimulus ambiguity permits the internal factors to dominate in perception, Abt nevertheless emphasizes that lack of stimulus structure results in heightened anxiety. This is so because the ambiguous stimulus field compels the individual to either utilize old and inadequate response patterns or to establish new behavioral sequences. It is the process of adapting behavior to a new situation which Abt sees as resulting in increased anxiety. Under such anxiety, the subject resorts to projection in the *projective* technique to control his anxiety.

Abt is partial to projective techniques that have minimal structure since it is under such stimulus conditions that such internal factors as wishes, impulses, fantasies, values, etc. will manifest themselves by influencing the perceptual process. Such internal factors will result in focusing on certain aspects of the stimulus situation through *"selective attention,"* a process which sensitizes the person to stimuli which support security and desensitizes him to stimuli that do not promote security. Projective techniques are seen as tools to maximize the operation of internal factors in perception.

Thus, while Abt advocates a new projective psychology, it is evident that his orientation is deeply embedded in perception theory. With Bruner, he sees perception as a function of the stimulus (external) and of the subjects' needs (internal), but stresses the significance of the latter for projective methods. He draws upon the construct of self-concept as the prime regulator of perception. Projective techniques, because they are unstructured, arouse anxiety and thus they permit study of the degree of anxiety that can be tolerated and of the defenses used by the subject.

Eriksen (1954) has also attempted a general bridging between perception and projective methods. He observes that many of the projective techniques are essentially perceptual tasks that operate with the basic assumption that a subject's needs will to a great extent determine how he perceives the test material. He also notes that in addition to needs, defense mechanisms influence perceptual behavior and may in fact serve to mediate between needs and perception.

Eriksen emphasizes that research in perception has supported some of the clinical assumptions underlying projective methods. However, it is necessary to distinguish such confirmation of projective theory from endorsement of specific methods. He criticizes the absence of sufficient norms for interpreting projective data and observes that without norms one cannot determine the ambiguity of test stimuli. He criticizes projective methods for failing to afford opportunities for the expression of a wide variety of needs. He also raises a question concerning the various types of needs that can achieve projective expression and concludes that it is the acceptable, although frustrated needs, that are most frequently expressed in projective material. He urges caution in the interpretation of need strength from projective data inasmuch as defense mechanisms may intervene.

Eriksen has been directly involved in research relating perception and projective techniques. One study (Eriksen and Lazarus, 1952) demonstrated a relationship between emotional disturbance in a motivational area and rejection of Rorschach responses related to that area. This study thus supported the idea that perceptual defense operates in the Rorschach. In another study, Eriksen (1951) demonstrated that subjects manifesting perceptual sensitivity to aggression told more overtly aggressive stories to TAT pictures than did subjects displaying perceptual defense to aggression.

Eriksen thus stresses the role of defenses in intervening between the projective stimulus and the response and correctly cautions against the direct measurement of need strength from responses to a projective technique. He also raises the interesting question of whether projective techniques are capable of assessing the entire range of human needs or whether they can effectively do this for certain kinds of needs only. It is his conclusion that projective methods are most effective in revealing acceptable, frustrated needs.

While there seems little disagreement with perception theorists that perception is a central process in projective techniques, the clinicians' hunger for guidance from perception theory remains essentially unfulfilled. General statements about the role of perception abound in the papers by Bruner, Abt and Eriksen, but there is little provided that can be utilized practically. However, there are important conceptual issues that are raised. There is general agreement that projective methods are a specific area for the operation of perception and that these methods do not require a special perceptual theory. There is general recognition that projective techniques provide the opportunity to study a subject's style of perception, both perceptual defense and perceptual sensitivity. There is also agreement that the less structured a stimulus is, the more internal needs will determine the final perceptual response although they recognize that defenses serve to mediate between stimulus and response. Bruner, however, criticizes the Rorschach as a method of studying perceptual defense because the blots lack intrinsic meaning. It is his conclusion that perceptual defense can be most effectively studied with stimuli that are structured for the content which is to be defended against. This is similar to the thinking of Epstein (1966) described earlier and thus places Bruner among those who deplore the absence of relevant structure in projective methods. While there is agreement on the role of needs and motives in perception, it is Abt who is more explicit in focusing on the self-concept as the regulator of perceptual behavior, i.e., what is perceived must be consonant with the individual's self-concept. Abt also offers the important observation that minimal stimulus structure increases the anxiety for the subject because it demands a new adaptation. It is this quality of the projective technique which makes it possible to study the subject's manner and effectiveness in the handling of anxiety.

Cognitive Theory

A relatively recent attempt to relate psychological theory and projective techniques has been via cognition, which draws upon information theory, decision theory and computer simulation techniques. A recent exposition of this view is that of Fulkerson (1965). According to information theory, information processing depends upon the input, e.g., stimulus characteristics and background effects operating when the stimulus is presented. Here, too, is a familiar criticism that insufficient consideration has traditionally been given to the stimulus dimensions by projective test users.

Decision theory approaches the problem of the stimulus by focusing on the *choice* behavior of a subject. Decision theory sees choice behavior as occurring under conditions of certainty, risk, uncertainty or a combination of uncertainty and risk. Responses to projective stimuli can thus be characterized as choice behavior in response to a stimulus that confronts the subject with some degree of uncertainty. The strategies utilized by the subject in making choices in the face of uncertainty may be different from those utilized under conditions of risk or certainty. Atkinson (1957) and Rotter (1960), in their work, support the notion that people behave in experimental situations according to decision theory expectations.

Following decision theory, Fulkerson gives the example of the subject confronted by an inkblot and experiencing a number of sources of uncertainty. The subject may not know the range of possible percepts available to him, he may not be able to evaluate the possible outcomes or consequences of any given response, and/or he may not be able to predict the likelihood that any given outcome or consequence will occur. If subjects vary as to how uncertain they find an inkblot, then a new interpretative approach becomes necessary. The test interpreter must determine the degree of risk or uncertainty of the test situation for the subject, interpret responses in the context of such knowledge of risk or uncertainty, and predict extra-test behavior in situations involving the same degree of risk or uncertainty.

Fulkerson describes a model of general cognitive theory applicable to projective techniques. According to this model, any stimulus confronts the perceiver with a series of choices under conditions of uncertainty. These choices are part of *information processing*. An *encoding* process requires clarity of *input* (the stimulus must be cognitively clear). A *scanning* operation then ensues. As a function of variables such as instructions or motivational states, a set of expectancies (an internal image equivalent to the notion of "apperceptive mass") are generated. This "apperceptive mass" is called the *image* by Miller, Galanter and Pribram (1960) and serves as the criterion against which input can be compared. The selection rules which govern this comparing process are called the *planx* by Miller, et al. They deal with only one aspect of the selection process, the comparison, calling this the *TOTE* unit. This involves a sequence which starts with testing to see if the input matches expectancy, followed by internal operations aimed at reducing the discrepancy, followed by another testing, etc., until consonance between input and image is achieved. At this point, the process leads to a response and terminates (Coombs, 1964). Simon (1957) has indicated the scanning operation of the testing situation may not be lengthy since human search patterns have a tendency to stop when the first satisfactory response is found unless motivation to procure an optimal response is very high.

The individual must assess the risk of each possible action, which under conditions of uncertainty can never be done with absolute accuracy. Thus, the subject must select a satisfactory strategy in the face of uncertainty. According to decision theory, the optimal strategy under such conditions is to delay a response until more complete information is available. If such delay is not possible, then the alternative strategy is to minimize possible risks by assessing the worst that can happen and to select that action which has the least unsatisfactory outcome. The subject may use a cautious strategy or a strategy of giving socially acceptable answers. Thus, Fulkerson gives the example of a patient confronted with an uncertain interviewing situation. He might ask himself which of two possible errors would be worse. He might overemphasize his symptoms in which case he might appear more disturbed and run the risk of very drastic treatment, or, minimizing his symptoms, he might appear less disturbed and run the risk of not receiving treatment. Within this context, defense mechanisms are "strategies in action" designed to minimize risks. Thus, knowledge of the defense mechanism a person is using provides information about the situation as perceived by the subject and not merely about the subject himself.

From an information processing point of view, the projective test simply confronts the subject with the necessity of dealing with an uncertain situation—to make a response in the face of insufficient information. The variables influencing responses to a projective test are identical with those influencing responses to any stimulus. The information processing steps are the same. It is Fulkerson's conclusion therefore that no special theory is required for projective techniques.

Fulkerson's applications of cognitive theory to projective techniques, by placing its stress on the strategies employed by an individual in a situation of uncertainty and risk, adds an interesting dimension to projective methods not emphasized by other theoretical positions. While his use of information processing theory is of interest, it is not likely to contribute much to the actual interpretation of projective data in the clinical situation. His process of comparison, of matching input to expectations, parallels Rapaport, Gill and Schafer's (1945, 1946) "cogwheeling" of perception and association described earlier.

Decision theory has its origins in the theory of games, which attempts to illuminate how a person should make decisions when he is a participant in a game or a market in competition with others (Von Neumann & Morgenstern, 1947). Statistical decision theory parallels game theory (Wald, 1950). Both game theory and statistical decision theory concern themselves with decisions to be made in the face of uncertainty. In the case of game theory, uncertainty arises from the actions of competitors while in statistical decision theory uncertainty arises from the random variation of events.

Decision theory, the study of rational behavior in the face of unknown conditions, is not only applicable to the understanding of the subject in the test situation who must make choices under varying conditions of uncertainty. The examiner, faced with the problem of making predictions from a subject's test performance, similarly must make choices under varying conditions of uncertainty. It has been Cronbach and Gleser (1965) who have made one of the most systematic applications of decision theory to the problem of the *examiner's* strategies and choices under conditions of uncertainty. In fact, tests are used precisely because decisions have to be made about people under conditions of inadequate information.

Fulkerson (1965), in discussing decision theory, raises the issue of the criterion to be used in assessing the validity of interpretations from a projective technique. He criticizes the classical goal of projective testing, which is to describe intra-psychic dynamics—"an internal reality." He sees this as an intermediate but not ultimate goal. Interpretations represent information and are needed only to make a choice. Therefore, he states that the ultimate goal of testing should be decision-making and the ultimate criterion some outcome variable.

It is therefore desirable that a theory of test construction and test usage consider how tests can best serve in making decisions. Cronbach and Gleser indicate that contemporary test theory does not consider the issue of how tests can best serve in decision-making. This is so because the test is viewed exclusively as a measuring instrument, and test theory is concerned primarily with accuracy of measurement while ignoring the ultimate purpose of testing, which is to arrive at decisions about a person. Obviously, the value of any test depends upon its accuracy, but many other considerations enter into establishing its value, including the relevance of the measurement to the decision that has to be made and the potential losses that can result from an erroneous decision. "Recommendations regarding the design, selection and interpretation of a test must take into account the characteristics of the decisions for which the test will be used since the test that is maximally effective for one decision will not necessarily be most effective elsewhere" (Cronbach & Gleser, p. 2).

Test theory must therefore be based on an examination of the kinds of decisions for which tests are used and what demands these place upon the test. Such test theory must consider the costs (including economic) and consequences (positive and negative) of decisions to be made from testing data, i.e., its utility.

There is a dilemma faced by both the test constructor and test user in terms of the choice between the careful assessment of a single variable and the more cursory assessment of a variety of variables. Drawing upon communications language, Cronbach and Gleser discuss this dilemma in terms of a choice between narrowband and wideband tests. In communications, wider bandwidth yields more information but the clarity or fidelity of such information is usually less than for the narrowband signal. Thus, wide bandwidth and high fidelity are mutually exclusive demands made upon a communication system. This has important parallels for testing. If the tester seeks information relevant to a single decision, he can be assured of a much more dependable answer than if he seeks information for a variety of decisions. On the other hand, he must answer all other questions on the basis of chance since he has not sought information beyond what is relevant for that single decision. In a decision-making situation, compromise is necessary between diversity of information (*bandwidth*) and precise, specific information (*fidelity*).

Following this rationale, Cronbach and Gleser offer several generalizations to assure maximum utility in making multiple decisions: 1) Testing time should be divided among several tests rather than spent on a single test where several decisions are contemplated. 2) The number of tests to be used should be a function of differences in test costs, the different contributions of the tests, and the intercorrelations between tests. Thus, it may be preferable to use a smaller number of tests than there are decisions to be made rather than dividing testing time to encompass all decisions. 3) There is an optimal number of tests and amount of time for each test. Where the tests are of uniform utility, time should be equally divided among the tests. Where the tests are not of uniform utility, time allocated to each test should be a function of its contribution per unit cost to the intercorrelation among the tests.

It is rare that a *quantitative* estimate is what is expected from testing. Rather, the decision-making process requires a judgment among two or more *qualitative* categories or treatments, and quantitative measurement and its accuracy is of utility only in aiding these qualitative decisions. Some have suggested that any test is a tool for locating persons in categories and consequently an important quality of a test is not so much how accurately it orders people but rather its ability to discriminate at the boundaries between categories.

One of the most important implications of decision theory lies in the new interpretation it offers for wideband procedures of which projective techniques are a prime example. A projective technique like the Rorschach assesses intellectual abilities, social relationships, sexual and aggressive attitudes, styles of cognition and many other attributes. While any single Rorschach may provide little or no information regarding some of these areas, every Rorschach provides information on some of them. Thus, a wideband procedure such as the Rorschach provides information for a variety of decisions.

Cronbach and Gleser compare two aspects of any kind of information sought: *exhaustiveness* and *dependability*. Exhaustiveness defines whether the information sought is sufficiently extensive to provide what is wanted. Dependability refers to the validity of such information. They indicate that a wideband procedure will make a greater contribution in some situations than would a narrowband procedure. The narrowband procedure provides valid information in regard to a single decision but provides no information for other decisions. However, even where a wideband technique may offer more information than a narrowband instrument, the decision maker must recognize that it will introduce more errors. Thus, Cronbach and Gleser recommend that the wideband instrument should be the first stage in a sequential process of testing, thus permitting the reversal of a tentative decision before it is finally implemented. Actually, much of clinical testing is of this sequential type, e.g., a Rorschach is administered, leads are developed, TAT cards are selected to test these leads, etc. The wideband technique directs subsequent observations that ultimately lead to enough data for a dependable terminal decision. While the evidence from wideband techniques may have lower reliability and validity, when used sequentially as above they focus attention on facts which might be neglected. They thus argue against conventional validity for wideband techniques.

It is their statement that inferences from projective tests may often be wrong, but they are correct more often than chance and they often suggest hypotheses which, when confirmed, are of great practical importance. They conclude by stating that the real issue is not whether wideband methods (e.g., projective techniques) are good or bad. The basic question for any given decision problem is what is the procedure that will provide the best information.

Decision theory, as applied to testing by Cronbach and Gleser, is unique in that it does not focus on the nature of stimuli or the interpretation of responses, but rather focuses on the considerations to be evaluated by the examiner in selecting the most appropriate techniques. Their criterion of utility or pay-off value in decision-making adds a much needed dimension to current test theory. Of unique significance are their concepts of bandwidth and fidelity which lead to their conclusion that wide bandwidth techniques, such as projective methods, may have low fidelity for specific information but high utility for decision-making.

In the area of cognition, decision theory looms as a powerful tool in illuminating certain major aspects of projective testing. For Fulkerson, its prime application is in understanding the behavior of the subject; for Cronbach and Gleser, it lies in understanding the task of the psychologist. The oft-repeated criticism of the projective tester's neglect of the stimulus is echoed by Fulkerson but his application of cognitive theory does not provide the projective tester with much substantive content for understanding the stimulus, as does the earlier reported work of Epstein (1966). Fulkerson's description of the projective stimulus as presenting a situation of uncertainty and risk which requires that the subject adapt strategies in his decision-making bears a familiar resemblance to Abt's (1950) description of the ambiguous stimulus as one that arouses anxiety which compels the subject to manifest his traditional defensive posture.

Cronbach and Gleser stress the criterion of utility in making decisions as the prime factor in determining the value of any test, including projective techniques. Their discussion of the relative merits of wideband as opposed to narrowband procedures is important for it recognizes the different uses of these two approaches and stresses the need to utilize different criteria in evaluating these two types of methods of assessment. Their applications of decision theory point to a common factor in the subject's responding to a projective test and the examiner's interpretation of these responses—both are operating under conditions of uncertainty. Their emphasis on sequential testing in which wideband procedures are used initially to develop hypotheses and narrowband procedures to test them is an important practical recommendation.

The prime problem that exists in applications of cognitive theory to projective techniques thus far is that it does not provide the users of these methods with differential substantive criteria. It fails to be of practical help in interpreting data from a Rorschach as opposed to data from a TAT since its major concern has been on stressing responses as a function of dealing with uncertainty—in a Rorschach or a TAT. This limitation is undoubtedly a function of the status of the theory at this stage of its development.

ADAPTATION LEVEL THEORY

The theory of adaptation level was developed by Helson (1947, 1948) to account for certain psychophysical and perceptual phenomena. He has broadened its application to encompass a variety of areas of psychology, including the study of attitudes, social psychology and personality (Helson, Blake, Mouton & Olmstead, 1956; Helson, 1955, 1959). According to him, adaptive behavior of an individual is a function of three sources of variation: 1) stimuli in the person's immediate focus of attention; 2) all other stimuli present and forming a background; and 3) residual effects of stimuli from past experience (all behavioral determinants within the organism). Individual differences in response to any stimulus are therefore seen as a function of the differential effects and interactions of the *stimulus* itself, the *background factors* operative at the time of exposure to the stimulus, and the *residuals* from past experience. Adaptation level is defined as that area on a continuum of response in which *no* response or a neutral response occurs as a result of the pooling of these sources of variance. This is similar to the concept of homeostasis. Adaptation level is different from person to person because these three factors and how they interact vary with different people. One can therefore talk of different *levels* of adaptation. It also varies from time to time for a given person as changes occur in these three factors. In other words, the adaptation level fluctuates as the three factors vary. A response is thus referable to an individual's adaptation level for the given situation and implies that for that individual the pooling effect of these three factors is such that the person has now moved from his adaptation level on the continuum of response. Further, responses below the adaptation level and those above it will be different from those at the adaptation level. It should be noted that Helson's approach is an attempt to correct for what he feels has been previously an inadequate emphasis in the study of personality—either a stress on factors within the individual or a stress on external or situational factors. It is his emphasis that his theory permits the study of both sets of factors in interaction while permitting evaluation of the relative contribution of each.

In attempting to understand the way in which the determinants of responses to projective techniques interact, Murstein (1959, 1965) has drawn upon Helson's theory of adaptation level. In applying Helson's formulation to projective techniques, Murstein identifies the three factors referred to above: 1) the *stimuli* in the test, a major property of which is ambiguity; 2) the *background stimuli,* consisting of both the psychological and the physical environment in which the test is being taken, and including the purpose of the testing from the point of view of the subject and the examiner, the sex, age, etc. of the subject and examiner; and 3) the *residuals,* or the personality factor, including organismic needs and learned needs and the totality of experience prior to testing. Murstein feels that the expression of such needs in a projective technique is a function not only of intensity of the need but also of the expectancy of satisfying that need. The dimension of expectancy is a central issue in Rotter's social learning theory (1954) and has been discussed earlier. According to this conceptual model (Murstein's modification of adaptation level theory), whether a response on the TAT is characterized by hostile content would be a function of the pooling of the three stimuli factors: the hostile pull of TAT picture as the immediate stimulus, other stimuli in the background, e.g., a hostile examiner, and the hostile needs of the subject (the residuals). The latter factor would also include the expectancy of whether the response would be accepted or punished. Murstein emphasizes that the stimulus and background factors can be objectively assessed without reference to the individual. A TAT card can be scaled for its stimulus pull for hostility. It is also possible to scale the background factors for hostility, e.g., ratings of examiner hostility. The most difficult variable to quantify is the residual or personality variables. The importance of the role of expectancy in determining whether a need will be expressed in the projective technique is discussed by Murstein by reference to the work of Brozek, Guetzkow and Baldwin (1951). They studied a group of subjects who had volunteered for a semi-starvation diet for 24 weeks and found that these subjects showed no significant increase in food responses on the Rorschach, although they talked about food to others. Murstein states that if a need such as hunger is aroused, and the expectancy for the satisfaction of hunger is not immediate, fantasy may serve to reduce the intensity of the need. In a choice between several kinds of fantasy, the one offering a more realistic solution of the need will be the one more likely to be used. Murstein then argues that the discussion of the satisfaction of hunger needs allows more gratification than the perception of food on the Rorschach. He predicts that food responses would have increased if the subjects had not been given the opportunity to talk about food.

Murstein's use of expectancy as a construct implies a volitional component with regard to the subject's determining his response. Murstein gives an example in the case of the person with a high hostile need who is not threatened by his hostilities. Such a person, in response to a Rorschach blot, may perceive "angry men" or "fierce-looking tigers." However, if such a person views himself as a friendly individual, he will not permit such responses to be expressed and will provide a response more consonant with his self-perception. Murstein therefore implies that a subject can identify those responses which are consonant with his self-perception, although there are individual differences in this capacity. While projective techniques have often been described as methods that do not allow the subject to be aware of what are adequate responses, Murstein states that few techniques have been developed which are completely beyond the understanding of the subject (Murstein, 1956, 1958a, 1958b). Murstein discusses the circumstances under which responses may occur outside the control of the subject. One such condition is when the stimulus is so clearly defined that the subject cannot alter this reality context. Another instance is when a need is so strong that the subject may not be able to censor his perception.

Thus, Murstein's application of adaptation level theory to projective techniques places emphasis on the interaction of stimulus, background and personality variables as determinants of responses to projective techniques. He is particularly emphatic about the need to know more about the rol of the stimulus in projective perception, in contrast to earlier advocates of projective methods who seemed to de-emphasize the stimulus variable. He particularly stresses the need to define the "stimulus pull" for stimuli, the direction in which Epstein's (1966) work, earlier reported, goes. His application of the expectancy thesis, following from Rotter (1954), raises important questions regarding the volitional component in a subject's responses. Two studies have been reported in which adaptation level theory has been applied to projective techniques (Block, 1962, 1963).

FIELD THEORY

Deutsch (1954) defines the projective test situation as a social situation and indicates that a subject's responses cannot be interpreted without consideration of the nature of this social framework. A subject's responses to a projective technique are mediated and determined by three factors: 1) the subject's personality tendencies; 2) the *objective* situation; and 3) the *subjective* definition of the situation by the subject. Deutsch's prime concern is with the last of these.

He describes the core notions in field theory that are relevant to understanding projective techniques. The first of these is that all psychological events (perceiving, thinking, remembering, dreaming, feeling, etc.) are to be thought of as a function of the person and the environment (*field*) viewed interdependently and not in isolation. Lewin (1951) has termed this the *life space*. The projective test situation consists not only of the stimulus material but also of interpersonal interaction between examiner and subject, the institutional setting in which the examination occurs, the cultural definitions of testing brought by the subject, and the immediate physical conditions under which testing occurs. The concept "individual" refers not only to the perceptual, drive, and cognitive systems, but also to the anticipations and expectations which the individual has about the projective situation.

The second core notion of field theory is that psychological events have to be explained in psychological terms. A subject's responses to a test can be understood only if one understands the subject's definition of the total situation, which may differ from the examiner's definition of it. To one subject, projective testing may be interpreted within an achievement-oriented framework, to another in terms of a playful situation, with each definition resulting in different response patterns.

The third core notion is that psychological events must be explained in terms of the psychological field existing at the time the events occur. A past event can create a condition which continues into the present, but it is inevitably influenced by the present psychological field.

Success in attaining one's goals in a social situation is dependent upon one's own actions and the actions and reactions of others. Parsons (1951) speaks of the "complementarity of expectations" which is the supposition that participants in a social situation are able to communicate through common symbols and that norms are present to define the range of appropriate actions and reactions on the part of both participants in the social interactive situation.

A basic requirement for the administration of any test is that the examiner be able to communicate to the subject what is expected of him and what is permitted and that the subject be willing and able to meet the examiner's expectations. Similarly, the subject must be able to communicate to the examiner and the examiner must be willing and able to record what the subject does.

It is Deutsch's thesis that the study of the subject's intentions and expectations with regard to the social situation of testing are required to interpret his responses to that situation. One of the values of the projective test lies in the fact that the subject has a range of possibilities for dealing with the task and for communicating what he does with it. His role in relation to the task is minimally defined. The norms permit him to select from a wide array of possible reactions to the test. Thus, he expresses through his choices certain value orientations, including what he considers valid judgments, appropriate affects, etc. In responding to the Rorschach card, his first response will be a function of such choices as whether to respond quickly, to deal with the whole blot or to parts, to use form or other determinants, etc., which are functions of his "value orientations." While some of these choices may be dependent upon the stimulus characteristics, many will be a function of his "value orientations." The projective technique is therefore a device for the assessment of "value orientations."

There are individual differences in the way people interpret the testing situation. Certain subcultural definitions of a testing situation differ from those held by individuals of the urban, schooled middle class. In western culture, as Schachtel (1945) has indicated, tests are closely related to authority, status and competition. For the middle class person, the projective test is therefore of value in understanding his reactions to situations which are relevant to achievement, authority and status. With groups who define a projective test situation in terms of its pleasureful or aesthetic possibilities, the projective test is less likely to reveal the individual reactions to situations relevant to achievement, authority and status.

Thus, Deutsch's thesis is of value in stressing the social nature of the projective test situation. In drawing upon field theory, he is indicating that the laws governing behavior in a social situation can be applied to the test situation. Of crucial importance in understanding behavior in any social situation is the subject's definition of the situation and his intentions with regard to it. His perception of the test situation will be a function of his personality, characteristics of the stimuli, the personality and expectations of the examiner, the relative social statuses of the two members, the setting, the purpose of the testing, and how the culture defines appropriate behavior in a testing situation. Deutsch's conclusions are important: predictions to the extra-test behavior require knowledge of how the subject has defined the test situation and how this definition corresponds to his definition of other situations. Mention should be made of one study (Rao & Ramadevi, 1958) which describes a method for representing TAT protocols in Lewinian topological constructs.

DEVELOPMENTAL THEORY

Amazingly little has as yet been done in linking developmental theory to projective techniques. One of the few attempts has been to analyze Rorschach location scores in terms of Werner's (1948) developmental theory. This is discussed by Hemmindinger (1960). Werner's approach is that developmental changes occur systematically and in orderly sequence. The principle describing how changes take place is: "When development occurs, it proceeds from a state of relative globality and lack of differentiation to a state of increasing differentiation, articulation and hierarchic integration" (Hemmendinger, 1960, p. 59).

There have been some attempts to apply developmental theory to such problems as differences in perceptual functioning between different clinical groups and normals, between subjects of different ages, etc. This research began with the work of Friedman (1952, 1953) who applied Werner's developmental approach to the structural aspects of Rorschach location scores. He developed a scoring system designed to assess developmental level based upon perceptual functioning in the Rorschach. These developmental location scores are based upon the structure of the percept, the adequacy of form level, the arrangement and integration of its parts, etc. The use of this method permits the ordering of persons on a scale of perceptual development, presumably reflecting personality development.

The research that has been done using this method indicates that development is always relative, in that adult perceptual functioning retains some of the properties that are characteristic of young children, and conversely, young children manifest traces of perceptual functioning which characterize more mature functioning. The data can thus be characterized as continuous rather than discrete.

Developmental theorists define regression operationally as the relative preponderance of lower levels of functioning which would be expected in pathological groups. According to developmental theory, clinical groups characterized by severe psychopathology should demonstrate such lower level functioning to a greater degree than groups characterized by less severe psychopathology. Research based on perceptual level in the Rorschach has validated a number of these formulations including character-istics of normal development as a systematic and orderly progression over ascending age levels (Hemmendinger, 1953). Friedman (1952, 1953) demonstrated the phenomenon of regression by showing that genetically early and genetically late features of perceptual functioning were present in schizophrenics, with the less mature features dominant. Siegel (1953) has demonstrated that perceptual impairment in different types of dis-orders parallels developmental progression. He demonstrated that the perception of paranoids is similar to that of children six to ten years of age (differentiated but minimally integrated perception) while the per-ception of hebephrenics and catatonics resembles that of children three to five years of age (global, amorphous perception). Thus the perception of the paranoid is closer to that of the normal adult than is that of the hebephrenic and catatonic. He further indicates that while the perception of the paranoid resembles that of the child of six to ten years, it is not identical to it, for paranoids show a combination of genetically early and late characteristics. Pena (1953) applied this orientation to the field of brain damage and demonstrated the applicability of perceptual regression here. These "level of regression" studies demonstrate that psychological integration has an important correspondence to developmental level.

Meili-Dworetzki (1956) describes research conducted in Europe deal-ing with the genetic aspects of Rorschach determinants. She studied perceptual development at different age levels using ambiguous figures and found that "manner of approach" changed according to principles of mental development: "differentiation," increased "complexity" and growth in "flexibility." She demonstrates that these perceptual changes occur developmentally in children's responses to the Rorschach and re-lates a number of response determinants, e.g., movement, color, shading, etc., to the principles of perceptual development. It is an important con-tribution to an understanding of the developmental approach to the Rorschach, although she does not provide a scoring scheme that is as functionally useful as Friedman's (1952; 1953).

Developmental theory has had minimal application to projective techniques and what application it has had is as yet limited primarily to one technique, the Rorschach, and to but one singular aspect of it, namely, the development of a system of scoring Rorschach responses to assess the level of an individual's development through analysis of the quality of his perceptions. It does not seem that developmental theory has had much to say as yet about the stimulus, the testing situation, and the internal processes to explain a response or the interpretation of responses. The rich and exciting developments occurring in developmental theory should ultimately be brought to bear more systematically on projective methods.

Kaplan (1963) indicates that the projective psychologist typically is concerned with the feelings, preoccupations, and motivations that lie behind the action of a person, rather than with the action itself. According to this orientation, the understanding of underlying personality processes —"the unseen"—is of primary concern, even to the extent of observing overt behavior in the test situation in order to illuminate these underlying processes. Overt behavior in the projective situation, according to Kaplan, is treated symbolically and interpreted in terms of its implications for covert personality. Thus, the "inner" personality is central and action (behavior) is peripheral.

Kaplan, in search of a theory of the meaning of action, considers the theory of social action of Parsons (1951) and existentialism (Sartre, 1956), both of which utilize concepts that Kaplan feels are significant in the interpretation of projective techniques. Kaplan was led to a theory of action by a series of experiments in which subjects were readministered the Rorschach under instruction that they were not to repeat the responses given previously. He indicates that subjects were able to give new sets of responses, equal in length and variety to the first Rorschach, but distinctly different from it (e.g., Kaplan & Berger, 1956). It was Kaplan's conclusion that this could be primarily understood not in terms of deep, underlying personality characteristics but rather in terms of the more immediate motivation of what the subject was trying to do.

He is critical of the interpretation of projective technique performance as being the product of a personality that is fixed. He feels that the experiments referred to above indicate that personality is capable of variability and that performance on a projective technique will be influenced not by fixed inner needs and tensions but by factors closer to the action itself. In other words, he views projective test performance as a function of *purposeful action,* of *choice* and *decision making.* This would therefore require that the psychologist look at action (behavior) in the projective test situation differently from the way he has usually viewed it.

Existentialism emphasizes that psychological existence is nothing more than action, which is the most extreme position with regard to human personality. Will, choice, intention and action are central concepts. Nothing exists which is not established by the action of the individual. The construct of personality is seen by existentialism not as a psychic reality of drives and personality structures but a product of actions taken by the person in creating his own existence.

Kaplan feels that projective psychologists have approached the interpretation of the Rorschach with incorrect attitudes. He feels that the Rorschach response should not be examined from the point of view of what it tells about the inner life of the subject, since this line of inquiry suggests that the psychologist is really interested in something other than the response (the action). What is appropriate to ask is what the response (the action) means as a choice that has been made and the kind of being that makes such a choice. In other words, it is the psychologist's task to understand the nature of the response as an action taken and what this implies.

One consequence of conceptualizing projective test responses in terms of action is that it makes it possible to view them in terms of the concepts social scientists have utilized in explaining everyday, purposeful behavior. Parsons (1951) explicates the problem of action in his theory which in many ways complements existentialist theory. This theory regards personality not as a function of fixed and stable characteristics but as what a person does. These actions (what he does) occur according to normative patterns. Norms determine behavior in every situation, including the projective test situation.

A dominant, but often neglected, aspect of the testing situation is the understanding by both subject and psychologist that the actions of the subject will be interpreted by the psychologist to define his personality. The subject is faced with the problem of what to tell the examiner and, in the process, what to tell himself. This problem is resolved by the subject resorting to normative patterns, i.e., both latent and explicit definitions of what are correct and incorrect actions. Kaplan gives as an example the expectation in our culture that a person manage his drives such that they be adequately controlled yet permit gratification. This is a cultural prescription and persons who have developed a conforming orientation act this way. Ego strength, from this point of view, is more than a product of past experience; it is a way of acting that the person consciously or unconsciously selects from a number of alternatives and can be viewed as a function of a conforming orientation.

Kaplan stresses that the motivation associated with the action has to do with what the subject perceives is expected, rather than with the action itself. Thus, if a subject indicates he is lazy, the motivation associated with this action cannot be explained primarily in terms of passivity or dependency, but rather with his rejection of the value that a person should be energetic and striving. This dimension of *conformity-deviance* is a major fulcrum of Parsons' theory. Conformity, within this framework, must be motivated, i.e., the individual makes the choice to act with conformity or deviance.

According to Kaplan, the subject who takes a Rorschach has some conscious or unconscious awareness of the alternative ways of acting (responding) that are available to him and of the social values that are attached to each of these alternatives. His choice of the alternative signifies the way he has decided to relate himself to the task. Kaplan points out that research on productivity on the Rorschach indicates that subjects have a normative expectation with regard to this variable. Interviews with subjects indicate concern about what constitutes an adequate number of responses. Productivity can easily be altered by specific instructions and this indicates that the subject is oriented and relating himself to normative prescriptions.

Kaplan stresses the need to focus on the subject's action in the testing situation as the prime object of study and is similar to a number of other theoretical approaches (e.g., Fulkerson, 1965) that have indicated that the subject is involved in making choices when he responds to test stimuli and that such choices can be conscious (e.g., Murstein, 1956, 1958a; 1958b). Here Kaplan has employed existentialism and sociological theory (Parsons) and stressed the importance of understanding a response not in terms of its implications for hidden dynamics but as a reflection of the choice being made, e.g., purposeful action. What is unique is the emphasis on choices which are dictated by normative expectations.

CONCLUSIONS

The previous sections have described various attempts to relate projective techniques to psychological theories. At best this report must be incomplete because of limitations of space. Some reference should be made of other efforts in this direction, e.g., Hanfmann's (1952) treatment of projective techniques within the framework of *organismic theory,* Holt's (1954) formulations of the relevance of Murray's *personology* to projective methods, Klopfer's (1954) discussion of the relation between *Jungian theory* and the Rorschach technique, and Holzberg's (1963) discussion of projective techniques within a *communications theory* model. There is also the volume edited by Rickers-Ovsiankina (1960) which describes contemporary psychological bases for the various Rorschach scoring categories.

It is clear that there is an abundant literature in this domain that must compel rejection of the notion that projective techniques are without foundations in psychological theory. What appears lacking is a single, encompassing theory that can illuminate all aspects of projective testing. But this is the problem of psychology—is there one single theory yet advanced that can account for all aspects of human behavior? Lindzey (1961) has correctly stated that the areas of projective techniques and psychological theory are ". . . neither alien nor are they on intimate terms" (p. 152). One can concur with his conclusion that there is much in psychological theory that is consonant with the assumptions and practices in projective testing. But he deplores what has been mentioned earlier, i.e., the absence of "coherent, explicit and illuminating" sets of formulations that will really integrate these two areas. What he notes are fragmentary formulations from theory that make a good fit to certain aspects of projective testing.

Yet, the diverse formulations described in this chapter are rich in their theoretical import and are unlimited in their practical application. We have noted theoretical attempts to understand the nature of the projective stimulus, the context within which testing occurs, the nature of the interaction between subject and tester, the "internal" process occurring after stimulus input, the nature of the response itself, the subject's expressive behavior, the interpretation of the response, etc. Surely these theoretical formulations can enlarge the context for the use of projective techniques in research and in clinical practice and, by being made explicit, permit the ultimate attainment of the goal of an integrated theory that can illuminate projective testing.

It was Lindzey (1961) who suggested that the need to relate projective techniques to psychological theory is rooted in the desire to establish another index of the validity of projective techniques. This chapter is ample testimony that such relatedness exists and should therefore provide another measure of confidence in these methods. There is the further observation that such relatedness opens a process of mutual influence such that psychological theory can be used not only to develop projective testing but projective techniques can themselves become the basis for further refinements and extensions of psychological theory. The latter may ultimately become the major contribution of this exercise in relatedness, for many of our theories are incomplete and possess serious limitations.

REFERENCES

Abt, L. E. A theory of projective psychology. In L. E. Abt & L. Bellak (Eds.) . *Projective Psychology*: *Clinical Approaches to the Total Personality*. New York: Knopf, 1950. Pp. 33-66.

Abt, L. E., & Bellak, L., (Eds.) . *Projective Psychology*: *Clinical Approaches to the Total Personality*. New York: Knopf, 1950.

Atkinson, J. W. Exploration using imaginative thought to assess the strength of human motives. In M. R. Jones (Ed.) . *Nebraska Symposium on Motivation—1954*. Lincoln: University of Nebraska Press, 1954. Pp. 56-112.

Atkinson, J. W. Motivational determinants of risk taking behavior. *Psychol. Rev.*, 1957, *64*, 359-372.

Atkinson, J. W., (Ed.) . *Motives in Fantasy, Action, and Society*. Princeton: Van Nostrand, 1958.

Auld, F. Contributions of behavior theory to projective techniques. *J. Proj. Tech.*, 1954, *18*, 421-426.

Block, W. E. Adaptation level theory: paradigmatic application to projective testing. *J. clin. Psychol.*, 1962, *18*, 466-468.

Block, W. E. Clinical validation of adaptation level theory as a framework for projective testing. *J. clin. Psychol.*, 1963, *19*, 304-309.

Blum, G. S. A study of the psychoanalytic theory of psychosexual development. *Genet. Psychol. Monogr.*, 1949, *39*, 3-99.

Blum, G. S. *The Blacky Pictures*: *Manual of Instructions*. New York: Psychological Corp., 1950.

Blum, G. S. Defense preferences in four countries. *J. proj. Tech.*, 1956, *20*, 33-41.

Brownell, M. H., & Goss, A. E. Stimulus-response analysis of inferences from projective test behavior. *J. Pers.*, 1957, *25*, 525-538.

Brozek, K., Guetzkow, H., & Baldwin, M. V. A quantitative study of perception and association in experimental semi-starvation. *J. Pers.*, 1951, *19*, 245-264.

Bruner, J. S. Perceptual theory and the Rorschach Test. *J. Pers.*, 1948, *17*, 157-168.

Clark, R. A. The projective measurement of experimentally induced levels of sexual motivation. *J. exper. Psychol.*, 1952, *44*, 391-399.

Coombs, J. W. *A Theory of Data.* New York: Wiley, 1964.

Cronbach, L. J., & Gleser, G. C. *Psychological Tests and Personnel Decisions.* Urbana: University of Illinois Press, 1965.

Deutsch, M. Field theory and projective techniques. *J. proj. Tech.*, 1954, *18*, 427-434.

Dollard, J., & Miller, N. E. *Personality and Psychotherapy.* New York: McGraw-Hill, 1950.

Epstein, S. The measurement of drive and conflict in humans: Theory and experiment. In M. R. Jones (Ed.). *Nebraska Symposium on Motivation—1962.* Lincoln: University of Nebraska Press, 1962. Pp. 127-206.

Epstein, S. Some theoretical considerations on the nature of ambiguity and the use of stimulus dimensions in projective techniques. *J. consult. Psychol.*, 1966, *30*, 183-192.

Eriksen, C. W. Some implications for TAT interpretation arising from need and perception experiments. *J. Pers.*, 1951, *19*, 282-288.

Eriksen, C. W. Needs in perception and projective techniques. *J. proj. Tech.*, 1954, *18*, 435-440.

Eriksen, C. W., & Lazarus, R. S. Perceptual defense and projective techniques. *J. abn. soc. Psychol.*, 1952, *47*, 302-308.

Erikson, E. H. *Childhood and Society.* New York: Norton, 1950.

Friedman, H. Perceptual regression in schizophrenia: an hypothesis suggested by the use of the Rorschach test. *J. genet. Psychol.*, 1953, *81*, 63-98.

Friedman, H. Perceptual regression in schizophrenia: an hypothesis suggested by the use of the Rorschach test. *J. proj. Tech.*, 1953, *17*, 171-185.

Fulkerson, S. C. Some implications of the new cognitive theory for projective tests. *J. consult. Psychol.*, 1965, *29*, 191-197.

Goss, A. E., & Brownell, M. H. Stimulus-response concepts and principles applied to projective test behavior. *J. Pers.*, 1957, *25*, 505-523.

Hanfmann, E. William Stern on "Projective Techniques." *J. Pers.*, 1952, *21*, 1-21.

Hartmann, H. Comments on the psychoanalytic theory of the ego. *Psychoanal. Study Child*, 1950, *5*, 74-96.

Helson, H. Adaptation-level as frame of reference for prediction of psychophysical data. *Amer. J. Psychol.*, 1947, *60*, 1-29.

Helson, H. Adaptation-level as a basis for a quantitative theory of frames of reference. *Psychol. Rev.*, 1948, *55*, 297-313.

Helson, H. An experimental approach to personality. *Psychiat. Res. Rep.*, 1955, *2*, 89-99.

Helson, H. Adaptation level theory. In S. Koch (Ed.). *Psychology: A Study of a Science,* Vol. 1. New York: McGraw-Hill, 1959. Pp. 565-621.

Helson, H., Blake, R. R., Mouton, Jane S., & Olmstead, J. A. The expression of attitudes as adjustments to stimulus, background and residual factors. *J. abnorm. soc. Psychol.*, 1956, *52*, 314-322.

Hemmendinger, L. Perceptual organization and development as reflected in the structure of Rorschach test responses. *J. proj. Tech.*, 1953, *17*, 162-170.

Hemmendinger, L. Developmental theory and the Rorschach method. In M. A. Rickers-Ovsiankina (Ed.). *Rorschach Psychology*. New York: Wiley, 1960. Pp. 58-79.

Holt, R. R. Implications of some contemporary personality theories for Rorschach rationale. In B. Klopfer, M. D. Ainsworth, W. G. Klopfer, & R. R. Holt, *Developments in the Rorschach Technique*, Vol. I: *Technique and Theory*. New York: Harcourt, Brace & World, 1954. Pp. 501-560.

Holt, R. R. The nature of TAT stories as cognitive products: A psychoanalytic approach. In J. Kagan & G. Lesser (Eds.). *Contemporary Issues in Thematic Apperceptive Methods*. Springfield, Ill.: Charles C Thomas, 1961.

Holt, R. R., & Havel, J. A method for assessing primary and secondary process in the Rorschach. In M. A. Rickers-Ovsiankina (Ed.). *Rorschach Psychology*. New York: Wiley, 1960. Pp. 263-318.

Holzberg, J. D. The relevance of personality theory for projective methods. *J. proj. Tech.*, 1954, *18*, 418-420.

Holzberg, J. D. The clinical and scientific methods: Synthesis or antithesis? *J. proj. Tech.*, 1957, *21*, 227-242.

Holzberg, J. D. Projective techniques and resistance to change in psychotherapy as viewed through a communications model. *J. proj. Tech.*, 1963, *27*, 430-435.

Kaplan, B. Projective techniques and the theory of action. *Merrill-Palmer Quart.*, 1963, *9*, 3-10.

Kaplan, B., & Berger, S. Increments and consistency of performance in four repeated Rorschach administrations. *J. proj. Tech.*, 1956, *20*, 304-309.

Klopfer, B. Rorschach hypotheses and ego psychology. In B. Klopfer, M. D. Ainsworth, W. G. Klopfer, & R. R. Holt, *Developments in the Rorschach Technique*, Vol. 1: *Technique and Theory*. New York: Harcourt, Brace & World, 1954. Pp. 561-598.

Korner, A. F. Theoretical considerations concerning the scope and limitations of projective techniques. In B. I. Murstein (Ed.). *Handbook of Projective Techniques*. New York: Basic Books, 1965.

Kris, E. *Psychoanalytic Explorations in Art*. New York: International Universities Press, 1952.

Lazarus, R. S. A substitutive-defensive conception of apperceptive fantasy. In J. Kagan & G. S. Lesser (Eds.) *Contemporary Issues in Thematic Apperceptive Methods*. Springfield, Ill.: Charles C Thomas, 1961. Pp. 51-71.

Lewin, K. *Field Theory in Social Science*. New York: Harper, 1951.

Lindzey, G. *Projective Techniques and Cross-Cultural Research*. New York: Appleton-Century-Crofts, 1961.

McClelland, D. C. Some social consequences of achievement motivation. In M. R. Jones (Ed.). *Nebraska Symposium on Motivation—1955*. Lincoln: University of Nebraska Press, 1955. Pp. 41-65.

McClelland, D. C., Atkinson, J. W., Clark, R. A., & Lowell, E. L. *The Achievement Motive*. New York: Appleton-Century-Crofts, 1953.

Meili-Dworetzki, G. The development of perception in the Rorschach. In B. Klopfer (Ed.). *Developments in the Rorschach Technique*, Vol. II: *Fields of Application*. Yonkers: World Book, 1956. Pp. 104-176.

Miller, G. A., Galanter, E., & Pribram, K. H. *Plans and the Structure of Behavior*. New York: Holt, 1960.

Miller, N. E. Experimental studies of conflict. In J. McV. Hunt (Ed.). *Personality and the Behavior Disorders*. New York: Ronald, 1944.

Miller, N. E. Theory and experiment relating psychoanalytic displacement to stimulus-response generalization. *J. abnorm. soc. Psychol.*, 1948, *43*, 155-178.

Miller, N. E. Comments on theoretical models, illustrated by the development of a theory of conflict behavior. *J. Pers.*, 1951, *20*, 82-100.

Miller, N. E. Liberalization of basic S-R concepts: Extensions to conflict behavior, motivation, and social learning. In S. Koch (Ed.). *Psychology: A Study of a Science*, Vol. 2. New York: McGraw-Hill, 1959. Pp. 196-292.

Murstein, B. I. The projection of hostility on the Rorschach and as a result of ego threat. *J. proj. Tech.*, 1956, *20*, 418-428.

Murstein, B. I. Nonprojective determinants of perception on the TAT. *J. consult. Psychol.*, 1958a, *22*, 195-199.

Murstein, B. I. Some determinants of the perception of hostility. *J. consult. Psychol.*, 1958b, *22*, 65-69.

Murstein, B. I. A conceptual model of projective techniques applied to stimulus variations with thematic techniques. *J. consult. Psychol.*, 1959, *23*, 3-14.

Murstein, B. I. Assumptions, adaptation level, and projective techniques. In B. I. Murstein (Ed.). *Handbook of Projective Techniques*. New York: Basic Books, 1965. Pp. 49-68.

Parsons, T. *The Social System*. Glencoe: Free Press, 1951.

Pena, C. D. A genetic evaluation of perceptual structuralization in cerebral pathology: an investigation by means of the Rorschach test. *J. proj. Tech.*, 1953, *17*, 186-199.

Postman, L., Bruner, J. S. & McGinnies, E. Personal values as selective factors in perception. *J. abnorm. soc. Psychol.*, 1948, *43*, 142-154.

Rao, S. K. R., & Ramadevi, T. Situational analysis of TAT responses. *J. All-India Inst. Ment. Health*, 1958, *1*, 18-25.

Rapaport, D. Principles underlying projective techniques. *Char. Pers.*, 1942, *10*, 213-219.

Rapaport, D. The Rorschach Test: a clinical evaluation. *Bull. Menninger Clinic*, 1945, *9*, 73-77.

Rapaport, D. The theoretical implications of diagnostic testing procedures. *Internat. Congr. psychiat. Rep.*, 1950, *2*, 241-271.

Rapaport, D. Projective techniques and the theory of thinking. *J. proj. Tech.*, 1952, *16*, 269-275.

Rapaport, D., Gill, M., & Schafer, R. *Diagnostic Psychological Testing: The Theory, Statistical Evaluation and Diagnostic Application of a Battery of Tests*, Vol. 1. Chicago: Year Book Publishers, 1945.

Rapaport, D., Gill, M., & Schafer, R. *Diagnostic Psychological Testing: The Theory, Statistical Evaluation and Diagnostic Application of a Battery of Tests*, Vol. 2. Chicago: Year Book Publishers, 1946.

Rickers-Ovsiankina, M. A. *Rorschach Psychology*. New York: Wiley, 1960.

Rogers, C. R. *Client-Centered Therapy: Its Current Practice, Implications, and Theory*. Boston: Houghton Mifflin, 1951.

Rorschach, H. *Psychodiagnostics: A Diagnostic Test Based on Perception* (4th ed.). New York: Grune and Stratton, 1942. (Originally published in 1921).

Rorschach, H., & Oberholzer, E. The application of the form interpretation test. In H. Rorschach, *Psychodiagnostics: A Diagnostic Test Based on Perception* (4th ed.). New York: Grune and Stratton, 1942. (Originally published in 1921). Pp. 184-216.

Rotter, J. B. *Social Learning and Clinical Psychology.* New York: Prentice-Hall, 1954.

Rotter, J. B. Some implications of a social learning theory for the prediction of goal directed behavior from testing procedures. *Psychol. Rev.,* 1960, *67,* 301-316.

Sartre, J. *Being and Nothingness.* New York: Philosophical Library, 1956.

Schachtel, E. G. Subjective definitions of the Rorschach test situation and their effect on test performance. *Psychiatry,* 1945, *8,* 419-448.

Schafer, R. *Psychoanalytic Interpretation in Rorschach Testing: Theory and Application.* New York: Grune and Stratton, 1954a.

Schafer, R. Some applications of contemporary psychoanalytic theory to projective testing. *J. proj. Tech.,* 1954b, *18,* 441-448.

Schafer, R. Regression in the service of the ego: The relevance of a psychoanalytic concept for personality assessment. In G. Lindzey (Ed.). *Assessment of Human Motives.* New York: Rinehart, 1958. Pp. 119-148.

Sears, R. R., Whiting, J. M. W., Nowlis, V., & Sears, P. S. Some child rearing antecedents of aggression and dependency in young children. *Genet. Psychol. Monogr.,* 1953, *47,* 135-234.

Siegel, E. L. Genetic parallels of perceptual structuralization in paranoid schizophrenia: An analysis by means of the Rorschach technique. *J. proj. Tech.,* 1953, *17,* 151-161.

Simon, H. A. *Models of Man.* New York: Wiley, 1957.

Von Neumann, J., & Morgenstern, O. *Theory of Games and Economic Behavior.* Princeton: Princeton University Press, 1947.

Wald, A. *Statistical Decision Functions.* New York: Wiley, 1950.

Werner, H. *Comparative Psychology of Mental Development* (rev. ed.). Chicago: Follet, 1948.

3

Psychopathology, Assessment, and Psychotherapy

MAX L. HUTT

The task of assessing the human personality is beset with many obstacles. As even the layman "knows," personality is highly complex. The psychologist has learned, moreover, from research and from clinical experience, that the personality may be conceptualized in many different ways, that it is a variable phenomenon in respect to both time and situation, and that the meaning of any component in the make-up of personality is highly dependent on other components and their organization. Any method of assessing "the personality" or aspects of the personality has serious limitations as well as possible virtues. The projective approach to assessment is, as we shall see, even more hazardous than many of the so-called objective methods of measurement; at the same time, the projective method has many advantages, chief among which, according to the present writer, is that it examines the personality "in process," i.e., while it is functioning (Hutt, 1945).

Our object is to examine and evaluate the interrelationships among the projective method of assessment, psychopathology, and psychotherapy. It is precisely because projective methods attempt to measure personality "in process" that it is necessary to understand something of that process. If we could assume that the human being invariably responds to similar stimuli in the same way, we would not have to be greatly concerned about "in process" phenomena. However, it seems well established that this is not the case (Hutt et al, 1966). Human personality can best be conceived as being in a constant state of flux, with only relative stabilities in behavior. And. over the years, personality changes do occur, sometimes slowly, and at other times with great rapidity. As Lewin (1935) and other gestaltists see it, personality does not "exist" within the individual; rather it emerges out of the ongoing interaction of the individual with his current life space. In this sense the individual does not "have a personality," but rather he manifests varying personality reactions from which we may infer some of the characteristics of his personality trends.

A specific illustration of these ideas may be helpful. The newspapers reported the case of an elderly man who was discovered to have been the murderer of a number of women whom he had dismembered and buried in his basement. In the village where this man lived and was well known, he was universally thought of as a kind, courteous, stable, well-controlled person. He had never been rude or otherwise unpleasant to either men or women. He had gone about his ways, quietly and efficiently, had seemed to like people, and was liked by them in turn. Yet, over a period of time he had killed a number of women and had mutilated their bodies. It is easy to say, in retrospect, that he suffered from some severe form of psychopathology; one might even guess at the specific nature of this psychopathology. Yet, it might have been impossible, or at least very difficult, to infer that such pathology existed on the basis of his known overt behavior. Or was it possible that his psychopathology developed out of certain events in either his internal life or external circumstances, or both? In any case, the outcome in overt behavior, at any given point in this man's life, was the result of underlying processes occurring in interaction with ongoing events in his external world.

Hutt (Carr et al, 1960) has phrased this position as follows: ". . . if we conceive of all overt behavior as the end-product of internal homeostatic processes designed to offer the individual maximal adjustment for him at any given moment to external as well as internal stresses, we cannot avoid the conclusion that, to borrow from a popular song, 'We can't have one without the other.'" Objective or highly structured tests probably maximize the assessment of specific, overt behaviors which the individual currently is likely to display. We can use such indices to infer underlying dynamics. However, projective or highly unstructured tests probably maximize the assessment of unconscious processes and ongoing processes. We can, of course, use such evidence to infer the probability that certain behavior will emerge as a consequence, although it would be better to make such predictions as contingency predictions, in which we specify the nature of the external conditions under which this will occur. Our point is that we need both kinds of test data—and much more besides—if we are to assess the individual in depth and characterize him in terms of both his potentialities and his current behavioral modes.

The user of projective tests obviously has a more difficult and complex task than the user of objective tests. He has the task of evaluating the projective protocol in terms, primarily, of potentialities. He must attempt to understand the *current* personality dynamics of the individual, and on this basis make certain predictions about his overt behavior under the *varying circumstances* of his life. He cannot assume that there is a fixed, unvarying set of behaviors that can be predicted regardless of external stresses. He cannot even assume that a given stimulus which has a normative value for others will necessarily have this same value for his subject; rather, he has to evaluate the probable value, realistic and symbolic, which such a stimulus has for the particular person.

One other asset of tests which enable the examiner to observe and evaluate process phenomena, and which is found in most projective tests, is that they lend themselves to the formulation of "sequential hypotheses" about the person (Carr, et al, 1960). In the projective test situation, we are usually able to follow the patient as he formulates his responses to successive test stimuli. For example, we can observe such phenomena as the following (in the Rorschach test situation) : 1) What is his initial adaptation to the test stimulus? 2) To what elements in the stimulus does he respond first? 3) Does he continue to make the same kind of response to recurring elements in later test stimuli? 4) Does he proceed to make better or poorer integrations of subsequent test materials? 5) Do certain kinds of test stimuli have a traumatic impact upon him? 6) If so, how does he recover? 7) What kinds of defensive behaviors does he display? 8) How, if at all, does he make use of the interpersonal context of the examination (becoming more dependent, seeking more support, adapting by the use of "distance," becoming more constricted and resistive, etc.). These are only a few of the phenomena we can observe during and after the testing.

On the basis of such observations, coupled with normative data for the test and anamnestic material, the examiner can develop a continuing series of hypotheses about the individual. Each successive response lends itself to a number of specific hypotheses about the person, including such evaluations as: nature of cognitive and affective controls and assests; accuracy of perceptual responses; awareness of reality; use of fantasy; types and hierarchies of defenses; nature of sexual identity; specific areas of conflict; nature of interpersonal needs; assets available for change and recovery, etc. As each successive response is evaluated, some of these hypotheses may be strengthened, others weakened; some may need modification; some may have to be reconciled with each other, while others may remain paradoxical or contradictory; some may have to be discarded. The specific source for such hypotheses in the data of each projective response need not be considered in the present discussion; this would involve the specific properties of each type of projective test, the rationale behind such tests, and the clinical and experimental experience with them. What we are stressing, nevertheless, is the possible utility of such an approach which projective test data tend to maximize.

PSYCHOPATHOLOGY AND ASSESSMENT

Now we can turn to the nature of the interrelationship between psychopathology and assessment. It is possible, of course, to use projective tests without any sophisticated understanding of psychopathology (although we do not recommend this). The examiner may score or evaluate the test protocol and then compare the test scores with published norms indicative of the type and severity of psychopathology. Such use of projective test data is precisely similar to the use of norms with objective tests. They both rely upon actuarial methods and are characterized by the values and limitations of such methods. Although the development of objective scoring of both objective and projective tests has shown considerable sophistication during the past decade, objective scores and evaluation by actuarial methods alone are likely to result in a number of serious limitations, among which we should like to highlight two: 1) they are based on the assumption that the meaning of a score (or a norm) is universal across the population, irrespective of variations in the configuration of responses leading to that score and irrespective of the unique developmental and experiential background of the specific individual; and 2) they fail to consider the idiosyncratic meaning of process phenomena. Let us examine the first limitation in some detail.

Configuration of responses and assessment

Speaking of the possible values of diagnostic testing in general, Rapaport (1954) said, "Psychodiagnostic tests can make an important contribution if only their limitations are not forgotten and if they are used *to clarify clinical findings rather than to replace them*" (italics ours). He was discussing the gain which might be obtained by the use of objective scoring of diagnostic tests, but sought to emphasize that objectivity was always relative. Objective tests and objective scoring seek to provide the advantage of sampling a well defined and well delineated segment of behavior, and of providing a highly consistent method of evaluating this behavior. Nevertheless, the test, can do no more than *attempt* to sample a particular segment and it can only *attempt* to provide an evaluation that has consistent meaning across the population. The test can provide a stimulus that is "objectively" constant for all subjects, but the perception of that stimulus as well as the response to it cannot be entirely predetermined. The effects of recent, especially emotionally charged, experience, of the unique socialization experiences of the individual, and of physical trauma and disease, as examples, may markedly influence these factors. The same comments apply, of course, to relatively unstructured or projective tests, but the examiner is more likely to be "on guard" with such tests and will not naïvely assume that the score measures what it is supposed to measure. The great "danger" of an objective score based on an objective test is that external, situational factors are not likely to be given much consideration and that, therefore, the usual or "average" validity of a score is interpreted at face value—precisely because it is assumed to be "objective" and hence inviolable.

This issue becomes even more significant when one attempts to assess psychopathology in an individual. Some commonplace examples of the influence of different kinds of psychopathology upon test behavior may be helpful. When an individual is severely depressed, his test responses are likely to be markedly constricted. Not only is it then difficult to obtain a "rich" protocol, but the meaning of the responses, apart from the obviously present depression, assumes quite different significance. Severe depression of recent onset may have quite different effects from long-term, insidious depression. As another example, consider the effects upon test performance of the "normal" turbulence which frequently accompanies adolescence. In such an instance, test responses may appear to be full of pathology, yet the skilled clinician who knows something of the nature of both normal and pathological adolescence, should be able to distinguish between test signs of apparent pathology and evidence of true pathology. Or, consider the possible effects of malingering upon test results. The very clever malingerer may do much to give the impression of pathology when he wishes to do so, and his test scores may reflect such pathology, but here again, the sophisticated clinician will examine the record for inconsistencies and will frequently be able to interpret the "pathology" as feigned—no matter what the objective scores may say.

A more complex example may provide additional emphasis to the contention that a test score does not necessarily have universal significance. Suppose we are trying to assess whether or not an individual has some organic pathology. He is given a test, or a battery of tests, as part of this assessment. The test, or each test in the battery, may typically yield some "sign" of organicity. Yet, neither the presence of a "sign" nor its absence is necessarily diagnostically significant. Even the presence or absence of a group or configuration of signs is not necessarily significant, although groups of signs tend to have greater validity than single signs. The so-called test signs of organic pathology have to be evaluated and interpreted on the basis of a number of contingency factors. In the first place, the personality of the patient (or his general psychopathology) may and usually does markedly influence the occurrence of the test sign. Then, the nature of the location of the supposed organic defect, whether in the right or left hemisphere, whether highly localized or more diffuse, and whether at a higher or lower neurological level, will influence the appearance of certain signs in test behavior. And then, the duration of the organic deficit will contribute to the appearance of test signs. Finally, the type of organic damage (whether, for example, constant and highly localized or whether progressive and more widespread) will influence test behavior. The clinician cannot count upon some objectively determined test signs as the sole, or even the major, basis of his evaluation of possible organic damage. He must take into account the possible influence of the kinds of factors we have just enumerated. Beyond this, he must also be cognizant of the values and limitations of each test in his armamentarium for assessing possible brain damage—since different tests have differential utility in this respect (Hartlage, 1966). And then, he must evaluate test findings in the light of the specific history of each patient. All of this constitutes no simple problem, nor will the avid seeker of objective test signs find solace in such a state of affairs. On the other hand, the clinician who relishes the intellectual challenge will find much in this kind of problem to intrigue and stimulate him.

Thus we see that the user of projective tests begins his diagnostic assessment of an individual with an acute awareness of the complexity that confronts him. In attempting to assess psychopathology he relies upon more than the presumed validity of his tests. To begin with, he attempts to learn all he can about the values and limitations of each of his tests. Beyond this, he attempts to learn all he can about the clinical and theoretical meanings of various forms of psychopathology. And then, he utilizes his growing clinical experience as a means of *assessing* what has been assessed, i.e., he makes a careful clinical evaluation of the test responses in the light of: 1) himself as a sensitive observer of the behavior afforded by the test situation; 2) hypotheses that can be formulated provisionally about the probable significance of test data and of concurrent behavior; and 3) the evidence and the inferences that seem probable in terms of the specific individual's life history, physical condition, and his present life setting (including his motivation for taking the test).

Without a sophisticated understanding of the nature of various forms of psychopathology, which implies knowledge of the theories of psychopathology, the clinical and other empirical evidence upon which such theories rest, and the variations in clinical manifestation which each type of psychopathology may show, he would be more of a clerk than a diagnostician. However, with such sophistication, he not only can evaluate the clinical material for possible leads, but he can utilize the experience that emerges with each case to challenge existing nosologies of psychopathology or to enrich them with further data and new understanding.

Knowledge of psychopathology serves other useful purposes for the projective tester. It assists him in selecting the specific projective instruments that are likely to be most helpful in understanding a particular patient. For example, he will select tests that will offer the best sample of segments of behavior for exploring the particular problem that confronts him. If the patient apparently suffers from depression, he may wish to assess inhibitions of cognitive functioning, areas of conflict, severity of pathological defenses and the like. The Rorschach test may, in some instances, fail to yield much evidence of such areas if verbal communication is severely limited. In such cases, non-verbal techniques or modified verbal techniques, such as the Hutt Adaptation of Bender Gestalt (HABGT) (Hutt & Briskin, 1960), or Human Figure Drawing Test (Machover, 1949) may be quite useful. The projective use of the WAIS may serve to highlight the kinds of inhibitions and impairments in intellectual functioning better than the usual projective device. Similarly, if the major concern in diagnosis is to delineate content areas of conflict, such tests as the TAT (Henry, 1956), or Sentence Completion (Rhode, 1957) may be needed. Different tests highlight different components in the personality and hence their selective use in a battery in order to focus the diagnostic material on the specific problems to be delineated may be preferable to the the the routine use of a standard battery of tests (Hutt, 1958; Wallen, 1956).

Knowledge of theories and clinical manifestations of psychopathology can greatly assist the diagnostician in carefully evaluating the meaning of test responses and test behavior. Any kind of pathological behavior (or seeming pathological behavior) can have many alternative meanings. The examiner must carefully consider all possible meanings before accepting some and discarding others. For instance, in the case of the HABGT with which the writer has, perhaps, greater clinical familiarity than with other tests, the patient may show the phenomenon of some type of *perseveration* in his test behavior. (On design 2 of this test, consisting of 12 equidistantly placed dots, perseveration might be manifested when the patient draws 18 dots across the page instead of the required 12.) Empirical evidence has demonstrated that the phenomenon of perseveration is most frequently associated with some types of organic pathology, with regressive states in schizophrenia, and with some forms of mental retardation (Hutt and Briskin, 1960). The sophisticated clinician knows not only that these conditions are associated with the test sign of perseveration, but he also is aware of the reasons (or suspected reasons) such a phenomenon occurs. Hence, when the test sign does appear in a particular protocol, he seeks to determine whether 1) there is additional evidence in the test record or elsewhere to support the hypothesis that the sign means what it is supposed to mean, and 2) there is some alternative explanation for the phenomenon in the particular case.

One of the special procedures, which this writer first introduced for the Rorschach test (Hutt, 1947), to test the meaning of a particular sample of test behavior is that of "testing-the-limits." In the case of the Rorschach test the procedure involved the experimental manipulation of the degree of ego support offered the subject, *after the regular administration of the test had been completed,* in order to assess the subject's capability of modifying or improving his response. Thus, if the subject had been unable to produce any movement responses, his potential for producing such responses was tested by offering defined degrees of general suggestions that might induce the giving of such responses. The failure of the subject to make use of such assistance or redirection was itself of great value in defining more emphatically the degree of type or pathology, i.e., organic patients and severe schizophrenics are most likely to fail in making improvement under these test conditions. Moreover, the degree and type of change in test response could be utilized to delineate more precisely the nature of the underlying pathology. In the case of the Bender test, the phenomenon of perseveration could similarly be tested by asking the subject to take this test item again (and under varying degree of ego support) to determine whether it did, in fact, represent the alleged test sign of a particular form of pathology.

This illustration also suggests that types of conditions other than those typically responsible for a test sign can produce the phenomenon in question. In the case of perseveration (and it might be noted in passing that there are several forms of perseveration with quite different meanings), the phenomenon might occur due to: 1) misunderstanding by the subject of the directions of the test; 2) prior educational or cultural experience which might have "conditioned" the response for reasons other than those which typically gave rise to it; 3) lack of attentiveness to detail other than inattentiveness associated with the suspected pathology; 4) oppositional or rebellious behavior of the subject in which there is some conscious wish to do things differently; and, 5) perception of the task in terms different from those intended (as for example, believing that if it is good to draw 12 dots, it is even better to draw 18). And, of course, there may be still other explanations. One of the responsibilities of the clinician is to attempt to determine which of such alternative explanations may apply in a particular case. The objective test response, by itself, *does not entirely define the probable meaning of the behavior*. The projective meaning of the test response is, therefore, an important part of this definition. Recently, Kornrich (1965) published a volume in which various authors suggest a rich variety of "test modifications" to help make the meaning of test behavior both more explicit and more useful clinically.

In this discussion we have only begun to explore possible relationships between the phenomena of psychopathology and problems of assessment. In considering the projective meaning of test behavior for possible pathology (as well as for possible health), the diagnostician will utilize, in addition to objective and normative data, such characteristics of the response as: obvious content and its meaning; symbolic content and its meaning; the style of the response, i.e., its qualities of consistency, structure, tempo, qualification; and adaptiveness of the response, i.e., the relative and progressive use made by the subject of successive test stimuli to which he is exposed.*

Process phenomena and assessment

Now let us turn to the second limitation of objective tests which we have stressed, and to the relative advantages which we believe projective tests have in this regard i.e., the phenomena of *process behavior*. By process behavior we mean, quite simply, the kinds of behavior which emerge in any interpersonal situation as the situation *develops*. The

---

*The interested reader may wish to consult two excellent book-length discussions of such projective uses of test responses, one by Schafer (1954), and the other by Sarason (1954).

transformations in behavior which occur as a situation develops may, and often do, significantly influence the meaning of the behavior to the observer if he is alert to them. If we were to conceive of an examiner who was so insensitive to this aspect of behavior that he never permitted it to influence his evaluations of the subject, we could recognize at once that, at least under such exceptional circumstances, this examiner's evaluations might be seriously distorted. For example, if while examining a child, the examiner did not recognize that the child was extremely fearful, that as the examination progressed the child became even more fearful and increasingly limited his responsiveness, this examiner could not possibly begin to estimate the probable distortion in test results which were being obtained, nor the possible need to deal with the fear in this child before proceeding with testing.

There are many aspects to the complex problem of process behavior phenomena, and we can do no more in the present discussion than to highlight a few of them. Let us start with the proposition that all test behavior occurs in an interpersonal context and that test behavior is influenced to some degree by the nature of this context. We shall see that projective test situations, far more than objective test situations, permit more ready assessment of the effect of the interpersonal context. We now know that many factors influence the subject's behavior. His perceptions of the purposes of the test and his initial motivations for the examination can greatly modify the nature of his responses (Cronbach, 1946; Hamilton & Robertson, 1966; Hutt et al, 1950; and Whittaker et al, 1952, as examples). We hardly needed research to prove this point, but many research studies have been done which have defined more precisely some of the variables involved in this aspect of interaction and the kind of influence they may have. Instead of summarizing this evidence, let us offer one illustration of the extreme influence the subject's motivations may have upon test performance—even in an objective test situation.

The writer had occasion to work with a middle-aged woman who was concerned with the great difficulties her child was manifesting in his behavior. Before coming to the writer both she and her child had been seen by a psychologist in a well-known clinic, and as part of this diagnostic consultation she had been given an individual intelligence test: the Stanford Binet Scale, Form L. In reporting on his findings, the psychologist had noted: "This woman of obviously retarded intelligence (she has an IQ of 68) has been unable to cope with her child largely because of her own intellectual inadequacies." However, this writer was impressed with this woman's good common sense, her relatively good insights about herself and her child, and her strong motivation in doing something to assist her child in his development. As part of his assessment of this woman, he attempted to gain some understanding of what he felt was the surprisingly low intelligence rating. The reason soon became quite clear. She had been given the intelligence test, she said, without any explanation of its purpose, saw no reason for taking it, wanted an opportunity to "tell someone about her problems" but seemed denied this opportunity, and was examined by a "cold fish of a man" who seemed to make no effort to empathize with her problem or to communicate any warmth or understanding. She stated that she paid little attention to his questions during the examination and made little effort to cooperate. Later, in his clinical work with this woman, the writer thought it would be advisable to secure an "objective" evaluation of her intelligence—if for no other reason than to "clear the record." He discussed this with her, gained her understanding and enthusiastic cooperation, and gave her the same test again: the Stanford Binet Scale, Form L. This time she obtained an IQ of 117! In discussing the test with her, after the examination, the writer asked whether she remembered some of the answers she had given during the previous testing. She remembered a few, and the following is an example of how her attitudes influenced her responses (and earned her the low IQ).

On Year level XIII, the first item is the so-called "Plan of Search" test. The examinee is shown a circle, with an opening in it, and is told: "Let's suppose that your purse with a lot of money in it has been lost in this big field. Take this pencil and start here (pointing) at the gate, and show me where you would go to hunt for the purse so as to be sure not to miss it." The woman said she responded by making some hurried marks with her pencil and saying, "Why should I bother? Let someone else look for it." The previous examiner had marked this response as a failure (as indeed he had on a number of other items, for similar reasons). In the present test situation, the woman carefully made a tight spiral and verbalized quite well why this plan would enable her to find the purse if it were in the field.

In this case, it is obvious that the woman's perceptions of the test situation and her motivations greatly influence her test behavior and the test findings. (It is equally clear that the examiner failed to be aware of, or take into account, the possible influence of such factors, for there was no qualification to his reported findings of "obviously retarded intelligence.") Although the examiner can become aware of such factors in any test situation, it will later become clear that he is even more likely to do so in projective test situations.

Another kind of process phenomenon is that which involves the psychologist's personality. Projective test results are relatively easily influenced by such aspects of this factor as his "warmth" and his "class bias" (Hamilton & Robertson, 1966; Shuey, 1958). Of course, even objective tests may show this result—as research evidence has demonstrated—but the very nature of projective tests makes them much more susceptible in this regard. The reason for this seems to be, primarily, that the test task calls for the examiner's projection i.e., his attribution of characteristics to the test stimuli, and since such tests are relatively unstructured they permit a greater degree of such projection.

This phenomenon might, at first, seem to be a disadvantage. It indicates that no test can be assumed to be impervious to the interaction of examiner and subject and it might seem to lead us to despair since we cannot, in this regard, completely standardize the test situation. On the other hand, this interaction has several advantages. It leads us to recognize the great variability in human personality and the need to take this into account in phrasing our evaluation. It has led some examiners to newer, more dynamic conceptions of personality which, in turn, have pointed the way to promising new research leads. And it can be of practical value in clinical assessment, for if the examiner's personality does affect test results, then what kinds of test situations and what kinds of people are most susceptible to such influences?

Both experience and research evidence have shown that projective test situations, far more than most objective test situations, mirror the effect of the interaction of examiner and subject. Aside from research findings which have explored this problem, clinical evaluations have been directly influenced by it. Examiners have become more sensitive to the impact of their personalities. In addition, they have learned how to evaluate extreme or deviant reactions on tests in terms of the personality characteristics or pathology of certain subjects. The sensitivity of projective tests to such phenomena has led to various direct and indirect "inquiries" with the subjects about the meaning and significance of his test responses. These kinds of data can more clearly define both the types of psychopathology and the probable limits of predictions made upon the basis of test data. Such an orientation, which views the person less as a machine and more as a dynamic organism, can lead to more meaningful, deeper analysis of the personality than might otherwise be possible. Stated in other terms, it has led to the view that predictions about the person have to be phrased *in terms of the specific conditions under which they were obtained.* And this means, in turn, that no test result, no matter how "valid," can be improperly generalized to describe how the individual will operate under varying circumstances. There always has to be some well-defined evaluation of the nature of such significant circumstances. If projective tests tend to make us more cautious in this regard, then, in the end, they will have served the highly important function of destroying the myth of "a general validity" of any test.

In addition to such phenomena as those we have been discussing, there is another class of process phenomena, pertaining to how the individual successively adapts to various test stimuli and how he organizes his adaptive behavior. It is in this developing behavior, which the individual utilizes as he continues to grapple with the test situation, that many clues about his personality reactions may be found and many aspects of his functioning highlighted. There are many issues presented by this problem: 1) How well motivated is the individual in this test situation? How much effort does he bring to this task? 2) How does he react to his difficulties and to frustration? Does he meet failure with renewed effort and effectiveness, or does he give up easily and become less effective? 3) How well do his defenses hold up under stress? Does he tend to cope better as stress continues or does he regress or become more disorganized? 4) Does the pattern of defenses change as the test progresses or does it remain relatively fixed? 5) Does he respond differentially to different types of stress? 6) Does he depend upon the examiner and seek his support or does he withdraw from continued interpersonal contact? 7) Are the different areas of his personality (such as the cognitive and the emotional) differentially affected under stress?

Phenomena such as these occur, of course, in objective test situations but they tend to be obscured by the nature of the situation itself, for we are likely to be concerned primarily with the final outcome—the score—and we have difficulty in either observing or assessing the developing situation. That stress does, indeed, have a differential effect even upon intelligence test scores has been demonstrated by the relative indifference of well-adjusted individuals to the increasing frustrations of successively more age-scale test items on the Stanford-Binet Scale, in contrast to the highly significant and intellectually depressing effect upon poorly adjusted individuals (Hutt, 1947). More than this, for poorly adjusted individuals, at least, the standardized procedure for giving this test produced less valid measures of intellectual potential than an "adaptive" method, which did not make any of the test items easier but alternated easy and difficult items. In this research study, one implication was that systematic variation in testing method could improve test prediction!

One great virtue of projective test situations is that they "compel" the subject to organize his response—usually to a relatively unstructured test situation. Moreover, especially if the test is given individually, they enable the examiner to observe the subject's behavior and test reactions as the test progresses. These observations and test data can be codified, scored, and weighted after the test has been completed. In any case, this type of test situation provides a wealth of data concerning this whole aspect of personality reactions. They enable the examiner to develop and test clues to the specific defense hierarchy of the subject. They provide valuable insights concerning specific areas of conflict. And they offer valuable evidence concerning the type and severity of the psychopathology. Conversely, as we have stated earlier, the examiner with a sophisticated understanding of psychopathology can more rigorously determine which of several psychopathologies might properly account for a particular subject's responses. Several volumes offer detailed examples of procedures of this kind (e.g., Blank, 1965; Hutt & Briskin, 1960; Knight & Friedman, 1954; Sarason, 1954; Shafer, 1954).

Historically, clinical psychologists first had little occasion to utilize psychological assessment for specific psychotherapeutic purposes. In the early days of clinical psychology, assessment was used mainly for purposes of assisting in assigning the patient to a nosological category. Other purposes usually included, as a major aim, assisting in some process of classifying the individual: retarded versus non-retarded, delinquent versus non-delinquent, neurotic versus psychotic, and so on. Many of the findings of the clinical psychologist, even in a psychiatric setting, were used to assist other specialists, usually physicians, in arriving at various administrative decisions about the patient: should he remain in the hospital; was he a suicidal risk; is there any evidence of psychological stress which warrants psychiatric treatment; does he require closed or open ward treatment; how much danger is there of "acting out"; is there evidence of organic brain damage which requires neurological referral, and so on. Although these services of the psychologist were, and still are, useful in many ways, they were seldom related specifically to the problems of the therapeutic process *per se*. Indeed, in earlier days, clinical psychologists had little interest in psychotherapy, were only infrequently trained in its theories or practices, and had little occasion to use the findings from their psychological tests for purposes of predicting the probability of successful change that might attend psychotherapy or of assisting the therapist in the strategy or tactics for a particular patient.

All of this has changed drastically over the past two decades. Increasingly, clinical psychologists have been seeking roles as psychotherapists or, at least, as part of a team involved in the psychological treatment of emotionally disturbed individuals (Sargent & Mayman, 1959). Moreover, as interest in psychotherapy increased, clinical psychologists often lost interest in psychological testing. Frequently, the argument was heard, and not without some justification, that the tests contributed little either to the therapist's understanding of the patient or to the therapeutic strategy. It was interesting to this writer that, most often, this kind of comment was made by diagnosticians who used the tests primarily to obtain a general score of psychopathology or to place the patient in some nosological category, rather than to attempt to understand him more fully in terms of *areas of conflict, nature of defenses, motivations for behavioral change,* and other problems of this kind. Sometimes the psychologist was interested primarily in using tests to obtain some measure that would predict length of therapy or some aspect of therapeutic outcome.

During the past few years, another change has occurred in which increasing and more sophisticated use has been made of psychological tests in many aspects of the therapeutic endeavor. As psychologists gained greater sophistication about psychotherapy, many of them also gained greater sophistication concerning the possible uses of psychological tests, and especially projective tests, in *understanding the patient more deeply, in highlighting aspects of his functioning,* in *clarifying the meaning of his behavior in therapy,* and in *predicting the chances for the success of psychotherapy.* Along with this has come greater sophistication concerning the uses of psychological tests in research on psychotherapy in terms of both process and outcomes.

It would be helpful if we were to conceive of psychotherapy more broadly than we have heretofore been accustomed to doing. The term has usually been reserved for special forms of treatment in which the aim was to induce a change in the individual's psychodynamic balance through the process of uncovering and resolving conflict. In this respect it was often distinguished from "counseling" which was frequently thought of as less "deep" and as more related to external or situational problems than to internal problems. It was also differentiated from those methods of behavior change relying primarily upon experiential change, conditioning procedures, and other forms of learning. Although each of us may have his preferences (biases, if you will) concerning the method of psychotherapy he thinks is most effective, the evidence concerning the relative effectiveness of the various methods of inducing behavioral change, whether simple or complex and whether "deep" or symptomatic, is far from conclusive. A great amount of continuing research effort will be needed before really convincing evidence is available to "explain" which theories and which methods are most appropriate and most effective for which conditions under which circumstances. It might, therefore, be best if we either subsumed under the general rubric of psychotherapy *all* of the diverse methods of inducing change in behavior, or else coined another term to include all of these methods. In any case, our further comments in this section are intended to apply to all forms of psychotherapy, broadly defined—in other words, to all forms of inducing behavioral change.

Prediction of psychotherapeutic change

If psychotherapy is to be undertaken, it is with the expectation that some change for the better in behavioral functioning will occur. Hence, it would be useful if we could predict which individuals would be most likely to profit from a particular form of psychotherapy. The clinician must, therefore, have some understanding of the various types of psychotherapy if he is to utilize the findings from his assessment of the patient. Neither a test score nor a general personality description alone will suffice for such purposes. The test score might be found to correlate with length of stay in psychotherapy (Gibby et al, 1953), or with amount of change induced in psychotherapy (Rogers, 1953), for example, but neither type of prediction can have any significant meaning *unless* the type of psychotherapy *and* the type of patient is carefully specified. Failure to keep these provisos in mind may explain why, in some instances, a prediction score based upon the Rorschach protocol (Klopfer's Rorschach Prognostic Rating Scale) which has usually proved to be successful in this regard (Endicott and Endicott, 1964), is sometimes quite unsuccessful (Fiske et al, 1964). Not only do individuals differ in the kind of psychopathology they manifest, but the different forms of psychopathology are differentially related to probable success when exposed to different forms of psychotherapy. The prognosticator, therefore, must attempt to relate his specific test findings to specified approaches for producing change.

It seems to be true that persons with less psychopathology (or with better psychological health) are more likely to improve with almost any form of psychotherapeutic experience. Indeed, such persons are probably even more likely to improve if they are given no psychotherapy at all (O'Connor et al, 1964)! It might therefore seem that the psychologist is on relatively safe ground if he simply bases his prediction of probable therapeutic improvement on some measure of the severity of psychopathology or some measure of health, such as ego strength. But such predictions, even if they are better than chance predictions for *some classes of individuals,* may prove to be highly inaccurate or even worse than chance predictions for certain individuals. One can guess at some of the factors that could account for such phenomena. For example, if the therapeutic method involves prolonged exposure to anxiety-laden experiences in therapy, as psychoanalysis and other forms of "uncovering" therapy do, those individuals who are low in anxiety tolerance (no matter what the general level of their psychopathology is) or who are poorly motivated for prolonged and sometimes painful therapeutic experience may fare badly in such programs. On the other hand, some of these individuals may be able to make significant gains (temporarily, if not fundamentally) when provided with therapy that relies primarily upon supportive measures or upon conditioning procedures. Moreover, since psychotherapy typically involves the *interaction* of a therapist with a patient (or group of patients), the nature of the therapist's personality may differentially influence the course of therapy, so that a given method of therapy may be effective for some individuals with a given form of psychopathology, yet ineffective for other individuals with the same psychopathology (but different personality characteristics), depending upon the specific interaction with particular psychotherapists.

There are, therefore, at least two general classes of predictions concerning the probable effectiveness of therapeutic improvement. One concerns the general likelihood that an individual's adjustment will improve. The other concerns the likelihood that he will respond to a specified type of psychotherapy or the personality of a particular therapist. General scores of degree of psychopathology or of motivation for change may be more helpful for the first category of predictions.

The use of projective tests in therapeutic management

Projective tests have found a wide use in assisting the therapist in his management of the case. Sometimes such tests are given before psychotherapy is undertaken in order to assess the nature of the patient's problems and the probable values of alternative methods of dealing with them. Sometimes they are administered during the course of psychotherapy to assist the therapist in dealing more effectively with the patient, and sometimes they are given at or after the conclusion of therapy to help evaluate the degree and nature of change or, as in research studies, to help evaluate the effectiveness of the therapeutic approach. Discussion of each of such uses would require far more room than one chapter can provide, but we shall attempt to illustrate and highlight some of the problems for each of these kinds of uses.

Typically, when projective tests are administered before psychotherapy is undertaken they are given in order to determine whether the patient is a "suitable candidate" for psychotherapy or whether any form of psychotherapy is indicated (Sargent & Mayman, 1959). In such instances the problems involve the determination of the presence and degree of severity of psychological disorders, and such related problems as whether the patient requires inpatient treatment, supportive or "uncovering" therapy, and the probable duration of therapy. The importance of careful assessment of each of these problems should not be minimized. But it is probably true that methods other than projective testing can offer at least as much assistance and are usually far less consuming of time and money. The sophisticated clinician will not rush into the "blind use" of projective tests, in such cases, merely because he likes them, but will give consideration to the use of objective tests, appraisal of history, and interview and observational methods.

When projective tests are used to generate hypotheses or furnish evidence about the individual dynamics of the patient their therapeutic value is most apparent. Such tests as the Rorschach can reveal *underlying pathology* that is not readily observable in early therapeutic sessions; such information can be of great value to the therapist as a "warning" to use caution in interpreting or uncovering conflicts when the patient cannot be expected to deal with them in a constructive manner. Tests like the Hutt Adaptation of the Bender Gestalt Test can indicate the presence of an organic factor that might otherwise not be suspected and can alert the therapist to the need for medical evaluation. But beyond such general values in therapeutic strategy which are related to the kinds of and depths of pathology, projective tests can furnish a description in depth of the patient's dynamics, which can lead to important hypotheses concerning specific conflicts, defense styles, adequacy of reality testing, and the like. Recently, Blank illustrated the use of tests in the management of ten cases (Blank, 1965). Some years ago, Spiegelman and Klopfer (1956) demonstrated in detail the possible values of the Rorschach in therapy with a child. And Schafer (1954) has shown how the Rorschach can be interpreted from a psychoanalytic frame of reference to yield rich and varied findings about both personality structure and functioning which, in turn, can be meaningfully related to therapeutic management.

Some of the areas of functioning and structure which may be elucidated by projective tests are listed below. No claim is made for the exhaustiveness of this list or for the independence of each of the several items. Rather, the list is suggestive of the kinds of findings which may be obtained from such tests. Moreover, some projective tests are far more effective in elucidating certain areas of functioning than are others, and in common clinical use a combination of tests (in addition to objective-type tests) may be desirable.

Structure of the Personality

1. Ego strength (ego control)
2. Superego strength
3. Types of defenses
4. General style of adaptation
5. Perceptual maturity
6. Cognitive style
7. Reality testing
8. Level of affect
9. Capacity for fantasy
10. Personality style (obsessive, hysterical, etc.)
11. Field dependent or field independent (or perceptually abient or adient)

Personality Dynamics

1. Types of conflicts
2. Nature of self-concept
3. Sexual identity
4. Severity of regression
5. Nature of fantasy life
6. Motivations and needs
7. Nature of interpersonal and object relations
8. Nature and strength of aggression
9. Nature and strength of dependency
10. Level of creativity
11. Type of self-insight
12. Reaction to stress

As has been suggested, different projective tests tend to tap different *levels* and different *areas* of the personality. In general, the more unstructured the test stimuli, the greater is the likelihood that deeper and more symbolic levels and areas will be tapped (Stone, 1953). One example of the varieties of test findings that can be derived from different projective tests is found in the book by Shneidman (1951) in which the Rorschach, Draw-a-Person, Bender-Gestalt, Thematic Apperception Test,

Minnesota Multiphasic, and the Wechsler-Bellevue scale, administered to a single patient, were analyzed by clinicians who were regarded as expert with each instrument.

A great deal of research has gone into the development of specific test scores and indices which can be of value to the therapist. It would take us too far afield to summarize and evaluate such studies, but a few examples may offer some idea of the scope of such efforts. Hertzman and Pearce (1947) evaluated the personal meaning of the M response on the Rorschach as revealed in therapy. The use of the Rorschach in predicting continuation in therapy was studied by Auld and Leonard (1953). Piotrowski and Schreiber (1952) applied the perceptanalytic method of analyzing the Rorschach to measure changes in the course of therapy. Sexual identification was explored with figure drawings by Armstrong and Harrock (1961). The relation of a perceptual measure of adience-abience to behavioral change was reported by Hutt and Fuerfile (1963). These few illustrations cannot, of course, suggest the wide scope of studies in this field. Excellent summaries of the utilization of projective tests in connection with therapeutic programs may be found in some of the issues of *Annual Review of Psychology* (1950—).

Often, projective tests are given before and after psychotherapy to help assess the nature and stability of the change that may have occurred. Of course, such differences cannot be ascribed entirely or even primarily to the effects of psychotherapy. Individuals change even without psychotherapy! Situational factors, rather than psychotherapy may have accounted for the change. It is for reasons such as these, and for other reasons, that research studies have attempted to evaluate more precisely the probable effects of particular forms of psychotherapy.

Systematic research study of the nature and the effects of psychotherapy utilizing a variety of measures of process and outcomes began in about 1950 with the research project initiated by Rogers and co-workers and culminating in the book, *Psychotherapy and Personality Change* (1954). Prior to this time some investigators had attempted limited research work on isolated factors connected with therapy or on the "general" effects of psychotherapy. Rogers' program initiated the study of many aspects of therapeutic process and therapeutic outcome. It used a variety of measures, among which were some based upon the Rorschach, the Thematic Apperception Test, and Stein's Sentence Completion Test. It was learned that these tests could yield measures which were correlated with amount and type of change related to the therapeutic experience. Since that time many investigators and a number of comprehensive research programs have undertaken to study both process and outcome, and many have utilized projective tests for such studies.

As we have noted, research work has been directed at the problems of outcome as well as process involved in psychotherapy. Such variables (or complexes of variables) as degree of psychological maturity (or freedom from psychopathology), sexual identity, self-concept, impulse control, self-awareness, and freedom from conflict have been studied. The TAT has been used frequently in such studies (e.g., Rogers & Dymond, 1954), but other projective tests have also been employed. Projective tests have been used to obtain personality evaluations of the patient, the therapist and patient-therapist interaction. They have also been employed to study the effect of particular therapeutic techniques (such as social reinforcement, increase in empathy between patient and therapist, emotional climate) upon therapeutic movement (Weiss et al, 1964; Pope & Siegman, 1964). They have been employed to predict or evaluate changes in the dynamic patterns of functioning and changes in the nature of the patient-therapist relationship (Kutash, 1951; Goertzel, 1953; Rioch, 1949).

Projective tests seem to be especially valuable in assessing covert factors which operate in the course of therapy. They are less successful in delineating or predicting overt behavior which is likely to be the end-product of many intervening factors and which, perhaps, can be better predicted from measures relying primarily upon other samples of overt behavior during an interview, on self-rating scales, and on objective tests (Carr et al, 1960).

We must end on the same kind of note with which we began. Projective tests tap underlying features of the personality. To use them wisely the clinician must know a great deal not only about the nature of these tests—their theory and their clinical and experimental history—but a great deal about psychopathology and about the nature of behavioral change. The intricate and complex interactions between psychopathology and therapeutic change as well as the intricate interrelationships between test data and the phenomena of behavior provide a challenge to the competent clinician and a rich source of gratifying insights as well. The values of such insights need to be tested in the crucibles of both clinical experience and well-conceived research studies.

REFERENCES

Annual Review of Psychology. Palo Alto, California: 1950 and each year thereafter.

Armstrong, R., & Harrock, P. Sexual identification and the first figure drawn. *J. consult. Psychol.,* 1961, *25,* 51-59.

Auld, F. J., & Leonard, D. The use of Rorschach scores to predict whether patients will continue in psychotherapy. *J. consult. Psychol.,* 1953, *17,* 104-109.

Blank, L. *Psychological Evaluation in Psychotherapy: Ten Case Histories.* Chicago: Aldine, 1965.

Carr, A. C. et al. *The Prediction of Overt Behavior through the Use of Projective Techniques.* Springfield, Ill.: Charles C Thomas, 1960.

Cronbach, L. J. Response sets and test validity. *Educ. Psychol. Meas.,* 1946, *6,* 475-494.

Endicott, N. A., & Endicott, J. Prediction of improvement in treated and untreated patients using the Rorschach Prognostic Rating Scale. *J. consult. Psychol.,* 1964, *28,* 342-348.

Fiske, D. W., Cartwright, D. S., & Kirtner, W. L. Are psychotherapeutic changes predictable? *J. abnorm. soc. Psychol.*, 1964, *69*, 418-426.

Gibby, R. G., Stotsky, B. A., Miller, D. R., & Hiler, E. W. Prediction of duration of therapy from the Rorschach Test. *J. consult. Psychol.*, 1953, *17*, 348-354.

Goertzel, V. *Shifts in Personality in the Rorschach Test and in Psychotherapy.* Unpublished doctoral dissertation, University of Michigan, 1953.

Hamilton, R. G., & Robertson, M. H. Examiner influence on the Holtzman Inkblot Technique. *J. proj. Tech. & Pers. Assess.*, 1966, *30*, 553-558.

Hartlage, L. Common psychological tests applied to the assessment of brain damage. *J. proj. Tech. & Pers. Assess.*, 1966, *30*, 319-338.

Henry, W. E. *The Analysis of Fantasy.* New York: Wiley, 1956.

Hertzman, M., & Pearce, J. The personal meaning of the human figures in the Rorschach. *Psychiatry*, 1947, *10*, 413-422.

Hutt, M. L. The use of projective methods of personality measurement in Army medical installations. *J. clin. Psychol.*, 1945, *1*, 134-140.

Hutt, M. L., & Shor, J. Rationale for routine Rorschach "Testing-the-Limits." *Rorschach Research Exchange*, 1946, *10*, 70-76.

Hutt, M. L. A clinical study of "consecutive" and "adaptive" testing with the Revised Stanford-Binet. *J. consult. Psychol.*, 1947, *11*, 93-103.

Hutt, M. L., Gibby, R. G., Milton, E., & Potthurst, K. The effect of varied experimental "sets" on Rorschach test performance. *J. proj. Tech.*, 1950, *14*, 181-187.

Hutt, M. L. The psychodiagnostic test battery: general considerations. In D. Brower & L. E. Abt (Eds.). *Progress in Clinical Psychology*, volume III. New York: Grune and Stratton, 1958.

Hutt, M. L., & Briskin, G. J. *The Hutt Adaptation of the Bender-Gestalt Test.* New York: Grune and Stratton, 1960.

Hutt, M. L., & Feuerfile, D. The clinical meanings and predictions of a measure of perceptual adience-abience for a deaf-retarded group. Paper presented at the American Psychological Association, Philadelphia, Pa., 1963.

Hutt, M. L., Isaacson, R. L., & Blum, M. L. *Psychology: The Science of Interpersonal Behavior.* New York: Harper & Row, 1966.

Knight, R. P., & Friedman, C. R. (Eds.). *Psychoanalytic Psychiatry and Psychology.* New York: International Universities Press, 1954.

Kornrich, M. (Ed.). *Psychological Test Modifications.* Springfield, Ill.: Charles C Thomas, 1965.

Kutash, S. B. The Rorschach examination and psychotherapy. *Amer. J. Psychother.*, 1951, *5*, 405-410.

Lewin, K. *A Dynamic Theory of Personality.* New York: McGraw-Hill, 1935.

Machover, K. *Personality Projection in the Drawing of the Human Figure.* Springfield, Ill.: Charles C Thomas, 1949.

O'Connor, J. F., Daniels, G., Karush, A., Moses, L., Flood, C., & Stern, L. O. The effects of psychotherapy on the course of ulcerative colitis—a preliminary report. *Amer. J. Psychiat.*, 1964, *120*, 738-742.

Piotrowski, Z. A., & Schreiber, M. Rorschach perceptanalytic measurement of personality changes during and after psychoanalytically oriented psychotherapy. In G. Bychowski (Ed.). *Specialized Techniques in Psychotherapy.* New York: Basic Books, 1952.

Pope, B., & Siegman, A. An intercorrelational study of some indices of verbal fluency. *Psychol. Rep.*, 1964, *15*, 303-310.

Rapaport, D. The theoretical implications of diagnostic testing procedures. In R. P. Knight & C. R. Friedman (Eds.). *Psychoanalytic Psychiatry and Psychology*. New York: International Universities Press, 1954.

Rhode, A. R. *The Sentence Completion Method*. New York: Ronald Press, 1957.

Rioch, M. J. The use of the Rorschach test in the assessment of change in patients under psychotherapy. *Psychiatry*, 1949, *12*, 427-434.

Rogers, C. R., & Dymond, R. F. (Eds.). *Psychotherapy and Personality Change*. Chicago: University of Chicago Press, 1954.

Rogers, C. R., & Hammond, K. R. Predictions of the results of therapy by means of the Rorschach test. *J. consult. Psychol.*, 1953, *17*, 8-15.

Sarason, S. B. *The Clinical Interaction*. New York: Harper, 1954.

Sargent, H., & Mayman, M. Clinical psychology. In S. Arieti (Ed.). *American Handbook of Psychiatry*, Volume 2. New York: Basic Books, 1959.

Schafer, R. *Psychoanalytic Interpretation in Rorschach Testing*. New York: Grune and Stratton, 1954.

Shneidman, E. S. (Ed.). *Thematic Test Analysis*. New York: Grune and Stratton, 1951.

Shuey, A. M. *The Testing of Negro Intelligence*. Lynchburg, Va.: J. P. Bell, 1958.

Spiegelman, L., & Klopfer, B. Rorschach reactions and child therapy: a case study. In B. Klopfer, et al. (Eds.). *Developments in the Rorschach Technique*, volume 2. New York: Basic Books, 1956.

Stone, H. The relationship of hostile-aggressive behavior to aggressive content on the Rorschach and the TAT. Unpublished doctoral dissertation, University of California at Los Angeles, 1953.

Wallen, R. W. *Clinical Psychology: The Study of Persons*. New York: McGraw-Hill, 1956.

Weiss, R. L., Krasner, L., & Ullman, L. Responsivity of psychiatric patients to verbal conditioning: "success" and "failure" conditions and patterns of reinforced trials. *Psychol. Rep.*, 1964, *15*, 303-310.

Whittaker, E. M., Gilchrist, J. C., & Fisher, J. Perceptual defense or response suppression? *J. abnorm. soc. Psychol.*, 1952, *47*, 732-733.

4

Problems of Validities

BERTRAM P. KARON

In this chapter, I shall not attempt to review all the issues of validity of projective tests and the evidence relevant thereto. (That would take several volumes, rather than a chapter. One can summarize the literature briefly as follows: There are hundreds of articles on projective techniques which show them to be valid and hundreds of articles demonstrating them to be invalid.) Rather it is my intention to discuss some issues of validity both in clinical and research uses, to point out some of the considerations in the appropriate use of projective techniques in both settings, and to describe some of the common misconceptions which have led to confusion, conflicting evidence, and inappropriate conclusions.

I shall discuss the determination of validities (including a differentiation of the various kinds of validities commonly used by psychologists) with emphasis on some of the clinical issues, and finally present some surprisingly little-known statistical methodologies which make it easier for the clinically-oriented psychologist to do research which does not violate his feeling about what it is he wishes to investigate in the first place. Included will be a discussion of the notion, widely held, that reliability is essential to validity, and a mathematical demonstration of the fallacy of that notion. The appropriate use of the matching test, Tau', the product moment r as a non-parametric statistic, and chi-square with expected values less than 5 will be described. Finally, the overly rigid interpretation of Stevens' four types of scales, and the statistics appropriate thereto, which has prevented psychological researchers from using the most straightforward—and most powerful—statistical techniques, will be discussed so as to remove this unnecessary methodological straightjacket.

KINDS OF VALIDITIES

We commonly think of the validity of a test as meaning the degree to which the test measures what it purports to measure. But when we begin to examine validity, it becomes obvious that this is a complicated question.

The American Psychological Association's *Standards for Educational and Psychological Tests and Manuals* (French, Michael, et al, 1966) describes three different types of validity—*content validity, criterion related validity,* and *construct validity.* It is also useful to distinguish *concurrent* from *predictive validity, clinical* from *research validity,* and *intrinsic* from *extrinsic validity.* In making these distinctions, it is important not to be misled into believing that these represent disjoint categories, or that they are necessarily exhaustive. They do emphasize different aspects of determining validity, all of which may not be involved in any one test used for any one purpose.

Content validity

Content validity refers to a test which is said to measure something because an expert judges the test's content to be representative of that which is to be measured. According to the APA *Standards* (p. 12) this type of validity is appropriate when "the test user wishes to determine how an individual performs at present in a universe of situations that the test is claimed to represent." Thus, for example, a final exam in a college course would be such a situation: it attempts to measure how much of the content of the course has been mastered. Content validity would be established if expert opinion considered the items to be a reasonable sampling of the course material.

Content validity, which is considered not only useful, but necessary, in evaluating measuring instruments in the rest of psychology, is often neglected in discussions of projective tests. The underlying assumption that would explain such neglect can only be that there is no body of theory and practice in clinical psychology that would justify considering anyone an expert. This is sometimes stated explicitly, and is always based on ignorance of the literature. Thus, for example, a large number of students reach graduate school without ever having heard about even a single laboratory experiment in which unconscious processes were demonstrated (e.g., Diven, 1937; Haggard, 1947; Lacey, 1964; Reyher, 1967; etc.), let alone the wealth of clinical data which exist.

There is, of course, an extensive body of clinical theory and data, and the competent clinician can derive from theory what is appropriate content. Content validity is particularly important for projective techniques when measuring something for which there is no alternative simple measure. For instance, the existence of a particular unconscious fantasy may have no other good measure. In clinical uses, the wide variety of facets of personality in which the clinician may be interested will usually not have had the necessary research to establish convincingly, on a correlational basis, the validity of the measure, largely because of the number of such facets and the difficulty of doing such research. But content validity, i.e., the judgment from theory of a competent clinician, turns out to be a powerful tool, as will be illustrated later on.

Of course, in developing a better set of theories, systematic research is useful; that is, research in which variables are controlled as opposed to naturalistic observation. But in clinical psychology such research, in general, merely has provided firmer evidence for theories already developed from clinical observation. For many problems of psychology, it may be a long time, if ever, before relevant laboratory experiments are possible.

To reiterate: the competent, adequately trained, and experienced clinician has a powerful set of theories and clinical observation to fall back on, and the vast difference between the judgment of such an expert and the judgment of a first-year graduate student is often neglected in research studies that obtain negative findings with respect to validity.

Criterion-related validity

Criterion-related validity is what one most commonly likes to use. Here one evaluates the validity of the test by its ability to agree with some other measure (criterion). According to the APA *Standards,* this is appropriate when one wishes to forecast an individual's future standing or present standing on some variable of significance different from the test. "This is demonstrated by comparing a test score with one or more variables considered to be a direct measure of the characteristic or behavior in question" (p. 13). This type of validity seems most direct. Unfortunately, there may not be a better measure available of the variable to be predicted than a projective test.

The other problem with criterion-related validity lies in the nature of the criterion. Very often, in research on projective tests, the failure of prediction is due to a poorly understood criterion rather than a failure of the test. Thus, one may not be able to predict the performance of a group of Air Force pilots from the Rorschach, not because one cannot interpret personality characteristics from the Rorschach, but because one has never had any clinical experience with successful and unsuccessful pilots and hence has only a stereotyped or mythological understanding of what kinds of personalities tend to be successful or unsuccessful pilots.

The criterion problem. This problem is one of which industrial psychologists are well aware, but one that both academic and clinical psychologists often ignore; namely, that failure of prediction may be due not to inadequacies of the measuring instruments, but to failure of the criterion. The criterion is rarely as simple as it seems.

The most obvious examples are the failures of projective techniques to predict psychiatric diagnosis. But an examination of the criterion readily shows that psychiatric diagnosis varies from hospital to hospital, and from psychiatrist to psychiatrist within a given hospital. An uncertain and shifting criterion is not going to be predicted easily.

As long ago as the first book on the TAT (Tomkins, 1947, p. 266) it was suggested that the psychiatric entities "do not, in our opinion, represent homogeneous entities even at the level of symptomatology. It is for these reasons that correlations between TAT results and these entities cannot be far reaching. Such effort would be better applied to the reclassification of mental disease on the basis of homogeneous test patterns."

This suggestion has generally been ignored. The one major exception is Beck's derivation of six sub-types of schizophrenia on the basis of the Rorschach (Beck, 1954).

A pretty example was brought to light by Lacey, Bateman, and Van Lehn (1952) in which an apparent failure of the Rorschach to predict was based on an inadequate analysis of the criterion. Using classical Rorschach theory, they employed $C + CF - FC$ as a measure of uncontrolled emotionality. They correlated this with a number of physiological measures (PGR, heart rate, heart rate variability, etc.) under a number of stress situations. For any one physiological measure in any one stress situation, the correlation with this Rorschach variable was trivial and not statistically significant. If they had stopped there, they would simply have added another negative finding to the Rorschach literature. However, they did not change the Rorschach measure. They did ask more about the criterion. They added the psychological fact that not all people react to stress with the same physiological system. For each stress situation and each physiological measure, they changed the scores to standard scores. (This made the different kinds of scores comparable, since they now all had the same mean and variance.) For a given situation and for each individual, they used that physiological system on which his standard score was highest. Statistically, this should have had no effect on the correlations except to make them even smaller, since the range of variation was decreased by the elimination of very low scores. But, psychologically, if each person has a characteristic stress system and if the Rorschach score is valid, then the correlation should increase. Indeed, that is what happened.

They then added the further psychological fact that a particular stress situation may not be equally stressful for all people. For example, some react to physical pain more than psychological stress, while for others it is reversed. Therefore, for each subject they used the maximal standard scores, not only across physiological systems, but also across stress situations. Again, statistically, the only effect should have been to lower the correlation because of restriction of the range of variability. But, psychologically, if people do react differently to different kinds of stress, and if the Rorschach score is valid, then the correlation should increase.

Again, that is what happened. The findings were clearly statistically significant.

This study is impressive, not because it found validity for one Rorschach measure, but because it demonstrated why other studies had not. The key lay in the psychological analysis of the criterion.

This is true both for clinical and research studies. Thus, if you ask someone to predict who will be a good Air Force pilot or a good clinical psychologist on the basis of the Rorschach, one must first know what are the characteristics of a good Air Force pilot or of a good clinical psychologist. One's stereotyped abstract ideas are apt to be very misleading.

But surely clinical psychologists know the characteristics of a good clinical psychologist! Surprisingly, it does not seem so, and it is my belief that this accounts for the reported inability to predict success in clinical psychology from projective tests.

Another example of the criterion problem, combined with the theoretical analysis of the projective measure, lies in the ambiguous findings of the Rosenzweig Frustration Picture test in predicting assaultiveness in delinquents. If we examine the test we notice that it only uses the handling of verbal aggression. ("What does he say?") "Aggression," like most personality characteristics, is to a large extent an arbitrarily-defined construct. The relationship of the handling of verbal aggression to the handling of physical aggression is not the same for all people.

This may be illustrated by citing an example of a very assaultive delinquent who was arrested for "mugging." He would literally give me sermons about how "immoral it was to hate," how he could "never hate anyone," and he could not understand "how anyone could be so immoral as to hate." Once he said that he might "dislike someone a little bit," and if "I disliked him enough, I might kill him, but I cannot understand how any one can be so immoral as to hate." This verbal pacifist had been arrested for a "mugging" so brutal that even his accomplices were sickened and pulled him off the victim. (Needless to say, no one who earns a living by mugging is apt to be squeamish about brutality.) The victim's skull had been fractured in seven places, and there were injuries on the rest of the body of similar severity, all of which had been inflicted not with weapons but simply by hitting or kicking the victim. Yet, he was very inhibited in the expression of verbal aggression.

In my experience this is not an occasional paradox, but rather a frequent occurrence. The inability to tolerate conscious anger was characteristic of those patients who were homicidally dangerous, and psychotherapy which increased their tolerance for aggressive feelings, fantasies, and verbalizations also increased their capacity to control their physical aggression.

If one has clinical experience with assaultive delinquents, one finds typically that they are not verbally aggressive. On the contrary, they are often verbally impotent and explode physically to express the anger which may not be dischargeable otherwise. Indeed, it may not even be conscious. One would not expect their behavior to be predicted by a test of fantasy which measures only, "What does he say?"

In studying psychotic depressives, one finds that their TAT protocols do not especially contain stories filled with depression, sadness, or guilt, but rather psychotic depressives tell short stories which contain surprisingly little mention of affect. In one study of psychotic depression, we found that whenever a patient yielded a protocol full of depression, sadness, and/or guilt, he was almost inevitably re-diagnosed by the clinical staff as paranoid schizophrenic very shortly thereafter. One could talk about "lack of validity," but if one does, one misses the chance to discover something of importance—that affect is missing. This suggests that affect is missing as a defensive process against intolerable anguish. The awareness of this possibility led to interesting theoretical questions about the nature of psychotic depression and of the affect system (Tomkins, 1963).

To return to the Rorschach: one ordinarily assumes that dark shading relates to depression specifically, and that color relates to affect. It is well known, however, that psychotic depressives do not typically give either dark shading or color, but a simple protocol with good form quality, few responses, primarily form dominated. One possibility is to assume that the projective assumptions are invalid, since the patient is obviously "depressed." Another psychologically more fruitful approach is to assume that perhaps the projective assumptions are not invalid, that the individual is portrayed accurately, maintaining normal functioning within a highly restricted range (good form quality, but few responses), and that the psychotic depressive is not suffused with conscious depression, but is again affectless, as a defense against intolerable anguish, reinforcing the TAT findings. But such fruitful use of projective tests to discover new information is impossible if one is unwilling to re-examine the criterion.

Clark and Sensibar (1955) began by using a McClelland-like approach to study the need for sex in the TAT. They showed one group of male college students pictures of innocuous landscapes and another group sexy nudes. One might have expected that the group viewing the nudes would be sexually aroused, and one could then validate the need sex by scoring the increase in sexual fantasy. But that is not what happened. The aroused group gave less overt sexual content in their stories. One might have concluded the TAT was invalid. In this instance the authors instead analyzed the criterion, and as a consequence shed light on a controversial area of psychological theory.

Clark and Sensibar suggest as an alternate hypothesis to the simpleminded one that the TAT is invalid, that the subjects were sexually aroused, but that this sexual arousal also aroused anxiety and guilt over sex, which inhibited the expression of even the usual amount of sexual content in the fantasies. To check on this, the arousal condition (sexy-nude pictures) was repeated at a fraternity beer party where the social setting and the alcohol would decrease the anxiety and guilt. As predicted, the amount of overt sexual content was clearly increased over the other two conditions.

Having confirmed their theoretical understanding of the first apparently negative finding, the authors realized that they had the data for resolving an important issue. Freud (1950), and Ferenczi (1950) even more clearly, speak of dream symbolism as being used for defensive purposes, to disguise the meaning of the content from the dreamer. As diverse theorists as Jung (1920), Fromm (1951), and Hall (1953) have suggested an opposing view: symbolism is a primitive language peculiar to dreams and fantasy which is not used particularly to disguise, but simply to express what needs to be expressed. The first view leads to the prediction that sexual symbolism should be most striking in the fantasies of subjects who were sexually aroused, but who were inhibiting the expression of sexual fantasies because of anxiety and guilt, and should be least present when the sexual content is expressed most overtly. The Jung-Hall-Fromm formulations lead to the opposite prediction: the symbolic sexual content should vary with the overt sexual content. This is an issue about which bright and competent people can obviously disagree on the basis of clinical observation. But Clark and Sensibar's finding bears out Freud and Ferenczi. As before, a careful analysis of the criterion leads not only to a better understanding of the projective techniques, but more important, new information about the nature of human beings.

In general, the research use of projective techniques requires objectively described knowledge of the criterion to be predicted, and the valid clinical use of the projective tests requires relevant clinical experience.

Concurrent vs. predictive validity. In determining criterion-related validity, one needs to be concerned with another distinction: concurrent vs. predictive validity. Concurrent validity refers to examining the relationships to a criterion at a single moment in time. Predictive validity refers to checking whether the test predicts differences at a future time. One may accept concurrent validity as being all that one can obtain with reasonable effort, but there is always the possibility that concurrent validity may not be predictive validity.

For example, amount of overt homosexual experience will undoubtedly differentiate incarcerated criminals from individuals of the same age, sex, education, IQ, and social class, who have no criminal records. But there is no evidence that this variable among non-incarcerated individuals would predict who will commit crimes in the future (inasmuch as homosexual activity is the consequence of being in prison without women as a result of committing a crime) . Similar, though unfortunately less obvious, problems continuously arise in research.

Construct validity

The third type of validity mentioned in the APA standards is construct validity. This is postulated as appropriate when the examiner has a theory that the test measures some trait or attribute, but there is no single alternative criterion which measures that trait or attribute. Here sets of correlations with other variables that should correlate with the postulated trait, and differences in behavior in experimental settings which should occur for people differing in this trait are used to investigate the adequacy of the formulation. Appropriately, the APA manual (p. 15) stresses that a combination of logical and experimental investigation is involved, and that one should bring to bear all available evidence in trying to establish construct validity. Obviously relevent, but not mentioned by the APA manual, is clinical observation.

Clinical vs. research validity

Clinical and research validity may also be differentiated. An instrument is usually valid for research purposes if it measures some one or few traits consistently. It is possible for the test to include a great deal of random error (that is, random with respect to the variables under consideration in the experiment) and still be useful, if there are large enough numbers of subjects. Clinical validity, on the other hand, usually involves a very special prediction, often very precise, but frequently not exactly reproducible. Usually the measuring instrument is a test plus a clinician. It is important to make this distinction because some of the considerations which go into evaluating the validity of an instrument are different for the two uses (as well as many consideration which are similar) .

An example which may illustrate this distinction is that of a patient who came to see me for "vocational counseling." He prided himself on the "sweet reasonableness" of his apparently untroubled marriage. Projective techniques, however, indicated that there were serious problems. His TAT had a number of stories in which the hero seriously contemplated or attempted suicide. In each such story, the suicide or suicidal impulse was precipitated by loss of a love object. In the stories in which the hero didn't commit suicide (the majority of them) it was because it would be unfair to his or her child or children and/or that "no one would care anyhow." The heroes who committed suicide were all childless.

After obtaining this TAT, I asked the patient whether he had ever considered killing himself. He said no, that his only problem was his inability to stick to one career, or to finish graduate school.

Approximately one month after the patient had begun therapy, his wife informed him that she was leaving him. He went downstairs to the kitchen, felt depressed, decided to kill himself, then went to his child's room, decided it would not be fair to the child, and anyway "no one would care." He then kept his appointment the next day and recounted the events. How do you research prediction of this complex sequence of thought? It can be done, but not easily.

Clinical validity vs. clinical "fudging"

The projective test is often at its most impressive in its clinical uses. In the hands of a skilled clinician it becomes a powerful and sensitive tool providing accurate description of important traits. However, this is not necessarily typical. All too often the aim of the clinician is to never say anything which can be disproved. The protocol is often filled with material so vague that one could not tell whether it fit any given individual or not, or with material which from theory thought to be universal ("There is evidence of an Oedipus complex"). Such reports are less than worthless.

An impressive study of the possibility of "fudging" was carried out by Sundberg (1955). He composed two all-purpose personality descriptions, and found that subjects, and relatives and/or friends of subjects were as likely to accept the all-purpose description as they were to choose the actual description written from an MMPI. While this research did not involve a projective test, the principle is the same.

ON THE NATURE OF CLINICAL UNDERSTANDING

In view of the frequently global nature of personality descriptions from projective techniques, one type of experimental methodology that seems appealing is the Q-sort or Checklist. The diagnostician is asked in the Q-sort to sort a variety of items in terms of how clearly they describe the individual tested or to sort the items in the way the subject would sort the items in describing himself. The items are arranged in piles which approximate a normal distribution and may be correlated with the way the same items are sorted by the subject or by an expert judge on the basis of other information. Similarly, the projective tester may be asked to fill in an inventory or Checklist as the subject would, and this is compared with what the subject actually fills in the questionnaire. Research using such techniques is often disappointing. One reason for this is the critical nature of the choice of the particular items or statements used. The items chosen may not be of interest to the clinician, and what may be of interest to the clinician may not appear on the Q-sort. The aspects of personality which may be conceptualized are literally infinite; what a particular clinician means by "understanding" a particular patient is not a random selection of all possible facets of personality.

Typically, clinical data consists of a vast amount of information with literally infinite facets which could be examined, from which the clinician extracts what is most pertinent to him for some purpose. This is a model difficult to encompass in traditional psychometrics.

Thus, a Q-sort or Checklist is useful as a measure of validity only if the items are those of real interest to the projective tester and reflect aspects of personality about which he is used to making inferences.

The Use of the Clinical Projective Tester as Research Instrument

One can use, and many people have used, the clinical projective test as interpreted by an expert clinician as a research tool. This makes good sense as a procedure, but does cause malaise in some of the rigorous-minded. One desideratum of experimental procedure in such research is that the interpretations be made "blindly," that is, without knowing as to which group the subjects belong. There have been attempts to validate the uses of clinically interpreted projective techniques in research. Thus, Kardiner and Ovesey (1951) examined each subject with 25 to 100 psychoanalytic interviews and also administered to each subject a Rorschach and a TAT. The three sources of data were analyzed independently. The results were strikingly congruent. Of course, this may not satisfy the reader who wants every statement phrased as a numerical index. Moreover, only over-all conclusions are stated in the book, and one may want case-by-case correspondence in order to be convinced. Perhaps more useful for the skeptical are the non-numerical data presented by Gladwin and Sarason (1953). Examining their data is a particularly valuable experience for the reader who has never had the chance to observe in a clinical setting a close congruence between clinical interpretations of projective tests and other data.

Gladwin and Sarason have published a series of Rorschach and TAT interpretations by a psychologist, arrived at blindly from projective protocols obtained by an anthropologist from 23 people—12 men and 11 women—on the island of Truk. The correspondence between the individual personality descriptions from the Rorschach and TAT alone and those made by the anthropologist on the basis of first-hand observation is impressive. While this correspondence is not reduced to a set of statistical coefficients, it is obvious that there is a striking one-to-one correspondence and that the personality descriptions could not be paired differently without destroying that correspondence.

For many research purposes it is useful to make a distinction between what may be termed intrinsic and extrinsic validity of the projective test. Intrinsic validity refers to experimental situations where the theory being tested in itself predicts the specific response on the projective test. Extrinsic validity refers to experimental situations where the projective response is not predicted by the theory being tested, but by a special theory of the projective test, like the color-affect hypothesis on the Rorschach, or by some correlational study, such as McClelland's definition of the need for achievement.

It is my general feeling that intrinsic validities are apt to be more directly scientifically useful than extrinsic validity studies, particularly when there are negative findings. In the case of extrinsic validity, given negative findings one is never sure whether the theory being tested or the special theory of the test is inadequate. Nonetheless, many extrinsic studies have been very valuable, for instance, the Lacey, Bateman, and Van Lehn study (1952) cited above.

Examples of correlationally determined external validity are McClelland's (1953) work on the need for achievement or Schwartz's (1955, 1956) work on castration anxiety. McClelland (1953) experimentally induced a "need for achievement" in one group and not in another, and assumed that what changed in TAT stories must be the "need for achievement." But clinical experience reveals clearly that the strongest need for achievement occurs in people for whom it is not situationally determined, who must achieve irrespective of the situational demands. In some cases, it is almost impossible to even temporarily turn them off. Such motives are not tapped by the extrinsically defined "need for achievement."

Schwartz scored TAT's of subjects before and after they viewed a film of an Australian sub-incision ceremony. The assumption was that watching the film aroused castration anxiety. Whatever increased was taken as a measure of castration anxiety, and used in further research. Interestingly, fantasies involving mutilation, castration, or appendages being cut off are reported as not increasing. This is a surprising finding whose meaning it might have been profitable to investigate, particularly since such fantasies do occasionally occur in clinical protocols (e.g., Tomkins, 1947, pp. 270-271). By contenting himself with extrinsic validity, the investigator has overlooked an interesting problem.

Examples of intrinsic validity are the Clark and Sensibar study on sexual symbolism cited above, where the theory or theories being tested predicted the projective test responses. Another example is a study, using a modified Blacky castration card, (Karon, 1964) of which parent is seen as the castrator in the fantasies of schizophrenics. The assumption that fantasies concerning a dog's tail being cut off would reveal the structure of castration fantasies is an integral part of the theory being tested. (The finding was that both parents were fantasied as castrators, but that the father-castration fantasy served as a defense against the more frightening mother-castrator fantasy.)

A more recent study (Meyer & Karon, 1967) in which the theory predicted the fantasy itself, and in which this use of intrinsic validity permitted demonstration of a theory that psychotherapists who work intensively with schizophrenics have maintained for a long time, but which has been disputed in the research literature, may be summarized as follows:

On the basis of clinical experience it seemed clear that a critical aspect of psychologically destructive mothers seemed to be the way in which they have used their children to satisfy their own needs when their needs and the needs of the children conflicted. Direct questions did not seem promising as a research technique, since mothers whose involuntary and unconscious interactions with their children were extraordinarily destructive will consciously hold enlightened child-rearing opinions and good intentions (Karon & Rosberg, 1958). It seemed logical that the TAT should provide a measure of the motivational basis for this destructiveness.

Six mothers of schizophrenic children and six mothers of normal children were administered TAT's. Each story was typed on separate sheets of paper. All stories were shuffled, and scored blindly as follows:

1. Is there an interaction between a dominant and a dependent individual with somewhat conflicting needs? If not, the story is considered Unscorable.

2. If such an interaction occurs, does the dominant person take the dependent person's needs into account? If so, the story is scored as Benign (B). If not, the story is scored as Pathogenic (P).

The protocols were then re-assembled, and for each one there was computed a Pathogenesis score: $P/(P + B)$, where P is the number of pathogenic stories and $(P + B)$ is the total number of scorable stories, that is, the number of pathogenic plus the number of benign stories.

The samples were clearly separated; mothers of normals scored from .25 to .69 with a mean of approximately .35, mothers of schizophrenics varied from .65 to .95 with a mean of .75. This was replicated with samples of 20 mothers in each group by Mitchell (1966).

SOME HINTS ON CODING FANTASIES

In the analysis of TAT protocols for research purposes, the problem of coding is a serious one. The facets of personality which are of possible importance are literally infinite, and it is impossible to devise a universal coding scheme that would be suitable and accurate for all possible purposes.

The attempt to devise widely applicable coding categories usually leads to vagueness. For example, in the category of "suicidal stories," one might lump stories in which a character commits suicide, considers suicide but doesn't commit it, stories in which the hero merely thinks of suicide, and stories which are taken to be symbolic of suicide. Lumped together as if they were equivalent might be stories in which the hero is very similar in age, sex, and life circumstances to the teller of the stories, and stories which are distant in age, sex, time, place, circumstances and special states (alcohol, hypnosis, etc.). Such gross categories are not of much use, and typically do not predict sucide. The differentiae need to be carefully considered; e.g., in my experience the most dangerous stories are those where a hero of the same age, sex, and life circumstances as the teller not only considers, but actually carries out the suicide. Stories about the suicidal thoughts predict not suicide, but suicidal thoughts. Stories in which suicide seems to be represented symbolically do not predict suicide any more than stories containing symbolic sex predicts sexual acting out. On the contrary, the symbolic impulse is one which is ego-alien, whether sexual or suicidal.

In clinical practice, one usually dispenses with categories, and a wide variety of possible conceptualizations may be rapidly considered by the clinician. In research uses, one is ordinarily concerned with a delimited concept. Here one can, and should, draw up a specific code. In my experience the optimal procedure is to actually list the specific words to be coded in a given manner. Arbitrary decisions are made once and for all. Scorer reliability is achieved easily, but with work.

Whenever clinical judgment (or indeed any non-objective judgment) is to be used in research, it is imperative to have the judgments made blindly, that is, without the scorer knowing to which sample a particular protocol belongs. It is usually best to randomly intermix protocols so as to minimize the possibility that the batch of data may become identified.

RELIABILITY: PARADIGM OR PARADOX?

A supposed lack of reliability is often pointed out as demonstrating the scientific inadequacy of projective tests. This argument derives from the inappropriate but widely embraced psychometric theory of reliability, which holds that low reliability implies low validity. But it can be readily demonstrated mathematically that no limitation on validity necessarily follows from zero inter-item correlations. This proof is given below, as well as some of its implications for projective tests.

Temporal consistency

Of course, internal consistency is not the only operational meaning of reliability. Consistency over time is the alternative empirical measure of reliability. But such repeat reliability, that is, temporal consistency, is relevant only if the characteristic being measured does not fluctuate with time. Many of the characteristics which projective techniques are intended to measure are motivational or emotional, and there is no reason to assume that these characteristics are temporally stable. On the contrary, it is clear for some motives that a temporally stable measure must be invalid. Thus, a measure of hunger, or of mood, which never fluctuated, could not possibly be measuring the appropriate variable. For most personality variables, it is an empirical question, to be answered by appropriate measuring instruments, as to what extent they are temporally stable or unstable, and what temporal patterning there may be to the changes, such as the cyclical variation one would expect with hunger. Thus, temporal stability or regularity must be investigated rather than assumed.

Temporal consistency, consequently, cannot be a criterion of the measuring instrument unless it is already known (as is rarely the case) that the characteristic being measured is itself temporally stable.

Internal consistency

This is not a new argument, and its implications are usually that repeat reliability is conservative (too low) as a result of changes in the trait measured, and that internal consistency is a more accurate index of reliability. Moreover, internal consistency is generally easier to obtain, and hence is frequently the only measure of reliability reported. It is often assumed that internal consistency must be higher than temporal consistency, a conclusion which is as false as the assumption that internal consistency limits validity. One need only substitute the score on a later administration of the test in place of the criterion measure in the mathematical argument below, and it immediately follows that there is no necessary relationship between these two types of reliability.

At this point, it is worthwhile to present the simple mathematical argument which rigorously demonstrates that low internal consistency does not limit validity. It is only necessary to define a test with the lowest possible internal consistency, that is, zero, and investigate what validity is possible. Classical reliability theory would hold that the maximum validity attainable in such a case is also zero. (The non-mathematical reader may prefer to skip at this point to the "Implications.")

Mathematical argument

To investigate the consequence of zero internal consistency, define a score S_i, the score of individual i, as a function of a set of elements (for example, the sum of his scores on a set of items) :

$$S_i = f(a_{1i}, a_{2i}, \ldots, a_{ji}, \ldots, a_{ni}) \tag{1}$$

where f is some function, for example, the sum; and a_{ji} is a component element, for example, the score of individual i on item j.

Now add the condition of zero inter-item reliability, that is, that each item has no correlation with any other item:

$$r_{a_j a_k} = 0, \text{ for all } j \neq k \tag{2}$$

where $r_{a_j a_k}$ is the correlation between item j and item k.

Finally, define a criterion value C_i for each individual i. In order to explore what is possible, one may arbitrarily define a criterion value, C_i, which is itself a function of a set of component elements, as follows:

$$C_i = g(A_{1i}, A_{2i}, \ldots, A_{Ji}, \ldots, A_{mi}) \tag{3}$$

where g is some function, and A_{Ji} is an element of the criterion.

At this point the maximum possible value of the validity coefficient r_{sc}, that is, the maximum possible correlation between S and C, given zero inter-item correlation, may be readily determined. If f (x) should happen to be the same function as g (x), and if each a_{ji} should happen to correspond exactly to a corresponding A_{Ji}, then the correlation r_{sc} will equal unity. Indeed, S and C will be identical. Stated as equations,

$$\text{If } f(x) = g(x) \tag{4}$$

$$a_{ji} = A_{Ji}, \text{ for all values of } j \text{ and } J \tag{5}$$

$$n = m \tag{6}$$

$$\text{then } S_i = C_i \tag{7}$$

$$\text{and, of course, } r_{sc} = 1 \tag{8}$$

Implications

Obviously, zero inter-item reliability implies no upper limit to validity, without further assumptions. Where then did the idea originate that reliability limits validity? From classical test theory (e.g., Gulliksen, 1950, pp. 4-38), which divides the variance of test scores into two components, true score and error, and defines error as being uncorrelated with anything. If that assumption were true, then reliability would indeed limit validity. That human performances contain such error, uncorrelated with anything, is uncongenial to much of personality theory (e.g., Freud, 1949), but it has useful implications. In particular, many equations in test theory become much simpler (e.g., the Kuder-Richardson, Spearman-Brown, and many other formulas). In many domains, particularly intelligence testing, these equations have proved useful. Even the concept that reliability limits validity has proved useful; test constructors, despite imperfect criteria, have in many instances been able to raise all validity coefficients by increasing reliability, just as predicted by classical test theory.

Why then abandon an assumption, which, if not absolutely accurate, is sufficiently so for all practical purposes? Even if, in the abstract, validities in excess of reliability are mathematically possible, are they ever, in fact possible in psychology? Obviously, they are, or this section would never have been written.

It may be instructive to take an example from physics. A "clinical" physicist decides he is interested in one characteristic of a number of objects. He terms this characteristic V. After looking at these objects, he decides that a characteristic A has something to do with V and would make a good item. He also decides that two other characteristics, B and C, have something to do with V. He then measures A, B, and C on a number of objects. He asks the advice of one psychometrician who says to him, "What is the reliability of your test?" The physicist then computes the correlations between each of his items and finds that

$$r_{AB} = 0, r_{BC} = 0, \text{ and } r_{AC} = 0. \tag{9}$$

He is then advised that he has a terrible test, which he ought to abandon.

But our "clinical" physicist is unhappy with such advice. It conflicts with his experience, so he goes to another psychometrician. This fellow says, "The devil with reliability. Run your validity, and then we'll talk." The physicist does this and finds that the correlation between V and the sum of A, B, and C is actually extraordinarily large. When the new psychometrician points out that many variables in psychology have simpler relationships when transformed to logs, the physicist tries transforming all his variables to logarithms, and then finds the correlation is now 1.00 between log V and the sum of log A, log B, and log C, since V was the amount of water that could be stored in rectangular containers, and variables A, B, and C were the length, width, and height of the containers.[1]

But what does this physical example have to do with psychology? In the area of personality, particularly projective tests, one regularly encounters similar phenomena. The correlation between a variable measured on one card, let us say, of a TAT, is apt to be low when compared with the same variable measured on another card.

What accounts for the low correlations between cards on the TAT is this: Personality characteristics are, for the most part, abstractions for some purpose, to a large extent arbitrarily defined (Karon, 1958, pp.

[1] One psychologist, on reading a draft of his chapter, argued that volume is a derived measurement, and hence "not the kind of measurement we need in psychology," while length, width, and height are "fundamental" measurements. Weight, however, is a fundamental measurement and the same relationship holds between weight and length, width, and height, inasmuch as weight is simply volume multiplied by a constant for the particular substance.

55-59). Thus, for example, it is for many purposes useful to speak of "aggression," yet it is clear that for different people verbal aggression, physical aggression, and thought aggression are handled similarly, inversely, or independently; for different individuals aggression toward superiors and inferiors, toward family and toward strangers, etc., may or may not be handled similarly.

As previously mentioned, much of the confusion about the validity studies of the Rosenzweig Picture Frustration Study may be readily resolved when one realizes that it only directly measures the handling of verbal aggression, "What does he say?" and that the relationship between the handling of verbal aggression and the handling of thought aggression and of physical aggression is not the same in all people. Thought aggression is, on the whole, more closely related to verbal aggression than it is to physical aggression.

It is clear that for some purposes it is essential to distinguish the subtypes of aggression. It is also clear that psychoanalysis would never have learned what it has about displacement and other techniques of handling aggression if it were necessary to exactly specify the subtype every time one talked about aggression. Moreover, the distinctions that could be made are limited only by human ingenuity. Thus, what distinctions one makes depend on one's purpose.

Whatever the final delimitation of the concept to be used, it will almost always include uncorrelated components. What is measured on a particular card, say, on the TAT, is the reaction to a particular situation. Whether this is positively related, negatively related, or independent of another situation is a matter that usually differs from person to person.[2] There is thus no reason to assume that the components of meaningful personality constructs are necessarily positively correlated with each other, or that the components of tests that measure these constructs are necessarily correlated with each other. Indeed, valid measures of constructs which include uncorrelated components (as do most personality variables) will tend to derive from tests which similarly include uncorrelated items.[3]

[2] There are, in addition, systematic, if peculiar, effects: For example, there is a see-saw effect whereby, if a variable is high on one card, it will be low on the next, and high on the third, etc. (One possible way of explaining this is by taking the "need" model seriously, whereby a fantasy partially satisfies the "need," hence, it is lower on the next card. Not having been expressed, it now has recurred for the following card, etc. The important point is that appropriate models for these kinds of instruments must be evolved.)

[3] Such situations are by no means exclusively limited to projective tests. Thus, if one administers tests of competence in statistics to graduate students in psychology, one almost invariably finds that items having to do with chi-square tend to have little or no correlation with items having to do with t-tests or analysis of variance. It is obvious that eliminating chi-square from the test would increase the reliability and decrease the validity and usefulness of the test.

This conclusion is restated more rigorously by using equation
(3):

$$C_i = g \ (A_{1i}, A_{2i}, \ldots, A_{Ji}, \ldots, A_{mi} \tag{3}$$

where C_i is the value of individual i on the criterion C, which can now be defined as that particular specified characteristic which is to be measured. The equation simply states that the criterion C_i is some function g of a set of components A_J. For most personality variables it is not now known what the components A_J really are, nor, obviously, is it likely that there will be measures which correspond to all of these elements A_J. But insofar as one has measures of some element a_j (in this case, responses to a particular card) which correspond to some element or elements A_J, there will be some correlation between S_i and C_i. If one has additional elements a_j corresponding to more of the elements A_J of the criterion, the correlation will improve.

Conclusion about reliability and validity

In short, what is implied by this whole discussion is that for projective tests, validity coefficients are important and that reliability is largely an irrelevant consideration.

A Measure of Reliability for Those Who Insist on It

But what can one advise the student or colleague in this era when "reliability" is a good word, and everyone is made "sophisticated" by his elementary (or advanced) texts into suspicion of anyone not reporting "reliability"? It is really very simple. He should enter mental test theory at the point most advantageous to him.

If classical mental test theory were applicable, then no "validity" coefficient could exceed the square root of the reliability. ("Validity" coefficient as used in this sentence means simply a correlation coefficient between the test and any other independent measure of any variable, and not the more specific meaning of validity as correlation with the particular, specified characteristic that the test is supposed to measure.)

This may be equivalently stated as: the reliability must be greater than the square of any "validity" coefficient. There is no way for this relationship not to hold, if the assumptions of classical test theory apply. This procedure for determining a lower bound to reliability is a well-established part of classical mental test theory (Gulliksen, 1950, pp. 23-28).

Therefore, students who work with projective tests may take the highest validity coefficient (the highest correlation of their test score with anything), square it, and report this estimate of a lower bound to the reliability, which indeed it is. That this lower bound to the reliability, so estimated, is frequently higher than the internal consistency directly measured, is simply evidence of the fact that mental test theory, with its assumption of random error uncorrelated with anything, does not apply to their domain. If the theory were not Procrustean, such discrepancies would be impossible.[4]

Preferable, however, is the more straightforward recommendation that the student simply report the validity coefficients, and let these coefficients speak for themselves.

A useful consideration from classical test theory

One aspect of classical test theory which is useful and often ignored is the clear-cut statement of the consequences of homogeneity and heterogeneity of variance on validity; that is, how large are the differences to be predicted. According to classical test theory (Gulliksen, 1950), the more varied the population, the greater will be any correlation coefficient (reliability or validity). Although the assumption of pure random error is not justified, this particular conclusion does hold, and one can regularly obtain greater or lesser correlation coefficients by changing the variance of the population. It is thus important to keep an eye on the spread of the population measured in comparing studies.

This is true not only in research uses, but also in clinical settings. Thus, in some settings the projective testers regularly have difficulty in clearly assessing most patients. But, only patients difficult to assess are referred to the psychologist. The projective tests are generally clearer than other sources of information, but only very puzzling patients are ever referred for psychologicals. This is not an unreasonable clinical procedure, but it leads to unduly pessimistic feelings in such settings about the certainty of making inferences from the projective tests.

Some useful statistical techniques

Appropriate statistical methodology for assessing the validity of projective techniques is not always obvious: it is my intention to present some useful possibilities which are not as widely known as perhaps they might be. Included here will be a discussion of the matching test, Tau', the use of chi-square for contingency tables with expected values less than 5, the product-moment correlation coefficient as the most efficient completely non-parametric test of association, and some comments about the over-restrictiveness of Stevens' injunctions about the four types of scales and the statistics appropriate thereto. The aim of this discussion will be to free the researcher by making him aware of possibilities for statistical analysis, since the data from projective tests do not always come in such fashion as to make quantification easy.

---

[4] Of course, this is not to advocate capitalizing on chance by scanning 100 validity coefficients and choosing the largest. But, in the ordinary course of research, one has one, two, or three validity coefficients, and capitalizing on chance is not a problem.

The matching test. The obvious way to examine global predictions is by matching procedure. Thus, individuals (or personality descriptions of individuals) are matched with the projective protocols (or personality descriptions written from the projective protocols). Similarly, the individuals may be grouped into categories (e.g., diagnoses, prognoses, personality types, etc.) and again the problem is matching them, that is, categorizing them in the same way. Significance tests are described by Gilbert (1956).

Where individual descriptions are to be matched (i.e., each category consists of one individual), the expected or average number of correct matches by chance will be one, no matter how large the sample size. (The probability of any one individual's being correctly matched by chance is $1/n$. Thus, as the sample size increases, the probability of any individual's being correctly matched by chance decreases proportionally.) Significance levels are very simple to determine as follows:

Significance Levels for Matching Experiments (Gilbert, 1956)

Sample Size	3 Matches	4 Matches	5 Matches
4	cannot occur	.04	
5	.09	cannot occur	.008
6	.08	.02	.001
More than 6	.08	.02	.004

For experiments where the individuals are divided into categories (diagnoses, prognoses, personality types, etc.), if the number of individuals in each category is the same, the determination of significance levels is equally simple. If the projective tester is told the categories and the fact that the number of cases is the same in each category, the expected (or average) number of correct matches by chance is equal to the number of individuals in one category. If we call this number m, and number of categories c, then

$$n = cm = \text{total number of cases}$$

$$\sigma^2 = \frac{m\ (n-m)}{n-1} \tag{10}$$

where σ^2 is the variance of the number of matches by chance.

The significance level may be readily approximated by:

$$Z = \frac{M - m - .5}{\sigma} \tag{11}$$

where M is the number of correct matches, and $-.5$ is a correction for continuity which should be used except when there are only two categories, in which case the correction for continuity is -1.

Z is approximately normally distributed, and hence 1.64 is the .05 level, and 2.33 the .01 level of significance. (These are one-sided probabilities since almost always one is concerned only with the possibility that there are more correct matches than would occur by chance.)

If the projective tester is not told that the number of cases in each category is equal, in which case he will not place the same number of individuals in each category, the research design is less sensitive. However, formula (11) still applies; the expected number of matches by chance is still m, the number of cases in each category for the classification where this number is equal, but the variance is slightly different:

$$\sigma^2 = \frac{m\ (n^2 - \sum m_i^2)}{n\ (n - 1)} \tag{12}$$

where m is the number of cases in each category for the classification where they are equal; n_i is the number of cases in category i of the classification where they are unequal; and n is the total sample size, i.e.,

$$n = cm = \sum n_i \tag{13}$$

If the number of cases in each category are unequal, but the rater is informed, the equation becomes slightly more complicated:

$$m = \frac{1}{n} \sum n_i^2 \tag{14}$$

where m is the expected number of matches by chance; n_i is the number of cases in category i, and n is the total number of cases. The variance is given by:

$$\sigma^2 = \frac{1}{n^2\ (n-1)} \left[(\sum n_i^2)^2 - 2n \sum n_i^3 + n^2 \sum n_i^2 \right] \tag{15}$$

Gilbert gives procedures for all possible numbers of categories and numbers of cases in each category in each classification. He points out that the most sensitive test is provided by informing the rater as to the number of cases in each category.

Chi-square. The matching tests described above require the same categories for both classifications and ask only how many "matches" occurred; more general is the use of chi-square with categorical data, which can ask whether there is any non-random relationship between two sets of categories, which need not be the same. The fact that almost any kind of data can be cast into a set of categories has made chi-square a trusted tool of the projective tester. Most clinicians, however, still feel that the old injunction that one must have an expected values of at least 5 in every cell of the contingency table is still valid.

For the 2 x 2 table it is well known that the most exact test is Fisher's Exact Test, which makes no such restriction. But Cochran has shown that chi-square (with Yates correction for continuity) may be used with expected values of less than 5 in one cell of a four-fold table, if the total sample size is at least 40.

More important, Cochran (1952, 1954) has shown that chi-square may be appropriately used for contingency tables with more than one degree of freedom with expected values as low as 1. This is an experimental situation for which simple alternative analyses were not readily available. Previously, the ordinary recommendations were to combine rows or columns so as to bring the minimum expected value for any cell up to 5. But this often throws away too much information. Craig (1953) has provided appropriate formulas for combining individual cells which are adjacent to each other; this was a considerable improvement, but is no longer necessary for most experimental situations.

As Cochran points out, if less than one-fifth of the cells have expected values less than 5, but equal to at least one, one can simply compute chi-square in the ordinary manner.

If more than one-fifth of the cells have expected values below five, but equal to at least one, one only needs to correct for continuity. The procedure with more than one degree of freedom is as follows:

1. Compute chi-square as usual.

2. Keeping the marginal totals constant, change one observation so as to determine that value of chi-square which could have occured which is smaller, but as close as possible to the actual chi-square.

3. The average of these is the value of chi-square to be used in determining the significance level, since it has been appropriately corrected for continuity.

In most cases the correction will be small.

If all cells have expected values less than 5, the minimum expected value per cell should be 2, and one should correct for continuity as above.

If there are more than 30 degrees of freedom, and if most or all the cells have expectations less than 5, Cochran recommends using a normal approximation to the distribution of chi-square with a theoretical mean and variance computed using the formulas given by Haldane (1939).

Before we leave the topic of chi-square: Anyone familiare with the psychological research literature cannot help but repeat the elementary, but still widely violated, assumption that each observation in the frequency counts in each cell in a contingency table from which chi-square is to be computed must be experimentally independent. To cite examples which have appeared in the literature, the number of individuals (number of people) who give a particular response on the Rorschach or who report a given type of dream is the appropriate kind of frequency for the cells of a contingency table from which chi-square is to be computed.

Yet studies exist where the entries represent the frequency of a given type of response (W, S, etc.) in a group of subjects, or the frequency of a given type of dream (e.g., dreams where male figures predominate, etc.)

in a group of subjects. The number of such Rorschach responses or dreams may consist of several from one subject and one from another subject.

The psychological meaning of the statistical requirement of independence is clear upon reflection: an individual who has a particular kind of dream, gives a particular Rorschach response, or indeed any kind of response, for that matter, is more likely to give similar responses than is someone else; that is, additional responses from the same individual are apt to be more alike than responses obtained from separate subjects. To take an extreme example, suppose two groups of ten subjects are compared, and it is found that there are ten M responses in one group and none in the other. If those ten responses all came from the same subject, the finding should not lead to any conclusion about the difference between the populations from which the samples came, that is, the finding is not statistically significant when appropriately analyzed. On the other hand, if those ten M consist of one M per subject in one sample while there were none in the other sample, this is clearly statistically significant, and one would be willing to draw some inferences about such a finding.

If chi-square cannot be used to analyze such data, what should one do? Use the number of such responses per person as a score. The scores may then be analyzed by t-tests, analysis of variance, Kolmogorov-Smirnoff, correlation coefficients, or any other significance tests which the researcher is accustomed to using. An alternative appropriate procedure is to sample one response per subject, if one insists on using chi-square.

Tau'. Sometimes one has two sets of categories, but the categories are ordered. For example, one might wish to correlate outcome of psychotherapy, categorized as "Improved, No change, Got worse," with a set of prognostic categories such as "Extremely likely to benefit, Likely to benefit, Not likely to benefit, Likely to deteriorate." One gets a more sensitive test of significance of the relationship than chi-square if one takes the ordering into account. This can be accomplished by testing the significance using Kendall's Tau coefficient of rank correlation (Kendall, 1948). The test of significance does not require modification. For most such situations, however, Tau as a descriptive correlation coefficient will not have +1 or −1 as attainable upper or lower limits. A modified Tau coefficient, Tau', has been described which will always have +1 as an upper limit for as perfect association as the experiment will permit, and 0 as its expected value by chance, and which is applicable to describing the association between any two sets of ordered categories no matter how disparate (Karon & Alexander, 1958).

The product-moment correlation coefficient. For data which can be cast in the form of two sets of measurements, the product-moment correlation coefficient is the most frequently used measure of association. Recently, there have been some qualms on the part of researchers on the basis that the bi-variate normality assumption is dubious. But Pitman (1937) has shown how the product-moment correlation coefficient may be used as an absolutely non-parametric test of association. He used the randomization criterion in place of the usual assumption of sampling from a bi-variate normal population; that is, he assumed that the numbers which occurred in the experiment are fixed, but considers all possible ways of pairing them. For any set of pairings one could compute a product-moment correlation coefficient. Thus, one generates a population of possible values of the correlation coefficient. The most extreme values of this population of correlation coefficients may then be taken as significant. The procedure is obviously non-parametric, but it is laborious. However, Pitman has also shown that, as the sample size increases, the distribution of the correlation coefficients approximates that generated by normal curve theory, and, further, that ten cases is a sufficiently large sample with which to use this approximation for all practical purposes. Hence one may safely use the conventional tables of significance for the product-moment correlation coefficient as the most efficient non-parametric test of association for samples of 10 or greater.

Scales of Measurement

Finally, let us consider the overly rigid description of which statistics are appropriate for various kinds of measurements. Projective testers are apt to be hampered by these restrictions, since it may not be clear whether numbers derived from those tests represent ordinal, interval, or ratio scales. As long as the formulations of Stevens (1951), Siegel (1950), etc., are widely accepted, appropriate and sensitive procedures for analyzing data may be ignored.

As any graduate students knows, Stevens defined four types of scales —nominal, ordinal, interval, and ratio—and described the types of mathematical operations which were legitimate for each. Thus, according to this view, nothing but counting the number of cases at each value is appropriate for a nominal scale; only greater-than or less-than relations are appropriate on ordinal scales, but not addition or subtraction; addition or subtraction may be performed on interval scales, but not multiplication or division.

Siegel (1950) in his book on non-parametric statistics confuses the original meaning of "non-parametric," that is, "not assuming a normal distribution" with assumptions about the nature of the scale of measurement. As Lubin (1963) has pointed out, nothing in the development of significance tests assumes anything about the scale of measurement. Non-parametric statistics merely refer to statistics without a normality assumption.

Numbers do not know where they came from. Lord (1953) has described a situation where it was appropriate to test the significance of the mean of a set of football numbers, an obviously nominal scale. We ordinarily have no hesitation in computing means and variances and doing *t*-tests on interval scales, like temperature, even thought this involves multiplication and division, which are supposed to be illegitimate without a fixed meaningful zero point. But we rationalize this on the basis that it doesn't make any difference in the outcome, that the multiplication and division are intermediate steps. So, too, the calculation of means, variances, *t*-tests, etc., on an ordinal scale is perfectly justified to test if two samples are from the same population or a different one. The only consideration is the conclusion we draw after the statistical tests are done; i.e., on a nominal scale, the conclusion is "different from"; on an ordinal scale "greater or lesser than"; on an interval scale "greater by so many units"; on a ratio scale "so many times as great."

The case of greatest interest will be the ordinal scale. As long as one can make reasonable guesses as to the sampling distribution (and the powerful conventional tests such as *t*-test and analysis of variance are fairly robust, i.e., relatively insensitive to departures from a normal distribution), one may readily use any ordinary computation. That one's final conclusion must be stated simply as "A is greater than B" is usually no hindrance, since in most psychological experiments that is as precise a conclusion as the experimenter wishes to reach in any event. For a fuller discussion the reader is referred to Lubin (1963).

CONCLUSION

After surveying a number of disparate issues, and providing some hopefully helpful methodological suggestions, what can we say about the future?

First, projective techniques will continue to be used clinically, for there now exists no adequate substitute for them. Secondly, they have yet to play their full role in research. Partly this is due to the behavioristic emphasis in much of American psychology for so long. For a behaviorist there are no questions about human beings for which a projective technique is an appropriate investigative tool: the problems are solved by defining them as non-existent. As more clinically experienced psychologists get more involved in basic research, and insofar as the explanation of thought processes, fantasies, impulses, affects, and defenses, conscious and unconscious, become more regularly and legitimately the prime concern of psychology, the projective techniques must play a greater role in basic research. This, I believe, is the inevitable road ahead.

REFERENCES

Beck, S. J. *The Six Schizophrenias*. New York: American Orthopsychiatric Assn., 1954.

Clark, R. A., & Sensibar, Minda Rae. The relationship between symbolic and manifest projections of sexuality with some incidental correlates. *J. abnorm. soc. Psychol.*, 1955, *50*, 327-334.

Cochran, W. G. Some methods for strengthening the common x^2 tests. *Biometrics*, 1954, *10*, 417-451.

Cochran, W. G. The x^2 test of goodness of fit. *Ann. math. Statist.*, 1952, *23*, 315-345.

Craig, C. C. Combination of neighboring cells in contingency tables. *J. Amer. statist. Assn.*, 1953, *48*, 104-112.

Diven, K. Certain determinants in the conditioning of anxiety reactions. *J. Psychol.* 1937, 291-308.

Ferenczi, S. The ontogenesis of symbols. *Sex in Psychoanalysis: Selected Papers*, Vol. 1. New York: Basic Books, 1950. Pp. 276-281.

French, J. W., Michael, W. B., et al. *Standards for Educational and Psychological Tests and Manuals*. Washington: American Psychological Assn., 1966.

Freud, S. *The Interpretation of Dreams*. New York: Macmillan, 1950.

Freud, S. *The Psychopathology of Everyday Life*. London: Benn, 1949.

Fromm, E. *The Forgotten Language*. New York: Reinhart, 1951.

Gilbert, E. J. The matching problem. *Psychometrika*, 1956, *21*, 252-267.

Gladwin, T., & Sarason, S. B. Truk: Man in Paradise. (Viking Fund Publications in Anthropology, 20) . New York: Wenner-Gren, 1953.

Gulliksen, H. *The Theory of Mental Tests*. New York: Wiley, 1950.

Haggard, E. A. Some conditions determining adjustment during and readjustment following experimentally induced stress. In Tomkins, S. S. (Ed.) . *Contemporary Psychopathology*. Cambridge: Harvard University Press, 1947. Pp. 529-544.

Haldane, J. B. S. The mean and variance of x^2 when used as a test of homogeneity when expectations are small. *Biometrika*, 1939, *31*, 346-355.

Hall, C. S. *The Meaning of Dreams*. New York: Harper, 1953.

Jung, C. G. *Collected Papers on Analytical Psychology*. London: Balliere, Tindall & Cox, 1920.

Kardiner, A., & Ovesey, L. *The Mark of Oppression*. New York: Norton, 1951.

Karon, B. P., & Rosberg, J. Study of the mother-child relationship in a case of paranoid schizophrenia. *Amer. J. Psychother.*, 1958, *12*, 522-533.

Karon, B. P. *The Negro Personality*: *A Rigorous Investigation of the Effects of Culture*. New York: Springer, 1958.

Karon, B. P. An experimental investigation of parental castration fantasies in schizophrenia. *Brit. J. Psychiat. (J. ment. Sci.)* , 1964, *110*, 67-73.

Karon, B. P., & Alexander, I. E. A modification of Kendall's Tau for measuring association in contingency tables. *Psychometrika*, 1958, *23*, 379-381.

Kendall, M. G. *Rank Correlation Methods*. London: Griffin, 1948.

Lacey, J. I., Bateman, Dorothy E., & Van Lehn, Ruth. Autonomic response specificity and Rorschach color responses. *Psychosom. Med.*, 1952, *14*, 256-260.

Lacey, J. I., Smith, R. L., & Green, A. Use of conditioned autonomic responses in the study of anxiety. In Reed, C. F., Alexander, I. E., & Tomkins, S. S. (Eds.) . *Psychopathology*. New York: Wiley, 1964. Pp. 275-288.

Lord, F. M. On the statistical treatment of football numbers. *Amer. Psychol.*, 1953, *8*, 750-751.

Lubin, A. Statistics. *Ann. Rev. Psychol.*, Vol. XIV. Palo Alto: Annual Reviews, Inc., 1963. Pp. 345-370.

McClelland, D. C., Atkinson, J. W., Clark, R. A., & Lowell, E. L. *The Achievement Motive*. New York: Appleton-Century-Croft, 1953.

Meyer, R., & Karon, B. P. A study of the schizophrenogenic mother hypothesis by means of the TAT. *Psychiatry*, 1967, *30*, 173-179.

Mitchell, K. E. An elaboration of a study of the schizophrenogenic mother concept by means of the Thematic Apperception Test. *J. abn. Psychol.* (in press) .

Pitman, E. J. G. Significance tests which may be applied to samples from any population. II. The correlation coefficient test. *Suppl. J. roy. statist. Soc.*, 1937, *4*, 225-233.

Reyher, J. Hypnosis in research on psychopathology. In Gordon, J. (Ed.) . *Handbook of Clinical and Experimental Hypnosis*. New York: Macmillan, 1967. Pp. 110-147.

Schwartz, B. J. The measurement of castration anxiety and anxiety over loss of love. *J. Pers.*, 1955, *24*, 204-219.

Schwartz, B. J. An empirical test of two Freudian hypotheses concerning castration anxiety. *J. Pers.*, 1956, *24*, 318-327.

Siegel, S. *Nonparametric Statistics for the Behavioral Sciences*. New York: McGraw-Hill, 1950.

Stevens, S. S. Mathematics, measurement, and psychophysics. In S. S. Stevens (Ed.) . *Handbook of Experimental Psychology*. New York: Wiley, 1951. Pp. 1-49.

Sundberg, N. P. The acceptability of "fake" versus "bona fide" personality test interpretations. *J. abnorm. soc. Psychol.*, 1955, *50*, 145-146.

Tomkins, S. S. *The Thematic Apperception Test*. New York: Grune and Stratton, 1947.

Tomkins, S. S. *Affect, Imagery and Consciousness*. New York: Springer, 1963.

ASSOCIATION
TECHNIQUES
(Inkblots)

The two chapters in this section deal with inkblot association methods—one old, one relatively new. Word association techniques should also appear in this section of the book, but for the sake of brevity and convenience, a discussion of this promising method may be found in Part IV (Chapter 9).

Rorschach's ten standard inkblots are probably the best known projective stimuli. There are five black inkblots (including shading), two black-and-red, and the remaining three, multicolored. The instructions direct the subject to tell the examiner what he sees in each card: "Be sure to tell the examiner everything that you see on the card as you look at it." Although the stimulus material is standard and fixed, the subject's response is free. He may look at the card as long as he wishes, give as many responses as he cares to, and react as quickly or slowly as he may be inclined to do. The procedure is divided in two parts: 1) The *free association* period during which the subject gives the responses and the examiner is the passive listener and recorder; and 2) the *inquiry* period, during which the examiner investigates the nature of each response.

Essentially, three questions need to be answered concerning each response: "What?" "Where?" and "Why?" The first question, concerning the *content,* is usually answered during the association period. The subject states what he sees—a human (H), an animal (A), a landscape (Ls), etc. Answers to the other two questions that do not refer to content, but to the perceptual mode of the subject, must be obtained during the inquiry.

The answer to the question "Where?" refers to *location.* There are three main possibilities, according to the Rorschach system. First, the subject may use the whole blot (W) as his stimulus; second, he may use a common, usually large detail (D) which is part of the total blot;

and third, he may point to a tiny and rarely used detail (Dd) as representing the content with which he responded. A special notation is also used when the entire response, or part of it, is located in the white space of the card (S).

Most complicated is the inquiry with respect to the third question ("Why?")—the determinant of the response. It involves a certain amount of reflection and introspection on the part of the subject. The most common determinant of inkblot responses is form (F). The subject indicates, in these instances, that the formal characteristics of the whole, or part of the blot, led him to the content with which he responded. Form may be good (F+), i.e., corresponding well to the content, or may be poor (F−), i.e., deviant, far-fetched, with little correspondence to the object seen. Other major determinants are movement (M), color (C), and shading. Form may be combined with the latter two determinants. For instance, color may be primary and form secondary in the determination of the response (CF), or vice versa (FC). The location, determinant, and content, therefore, combine in the characterization of each response. A final summary of these variables serves as the basis for the interpretation of the total record.

For a more thorough understanding and knowledge of Rorschach testing, scoring and interpretation, the reader may turn to one of the specialized texts on this subject (see references of Chapters 5 and 6).

During the past two decades, a great many studies have raised important questions with regard to the reliability and validity of the Rorschach and its underlying interpretive hypotheses. Dr. Beck's chapter concerns itself with many of the theoretical and methodological issues which have been brought into question. The author comes to grips with these problems and ranges beyond—to issues of concern to those involved in the study of personality in general and its relationship to perceptual and cognitive processes interlaced in the Rorschach method.

In the next chapter, a derivative of the Rorschach method, the Holtzman Inkblot Technique (HIT) is introduced by the originator. This method is entirely new as far as the stimulus material is concerned. It employs many of the Rorschach variables and introduces some new ones, based on some of the research literature. In contrast to the Rorschach, the HIT is based on psychometric principles, minimizing some of the subjective aspects involved in the traditional Rorschach testing. Dr. Holtzman presents a systematic account of this technique and a detailed review of the research and clinical applications of the method to date. He attempts to avoid the methodological pitfalls of the older method and the criticism to which it is subjected.

5

Reality, Rorschach and Perceptual Theory

SAMUEL J. BECK

I.

The psychologist setting out to study the human personality faces a dilemma. The knowledge he seeks is about men, women, children, as we know them in their real lives—their thinking, emotions, anxieties, moods, their daydreams, purposes, gratifications—all that fusion of mental experience which, at any particular moment, is a total human being. This is the psychologist's objective. His disciplined habits of research follow the precept that Descartes formulated as the second of his four guidelines which, from the age of twenty-three on, he used in directing and criticizing his own thinking. It is, he writes, "to divide each of the difficulties that I shall be examining into as many parts as possible and as will be requisite the better to resolve them" (Descartes, 1943; p. 88) .*

The dilemma is compounded by the circumstance that any total human being is divisible into so many parts. The psychological variables manifest in overt behavior seem endless. Just as no two persons are the same in physical features, neither are they similar in their psychological features—the way they walk, talk, eat breakfast, dress, and all the habits that make up one's way of life. This variegation is stock in trade for the psychopathologist. The patient in the mental hospital may be reacting with symptoms which to the observer are quite different from those of the patient in the next bed. Yet the diagnosis of the two may be the same.

Dissimilar though the manifest symptoms are, the psychological forces

The reasoning in this article grew in part out of research carried out under grant no. 17156, Department of Mental Health, State of Illinois.

*My published translation does not seem to me to render Descartes' meaning adequately for this passage. The French reads: "Le second, de diviser chacune des difficultes que j'examinerais en autant de parcelles qu'il se pourrait et qu'il serait requis pour les mieux resoudre."

of which they are the expression are similar or the same. The problem for the psychologist is to ascertain these psychological forces. They are the unseen realities that become the seen realities or the symptoms. This reasoning extends from the various clinical pictures to the population generally. The visible behaviors of any two or more persons will differ in the eyes of those about him. Yet of anyone whom we know, we know generally how he will act, given certain circumstances. We take for granted certain constancies in each person. In everyday language, these are his character traits, the sources of the style of life which we take for granted in our friends, our wives or husbands, our children, the associates in our vocations; and, insofar as their public images are delineated, those of our national leaders.

The task before a psychology of personality is to delineate the forces, the constancies, (hypothetical constructs, to be sure) that are the sources of the observables. A corollary from the hypotheses of the constancies is that they enable us to predict the behavior of others. This inheres in the sheer fact that they are constants. In our transactions with one another we are, in fact, always predicting. We are pretty sure regarding what a person is likely to do, sure that what he does today he will do tomorrow, and on another morrow. These are the judgments of everyday life and its wisdoms.

Yet we do not normally break the person down into his component character traits, i.e., into his several psychological processes. The psychologist, on the other hand, is on a search. He asks now, "Can the hypothetical constructs, the processes, be verified? What is the connection between the processes and the person as we see him with his everyday behaviors and his lifetime character patterns?" Is there any method whereby these questions can be answered?

The Rorschach test, as its exponents claim, cuts across intellectual and emotional variables. Its critics question or reject this claim. In this chapter, I propose to examine Rorschach test theory in the light of some perception theory. Let it first be noted here that Rorschach did not discover new mental processes. The separate psychological areas to which the concepts of the test are referred are familiar to psychology. The intellect and the emotions have long been the provinces of the laboratory and the former a large enterprise of the clinic. Imaginative activity has been more elusive, but ventures into it have been undertaken. Those very human devices, the defenses, have grown out of psychodynamic insights with special credit due to psychoanalysis, particularly to the writings of Anna Freud and of Fenichel. Rorschach did not discover any of these, though they are the foundations of his test. He did discover ways of searching for and recognizing these psychological activities or experiences. Nevertheless, emphasis needs to be placed on the penetration of his test to fantasy activity. This was a discovery original with him, and a most important one from a viewpoint of whole personality research.

The great advance in the exploration of personality that Rorschach achieved is in enabling us to judge the effects of the intellectual and the emotional processes on one another. A set of objective stimuli mirrors the individual's use of his mental resources and their fusion into that unit which is the person that we see, the individual striving to adapt to his circumstances, as he, at that point in his life, perceives them. This is what Rorschach did that was new.

II.

The psychological field in which a Rorschach test concept can most definitely be observed is that of perception. In the subtitle to his *Psychodiagnostik* he uses the expression: "a perception-diagnostic experiment" (*Ergebnisse eines Wahrnehmungsdiagnostischen Experiments*). Visual phenomena are stressed by von Fieandt as the principal source by which we know external objects. In a paper, "Toward a Unitary Theory of Perception" (1958) he says, "The conditions of object perception can consequently be reduced by operations not exceeding the optical sphere." He points to the dependence of other modalities on the visual. Regarding tactual experience he writes, "Only men with normal visual images (not the born blind) are able to objectivize their exclusively tactual impressions." He adds a similar observation concerning the sense of hearing; it ". . . can mediate thing impressions only if the auditory stimulation comes combined with optic or haptic stimuli simultaneously and is localized in the same direction." At still another point he comments, "For man, undoubtedly the world of sight is the most important, but," he adds, "surely a purely visual world would be an abstraction. Such a thing is never found in empirical reality."

Rorschach's inkblots are, of course, visual stimuli. The associations that they elicit point to memory images held by the subject, and as such, they report a former visual experience on the part of the subject. He must have seen the "man," "butterfly," "tree" at some time in order to extract these forms from the Rorschach test figures. His associations then report a reality with which he has once interacted. This is to say that the Rorschach inkblots yield information regarding the subject's realities. These are the phenomenal realities, or "experienced reality," using von Fieandt's pertinent language.

The clinical observer cannot, however, be content with his patient's phenomena. The things which the patient says he sees are the measure of his ability to know reality. Here we must be crystal clear about what we mean by "reality." The patient's phenomena may be unmistakably vivid to him, sharp in outline. As a clinical example, the animals, elves, and other creatures of delirium tremens are terribly real to the patient. Yet doctor, nurse, ward attendants go their merry way unaffected by these horrors: the patient's reality is private and his own. In our everyday comings and goings we deal with numerous objects to which most people react in about the same way. These are the realities of our external world.

Rorschach did his perception experiment within this modality by which we take in most of our information. He invented, in fact, a totally new visual world. It is a simple experiment in what each person sees, and it uncovers "the experienced reality of the individual." But Rorschach's invention went a giant step further. The test contains a technique for judging the subject's experienced reality using as a frame of reference the reality experienced by his society generally. In processing th Rorschach form associations—and by far the greatest number of the associations are wholly or partially determined by form—we mark some F+ for good form, and some F—, for poor form. Although the terms "good" and "poor" have social significance as behavior acceptable or undesirable, the scoring does not make social value its criterion.

The criterion for F+ is the empirical, objective one: do people of average or higher intelligence, normally behaving in their environments, see this "man," "alligator," "lake," and the rest when looking at this inkblot? These are the people that establish a community's realities. They usually make the correct decisions in their affairs with those about them; they know how to protect and care for themselves, whether in physical hazards or social ones. What they do brings them through the vicissitudes of life with the success that is the lot of the majority of us. So the way they see things, physical objects as well as societal values, is the measure of everyday pragmatic reality. I return to this point below.

It follows that anyone who behaves as these "normally behaving" people do, in the major matters of life and in a large enough proportion of his activities, knows reality. Important implications concerning ego follow, therefore, from the F+ concept. It was by the associations of these people that we established the Rorschach realities, i.e., what is F+ and what is F—. When a person perceives in the test a large enough number of forms that agree with these criterion percepts, we can predict of him that he will be a realist in a world external to himself.

The Rorschach perceptions are explicable from phenomenological theory if we simply inspect any one response taken by itself. The F+ concept as societal reality points up the inadequacy of phenomenology for purposes of judging the person in the context of a social setting. Phenomenology does not provide a frame of reference whereby one can evaluate one's ability to know the realities outside oneself, those hard and sometime terribly uncomfortable realities with which the world confronts us. Whatever a person's inner experience may be when he says "two clowns" (fig. II) or "a bear climbing on some rocks" (fig. VIII) it is his private experience. It cannot, as Mandler and Kessen point out, be subjected to public tests (1959, p. 38). They say on a later page, "It should be obvious by now that private events, mental operations or not, cannot be adequately named in the language of science. Our discussion of phenomenology is directly relevant to this point . . ." (Mandler & Kessen, 1959, p. 113) .

However truly a subject's percept reports the phenomenal appearance to him of a thing, i.e., his experienced reality, we have no way of knowing whether what he sees is what healthy people see in that object. We cannot say whether within certain conditions he will behave as the healthy do in regard to whatever social values will be involved; whether he will come through a peril unhurt, or will survive. From the fact that most healthy individuals do see in fig. II of the Rorschach test "two clowns" or the "two animals" (above) , and many other associations in any accumulated F+ lists (see Beizmann, 1966) we can make plausible predictions concerning our subject under scrutiny and can do so within a pragmatic range of accuracy. This reasoning is of critical significance to the clinical psychologist. An experiment in perception, Rorschach or other, that cannot reveal to what degree the person's experienced reality conforms to the realities with which he will collide is of only academic value to the clinical investigator. It may be added here that the "practical man" in industry or in politics would not expect to survive long if he rested only on his own, private, phenomenal realities. His is a reality which is being constantly put to the grim test of a competitive world. Thus it is that Rorschach perceptions correct for the inadequacy of phenomenology. The test has a technique for appraising the perceiver's realities as public events.

Let us say that a certain number of the S's responses are designated F−. Where most persons see a human form (e.g., in the central detail of fig. I) he sees "a scorpion." This is phobic thinking. As a clinical symptom it is likely to be evidence that the patient carries a fearful attitude about some particular person. Concerning no one else does he react with the idea, "a scorpion." The subject's transactions with this particular person are thus likely to cause that person some disagreeable moments. The percept is, however, reality only to the subject, his private reality. As F− it has not stood the test of reality when subjected to public scrutiny. To no one else is any person a scorpion. Thus the F+ procedure assays the public quality of a private reality.

The decision on any Rorschach association as F+, F− should be a simple enough undertaking. Two steps are necessary. First, the test is administered to other S's, a criterion population sample. Their responses are listed. A statistical gauge is worked out, and the new response is checked against the list so constructed. Second is clinical validation. The patient's overall reality perception is estimated from his Rorschach pattern. This is scrutinized from a perspective of the clinical investigation. How nearly do they conform to each other?

III.

A most illuminating paper on perception theory, and one which I see as fitting the F+, F— concept, is Bruner's "On Perceptual Readiness" (1957). To the Rorschach student, it is exciting to recognize so much of Rorschach's explicit principle in Bruner's thinking. Here is one theory of perception within which Rorschach's psychology fits comfortably.

Rorschach sets up four criteria for an F+ percept. In the second of these he refers to the memory impression, *Engramme,* which a person must possess. The third reads "The ability to evoke these memory images, to awaken them, to bring them to consciousness" (Rorschach, 1932, p. 61). Bruner's point of departure concerning perceptual readiness is each person's "differential use of cues in identity categorizing [an object]" (p. 124). His description and detailed discussion of the cues constantly awaken recognition in anyone familiar with the associational activity that goes on in responding to the test.

Bruner's "cues" are Rorschach's *Engramme.* The subject is using the cues that emerge from the inkblot figure in order to identify and categorize the object that come to his mind. In the act of categorizing, i.e., in the associational content, he states a meaning that the percept has for him. The "bat," "animal skin," "women, girls" have the potential in them for a certain experience on his part because of the general class or category in which these objects belong. So these percepts demonstrate one of Bruner's postulates, ". . . that all perception is generic in the sense that whatever is perceived is placed in and achieves its 'meaning' from a class of percepts with which it is grouped" (p. 124). Implicit always in the "meaning" of the class is the effect which the object seen may have on the subject. Some objects are, by reason of the general properties of the class, known to be benign, gratifying; some are noxious. Whatever the meaning is, the subject reacts adaptively. When Bruner, in the paragraph preceding, makes the "bold assumption" that ". . . all perceptual experience is necessarily the end-product of a categorizing process" he is stating implicitly a dynamic principle: perception serves the adaptive urge. One's percepts have meaning to him insofar as the object in the percept is something good or bad for him.

However, Bruner is, in this article, interested in perception theoretically—what it is as a cognition process. But the clinical psychologist wants to know whether his patient judges the object before him using the same frame of reference as his society generally. Does the patient use the presented cues as others do? Does he categorize accurately? Is his experienced reality that of his fellow citizens?

The empirical facts are that some persons using these same cues perceive objects deviating in form, hence in category, and hence in meaning from those of the norm population. The cues, i.e., the stimuli, are the same but in Rorschach language the percept is F—. The cognition of the subject is deviant. This is the important differential which the test achieves for us in the F+, F— concept. Call his cognition good-bad, accurate-erratic, realistic-dereistic. Whatever one calls it, the clinical investigator has a clue as to how this patient is likely to react in the universe outside the test: in bad social form, making poor judgments, being unrealistic. At the dynamic level he has a clue to ego functioning.

The diagnostic information that is being unearthed is what principally interests the clinical thinker. Recall that Rorschach called his test one of both perception and diagnosis. The obvious indications are that either the persons did not attend to and use the portions in the inkblot figures, the cues, that the norm population uses, or he did attend to these but his own *Engramme,* the cues which the blot figure awakened in him, differed from those in the population generally. This is still reasoning within cognition, not clinical, theory. The clinician's questions from the F— alone (and disregarding for the moment the other information in the particular Rorschach pattern) spread out in the following directions:

1) The subject does not possess the cues for the "bat" or the other F+ percepts. If so, it is because 2) he has not learned them; which could be because 3) he is too young, has not been exposed to the objects in the class "bat" or "skin" and others. Or again 4) he does not have the brain tissue with which to fix the memory cues, and neved did have it. He is one of those unfortunates who was born mentally defective. Still again 5) he did at one time possess the brain tissue necessary for such cognitive processes, but he suffered the misfortune of an illness or an accident, either of which impaired the functioning of the brain. He lost his intellectual ability, his memory, and the other cognitive processes. These deficits may also be due to senility.

All the foregoing inadequacies are related to brain pathology. But in the majority of patients no such pathology can be established. The person may well be grown up in years and intellect, an adult or an adolescent, and with an IQ of 130 or even more. He has learned the cues to the object "butterfly" and "animal skin" and the others. That is, he has always had, and he still has, adequate brain tissue with which to categorize the objects that life presents before him. He can do so for the Rorschach test figures. One presents these stimuli to him and he sees a "spider" (fig. I) or a "snowflake" (fig. VI) or a "mask" (fig. X). What has happened to his cognitive cues for the "good" or "correct" percept? The answer: he still possesses these and he also possesses the cues for spiders and the other F—. Something in his psychological makeup activates more valence on his part for these deviant associations. The clinical student recognizes here the psychodynamic factor, i.e., the factor of personality—or if you prefer, the concept of need (Murray).

A person's perception, his cognitive functioning, is in instances erratic because he distorts the object. He sees it not as it is, meaning not in accordance with the experienced reality of a normative segment of the population. That is, he sees it not as *it* is, but as *he,* the patient, is. Here we enter on the problem of the whole personality as a psychological determinant.

Theorists, as cited by Bruner, are aware of perceptual experience as something dynamic. Thus: "Gibson like Titchener before him, urges a distinction between the visual field and the visual world, the former the world of attributive sense impressions, the latter of objects and things and events. Pratt urges that motivation and set and past expereience may affect the things of the visual world but not the stuff of the visual field" (p. 125). Von Fieandt in his article (1958) also focuses on this distinction: " 'Pure sensation' is never found in natural surroundings. It can only be experienced in laboratories as a result of artificial refinements." We may recall his comment that a purely visual world is never found in reality. He puts his finger on the psychodynamic factor in stating essentially a Rorschach thesis: "The psychological side of the process implies that the organism reacts as a whole to a relational system of stimulus effects."

Von Fieandt is saying that it is the person as such who does the perceiving. This view corresponds with those of the writers above cited from Bruner. In the Rorschach test the F— percepts are the person mirrored in his unique, at times idiosyncratic, percepts. Some of his F— responses result from inadequate size of, or damage to, the brain; some from foggy mental state (drug influence); some from flighty attention caused by undirected spontaneity. In some it is the psychological person: his self distorted, he distorts his percepts.

Bruner, too, when he discusses perception as varyingly veridical, expresses a Rorschach proposition. He is formulating what the generic meaning of F+ is, as it can be empirically demonstrated in clinical findings. "What we generally mean when we speak of representation or veridicality is that perception is predicted in varying degrees," and, ". . . the categorical placement of the object leads to appropriate consequences in terms of later behavior directed towards the perceived object; it appears as an apple and indeed it keeps the doctor away if consumed once a day" (p. 126).

This reasoning is validated in F+ experience as follows: 1) From my rationale concerning the adaptive significance of F+, it follows that in the associations of the subject so scored, he is categorizing the object correctly for the consequence to be expected later. 2) Experience with the test in the several personality pictures in the normal population is that individuals in differentiated groups respond with varying percentages of F+. Their perception is varyingly veridical. 3) In the clinical groups, the F+, F— variances consistently follow clinical logic. The more disturbed a patient, the lower his F+ percent; the more integrated, the higher this finding. An overview of these differentials is presented in the accompanying table (see Table 1).

Table 1. F+ Trends in Various Personality Groups

Personality Groups	F+ Percentage
Normal adults	
Superior intelligence	85 to 95*
Average intelligence	75 to 90
Inferior intelligence	60 to 75
Children	
Ages 10 and up	60 to 85
Ages 6 to 9	58 to 70
Ages 5 and below	55 and lower
Simple feeble-minded	
Medium deficiency	45 to 70
Severest deficiency	40 and lower
Affective psychoses	
Manic depression	
manic	40 to 70
Manic depression	
depressed	up to 100
In two patterns of schizophrenia	
Very disordered	
paranoid	below 60; varying with degree of disorder
In one pattern of schizophrenia	
Intellectually cramped,	
rigid; emotionally bland	65 to 85
In transition schizophrenics	50 to 75
Organic psychoses	varies downward with degree of deterioration

For healthy adults, all intelligence levels, mean percent is 83.91; SD 8.12. Critical minimum for healthy is 60.
*All ranges are approximate.

The general statement from findings in normal and in clinical groups is: F+ varies directly with veridical perception. The persons who manage their affairs successfully in life, those who accurately perceive the meanings of objects and accurately predict consequences to follow from confrontation with these objects, are those (assuming always certain other Rorschach data in their total patterns) whose F+ percentages range between 75 and 90. Quoting this generalization in Bruner's language: "In fine, adequate perceptual representation involves the learning of appropriate categories, the learning of cues useful in placing objects appropriately in such systems of categories" (p. 127).

Empirical F+ findings for the persons in the healthy population samples are consistent with another detail of Bruner's theorizing. He speaks, at several points, of learning that goes on in perceptual categorizing: "Learning how to isolate, weigh, and use criterial attribute values . . . In learning to perceive we are . . . *learning to predict and to check what goes with what* . . ." (p. 126, Bruner's italics). He reasons: "The most appropriate pattern of readiness at any given moment would be that one which would lead on the average to the most 'veridical' guess about the nature of the world around one" (p. 130). These excerpts, and also the one below concerning "the most ready perceiver, etc.," exactly describe the persons with F+ percentages in the 75-95 levels. Using my results (Table 1) as point of reference and assuming the validity of the F+ concept, I may put it that the Rorschach data support Bruner's theorizing.

A word is in order here concerning the way I constructed my normative F+ lists. In my early years with the test I tried it out on many persons with whom I had professional contact. Principally, there were psychologists, psychiatrists, social workers, people in academic positions, others in business or in public affairs. All were of mature but not advanced age. These persons, (51 in all; their responses collected in the years 1929-32) all necessarily of superior intelligence, were my original criterion population. I always felt a pressing need for an average population with which to test out this list obtained from a group at the upper end of the intelligence curve. The opportunity came in 1948-49 on an NIH grant. Rorschach response records were collected individually from 157 persons. This is the Spiegel sample composed of employees in a large mail-order house from the lowest work classification to a sub-executive group. In the report for this research (Beck, et al, 1950) we describe the method whereby I set up the original F+ list (the superior group) and the corrections that were indicated by the findings in the 157 men and women representative of the mid-range of the population in Chicago.

The F+ list that I have been using in recent years rests on two foundations. One is the percepts of my superior persons intellectually, persons functioning effectively in their respective fields and presumably healthy. Among them were a university professor who later became president of a university and is now directing a leading scientific institution; a woman professor in another university; a woman filling an important governmental post when she took the Rorschach and who continued to serve in that post for more than 30 years—these individuals and their full test records I have reported (Beck, 1967).

My theory is that brighter individuals of a society are the first to perceive the realities of that society's universe. They "know the properties of objects and events we encounter," to use Bruner's language. They invent the complex tools and they grasp the social values. They are "the brains" in the literal as well as the figurative sense. On their growth and thinking depends their society's survival. The principle is as old as Biblical wisdom: except the leaders have vision, the people perisheth. However, the vision of its leaders are not yet the people's realities. The percepts must also become the experienced realities of the greater portion of the people, in the middle range; in statistical jargon, those within two sigma on each side of the mean. The intellectual discovers the realities. The middle two-thirds are the final authority regarding what are to be the current realities. What they accept as of now, *goes*, is *true*, is *real*.

Therefore, we subjected our original F+ list (as obtained from the superior adults) to the scrutiny of the authority. We gave the test to the sample out of the middle two-thirds of the population. This is the second foundation for the F+ norms which I presently use. By the associations so gathered we corrected and enlarged the original list. It is of interest that Beizmann's manual, which I received only in June of 1966, from Paris, is a compilation of the F+, F− scorings as published by Rorschach, Loosli-Usteri, and myself (1966). The Beizmann manual is likely to become an international standard reference source.

The corollary of all the foregoing is that F+ is a major index to the ego's functioning. A person responding within the healthy F+ range (75 to 95 percent) knows the realities of his society. He knows the "*criterial attribute* values required of an instance to be coded in a given class . . ." (p. 131, Bruner's italics). That is, he knows what to do in most exigencies presented by daily life. It may be only that he can fix a minor defect in one of the numerous electrical appliances that now make up a household; it may be that he pays his bills with reasonable promptness; or it may be that in his interpersonal transactions he has due regard for the rights and dignity of the other. He has acquired both the pragmatic know-how available to most persons in the middle two-thirds of the population, and he is sensitive to the values of his group culture. To the extent that he carries on practically and lives by those values—again, it takes variables in addition to F+ to indicate that he does so—he has the esteem of those about him. His awareness that he has that esteem is the psychodynamic source of his own self-esteem. And the measure of one's self-esteem is the measure of one's ego. One's F+ percent, as a principal measure of self-esteem, is a principal dimension in measuring one's ego.

Some other of Bruner's attributes of the perception process are recognizable in the Rorschach concept. Bruner writes, "Where the fit to accessible categories is not precise, or when the linkage between cue and category is low in probability in the past experience of the organism, the conscious experience of cue searching occurs. 'What is that thing?' Here, one is scanning the environment for data in order to find cues that permit a more precise placement of the object" (p. 131). He is here stating the fourth of Rorschach's four criteria for F+, that is, critical discrimination. Rorschach puts it this way: "Fourth is the ability to select out the most similar among the memory images that present themselves. This is in the main a many sided associational process which again itself depends on the attention. This must be directed now not only to the external stimulus but also on the mobilizing memory images, in order to enable one to control the perception activity and to criticize his perception" (Rorschach, 1932, p. 61). (The German word is *Deutung*, literally "interpretation"; in this context better rendered as "perception").

Bruner writes, "The most ready perceiver would then have the best chances of estimating situations most adequately and planning accordingly" (p. 130). In taking the Rorschach test, the persons in the high-average to superior intelligence ranges speedily associate with the usual F+ percepts, as indicated in the measured time per first response and average time for all responses. They disclose their planning and foresight abilities in the high level at which they grasp relationships between their percepts, (the organization activity, z) an ability that varies directly with levels of intelligence in integrated individuals.

The accessibility of categories is another feature of perceptual readiness in Bruner's theorizing, and he adds, "The more frequently in a given context instances of a given category occur, the greater the accessibility of the category" (p. 132). The category most accessible in the Rorschach test stimuli is the animal forms. This is universal experience with the test. Human forms are next in frequency, i.e., they are next in accessibility. The empirical fact is that the higher the intelligence of the person, the smaller the animal percentage in his associational content, and the greater the number of his human forms. Cues are available for both animal and human percepts. The test, as it taps these two most accessible categories, differentiates those of higher intelligence insofar as they utilize the less common cues. By associating more about humans, they disclose a broader interest in their fellows.

The identification of things realistically, important as it is towards getting on in one's world, is not the first step in the perception process. Before one categorizes the object, one must attend to it. The Rorschach test technique for any S's attention pattern is the proportion in which he selects wholes, major details, and minor details of the inkblot figures (respectively designated as W, D, Dd). Regarding this variable I had for many years been perplexed by my readily obtaining data that conflicted with Rorschach's formulated theory. It took a paper by Roger Brown, "How Shall a Thing be Called" (1958) to help clear what was a theoretical roadblock.

Rorschach writes: ". . . the number of W is before all index to the energy available for the drive to associate. Often it is also an index to the conscious or unconscious wish for complex achievement, of abstracting or synthesizing. Large number of good, primary W responses are frequently found in the philosophically disposed while larger number of good, synthesized W responses are frequently produced by those with imaginative talent. These abilities when optimally found are additional components of high intelligence" (1932, pp. 63-64). While, to be sure, Rorschach also describes various kinds of W, some which would be inconsistent with high intelligence, my own empiric data stubbornly insisted that some persons responded with many W who could not be of high intelligence. The very young child consistently associates to the whole test figure. The feeble-minded do so and, what is even more perplexing, the lower the intelligence rating, the more W's I have been finding in some; occasionally a feeble-minded subject in the lowest range would produce 10 W, one for each blot figure. Differentiating features, to be sure, emerged in the framework of the response record in its entirety and valid diagnostic pictures could be drawn. This was pragmatic method, based on empiric results. Theory remained obscure.

Brown's article (1958) provided the clarifying leads. Citing an older study (M. E. Smith, 1926) on the topic of children's vocabulary, he writes, *"Fish* is likely to be learned before *perch* and *bass. House* before *bungalow* and *mansion; car* before *Chevrolet* and *Plymouth.* The more concrete vocabulary waits for the child to reach an age where his purposes differentiate kinds of fish and makes of cars" (p. 18). Thus the child first learns the name of the class as a whole. He reacts to a category of objects before he discriminates the particulars that enter them. "The child over-generalizes the use of a conventional word," wrote Brown. "The word *dog* may, at first, be applied to every kind of four-legged animal. It sometimes happens that every man who comes into the house is called *daddy"* (p. 19).

The child in his earlier learning phases reacts to whole classes. It is what he does with his Rorschach test stimuli. He responds to them holistically. At the older ages, the attention distributes to details; perceptions is now more discriminating. This shift in the W-D selection can be traced also in the feeble-minded but later in the chronological ages and varying directly with the degree of mental deficiency. Some patients with brain pathology also associate excessively to wholes and an occasional depressed person does so. The ability to discriminate the salient elements of one's environment, as the ability to recognize the particular individuals in it, develops thus with chronological growth, and depends on a healthy brain in an individual psychologically liberated.

Brown's observation about naming the class is exemplified also in Rorschach test experience. Younger children more frequently associate "an animal," "a bird," "a man," than they do "an elephant," "a clown," "a dancer." "The best generalization," comments Brown, with regard to vocabulary growth, "seems to be that each thing is first given its most common name. This name seems to categorize on the level of usual utility . . ." (p. 19). Once again, then, a Rorschach test procedure is comfortable in a theoretical bed made for a particular component in perception, namely, the attention process.

This support can be found also in the position which Brown takes relative to cognitive development. "The primitive state in cognition is one of comparative lack of differentiation. Probably certain distinctions are inescapable; the difference between a loud noise and mere silence; between a bright contour and a dark ground, etc. These inevitable discriminations divide the perceived world into a smaller number of very large (abstract) categories. Cognitive development is increasing differentiation. The more distinctions we make, the more categories we have and the smaller (more concrete) these are" (Brown, 1958, p. 19).

In the Rorschach test experience, the order of W findings is: 1) the young child's wholes, a monolithic, nondiscriminating percept; 2) attention to component details, and in some responses a reorganizing of them into wholes—the themes are not likely to be unusual, rather, they are in categories frequently produced; 3) much distribution of the attention both to wholes and details, including fine details—after the blot figure is thus broken down, it may be energetically re-synthesized into a meaningful unit, usually of original content. The university president (Beck, 1967) is the exemplar, but similar responses form the associational products of many men and women at leadership levels in their professions.

These persons are the abstract thinkers in the sense that Rorschach uses the term. They are the ones who detect the commonalities in varied events and penetrate to the general force or principle inherent in the many instances. Thus are hypotheses created in science. Newton grasped that the falling apple and the planets revolving around the sun exemplified the same law; in a similar manner did Darwin hypothesize in his observations about the habits of giant turtles and wingless locusts; and so did Freud concerning a young woman's aphonia and a young man's hostility to his fiancee. Gravity, Evolution, the Unconscious were their respective abstractions.

Brown erroneously construes the vocabulary of the very young child as abstraction. When the child says "fish," "house," "car" he is not abstracting in the sense of penetrating and understanding the properties that make them the one class that they are. What the child is reacting to is what he can see, eat, touch. This is so when all dogs are just "dog" and all men are "daddy." This is not abstract but decidedly concretistic cognition. Brown is only partly right when he says: "Cognitive development is increasing differentiation" (p. 19). It is that and in another, later developmental stage, and more rarely achieved, it is a re-synthesizing of the differentiated and an abstracting out of general significance.

The Rorschach test offers important evidence concerning the development of the thinking process. The course of W as an index to undiffer-entiated holistic perception, then to discrimination of parts and wholes, and then to abstraction at the highest level, parallels the chronological growth of the child. And as Brown notes, "The school boy who learns the word *quadruped* has abstracted from differentiated and named sub-ordinates . . ." (p. 20).

IV.

Now about an opportunity that is being missed by academic, experi-mental psychologists, that is, the opportunity to be both psychologists and scientists. I assume that we psychologists are engaged in our partic-ular work because of our interest in human nature. I assume this for all psychologists, whether in the laboratory or in the clinic, whether watching the rat in his maze, the human being in his neurosis, the dog responding to a bell, or the man to a red light on the street corner; the bee or the ant societies toiling and swarming in their nests and their hives, or *homo sapiens* wasting himself and striving in his conglomerate, competitive society. On whichever of these areas we concentrate, our interests as psy-chologists ultimately root back to one source: What makes the most in-telligent of all animals behave as he does? What are the mainsprings and what are the inner works of human behavior?

One of our difficulties is that we feel the Socratic doubt: What can we really know? Which is to say, what is the truth? And an even more difficult question, what is the truth about human nature? The laboratory psy-chologist rigorously controls all variables but one. But how much does he see? The clinical psychologist "feels" himself into his fellow human being. But how clearly—or rather, how dimly does he see that being? It is the dilemma of the psychologist: he can be either rigidly accurate and know less, or he can venture farther and lose his way. On the other hand, each one of us, whatever our interest area, is making some real advance in psychological knowledge even though none of us can appre-hend truth in its entirety. This is aside from the circumstance that "all our truths are only relative truths, truths but relative to man and to all other aspects of truth, and yet the nearest thing to absolute truth that man can obtain; that absolute truth is, in fact, at least insofar as man is concerned, a semantic confusion" (Huskins, 1951, p. 688). Truth to its pursuer is, in fact, what in Keats' "Ode on a Grecian Urn" the maiden is to the lover:

> Bold Lover, never, never canst thou kiss,
> Though winning near the goal—yet do not grieve;
> She cannot fade, though thou hast not thy bliss,
> For ever wilt thou love, and she be fair!

The pursuit goes on then. On the stage of personality research, prior to the time that the Rorschach test made its bow, a number of actors had made their entrances and their exits. There were the Kent-Rosanoff list, sundry questionnaires and personality inventories, the eidetic imagery of the Jaensches, the constitutional types out of Marburg, Jung's extrovert hypothesis out of Zurich.

Yet we in clinical psychology and the people in our sister disciplines —psychiatry, social work, or the specialized ones, such as delinquency —were not happy with our results. Something was amiss. Findings were fragmentary. They turned up information about part functions of the individual which remained static descriptions. The investigators did not dare reason, or even speculate, about how the individual uses these functions in his overall adaptive struggle. Rorschach and his test turned a corner in the history of the exploration of personality. It is an instrument that comes near to being one that can trace out a behavior pattern both in breadth and in depth. With its entry on the stage of personality exploring, let us say that Act One closed.

The curtain rises on Act Two, and some new characters enter on the scene. The statisticians have sharpened their daggers. Let us not call them the villains of the piece—we need them. I prefer to look on them as the Loyal Opposition. Their methodology and logic are ever essential for the inspection of our data. They worm their way through our errors and provide the compass with which we set the new directions of our research. The trouble with so many statisticians is that they want to put the statistical cart before the psychological horse. They criticize results on the ground that they do not fit the cut prescribed by this or that statistical rule.

There is a hazard in the tight constraint effected by the reins of statistics. The result can be to snaffle scientific venture and freedom. We bend the knee before the authority of the coefficient of correlation, of chi square, of the t-test, and then there is the statistical test with two tails. Research reports close with an affirmation of faith: "The results are significant at the .01 or the .001 or the .05 degree of confidence." Critically essential as statistics are as correctives in any scientific endeavor, the question is in order whether the statistician always remembers that his rationales are *aids* to science, but not science, in the sense of observing events in nature. Statisticians may in fact be vulnerable to an occupational hazard. In becoming so enamored of their own brain child, they lose sight of its relationship to the data which it helps to illuminate. It may be their escape from reality.

Authoritarianism in science is of course nothing new. Where the danger lies, again citing the Huskins paper, is in "the desire to accept authority." That is, the younger recruits in the field, in their yearning for security, cling to the rules and the formulae for dear life. Becoming compulsively bound, the loss which they take in terms of scientific imagination may be irreparable. The freedom to err is the price of creativity.

But freedom can loosen into license and license degenerate into anarchy. The Rorschach scene is at present a chaos of sights and a cacophony of sounds, with very little sign of real order. With few exceptions, so far as I can judge from published reports of Rorschach test material, everyone using the test does that which is right in his own eyes. Examiners ignore rules of administration. In evaluating responses they disregard such statistical norms as have been worked out. Many use the test simply for the thematic content which it evokes. Since there are no established guidelines to semantics of theme, what these examiners are doing is no more than free associating to the patient's free associations. They thus evade the task of identifying the formal variables and of doing the structural analysis. Such method of analysis is the most important contribution the Rorschach has made toward the objective exploration of a personality. It is a demanding task but psychologists by-pass it. The Rorschach scene can thus be described in the words of another writer in the "American Scientist" (Stern, 1956) and I use his Latin: *Quot capita tot sensus*. Freely rendered, "The number of heads is equal to the number of Rorschach methods."

For relief from this turbid scene we turn to the statisticians. The questions they have been opening up concerning the principles of the test, its assumptions, its claims, are welcome ones to serious workers with it. They are challenges which, when met, must lead to discarding what is not valid, confirming what is. Accepting these challenges, we ask them to meet our request: to devise a statistical method that will aid us in solving our problem. As statisticians progress towards that end they will be advancing their own science toward a new, creative phase. As they progress they will aid the clinician in eschewing his own occupational hazard: the bias which enters into any psychological judgment. In point here is the caution in the Huskins (1951) paper: "The biologist, beyond all other scientists, has to recognize that all his data, all his conclusions, are part of a web of which he himself is a component, his experience strands therein; he is never on the outside looking in, but always a part of the problem he is seeking to solve" (p. 691). If this is so about a presumably objective science such as biology, how much more true is it in the field of psychology, and more especially in the field of personality!

V.

What are the research opportunities in general psychology arising out of Rorschach test concepts? I list here, in condensation, some suggestions to be undertaken by laboratory—not Rorschach—experimental techniques set up *ad hoc*. Rorschach test principles and insights are certain to profit as these are carried out and general psychological knowledge is thereby extended.

DW, DdW, DdD. These are the responses in which S attends only to a detail (DW) and refers the meaning (categories) to the entire blot figure. Or S does so although attending only to a rare detail (DdW). In instances he attends to a rare detail and refers the meanings to a larger detail of which it is a part, (DdD). Some questions for general psychology are: What are the variances in the amount of cue used by S's in categorizing an object? What variances in accuracy of the percept go with variances in the amount of cue used? Among relevant theoretic questions in perception are: Do some persons perceive the part as a whole? Do some persons reason regarding the whole from the part? What is the relation of speed in categorizing to accuracy?

W. The ability to comprehend objects as units. The experimental stimuli will need to be constructed so that S may be free to attend to parts or the wholes. The stimuli are to vary in difficulty. The population sample is to consist of children ranging in age from earliest years into adolescence. This experiment is especially applicable to Brown's theorizing.

Z. The ability to relate percepts meaningfully. Two or more percepts are organized into a new form. The new categorizing obtains in none of the parts alone, only in the new unit. While W is one form of Z, the mental process involved in Z is more complex. It frequently consists first in breaking down the whole stimulus and then organizing—an analytic-synthesis activity. Gestalt principles are demonstrated in Z, as I have shown (Beck, 1933). The population sample for Z is to be principally adults; if tried in children psychometric ratings should be available. The results are to be studied for their variance with generalizing and abstracting abilities in the respective persons.

The personal F—. Erratic perceptions that can be shown as mirroring interests or needs of serious personal importance to the subject. The individual distorts what he sees under pressure of intense emotions. Gombrich, in his *Art and Illusion,* asserts the primacy of the person in what one sees. Quoting from a review of Gombrich's book by Wollheim, "Perception, he [Gombrich] argues, is conditioned by the attitude and expectations, by the 'mental set' of the observer: and what the observer sees cannot be dissociated from the *schemata* or patterns he imposes upon experience" (1960).

The psychologist's experimental technique may well be tachistoscopic and should be a simple one to set up. The difficulty will lie in the validating source. Could a word association list be set up—one in which the content of the responses suspected of being personal F— would be interspersed with the neutral words?

The white space (s). The valence for attending to empty, rather than filled, space in the stimulus figure. Gestalt psychology has of course provided a considerable background pertinent to this phenomenon; the figure-and-ground experiments. The psychodynamic interest in the preference for these white spaces has to do with their projecting self-will, obstinacy, negativism. As in the case of the personal F—, the important question is that of a validating criterion.

The textural determinant (T). This variable, first reported by Klopfer (1956) is more important than the research attention it has received in Rorschach test investigations. There are reasons for this scanty effort. One is the fact that the responses thus scored are rare. Second is the more than usual uncertainty in identifying this determinant. It derives from the shading quality in the stimulus with which the person associates as if with a tactual experience. When S so associates it may be dynamically important when interpreted as stemming out of erotic hunger. Harlow's researchers on the maternal behavior in monkeys come to mind (1958); also Liddel's on sheep (1956). The skin, it has been observed, is probably the largest organ in humans. It is the agent most involved in personal interaction from earliest infancy on. In respect to texture, then, the opportunity is an exceptionally inviting one, all the more so because the area has been so little explored. Validating information will of course be a major task.

The fantasy association (M). Much has been written about this very important of Rorschach's concepts. On the basis of his theory concerning its significance it would seem untestable by experimental method. For, M is a window into the unconscious and *ex hypothesis* the unconscious cannot, in working life (when psychological experiment would be carried on) be brought to consciousness. Bruner (1957), to be sure, uses the term "unconscious" in connection with the "silent process in perception as once identified by Helmholtz." However, the unconscious which Bruner describes is not the unconscious of Freud or of psychoanalytic theory. It is the preconscious.

When that world of our dreams, from which we are so hermetically sealed in our waking hours, can be investigated by non-Rorschach sources, we will be in a position to validate or refute the claims for M. The assertions concerning the significance of M are so far-reaching, its dynamic potential for exploring the deeper motivations of human behavior so large, that the psychologist who devises the method may himself be turning a corner in personality study.

Defensive blocking. The Rorschach test evokes this in a number of its variables: low productivity (R), heightened perceptual accuracy (F+), increased attention to details (D), increased perception of animal forms (A), reduction of the organizing ability (Z). The individual is reducing influx of stimuli and so staves off excitation. An experiment which in varying degrees cuts down the influx of stimuli should be a simple one for the psychology laboratory. This could directly test out the varying incidence of the Rorschach test variables which I here note.

Color shock and shading shock. The novel stimulus evokes the maximum response. This too is defensive, shuts out more stimuli, and reduces excitement. Are there learning experiments or even sensory (pupillary, auditory) methods of research that educe measurable variation in re-sponse with variation in novelty of the stimulus? And does the measure return to normal as the novelty wears off? As the subject becomes accli-mated to the novel stimulus first presented, does he then react within his normal measure to any other new stimuli? This kind of research would be a direct experimental check on Rorschach theory concerning color shock and shading shock.

Such are some of the opportunities for psychological investigation that the Rorschach test sphere presents, with promise of fruitfulness for general psychology. To the Rorschach test student they will provide critical information both at the practical and the theoretic levels. The suggested experiments do not exhaust the list of opportunities. There are also the color phenomena, the several shading variables, the experience balance (EB) and the experience actual (EA); the total personality pattern conceived as a functional proposition (Beck, 1966; Rapoport, 1952). It is up to the younger generation of psychologists to push back the horizon.

In closing one can but remember how brief was the life of Hermann Rorschach. Had he lived, it is certain that he would have himself under-taken some laboratory testing of his ideas. He in fact outlines some ex-periments: the stimulus is a cat painted in the color of a frog; a frog in the color of a finch. He also discusses control series for the present original blot figures (see Rorschach, 1932, pp. 57-58). For the clinical psychologist, Rorschach's great contribution is that he closed the gap between psychometrics and depth personality testing. More important, he made it possible to bridge the gulf between two minds, that of the examiner and his patient, to bring out into the open regions of the mind otherwise stored away, veiled from the patient and the therapist. One can only speculate how much further Rorschach's fertile mind would have carried this task, had he lived longer.

REFERENCES

Beck, S. J. Configurational tendencies in Rorschach responses. *Am. J. Psychol.*, 1933, *45*, 433-443.

Beck, S. J. *Rorschach's Test, Vol. II, A Variety of Personality Pictures*. New York: Grune and Stratton, revised edition, with H. B. Molish, 1967.

Beck, S. J., Rabin, A. I., Thiesen, W. G., Molish, H. B., & Thetford, W. N. The normal personality as projected in the Rorschach test. *J. Psychol.*, 1950, *30*, 241-298.

Beck, S. J. *Psychological Processes in the Schizophrenic Adaptation*. New York: Grune and Stratton, 1965.

Beck, S. J. Emotions and understanding. In *International Psychiatry Clinics*, Vol. 3, No. 1. Boston: Little, Brown, 1966. Pp. 93-114.

Beizmann, C. *Livret de Cotation des Formes dans le Rorschach*. Paris: Centre de Psy-chologie Appliquée, 1966.

Brown, R. How shall a thing be called? *Psychol. Rev.*, 1958, *65*, 14-21.

Bruner, J. S. On perceptual readiness. *Psychol. Rev.*, 1957, *64*, 123-152.

Descartes, R. *Discours de la Méthode*. Paris: Editions de Cluny, 1943.

von Fieandt, K. Toward a unitary theory of perception. *Psychol. Rev.*, 1958, *65*, 315-320.

Harlow, H. F. The nature of love. *Am. Psychologist*, 1958, *13*, 673-685.

Huskins, C. L. Science, cytology and society. *Am. Scientist*, 1951, *39*, 688-699, 716.

Klopfer, B. et al. *Developments in the Rorschach Technique*, Vols. I and II. World Book, 1956.

Liddell, H. S. *Emotional Hazards in Animals and Man*. Springfield, Ill.: Charles C Thomas, 1956. Pp. x-97.

Mandler, G., & Kessen, W. *The Language of Psychology*. New York: Wiley, 1959.

Rapoport, A. What is semantics? *Am. Scientist*, 1952, *41*, 123-135.

Rorschach, H. *Psychodiagnostik*: *Methodik und Ergebnisse eines Wahrnehmungsdiagnostischen Experiments* (ed. 2). Bern: Huber, 1932.

Stern, A. Science and the philosopher. *Am. Scientist*, 1956, *44*, 281-295.

Wollheim, R. Visions of the truth. (Review of E. H. Gombrich, *Art and Illusion*). In The London *Observer*, April 3, 1960.

6

Holtzman Inkblot Technique

WAYNE H. HOLTZMAN

Drawing heavily upon studies with the Rorschach, the Holtzman Ink-blot Technique (HIT) is a new projective method designed to overcome psychometric limitations in the Rorschach by constructing completely new sets of inkblots.[1] Unlike the Rorschach, which has only ten inkblots in a single form, the HIT consists of two parallel forms, A and B, each of which contains 45 inkblots constituting the test series and two practice blots, X and Y, that are identical in both forms. Thus, standardized responses can be obtained from a total of 92 different inkblots rather than just ten.

The HIT differs from the Rorschach in several important respects other than merely the number of inkblots. 1) The characteristics of the HIT stimuli are richer and more varied in color, form, and shading. 2) The blots vary considerably in degree of symmetry or balance, providing a new stimulus dimension for analysis. 3) The subject is encouraged to give only one response per card rather than as many as he wishes, thereby holding more constant the number of responses given. 4) A brief, simple inquiry follows immediately after each response. 5) Carefully matched, parallel forms of the HIT are available, permitting the use of test-retest designs and the study of change within the individual. 6) Standardized percentile norms are provided for 22 inkblot scores on a variety of populations, facilitating interpretation and analysis. 6) Group methods of administration and computer scoring make it possible to use the HIT for rapid, large-scale screening as well as for individual diagnosis and assessment.

Development of the HIT was prompted by the growing number of experimental studies following World War II which were critical of the Rorschach. The vigorous post-war growth of psychodiagnostic testing and the resulting fusion of academic and clinical psychology produced a flood of dissertations and related studies evaluating the Rorschach. Al-

[1]Much of the material presented in this chapter is adapted from the extensive monograph, *Inkblot Perception and Personality,* by Holtzman, Thorpe, Swartz, and Herron (1961). The author wishes to thank Jon D. Swartz for his critical reading of this chapter and his various suggestions to improve it.

though much of this research was irrelevant or too poorly conceived to provide an appropriate evaluation of the Rorschach method, an impressive number of carefully designed validity studies yielded negative results. In the wake of these experimental studies came the growing realization that the Rorschach had inherent psychometric weaknesses, which cast considerable doubt on the interpretation of its quantitative scores.

Such critics as Cronbach (1949), Zubin (1954) and Hertz (1959) have pointed to major difficulties in the Rorschach arising from the following: 1) The examiner-subject interaction and variations in style of inquiry; 2) lack of satisfactory internal consistency or test-retest reliability for many scores; 3) lack of agreement as to scoring criteria for different variables; and 4) the widely varying number of responses often obtained for the ten Rorschach cards. The complex, curvilinear relationship between number of responses and most other scores on the Rorschach makes it impossible to establish adequate norms for most Rorschach scores, forcing the clinician to fall back upon rough rules of thumb for interpretation.

Once one abandons the basic idea of using only ten inkblots, of permitting the subject as few or as many responses as he cares to give, and of conducting a highly variable inquiry for purposes of illuminating the scoring categories, most of the weaknesses inherent in the standard Rorschach can be overcome. The fundamental issue is how to alter the task and develop psychometrically sound scoring procedures for responses to inkblots while still preserving the rich projective material for which the Rorschach has been quite rightly recognized.

Exploratory studies indicated that, in general, the first response to an inkblot contained sufficient richness and variety of style, organization, determinants, and content to provide scorable information for all the major variables employed in the prevailing Rorschach systems. By limiting the subject to one response per card and greatly increasing the number of inkblots in the series, it was possible to increase the length of the test and therefore the reliability of resulting scores.

The development of the HIT took place in six stages over a period of five years prior to the existence of any large-scale reliability or validity studies. First, techniques for producing inkblots were perfected, taking advantage of modern inks, papers, and artistic approaches. Second, many hundreds of inkblots were screened by actual administration to subjects and evaluation of the outcome. Third, a conceptual framework and objective scoring procedures were developed by which the inkblots (test "items") could be selected. Fourth, matched pairs of inkblots were established on the basis of item analyses and randomly assigned to Form A or Form B to assure the exact psychometric equivalence of the parallel forms. Fifth, preliminary studies were made using the original inkblots to perfect the scoring system and to produce the evidence needed to justify the great expense of mass production for general use. And sixth, the final engraving and printing of the 92 inkblots was carried out with high precision to assure the fidelity of the copies released for experimental use and eventual clinical application. Only after these major developmental stages were completed was it feasible to undertake large-scale, systematic studies of possible variance due to examiners, inter- and intra-scorer agreement, the internal consistency of scores, test-retest reliability using parallel forms, the correlates of inkblot variables, the similarities and differences between the Rorschach and the HIT, group differences for diagnostic purposes, and experimental or clinical applications.

The construction and initial testing of inkblots was divided into three cycles for purposes of gathering data, with each cycle containing a set of 45 untried inkblots. The order of presentation of the inkblots was shuffled randomly for each subject so that every blot had an equal opportunity to appear anywhere in the order. Three preliminary samples, each containing 45 college students and 45 patients from a state mental hospital, were used for the initial item analysis. Thus a maximum of ninety responses was available for each of the 135 inkblots. Two kinds of criteria were used to determine the "goodness" of a given blot: 1) the extent to which the blot discriminated between the two extreme populations of college students and mental patients, and 2) the amount of information contributed by the blot toward total scores in both populations on such variables as location, color, shading, and movement. The best of the 135 inkblots were arranged in matched pairs and selected according to overall ratings of "goodness" until the forty-fifth pair was reached. The members of each pair were randomly assigned to either Form A or B, thus assuring random distribution of any stimulus qualities left unmatched and increasing the likelihood of obtaining truly parallel forms. Two "easy" inkblots with popular concepts were placed in front of the 45 inkblots in each form as practice blots to help establish the appropriate instructional set.

The conceptual framework for devising a scoring system departed somewhat from traditional approaches to the scoring of inkblot responses while preserving the essence of much previous work on the Rorschach. Four criteria were employed for inclusion of a variable in the scoring system. First, the variable had to be one which could be scored for any legitimate response to an inkblot. Second, the variable had to be sufficiently objective so that trained individuals could achieve high inter-scorer agreement. Third, the variable had to show some promise of being pertinent to the study of personality through perception. And fourth, each variable had to be logically independent of all others wherever possible, even though empirical relationships might show up later. Twenty-two variables met these criteria sufficiently well to be included in all the subsequent normative, reliability, and validity studies as reported in the extensive monograph by Holtzman, Thorpe, Swartz, and Herron (1961) describing the HIT and its development.

Standard materials for the HIT consist of the two parallel series, Form A and Form B, the accompanying printed Record Forms and Summary Sheets, and the *Guide for Administration and Scoring*. Sets of 35 mm. slides are also available for use with the group method of administration.

The inkblots are printed on thin but tough white cardboard 5½ by 8½ inches in size. Cards X and Y contain practice blots that are usually not scored. These two cards appear at the beginning of both Forms A and B. Card X is a massive achromatic blot which looks like a bat or butterfly to most people. Very few individuals reject this card although some prefer to use a smaller area rather than the whole blot. Card Y is suggestive of a person's torso to most people. Red spots of ink introduce the subject to color and often evoke responses such as "spots of blood," either given alone or integrated with the torso.

Cards 1 and 2 in both A and B are achromatic and sufficiently broken up to make a whole response difficult unless there is integration of detail, or unless the subject gives a very vague concept or one in which the form of the concept fails to fit the form of the inkblot. Both cards have popular responses in smaller areas of the blot, helping to break up a response set to give only wholes. Card 3 is irregular in form and has a large red "sunburst" splotch overlaid on an amorphous black inkblot. It is very difficult to give a form-definite, form-appropriate whole response to Card 3 because of the chaotic, unstructured nature of this inkblot. Card 4 is just the opposite, containing several finely detailed popular concepts that can be interrelated, together with color and shading that produces a vista-like effect. A "battle scene" or "cowboy watching a sunset" are typical of Card 4A, and "knight carrying a spear and shield" is typical of Card 4B.

Cards 5A and 5B are asymmetrical, grayish-colored blots unlike any in the Rorschach. By penetrating the charcoal-like quality of these blots, one can distinguish a number of detailed objects. Together with several similar, rather wispy, amorphous, asymmetrical blots later in the series, these cards are difficult, particularly for the individual who is searching for definite concepts having good form or who wishes to use the entire blot.

The remaining inkblots cover a wide range of stimulus variation, giving the individual ample opportunity to reveal certain aspects of his mental processes and personality by projecting his thoughts onto otherwise meaningless inkblots. Twelve of the inkblots in Form A are black or gray, two are monochromatic, eleven are black with a bright color also present, and the remaining twenty are multi-colored. Most of the blots have rich shading variations which help to elicit texture responses. A similar distribution of color, shading, and form qualities is present in Form B.

CHAPTER 6 · Holtzman

Standard procedures have been developed for administering the HIT so that published normative data may be used as an aid to interpretation. Instructions to the subject have been designed to make the task as simple as possible while eliciting sufficient information to score major variables reliably. The basic problem is one of encouraging the subject to respond fully without at the same time revealing to him the specific nature of the variables to be scored. The standard instructions differ from those for the Rorschach inkblots in several ways. First, the examiner instructs the subject to give only one response to each card. Second, the brief inquiry is given immediately after each response. And third, the permissible questions by the examiner during inquiry are limited in scope and are asked rather regularly to avoid inadvertent verbal conditioning of certain determinants or content.

A Record Form and a Summary Sheet are available for the examiner to use in recording responses and scoring. Space is provided on the front page of the Record Form for the subject's name, age, sex, and other identifying data. To facilitate the recording of location, schematic diagrams for the inkblots are included. As each response is given, the examiner outlines the specific area used. Adjacent to the diagram is a blank space for recording the verbatim response or a shortened version of it. Scores for the 22 variables are recorded in the appropriate boxes on the Summary Sheet. Reaction Time is entered on the Record Form at the time of administration and transferred later to the Summary Sheet. Extra boxes are provided on the Summary Sheet to take care of any additional variables.

After making appropriate introductions and establishing rapport, the examiner sits next to the subject where he can easily see the area of the inkblot used and can readily follow any elaboration given by the subject. The stack of 47 inkblots is placed in front of the examiner, face down in serial order with the first trial blot (X) on top. The number of the blot appears on the back of the card along with an A or B to identify form. The examiner picks up the cards one at a time, handing each one in upright position to the subject. The instructions given the subject should be informal and should stress the following points: 1) These inkblots were not made to look like anything in particular; 2) different people see different things in each inkblot; and 3) only one response for each card is desired. Although the exact wording used may vary from one type of subject to the next in order to avoid stiffness and maintain rapport, the above points should be emphasized in a standard manner.

After an examiner has become familiar with the materials, he may prefer to score certain variables while administering the inkblots rather than waiting until later. Of course, where such scoring is done concurrently with administration, care must be taken to do the scoring unobtrusively; even then it may be unwise with certain subjects. Most of the variables can be scored just as easily at a later time. However, one variable, Form Appropriateness, is actually easier to score at the time the response is given.

Early in the session, the subject will frequently ask such questions as, "Can I turn the card?" or "Should I use the whole inkblot?" The examiner should always answer with a noncommittal remark such as, "That's entirely up to you." When the subject gives a response with the inkblot inverted or turned sideways, particular care should be taken to record the card position on the Record Form alongside the response.

Immediately following each response, a brief inquiry is made by the examiner to check on certain aspects of the response and to obtain additional information helpful in scoring. Three kinds of questions are permissible in the standard administration: a question to clarify location (Q_L), a question regarding characteristics of the percept (Q_C), and a general question encouraging elaboration (Q_E). The actual wording used can vary a great deal so that the inquiry becomes a natural part of the conversation between examiner and subject. Typical phrasing would be as follows:

Q_L: "Where in the blot do you see a ....?"
Q_C: "What is there about the blot that makes it look like a ....?"
Q_E: "Is there anything else you care to tell me about it?"

Usually the subject comprehends the nature of the task very quickly and the actual inquiry can be kept to a minimum. In any event, it is unwise to ask pointed questions or to stray from the very simple, general inquiry illustrated above. The examiner will occasionally be tempted to ask a specific question to help clarify a particular determinant that may be unclear from a rather cryptic response. It is better to leave well enough alone in such instances because specific inquiry tends to alter the subject's verbal response to the inkblots that follow. Of course one can repeat a general question with different phrasing, if the response is still very ambiguous. Another technique an examiner might use is to pretend to be obtuse, as though he does not understand or did not hear correctly. It is also sometimes helpful to have the subject trace with his finger the outline of the percept. The important thing is to encourage the subject to talk about his response without giving him cues that alter his subsequent responses. A skilled examiner, sensitive to subtle nuances in the examiner-subject interaction, can control the flow of conversation by stimulating a reticent individual and slowing down a verbose person.

A few subjects may disregard the instructions to give only one response per card. Such failure to conform to instructions may take several forms which can have diagnostic significance in their own right. Some disturbed patients, for example, may give a steady stream of different associations to the same inkblot, being unable to focus on any one percept. In such cases, the examiner can often reinforce his instructions by replacing the inkblot with the next in series as soon as the subject shifts his focus to a new response, and by making such remarks as, "Just a minute, let me get that down." If the examiner tries to write down everything the subject says, regardless of its relevance to the primary response, he may inadvertently encourage the subject to give more and more associations. In such cases, the subtle behavior of the examiner, rather than any amount of direct verbal instruction, is more likely to determine whether the subject conforms to the standard instructions.

Another, less pathological, deviation from standard behavior occurs when a subject gives two competing responses almost simultaneously. In every case, it is important to determine which is the primary response. Usually the primary response is the first given, particularly when there is any development or elaboration of the initial percept. In such cases, the second response is ignored except for the possible scoring of Pathognomic Verbalization. Sometimes, however, a subject will give a premature association, as though thinking out loud while organizing what he intends to be the primary response. In all such cases, the subject will move on rapidly and spontaneously to his main percept before the examiner has a chance to make any inquiry about the initial association. When in doubt, a simple question such as, "Which did you mean to give me as your response?" will usually clear up the matter.

Still a third failure to conform to instructions occurs when a subject rejects an inkblot, claiming that he can see nothing in it. Several such rejections within a single protocol are fairly common, making the number of rejections (R) a variable of some interest in its own right. An effort should be made, however, to keep the number of rejections at a minimum by giving the subject plenty of time and encouragement. If a subject fails to respond after one minute and is still looking at the inkblot, the examiner can give a word of encouragement such as, "Some are more difficult than others," or, "Does it suggest anything to you?" If a subject rejects an inkblot without looking at it for at least a minute, the examiner should encourage him by saying, "Would you like to look at it a bit longer?" If a subject persists in rejecting subsequent inkblots after several such encouragements, the examiner should abandon further attempts to obtain a response and let him reject as many as he wishes.

There are a number of experimental variations of administration that need to be studied more thoroughly. In spite of the many interesting variations in test administration that can be attempted, there is much to be said for adhering closely to the standard method of administration. This method has proved highly practical and yields objective, reliable scores on a number of variables worthy of serious study. Currently published normative data and statistical studies of value in the interpretation of the protocols assume close adherence to the standard method of administration.

In the course of standardization, an attempt was made to develop quantitative variables which it was believed would cover nearly all of the important scoring categories and dimensions commonly employed with the Rorschach. After an exhaustive review of previous systems for the Rorschach and preliminary studies to determine inter-scorer agreement, 22 variables were finally carried forward for standardization and analysis. Two variables, Location and Space, deal with the particular parts of the inkblot used by the person in organizing his response and the figure-ground relations of these parts. Form Definiteness, Form Appropriateness, Color, Shading, and Movement are closely related to the stimulus qualities often referred to as the determinants of the response. The more important kinds of content are coded into Human, Animal, Anatomy, Sex, and Abstract. The quality of the response content is captured in part by such scores as Anxiety, Hostility, Barrier, Penetration, and Pathognomic Verbalization. Integration, Balance, Popular, Reaction Time, and Rejection complete the set of 22 variables for which standardization data have been compiled. A twenty-third variable, Affect Arousal, was included in many of the earlier studies although it proved to be too sensitive to examiner differences for normative purposes. A very brief definition of each variable is given below:

Reaction Time (*RT*) — the time, in seconds, from presentation of the inkblot to the beginning of the primary response.

Rejection (*R*) — score 1 when the subject returns the inkblot to the examiner without giving a scorable response.

Location (*L*) — tendency to break down the inkblot into smaller fragments; score 0 for use of whole blot, 1 for use of a large area of the blot, 2 for use of smaller areas of the blot.

Space (*S*) — score 1 for response involving a figure-ground reversal where white space constitutes the figure and the inkblot is the ground.

Form Definiteness (*FD*) — a five-point scale ranging from a score of 0 for a concept having completely indefinite form ("squashed bug") to a score of 4 for highly specific form ("man on horse").

Form Appropriateness (*FA*) — goodness of fit of the form of the concept to the form of the inkblot; score 0 for poor, 1 for fair, and 2 for good form.

Color (*C*) — importance of both chromatic and achromatic color as a determinant; score 0 when not used, 1 when used only in a secondary manner (as in the Rorschach FC), 2 when color is a primary determinant but some indefinite form is present or implied (as in the Rorschach CF), and 3 when color is primary and no form is present (as in the Rorschach C).

Shading (*Sh*) — importance of shading or texture as a determinant;

score 0 when not used, 1 when used only in a secondary manner, and 2 when shading is a primary determinant.

Movement (*M*) — a five-point scale for measuring the degree of movement, tension, or dynamic energy projected into the percept by the subject, regardless of content; score 0 for none, 1 for static potential (sitting, looking, resting), 2 for casual movement (walking, talking), 3 for dynamic movement (dancing, weeping), and 4 for violent movement (whirling, exploding).

Pathognomic Verbalization (*V*) — a five-point scale ranging from 0 (no pathology present) to 4 (very bizarre verbalizations) for measuring the degree of disordered thinking represented by fabulations, fabulized combinations, queer responses, incoherence, autistic logic, contaminations, self references, deteriorated color responses, and absurd responses.

Integration (*I*) — Score 1 when two or more adequately perceived blot elements are organized into a larger whole.

Human (*H*) — Score 0 for no human content present, 1 for parts of human beings, featureless wholes or cartoon characters, 2 for differentiated humans or the human face if elaborated.

Animal (*A*) — Score 0 for no animal content, 1 for animal parts, and 2 for whole animals.

Anatomy (*At*) — Score 0 for no penetration of the body wall, 1 for X-rays, medical drawings, or bone structures, and 2 for viscera or soft internal organs.

Sex (*Sx*) — Score 0 for no direct sex references, 1 for socially accepted sexual activity and expressions ("buttocks," "kissing"), and 2 for blatant sex references ("penis").

Abstract (*Ab*) — Score 0 if no abstract concept is present, 1 if abstract elements are secondary, and 2 if the response is wholly abstract, e.g., "Reminds me of happiness."

Anxiety (*Ax*) — A three-point scale for rating the degree of anxiety apparent in the content of the response as reflected in feelings or attitudes ("frightened animal"), expressive behavior ("girl escaping"), symbolic responses ("dead person"), or cultural stereotypes of fear ("witch"); score 1 when debatable or indirect and score 2 when clearly evident.

Hostility (*Hs*) — A four-point scale for rating degree of hostility apparent in the content of the response, with increasing score as hostility moves from vague or symbolic expressions to more direct, violent ones in which human beings are involved.

Barrier (*Br*) — Score 1 for reference to any protective covering, membrane, shell, or skin that might be symbolically related to the perception of body-image boundaries.

Penetration (*Pn*) — Score 1 for concepts symbolic of body penetration.

Balance (*B*) — Score 1 where the subject expresses concern for the symmetry-asymmetry dimension of the inkblot.

Popular (*P*) — Score 1 if a popular response is given, popular responses being defined statistically for specific areas of the inkblots in earlier normative studies of the HIT.

The total score for each of the 22 variables is obtained by summing across the 45 cards, using the Summary Sheet as a convenient form for this purpose. In addition to the total scores, it is a simple matter to derive a number of other special scores from the basic elements coded for each blot. For example, the number of W, D, or d responses in Rorschach terms can be determined by counting the number of cards coded 0, 1, or 2, respectively, on Location. If the number of human movement responses is desired, one need only count the cards in which Movement is coded 2 or higher and Human is coded 1 or 2. The number of FC, CF, or C responses in the Klopfer system for the Rorschach can be readily derived by merely counting the number of chromatic cards coded 1, 2, or 3, respectively, for Color. Such configural scoring is easy from the Summary Sheet and opens up a large number of special-purpose scores, some entirely new and others highly similar to scores in the several Rorschach systems.

Three of the variables, Form Definiteness, Form Appropriateness and Pathognomic Verbalization, should be corrected for the number of cards rejected, using the formula,

$$CS = \frac{45}{(45 - R)} S$$

where CS is the corrected score, S is the uncorrected score, and R is the number of rejections. The purpose of this correction is to estimate what the score would have been if the subject had responded to the rejected cards in the same manner as he did to the others. Unlike most of the other inkblot variables, where automatic scoring of 0 for rejected cards presents no serious problem, Form Definiteness, Form Appropriateness, and Pathognomic Verbalization have quite different factorial structure in the raw score and corrected versions.

Detailed scoring instructions and examples are provided in both the *Guide* and the monograph accompanying the HIT. The brief definitions given above serve only to introduce the reader to the kinds of inkblot variables scored. It is important to study carefully the detailed scoring guide before attempting to score the HIT.

Nearly all of the scores developed for the HIT are based upon earlier studies with the Rorschach. Because of the greatly increased number of cards in the HIT, most of the scores have higher reliability than is attainable with only the ten cards in the Rorschach. Rejection, in particular, becomes a variable of some significance in its own right. The total score on Color is rather similar to the weighted Sum C score on the Rorschach. Movement is similar to the dynamic energy level scores proposed by Sells (1952) and Zubin (1953) for the Rorschach. Pathognomic Verbalization is a refinement of the system developed by Rapaport (1946) for interpretation of deviant verbalizations. Integration is taken directly from the work by Beck (1949) and Phillips, Kaden and Waldman (1959). The five content variables are rather similar to some of Zubin's (1953) special content rating scales. Anxiety and Hostility are adapted from the studies by Elizur (1949) and Murstein (1956). The two body-image scores, Barrier and Penetration, are taken directly from the extensive studies of body image and personality by Fisher and Cleveland (1958). Balance is a completely new variable made possible by the varying degrees of asymmetry in the HIT blots. And Popular is defined conventionally as responses which occur with a frequency of at least one in seven over a large normal population. Using a sample of 304 cases for Form A and a sample of 309 cases for Form B, this statistical definition yielded 25 inkblots in each form with popular percepts, testifying further to the precise equivalence of the parallel forms.

No doubt there are other variables which can be scored for standard HIT protocols. Indeed, several investigators have already developed new scores for special purposes. The standardized set of 22 variables, however, covers most contemporary systems for measuring dimensions present in inkblot perception and includes several new variables of interest.

A useful procedure for mastering the subtleties of the HIT scoring system is to practice administering the inkblots to several individuals after a careful reading of the *Guide*. These protocols can then be scored, one or two variables at a time, to gain familiarity with the system. Samples of difficult responses already scored are given in the monograph, providing additional practice for the beginner. While the first several protocols will take hours for the novice to score, it is common experience that after ten or twelve protocols an individual can score a protocol in twenty to thirty minutes with reasonably high reliability.

RELIABILITY OF INKBLOT SCORES

The original standardization studies for the HIT were carried out on fifteen different samples totalling 1334 individuals and 1642 protocols. Among normal populations, the samples ranged from five-year-olds through elementary and secondary schools to college students, housewives, and working-class men. Among the abnormal populations were samples drawn from chronic paranoid schizophrenics, general schizophrenic patients, mentally retarded individuals, and mentally depressed adult patients. Studies of both intra-scorer and inter-scorer consistency were carried out for several of these samples. Determinations of test-retest reliability or intra-subject stability over time intervals ranging from one week to one year were made for four of the normal samples. And estimates of internal consistency or immediate intra-subject stability were routinely obtained by the split-half method for each variable in every one of the fifteen samples.

Highly trained scorers concur to a large degree on nearly all the 22 variables, according to one study of inter-scorer consistency on a sample of 40 schizophrenic protocols. The inter-scorer correlations ranged from .89 to .995, with a median value of .98. But what about the average person who may be scoring HIT records? What kind of accuracy can he hope to achieve? One study aimed at answering this question involved four examiners, nine inkblot variables, and 96 protocols. Each examiner collected 24 protocols assigned randomly from the pool of subjects. He scored his own protocols immediately and once again three months later. In addition, each examiner scored 24 protocols drawn in a balanced manner from those collected by the other three examiners. The examiners varied in experience from one highly trained person to two moderately trained persons to an intelligent secretary who read the *Guide,* learned the system as best she could by herself and then served as an examiner in the experiment. The average inter-scorer consistency for these four examiners is given in Table 1, together with similar correlations for intra-scorer consistency.

Table 1. Average scoring consistency for nine variables.

Variable	Intra-Scorer	Inter-Scorer
Form Appropriateness	.92	.73
Color	.97	.89
Shading	.93	.84
Pathognomic Verbalization	.95	.81
Integration	.95	.87
Anxiety	.93	.86
Hostility	.95	.88
Penetration	.89	.84

While the inter-scorer agreement is appreciably less than that obtained when only highly trained scorers are used, in most cases it is sufficiently high to indicate that moderately well-trained scorers can agree very well. The untrained scorer did almost as well as the moderately well-trained ones, demonstrating that a neophyte can master most of the system fairly well entirely on his own. Ranging from .73 for Form Appropriateness to .89 for Color, the average correlations in Table 1 are probably conservative. At the time the study was conducted, the scoring manual was incomplete and only the highly experienced examiner had sufficient experience to incorporate all of the subtle but important scoring criteria which are now explicitly outlined in the *Guide.* Since then, however, others have obtained inter-scorer correlations at least this high on various populations and under varying conditions. Whitaker (1965) reported inter-scorer agreement of .81 for Pathognomic Verbalization, and Megargee (1965a) obtained agreement coefficients ranging from .73 to 1.00, with a median value of .96, in scoring all 22 variables.

As one would expect, the intra-scorer consistency is somewhat higher, ranging from .89 for Penetration to .97 for Color. There is generally high agreement between the examiner's scoring done immediately after collecting the protocol and the same person's scoring three months later.

This study was also designed to determine how much the examiner may be a factor influencing the performance of the subject. Two of the examiners were men and two were women; each differed greatly from the others in personality and appearance; and, of course, they varied considerably in experience. Since the subjects were randomly assigned to examiners, and since every protocol was scored three times in a balanced design, any significant sources of variance due to examiners or due to scoring could be isolated and interpreted. Only two variables—Color and Pathognomic Verbalization—showed significant examiner bias for the rescored records. In each case the source of bias was the untrained examiner, the secretary who had tried to learn the system on her own.

In a more recent study by Megargee, Lockwood, Cato, and Jones (1966), three inexperienced female examiners each gave the HIT to 30 college students, half women and half men, a total of 90 cases. For one-half of the cases each examiner assumed a positive, pleasant, reassuring role, while for the other half she tried to be negative and foreboding. Unlike Lord's (1950) study with the Rorschach where both the examiner and the tone of administration proved to be major factors influencing responses, the HIT was quite free of situational influences with two minor exceptions—small examiner differences in Rejection and Shading. Together with the earlier studies, these results indicate that the examiner is not an important source of variance in the HIT.

By using the parallel forms of the HIT in a test-retest design, the amount of intra-subject stability over time can be determined. This design was employed in four of the standardization samples—139 college students with an interval of one week between testing sessions, 72 eleventh-grade high school students with a three-month interval, 42 elementary pupils with an interval of one year, and 48 college students with a one-year interval. This same design has also been employed more recently in a longitudinal study of school children who are being tested annually for a period of six years, alternating Forms A and B from year to year (Holtzman, 1965a). Test-retest coefficients for the first three years of this study, based on 691 cases ranging in age from six to 14 years, are very similar to those obtained in the earlier studies by Holtzman, et al (1961).

The most stable scores over time are Reaction Time, Location, Movement, and Human. Test-retest correlations for these scores run in the sixties and seventies even after a one-year interval. The most unstable scores for normals over a period of one year are Popular, Anatomy, Space, Sex, Abstract, Balance, and Pathognomic Verbalization, usually with coefficients in the twenties or thirties. The remaining eleven scores are

moderately stable over a year's time, generally yielding test-retest coefficients in the forties or fifties. As indicated in Table 2, test-retest
coefficients are slightly higher for an interval of only one week. In general,
it can be concluded that the stability of most scores is sufficiently high to
justify use of the HIT to study changes in perception and personality over
a period of many months.

In all of these studies using both Forms A and B with the same subjects, statistical tests were also made to determine the equivalence of the
parallel forms. In every instance, neither means, standard deviations nor
intercorrelations of any inkblot scores differed significantly from Form A
to Form B, testifying further to the precise equivalence of the two forms.

Another approach to reliability is the computation of split-half reliability coefficients as measures of internal consistency or immediate
intra-subject stability. Six of the variables—Reaction Time, Location,
Form Definiteness, Form Appropriateness, Animal and Popular—have
good, reasonably normal distributions in all of the standardization samples. For these variables, the reliability estimates should be generally
accurate. Color, Movement, Human, Hostility, Anxiety, and Barrier have
good distributions in all the normal samples but are sharply skewed in
one or more of the abnormal samples. Shading, Integration, and Penetration have good distributions only in the samples of college students.
The remaining eight variables are sharply skewed or truncated in every
sample, making somewhat questionable the accuracy of the reliability
estimates using the split-half method. The range and median reliability
values for the 15 samples and 18 of the variables are given in Table 2.

Table 2. Split-half reliability and test-retest stability of inkblot variables

Inkblot Variable	Split-Half r's for 15 Samples		Test-Retest r with Interval of 1 Week (139 College Students)
	Range	Median	
Reaction Time	.95—.98	.97	.77
Rejection	.79—.98	.93	.76
Location	.86—.94	.91	.82
Form Definiteness	.81—.96	.88	.68
Form Appropriateness	.44—.91	.85	.55
Color	.70—.94	.88	.59
Shading	.62—.94	.78	.70
Movement	.71—.93	.81	.70
Pathognomic Verbalization	.49—.96	.87	.68
Integration	.59—.84	.79	.70
Human	.66—.93	.79	.67
Animal	.53—.95	.70	.38
Anatomy	.54—.94	.71	.53
Anxiety	.31—.91	.66	.54
Hostility	.54—.89	.71	.61
Barrier	.47—.85	.70	.45
Penetration	.41—.92	.62	.54
Popular	.00—.77	.51	.39

Reaction Time, Rejection, Location, Form Definiteness, and Color have consistently high reliability, a large number of coefficients being above .90. Most of the remainder are also highly satisfactory, only Popular proving to be generally low. Complete tables are given in the monograph by Holtzman, et al (1961), including standard errors of measurement as well as means, standard deviations, and reliability coefficients for each variable and population studied. These data are useful in establishing a confidence interval for an individual score prior to interpretation.

DIMENSIONS PRESENT IN INKBLOT SCORES

What can be said about the psychological meaning of inkblot variables, granted that they can be reliably measured? How do such variables relate to each other and to independent measures of personality? Are they of value in the differential diagnosis of mental or emotional disorders? What do they tell us about developmental processes? Before examining the validity of inkblot variables for different purposes, it may be instructive to look at the intercorrelations among the 22 HIT variables and the major dimensions they have in common.

Complete intercorrelation matrices of all inkblot scores were computed routinely for each of the samples in the standardization program. While correlations between any two inkblot scores may be of some interest when replicated over many samples, a more efficient way of examining the relationships among inkblot variables is to employ factor analysis and factor matching across samples. In nearly every case, six factors account for all the significant common variance present among the 22 variables. The first three of these have appeared in a number of factor-analytic studies of HIT variables, including some on samples from other countries. The last three tend to be less stable, shifting somewhat in composition according to the kind of population studied. The major patterns that have clearly emerged are as follows:

Factor I: Perceptual maturity and integrated ideational activity. Invariably defined by Movement, Integration, Human, Barrier, and Popular, Factor I usually accounts for more variance than any other. Anxiety and Hostility may also have moderately high loadings on Factor I, particularly among children or mentally retarded adults. A high amount of this factor would be indicative of well organized, ideational activity, good imaginative capacity, well differentiated ego boundaries, and awareness of conventional concepts.

Factor II: Perceptual sensitivity. Defined primarily by Color and Shading, and to a lesser extent by Form Definiteness (reversed) this bipolar factor involves sensitivity to the stimulus qualities of the blots. Balance also shows significant loadings in some populations, most notably adult schizophrenics. The positive pole of this factor would indicate over-reactivity to the color, shading, or symmetrical balance of the inkblot, while the negative pole would indicate primary concern for form alone as a determinant.

Factor III: *Psychopathology of thought.* Pathognomic Verbalization is the best single variable for defining this factor, although Anxiety and Hostility frequently have high loadings. Among children, Penetration is often a significant contributor to this underlying dimension, and in many abnormal populations Form Appropriateness (reversed) has appreciable loadings. A high amount of this factor would be indicative of disordered thought processes coupled with an active, though disturbed, fantasy life.

Factor IV: *Perceptual differentiation.* Although not as well defined because of the overshadowing influence of the first three factors, in most samples, particularly among children, Form Appropriateness and Location serve as defining variables. The factor is bipolar, the positive pole tending to indicate perceptual differentiation coupled with a critical sense of good form.

Factor V. Reaction Time, Rejection, and Animal (reversed) are the primary variables defining this factor. While Reaction Time and Rejection tend to go together in nearly every population, other scores vary in their contribution to this pattern making it difficult to generalize from one sample to the next. A high score on this factor may reflect either strong inhibition or inability to perceive concepts in the blots, depending on other factors present.

Factor VI. In about half of the populations studied, this residual factor takes the form of a minor pathological dimension defined by Penetration, Anatomy, and, where present, Sex. This particular pattern signifies a dimension indicative of bodily preoccupations independent of pathological components noted in Factor III.

After accounting for most of the common variance across the 22 variables by these six underlying dimensions, there still remains sufficient unique, reliable variance in many of the scores to justify their individual consideration. Most notably, Reaction Time, Location, Form Definiteness, Form Appropriateness, Color, Shading, and Pathognomic Verbalization show consistently significant residual variance. Only Popular, Penetration, and Integration are sufficiently well represented by one of the major factors to leave little or no residual unique variance. Consequently, it is recommended that, for most purposes, the individual scores be used for interpretation and analysis rather than only the factor scores representing these six dimensions. Where it is desirable to have only two or three broadly based dimensions for analysis, factor scores for the first three factors—Perceptual Maturity, Perceptual Sensitivity, and Psychopathology of Thought—can be crudely computed by simple, weighted combinations of the defining inkblot variables. Factor loading tables for each population are presented in the HIT monograph for those who wish to develop factor scores.

COMPARISON OF THE HIT AND THE RORSCHACH

Any new technique such as the HIT is likely to be viewed rather critically by clinicians or research psychologists who have built up a wealth of experience in the use of an established projective method such as the Rorschach. Quite rightly, they wish to know what advantages are to be gained by adopting the HIT, what information may be lost by substituting it for the Rorschach, and how similar the two methods are with respect to the projective, qualitative material elicited as well as the more quantitative, psychometric variables. Quite aside from the similarities and differences noted earlier, several studies have been reported which throw considerable light on these questions.

The first systematic comparison of the HIT and the Rorschach was conducted in a cooperative study involving Beck, Haggard, Bock, and Holtzman (Holtzman et al, 1961). Both Rorschach and Holtzman inkblots were administered twice to 72 high school students by Mrs. Samuel Beck—a total of four protocols per subject. The Rorschach always preceded the Holtzman by about three weeks, with an interval of approximately three months between original and retest sessions. The Rorschach protocols were scored by Mrs. Beck, using Beck's system of analysis (see Chapter 5, pages 115-135), and the HIT protocols were scored by Holtzman's research staff.

Eight scores within the two systems were sufficiently comparable in *a priori* definition to justify computing correlations between them. Variability in number of responses on the Rorschach was partially controlled by converting raw scores on other variables into average values per response. Since the true relationships between the Rorschach and Holtzman systems are attenuated by several sources of error, most notably the unreliability of scores, corrections for unreliability were applied to each validity coefficient, using the Spearman-Brown formula and split-half reliability estimates from the HIT. Corrected correlations across the two methods ranged from lows of .51, .57, and .66 for Shading, Human Movement, and Color, respectively, to values greater than 1 for Human and Animal, the two content scores. More recently, Whitaker (1965) has obtained a correlation of .76 (uncorrected for unreliability) for Pathognomic Verbalization when scored on Rorschach and HIT protocols.

The stimulus qualities of the Rorschach and Holtzman inkblots with respect to associative value have been studied systematically by Otten and Van de Castle (1963). The ten Rorschach cards and 45 HIT cards in Form A were mixed into one series which was rated using 14 semantic differential scales consisting of bipolar adjectives like clean-dirty, heavy-light, and active-passive. The connotations of the Holtzman cards were more varied, while at the same time covering all the "meanings" associated with the Rorschach cards. It was also discovered that some Holtzman cards tap patterns of meaning not found in the Rorschach cards, although the reverse was not true.

Rigorous comparisons between the Rorschach and Holtzman systems dealing with the subtle, qualitative aspects of the methods are more difficult to make. To the extent that one leans heavily upon sequential analysis of multiple responses to a single inkblot, the one-response-per-card format of the standard HIT is unsuitable. Intensive analysis of single responses is also less satisfactory on the HIT than on the Rorschach. Of course one can select a subset of HIT inkblots and administer them in a manner similar to the Rorschach; but such a procedure is not generally recommended since all the advantages of the HIT method are lost. Where there is considerable interest in multiple responses and depth analysis of single responses, it would be better to administer a subset of inkblots from either the same or parallel form of the HIT in a second testing session using the Rorschach method following the standard HIT. In this way one would have the advantages of both methods, plus the flexibility of specially derived subsets for intensive analysis.

Most clinicians who use the HIT, however, find that it yields ample qualitative material of a projective nature for depth analysis. An illustration of a case analysis involving the integration of both qualitative and psychometric approaches is given in the HIT monograph.

In general, the studies to date indicate quite conclusively that the Rorschach and Holtzman systems have a great deal in common as far as the underlying meaning of their respective variables is concerned. The important difference between the two methods is the psychometric advantage of the HIT with respect to standardization, reliability, clearer interpretability of quantitative scores, and the availability of truly parallel forms.

EXTERNAL CORRELATES OF INKBLOT SCORES

A considerable amount of information has accrued in the past five years bearing upon the relationships between inkblot scores from the HIT and independently obtained behavioral, personality, cognitive, perceptual, developmental, sociocultural, and psychodiagnostic measures. The findings from these many studies will be summarized first with respect to correlations with measures of cognition and perception. Then correlations with personality tests will be discussed, followed by a presentation of evidence bearing upon behavioral correlates. Developmental trends in children and major inter-group differences related to differential diagnosis and sociocultural factors complete the discussion.

Correlations with cognitive and perceptual measures

Correlations between HIT scores and standard measures of intelligence, scholastic achievement, and convergent thinking are low though statistically significant. In a sample of 197 seventh-grade children collected as part of the standardization study for the HIT, a large number of significant correlations ranging from .20 to .31 were obtained between Rejection (reversed), Location, Form Appropriateness, Shading, Movement, Integration, Anxiety, Hostility, and Barrier, on the one hand, and ten mental ability tests on the other. Measures of intelligence and social status were found by Thorpe and Swartz (1963) to be related to Rejection, the number of rejections dropping from an average of 12 to an average of six per protocol in going from low to high IQ groupings of seventh-grade children. Holtzman, Gorham, and Moran (1964) found similar significant but low correlations between Wechsler-Bellevue Vocabulary and Integration, Movement, and Form Appropriateness in a sample of 99 chronic, paranoid schizophrenic men. Preliminary results from the Austin longitudinal project based on 370 school children tested twice, one year apart, (Holtzman, 1966) yielded correlations between WISC Vocabulary and Movement ranging from .14 to .45 with a mean value of .27. The same relationship exists for Form Definiteness, Integration, Human, Hostility, Barrier, and Popular. Clearly, inkblot scores, particularly those defining the Perceptual Maturity Factor, do relate significantly to general intelligence, though at a low level.

Tests of divergent thinking, creativity, and other forms of cognitive functioning also correlate with inkblot scores in a meaningful manner. Using Guilford's tests of divergent thinking, Clark, Veldman, and Thorpe (1965) found that junior high school students who were high in divergent thinking ability gave more whole responses and got higher scores on Movement, Anxiety, Hostility, Color, and Penetration than did students who were low in this ability. They concluded that divergent thinkers give freer rein to imaginative production, have higher verbal facility, and are more responsive to the stimulus characteristics of inkblots. In a study of attitudes toward the imaginary, Codkind (1964) found that individuals with a high degree of fantasy acceptance have more complex cognitive organization and a greater openness to experience as shown by significantly higher scores on Integration, Abstract, Popular, Form Appropriateness, Color, Movement, Anxiety, Hostility, and Fabulation, and significantly lower scores on Location and Rejection.

In a factor-analytic study of schizophrenic thought processes, Holtzman, et al (1964) obtained eight orthogonal dimensions, five of which had high loadings from HIT variables as well as cognitive measures—Verbal Ability, Integrated Ideation, Stimulus Sensitivity, Pathological Verbalization, and Conceptual Autism. Gardner and Moriarty report several significant correlations between cognitive style dimensions and

HIT factor scores.[2] High Conceptual Differentiation (number of groups in the Object Sorting Test) is related to low Psychopathology of Thought (Factor III) in the HIT, a finding that has since been replicated for adolescents in the Austin longitudinal study. Other correlations between HIT and cognitive style variables are more tentative, varying inconsistently across different samples. Partially confirming the earlier studies by Witkin, Young (1959) found a different pattern of correlations between HIT scores and cognitive style variables for men than for women. From a recent review of perceptual-cognitive style and the HIT by Holtzman (1965b), it is obvious that more extensive investigation is needed to clarify these relationships.

Correlations with personality tests

Various paper-and-pencil approaches to the study of personality by self-inventory have been studied for possible HIT correlates but without much success. Among the variables included in the extended correlation matrix for the 197 seventh-grade children in the HIT standardization study were 12 scores from Cattell's Junior Personality Quiz. Only one of the correlations between inkblot scores and the personality scales proved highly significant statistically—a correlation of -.25 between Human and Neuroticism, a relationship that is at least in the expected direction. Similar negative results have been obtained for the Minnesota Multiphasic Personality Inventory and the Edwards Personal Preference Schedule when related to HIT variables in a group of 106 Peace Corps trainees (Holtzman, Santos, Bouquet, and Barth, 1966). A positive relationship was found, however, between a Guilt scale on the MMPI and Anatomy, Pathognomic Verbalization, and Form Appropriateness (reversed) in a study by Moseley, Duffy, and Sherman (1963) using depressed patients.

The more limited area of anxiety and hostility has been studied by Ruebush (1960), by Barger and Sechrest (1961), and by Swartz (1965), using such measures as the Manifest Hostility Scale of the MMPI, Taylor's Manifest Anxiety Scale, or Sarason's Test Anxiety Scale for Children. No significant relationships were found between self-inventory scores and inkblot scores of Anxiety and Hostility, although Swartz reported that children with high test-anxiety gave significantly lower scores on Movement and Barrier and higher scores on Rejection and Affect Arousal. It is apparent that the symbolic content scales, Anxiety and Hostility, in the HIT are strictly ratings at the fantasy level which are unrelated to self-inventory measures.

One major exception to the generally negative findings concerning

[2] Unpublished manuscript by Gardner, R. W. and Moriarty, A. entitled, "Personality development at preadolescence: an exploratory study of structure formation." (1965)

the relationship between HIT scores and self-inventory personality measures is the study by Richter and Winter (1966) in the field of creativity. Using scores on the intuitive-perceptive scales of the Myers-Briggs Type Indicator for defining high and low groups of women, they discovered that women with a high amount of this kind of creativity give significantly more Form Definiteness, Color, Movement, Human, Integration, Pathognomic Verbalization, Anxiety, Hostility, and Abstract. *A priori* predictions from the earlier Rorschach work and the studies by MacKinnon and his associates were confirmed in a striking manner by these results, indicating that the HIT is a useful instrument for measuring important aspects of creative potentiality.

Correlations with behavioral measures

Investigations involving specific behavioral measures of personality as they relate to HIT variables are rather scarce, although a number of studies have been reported demonstrating the effectiveness of the HIT in classification of groups or in differential diagnosis, studies in which behavioral ratings or manifestations often play a determining role in the criterion classification. The latter findings will be reported in later sections dealing with differential diagnosis and cross-cultural differences.

High Barrier appears to be related to more effective communication in small group settings, according to Cleveland and Morton (1962) who studied 70 psychiatric patients in a group therapy program. An extensive review of empirical work on both Barrier and Penetration has been made by Fisher (1963) who reports a number of interesting behavioral correlates. More recently, Megargee (1965b) found a significant, though low, relationship (.23) between Barrier and ratings of aggressiveness in 75 detained juvenile delinquents, indicating that the most seriously delinquent adolescents had lower Barrier scores.

Sociometric peer ratings within normal groups generally fail to show any relationship to inkblot scores (Barger & Sechrest, 1961; Holtzman et al, 1966). And yet, ratings by skilled observers or field performance ratings do show significant, meaningful correlations with inkblot variables. Barrier and Color scores, combined with scales from the Edwards Personal Preference Schedule, effectively predicted the rated performance of Peace Corps volunteers in villages of Brazil fifteen months after psychological testing (Holtzman et al, 1966). Mueller and Abeles (1964) found a correlation of .44 between Movement and judged degree of empathy. Megargee (1966a) reported that extremely assaultive adolescents give significantly fewer pure color responses (those coded C 3) than do moderately assaultive boys, a finding consistent with his theory that the infrequent violent act results from high control coupled with high aggression which finally reaches the breaking point. In a recent unpublished study, Megargee and Cook (1967) report low but significant correlations between Hostility and behavioral criteria of aggression for 76 juvenile delinquents. In addition, they found correlations of about .40 between several similar scales of Hostility in the HIT and in the Thematic Apperception Test, providing further evidence of the consistency of fantasy productions and symbolic hostile content from both apperception and inkblot methods. And finally, Brown, Harkness, and Proctor[3] found a correlation of .50 between interviewer's ratings of hostility and Hostility scores on the HIT. These results are sufficiently promising to warrant their being extended to other situations and populations.

Developmental trends in children

Following the lead of earlier Rorschach studies, several major investigations have been reported which demonstrate a strong relationship between HIT scores and developmental level. Thorpe (1960) derived 29 basic pattern scores using elements in the Holtzman scoring system drawn primarily from Location, Form Definiteness, Integration, Movement, Color, Shading, Human, Animal, and Pathognomic Verbalization. Highly significant age trends were found for all but two of the individual scores and for many of the pattern scores across four of the normal populations included in the HIT standardization studies. Thorpe and Swartz (1965) refined this preliminary study by repeating the analysis using groups balanced for sex and ranging in age from five to 20 years. While no significant sex differences or sex-by-age interactions were discovered for this large sample of 586 normal subjects, a number of striking age trends were noted, all of which are highly consistent with developmental theory. Integration, Movement, Human, and Shading showed a regular increase with increasing age throughout the age span studied. Color and Pathognomic Verbalization generally decreased with age. Form Appropriateness, and Form Definiteness rose fairly rapidly in pre-adolescent years, levelling off thereafter. Location increased steadily until the college years when it dropped to a new low.

Analysis of the pattern scores indicates that this curvilinear trend for Location is due to a shift in the way in which Location, Form Definiteness, Form Appropriateness, and Integration interact to form the response. The young child tends to give wholes without much attention to Form Appropriateness or Form Definiteness. By the age of ten, the child is more reality-bound and tends to achieve satisfactory definiteness and appropriateness of form by choosing smaller areas of the inkblot. As he grows older he is able to maintain good form while increasing the area of the blot used, integrating smaller parts into a larger whole. By the time he is in college, his perceptual organization, his ability to differen-

[3] Unpublished manuscript by Brown, G. D., Harkness, R. B., and Procter, D. E. entitled, "The Holtzman Inkblot Technique as a measure of anxiety and hostility."

tiate parts which are then integrated into larger wholes, his concern with reality, his focus on human interaction, his ability to project dynamic quality into his percept, and his sensitivity to the color, shading, and symmetry of the stimulus are all manifest at their peak in the developmental trends noted here.

Largely because of the striking and provocative findings in these basic studies of developmental trends across different age groups, a major longitudinal study was undertaken in Austin, Texas, involving about 140 first-graders, 140 fourth-graders, and 140 seventh-graders who were tested initially in the 1962-63 school year. Consisting of a variety of perceptual, cognitive, and personality measures in addition to the HIT, the test battery was administered to each child in each of the three groups at precisely the same age—initially 6 years 8 months, 9 years 8 months, and 12 years 8 months. Annual testing takes place on the anniversary date of initial testing until six years of repeated measurment have been completed. Other data from parental interviews, school records, and sociometric ratings are gathered periodically to shed light on the environmental, sociocultural factors that interplay with psychological development. In addition, the Austin longitudinal project is being carefully replicated in Mexico City under the direction of Rogelio Diaz-Guerrero and his associates to examine developmental trends cross-culturally. Several preliminary reports of this work have been published, although the definitive analysis remains to be done after completion of the testing program. Analysis of the first year in the Austin project yielded results essentially identical to those reported above for the standardization samples (Thorpe & Swartz, 1966).

A somewhat different approach to the concept of developmental level is to apply genetic-level pattern scores to the study of severity of disorder in schizophrenic patients. Steffy and Becker (1961) applied such pattern scores on the HIT to 36 schizophrenic patients in a VA hospital and correlated the overall scores with ratings on the Elgin Prognostic Scale. When duration of hospitalization was held constant, a correlation of -.46 was obtained between the HIT and the prognostic rating, indicating that low genetic pattern scores are associated with poor prognosis for outcome in schizophrenia.

Differential diagnosis

One of the primary uses of the HIT is to provide information of value in the differential diagnosis of various kinds of psychiatric patients or behavior disorders. Because of the qualitative nature of nosological systems, the external correlates of inkblot scores are represented by inter-group differences rather than correlation coefficients. The most extensive information bearing upon differential diagnosis is given in the monograph by Holtzman, et al (1961), which contains standardization data on fifteen different populations. Percentile norms are presented for eight major reference groups, five of which are different developmental levels ranging from five-year-olds to superior adults and three of which deal with psychiatric classes—chronic paranoid schizophrenics, depressed neurotics and psychotics, and mentally retarded individuals. The reference groups of average adults and elementary school children provide excellent control groups for comparison with the three abnormal populations.

Chronic schizophrenics differ significantly from normal controls of similar age and social background in a number of inkblot variables. Schizophrenics get higher scores on Rejection, Pathognomic Verbalization, Penetration, Anatomy, Sex, and lower scores on Location, Form Definiteness, Form Appropriateness, Shading, Movement, Integration, Human, Barrier, and Popular. While the means for Color, Anxiety, Hostility, and Animal are just about the same in schizophrenics and normals, the variances are much greater for schizophrenics, who tend to show either a lot of uncontrolled color and symbolic or animal content or none at all. Only Reaction Time, Space, Abstract, and Balance fail to discriminate between normals and schizophrenic patients. Using 100 schizophrenics and 100 normals from the HIT standardization samples, Moseley (1963) applied linear-discriminant-function analysis to develop weights for use in separating schizophrenic from normal protocols. All 16 of the HIT scores that he used, except Reaction Time, contributed significantly to the analysis, resulting in a classification by formula that was 88 percent correct. The procedure held up completely when cross-validated on a second sample of schizophrenic and normal cases, indicating that it can be used with some confidence in the diagnosis of schizophrenia.

Differentiating schizophrenics from depressed patients is a much more difficult task than separating schizophrenics from normals. When Moseley applied discriminant-function analysis to develop procedures for the differential diagnosis of schizophrenics and depressives, the results were almost as good as in the case of schizophrenics and normals: the percent correctly classified was 78. Depressives differ most markedly from schizophrenics by getting higher scores on Reaction Time, Location, Form Definiteness, Form Appropriateness, Movement, Human, Integration, Hostility, Barrier, and Popular and lower scores on Rejection, Color, and Pathognomic Verbalization. Depressives can also be distinguished from normals using Moseley's discriminant-function weights, though the accuracy of classification is somewhat less: 71 percent. The chief differences here are due to higher scores by depressives on Reaction Time, Pathognomic Verbalization, Sex, and Penetration and lower scores on Rejection, Color, and Movement.

Use of the HIT for differential diagnosis of other disorders has been tried by other investigators with equally good success. Barnes (1963) was able to discriminate between brain-damaged individuals and normal controls with about eighty percent accuracy. Megargee (1965a) published norms for male juvenile delinquents tested while in custody. He obtained a number of significant differences on HIT scores when comparing them with several normal control groups. And Connors (1965) reported a number of highly significant differences between emotionally disturbed children seen in an outpatient clinic and normal controls of the same age and background. In Connors' study, disturbed children got higher scores on Rejection and Anatomy and lower scores on all other variables except Pathognomic Verbalization, Sex, Abstract, Hostility, Penetration, and Balance. Using HIT factor scores, Connors found that neurotic children appeared to be more differentiated in response (Factor IV) and more inhibited (Factor V) than did hyperkinetic children. Cleveland and Fisher (1960) differentiated sharply between arthritic patients and those with ulcers, using only the Barrier score; the arthritics got much higher scores, confirming their hypothesis concerning the meaning of Barrier. Cleveland and Sikes (1966) discriminated between alcoholics and non-alcoholic patients using Penetration and two new inkblot variables, Decadence (all responses involving decay) and Water (all references to water), all of which are higher in alcoholics.

The HIT appears to be well suited for improving differential diagnosis and psychiatric screening, particularly when appropriately combined with other valid techniques. While most of the studies cited have not been concerned with the problem of controlling base rates, it is obvious that inkblot scores provide a powerful tool for diagnostic purposes. Considerable work now in progress at various hospitals and clinics will make it possible to develop a series of diagnostic weights that should be highly useful for the practicing clinician as well as the individual concerned with psychiatric screening.

Cross-cultural correlates

Because of the non-verbal, "meaningless" nature of inkblots and the standard, simple instructions to give only one response per card, the HIT is ideally suited for cross-cultural studies ranging from industrialized societies to primitive, non-literate tribes. During the past five years the method has been used successfully in many countries under widely varying conditions. Most of these studies are just beginning to appear in various publications.

One of the most extensive cross-cultural studies involving the HIT is the Austin-Mexico City project briefly described by Holtzman (1965a) in a theoretical analysis of cross-cultural research on personality development. Conducted in collaboration with Diaz-Guerrero and his associates, the project involves careful matching of Mexican and Texas samples on sex, age, father's education and occupation. A first report of cross-cultural findings on the HIT has been given by Swartz (1966). Protocols from

516 six-, nine-, and 12-year-olds were analyzed for 17 HIT scores across sex, age, father's occupational level, and culture. Quite aside from a number of highly significant interactions involving culture and the other three major factors studied, the Mexican children obtained generally lower scores on most HIT variables. Taken together with the findings from other tests in the cross-cultural project, these results are highly consistent with Diaz-Guerrero's theory concerning the different socio-cultural premises underlying Mexican and American personality development—the Mexicans are more passive and resilient while the Americans are more active and direct in their style of coping with stress.

Almost identical results were obtained by Tamm (1966) who studied 90 children in the first, fourth, and seventh grades of the American School in Mexico City. Although every child could speak both English and Spanish, half came from well educated Mexican families and half from American. The HIT and WISC were given to each child by a bilingual examiner in either Spanish or English, whichever language happened to be the dominant one. In spite of the common school system and similar general environment, Mexicans were higher on Location and lower on Color, Movement, and Pathognomic Verbalization at all ages. Several age-by-culture interactions were found, but the Mexicans and Americans were still as distinctly separate in the seventh grade as in the first, suggesting that the cultural difference is fairly fundamental, being relatively unaffected by formal schooling.

A somewhat different approach to cross-cultural research using the HIT has been taken by Gorham, Moseley, and their associates. Working with group-administered protocols collected in the native language, they have obtained large amounts of data from over a dozen different cultures throughout the world. A special computer-scoring system which they have perfected expedites data analysis and assures comparability of results across any languages for which scoring dictionaries have been compiled. Moseley (1964) reported a number of interesting differences and similarities among college students from Mexico, Panama, Hong Kong, and the United States. In a more recent study of college students from Argentina, Colombia, Venezuela, Panama, Mexico, and the United States, Moseley (1966) applied the powerful methods of multiple-discriminant-function analysis to the problem of separating respondents from different cultures. Particularly interesting was the way in which students from each country were misclassified since this pattern illustrated traits shared in common by the various cultures involved. Of the 100 Mexicans, for example, 81 were correctly identified; but more significant is the fact that all but two of the misclassified students were mistakenly called Americans rather than Colombians or Venezuelans, indicating rather dramatically that Mexican students are closer in personality structure to North Americans than they are to South Americans in spite of the common linguistic and cultural ties throughout Latin America. In a similar manner, all but four of the 35 misclassified Americans were mistakenly labelled Mexican.

The HIT has also been used in a search for transcultural universals rather than differences. Knudsen, Gorham, and Moseley (1966) derived popular concepts using the same statistical methods and criteria employed in the derivation of Popular for the standard HIT. The majority of populars appeared universally in all five cultures that were studied—Denmark, Germany, Hong Kong, Mexico, and the United States. While interesting idiosyncracies were noted in each culture, only one of the 25 original populars failed to appear in at least two of the samples.

CLINICAL APPLICATIONS

Compared to the Rorschach, on which a great deal of clinical material has been amassed, the HIT is a relatively new projective technique. And yet, it draws so heavily upon the Rorschach for its basic method and rationale that many clinicians find it valuable to combine the quantitative approaches stressed in the previous discussion with qualitative content analysis frequently employed with the Rorschach. Certainly there is sufficient continuity between the extensive work on the Rorschach and the recent studies employing the HIT to justify considerable generalization from one to the other. Quite understandably, most of the published material on the HIT deals with reliability, validity, basic experimental investigations, and other exploratory or evaluative work rather than clinical applications *per se*. Widespread application of a method should await thorough evaluation. The current review of recent work strongly suggests that a sufficient mass of promising evidence has now accrued to justify use of the HIT in practical, everyday assessment situations of a clinical nature.

Percentile norms for each of the 22 variables are presented in the standardization monograph as well as the *Guide,* making it possible to develop an individual profile of scores for assessment purposes. The norms are given separately for eight reference groups—five normal ones, ranging from five-year-olds to superior adults, and three abnormal ones: schizophrenics, depressives, and mental retardates. Norms have also been published for male juvenile delinquents (Megargee, 1965a), and other norms are being compiled. When dealing with the assessment of a particular individual, comparisons can be made with any of the reference groups, selecting first that group which is most similar to the reference population to which the individual belongs. A detailed illustration of the use of percentile norms in combination with Moseley's multivariate statistical approach to psychodiagnosis is given in a case analysis by Holtzman, et al (1961).

As computers become more routinely accessible to clinicians, the multivariate approach possible with the HIT will become sufficiently effective as an assessment tool to find extensive application in practical situations. Of course there is still a wealth of information in inkblot responses that remains uncoded in the 22 standard variables. At least for the immediate future there is no good substitute for a skillful, experienced clinical analysis which can incorporate both the quantitative and qualitative aspects of HIT protocols.

Variations in the Standard Method

Unlike the Rorschach, the HIT is particularly well suited for group administration because of the simple format involving only one response. The group method is more economical since almost any number of individuals can be tested at once, using colored slides projected on a screen and having each individual write out his responses on the Record Form. There is a slight restriction imposed by presenting inkblots only in an upright position, but most individuals fail to give inverted responses even in the standard individual method where they can turn the card. There is also some loss of information which can be gained only through the personalized, verbal interaction of the examiner and subject, thereby increasing the difficulty of scoring some variables. For use in large-scale psychiatric screening or research projects, however, the advantages of the group method far outweigh the disadvantages.

Details concerning the standard method for group administration are given by Swartz and Holtzman (1963). Based on a series of studies aimed at developing a procedure to insure scores comparable to those obtained with the individual method, the group method involves reading special instructions to the subjects, using trial inkblots X and Y to illustrate the technique, and projecting colored slides at exposure times of 75 seconds per blot after slightly longer exposures for the first nine cards. With the exception of Reaction Time and Balance which are lost in the group method, all of the inkblot variables are scored in the usual manner.

Split-half reliability and test-retest stability using parallel forms with a one-week interval are essentially as high for the group method as for the individual. Using a latin-square design involving Forms A and B given to large numbers of students by both the individual and group methods one week apart, Holtzman, Moseley, Reinehr, and Abbott (1963) made a systematic comparison of the group and individual methods of administration. Only five of 18 inkblots scores studied showed any significant mean differences attributable to method of administration. Location, Space, and Color scores were higher for the group method, and Barrier and Popular scores were higher for the individual method. Standard deviations of scores were the same for all variables except Anxiety which had a higher variance in the group method. Comparing the cross-method correlations in a multitrait-multimethod matrix revealed a striking degree of similarity across the two methods. From these studies it was concluded that the group method could be safely substituted for the individual method where one is dealing with subjects who can write out their own responses to the inkblots.

While the group method of administration is a far more economical way of collecting inkblot responses than is the individual method, there still remains the problem of scoring each record by hand, a task that takes at least 20 minutes per protocol. Gorham, Moseley, and their associates (Moseley, Gorham, and Hill, 1963; Gorham, 1964; Gorham, 1966) have successfully developed a method for scoring 17 HIT variables by high speed computer. A dictionary-building program was written for the IBM 7090 computer which alphabetizes words and counts their frequency of occurrence for any sample of protocols where the responses have first been properly key-punched. An empirically derived dictionary containing about 7,000 words has been compiled in several languages to facilitate cross-cultural studies. Each word in the dictionary is assigned multiple scoring weights by an individual experienced in scoring HIT variables. These weights are checked and refined by independent expert review before the dictionary is ready for use. Stored in the computer as a large table of scoring weights, the dictionary provides an automatic scoring system in any language for which words and weights have been compiled. Thus far, most applications have been restricted to English or Spanish. Some of the problems of translating Spanish HIT protocols into English have been outlined by Cook de Leonard (1965).

The amount of agreement between hand and computer scoring of the same protocols is surprisingly high in spite of the fact that syntax is only taken into account by the computer program in a rudimentary way. Intercorrelations between the two methods of scoring are high (above .80) for seven variables—Rejection, Location, Movement, Human, Color, Form Definiteness, and Animal. Cross-method correlations for Hostility, Popular, Anxiety, Anatomy, Shading, Penetration, Abstract, Sex, Barrier, and Integration range from .50 to .75. These results were achieved in a cross-validation of the scoring method by applying it to 101 Form A protocols obtained from college students tested by Swartz and Holtzman (1963). Cross-validation on 84 Form B protocols yielded equally high correlations between computer scoring and hand scoring of the same records.

In some situations it is not possible to set aside a minimum of one hour for administration of the HIT. Some interest has been shown in a short form containing the first thirty cards in either A or B. Herron (1963) conducted a study to determine the loss of information resulting from a 30-item HIT. He discovered that if .70 is accepted as a minimum value for adequate split-half reliability, the Short Form may be used successfully for at least the following variables: Rejection, Location, Form Definiteness, Form Appropriateness, Color, Pathognomic Verbalization, and Human. The same can probably be said for factor scores since they are derived from more than one inkblot variable.

Each of the above variations in the standard method still has as a major goal the production of inkblot protocols and scores which are as close as possible to the standardized individual method in their psychological meaning. Where one has special purposes in mind, several other variations are possible. Special subsets of inkblots can be drawn up using published item statistics for the 90 inkblots as a basis for selection. For example, figure-ground reversals (Space) occur rather rarely in the standard version of the HIT. But it would be a simple matter to select a dozen inkblots which have a high degree of "card pull" for such responses and then ask the subject to give two responses per card rather than one. The resulting scores on Space as an inkblot variable would be better distributed and more reliable, permitting special study of the psychological meaning of figure-ground reversals. On the basis of experimental studies dealing with the arousal of affect by color, Hill (1966) has proposed that the ten most brilliantly colored inkblots in the HIT be considered a special subset for measuring affective response to color.

In studies where many repeated measures of inkblot perception are needed, the 90 inkblots can be divided into smaller parallel subsets containing 10 or 15 blots each. Palmer (1963) and Simkins (1960) have employed this procedure quite successfully in several experiments. Two, or even three, responses per card can be required of each subject if necessary to insure sufficient information for reliable measurement. Still another possibility that has not been sufficiently explored as yet is the development of special-purpose multiple-choice forms for measuring variables of particular interest. A multiple-choice test would have the advantage of complete objectivity, although such a derivation would probably bear little resemblance to the standard individual method.

OTHER EXPERIMENTS

Most of the reported research on the HIT has been discussed under other headings. A few studies, however, deal with such topics as the basic qualities of the stimuli, or use of the HIT to produce atmosphere effects in social experiments.

Working with achromatic reproductions of eight chromatic cards as well as the originals, Van de Castle and Spicher (1964) determined the degree of subjective disturbance elicited by each card by means of a semantic differential composed of 16 pairs of bipolar adjectives. Both high and low scorers on tests of anxiety and neuroticism rated the chromatic cards in more favorable terms than the black and white ones. This finding, when combined with failure to find significant differences in the two groups of subjects, led to the conclusion that "novelty shock" was a more appropriate term than "color shock" in dealing with affective reactions to inkblots.

Using item statistics published in the HIT standardization monograph, Block and Greenfield (1965) selected a chromatic series of 12 cards graded according to the frequency of color responses which was assumed equivalent to the color stimulus value of the card. All 12 cards had low frequency of shading responses. Various combinations of order of presentation, context, and stimuli were tried, including achromatic reproductions of the colored cards, in experiments dealing with adaptation to inkblot stimuli, using bipolar pleasant-unpleasant scales for making judgments. Adaptation in the chromatic series was not only more complete but also at a higher hedonistic level than in the achromatic series. Significant interactions between determinants revealed that the hedonistic effect of color varied inversely with the degree of form definiteness or card structure.

When the HIT is presented to subjects as a test of intelligence in a formal atmosphere, there is a slight "tightening up" of the cognitive-perceptual process, according to Herron (1964). Under this particular instructional set as contrasted to the standard method of group administration, college students who were led to believe the HIT measured fundamental aspects of intelligence got lower scores on Penetration, Pathognomic Verbalization, and Hostility.

Using the standard group method, Herron (1965) gave the HIT to 16 students who had acquired a conditioned eyelid response and to 16 students who could not be conditioned in an earlier laboratory experiment. The conditioned-response group obtained significantly higher scores on Integration and Anxiety, extending to a projective technique the results of previous research showing conditionability to be related to paper-and-pencil measures of anxiety. Brasfield and Papageorgis (1965) formed high and low anxiety groups on the basis of a self-inventory anxiety scale and then studied the atmosphere effect upon self-ratings of contrived "personality evaluations" presumably based on HIT performance. In this case there was no analysis of HIT protocols, the sole purpose of the HIT being to provide a credible basis in the eyes of the student for the misleading interpretations.

Response length on the HIT has been linked to some inkblot scores in a series of studies by Megargee (1966b). The mean number of words used per response proved to be significantly correlated with Movement, Anxiety, Hostility, and Barrier in two different studies, suggesting that verbosity may play an important role in determining scores on these particular inkblot variables. This finding should be followed up by additional experiments designed to determine how much the obtained scores on HIT variables can be influenced by word fluency and other verbal factors which may be artifacts that must be controlled.

CONCLUSION

The rapidly expanding literature on the Holtzman Inkblot Technique shows considerable promise for the method when used appropriately. The availability for the first time of a large number of standardized inkblots opens a whole new field of research in this important area. While it is unlikely that all 22 standardized variables will remain unchanged in the face of new evidence from research, there is much to be said for adhering carefully to the detailed instructions for administration and scoring. Only in this manner can one take full advantage of the established norms and related procedures for interpretation.

Several promising variations in the method of administration and scoring have been developed recently which appear to adhere fairly closely to the original aims of the technique. It remains to be seen, however, whether group administration and computer scoring alter the qualitative aspects of the HIT to such an extent that its value is diminished in personality assessment. As with any new technique for the assessment of personality, the final verdict of its utility can be reached only after much investigation in a wide variety of situations, both experimental and clinical.

REFERENCES

Barger, P. M., & Sechrest, L. Convergent and discriminant validity of four Holtzman Inkblot Test variables. *J. psychol Stud.*, 1961, *12*, 227-236.

Barnes, C. Prediction of brain damage using the Holtzman Inkblot Technique and other selected variables. Unpublished doctoral dissertation, University of Iowa, 1963.

Beck, S. J. *Rorschach's Test, Vol. I, Basic Processes.* (Second edition, revised) . New York: Grune and Stratton, 1949.

Block, W. E., & Greenfield, L. Adaptation to inkblot stimuli: effects of order of presentation, context and stimuli characteristics. *J. clin. Psychol.*, 1965, *21*, 301-304.

Brasfield, C., & Papageorgis, D. Manifest anxiety and the effect of a dissonant self-relevant communication on self-perception. *Proc. 73rd ann. Conv. Amer. Psychol. Assoc.*, 1965, 193-194. Washington, D.C.: APA.

Clark, C. M., Veldman, D. J., & Thorpe, J. S. Convergent and divergent thinking of talented adolescents. *J. educ. Psychol.*, 1965, *56*, 157-163.

Cleveland, S. E. Body image changes associated with personality reorganization. *J. consult. Psychol.*, 1960, *24*, 256-261.

Cleveland, S. E., & Fisher, S. A comparison of psychological characteristics and physio logical reactivity in ulcer and rheumatoid arthritis groups. *Psychosom. Med.*, 1960. *22*, 283-289.

Cleveland, S. E., & Morton, R. B. Group behavior and body image: A follow-up study. *Hum. Relat.*, 1962, *15*, 77-85.

Cleveland, S. E., & Sikes, M. P. Body image in chronic alcoholics and non-alcoholic psychiatric patients. *J. proj. Tech. pers. Assess.*, 1966, *30*, 265-269.

Codkind, D. Attitudes toward the imaginary: Their relationship to level of personality integration. Unpublished doctoral dissertation, University of Kansas, 1964.

Connors, C. K. Effects of brief psychotherapy, drugs, and type of disturbance on Holtzman Inkblot scores in children. *Proc. 73rd ann. conv. Amer. Psychol. Assoc.,* 1965, 201-202. Washington, D. C.; APA.

Cook de Leonard, C. Problems in the translation of Spanish (Mexican) protocols into English. *Proc. Ninth Cong. Interamer. Soc. Psychol.,* Miami, Fla., 1964, 271-277.

Cronbach, L. J. Statistical methods applied to Rorschach scores: a review. *Psychol. Bull.,* 1949, *46,* 393-429.

Elizur, A. Content analysis of the Rorschach with regard to anxiety and hostility. *Rorschach Res. Exch.,* 1949, *13,* 247-284.

Fisher, S. A further appraisal of the body boundary concept. *J. consult. Psychol.,* 1963, *27,* 62-74.

Fisher, S., & Cleveland, S. E. *Body Image and Personality.* Princeton, N. J.: Van Nostrand, 1958.

Gorham, D. R. Development of a computer scoring system for inkblot responses. *Proc. Ninth Cong. Interamer. Soc. Psychol.,* Miami, Fla., 1964, 258-270.

Gorham, D. R. Validity and reliability studies of a computer-based scoring system for inkblot responses. *J. consult. Psychol.,* 1967, *31,* 65-70.

Herron, E. W. Psychometric characteristics of a thirty-item version of the group method of the Holtzman Inkblot Technique. *J. clin. Psychol.,* 1963, *19,* 450-453.

Herron, E. W. Changes in inkblot perception with presentation of the Holtzman Inkblot Technique as an "intelligence test." *J. proj. Tech. pers. Assess.,* 1964, *28,* 442-447.

Herron, E. W. Personality factors associated with the acquisition of the conditioned eyelid response. *J. pers. soc. Psychol.,* 1965, *2,* 775-777.

Hertz, Marguerite R. The use and misuse of the Rorschach method. I. Variations in Rorschach procedure. *J. proj. Tech.,* 1959, *23,* 33-48.

Hill, E. F. Affect aroused by Color, a function of stimulus strength. *J. proj. Tech. pers. Assess.,* 1966, *30,* 23-30.
Bull. Menninger Clin., 1963, *27,* 84-95.

Holtzman Inkblot Technique. The Psychological Corporation, 304 East 45th Street, New York, N.Y.

Holtzman, W. H. Inkblot perception and personality: the meaning of inkblot variables. *Bull. Menninger Clin.,* 1963, *27,* 84-95.

Holtzman, W. H. Recurring dilemmas in personality assessment. *J. proj. Tech. pers. Assess.,* 1964, *28,* 144-150.

Holtzman, W. H. Cross-cultural research on personality development. *Hum. Develpm.,* 1965a, *8,* 65-86.

Holtzman, W. H. Personality structure. *Annu. Rev. Psychol.,* 1965b, *16,* 119-156.

Holtzman, W. H. Intelligence, cognitive style and personality: a developmental approach. In Brim, O. G., Jr., Crutchfield, R. S. & Holtzman, W. H. *Intelligence: Perspectives 1965.* New York: Harcourt, Brace, & World, 1966.

Holtzman, W. H., Gorham, D. R., & Moran, L. J. A factor-analytic study of schizophrenic thought processes. *J. abnorm. soc. Psychol.,* 1964, *69,* 355-364.

Holtzman, W. H., Moseley, E. C., Reinehr, R. C., & Abbot, E. Comparison of the group method and the standard individual version of the Holtzman Inkblot Technique. *J. clin. Psychol.,* 1963, *19,* 441-449.

Holtzman, W. H., Santos, J. F., Bouquet, S., & Barth, P. *The Peace Corps in Brazil.* Austin, Texas: University of Texas. 1966.

Holtzman, W. H., Thorpe, J. S., Swartz, J. D., & Herron, E. W. *Inkblot Perception and Personality*. Austin, Texas: University of Texas Press, 1961.

Knudsen, A. K., Gorham, D. R. & Moseley, E. C. Universal popular responses to inkblots in five cultures: Denmark, Germany, Hong Kong, Mexico, and United States. *J. proj. Tech. pers. Assess.*, 1966, *30*, 135-142.

Lord, Edith. Experimentally induced variations in Rorschach performance. *Psychol. Monogr.*, 1950, *64*, No. 10 (Whole no. 316).

Megargee, E. I. The performance of juvenile delinquents on the Holtzman Inkblot Technique: a normative study. *J. proj. Tech. pers. Assess.*, 1965a, *29*, 504-512.

Megargee, E. I. The relation between Barrier scores and aggressive behavior. *J. abnorm. Psychol.*, 1965b, *70*, 307-311.

Megargee, E. I. Undercontrolled and overcontrolled personality types in extreme antisocial aggression. *Psychol. Monogr.*, 1966a, *80*, No. 611, 1-29.

Megargee, E. I. Relation of response length to Holtzman Inkblot Technique scores. *J. consult. Psychol.*, 1966b, *30*, 415-419.

Megargee, E. I., Lockwood, V., Cato, J. L., & Jones, J. K. Effects of differences in examiner, tone of administration, and sex of subject on scores of the Holtzman Inkblot Technique. *Proc. 74th ann. Conv. Amer. Psychol. Assoc.*, 1966, 235-236. Washington, D. C.: APA.

Megargee, E. I., & Cook, P. E. The relation of TAT and inkblot aggressive content scales with each other and with criteria of overt aggressiveness in juvenile delinquents. *J. proj. Tech. Pers. Assess.*, 1967, *31*, 48-60.

Moseley, E. C. Psychodiagnosis on the basis of the Holtzman Inkblot Technique. *J. proj. Tech.* 1963, *27*, 86-91.

Moseley, E. C. Some results of cross-cultural computer scoring of Mexican, Panamanian, Chinese and American students. *Proc. Ninth Congr. Interamer. Soc. Psychol.*, Miami, Fla., 1964, 277-281.

Moseley, E. C., Duffey, R. F., & Sherman, L. J. An extension of the construct validity of the Holtzman Inkblot Technique. *J. clin. Psychol.*, 1963, *19*, 186-192.

Moseley, E. C., Gorham, D. R., & Hill, E. Computer scoring of inkblot perceptions. *Percept. mot. Skills*, 1963, *17*. 498.

Moseley, E. C. Paper given in symposium on transcultural research at the Tenth Inter-American Congress of Psychology, Lima, Peru, April 3-7, 1966.

Mueller, W. J., & Abeles, N. The components of empathy and their relationship to the projection of human movement responses. *J. proj. Tech. pers. Assess.*, 1964, *28*, 322-330.

Murstein, B. I. The projection of hostility on the Rorschach, and as a result of ego-threat. *J. proj. Tech.*, 1956, *20*, 418-428.

Otten, M. W., & Van de Castle, R. L. A comparison of set "A" of the Holtzman inkblots with the Rorschach by means of the semantic differential. *J. proj. Tech. & pers. Assess.*, 1963, *27*, 453-460.

Palmer, J. O. Alterations in Rorschach's Experience Balance under conditions of food and sleep deprivation: A construct validation study. *J. proj. Tech. pers. Assess.*, 1963, *27*, 208-213.

Phillips, L., Kaden, S., & Waldman, M. Rorschach indices of developmental level. *J. genet. Psychol.*, 1959, *94*, 267-285.

Rapaport, D., Schafer, R., & Gill, M. *Diagnostic Psychological Testing*, Vol. II. Chicago: Year Book Publishers, 1946.

Reitman, E. E. Changes in body image following sensory deprivation in schizophrenic and control groups. Unpublished doctoral dissertation, University of Houston, 1962.

Richter, R. H., & Winter, W. D. Holtzman inkblot correlates of creative potential. *J. proj. Tech. pers. Assess.*, 1966, *30*, 62-67.

Ruebush, B. K. Children's behavior as a function of anxiety and defensiveness. Unpublished doctoral dissertation. Yale University, New Haven, Connecticut, 1960.

Sells, S. B., Frese, F. J., Jr., & Lancaster, W. H. Research on the psychiatric selection of flying personnel. II. Progress on development of SAM Group Ink-Blot Test. Project no. 21-37-002, no. 2. Randolph Field Texas: USAF School of Aviation Medicine, 1952.

Simkins, L. Examiner reinforcement and situational variables in a projective testing situation. *J. consult. Psychol.*, 1960, *24*, 541-547.

Steffy, R. A., & Becker, W. C. Measurement of the severity of disorder in schizophrenia by means of the Holtzman Inkblot Test. *J. consult. Psychol.*, 1961, *25*, 555.

Swartz, J. D. Developmental aspects of perceptual-cognitive functioning: preliminary findings from the first two years of a six-year longitudinal study. *Proc. Ninth Congr. Interamer. Soc. Psychol.*, Miami, Fla., 1964, 249-257.

Swartz, J. D. Performance of high- and low-anxious children on the Holtzman Inkblot Technique. *Child Develpm.*, 1965, *36*, 569-575.

Swartz, J. D. The roles of culture, age, sex, and father's occupational level in children's responses to the Holtzman Inkblot Technique. In Hereford, C. F. and Natalicio, L. (Eds.). *Aportaciones de la Psicología a la Investigación Transcultural.* México 1, D.F.: Editorial F. Trillas, S.A., 1967. Pp. 130-142.

Swartz, J. D., & Holtzman, W. H. Group method of administration for the Holtzman Inkblot Technique. *J. clin. Psychol.*, 1963, *19*, 433-441.

Tamm, M. Resultados preliminares de un estudio transcultural y desarrollo de la personalidad de niños mexicanos y norteamericanos. In Hereford, C. F. and Natalicio, L. (Eds.). *Aportaciones de la Psicología a la Investigación Transcultural.* México 1, D.F.: Editorial F. Trillas, S.A., 1967. Pp. 159-164.

Thorpe, J. S. Level of perceptual development as reflected in responses to the Holtzman Inkblot Technique. Unpublished doctoral dissertation, University of Texas, 1960.

Thorpe, J. S., & Swartz, J. D. The role of intelligence and social status in rejections on the Holtzman Inkblot Technique. *J. proj. Tech. pers. Assess.*, 1963, *27*, 248-251.

Thorpe, J. S., Swartz, J. D. Level of perceptual development as reflected in responses to the Holtzman Inkblot Technique. *J. proj. Tech. pers. Assess.*, 1965, *29*, 380-386.

Thorpe, J. S., & Swartz, J. D. Perceptual organization: A developmental analysis by means of the Holtzman Inkblot Technique. *J. proj. Tech. pers. Assess.*, 1966, *30*, 447-451.

Van de Castle, R. L., & Spicher, R. S. A semantic differential investigation of color on the Holtzman. *J. proj. Tech. pers. Assess.*, 1964, *28*, 492-498.

Whitaker, L., Jr. The Rorschach and Holtzman as measures of Pathognomic Verbalization. *J. consult. Psychol.*, 1965, *29*, 181-183.

Young, H. H., Jr. A test of Witkin's field-dependence hypothesis. *J. abnorm. soc. Psychol.*, 1959, *59*, 188-192.

Zubin, J., & Eron, L. *Experimental Abnormal Psychology* (Preliminary edition). New York: New York State Psychiatric Institute, 1953.

Zubin, J. Failures of the Rorschach technique. *J. proj. Tech.*, 1954, *18*, 303-315.

CONSTRUCTION

TECHNIQUES

As Lindzey suggests (see Chapter 1), construction techniques make relatively more complex demands upon the subject than do the association methods described in Part II. In this instance the subject is expected to *make up, create,* or "construct" a story in response to relatively more structured stimuli. The Thematic Apperception Test (TAT) is of course the prototype. Two chapters constitute the present section; one on the TAT and another on the various derivative methods based on Murray's TAT pattern and principles.

In Chapter 7, Dr. Rosenwald presents the important "theoretical considerations" of the TAT, which are followed by a description of the testing procedure and examples of stories and their interpretation ("clinical applications"). The chapter concludes with a section in which research concerning a number of the important assumptions of the test is reviewed. (The reader who is completely unacquainted with the TAT would do well to read the section on "clinical applications" first.)

Dr. Neuringer's chapter concentrates on several of the more important derivatives of the TAT. Its contribution extends beyond an examination of pictorial methods, such as the Children's Apperception Test, the Michigan Picture Test, etc., which were devised for special age groups: He also touches upon thematic methods which involve non-visual modalities, such as audition (Auditory Apperception Test). Included also are pictorial apperceptive techniques which are closely associated with personality theories; e.g., the Blacky—with orthodox psychoanalysis, and the Object Relations Test—with Fairbairn's theoretical system.

All in all this section is rich with descriptive and substantive material on the TAT and some of its modifications. This section also offers the reader some critical evaluations and selective reviews of pertinent research publications with these methods.

7

The Thematic Apperception Test

GEORGE C. ROSENWALD

Since its design in the mid-thirties, the TAT has risen to a preeminent postition among instruments of assessment. It has been used more widely than any other projective technique in the scientific investigation of motivation, and clinicians continue to rely on it heavily in coping with diagnostic problems of everyday practice. It has held its own so well in competition with the Rorschach test and the many other techniques described in this book for several reasons. Perhaps the foremost is that the manifest material yielded by the TAT is not mysterious in appearance. The comparatively untrained person can appreciate fabricated stories and fantasy tales; he needs no acquaintance with technical symbols and test scores to obtain at least a superficial feeling for the moods and perspectives of the subject who produced the stories, and even the experienced tester profits from this property which differentiates the TAT from other tests.

A second reason for the TAT's appeal, especially to the nonclinical investigator, is its origin. Unlike most projective tests, it is of academic-humanistic origin. It was first conveyed to the public through the work of Henry Murray and his associates at the Harvard Psychological Clinic, where it was employed in the case-study exploration of normal personalities. It was one of about thirty observational techniques and impressed these investigators as perhaps the most useful of all. This recommendation, sometimes together with Murray's theory of personality, has proved consistently attractive to a generation of investigators concerned with the study of personality.

There are perhaps a number of further reasons for the test's widespread appeal, but only one will be discussed in detail, namely the TAT's virtue as a "wideband" medium, that is, a medium through which a more comprehensive (not merely deeper) view of personality may be had than through other projective techniques (Cronbach, 1960). This

I wish to express my gratitude to Drs. Mary Engel, Martin Mayman and Roy Schafer for reading a draft of this chapter and making a number of valuable suggestions.

feature of the test will first be discussed in theoretical terms in the opening section of this chapter and will then be illustrated with the analysis of a sample case protocol in the second section. In the last section of the chapter, a survey of research is presented in which the "wideband" concept will again be implied by the broad range of psychological phenomena to which TAT performance is related.

The TAT's "wideband" quality explains in part how *one* means of understanding, describing, and classifying personality found favor with psychologists of greatly differing orientations. But it skirts another, more fundamental question which will haunt us throughout these pages: *Why does story-telling implicate the personality, and why does it implicate it so comprehensively?* Positivists may shrug this off as a needless concern, but it remains to be seen if the answer, if even the beginning of an answer, will not add substantially to what we know. To put it bluntly, direct investigations of the TAT itself have done very little until now to provide an answer. Instead, theories of fantasy have been invoked which stem largely from Freud's analysis of the dream and from subsequent extensions and elaborations of his analysis. While it is probably undesirable to construct a theory specifically for the TAT and without attention to developments in the rest of psychology, it is equally unrewarding to let matters rest at a comparison of the TAT and the dream or daydream. Such efforts help in the initial formulation of problems but cannot be regarded as shedding light on unknown factors. These will have to be studied directly.

THEORETICAL CONCEPTIONS

In the initial theoretical section, the TAT will be evaluated from three viewpoints. The first is *utility,* and deals with the tasks to which the TAT can be gainfully applied. The second is *components,* dealing with the aspects of personality which can be reconstructed from TAT stories. It is in this second evaluation that the "wideband" concept will be of use. The third is *process,* and is concerned with the forces and conditions of the psyche which operate in the production of stories to pictures. There is no process theory of the TAT currently available. For this reason the involvement of the personality in story-telling is only vaguely understood. The present chapter will, therefore, propose some methodological guidelines for an *independent* theoretical reconstruction of the TAT.

Utility

Various views have been propounded about the proper use of the TAT. At one time the TAT was regarded as the mirror of a person's motives and of their configuration. Somewhat later it began to have appeal as a clinical diagnostic device (Lindzey, Bradford, Tejessy &

Davids, 1959) . More recently, as batteries of tests represented the standard of good diagnostic practice, the TAT was relied upon to gauge the subject's conscious and preconscious fantasy contents. And finally it has been widely recognized, and will be proposed in this chapter, that the TAT has certain specialized functions, but that these are not in principle beyond the scope of other instruments, and that these others do not have exclusive areas of competence to which the TAT can never contribute. Thus, the TAT may be especially effective in furnishing the tester with insights regarding the subject's fundamental conceptions of, and patterns of interaction with, other significant figures in his life. But the Rorschach test cannot, therefore, be excluded as a source of similar insights. On the other hand, it is also true that the TAT is not, in the main, a means of assessing a person's fund of knowledge. Yet one can often draw inferences from it regarding this variable. Several schemes for personality description on the basis of the TAT have been circulated over the years (Bellak, 1954; Henry, 1956; Holt, 1951; Rapaport, Gill, & Schafer, 1946; Tomkins, 1947; and Wyatt, 1947) . For example, Henry details eight areas: 1) Mental approach; 2) imaginative processes; 3) family dynamics; 4) inner adjustment; 5) emotional reactivity; 6) sexual adjustment; 7) behavioral approach; and 8) descriptive and integrative summary.

It is not necessary to combine these various schemes, nor must one choose among them. They merely suggest what the tester commonly seeks to describe. As we shall see by reference to examples, these are not *all* the categories, and it is undoubtedly futile to set limits on relevant dimensions. At best, these categories represent a minimum of coverage.

Components

The evaluation of the TAT from the viewpoint of components cannot be undertaken without a closer examination of the "wideband" concept. This, together with the assumption that the TAT yields optimal results when included in a battery of tests, will serve as the basis for the remainder of this chapter. That is to say, it will be assumed that the TAT is immensely versatile, but not self-sufficient. The "wideband" concept has several applications to the TAT, and the first of these can be broached by presenting a rough outline of the structure of *any* individual-expressive thought product, including spontaneous daydreams, deliberate and inadvertent puns and jokes, creative insights or syntheses, dreams, free associations, and responses elicited by certain test stimuli.

With certain reservations, it may be said that all of these thought products are prompted and shaped more by inner impulses and tensions than by independent outer reality, and that their completed, manifest form is the last link in a chain of implicit, sometimes symbolic, events. They reveal personality with a degree of clarity inversely proportional to the degree to which *external* constraints guide and limit the individual's expressiveness. This inverse relationship constitutes the value of so-called unstructured tests.

Objective reality, that is, stimulus factors, is far from unimportant. It constitutes an adaptive requirement for the subject which would be almost completely eliminated if we asked him to tell any story which comes to his mind without reference to picture, instruction, or situational factors. Indeed, some subjects elevate the management of these realities to a higher level of importance than the self-expressive opportunities which the test furnishes. They deal with the TAT as though it were, above all, a cognitive-intellectual task. But this does not in principle negate the subordinacy of purely cognitive factors to individual-expressive ones. Most subjects sense that the TAT is an outlet for themes, visions, and values which are deeply significant, and often pressing, in their inner lives.

That a deep central force initiates and guides individual-expressive thought products is generally acknowledged. It is usually granted that deep contents lie at the base of TAT stories. However, the meaning of "deep" varies from author to author. Murray (1951) in a review of the TAT's utility, states that the test's "peculiar virtue will be found to reside not . . . in its power to mirror overt behavior or to communicate what the patient knows or is willing to tell, but rather in its capacity to reveal things which the patient is unwilling to tell or is unable to tell because he is unconscious of them." A somewhat different two-fold definition is offered by Rapaport. The TAT is discussed as an instrument specifically suited to the assessment of *ideational content,* as distinct from conceptual, intellectual, and formal assests and liabilities of thought. Secondly, the definition states that "the rationale basic to interpreting the TAT [is]: figures described, attitudes attributed, actions related in stories one makes up *are drawn from "memory"*—that is, from past experience; therefore, unless they are clichés accumulated in past experience, they directly represent the real or fantasied figures of personalities, the attitudes, feelings, and actions of which loom large in the subject's world." (p. 420) The expression "drawn from memory" is an implicit reference to another sort of depth. Rather than asserting that the TAT reflects ideational content which is unavailable to the individual's spontaneous experience or description of himself, Rapaport leaves the door open to a multilayered conception of past experience, recognizing that its record in memory is partly preconscious and partly unconscious.

The components fused and elaborated in most individual-expressive thought products fall along a broad continuum of accessibility, from deeply repressed and practically unavailable, through a range of relative latency, to a terminus of easy potential access. The TAT is a "wideband" instrument in the sense that we are about as likely to discover the traits which the subject could comfortably corroborate as we are likely to discover ones which are at the farthest remove from his acknowledged self-image.

There is a second meaning of "wideband" which is especially relevant to the TAT. The psychoanalytic conception of personality development posits that deep-lying, discharge-oriented drive tensions constituting the id undergo complex processes of binding, control, and defense under the aegis of the ego as they are guided to points of discharge, and that these more restrained and socialized derivatives are the basis for mature and stable interests, talents, attitudes, and personal relations. The metamorphosis of the most primitive into the fully evolved is a process of many stages, which are not discriminable under normal circumstances, but attract the clinician's attention when pathology interrupts the progression at intermediate points and lays the process open. To be more schematic, the individual's most elemental drive tensions are channeled in infancy and childhood into relationships with particular figures. These may be fused images of real and imaginary persons. Such channelings, or cathexes, are particularly enduring, and later adult relationships are often based on them. The mediational processes which lead from the early to the later relationships involve, among other mechanisms, defenses in layered arrangements. TAT stories frequently give evidence of 1) the person's most exigent drive tensions, 2) the prototypical relationships of infancy into which these were channeled, 3) the nature of the fear which brought about the repudiation or modification of these early relationships, and 4) the particular sort of avoidance or mastery which has since supplanted the early pattern and become characteristic of the adult. Since this progression is mainly a developmental one, the TAT story can be said to reflect "memory." However, since these four points are also represented in the subject's *current* personality organization, the test is once again a wideband instrument in the sense of encompassing a "vertical" progression of psychic organizations.

The TAT's wideband quality applies not only to object relations. A 28-year-old patient seeking treatment for a work inhibition told several TAT stories with obvious themes of Oedipal rivalry ending in distress, isolation, and remorse for the competitive hero. It was a noteworthy aspect of his performance on the TAT and elsewhere that his esthetic sense was highly refined and erudite. He made apt references to novelists, musicians, and sculptors and thereby enriched or deepened some of his themes and images. Also he observed the TAT instructions with meticulous, but not obsequious, care so that inquiry and prompting were rarely necessary.

These findings can be integrated as follows. The impulse to rival and dispossess the father-figure meets with strictures of guilt feeling so intense as to paralyze the patient in dealing *directly* with people whose authority rearouses this conflict. He neither competes nor submits. (The same conflict also freezes his productive work capacity.) Although there is no evidence of submissiveness as a pronounced pattern in his personal relations, his cultivation of the high life of the mind, his veneration of cultural forefathers, and his easy submission to rules of procedure are a partial resolution of the family conflict in the sphere of values and aesthetics. This case demonstrates the TAT's access to the wideband, stretching all the way from unacceptable impulses first felt in infancy to current *values,* and not just *personal relations* in the narrower sense.

To summarize, the TAT's special advantage lies in its comprehensiveness along three wide bands. One is the "vertical" band stretching from the infantile and primitive to the adult and derivative. Another stretches "horizontally" across the countless surface traits and trait-complexes relevant to personality appraisal: intellect, values, personal relationships, self-image, strivings, fears, hopes, preoccupations, defenses, styles, and many others. This will be demonstrated in the second section of this chapter. The third band stretches "diagonally" across these domains and across their respective levels of organization and development. This is the band of experiential access which includes what the subject is acutely aware of, as well as that of which he does not even dream.

Process

The third and least often presented theoretical viewpoint for evaluating the TAT is that of process. A paper by Holt (1961) presents the factual background for a process theory of the TAT. To understand what chain of inner events leads to a story would be of immense importance. It would allow a more realistic estimate of the TAT's utility for various tasks and a more empirical analysis of the specific personality components implicated within the stories' construction. The remainder of this theoretical section will be devoted to a proposal for a TAT process theory. Freud's theory of dream formation is an exemplary process theory. It assigned implicit relative weights to various factors as drives, unconscious memories, primary process dynamisms, day residue, preconscious memory, striving for intelligibility, secondary revision, and others. Another process theory is that provided by Hermann Rorschach for his test. Having isolated several response factors (e.g., whole, movement, color, animal responses, approach-type, perceptual accuracy) he instructed various subjects to increase one of these deliberately after having administered the test with the usual instructions. For each of these experimental instructions, he observed 1) the extent to which the factor in question was manipulable at will; 2) how such manipulation affected the remaining factors; and 3) what individual differences there were in each factor's manipulability. This process served as a basis for specifying and understanding the psychological mechanisms and dispositions which each response factor represented. The reader will find this an enlightening few pages (Rorschach, 1921). No such theory exists for the TAT, partly because no scheme for analyzing and scoring response factors has found widespread acceptance. It would be of great value to objectify stories' length, originality, vividness, clarity, emotionality, spontaneity, interest, to name only a few formal characteristics as well as to classify various theme contents. What would then be the effect of instructing subjects to tell long, original, or emotional stories, or stories about fame, intrigue, immorality, destruction? What if the subject were asked to tell a story about everyday life? What if he were asked not to tell the first story he thinks of, but the one after that? Would biasing the *content* of TAT stories influence formal factors, and *vice versa*, and would it do so equally for all subjects? Answers to such questions would constitute the basis of a process theory, linking specific personality factors and configurations to specific response factors and configurations.

It is usually assumed that individual-expressive thought products come about through processes somewhat akin to the one Freud proposed for dreams. Bellak (1954) states that other processes differ from the dream process in that the ego participates to a greater extent and in different ways. Dreams and imaginative test productions involve distinctly different kinds of control. Thought products composed while the individual is engaged in a rationally directed activity are more restrained as regards the expression of primitive, idiosyncratic fantasies. What is perhaps even more problematic than the control aspect, in the case of the TAT, is the nature of attention processes. Bellak points out that the ego must oscillate between control and attention. By "control" is meant the relationship between ego on the one hand and id and superego on the other. "Attention" stands for the ego's appraisal of the physical and social reality surround. How does consideration of reality enter the TAT process? Stories do not excel, in the main, because they fit the stimulus requirements, but because they are expressive and individualized. A consistent, clear orientation to the demands of the testing siuation and a consensual treatment of what is depicted on the cards is, of course, expected of the subject. But this constitutes a minimal standard, not a criterion of interpretive usefulness. The more complexly expressive the story, the more exacting such requirements will become. But even then we take the apperceptive and narrative adequacy of the story for granted, and when it is not adequate, we assume that the needs and visions expressed by the subject fall short of stability and adaptive success.

For subjects whose psychological functioning is relatively stable and adaptive, the TAT is an opportunity for the discharge of tension, the rehearsal of significant images of themselves and others, the exercise of various skills and defenses, and the implementation of important values. To speak of the TAT as an *opportunity* is to pinpoint the motivating aspect in the story-telling process. One often observes subjects taking an interest in the development of their stories as though these had an external origin. But this does not appear to be a matter of taking plea-sure in the sheer exercise of intellectual functions. The interest of the TAT lies more in its substance. Matters lie differently in the case of problem solving, where considerations of reality not only guide the process, but set it in motion and provide its interest. Idiosyncratic gratifications cannot be ruled out, but they are at most of secondary importance. Most of the pleasure in problem solving stems from hav-ing come to terms with a puzzling bit of reality. Subjects who are examined with the TAT do not feel pleased over having understood the instructions, having adequately accounted for all that is shown on the TAT card, or having conveyed the story to the tester in intelligible terms. These factors are too deeply ingrained in the subject's fundamen-tal wholeness to be singled out for self-congratulation. And if someone does take a delight in telling stories, this must usually be viewed in terms of specific themes or particular defensive strategies. In short, both motivational and cognitive factors are requisite for the emergence of TAT stories, but it appears that the former provide, as it were, the interest of the task.

The *motivational forces* which are set off by the TAT are 1) the relationship with the tester; 2) the instigation of the task as such; 3) the libidinal and aggressive drive derivatives aroused by specific test stimuli; and 4) the defensive and adaptive strivings mobilized by the first three sets of motives and by the themes and configurations in which these strivings are embedded.

It should be made clear that the relationship with the tester can be positive, indifferent, evasive, obstructive, and so forth. The instigation of the task as such can also take many forms. For instance, the subject can feel keenly challenged, gravely menaced, or casually entertained. How-ever, for a pertinent set of responses to emerge from the administration of the test, there has to be a minimal complementarity between the sub-ject's *interest* in the task and the tester's own expectancies. The term "interest" is here used in the same sense as in "self-interest," "vested interest," "disinterest." While it has mainly motivational connotations, it is not without cognitive implications in that the satisfaction of an interest depends on an orientation to the object. To take an interest in something signifies in common usage that, though the object may be *public* and freely accessible, one endows it with a personal meaning by bending it to a *private* use. This is an important aspect of "TAT be-havior": subjects take pleasure in observing the cards' objective reality and yet appropriating them for their individual-expressive ends. The task also sets in motion certain *cognitive processes* of orientation 1) to the tester; 2) to the story-telling task; 3) to particular stimuli; and 4) to stimulus settings.

Once again, it must be emphasized that orientation is contingent on a motivational premise. One orients oneself to something in preparation for some further transaction. In the TAT the orientation to the task and to particular stimuli is an implementation of the test's sustaining interest. Without a grasp of the task's requirements and of the stimulus dimensions, interest cannot be fully developed. For this reason, the separation of motivational and cognitive factors is justifiable only as a simplification. The TAT does not become interesting until it has been apprehended, and it is apprehended because it is potentially of interest. Subjects who are tested without their consent, for instance, prison inmates, are apt to listen to the instructions with only half an ear and to look at the cards quickly and superficially. As a consequence, their stories are impoverished not only from a lack of interest in story-telling, but from inadequate orientation to task and stimuli.

Does the focus on interest and on the process of orientation imply a psychology of will? Much of what is assayed in the formal features of TAT stories can be viewed as the persistence and harmony of the subject's intentions—both within the story and in its telling. This will shortly be illustrated with examples. Yet it would be wrong to imply that interest is always a discernible affective state or felt as such by the subject. Often it must be inferred from the cohesiveness of a plot, from the uniformity and convergence of the several plots produced by one person, or from the pulse and vigor of the narrative. Especially in testing subjects who affect exaggerated indifference, such as adolescent rebels, the level of manifest interest may be a good deal lower than that of inferred interest. Despite elaborate shows of indifference, their stories may be tightly plotted, lucidly told, and carefully observant of card detail.

As has already been pointed out, interest may at times have a negative prefix, for instance, when the subject is frightened, depressed, suspicious, or grossly self-centered. How prevalent negative interest is can often be inferred from the subject's effort to complete the story. If he ignores the instructions, leaving the story incomplete, this may be interpreted as a lapse of interest. What needs then to be determined is whether this lapse was caused by a particular stimulus, by the task as a whole, or by even more general endogenous factors. Some subjects describe outcomes and characters' feelings in some and not in other stories; other subjects never do so spontaneously. In the former case, the tester seeks a content-specific explanation; in the latter case, the lapse of interest must be derived from more pervasive factors.

The communication of the story is a second aspect of interest, no less important than its plot. Some subjects tell disjointed stories or stories containing *non sequiturs* and gaps. Sometimes references to characters are not made clear, the time sequence of the plot's action is indistinctly related, or the actions and feelings of various characters are left unclear. This can be a sign that the subject has little interest in making things clear to himself, let alone to others. However, it cannot be stressed enough that *none* of these lapses can *always* be ascribed to interest factors. Severely disturbed subjects are often confused for reasons of cognitive defect. In that case we seek direct evidence of weakness in attention or orientation. Apart from this, giving an intelligible account of one's thought products feels like an inviolable obligation to most subjects and is usually less influenced by the content to be related than by the liveliness of their interest and by the nature of their rapport. This question requires empirical research.

A third aspect of story-telling which comes under the influence of interest is what one may call the pleasure in story-telling. Hermann Rorschach discussed this as *Deutungslust* in reference to his own test and noted that depressed and blocked paranoid patients tend to experience displeasure. That is to say, interest is curtailed in persons showing a symptomatic loss of affective output and energy. Before applying this finding to the TAT, another factor should be added as well. This is what Rorschach referred to as *Deutungsbewusstsein,* the self-consciousness of the subject regarding the projective, or individual-expressive, process itself. Pedantic, compulsive, and depressive subjects are especially aware that their responses are only provisional and that other possible interpretations exist. This latter dimension is, of course, applicable to the TAT too. Some subjects become involved in story-telling without hesitation and with hardly a word or gesture about the relativity of it all. Others spend much effort in covering themselves against the possible reproach of not having mentioned every conceivable plot. By and large, those who experience the greatest pleasure in interpretation are also least self-conscious about the projective process. What sustains this ingenuous pleasure is interest, a generalized motivational force. One may observe the subject's level of interest *while* giving him the instructions and *before* showing him the first test card. His reaction to the TAT may differ appreciably from that to other tests administered before or after. Undoubtedly, this initial reaction is based on what the subject senses about his own defensive and adaptive patterns and may provide the tester with the first, and most succinct, cost analysis of gratifications and restrictions which the subject anticipates. In Rorschach's test, and probably in the TAT as well, apperceptive pleasure is positively, and apperceptive self-consciousness negatively, related to the subject's infusion of individual-expressive themes into the response process and to his overall productivity, which are, in the sense of the present discussion, collateral evidence of interest. All signs of interest vary from subject to subject as well as from story to story, indicating quasi-permanent as well as theme-specific personality dispositions. When fluctuations of this kind occur with great frequency or amplitude in a subject's stories, endogenous and, more specifically, autistic factors should be considered.

Four principal factors produce lapses or reductions in interest level:

1. Defensive inhibition of interest in the task. Specific themes or skills are defensively blocked.

2. Lack of interest in self-expression. Ego-identity includes values of stoicism, self-sufficiency, or rigid realism.

3. Lack of interest in other people's solicitude. Self-punishment and vindictiveness dominate the personality.

4. Loss of interest in the objective world. Withdrawal and apathy limit the subject's adaptive vitality.

To recapitulate, the level of interest and involvement, over the long run of testing and from moment to moment, and in the manifest as well as in the hypothetical sense, is of importance in the evolution of TAT stories. Interest level is reflected in the observance of the instructions as they pertain to the completeness of the plot, in the clarity with which the story is told to another person with whom the subject has a (passing) personal relationship, and in the pleasure and naturalness with which he produces individual-expressive themes in his stories. The concept of interest is here offered not only for its own sake, but as an example. It is a possible approach to a process theory of story-telling.

Orientation

In addition to a consistent level of productive interest, a fundamental adequacy of cognitive orientation is expected in TAT stories. As will become apparent, this orientation has comparatively subtle aspects. From the standpoint of process, certain nearly universal adherences to standards and other uniformities of orientation present a theoretical challenge. The subject usually identifies correctly the sex and age of figures depicted on the cards. But these consensual identifications are comparatively crude from the cognitive viewpoint. Tabulations are available for the common plot outlines elicited by each card. What perceptual and situational factors insure this homogeneity? Clearly a plot does not immediately follow from the "correct" identification of figures' sex, age, and posture. To take an example, card 6 BM often produces stories about a mother and her son who is either taking his leave from her or informing her of some misadventure or calamity. Why are plots about a strange young man rarer, and why does one never hear plots involving a young salesman and an elderly housewife? Another example: The girl shown on card 3 GF is almost always seen as weeping or sick because of her bent posture. Why is she hardly ever seen as doubled over with laughter? Why are stories rarely trivial in content (unless they are also impoverished in form)? This is the question alluded to earlier in mentioning orientation to stimulus settings. In short, the subjects' standard responsiveness to posture, moods, carriage is compelled by factors which are only partly known. There is nothing obvious about the appearance of the cards to militate against a variety of unusual plots, but these simply do not appear with appreciable frequency except in the records of subjects who are suffering from marked disturbances in adaptation.

Within the wide limits of adequate interest and orientation, there is room for personal styles. Halting simple stories elicited with generous help from the tester reflect one style. Fanciful, exotic stories and tiresome elaborations of trite and hackneyed themes reflect others. Insofar as any one of these styles is persistent and plausibly embedded in the compass of the personality, it reflects an integrated character structure. Insofar as orientation fluctuates or interest waxes and wanes, instabilities and permeabilities in overall functioning are indicated.

The development of a story hinges on factors other than adequate identification of figures' age and sex and consensual plot choice. Most subjects choose one of the available plot alternatives and develop it into a story. When a subject suddenly swerves from his accustomed procedure to deliberate over alternatives, a deviation may be said to have occurred in the level of interest with subsequent efforts at re-orientation (or non-orientation). As the story proceeds, the subject usually remains within the boundaries of congruence. That is, once a plot has been selected for development, other alternatives fade into the background as irrelevant, and the implications of the chosen plot are followed through. Occasionally, this does not happen. For example, a young borderline schizophrenic patient contemplated card 15 for some minutes before deciding that the figure depicted on it must have recently attended a costume ball wearing a New England pilgrim's costume, that his appearance had somehow reminded him of his deceased wife, that he had taken a taxi cab to the cemetery, and that he was now looking at her grave. The development of this plot violates the emotional aura of both a *masked ball* and of a *graveyard scene*. This is a subtler disturbance of orientation than a misperception of the figure's sex would have been. Even subtler is the disturbance of cognitive orientation implied in the following plot outline produced in response to card 12 M: A hypnotist is curing the young man of a long-standing psychological condition which has resisted all other treatments: sleeping sickness. The distortion, akin to what is called a contamination in Rorschach testing, consists of over-interpreting the figure's recumbent posture. This suggests that two half-completed plots were condensed by a patient whose thinking is pervaded by primary process mechanisms.

While it may be true that inconsistencies and anomalies in plotting the story are largely the result of disturbances in orientation, and that flaws in the clarity and completeness of the narration result from disturbances of interest, this distinction becomes more difficult in classifying subtle disturbances. The last-mentioned example of quasi-contamination presents just such a difficulty. Is the subject deficient as regards conceptual sharpness, or has he permitted himself this conceptually loose formulation out of negligence? The answer does not lie in a better understanding of the TAT process alone. Psychological events as well as many sorts of overt behavior pose the same question. For instance, the patient whose mind wanders during the gathering of his personal history, thereby rendering his account confused, is not merely showing an unstable *interest* in the interviewer's requests, but may be momentarily *attending* to irrelevant stimuli associated with his pathology, such as hallucinatory phenomena, recurrent worries, and so forth. It is his *orientation* to these irrelevancies which absorbs and deflects his *interest*.

There is probably no way in which the finished TAT story, or the adaptive shortcomings discerned in such a story, can be reduced to a small number of process factors. Interest and orientation have been singled out in these pages as examples and to point the way which analysis and research can take so as to arrive at a theory of process. Undoubtedly the relevant psychological factors contributing to any individual-expressive thought product are many and their interaction is complex, as the analysis of interest and orientation has so clearly shown.

CLINICAL APPLICATION

Before the clinical interpretation of the TAT can be discussed, some notes on test administration are in order. As for the test stimuli themselves, it has become a practice not to administer all twenty cards which Murray intended for each subject. (The entire set contains thirty-one cards. Some of these are appropriate for all subjects; others are administered according to the subject's age and sex.) For reasons of economy and because the TAT is usually administered as part of a battery of tests, thirteen or fourteen cards represent a common choice. It is wise to settle gradually on a standard selection, which one administers to all subjects with appropriate modifications for age and sex, rather than to select cards which will "bring out" the subject's suspected areas of difficulty. This latter practice is usually based on the belief that the TAT is most suited for the discovery of certain prototypical peer, authority, and family relationships; it minimizes the wideband potentialities mentioned earlier in this chapter as the outstanding virtue of the TAT and also sacrifices the advantage of standardization which test procedures enjoy over other forms of appraisal such as interviews, free associations, and the like.

It is best to begin the test battery with some general remarks about the purpose and usefulness of psychological tests to the effect that they add further information, each test in a different way, to what the subject (or patient) has already told about himself, that this is a way of getting to know him better and to help (or understand) him more effectively.

The TAT can be introduced as follows: "I am going to show you some pictures, and I want you to make up a story about each of these, the outline of a plot. Tell me what might be going on there, what led up to it, and what the outcome will be. Tell me about the people, what their thoughts and feelings are. You don't need to make it long or elaborate. An outline of a plot is what I would like. Please don't speak too fast, because I shall write down what you tell me." Parts of the instructions may have to be repeated in the course of testing if the subject seems to have forgotten them or is inattentive to them. The cards are then presented in their appropriate order, the response latency is recorded, and a verbatim record of the story is taken down including pauses, gestures, false starts, off-the-record remarks, and questions, as well as the tester's own questions and comments to the subject.

The TAT's wideband usefulness is a function of the complex task-demands weighing on the subject. Aside from basic apperceptive and narrative exigencies, which are exceedingly intricate, he must satisfy the four points of the instructions and pace his speech to the tester's recording. This latter adjustment is a direct demonstration of the subject's empathy, tact, self-restraint and circumspection. For this reason, it is valuable to record the stories in writing, thus requiring his adaptation to the tester's needs, even if tape recorders are available. For the same reason, it is better to let the subject tell his stories than to have him write then out.

The total time spent on each card is recorded as the subject surrenders the card. If inquiry is to be performed, this should be done immediately after each card when the story is still fresh in the subject's mind. Gaps, vaguenesses, and mix-ups in the narrative should be clarified first. Then one may collect elaborations of particularly striking details of content. What is obtained from inquiry is interpretively less valuable than what was produced spontaneously. For this reason, inquiry designed to cover any of the four points of the instructions, which may have been ignored in the story, is relatively less useful for the rounding-out of the particular story than it is for reminding the subject of the instructions with a view to subsequent cards. In this sense, inquiry on the TAT, as opposed to the Rorschach test, is meant to be self-eliminating. If the subject does not, from the first, tell self-contained stories, inquiry should have the effect of inducing him to do so until the tester can function as a mere scribe. This does not apply, of course, to obscurities in the plot or narrative which the inquiry is intended to clarify.

Some subjects, when asked to supply an outcome to their story, ask to look at the card once more. It is often educative for the subject if one does not comply with this request. Asking the subject to "just make it up" emphasizes that the story must issue more from his imagination than from the picture's detail. It is a useful practice also because it encourages the subject to take responsibility for the completion of the story, rather than to depend on the tester's inquiry.

This standard procedure may have to be modified in two cases. If a subject, such as a very depressed or blocked patient, cannot summon up a story, more weight has to fall on the tester's inquiry. What emerges in such a pulling of teeth is not interpretively as useful as a spontaneous story. But the formal aspects of perception, judgment, and reasoning which emerge in this way may be important for differential diagnostic purposes. The second case in which inquiry may have to be especially adapted is that of subjects who are only reluctantly agreeable to the task. As discussed earlier, some subjects undergo testing against their wishes, some are wary of their imagination and of self-examination, and some are acutely anxious and labile. In such cases, inquiry should be delayed until the end of the test, all the more so if it might alarm or irritate the subject and imperil the continuation of testing. For a more specific treatment of administration the reader is referred to Rapaport, Gill, and Schafer (1946).

A TAT record obtained from Mr. A, thirty years of age, will now be presented together with interpretive comments. The subject was originally assessed with a comprehensive test battery. For lack of space, three TAT stories had to be deleted from the protocol below.

> (After the usual instructions:) Should I compose it, or say it out as it comes up?

The initial question raised in the subject's mind by the test instructions concerns spontaneity or improvisation as against deliberateness and advance planning. To *compose* is an active, diligent verb in this context. To *say it out* is, by contrast, all the more passive-detached. For some subjects the TAT is a challenge not because it will expose particular private thoughts, but because self-expression as such is a difficult "genre" for them. To relinquish censorship and selectiveness is perhaps a threat to this man. This is all the more likely as he expects *it to come up*. The implication is that "it" has a motion, a tendency of its own, to which he need not necessarily apply any effort. The phrase also hints that he expects to tell things which are not already accessible to his awareness. Though this may seem obvious to the sophisticated reader and therefore banal, it is not. Many subjects assume that the story is *already* contained in the picture, and that a searching inspection of the card, seasoned with felicitous guesswork, will educe "it." For both of these reasons, it may be assumed that what is not yet there and will emerge by itself, may contain surprises. Is this what the subject wishes to forestall? Or, more accurately, is this what the subject needs the tester's permission *not* to forestall? At any rate, his self-consciousness reflects defensive instability. Leaving the decision to the tester bespeaks passivity and perhaps a wish for absolution from the guilt about impending breakthroughs of impulse.

The question furthermore reflects introspectiveness and sophistication. The very alternative is psychological-minded.

Card 1. 5″ A child . . . the parents are forcing him to take music lessons . . . and who might at the moment be considering what else he could do with his time as opposed to playing the violin. I presume that in time he'll develop his skill in the violin, although it might be a little painful. 1'20″ (what are his feelings?) He was not overjoyed at the prospect of the violin again.

The gross plot of the story is a common one, and yet its detail is individualized. Many subjects tell stories about a conflict between the parents' dictates and the child's wishes. What distinguishes Mr. A's story is that, whereas the parents' role is acknowledged, the opposition of the child is only vaguely, tentatively formulated. We are not told with what wishes of the boy the parents are interfering. Rather, the boy seems to be casting about for something else to take up his time. This difference, although stylistically small, is weighty from the viewpoint of interpersonal relations. Usually the boy's autonomy is infringed. Very often he is spatially hemmed in; for instance, he has to practice against his will, but would rather be outside playing ball. Rebellion against parental authority is then pitted against obedience, willfulness against renunciation. Mr. A's boy is in a different predicament. He has not yet found a purpose of his own, and is now seeking one as a reaction against being forced. Rather than the parents interfering with his desires, it is *he* who is about to distract himself from *their* prescription.

Could the spirit behind this story be that of a man who dislikes having others make plans for him even when he has none of his own? Three considerations argue against a freedom-fighter hypothesis. One is the already mentioned vagueness of the boy's counterplan, the second is the outcome of the story, and the third arises from certain expressive considerations. To begin with the first, that the boy is *considering*, suggests a relatively passive avoidance of the task. The boy is not about to *do* anything. Perhaps, we may speculate, he is daydreaming, for which the expression "considering" would be a euphemism. At any rate, the tone of this consideration, together with the earlier observation of cautiousness in regard to self-expression, suggests that we are dealing with only a mild form of defiance or avoidance.

As to the outcome of the story, its sense is to comply with the parental objective. Foiling it does not occur to the subject even as an unacceptable choice. Many subjects pose an alternative: "It could be that he never really learns how to play the violin, or maybe as he grows older, he realizes that he has an interest in music after all." That Mr. A settles on the compliant solution without considering alternatives, and that he does so without transition from the immediately preceding consideration, indicates a submissive and, in this instance, constructive facet of his self-image; this prevails over temptations to shirk duty. Indeed, one may wonder whether the balance is so weighed down on the side of restraint that Mr. A avoids legitimate self-assertion and is incapable of making selfish choices. That he minimizes his role of active protagonist was already implied in letting *it* come up and in deferring to the tester regarding his own individual-expressive freedom.

The third consideration which renders the assumption of an active rebel unlikely stems from Mr. A's choice of words. The development of musical skill, he says, will be gradual and a little painful. This is a disheartening prospect. Because it is an unusual and poignant statement, given the basic plot of his story (which is not unusual in itself) it is worth speculating about. Plaintiveness and self-pity are indicated by such statements as this. One is as likely to hear them from spoiled children, who are accustomed to softness and concessions, as from subjects whose lives are full of dissatisfaction. Mr. A's reply to inquiry suggests by its tone—most readily apparent if read aloud—that he leans in this latter direction. The terminal *again* conveys the merciless repetitive quality of his duties. It is all the more remarkable that the little boy makes no move or gesture to free himself. *Not overjoyed* is a minimization of the drudgery which is clearly implied. Withal, *he'll develop his skill in the violin.* Dreariness and pain do not deter him, and the inclination to stray from the task is not ultimately an instrument of defeatism. It is possible that Mr. A needs a measure of dissatisfaction to sustain him in the course of his achievements.

A last comment pertains to *his time* and *in time*. Mr. A appreciates the temporal expanse before him, and yet his time is not naturally filled with interests and occupations. It seems hazy before him and perhaps a little painful, filled with recurrent distress. This ennui and the search for something to fill the vacuum suggest a pent-up drive state, an incomplete repression making indistinct demands on his mind and giving rise to restive and frustrated moodiness (Fenichel, 1953). Taboo masturbatory wishes are often concealed when time hangs heavy on one's hands, but other erotic tensions may be involved as well. This cannot be gleaned from the material available so far.

Card 5. 20″. This would be the mother of a family walking into the living room of a home. She somehow gives the impression she just came up the stairs and is either annoyed or startled at something she has seen . . . and . . . perhaps saddened . . . Of course, it's very difficult to think what the future might be, but there is nothing to indicate it wouldn't be resolved, no major difficulty. Maybe she spotted a lamp that one of the kids had knocked over or something of that kind. 2′10″

This is a common plot, conceived and told without normative distortion. As a matter of second thought, it is perhaps too common and lacking in a personal twist, considering that Mr. A's verbal IQ was 128. The story is pale and somewhat undeserving of the term "plot." It contains only one major figure as was also the case in the previous story. While it is true that only one figure is depicted on each card, many subjects contrive actions which transpire between people. Card 1 often elicits stories with a more detailed description of the boy's parents, teacher, or idols. Stories told to card 5 often concern a husband, young people who are necking, burglars, unexpected guests, and so forth. Mr. A makes only the slightest reference to the *parents* (story 1) and to *one of the kids* (story 5). Perhaps the most significant events in his life are not the overt interactions between himself and other people, but the private transactions within his own mind, where he deals with painful duties and enervating families through the medium of fantasy.

More sharply than many subjects, he focuses on the internal state and processes of the depicted figure. In this story he begins by raising hopes for an event-filled interaction. *Annoyed, startled,* and *saddened* are affects which cry out for a discrete cause or instigation. But Mr. A dissipates the story's initial tension (*she just came up the stairs*) and ends instead on a hesitant note. The progress and rhythm of TAT stories reflect the subject's accommodative and defensive responses to his own excitement. In this story, he seems to have gotten off to a start with which his tolerance for action, especially irritated action, could not keep pace. Thus, he becalmed himself. Neither of the stories so far analyzed clearly acknowledges a conflict of interests between the main figure and anyone else.

Our deduction from the subject's initial question regarding spontaneity versus deliberateness is on somewhat firmer footing now that one of his heroines has grown emotional over disarrayed furniture. Perhaps Mr. A's personality is organized around reactive defenses against messy and destructive impulses with the result that he favors order and the avoidance of hostile encounters. If borne out, this speculation would alert us to other possible signs of an obsessive-compulsive character structure. His already mentioned superior intellectual endowment, but without commensurate creative deployment, is a factor consistent with that syndrome.

Why is it *very difficult to think what the future might be?* Mr. A did not find it difficult to read present emotions into the picture. Nor did he hesitate to report his impression of the woman's recent arrival on the floor. Once again, as in the previous story, time lies before him indefinite, *painful, difficult to think about.* However, unlike the little boy's, this mother's future—perhaps *because* she is a mother—will present *no major difficulty.* Where it occurs in this story, this seems an arbitrary assertion, designed to provide reassurance for any apprehensions aroused by the earlier description of affect. With this statement, an orderly progression of events is guaranteed: there is nothing to worry about. One is left to wonder whether the subject's prototypical image of the mother-figure is that of a woman to whom no major upset can occur, who overcomes intercurrent reversals with efficiency and orderliness, and whether, if this is his image, it is *systematically* different from that of the little boy. Have these two stories yielded an insight into the subject's own imagined or remembered interactions with his mother?

All in all, this is an ill-constructed story. Its progression is aborted. From *startled at something she has seen* via *no major difficulty* to the *knocked over lamp* leads a defensive path. Isolation and denial are the mechanisms by which he neutralizes his initial arousal. The story suggests that Mr. A is protecting both the woman as she makes a startling discovery and himself as participant story teller. The full significance of this pacification is not clear. One of the kids causes an accident, is discovered by his mother (*she just came up*), causes her sadness and agitation, but she is in control and handles the situation with poise. How does Mr. A feel about the composure of mothers? Does he bemoan it, does he wish it were more solid, or does he suspect its superficial appearances? Nor is it clear to what life themes or historical images the knocked over lamp refers. Insofar as the kid represents Mr. A's own infantile mischief or disorderliness, he takes care to minimize it. A more serious transgression, capable of bringing the mother onto the scene quickly and arousing intense emotion, has been glossed over. The implication is that nothing serious has happened after all. To be caught off-guard in the pursuit of taboo activities, for instance, masturbation, might lead to such dissembling. Finally, it should be pointed out that "mother of a family" has an odd ring. What the phrase probably mirrors is the subject's awed view of the mother as head of the family. Her emotional reactions described in the story itself bear out her impressive stature. At the same time it should be considered that what takes place *between* people in TAT stories also reflects constellations *within* the individual psyche. The mother-figure has a representation in the subject's mind even after she has ceased to be directly influential as a real person. Dissemblance is then aimed at ego and superego.

Of the several adjectives describing the woman's emotional state, one is worthy of special mention. That she is seen as sad is unusual in the normative sense; it is also gratuitous given the remainder of the story. This suggests tentatively that dejected moods are characteristic of Mr. A.

Card 15. 8″ This is a man who is very sad, who might be on this occasion commemorating the death of those who are close to him . . . sort of a grisly scene. It might suggest that he is a member of a concentration camp who has come after the war to pay his respect to those who weren't so fortunate. He is rather gaunt and aged, which would suggest an old man. He seems to be quite deep in his thoughts of things before, thinking of past times, sorrowfully perhaps . . . an expression of tragedy, the tragedy suggested by the tombstones. One could speculate many things about the future, but presumably he'd retreat from this environment to live out his life as best he could although it suggests that he could never completely forget this tragedy, whatever it was. 3'15"

The first, most general impression is of manifest dejection and loneliness—in much more pronounced degree than *a little painful* or *perhaps saddened*. The subject's despondency may be clinically conspicuous. This plot is better constructed than the first and second. Mr. A goes into explicit detail regarding the hero's emotional response. In contrast to the second story, he states that *one could speculate many things about the future*. To be sure, he does not in fact provide much more material concerning the future than he did in the preceding story, but his announcement stems from his feeling of comfort with the plot he has chosen, despite its depressive mood.

It is a good assumption, based on earlier speculation, that Mr. A's negotiation of card 15 is successful because the *scene is grisly,* not despite it. The card does, of course, present a graveyard scene, to which most subjects tell stories about mourning or about ghosts. This subject exceeds that baseline considerably by referring to a theme of atrocity and genocide. The choice of this reference gives his story an individualized significance and probably reflects the sado-masochistic fantasies commonly found in obsessive-compulsive patients. Although other test information, especially Rorschach findings, is of great use in predicting the relative significance of sadistic as against masochistic wishes, it seems, from the three stories so far presented, that Mr. A emphasizes passive victimization relatively more than active infliction of pain upon others. The source of pain is elsewhere than in the hero. Either, as in story 1, it emanates from the dictates of other people, or, as in story 5, it is only vaguely derived. In the present story, the stress is again on the tragedy of the victims and of the survivor, not on the bestiality of the camp authorities. The expression "member of a concentration camp" is, however, ambiguous; the terms "inmate" or "victim" would have left less doubt concerning the active or passive role played by the character.

It is noteworthy that the last three words of the story represent its only incongruity. He begins the story with a forthright statement of emotion (*sad, grisly*) but lapses into more restrained descriptions of affect and even derives the tragedy from the tombstones, seeking perceptual support for the initial spontaneous impression. Finally, having specified in patently psychological terms what led up to the present events and what the figure is thinking and feeling, the subject now wishes to make uncertain what he has already asserted. This is not unlike the more drastic discontinuity observed in the preceding story. In short, the subject's masochistic impulses are readily aroused, but only briefly sustained before they are covered over with haziness and generality. Especially in forecasting the future, he tends to be more hopeful than downhearted as though to say, the future will be grim, but not entirely unprofitable. Perhaps Mr. A is the sort of person who does not flaunt his misery, but wears a stiff upper lip and suffers silently.

Defensive generality is also evident in the story in a more fundamental sense. The tragedy which is related by the subject and which has impressed itself indelibly on the hero's memory, causing him to *retreat from this environment to live out his life as best he could* is an impersonal tragedy. Even in the setting of a concentration camp story, it is possible to speak about a man's *mourning* his *loved ones* who perished. Instead, the hero *pays his respects* to *those who weren't so fortunate*. The initial statement concerning the *death of those who were close to him* is dropped, and the collective tragedy *suggested by the tombstones* takes its place. Multitudinous pathos robs the hero of his peace of mind, and it seems doubtful that he could ever recover it. In our day, references to concentration camps are frequently concretizations of evil-in-the-world, or man's-inhumanity-to-man. It is ironic that by their enormity these crimes transcend what one can experience emotionally and survive as pale mementos and moral exhortations. In line with his obsessive coolness, Mr. A takes advantage of this irony of human comprehension. Theoretically speaking, "concentration camp" is both a representation of sado-masochism and a sufficiently abstract notion to serve the defense of affect isolation.

The first three TAT stories told by Mr. A reflect a tenuous engagement, whether positive or negative, with other people. The plots transpire in the solitude of individual minds and are affected by other people only from afar and in secondary ways. If the *retreat from this environment* constitutes a characteristic theme of life-management, the tester should concern himself with the question of schizoid features.

The position of the sole survivor, the exception to the rule (Freud, 1924 [1915]) is precarious with respect to self-esteem. As the study of traumatic war neuroses has shown, a heavy charge of guilt is often carried forward. Another likely outcome is the conviction of one's own excellence in the eyes of fate, an excellence which is dear and must be cultivated. We do not know from what peril in his past Mr. A emerged unscathed, nor do we know whether this peril is based on historical fact or on infantile irrealism. But his hero is haunted by the memory of an escape and this must have its counterpart in Mr. A's psychic life.

Card 14. 12″ This might be a prisoner with his background representing something not necessarily evil, but undesirable. He is looking to the future, thinking of better times ahead, escaping from what it is in his past. He might not be physically a prisoner although the large black area would suggest a void of negative past and his looking out the window would suggest a brighter future. The open window might suggest that he had found a way to escape the past. 2'5" (what led up to this?) Presumably something which he considers undesirable. I first thought of a criminal who had been committed for some crime, some legal crime.

Card 14 usually elicits stories of peaceful contemplation, repose, loneliness, insomnia, or longing. Sometimes despair is the chief mood. The theme of a prisoner is uncommon. As told by Mr. A, this story is neither clearly symbolic nor a concrete plot as were his first three stories. In fact, it fluctuates somewhat, sometimes approaching symbolism (*his background representing evil, not physically a prisoner*) sometimes realism (*a prisoner, looking out the window, committed for some legal crime*). Symbolic stories found in the records of intelligent subjects usually indicate that these subjects emphasize internal fantasy trans-actions more than vital exchange with other people. In the present sub-ject's case, we have already noted a paucity of interpersonal themes. The hypothesis of minimal schizoid aloofness cannot be dismissed.

Apart from these formal-diagnostic considerations, the story is evi-dently a dramatization of how guilt contracted in the past weighs on the subject's mind at present and limits his emotional freedom. As such TAT dramatizations go, this one is unusually direct and transparent. More often, the dramatization takes the form of a story with a beginning, a middle, and an end. Usually, the crime of the hero is spontaneously specified and his come-uppance takes the form of remorse, apprehension by the police, or fateful retribution. Mr. A has not gone so far as this. His story does not draw on freely participating fantasy. It rings as though by a mere change to the first person singular, it could be converted into a plausible account of his own subjective experience. One has the feeling that he might admit uneasiness or downright guilt over wickedness in his past. He might even go on to describe how these feelings limit his life or wall him off from other people.

Is this lack of concealment a sign of insight? Probably not. Just as intelligence *alone* does not ordinarily promote symbolic stories, so in-sight *alone* does not promote undisguised ones. The insightfulness of people who are by nature in contact with their inner lives or who have learned to experience themselves more fully in the course of psycho-therapy does not prevent them from making up stories as the TAT instructions demand. It is well to keep in mind that these instructions do not call for personal reminiscences, nor for a report of one's symptoms, nor for an exposition of one's psychological insights. In the main, genuine stories are much more useful to the tester than the subject's own psychoanalytic shortcuts or autobiographical hints.

Stories which are temptingly revealing are usually pat and mislead-ing. For this reason, the tester is not content with the above dynamic interpretation concerning the limitations imposed on life by remnant guilt feelings. It is quite likely that the positive, perhaps exciting, effects of guilt have been omitted from the subject's account. His fondness for painful and grisly themes suggests this.

We are now in a position to draw together some interpretive conclusions pertaining to Mr. A's time perspective. The *future* seems difficult to fathom and a little painful; the *present* is rather grey and vacant; and the *past* is evil and inescapable. In each of the last two stories, a tragic or evil history intrudes into the present and renders the future uncertain. The effect of this vision is likely to be regressive; at least it arrests the progression of life. One may wonder whether Mr. A's lack of spontaneity, noted earlier, is based on a horror of his own past's catching up with him. Interpersonal transactions are accordingly attenuated in favor of fantasy and social retreat. Such regressive accommodations to guilt are not without their compensating satisfactions, and these are perhaps what is concealed behind this "obvious" story of crime and punishment. If so, then his version of past suffering or wickedness is more a self-protective slogan than an integrative insight. He is apt to cling to it.

As regards the reference to a *brighter future,* it represents a somewhat magical forecast. Stories in which the hero, stopped by specific obstacles, works toward equally specific resolutions or circumventions are more indicative of real life energy and purposefulness. As the story stands, the imprisonment theme is more palpable than the escape theme.

No matter how realistic or wishful the plans for emancipation, one is impressed by the subject's wish to escape what he poignantly, though awkwardly, calls the *void of negative past.* In brief, it is likely that this lunge forward conflicts with the regressive, conservative pull discussed earlier. Mr. A probably perpetuates past modes of adaptation and defenses against arousal and guilt, but is sporadically and spasmodically overcome by restlessness and then wishes to crack through his inhibitions and set himself free from a dreary depressing life situation.

Card A. 10″ These are two old men who represent the elements and who appear to be having a quarrel at the current time. The one on top may represent climate and wind. The ravages of his past years are reflected in a tree that is twisted and bent. The lower figure might represent mankind with a heavy burden on his back and moving ahead against these obstacles, and the quarrel that's going on now would certainly represent an eternal quarrel and would unquestionably go into the future, an unending battle. 3′30″

(This card, presenting an eerie, white-on-black line drawing of two old men, is not part of the current edition of the TAT; it was included in the first Harvard Psychological Clinic edition, and is shown as picture

10 on page 400 of Rapaport, Gill, and Schafer, 1946.)

The ravages of the past are again pivotal in this story as they were in stories 15 and 14. The setting of the plot, the personages, and the timeless outcome provide an epic scope and suggest that in this subject's conscious account, that is, in his personal mythology, the past is blamed outright. The echoic return of this theme in three successive stories tends to confirm the hypothesis that the subject is making a tendentious use of his past, that is, that he is reaping instinctual and/or defensive benefits from this formula of suffering.

Like story 14, this one is half symbolic and half allegorical. This is not uncommon for this card. What is, however, noteworthy is the ease and comfort with which the subject tackles it. His reaction time is no longer than for other cards. Furthermore, he has shed the tentative diction of earlier stories *(certainly, unquestionably)*. We shall see that Mr. A is more adept with the abstract and farfetched than with certain day-to-day realities. Making one of the old men into the climate and letting the other represent that which he is, namely a human being, may be another of the subject's tactics to avoid an interaction between two real people. At first, the two old men both represent the elements. This is dropped, and the unending battle between man and the elements takes its place. The changes in Mr. A's theme developments make for a certain looseness of formal organization. The stories are not clearly conceived or well-aimed. This bespeaks a somewhat dreamy irresolute intellect: Mr. A does not strike one as a practical man.

The symbolic significance of the elements, the wind, or the climate may be found in their eternal, indomitable quality. This likens them to the stirrings of untamed libidinal and aggressive impulses. For those who do not make peace with these storms, the struggle can seem eternal. Mr. A further suggests that they can bend and twist life. The ravages of the past years cause irreparable damage.

Speculating on the nature of the burden on the man's back, it is reasonable to cite the impositions, annoyances, wickedness and guilt feelings which have bowed down the other heroes of Mr. A's stories. Despite the speculations about schizoid features in the subject's make-up, there can now be little doubt that his chief syndrome is obsessive-compulsive. His central concerns are activity versus passivity, self-accusation versus exculpation, confinement versus liberation, and affliction versus poised mastery.

In the previous story, Mr. A focused on a stimulus characteristic of the card *(the black)* and in this story again he draws attention to a perceptual detail, namely, the twisted trees. Both references are of depressive significance and suggest that Mr. A discerns reminders of life's drabness or futility not only in his inner tensions and emotional states, but, by a selective process, in his surroundings as well.

Card B. 10″ I identify the couple as Adam and Eve, but that doesn't tie them into the story. The boy is probably a son of her who is holding the child. He's come of age and has found himself a wife, and at the moment there might be some tension between his mother and his own plans. The mother has an infant. Perhaps she hasn't fully reconciled herself that her older son has grown to manhood. The general environment is probably one of poverty or misery. That would be carried through by the drawings on the wall. I presume, as time goes on, they'll adjust, and a new family will be established, and old ties adjust to this new relationship. 3′10″ (What exactly did you have in mind about the drawings?) The young couple was without clothes, and the mother had no shoes, and there were two drawings on the walls, one perhaps mounted and one below it that seemed to mimic it and was perhaps drawn directly on the wall. Both contained figures that seemed despondent, seemed unhappy. So I received the impression that it might be some primitive or peasant-type society.

(This card, adapted from Picasso's *La Vie*, is picture 8 on page 400 of Rapaport, Gill, and Schafer, 1946.)

The abortive reference to Adam and Eve evokes the theme of original sin, expulsion from infantile bliss, and eternal expiation (cf. story 15). Mr. A utters this false start, even though a moment's reflection would have led him to recognize that he could not tie the second woman and child into the story. This mildly impulsive opening reminds one of the fascination which this theme holds for him.

This story reveals a good deal about the subject's felt relationship with his mother and about his attitude toward adult manliness. The mother-figure is seen as possessive and inflexible. She seeks to prolong the son's dependent status. As for the son himself, he is uncertain and hesitant himself. First, he does not wish forcefully for the responsibilities of adulthood. That is, we hear nothing about any feelings of love: *he has found himself a wife*. Second, it is suggested that adulthood has overtaken him all at once (*he's come of age*). Third, the apperception of the babe-in-arms as a sibling makes the hero *her older son* and thereby emphasizes his relative youth. (More often the baby is seen as the young couple's offspring in the arms of its grandmother.) Taken together these considerations suggest that not only the mother-figure, but also the hero-figure is *not fully reconciled* to his manhood.

Once again the future is conceived as a period of patient (and a little painful?) adjustment. The assumption of autonomous responsibility does not take place smoothly as a matter of course. Old ties and reminiscences tend always to intrude into the evolving present. For the first time, we have a fairly specific suggestion regarding the past. It is possible that Mr. A has formulated the persistent regressive yearning as a trap set by a jealous domineering mother so as to ignore his own reluctance to move forward. There is a great deal of imagery in our culture, amounting to cliche, which allows us to blame overwhelming mothers for the male's retreat from adulthood and active independence. Snug Oedipal warmth is gladly denied and the catchphrase of a matriarchal gaolkeeper is put in its place. The TAT can tell us nothing reliable about what Mr. A's mother was really like, but his massive denunciation of his past directs attention to this alternative reconstruction. (For similar reasons, paradise takes on sinister aspects *because* man was expelled from it, and the survivor of the air battle or of the concentration camp may wish that he had not escaped!)

The subject's response to inquiry contains one *sequitur* and one *non sequitur*. That primitive dress indicates a peasant society is thinkable, but that paintings of despondent people could point to this, is impressionistic reasoning. The best guess is that *poverty and misery* reflect the subject's persistent depressive mood, just as the *concentration camp* did, and that his rationale for these is given after the apperceptive fact. This deviation from logical discipline is not severe. But it is a further indication of his indifferent involvement with external reality. He is on the whole more attentive to his inner promptings than to outer ones.

While the first few cards had been administered by a male tester, the remaining ones were postponed to another testing session with a female tester.

Card 13MF 10″ This is the morning after a wild party. The prior evening he really hung it on with alcohol. He is fully dressed and drowsy. This is not too long an acquaintance with this girl. Her general posture suggests she's inclined to that sort of behavior. He is thinking how lousy he feels. He is shaking the cobwebs. If she is awake she is looking up into the black void which reflects the emptiness of her life. I presume in the future she will go on with her activities, and he will go on with his normal pursuits . . . Hollywood! 2′40″

This story introduces new elements into the accruing personality picture of the subject. Choice of theme and of language contrast with the decorous, restrained attitudes of the previous stories. The rapport with a female tester—a factor which was discussed under the heading of interest earlier in this chapter—may have brought about this change in theme development. What subtle satisfactions Mr. A may derive from this situational circumstance is not clear except in the general sense that telling a story of sexual exploits to a female tester provides a sort of flirtatious excitement for many male subjects. What stories 5 and B have suggested concerning the subject's attitude toward female authorities amounts to respect and solicitude as well as the wish to escape their control. The present story, insofar as it is a communication with a female authority, gives no clue to such an attitude.

The persistent depressive tone is here interrupted for the first time; yet the mood of the story is distinctly *counter*-depressive and not successfully so. Forced gay abandon opens the story, but forbidden oral self-indulgence with subsequent trespass and guilt are the main theme. The high mood cannot be maintained and soon deteriorates. *Emptiness* and *black void* once again determine the prevalent climate. Cynical attitudes about a happy life are reflected in the expression *Hollywood*, the most pertinent aspect of which is the pretense at contentment and fulfillment.

Card B, which portrays two nude figures and sometimes evokes stories of illicit affairs, did not appeal to the libidinous side of Mr. A. It is only now, in response to a card which very often elicits prurient stories, that he gives himself over, and with a good deal of initial verve, to a story of self-indulgence. Sexual and oral revelry are joined, but lead to compunctions. The subject takes liberal advantage of the stimulus to present another side of himself. He communicates that moral issues are for him relative and negotiable.

Apart from its significance as a communication, the story is remarkable in what it reveals about the subject's self-image. There is enough detail and specification in the story to suggest that it stems from inside knowledge. That is, Mr. A has either been in a similar situation or, at any rate, he has a feelingful, secondhand acquaintance with it from reading, hearsay, or fantasy rehearsal. Whatever the source of this familiarity, Mr. A is apparently not so consciously forbidding toward himself as he has seemed to be.

If plot and expressive style seem inconsistent with his previous productions, the moral tone does not. The story is editorialized as "Hollywood" so as to set it apart from Mr. A's vision of real life. The story is presented as an excursion into fantasy. The woman's life is roundly denounced as empty. The subject's tone is scornful, and he predicts that she will continue *that sort of behavior.* Her very *posture* informs him of her *inclinations.* As for the hero himself, he too is not engaged in *normal pursuits.* Only by dint of *alcohol* did he err; and to remove any remaining doubts, the subject strikes the hero with a hangover and with a *lousy feeling.* Stories of sexual adventure are not uncommon for card 13MF. The hero is often remorseful and the woman loose. But Mr. A identifies himself with her sufficiently to mention her *outlook into the black void.* This represents a mixture of sympathy and contempt. He spoke of a *void* in story 14 where it had the effect of shackling the hero as if in prison.

Themes of irresistible domination by bodily urges (sex, alcohol) with subsequent feelings of emptiness and depravity are often told by subjects who suffer from an addiction or who cannot stop themselves from committing private sins. In either case, the effectiveness of ego controls is weakened, and the subject protects his innocence with the excuse that he cannot help himself. This may represent the libidinal gratification which arouses the subject's guilt and which alternates with this guilt, making the progression toward maturity and integrity difficult. Mr. A remains frozen in an interpersonal and emotional near-vacuum. This is the first story in which an affect-laden exchange between two real people has taken place. But even here, Mr. A leaves no doubt about the unacceptability of this. He is either a man who only interacts with others, sexually or otherwise, if the setting is not a part of real life (*Hollywood*) or, as an alternative, he is a person who harbors a pervasive suspicion regarding all forms of personal closeness and regards these, when they do occur, as cheapening and tasteless. His removal from other people may therefore secure him against interpersonal temptations and guarantee him private fantasy satisfactions without compromising himself. Perhaps he copes best with his own *void of negative past* when alone and is then freer to *go on with normal pursuits*. It becomes evident that both characters in this story are representatives of Mr. A. This story contributes, above all, in revealing the self-indulgent side of the subject which may be of importance *clinically* at the present time, considering how astringent his morality is as a rule, and *historically* in that it may symbolize the instinctual misdeeds concealed in his *undesirable past* (story 14).

Card 4. 12″ This is Hollywood too! An attractive young couple whose lives have been more than usually glamorous. At this particular moment the young lady is expressing, is attempting to express her warm feelings to this man. His attention has been momentarily diverted. He is preoccupied with some more distant thing, as if he had an object which was more demanding than this immediate occasion. The setting might be a home, a kitchen, except that what appears to be a calendar is more risqué than is normally found in one's kitchen. I suppose in the best Hollywood tradition, things are bound to turn out well: she is too attractive for him to be occupied elsewhere for too long. This scene might be indicative of future times. She is attempting to draw him near and keep him home. He is attempting new pursuits that will take him away. 4′35″ (namely?) Whatever—he looks like a rough-and-ready guy—whatever he considers would bring him fame and fortune . . . a trip to the moon or something.

Mr. A's heroes are gradually becoming less and less constrained. In this instance, not even alcohol was required. Centrifugal strivings are directly asserted. Marital integrity is just barely preserved because the young woman is *too attractive*. Even this last-minute godsend is qualified as *Hollywood tradition*. The availability of erotic incentives at home is apparently what qualifies this story as make-believe. It is possible that

Mr. A, were he asked, would complain of feeling indifferent to his wife and of wanting to stray from his marriage, at least in fantasy. Because this concern is also fraught with more infantile meaning, it becomes all the more difficult to manage. That uncontrolled passions may be setting off an internal battle was suggested by story A, and that independent sexual assertion is an offense also against the jealous mother-figure, was suggested by story B. Under these pressures, the happiest outcome would be the faithful return to his marital obligation with a simultaneous guarantee of erotic satisfaction therein. The interpersonal inhibitions noted in several of Mr. A's TAT stories are perhaps also indicative of sexual impotence. The themes and styles of stories 4 and 13MF raise the question whether he may be attempting to cure this symptom with extramarital affairs or whether he is currently under stress because he wishes to control this urge (cf. his first question to the male tester at the beginning of the TAT.) Short of directly interviewing the subject, which is the most appropriate mode of assessing this point, the Rorschach findings should be consulted on this question. They would give the best estimate of the subject's impulse-defense balance, his sense of value and responsibility, and his access to the sluice-gates of direct drive action. But the TAT is not entirely silent as to this question. The subject's passivity with respect to his erotic and adventurous interests is evident in his expressive style: *his attention has been diverted* by an *object which was more demanding; to be occupied elsewhere; pursuits that will take him away . . . bring him fame and fortune.* He assiduously avoids mentioning what the hero wishes and thus belies the *rough-and-ready* disposition. This formula also provides insurance against guilt: *"I did not pursue it; it* attracted *me!"* This is akin to engaging in sexual adventures under the influence of alcohol and later repudiating one's own part as well as the partner's. In this light it seems probable that sexual adventures occur only in his daydreams. More than his other stories, this has the appearance of a day-dream. The hero will find glamor and erotic satisfaction at his very hearth where it is not *normally found.* The rough-and-ready temperament is not borne out either by the story's detail or by what we have previously deduced about the subject. Even in this day, a *trip to the moon* is still a boy's fantasy. In other words, Mr. A will become receptive to a woman's feeling and abandon puerile flights of fancy when Hollywood films become realistic.

Despite the wishful quality of the story, Mr. A derogates the invention as *Hollywood.* Not only is it implausible, he seems to say, but it is tawdry as well. What a way for him to treat a style of life which approximates the emancipation he sought in stories 14, B, and 13MF! Not to be imprisoned by his past was a cherished hope, and now that he has realized this, he belittles it. One may deduce that this *is* an important wishfulfillment and that defensive forces have been called into play because it is so important. Further, one may deduce that Mr. A practices self-denial in real life, entertains reveries about golden opportunities, prevents their realization with masochistic resistances against success, is not surprised that things never turn out well, rejects other people's sympathy and renews his daydreams.

Card 6BM. 5″ This suggests the older woman just learned something unpleasant. The young man is a police officer who has just come to inform her of some unpleasant event. Her husband or one of her children was killed in an automobile accident. Her previous life was quiet and pleasant around the home, as it is with an older woman. The man looks out of place. He is used to patrol-car detective work. This is an unpleasant occasion he has to face up to from time to time. He would return to his occupation and have no further association with this woman. The woman will have to learn to endure this new loss and sorrow whatever it might be. 3′ (feelings?) She seems resigned to this loss. She is mature enough to realize these things happen. (his feelings?) He is nervous, quite unhappy he brought this news to her . . . uncomfortable.

The woman in story 5 was described as capable of coping effectively with the source of her irritation, and this was in contrast with the pessimism and discomfiture of most of the other characters. The mother-figure in story B was also endowed with assertive, possessive characteristics. The woman in the present story is seen as *mature enough to endure this new loss,* but the tone of the narrative, as interpreted from the police officer's viewpoint, is not one of relaxed or compassionate confidence in the woman's strength. Rather, it is a rationalized confidence stemming from his looking, as well as feeling, *out of place* and from his fretting in this *unpleasant* situation. It would have been a more accurate reflection of the *tone* of the story, had the subject said: "The officer hopes desperately that the woman is mature enough, etc., and that his presence or help will no longer be required so that he can return to his occupation." The story highlights the subject's quite intense discomfort in situations requiring him to assume a responsible, active helper role and to convey or share someone else's distress. The hero is present by dint of his job, not because he is personally affected as a family member or even a friend of the deceased, and he looks forward to an early exit, leaving the victim to an uncertain fate. It is not evident from this story whether the subject provides support reluctantly only when female figures are involved or whether the attitude is general. But emotional distancing has so far seemed a consistent feature of all his stories. The subject's mention that the detective would have no further association with the woman is somewhat gratuitous and raises the question whether Mr. A is himself maintaining his distance from older women with some difficulty, both hoping for contact with them and avoiding closeness.

To these two factors—the mother's sturdiness and the hero's diffidence—must be added a third. Story 5 contained suggestive evidence that the subject is bent on protecting the mother-figure against undue excitement. What was there achieved by formal means, is here accomplished thematically. Unconscious introjects are cognitively organized by the primary process, and it is no contradiction that the mother-figure should be seen as authoritarian, possessive, mature, and masterful while at the same time requiring protection to make her strong (as though she were vulnerable). That she furthermore gets protection by a formal disruption (story 5) or by the retreat of the officer charged with protection, is another seeming contradiction. One may infer from all this that the mother's vulnerability is perceived by the subject and that he imputes qualities of strength or willfulness to her because they serve his own defensive ends, as was evident in connection with the slogan proclaimed in story 14.

Card 7BM. 7″ A young man and his father or some older man he confides in. Probably some crisis has arrived, and he is not fully able to cope with it. So he is accepting advice from the older man. The older man, who has lived the best part of his life, remembers times when he found it necessary to seek advice from someone. At the moment one gets the impression that the older gentleman expressed an opinion and that the younger is contemplating it. By the set of his mouth, he is not delighted with what he has heard. The future: the old man will go back to his normal life, whatever it might be. The younger one will have to weigh the advice, to consider, to reach some decision on the problem. 5′7″ (problem?) Perhaps dealing with his profession. He reached a turning point. There is more than *one* road he can pursue, but not *all*. He has to think which of these . . . a career as a public servant or as a private entrepreneur, to make money, or a third course which would give him more freedom but is less challenging.

A *crisis* having arisen, the hero decides to *confide* and to *accept advice*. We have analyzed these stories and not encountered one about wholehearted unashamed intimacy. In this story the subject gives a hint that his aloofness stems in part from the attitudes he attributes to others. Thus, he finds it necessary to make the consultation explicitly acceptable to the older man by letting him remember that he too has asked for such support in his lifetime. Do other people seem forbidding to Mr. A in his daily contacts? It is quite consistent with his previous descriptions of helping relationships that they need to be rationalized in some manner and that *the old man goes back to his normal life* just as the police officer did in story 6BM and a minister, in story 12M, after performing last rites over the victim of an accident. *Not delighted,* like *not overjoyed* in story 1, smacks of poorly contained bitterness—defense by minimization. Neither does the hero simply reject the uncongenial advice, but tries to weigh various alternatives against each other. This too is consonant with obsessive defenses.

To fill in the image of his future is once again the perplexing task before Mr. A. The TAT sheds light on the various alternatives confronting him. To serve the public is nearly always an attractive goal to a penitent; a man with a *void of negative past* wants to be of use. But it is also a difficult image for one who feels so *out of place* in the role of helper or caretakers. Private enterprise, that is, *to make money,* is inviting to someone who treasures self-sufficiency, as Mr. A does. But we have also seen that he is not at ease in his loneliness, in his imprisonment. He would like to be in better empathic rapport and to obtain satisfactions from others. Thus, he is pulled back and forth between introversive, conservative, regressive incentives and liberating, forward-looking, adaptable ones. This pull may be experienced in actual vocational dilemmas, as well as in the broader unresolved identity choices which face him as a *turning point.*

What occupies the deliberations of this hero should not be dismissed as classical obsessive rumination which has found its way from the subject's mind into that of his hero. Perhaps it is this, but a good deal more could be implied as well. Empty, irresolute shilly-shallying is usually seen in obsessive patients' story-telling *style* ("it could be this, it could be that; on the other hand . . ."). But when the irresoluteness is not only thematic (as against stylistic) but also articulated, as it is in this case, it is apt to represent an active, more or less focused, and conscious-conscientious perplexity in the subject's (current) life.

From what we have learned so far about Mr. A, it is more than tenable that the questions which plague his mind do not differ appreciably from those which plague the hero of 7BM. The TAT analysis we have presented also suggests, by its allusions to the subject's distortions of his history and of his contemporary self, what insights he lacks for an optimal understanding and resolution of these questions.

Rounding out and generalizing what has been indicated already about the hero's career dilemma, we may say that the conflict between freedom and challenge is pervasive in Mr. A's life and has a double meaning: one, freedom-to-stay-by-himself (social retreat) versus the challenge-of-making-contact (adaptive drive satisfactions) and two, freedom-from-his-private-entrapment (escape from infantile guilt) versus the challenge-to-be-good-to-himself (acknowledgement of his vitality).

Mr. A, a 30-year-old Catholic, father of four children, was an industrial engineer who sought intensive psychotherapy following an episode of acute anxiety and various psychosomatic complaints. Although generally productive, his work had been recently interfered with by flurries of excitement and fear. As a rule he got along well at home but blew up in anger when he was inconvenienced by family routines. A central symptom was the guilt he felt over his inability to restrain himself from masturbating "in his sleep." A number of sexual perversions, performed in adolescence, and some abortive extramarital affairs were noted in early stages of treatment. Insomnia, depression, mild episodes of depersonalization, nightmares, infrequent confusional states, and a recurrent worry that he might be crazy complete the symptom picture. He described his mother as a controlling, bitchy person and his father as a weak alcoholic. He improved considerably in psychotherapy.

The analysis of this record illustrates the wide band of the TAT. It covers a horizontal range of factors including interpersonal style, affective variety and intensity, preferred defenses, instinctual emphases, thought organization, adaptive aims and assets, and prominent identity-dilemmas. The analysis also yields a vertical perspective on infantile and primitive as well as on contemporary and evolved personality factors. Finally, it has illustrated the diagonal band which subsumes repressed and preconscious contents. In the process of analyzing the TAT stories, grossly normative, empathic, and theoretical considerations play equally important parts. This is admirably and lucidly illustrated by Schafer (1958). When the TAT record is part of a battery, this tripartite orientation becomes more complex still. One's attention wanders freely over the material and is not focussed on one test, much less one response, at a time. The stories are read over several times, nearly to the point of memorization, and are allowed to work on the tester's mind and sensibilities. In this way, configurations, contrasts, leitmotifs can begin to stand out. Nothing interferes so much with the tester's appreciation of patterns as the impatience to translate the test protocols, story for story and element for element, into a personality description. Whereas the grasp of theory and the backlog of normative experience come with time and application, the empathic feel for another person through his individual-expressive thought products is attained by a voluntary assumption of naïveté regarding test technology and experiences. The tester must let himself be surprised by what he hears as though each TAT story were the first of his career. Thus, erudition and analytic activity blend with ingenuousness and impressionable passivity.

OVERVIEW OF RESEARCH

In the last section of this chapter, systematic investigations involving the TAT will be sampled. The volume of TAT research is nearly beyond survey; only its outlines can be indicated. The interested reader should consult Zubin, Eron, and Schumer (1965), Murstein (1963), or Kagan and Lesser (1961). Morgan and Murray (1935) in their original article aimed at a psychiatric audience, described the method in modest terms. They expressed the hope that it might lay open the "regnant pre-occupations" of the story-teller. With these in hand one might gain quick access to a person's repressed fantasies and expedite the cure of emotional problems. Shortly thereafter, *Explorations of Personality* (1938) presented the TAT as part of a large program of individual case study with normal subjects. Once again, the authors made few claims beyond those documented in their volume. But claims or no claims, investigators soon set out to gauge the predictive, diagnostic, and descriptive potential of the instrument. A second phase of research took the test's psychometric refinement as its aim. How to maximize its yield was the paramount concern. Somewhat apart from these two trends, there arose a third, vigorous, and perhaps more edifying to the clinician and personality theorist. This dealt with hypotheses drawn from clinical lore, psychopathology, theories of motivation, and the study of personality.

Criterion research

The experimental literature reports research *on* the TAT and *with* the TAT. It will be surveyed in three sections. The first of these is criterion research. The broad questions underlying this are whether the TAT does in fact measure what it is said to measure, whether it does have the differential diagnostic capacity claimed for it, whether it does stand in a specifiable relationship to other, mainly behavioral criteria. In general, investigations within this category take Murray's TAT for granted. They do not seek to improve or refine it, nor do they concern themselves with *why* the test does, or does not, measure up to claims.

Investigations published in the first decade of the test's existence mostly demonstrated its usefulness in distinguishing different groups of subjects. Rarely did one study lead logically to another. Balken and Masserman (1940) discovered reliable linguistic differences among the TAT stories of patients with hysterical, obsessive-compulsive, and anxiety-neurotic symptoms. Harrison (1940) achieved considerable success when comparing his inferences, based on psychiatric patients' TAT stories, with their hospital records, including biographical facts, attitudes, personal conflicts, and even IQ's. Most of these findings had to be regarded as tentative, pending replication. Also from that early period stems what is perhaps the first full-scale cross-cultural study with the TAT, a comparative investigation of Hopi and Navaho Indians reported by Henry (1947).

Although a good many of these early demonstrations would have been more convincing, had they chosen better prediction and classification criteria, eliminated uncontrolled contamination, or included replications of findings, they gave rise to a growing sense of the TAT's utility. Much of this was also felt in clinical settings and was therefore difficult to formulate. In 1951 Shneidman, Joel, and Little published a demonstration case in a book entitled *Thematic Test Analysis*. Fifteen experts had been given a TAT protocol for blind analysis with only the subject's sex, age, and marital status as background information. Each of these experts had been selected because he had previously published a method for interpreting the TAT. Each expert explained and demonstrated his method, submitted his step-by-step working notes, and his final interpretation. The book also contains anamnestic material about the patient. The work is interesting for a number of reasons. First, it witnesses that by the time of its publication, at least fifteen different approaches to the TAT were extant. Second, unknown to the various experts, the patient in question was somewhat of a diagnostic problem to those in charge of his case. The contributions of the TAT experts, therefore, constituted a real service. Third, insofar as the TAT experts committed themselves to specifications of the patient's diagnostic status, they were in close agreement with each other, but not with the impression which the patient had initially made on the hospital staff. Only gradually, as his illness became more crystallized, did the TAT diagnoses appear accurate. This illustrates the saving of time which test analysis often affords the clinician. Fourth, several experts began their reports with *accurate* appraisals of the patient's fundamental personality structure and proceeded to sometimes quite *inaccurate* reconstructions of his past or of his overt manner and presentation. That is, those conclusions in which they had less confidence tended also to be less accurate. Instances of "clinical validity" like the one just mentioned led to the conclusion that the TAT "contains" some useful information (more or less accessible to all interpreters) ; therefore, it seemed desirable to nail down more objectively what it contained so as to exclude by omission what it did not contain!

Norms. In developing a new projective test, the establishment of norms is a matter of importance because it lightens the cognitive burden of the tester. His job may not *only* be to analyze a given protocol in terms of adherence to and deviation from norms, but it cannot do without such analysis. Eron presented thematic norms pertaining to men (1950) and women (1953). His analyses were based on the responses of normal subjects and dealt with the emotional tone, outcome, themes, specification of characters and objects, perceptual distortions, and unusual formal characteristics. Rosenzweig and Fleming (1949) administered series of twelve cards to matched groups of fifty men and women and presented apperceptive norms. For each card and each sex group they tallied the percentage of subjects identifying each TAT figure as to a particular sex, age, identity, and other characteristics. They also provided norms for outcomes and problems.

There is certainly a good deal to be gained from knowing how often men and women identify, for instance, the huddled figure on card 3BM as a female or a male before one draws inferences about the subject's sexual identification from his alleged distortion. Carefully collected norms regulate many such interpretations. Yet this orthodox normative approach has not shown much life in recent years. The reason may be that one cannot easily collect norms at a level of analysis which is relevant to *typical* interpretive procedures. Clinicians are apt to complain that they need norms, but not of the sort which is available.

Group comparisons. Norms alone were insufficient for those wishing to capitalize the TAT's differential diagnostic potential. They proceeded from clinical diagnosis, feeling that TAT comparisons of two or more groups of patients who had been diagnostically classified might yield useful signs which might then be applied in daily clinical work. Davison (1953) compared the TAT protocols of sixty hospitalized patients falling into various nosologic groups and discovered that depressive patients tell more stories containing hostile and ambivalent personal relationships than do other groups of patients, and that hebephrenic patients, more often than others, tell stories with indeterminate outcomes and involving relatively few personal relationships. Ritter and Eron (1952) attempted to differentiate among normal subjects and various clinical groups in the following way. They noted those themes, outcomes, and emotional tones which were produced by at least forty percent of normal subjects for each TAT card and then counted the cases in each group which departed from these standards. Using this deviation model, they found that non-hospitalized neurotic patients fell between the normal group and the hospitalized groups. Such findings as these are more useful for dealing with groups than with individual clinical cases. They raise the question whether equally meaningful results could be obtained by reversing the procedure. If at least forty percent of hospitalized psychotics produce what is considered typical of psychological disorganization, what proportion of various normal and clinical groups depart from the standard? Or is normality a more homogeneous condition than psychological illness?

How relative the interpretation of such findings often is, is shown in Silver's study (1963) comparing the TAT's of psychopaths with those of control subjects. Psychopaths told shorter stories filled with more forthright accounts of sexual themes, but lacking achievement strivings, guilt themes, and references to a wish for personal recognition. It is obvious that what the TAT teaches us about psychopathy depends on which factors of story-telling the analysis singles out and on the other subject groups (for instance, normals, psychotics, the feeble-minded, alcoholics) with whom the psychopaths are compared.

Signs. Besides this empirical-exploratory method, there is a second approach to the diagnostic exploitation of the TAT: the sign validation approach. Lindzey and his co-workers have investigated signs for anxiety (Lindzey and Newburg, 1954) aggression (Lindzey and Tejessy, 1956) and homosexuality (Lindzey, Tejessy and Zamansky, 1958). In each study, casual observations by clinical authors are translated into a scoring scheme. For instance, if a clinician ventured the generalization that a subject's overlooking the gun on cards 3BM or 8BM is often a sign of conflict about his intense aggressive needs, Lindzey might count the occurrence of this phenomenon in all his subjects and relate it, together with a dozen other such signs, to independent ratings of subjects' aggressiveness by a team of clinical observers, or to their own self-ratings regarding aggressiveness. Unfortunately, these studies are marred by a spirit of excessive literalness in holding clinicians to their word. Thus, the incidence of "violent stories" came to be included as a sign side by side with "avoidance of guns," "forceful language," and "misrecognition of objects and characters so as to avoid an aggressive theme." All of these signs are, of course, relevant to aggression, but to lump them together is to assume that they have the same significance for overt aggression, anxiety about aggression, and defense against aggression. In fact, two of the mentioned signs seem to avoid, and two seem to emphasize, aggressive themata. The correlations discovered by the aggression study reversed prior expectations in that the signs seemed to be in accord with the subject's own self-ratings, and not with the judgments of a diagnostic council. As for the individual signs themselves, none correlated so well as a global clinical judgment by the person administering the TAT. The sign validation studies, despite their conceptual limitations, represented a stage in the TAT's maturation. They opened up some questions which are still far from being answered today.

But before the strict diagnostic conception of the TAT is laid aside, Dana's work should be mentioned. In one of several studies (1956) the TAT records of 150 subjects falling into three equal groups of normal, neurotic, and psychotic were analyzed with regard to three easily objectified dimensions: Perceptual Organization, Perceptual Range, and Perceptual Personalization. The first of these refers to the subject's ability to follow the test directions. The second score reflects the extent to which he makes reference in his stories to certain stimulus features on each card. The third variable is scored for any formal deviations from normal narrative. All three groups were reliably distinguished in regard to the first two variables. Dana then established two cut-off points for each of the three variables. The three scale intervals created in this way allowed a sharp discrimination of the three groups. Eighty-eight percent of normal subjects fell in the first Perceptual Organization interval, 72 percent of neurotic subjects fell in the middle, and 88 percent of psychotic subjects fell in the third interval. This study is illuminating in that relatively simple *formal* indicators were sufficient for gross discrimination. But Dana's success in discrimination should be re-examined in the light of base rates in the population. Whereas an *unexamined* subject, picked at random, in his study was as likely to be neurotic as psychotic or normal, this is not the case in clinical settings, where differential diagnosis is urgent, nor is it the case in the population at large.

Criterion research on the TAT tends to establish the instrument as legitimate in very broad limits. Clinicians who make use of it in daily practice are likely to feel that these investigations do not nearly tap its full diagnostic capacity. As a result, criterion research has, in general, done little to advance test practice, however much it may have done to ease the minds of skeptics.

Psychometric research

After this sampling of criterion research, there remain two other chief categories, psychometric research and personality-theoretical research. The first of these is less concerned with the test's diagnostic or descriptive-predictive virtues than with its basic assumptions. The underlying question of this type of research is: What stimulus values of the test are most conducive to the elicitation of revealing stories? Telling-stories-to-pictures is treated as a genuine psychological topic like problem solving, attitude change, or transfer of training, but with the important difference that what is learned from such investigations can be put to practical use without requiring the usual great leap from the pure to the applied. In an important article, Lindzey (1952) attempted to make explicit 1) those assumptions which are common to all projective testing, 2) those which are basic in determining the revealing portions of TAT stories, and 3) those which are involved in making inferences from these revealing stories about other aspects of behavior. Further, he listed for each of these assumptions the available scientific evidence. On the whole, the scientific underpinnings of clinical TAT interpretation were shaky. For some assumptions it was possible to cite evidence, but without a sense of conviction. For example, it is assumed in interpreting TAT responses that the subject's dispositions, strivings, and conflicts are sometimes indirectly or symbolically expressed. Lindzey's evidence was drawn from experimental research on displacement and stimulus-generalization, doll play, and hypnotic dream studies. On a high level of abstraction these can well be regarded as pertinent evidence of a consistency of observations across media. But clinicians who are in doubt do not gain much reassurance from this.

The hero assumption. The TAT scene is less somber today than it was in 1952—light has since been shed on basic assumptions. One, cited in Lindzey's article, is the so-called hero assumption, the assumption that there is a figure in each story with whom the subject identifies himself and to whom he attributes his own wishes, strivings, and conflicts. This hero is thought to be the first person appearing in the story, the person doing most of the "behaving," or the person resembling the subject the most. Accordingly, the other figures in the story are assumed to represent the important others in the subject's real life. The contrary assumption is that all the figures in the story are equally representative of the subject. Lindzey asserts that to hold the latter view means to forego drawing interpretive inferences about the subject's view of and interaction with other people since these are not distinctly represented in the story, according to the counterhypothesis. These are not the only views one can take of the matter as shown by Piotrowski (1952) who suggests that the hero assumption can be dispensed with. Instead, Piotrowski assumes that the subject attributes his own *acceptable* traits and motives to TAT figures which resemble him, and his *unacceptable* traits and motives to dissimilar figures. Only a detailed theory of process can deal with this issue. Experience shows that subjects often tell stories in which a personage unlike themselves plays the central role, but is *not* endowed with repugnant characteristics. What can be meant by similar and dissimilar figures? Does this not depend on the choice of stimulus material? What would regulate the subject's attribution of his traits and motives to two or more figures when all of these are equally dissimilar from himself? Would he, like the proverbial ass, starve betweeen two piles of hay? On the other hand, it should be remembered that even the strict hero assumption is complicated by the subject's own distortions. The story is told by *him*, and figures, whether they represent himself or others, are portrayed by *him* alone. What one can say about the other people in the subject's life is therefore always limited. TAT personages are the concretizations of the subject's dynamically elaborated experience and memory—the reduction of these to *real* events and relationships is full of hazards.

Although the status of the hero assumption remained uncertain, several investigators concentrated on one of its corollaries. If subjects attribute their own motives, dispositions, and conflicts to a figure with whom they identify themselves the most, and if this is facilitated by the figure's superficial similarity to the subject, then it stood to reason that TAT cards portraying figures which resemble the subject would elicit more useful stories. This reasoning led to the development of a set of cards for Negro subjects (Thompson, 1949). But a study by Cook (1953) demonstrated that this rationale is too simple. He administered both the regular Murray TAT and the Thompson modification to a group of white subjects and a group of Negro subjects and came to the conclusion that "with either a Negro or a White subject it is of little importance, so far as the defensiveness of the subject is concerned, whether pictures of the TAT or Thompson are used" (p. 318). Cook's supposition had been that more direct instigation emanating from cards containing figures which were similar to a subject would be manifest in greater defensiveness in that subject's stories. Inquiry revealed that Negro subjects thought of the figures depicted on the TAT and Thompson as people in general. By contrast, white subjects thought of the Thompson figures as "Negroes." It is likely, in other words, that white subjects were less closely identified with the Thompson figures than the Negro subjects with the TAT figures. This may be the reason that white subjects told longer, less vague, less uncertain stories to the Thompson cards than did Negro subjects; where the instigation is lessened because of dis-identification, defensiveness is reduced. In addition, it was found that Negro subjects told less evocative, vaguer, and more uncertain stories to *both* sets of cards than did white subjects. Cook's study serves to remind one that the subject's indigenous predispositions and the TAT cards are not the sole factors determining the stories.

Card ambiguity. No single stimulus-dimension has received so much attention as card ambiguity, and investigations of this have led to findings which will play an important role in any theory of process. The question is: Do relatively ambiguous TAT cards produce more revealing stories than relatively suggestive ones? Two further questions must follow this: How does one define ambiguity, and how does one define revealingness? The earliest significant effort to deal objectively with revealingness is that of Weisskopf (1950a) who proposed a transcendence index. This expresses numerically the extent to which the subject supplies individual-expressive ideas when asked to *describe* a TAT picture. The index is based on eleven categories including feelings, inferences regarding what happened before or after the depicted scene, evaluations of the pictures, mention of symbolic meanings, and others. Its average value can be calculated for each picture described by several subjects or for each subject describing several pictures. In the latter case, care must be taken to base the index on card *descriptions,* as was originally intended, and not on *stories.* In her original investigation, Weisskopf found that TAT cards designed for male and female subjects evoked the same amount of transcendence in any one subject regardless of sex, although female subjects showed higher indices on all cards. In Murray's series the first ten cards portray relatively familiar situations while the second ten are somewhat more fantastic and fairy-tale-like. Yet the first ten cards produced greater transcendence indices than the second ten. This was an important finding because it bore indirectly on the matter of ambiguity—not that fantastic content is necessarily more ambiguous than realistic everyday content, but behind the supposed correlation of ambiguity and revealingness there is an implicit assumption that a minimum of reality support promotes the manifestation of a subject's inner life. This hidden process-theoretical supposition was exposed to doubt by Weisskopf's finding regarding the "everyday" and the "fairy-tale" cards. In a second study, Weisskopf (1950b) addressed herself to the matter of ambiguity more directly. Instead of the usual TAT cards, she presented pictures with incompletely traced outlines or underexposed photographs. Both methods of presentation resulted in reduced fantasy activity as measured by the transcendence index. This approach to ambiguity takes on greater meaning when it is compared with an alternate conception which has been utilized more recently.

Kenny and Bijou (1953) report the following study: Raters were asked to determine for fifteen TAT cards, how many interpretations were possible for each. On the basis of their pooled judgments, the cards were assigned to high, medium, and low ambiguity sets, with those cards considered most ambiguous which were judged open to the greatest number of interpretations. Three testers administered the three sets to altogether eighteen subjects, following which two judges rated the obtained stories on a nine-point normalized scale for revealingness. It was found that the five cards of medium ambiguity elicited the most revealing stories. The relationship between ambiguity and revealingness had therefore to be thought of as curvilinear, rather than directly proportional. These findings have since been replicated by other authors. An incidental finding was that, despite a routinized data collection procedure, one of the three testers elicited significantly longer and more revealing stories than the other two.

Relevant to both criterion and psychometric research strategies are several studies involving the induction of drive states by experimental means and the measurement of its effects with the TAT. There is the by now classic experiment of Clark on sexual arousal (1952). Later experiments by Atkinson, Heyns, and Veroff (1954) dealing with the affiliation motive, by Schwartz (1955) with castration anxiety, and by Stricker (1962) with aggression, all exemplify the approach.

The research strategies discussed so far aim at the psychometric exploitation of the TAT through the influence of stimulus factors and through the direct manipulation of the subject. However, it is also possible to increase the yield by exploring more systematically those *response* dimensions which have gone unattended.

Formal factors. Holt (1958), leaning on Rapaport's (1946) analysis of formal variables, achieved distinctive—and in its way, unprecedented—success in predicting supervisors' ratings of psychiatric residents' competence from *formal* TAT variables alone. Low-level dimensions like those used by Dana in his differential diagnostic studies would have been inappropriate for Holt's purposes. Mere compliance with the test instructions would not have yielded useful differences. Instead he examined stories for such variables as Comments on the mood, spirit, or connotation of the picture; Vulnerability to unpleasant mood of the picture; Vagueness, overgeneralization, or disjointedness of organization;

Evidence of zest and enthusiasm as against Automatism; Psychological-mindedness; and many others.

Even though the prediction of behavior from purely formal variables is still rarely encountered in the research literature, the use of content variables has become more sophisticated and is gradually being fused with formal analysis. Pittluck (1950) found that although patients' aggressive fantasy and aggressive ward behavior were positively correlated, prediction was not feasible unless one took control and defense manifestations into account. Subjects whose aggressive fantasies were modified by thematic displacement, denial, excuse, or incompleteness, tended to act less aggressively than those whose aggressive fantasies were primitive and unqualified.

A related and exemplary study is that by Lesser (1958) who succeeded in isolating aggression-related from aggression-anxiety-related elements in the stories of grade-school boys. Thematic aggression and thematic aggression-anxiety were coded separately, but neither score predicted teachers' ratings and peer nominations of aggressiveness as well as did the ratio of these measures: aggression-anxiety/aggression. It can be seen that psychometric research is today no longer as single-mindedly concerned with the design of more revealing cards and more profitable test instructions. Increasingly, the investigator's attention is drawn to the more sophisticated appreciation of story-telling dimensions, in the sense of story content *and* of formal style.

Psychometric research on the TAT tends more and more to be conducted in conjunction with criterion and personality-theoretical investigations. This became necessary because earlier, purer psychometric studies, like those dealing with ambiguity, were concerned with non-differential aspects of the test. But since the TAT's chief task is the discovery of an individual's patterned motives, abilities, values, and views, a categorical research approach was of limited significance. To be sure, if stimulus dimensions affected people uniformly, it would one day be possible to devise cards eliciting more easily interpreted stories. But we do not know whether this assumption is warranted; it is quite plausible that stimulus values which produce revealing stories in one subject will have the opposite effect on other subjects. This is the gist of current perceptual theory (Klein, 1956). It is more than likely, therefore, that investigators will continue their efforts to improve the TAT's yield in *specific* criterion-oriented and differential terms: yield for particular theoretical purposes, yield for particular group differentiations. And such efforts will inevitably provide further substance for a process theory.

Personality-theoretical research

The investigations summarized in the remainder of the chapter fall into the realm of personality-theoretical study. This is a massive heterogeneous category, ranging from the corpus of experimental research on motivation (e.g., Atkinson, 1958) which is of impressive volume and intricacy, to a large array of individual clinical case studies. The elementary usefulness of the TAT is usually taken for granted by the investigator as he proceeds to clarify empirical relationships of diverse psychological interest. Whereas the first two categories represent research *on* the TAT, this one represents research *with* the TAT. In other words, it is usually assumed that the test reflects something of the subject's enduring or momentary characteristics. How one might expediently maximize this reflection is, however, usually ignored. Needless to say, advances in our comprehension of personality dynamics ultimately redound to the practice of TAT interpretation, thus closing the circle of knowledge and skill. Lesser's study (1958), already mentioned, makes such a contribution. In the most significant studies, criterion, psychometric, and theoretical strategies are blended. The intricacy and multivariation of the expression of motive in a story-telling test can be gleaned from an investigation by Saltz and Epstein (1963) which included self-report measures of aggressive drive, guilt, and conflict over hostility, as well as measures of thematic hostility and guilt. A third dimension was the ambiguity level of the TAT pictures employed. "From a pool of 181 college males, extreme groups of 20 each were selected on each of the self-report measures. It was found that (a) self-reported hostility across levels of guilt was directly related to TAT-hostility on pictures of low relevance for hostility only; (b) TAT-hostility across pictures was directly related to self-reported hostility when guilt was low and inversely when guilt was high; (c) TAT-hostility was inversely, and TAT-guilt directly, related to self-reported guilt . . ." This order of complexity is chastening for the student who still entertains the primitive question, asked some years ago, whether drive-fantasy is an alternate outlet for motives and is therefore inversely related to drive-behavior or whether it is a collateral channel of expression and is therefore positively related. On the other hand, it is of course encouraging that psychometric and theoretical considerations have *jointly* raised new questions.

The TAT has been useful in the study of personality dimensions which are relatively more permanent than the rise and fall of motives. Dispositions which are deeply, quasi-organically embedded in the fabric of personality, emerge in the story-telling task. Epley and Ricks (1963) assigned ten degrees of foresight and hindsight to TAT stories depending on the time period ("less than an hour" to "a life span") covered in each story. High foresight scores were associated with independent measures of academic achievement, freedom from anxiety, and empathic involvement in other people. High hindsight scores were associated with creativity, sensitive imaginativeness, and openness to experience. It is clear from these findings that a simple breadth-of-time-span dimension may be inadequate for a number of psychological purposes. Furthermore, the seeming remoteness of independent and dependent variables points up the usefulness of the TAT in investigations which are unconcerned with test validation. Ervin reports a study (1964) in which a group of bilingual subjects were tested with the same cards in each of their two languages on two separate occasions. Among other findings relating to within-subject differences, she found that female subjects tested in English obtained higher need-achievement scores than they did when tested in French. The pattern of differences between French and English themes is closely in keeping with certain generalized cultural traits such as intra-familial attitudes toward aggression, stereotyped sex-role, and the like. The intriguing suggestion offered by this study is that expressive diction is not the final link in the story-telling chain, but that it rather structures the implicit cognitive, affective, evaluational categories within which the story's outline takes shape—once again an apparently deeply ingrained disposition.

Related to the above investigation of culturally derived categories is a study by Singer and Opler (1956) who, on the basis of anthropological and child-rearing premises, predicted and obtained reliable differences between Irish and Italian schizophrenics. As measured by the transcendence index, Irish patients told more imaginative TAT stories; they also showed a greater capacity for deliberate motor self-restraint and for delay of action; they were more cooperative and cautious than Italian patients. The theoretical network linking imaginativeness to motor restraint is furthermore rounded out with the datum that Irish patients produced more M responses on the Rorschach test.

Hypothesis testing. In one sense—the sense of conceptual distance between the variables—these three studies strike one as *tours de force*. Not all theoretical research shares this characteristic. Kagan and Mussen (1956) analyzed TAT stories for two kinds of themes: 1) those in which the hero sought help from another individual in solving a personal problem or was disturbed over the loss of a source of love or support, and 2) those in which the hero is given some help or gift (advice, food, money) *not* specifically requested. The subjects whose stories were scored participated in an Asch conformity experiment. It was found that subjects scoring high on the first type of theme were more likely to yield to conformity pressures in the Asch situation than subjects with low theme frequencies. Themes of the second type were not related to Asch performance. A common factor is implied in wanting help and in yielding to suggestion. Atkinson and Walker (1956) instructed subjects to designate the quadrant of the visual field which "stood out the most" in a subliminal exposure experiment. They found that high need-affiliation subjects pointed more often to the quadrant holding a human face than did low need-affiliation subjects. The TAT has also been used extensively in the systematic confirmation of hypotheses stemming from theoretical formulations. For instance, Schwartz (1956) confirmed that male homosexual subjects show a greater incidence of castration anxiety themes in their TAT stories than do normal control subjects. Silverman (1964) reported an investigation of thought disturbance in psychiatric patients as a function of fantasy-eliciting stimuli. TAT cards which were rated highly relevant to aggression produced stories with more formal disturbances than did more neutral cards. These findings shed light on the connection between content and form of thought—a topic which is constantly on the clinician's mind when dealing with various forms of intellectual disorganization as related to broader personality disruption.

Psychopathology and psychotherapy. The last category of theoretical research deals with psychopathology. The least complex research designs are those using the TAT to confirm psychodynamic characteristics commonly attributed to a nosologic entity, e.g., Matarazzo (1954) tested a generalization about essential hypertension to the effect that patients suffering from this condition are habitually inclined to inhibit the expression of aggressive impulses. Using a technique consisting of criticism and abuse, which had previously been shown by Bellak (1944) to be effective in producing an increase in aggressive TAT stories, he found that hypertensive patients did *not* show a smaller increase in such themes than normotensive controls, as had been predicted, and that indeed both groups showed a *decrease* in such themes. However, he found that hypertensive patients differed significantly from normotensive patients in that they refused to continue with the task when subjected to criticism. These findings are interesting in three respects: 1) They raise a question regarding expressive channels: When is low aggression-tolerance evident as task rejection and when as thematic defensiveness? 2) They raise a question of sampling: How are two groups of patients alike, one hypertensive and one normotensive, but different from Bellak's subjects, that is, from non-patients? 3) They suggest that the understanding of hypertensive psychodynamics may require certain assumptions regarding the threshold and not merely the tolerance for frustration. How else may one explain that one and the same drive-stimulus (assuming near-perfect replication) could be absorbed by normals, but not by hypertensive patients?

Two studies by Poser and Lee (1963) and by Weiss and Emmerich (1962) use the TAT to explore the psychopathology of gastrointestinal disorders.

A study by Welch, Schafer, and Dember (1961) is exemplary in its coverage of both formal and content dimensions for purposes of elucidating the similarities and differences between hypomanic and depressed patients. It was predicted that these two groups would have depressive features in common, but that the hypomanic patients would manifest denial of depressive content. This was confirmed by means of an objective scoring manual for themes of guilt, fear, unhappiness, lack of supplies, flow of aggression, feelings in the test situation, and expansiveness as against constrictiveness in the use of space and time.

Also of great interest in this connection is a study by Goldman and Greenblatt (1955). Forty-five schizophrenic patients were tested in the acute phase of the illness, and again just prior to discharge. Two psychologists rated the pair of TAT records obtained from each patient with respect to three dimensions: 1) Positive changes in interpersonal relations, that is, more definite role descriptions; greater immediacy (changing from "they-there-then" to "me-here-now" stories; "this is a midwest farmer" rather than "this is in Biblical times"); closer relationships ("mother and daughter" rather than "little girl and maid"); themes showing interaction ("she is talking to her" rather than "she is looking at her"). 2) Positive changes in attitude toward the world, that is, fewer fear and avoidance themes; greater compliance with test instructions (giving *specific* action, past, future, and thoughts and feelings, though not necessarily positive or hopeful in tone). 3) Positive changes in expression and control of emotions, that is, mention of feelings rather than flat, apathetic stories; using emotions as the basis for action in the plot ("he is leaving home because he is unhappy"). Interjudge reliability was satisfactory for the most part. Patients had been independently rated as to whether they were psychiatrically "markedly improved," "improved," or "non-improved." The first and third of these patient groups differed significantly from each other in regard to each of the three TAT dimensions of positive change. In combining "markedly improved" with "improved" and comparing them with "non-improved," significant differentiation could still be achieved with dimensions 2 and 3, but not with 1. This study is an excellent example of translating a theory of schizophrenia (and a theory of therapy for schizophrenia) into operational terms, while at the same time establishing the TAT as useful in measuring the relevant dimensions of personality change.

In this last section of the chapter, a number of studies have been reviewed, which raised the question of expressive channels in the TAT. We have had occasion to wonder about the priorities of content and style in the conveyance of personality dispositions, and we have also taken note of certain expressive phenomena which seem to bypass the TAT entirely, for instance, in the experimental frustration of patients with essential hypertension. Even earlier it was indicated that in clinical work the TAT is not always used by itself, but constitutes part of a test battery. It seems fitting, therefore, to conclude this section with the summary of a study which points up the TAT's usefulness in such employment. Leary (1956) conceptualized personality as distributed over five levels of integration. The first and second levels include how an individual appears to others and what he reports consciously about himself. The third level, to which TAT productions pertain, is the level of imaginative and fantasy expression. The individual reduces anxiety by complementing on this level what had to be omitted or distorted on levels 1 and 2. Leary administered his Interpersonal Checklist (level 2) and the TAT (level 3) to several individuals entering psychotherapy. By analyzing differences between level 2 and level 3 personality profiles, he was able to predict the *kind,* though not the *amount,* of change brought about by treatment. Once again, this is a research design which sheds light on a theory of personality, on the efficacy of psychotherapy, and on the test instrument employed.

What light have investigations of the TAT shed on the mysterious involvement of the personality in story-telling? This fundamental question, broached initially, is still unanswered. One can feel certain that personality *is* implicated, deeply and comprehensively implicated. But we know next to nothing about the involvement of specific personality factors in specific story factors. At best we can enumerate the personality components and forces which are represented in a story, but we cannot reconstruct the dynamic process of their involvement. That is to say, our understanding of story-telling as a psychological process is not nearly as articulate as our understanding of personality, incomplete and uncertain as *that* is. Past research has been bifurcated, one effort concentrating on the instrument with scant attention to individual-dynamic configurations, the other on criterial and dynamic-descriptive dimensions with too little concern for the mediational processes. What has been singularly missing, almost to the point of deliberate avoidance, is the systematic experimental manipulation and analysis of the factors of story-telling. Formal and content parameters need to be explored methodically, using subjects with known base-line performance, and with a sharp eye on the factors' susceptibility to various kinds of influence and on their empirical interrelatedness among themselves.

The orientation of this chapter has been the presentation of the TAT as a multipurpose and multidimensional technique whose immense promise is very widely recognized today. Yet the test is still far from completely understood; some of the assumptions made in the clinical use of the TAT do not yet rest on solid scientific ground. And what is even more astonishing is that much which *is* known on the basis of impeccable experimentation is still of rather indifferent value to the clinician for whose sake it is being ascertained. The clinical utilization of the TAT is making great strides nevertheless, and the knowledge gained about the test through systematic research continues to be of momentous importance for many fields of psychology. A test which is so securely established in our workshops can surely anticipate a future as illustrious as its history.

REFERENCES

Atkinson, J. W., (Ed.) . *Motives in Fantasy, Action, and Society.* Princeton, N.J.: Van Nostrand, 1958.

Atkinson, J. W., Heyns, R. W., & Veroff, J. The effect of experimental arousal of the affiliation motive on thematic apperception. *J. abn. soc. Psychol.,* 1954, *49,* 405-410.

Atkinson, J. W., & Walker, E. L. The affiliation motive and perceptual sensitivity to faces. *J. abn. soc. Psychol.,* 1956, *53,* 38-41.

Balken, E. R., & Masserman, J. H. The language of fantasy: III. The language of the fantasies of patients with conversion hysteria, anxiety state, and obsessive-compulsive neurosis. *J. Psychol.,* 1940, *10,* 75-86.

Bellak, L. The concept of projection. *Psychiatry,* 1944, *7,* 353-370.

Bellak, L. The Thematic Apperception Test in clinical use. In L. E. Abt & L. Bellak (Eds.) . *Projective Psychology.* New York: Knopf, 1950.

Bellak, L. *The TAT and CAT in Clinical Use.* New York: Grune and Stratton, 1954.

Clark, R. A. The projective measurement of experimentally induced levels of sexual motivation. *J. experim. Psychol.,* 1952, *44,* 391-399.

Cook, R. A. Identification and ego-defensiveness in thematic apperception. *J. proj. Tech.,* 1953, *17,* 312-319.

Cronbach, L. J. *Essentials of Psychological Testing,* Second edition. New York: Harper, 1960.

Dana, R. H. An application of objective TAT scoring. *J. proj. Tech.,* 1956, *20,* 159-163.

Davison, A. H. A comparison of the fantasy productions on the TAT of sixty hospitalized psychoneurotic and psychotic patients. *J. proj. Tech.,* 1953, *17,* 20-33.

Epley, D., & Ricks, D. R. Foresight and hindsight in the TAT. *J. proj. Tech.,* 1963, *27,* 51-59.

Eron, L. D. A normative study of the TAT. *Psychol. Monogr.,* 1950, *64,* no. 9.

Eron, L. D. Responses of women to the TAT. *J. consult. Psychol.,* 1953, *17,* 269-282.

Ervin, S. M. Language and TAT content in bilinguals. *J. abn. soc. Psychol.,* 1964, *68,* 500-507.

Fenichel, O. On the psychology of boredom. In *The Collected Papers of Otto Fenichel.* New York: Norton, 1953. (originally published in 1934) .

Freud, S. Some character types met with in psychoanalytic work. In S. Freud, *Collected Papers,* vol. IV. London: Hogarth Press, 1924. (originally published in 1915) .

Goldman, R., & Greenblatt, M. Changes in TAT stories paralleling changes in clinical status of schizophrenic patients. *J. nerv. ment. Dis.,* 1955, *121,* 243-249.

Harrison, R. Studies in the use and validity of the TAT with mentally disordered patients. II. A quantitative validity study. III. Validation by the method of "blind" analysis. *Character and Pers.,* 1940, *9,* 122-133, 134-138.

Henry, W. E. The TAT in the study of culture-personality relations. *Genet. Psychol. Monogr.,* 1947, *35,* 1-134.

Henry, W. E. *The Analysis of Fantasy.* New York: Wiley, 1956.

Holt, R. R. The TAT. In H. H. Anderson & G. L. Anderson (Eds.) . *An Introduction to Projective Techniques.* New York: Prentice-Hall, 1951.

Holt, R. R. Formal aspects of the TAT: A neglected resource. *J. proj. Tech.,* 1958, *22,* 163-172.

Holt, R. R. The nature of TAT stories as cognitive products: A psychoanalytic approach. In J. Kagan & G. S. Lesser (Eds.). *Contemporary Issues in Thematic Apperception Methods.* Springfield, Illinois: Charles C Thomas, 1961.

Kagan, J., & Lesser, G. S., (Eds.). *Contemporary Issues in Thematic Apperception Methods.* Springfield, Illinois: Charles C Thomas, 1961.

Kagan, J., & Mussen, P. H. Dependency themes on the TAT and group conformity. *J. consult. Psychol.,* 1956, *20,* 29-32.

Kenny, D. T., & Bijou, S. W. Ambiguity of pictures and extent of personality factors in fantasy responses. *J. consult. Psychol.,* 1953, *17,* 283-288.

Klein, G. S. Perception, motives, and personality. In J. L. McCary (Ed.). *Psychology of Personality.* New York: Logos, 1956.

Leary, T. A theory and methodology for measuring fantasy and imaginative expression. *J. Pers.,* 1956, *25,* 159-175.

Lesser, G. S. Conflict analysis of fantasy aggression. *J. Pers.,* 1958, *26,* 29-41.

Lindzey, G. TAT: Interpretive assumptions and related empirical evidence. *Psychol. Bull.,* 1952, *49,* 1-25.

Lindzey, G., Bradford, J., Tejessy, C., & Davids, A. TAT: An interpretive lexicon for clinician and investigator. *J. clin. Psychol. Monogr. Suppl.,* 1959, no. 12.

Lindzey, G., & Newburg, A. S. TAT: A tentative appraisal of some "signs" of anxiety. *J. consult. Psychol.,* 1954, *18,* 389-395.

Lindzey, G., & Tejessy, C. TAT: Indices of aggression in relation to measures of overt and covert behavior. *Amer. J. Orthopsychiat.,* 1956, *26,* 567-576.

Lindzey, G., Tejessy, C., & Zamansky, H. TAT: An empirical examination of some indices of homosexuality. *J. abn. soc. Psychol.,* 1958, *57,* 67-75.

Matarazzo, J. D. An experimental study of aggression in the hypertensive patient. *J. Pers.,* 1954, *22,* 423-447.

Morgan, C. D., & Murray, H. A. A method for investigating fantasies: The TAT. *Arch. Neurol. Psychiat.,* 1935, *34,* 289-306.

Murray, H. A. *Thematic Apperception Test.* Pictures and manual. Cambridge: Harvard University Press, 1943.

Murray, H. A. Uses of the TAT. *Amer. J. Psychiat.,* 1951, *107,* 577-581.

Murray, H. A., et al. *Explorations in Personality.* New York: Oxford University Press, 1938.

Murstein, B. I. *Theory and Research in Projective Techniques (Emphasizing the TAT).* New York: Wiley, 1963.

Piotrowski, Z. A. The TAT of a schizophrenic interpreted according to new rules. *Psychoan. Rev.,* 1952, *39,* 230-251.

Pittluck, P. The relationship between aggressive fantasy and overt behavior. Unpublished doctoral dissertation, Yale University, 1950.

Poser, E. G., & Lee, S. G. Thematic content associated with two gastrointestinal disorders. *Psychosom. Med.,* 1963, *25,* 162-173.

Rapaport, D., Gill, M. M., & Schafer, R. *Diagnostic Psychological Testing,* Volume II. Chicago: Year Book Publishers, 1946.

Ritter, A. H., & Eron, L. D. The use of the TAT to differentiate normal from abnormal groups. *J. abn. soc. Psychol.,* 1952, *47,* 147-158.

Rorschach, H. *Psychodiagnostik.* Berne: Hans Huber, 1921.

Rosenzweig, S., & Fleming, E. E. Apperceptive norms for the TAT: II. An empirical investigation. *J. Pers.,* 1949, *17,* 483-503.

Saltz, G., & Epstein, S. Thematic hostility and guilt responses as related to self-reported hostility, guilt, and conflict. *J. abn. soc. Psychol.*, 1963, *67*, 469-479.

Schafer, R. How was this story told? *J. proj. Tech.*, 1958, *22*, 181-210.

Schwartz, B. J. The measurement of castration anxiety and anxiety over loss of love. *J. Pers.*, 1955, *24*, 204-219.

Schwartz, B. J. An empirical test of two Freudian hypotheses concerning castration anxiety. *J. Pers.*, 1956, *24*, 318-327.

Shneidman, E. S., Joel, W., & Little, K. B. *Thematic Test Analysis.* New York: Grune and Stratton, 1951.

Silver, A. W. TAT and MMPI Psychopath Deviant Scale differences between delinquent and nondelinquent adolescents. *J. consult. Psychol.*, 1963, *27*, 370.

Silverman, L. H. Ego-disturbance in TAT stories as a function of aggression-arousing stimulus properties. *J. nerv. ment. Dis.*, 1964, *138*, 248-254.

Singer, J. L., & Opler, M. K. Contrasting patterns of fantasy and motility in Irish and Italian schizophrenics. *J. abn. soc. Psychol.*, 1956, *53*, 42-47.

Stricker, G. The construction and partial validation of an objectively scorable apperception test. *J. Pers.*, 1962, *30*, 51-62.

Thompson, C. E. *Thompson Modification of the Thematic Apperception Test.* Cambridge: Harvard University Press, 1949.

Tomkins, S. S. *The Thematic Apperception Test: The Theory and Technique of Interpretation.* New York: Grune and Stratton, 1947.

Weiss, P., & Emmerich, W. Dependency fantasy and group conformity in ulcer patients. *J. consult. Psychol.*, 1962, *26*, 61-64.

Weisskopf, E. A. A transcendence index as a proposed measure in the TAT. *J. Psychol.* 1950a, *29*, 379-390.

Weisskopf, E. A. An experimental study of the effect of brightness and ambiguity on projection in the TAT. *J. Psychol.*, 1950b, *29*, 407-416.

Welch, B., Schafer, R., & Dember, C. F. TAT stories of hypomanic and depressed patients. *J. proj. Tech.*, 1961, *25*, 221-232.

Wyatt, F. The scoring and analysis of the TAT. *J. Psychol.*, 1947, *24*, 319-330.

Zubin, J., Eron, L. D., & Schumer, F. *An Experimental Approach to Projective Techniques.* New York: Wiley, 1965.

8

A Variety of Thematic Methods

CHARLES NEURINGER

Since the introduction of the Thematic Apperception Test (TAT) in the middle 1930's (Morgan & Murray, 1935), the test has become very popular with the psychological community. It was not the first thematic apperception technique to be developed; Brittain (1907), Libby (1908) and Schwartz (1932) had all previously utilized pictures that served as stimuli for story productions. Van Lennep (1951) reported that his thematic-type test (The Four Picture Test) had been published in Holland in the early 1930's. However, the TAT seemed to capture the imagination of projective and personality-minded psychologists to such a degree that "offshoots" began to sprout almost immediately.

The TAT pretty much defined the parameters of the thematic apperception technique. The materials of a thematic apperception test usually consist of a set or series of pictures depicting either one figure, or a set of figures in some sort of relationship. The pictures are presented to a subject who is asked to use his imagination to construct or "make up" a coherent story associated with the stimulus material.

It was because of discontent with the stimulus characteristics of the TAT that other thematic apperception techniques were developed. Some psychologists felt that the TAT stimuli were too broad and general, and that the test could not be utilized to study personality dynamics in particular areas that were of special interest to them. While they acknowledged that the TAT could well serve as a general projective technique, it was further argued that it was not constructed so as to reliably

The author wishes to express his gratitude to the following authors and publishers for permission to quote from the publications listed below: Gwen Andrews and her co-workers, and Science Research Associates (*The Michigan Pictures Test Manual*); Gerald S. Blum and Psychodynamics Instruments (*The Blacky Pictures: Manual of Instructions*); Jerome Kagan and Grune & Stratton (A. I. Rabin and Mary S. Haworth (Eds.)., *Projective Techniques with Children*); Herbert Phillipson and Tavistock Publications (*The Object Relations Test*); Edwin S. Shneidman and Grune & Stratton (A. I. Rabin and Mary S. Haworth (Eds.)., *Projective Techniques with Children*); Bureau of Publications, Teachers College, Columbia University (*Symonds Picture-Story Test*).

yield data in many important areas of personality. These psychologists then developed other thematic apperception techniques whose stimuli were so arranged as to force the subject's attention towards certain kinds of fantasy production. A good illustration of this kind of thematic apperception test is the one developed by McClelland, Atkinson, Clark and Lowell (1953) to study the need for achievement motive.

Paradoxically, other psychologists developed thematic techniques because they felt that the range of fantasy evoking stimuli on the TAT was too narrow and confining. The TAT, they argued, was too restrictive and full projective fantasy was not possible with the test. Shneidman (1949) developed his thematic apperception technique in such a ways as to liberate the subjects from restrictive pictures and allow them to choose personally relevant stimuli.

It was also commonly felt that the TAT stimuli were not applicable to certain kinds of individuals (children, adolescents, Negroes, persons of low socio-economic class, etc.) because the pictures were meaningless, foreign and different for these persons and they, therefore, could not adequately identify with the figures on the cards. Bellak felt that a special thematic apperception technique was needed for children and developed a Children's Apperception Test (1949). Symonds (1948) developed a thematic test for adolescents and Thompson (1949) constructed a form for Negroes.

Very soon after the TAT's commercial publication (Murray, 1943) there appeared a bewildering number of thematic apperception techniques. The range of existent thematic methods is staggering. The greater number of them were developed for special research purposes. Lebo and Harrigan (1957) developed a pictureless TAT which used only Murray's (1943) verbal descriptions of the TAT cards. Special versions of the TAT have been developed for use with various racial and cultural subgroups. There is a TAT for Negroes (Thompson, 1949), Indians Henry, 1951) South African natives (Lee, 1953; Sherwood, 1957) and Pacific islanders (Lessa & Spiegelman, 1954). Thematic techniques exist (Chowdhury, 1960) American Indians (Alexander & Anderson, 1957; for work with the physically handicapped (Greenbaum, Qualtere, Carruth & Cruickshank, 1953; Moed, Wight, Feshbach, & Sandry, 1963; Weisskopf & Dunlevy, 1952) as well as certain vocational groups such as nuns (Lasaga y Travieso and Martinez-Arrango, 1946), naval personnel (Briggs, 1954), army recruits (Walker, Atkinson, Veroff, Birney, Dember & Moulton, 1958), parachutists, (Fenz & Epstein, 1962) and blue- and white-collar workers (Veroff, 1961). Other thematic materials have been developed to study family relationships (Howells & Lickorish, 1963), vocational interests (Goldstein, 1960), group cohesiveness (Libo, 1953), and teacher aptitude (Shapiro, Biber & Minuchin, 1957). Special forms have been developed to evaluate single motivational states such as need for achievement (McClelland, Atkinson, Clark & Lowell, 1953), need for affiliation (Atkinson, Heyns & Veroff, 1954) and need for dominance (Veroff, 1957).

In addition, special thematic tests for chilren have come into being. The child's perception of the family has been evaluated by thematic techniques developed by Alexander (1952), Amen, (1941), Cummings (1952), Finch (1955), Henry (1957), and Jackson (1950). Other forms for children dealing with attitudes toward teachers (Biber & Lewis, 1949; Malpass, 1953) and racial attitudes (Johnson, 1950) are available.

This chapter deals specifically with those techniques that are commercially available and which have had a somewhat wide usage in this country. They are: The Childrens Apperception Test (CAT), Picture Story Test (PST), Michigan Pictures Test (MPT), Blacky Pictures, Make-A-Picture Story Test (MAPS), Four Picture Test (FPT) and the Object Relations Test (ORT). Two special apperception techniques (Auditory Apperception Test and Three Dimensional Apperception Test) will also be reviewed. Although the Tomkins-Horn Picture Arrangement Test (PAT) is not strictly a projective technique, it points the way to a possible future direction for thematic techniques, and for this reason it is included in this chapter.

The Children's Appreciation Test (CAT) [1]

The Children's Apperception Test (CAT) was developed by Leopold Bellak in the early 1950's. It comprises 10 cards with animal figures portrayed in different situations. Several presentations and descriptions of the test are available to the reader (Bellak, 1954, 1949; Bellak & Bellak, 1949; Bellak & Adelman, 1960). The CAT was designed for the purpose of facilitating the gathering of thematic content material from children. Bellak feels that the CAT is best suited for children between the ages of three to ten. Children at age three, he believes, are verbal enough to participate and respond to projective techniques of the kind represented by the CAT. Adolescents, he argues, should be given the Symond's Picture-Story Test (Symonds, 1949) or the TAT. Adults should have only the TAT administered to them.

The CAT, Bellak claims, is particularly suitable for children because they have difficulty making adequate identifications with the adults pictured in the TAT. He feels that the use of animal figures rather than human stimuli makes it easier for the child to make identifications. The adult world is a place with which the child has had no experience. He (the child) can, however, identify with animals because they are smaller and are also "underdogs." The use of animal figures also allows for

[1] An extensive treatise on the CAT, including a review of the literature, clinical applications and some normative data, was published too late for discussion in the present chapter. The reader is referred to the book, by Mary R. Haworth, *The CAT: Facts About Fantasy*. New York: Grune & Stratton, 1966.

enough psychological distance from the adult world to permit the expression of latent trends, without guilt, anxiety, or fear of reprisal. Bellak bases this assumption upon an observation to this effect made by Ernst Kris, and a study by Bills (1950) which indicated that children gave more stories to animal pictures than TAT cards. In addition, Rorschach researchers reported that animal responses appear more often in the protocols of children than adults (Klopfer & Kelly, 1942; Cass & McReynolds, 1951).

The CAT was designed to "facilitate understanding of a child's relationship to important figures and drives" (Bellak, 1954, p. 149). In addition, the CAT can give clues as to the "child's structure, defenses, and his dynamic way of reacting to, and handling, his problems of growth" (Bellak, 1954, p. 149). Bellak feels that the test can yield information about the "universal" problems of childhood such as orality, sibling rivalry, attitudes towards parental figures (singly and in combination), aggression, acceptance by the adult world, fear of loneliness, etc. The author claims that the test is useful diagnostically, as a personality exploration method, and as a method of play therapy and for developmental research. As an aside, Bellak asserts that the test is somewhat culture free, since Negro and European children can react to animals without great cultural biases entering in.

The test was developed by sending a preliminary set of 18 cards to various psychologists and psychiatrists for use in their clinical work. The resulting protocols were analyzed by Bellak, and based on their productivity the number of cards was reduced to ten.

The CAT is administered in much the same way as the TAT. Because children are easily distracted, special efforts to establish good rapport are necessary. Bellak suggests structuring the testing situation as a game, to be played between the examiner and child. The child is told that he and the examiner are going to play a game in which he has to tell a story about a picture. The child is further told that it is best to start off by telling what is going on (i.e., what the animals are doing). Later on, the examiner may ask about what went on before and what will happen later. After the 10 cards are administered, the examiner can go over the stories for elaboration of unclear parts of the protocol and for more information about specific areas of interest. It is suggested the cards not in use be kept out of sight of the child because their presence is distracting and the child may wish to play with them.

The materials consist of ten cards in which animals are portrayed in various situations. A short description of the stimulus material and Bellak's proposed probable-themes-elicited-for-each-card is given below.

Card 1. *Chicks seated around a table on which there is a bowl of food. A large, dimly seen chicken stands off to one side behind the table.* This card may elicit oral themes, oral deprivation, sibling rivalry, relationships to mother and feeding problems.

Card 2. *Two bears pulling a rope in opposition. A smaller bear also pulls on one of the ends.* Themes elicited here concern aggressive fantasies, interparental conflict, parental preference, etc.

Card 3. *A lion with a pipe and cane is seated in a chair. A mouse is seen peering out of a hole.* Paternal identification and characterization, Oedipal difficulties, child-father relationships and general difficulties with authority are some of the themes that may be elicited here.

Card 4. *A kangaroo with a baby kangaroo in her pouch. A larger kangaroo child riding a bicycle.* Sibling rivalry, birth curiosity, maternal characterizations, regressive fantasies, striving for independence and autonomy, conflict between dependency and aggression, flight from danger, are content areas that may be given to this card.

Card 5. *A crib holding two baby bears in a darkened room with a large bed in the background.* Primal scene anxieties, sexual curiosity and sibling rivalry themes can be found here.

Card 6. *A baby bear lying in the front of a cave. Two dimly outlined larger bears lying on the ground behind the smaller bear.* This card may elicit primal scene anxieties, parental jealousy, rejection fears, etc.

Card 7. *A tiger leaping at a monkey.* Fear of aggression, aggressive tendencies, fear of parents may be associated to the card.

Card 8. *An adult monkey talking to a smaller monkey. In the background are two other adult monkeys sitting on a sofa.* Stories relating to family constellation problems, feeding, embarrassment and shame may be given to this card.

Card 9. *A dark room seen from inside a lighted one. A crib with 2 rabbits looking out can be seen in the dark room.* Fears of darkness, desertion, and curiosity themes may be highlighted.

Card. 10. *An adult dog sitting in a bathroom holding a smaller dog.* Anal problems, punishment concerns, maternal characterization themes may be given to this card.

Before interpreting the test protocols, the examiner should keep in mind that the young child's verbal level is not as sophisticated as that of the adult. The stories may not be clear-cut and cohesive. In addition, the child, because he is not straitjacketed by the conventions of language, may use symbols in an idiosyncratic manner. Bellak feels that children may be very productive in their stories because they use more symbol projection, and wish fulfillment themes are usually very manifest and readily given.

Bellak has provided an analysis blank (1954, pp. 160-165) which is a check sheet for summarizing eleven important variables. (Bellak has modified his check sheet and interpretive categories somewhat [Bellak & Adelman, 1960, pp. 69-75]. But the differences between the new and old check sheet are negligible). One check sheet is filled out for each card. The eleven variables used for interpretative purposes are summarized below.

1. *Main Theme*: Overall summary interpretation of story (e.g., If one competes with authority, one gets hurt).

2. *Main Hero*: Attributes of the hero (abilities, interests, needs, level of adequacy, etc.).

3. *Figures are seen as—*: This concerns how the child sees the persons around him (achieving, demanding, compliant, nurturant, etc.).

4. *Identification*: Identification figures of the subject (mother, father, sibling, etc.).

5. *Figures and External Circumstances*: A characterization of persons (other than the hero) and of the circumstances that surround the hero (punishers, deceivers, friend, enemy, food, teacher, etc.).

6. *Objects and Figures Omitted*: Here important omissions are checked off.

7. *Nature of Anxieties*: Here are noted the sources of fear and anxiety (physical harm, loss of love, rejection, being devoured, etc.).

8. *Significant Conflicts*: The major conflict areas are noted here (e.g., between superego and aggression, between autonomy and compliance) as well as the mode of resolution.

9. *Punishment for Crime*: The relationship between a crime and its punishment is categorized (just, severe, lenient, etc.).

10. *Outcomes*: The outcomes are described in terms of their affect and reality tones (depressed, cheerful, realistic, wishful, bizarre, etc.).

11. *Maturational Level*: Appropriateness of development is categorized here from a comparison of the level of language, thematic organization, moral and ethical development and emotional control on the CAT stories, and IQ or MA as ascertained from an intelligence test (Stanford-Binet or WISC).

After a perusal of the summary check sheets is made, the examiner then has the material for the writing of an interpretative report. No formal scoring system is used, but the summary check sheet serves as basic data and augments the examiner's skills and experience. Interpretative examples, given by Bellak, are framed in psychoanalytic theory.

Bellak has also devised another series of CAT cards which he calls CAT-S because the stimulus material is designed to deal with specific problems (disability, pregnancy, school, etc.) facing the child as opposed to the "universal" problems that are tapped by the CAT. The CAT-S may also be used as play material for an inhibited child. The examiner may prepare such a child for the CAT administration by letting him play with the CAT-S cards and coaxing him into giving simple stories.

Although Bellak presents a scheme for the collection of normative data (1954, pp. 242-268) for the CAT and CAT-S, very little work of this kind has been done. Lehman (1956) reported very few CAT interpretative category differences among children of various socioeconomic classes. Byrd and Witherspoon (1954) have made available the main themes of 80 preschoolers. That the CAT does discriminate between schizophrenic and children with cerebral palsy has been reported by Gurevitz and Klapper (1951). Haworth (1963) has developed a checklist of ten categories of defense and identification patterns for the CAT which successfully differentiated a clinical group from control school children.

The bulk of the research done on the CAT has concerned itself with Bellak's thesis that animal stimuli evoke greater productivity in children than do human figures. This contention has stimulated lively controversy and vigorous research. An overwhelming number of these studies did not support the contention that animal figures are superior to human stimuli in eliciting projective material. Some of the studies indicated quite the opposite (i.e., children gave longer and more meaningful stories to the TAT than to the CAT). This is not the place to review these studies, but the reader may find excellent accounts of the research on this problem in Bellak and Adelman (1960, pp. 66-68) and Murstein (1961, pp. 255-258; 1963, pp. 212-215) and Zubin, Eron and Schumer (1965, pp. 504-505).

The CAT has become very popular with clinical psychologists in the ten years since its publication. The mode of interpretation that Bellak suggests can fit into most personality theory orientations. The paucity of normative data and the dearth of validity and reliability studies detract from the test's proposed usefulness. The major rationale behind the test (i.e., that children will be more productive when dealing with animal stimuli in comparison to human stimuli) has not been supported by research. The test's greatest usefulness may be as a "play" type thematic apperception test that will relax inhibited and repressed children. It can also be wisely used as a set of stimuli that could evoke responses to specific conflicts and disturbances not readily elicited by other methods.

The Picture Story Test (PST)

The Picture Story Test (PST) was conceived by Percival M. Symonds (1948, 1949) in the late 1930's. Symonds felt that the thematic apperception technique was a good one for the study of the personality of adolescent boys and girls because it offered psychologists a good tool for getting at underlying wishes, impulses and attitudes through fantasy productions. He had a special set of story cards developed in which the central character or figure was an adolescent boy or girl. He felt that such stimulus material would ease the task of identification for adolescents and therefore bring forth greater fantasy production. Symonds conceived of his test as an extension of the TAT but gave it another name (Picture Story

Test) to avoid confusing it with the set of cards developed by Morgan and Murray.

Symonds developed several criteria for selection of thematic apperceptive type stimulus material for the ascertaining of adolescent fantasies, based on his previous work on the usefulness of ambiguous materials for projective fantasy study (1939). He argued that such stimulus cards should have a minimum of detail and be populated with adolescent figures with which boys and girls could make identifications. Following these strictures and on the basis of his observations of adolescents, he asked an artist to draw 42 pictures from specifications describing situations with which he felt boys and girls could easily identify.

The 42 pictures were administered to 40 normal adolescent boys and girls from junior and senior high schools in Elizabeth, New Jersey, in the early 1940's. All the adolescents were volunteers and subsidiary data (parent and teacher interviews, autobiographies, an interest and attitude questionnaire, and school records) were also collected for the subjects.

Analyses of these data indicated several things. Symonds reported the presence of a warming-up effect (i.e., story richness and productivity began to rise substantially after the 20th stimulus card was administered). He also found few sex differences and concluded that separate series were not needed for the different sexes. He further reported that male adolescents gave more themes of violent death, crime, imprisonment, love and money than did females. Girls tended to associate more themes of aggression by disobedience, rebellion and resistance and friendship than males. Younger children (under 14 years of age) gave more happy stories than older children, while 15-year-olds presented the researchers with more discouraging themes than the younger children. An inventory of the themes collected in this study can be found in Symonds' book on adolescent fantasy (1949, pp. 79-103). Normative frequency data for each of the themes in terms of quartile position can also be found in the same volume (pp. 94-104).

The twenty cards that 1) yielded the largest number of important themes and which 2) were also rated best by the research study examiners, were selected for the final form of the test. These cards are divided into two sets (A and B). Set B is reported to be the superior of the two in terms of meeting the selection criteria. Symonds suggests that if all the cards cannot be used for some reason, set B should be the series of choice.

Symonds gives no indication as to what particular themes the cards are best suited to elicit, and he does not offer any descriptions of the card material. The descriptions of the stimulus materials that follow were made by Jerome Kagan (1960, pp. 112-113).

A. 1. An adolescent boy holding a valise stands on an empty street.

A. 2. An adolescent boy knocks on a door.

A. 3. In the foreground an adolescent girl sits with a book in her lap; in the background a young couple are walking.

A. 4. An older man with a somewhat angry expression and money in his hands stares at an adolescent boy who has one hand out toward the man.

A. 5. An adolescent girl with books beside her sits on the ground.

A. 6. An adolescent boy walking in a house at night with a shadowy figure in the background.

A. 7. An older woman talks with an adolescent boy.

A. 8...In the foreground an adolescent girl stares foreward while in the back of her is a heavily made-up young woman.

A. 9. A young woman in a domestic uniform holds a broom.

A. 10. A young couple stare into a crystal ball with a fortune teller beside them.

B. 1. An adolescent boy with his fists clenched and the suggestion of an angry expression walks out of a door.

B. 2. An adolescent girl looks into a mirror and an older woman stands beside her.

B. 3. In the foreground an adolescent boy stares forward and in back of him is an older boy with a cigarette in his mouth and the suggestion of a sneer on his face.

B. 4. An adolescent girl is holding a flower, with an older woman and a younger girl beside her.

B. 5. In the foreground stands a woman with the back of her head to the subject; in the background a young woman talks to the first woman.

B. 6. An adolescent boy with the suggestion of an angry expression is slumped in a chair.

B. 7. An adolescent girl is climbing the stairs at night and a shadow of a figure is at the top of the stairs.

B. 8. An adolescent girl talks to an older man.

B. 9. An adolescent boy is in a prison cell.

B. 10. An adolescent girl holding a book is walking on a street with the outline of a man in the background.

Symonds suggests that the examiner engage the subject in a leisurely and friendly get-acquainted type of interview in order to establish rapport. This is particularly necessary with adolescents who may generally be suspicious of the motives of adults in a "testing" situation. The following instructions are given to the subject:

"This is a test of creative imagination. I want to find out how much imagination you have. Here are some pictures which I am going to show you one by one. These pictures are like the ones used in magazines to illustrate stories. Imagine yourself a story writer and tell a story in which the picture could be used as an illustration. Each picture will present a scene with people in it. Try to imagine what happened before this scene and what led up to it. What are the characters in the picture thinking, how do they feel, and what do they say? How is it going to turn out? Please do not feel that you must make your story commonplace and conventional. It can be as absurd, as wild, or as silly as you wish. I am the only one in school who is going to see your stories, so you can say whatever comes into your mind without any fear. I want you to tell me a story based on this picture.

I am going to be your stenographer and take it down as you tell it." (1948, pp. 6-7).

A criticism can be leveled against part of Symonds' instruction in that they very strongly suggest to the subject that he ought to give absurd and wild stories. Such suggestions may lead the subject into believing that he needs to give a preponderance of strange and bizarre stories, a situation which may lead the examiner into making erroneous interpretative inferences.

Reaction times should be noted for each story since they give the examiner a rough indication of the subject's acceptance of and adaptation to the test. After the PST is administered, the pictures are given back to the subject one by one and the examiner reads the story aloud to him. The examiner may inquire from the subject about where he got the idea for the story, what made him think of this or that, etc.

The PST protocols can be analyzed in terms of content and formal characteristics. Content analysis of the PST has to do with identification of the hero of the story, a description of his characteristics and the psychological forces emanating from, and influencing, him. The hero's relationships with other people and his interests and attitudes should also be analyzed. The type and mood of the story endings is also to be studied carefully. Symonds describes these categories in some detail (1948, pp. 8-16) but they are generally couched in intuitive terms. Only the reaction time variable, in the formal analyses suggested by Symonds, can be considered as objective. The other formal analyses categories are attitude toward test, special comments, significance of story, range of content, fidelity between story and stimulus, story structure, presence of details, emotional tone, style and level of language and inter-story consistency. The criteria for making the formal analyses are judgmental and the reader may have difficulty in making decisions about formal aspects of the stories.

No particular method of interpretation is suggested beyond the point that the psychologist should "understand the facts and principles of dynamic psychology and be conversant with the psychoanalytic theory of symptom formation" (1948, p. 16).

Symonds does provide some normative data (1948, p. 20) based on his standardizing study. He has presented the percentage of occurrence of certain themes for the twenty cards among the forty adolescents used to develop the test. The number of themes of a particular type is given in terms of its second and third quartile range. If a subject gives a number of stories greater or lesser than these limits, it is suggested that the subject is either overconcerned with or denying problems in this area. Themes whose frequency of occurrence was too low for consideration are not given in the norm tables.

Very little has been done with this test beyond the original study. Symonds and Jensen (1961) retested twenty-eight of the original subjects thirteen years later and reported that fewer themes of hostility were given than had appeared in the earlier study. The stimulus material has received a great deal of criticism. Kagan (1960), Murstein (1963) and Newton (1959) have all commented on the dismal and gloomy character of the drawings. Symonds (1949) noted this in his early study and felt that this would certainly influence the tone of the stories given to the cards. The drawings are such that one could easily expect an abundance of dysphoric stories irrespective of the mood of the subject. Kass (1959) felt that the normative tables were insufficient for adequate use since too many important themes were not included because they weren't given often enough.

The PST has not elicited great interest and has not been used very widely. This may be due to its poor standardization, insufficient norms and interpretative vagueness. However these criticisms can be leveled against many more popular projective tests. Its greatest drawback may be its similarity to the TAT. There is no evidence that it is superior to the TAT in terms of eliciting fantasy information from adolescents. In fact, Symonds reports from his study that adolescent figures are not necessary for a boy or girl to make identifications. He concluded that ". . . most adolescents find it possible to identify themselves with babies, with old men and women, with members of the opposite sex, with animals, and even with inanimate objects" (1949, p. 53).

THE MICHIGAN PICTURES TEST (MPT)

The Michigan Pictures Test (MPT) was developed jointly by psychologists at the University of Michigan and the Michigan Department of Mental Health in the late 1940's. This cooperative effort produced a thematic projective technique that is soundly based on quantified normative data. Using the auspices of the Michigan Department of Mental Health, over 1,400 children throughout the state of Michigan were given the test on an individual basis. The development and standardization of the test were carried out in such a manner as to allow the clinician some degree of confidence when making inferences from MPT data. The developmental, standarization and validation procedures, as well as a description of the test, can be found in Andrew et al (1951, 1953), Hartwell et al (1951) and Walton et al (1951).

The authors felt that thematic projective tests worked particularly well for children, but that the TAT cards with their human figures, and often stylized drawing, were too foreboding for children and impeded the gathering of stories. They argued that adequate stimulus material for children should be realistic, reflect everyday events and feature figures with which children can identify. Approximately 1000 pictures were pretested with school children and children who were undergoing treatment in mental health clinics. On the basis of their findings and with consultation with mental health workers, the authors developed a set of cards which they felt met the criteria of adequate stimulus material for children.

The purpose of the test is to "investigate and measure the emotional reactions of children in the preadolescent and adolescent stages of development" (Andrew et al, 1953, p. 25). The authors feel that the test is especially useful as a screening device for maladjustment in children, as a diagnostic indicator of neurosis in children, and as a source of therapy recommendations.

The MPT is composed of fifteen cards and one blank card. The cards are divided into two series (one for boys and one for girls) of twelve cards each. Eight of the cards can be used in common for both sexes and four cards apiece are only applicable for each of the sexes. Four of the common cards have been designated as "core cards." These core cards (to be described below) provided the basis for the standardization and validation studies and, therefore, also provided the material from which scoring and interpretations are made.

A perusal of the cards indicates that they have pretty well met the criteria that the authors developed for adequate stimulus material. They are more realistic than the TAT. In fact, except for one card which is from the TAT series and the blank card, they are all photographs of easily identifiable figures in everyday situations. A description of the cards is as follows.

Card 1: (Core Card). A family of four seated around a table. The man is reading a newspaper while a woman feeds a boy. A girl watches the proceedings.

Card 2: A boy and girl are standing together. The boy holds a straw hat and the girl looks away.

Card 3: A schoolroom scene with a teacher and pupils. One boy is standing.

Card 4B (for boys): A man seated with a boy standing beside him, with head bowed.

Card 4G (for girls): A woman and girl holding a doll are seated on a couch. (This is card 7GF of the TAT).

Card 5. A man with two naked boys in a bathroom.

Card 6: (Core Card). Six boys and girls playing checkers.
Card 7: Four boys walking on a country road.
Card 8B: A boy resting his head on his chin, staring upwards.
Card 8G: A girl with her head in her hands.
Card 9: (Core Card). Lightening on a black background.
Card 10B: A boy standing before a man behind a desk.
Card 10G: A man and a girl are seated. The girl is reading.
Card 11B: A policeman, woman and boy are standing in a doorway.
Card 11G: A girl sits alone in a classroom.
Card 12: (Core Card). Blank.

After comparing the stimulus values of several different thematic techniques, Kagan (1960) felt that the MPT would tend to evoke more themes of achievement and concern with peer affiliations than the TAT or Symonds Picture Story Test (PST), both of which tend to draw themes of aggression, rejection and sadness.

The test is applicable to children between the ages of 8 and 14. After rapport is established with a child, the cards are administered one at a time. The standard instructions to the child are:

"I am going to show you some interesting pictures. I'd like you to make up a story about each picture. Any kind of story will be all right. Just tell me what has happened in the picture and how it is going to turn out, just as if you were making up a whole story. You can tell me how the people in the story feel and what they are doing." (Andrew, et al, 1953, p. 61).

For the one blank card, the child is asked "Let's see how good your imagination is. This time make up any kind of story you like about this blank card" (Andrew et al, 1953, p. 61). Gentle urging and coaxing is recommended with reticent and inhibited children. An inquiry may be made in order to obtain additional material and for purposes of clarification. However, inquiry data is not used for scoring purposes.

Fourteen hundred children in the third, fifth, seventh and ninth grades in nine public school systems in Michigan and in eleven state child guidance centers comprised the standardization population. Socioeconomic status and geographical considerations were made in the selecting of the school systems so as to obtain a sample commensurate with census population characteristics. Each of the children was administered the whole test on an individual basis. Eight variables were selected for validation study. The children's teachers were asked to fill out a twelve-item Rating Scale of Pupil Adjustment (which the MPT authors developed) for each of their pupils. The scores on the rating scale comprised the validation criteria of emotional adjustment. There is, of course, a question about the procedure of using an unvalidated rating scale to validate an unvalidated projective technique. In this case, the authors have assumed that teacher's ratings are adequate indicators of their pupil's emotional adjustment levels. However, the development of the testing movement has come about precisely because of the failure of people like classroom teachers to adequately make judgments about pupils. One critic of the MPT (Krugman, 1959) has asked of the test developers, "Why it is necessary to attempt to develop a complex clinical instrument that accomplishes much less effectively what a simple rating scale used by classroom teachers is assumed to do much better?" (p. 150).

In any case, the authors divided the scores on the rating scale into high and low emotional adjustment scores (upper and lower thirds of the distribution) and decided whether the eight MPT variables could differentiate among high and low adjustment children, as defined by their rating scale scores. The clinic populations of children were also used for cross-validation purposes (i.e., would the MPT successfully identify well-adjusted children and clinic children, who were assumed to be poorly adjusted?)

On the basis of the data from the four core cards, it was found that only three variables (Tension Index, Verb Tense and Direction of Forces) could differentiate between the high and low adjustment children. The Tension Index is a global reflection of basic unresolved needs. From a list of seven basic psychological needs (love, extrapunitiveness, intrapunitiveness, succorance, superiority, submission and personal adequacy) decided upon by the authors on an *a priori,* intuitive basis, it was found that the well adjusted children made more references to love and personal adequacy needs than did the poorly adjusted children. On the other hand, more extrapunitive and submission needs were mentioned by the poorly adjusted than by the well adjusted children.

The authors also felt that the usage of various verb tenses would indicate maladjustment (e.g., past tense may reflect avoidance and regression). It was found that the maladjusted children used the past tense more often than the well adjusted, but that the present tense was more the favorite of the well adjusted children. No differences in frequency of future tenses was found between the groups. The Direction of Forces variable has to do with whether influences emanate from, or are directed against, the central character. Surprisingly, it was found that no differences in direction existed between the well- and poorly-adjusted children. What was reported was that the well adjusted children made overwhelmingly more references to both directions than did the poorly adjusted children. Of these three significant differentiators, the Tension Index seems to have stood up best, negotiating three separate cross-validation studies (Walton et al, 1951).

The authors also report fairly high interjudge scoring reliability coefficients (ranging from .91 to .98) for these three variables. The three successful differentiators naturally make up the bulk of the interpretative inference bases. Instructions and criteria for scoring the Tension Index, Verb Tense and Direction of Forces variables are given in the MPT manual (Andrew et al, 1953, pp. 66-73). Scoring criteria for the other variables are also given in the manual (pp. 73-79) with the suggestion that, although they are not discriminatory, they serve as sources for hunches about the child's personality.

After scoring the protocol, the examiner may turn to a series of tabled norms (Andrew, et al, 1953, pp. 81-87) for the three variables which were developed from the standardization population and which are arranged by grade level. Critical cutoff scores at each level are available for categorizations of the level of adjustment. A combined Maladjustment Index (the number of scores equal to or above the critical cutoff points) can also be computed.

While the psychologist is invited to interpret the data from the test in any way that is comfortable for him, the authors of the MPT point out that the validity of their test has only been established on three variables developed from four cards. They also feel that they have developed an objective measure of degree of maladjustment in children, using a projective technique.

The MPT has been carefully and thoughtfully developed by its authors. They have avoided the pitfalls of premature and hasty standardization and validation. They have gathered extensive norms. Although there is a question about the Rating Scale of Pupil Adujstment as the validating criterion, the inferences that can be drawn from the test about a child's level of adjustment seem fairly safe. Yet, the objectification and precisioning of a projective technique seems to diminish the amount of data from which adequate inferences can be made. This is specially true of the Picture Arrangement Test (to be described later). However, this need not be true for the MPT. With over 1,400 protocols available, an almost infinite variety of hypotheses could be tested. It is unfortunate that not more has been done with the MPT data. The extension of the kinds of data already available for the test would be a boon to psychologists. Once again one must say that more work needs to be done with this test.

THE MAKE-A-PICTURE STORY (MAPS) TEST

The Make-A-Picture Story (MAPS) test was constructed and developed by Edwin S. Shneidman (1947, 1948, 1949, 1952, 1960). It was designed to go one step further than the TAT in eliciting projective material by removing the stimulus demands of the figures on the cards.

Shneidman stated that the "MAPS test is essentially a variation of the TAT principle in which the backgrounds and figures are separated, so that the subject is faced with the task of selecting one or more cut-out-human-like figures from among many such figures, populating a background picture, and then (as he would in the TAT) telling his story. In a sense, therefore, the subject must respond to a stimulus situation which he has in part himself created, using a *dramatis personae* of his own choosing. The possibilities for vicarious psychodrama, in addition to the usual diagnostic uses of picture thematic materials, immediately present themselves to mind" (1960, p. 130).

The author argues that the MAPS allows the subject more freedom to participate and structure his world than does the TAT. By populating and manipulating the miniature world of the MAPS, the subject does not need to be hemmed in by the restrictions of the card stimuli, but can therefore reveal his own idiosyncratic style and personality.

The MAPS is thought to be applicable to children over six years of age and very well suited for adults. Spiegelman (1956) has used the test with three-year-olds. The utility of the test for psychotherapeutic play and psychodrama is strongly suggested by the work of Fantel and Shneidman (1947).

The test consists of 22 cards which usually depict background scenes without people. (There is a head in the corner of *dream* background and what might be a figure in the bed in the *bedroom* background.) The depopulated backgrounds are a *Living room, Street, Medical scene, Bathroom, Dream, Bridge, Bedroom, Forest, Closet, Camp, Doorway, Cellar, Landscape, Cave, Raft, Attic, Shanty, Cemetery, Nursery, School room* and *Stage.* A blank card is also utilized. Shneidman chose some of the backgrounds because he felt that they would give rise to specific kinds of contents (the *Bridge* should elicit depressive and suicidal stories; the *Bedroom* might bring forth contents having to do with sexual problems, hypochondriasis, dependency, etc.). Certain of the backgrounds are highly structured such as the *Living room* and *Street,* while others (*Dream* and *Blank*) are very ambiguous.

The subject may populate these backgrounds with any number of 67 cut-out figures. These figures are of children, animals, males and females, minority groups, legendary or fictitious characters all appearing in various costumes and states of undress, clearly or ambiguously drawn, expressive or blank faced, and standing up or lying down.

The test is administered by placing the *Living room* scene in front of subject and telling him that he is going to be shown pictures like this one at a time. The examiner then pours the figures on top of the card and further informs the subject that he will have these with which to work. It is pointed out to the subject that he can use one or more of the figures and that he should place them on the background picture as they might appear in real life. The subject is then instructed to put the figures out on the table, so that each will be visible. Supplementary instructions are then given, indicating to the subject that he should tell a story about the situation; tell about who the characters are, what they are doing, thinking and feeling, and how it all turns out. After each story, and before the next background is presented, the figures are put back into place on the table. For the blank card, the subject is asked to make up, or visualize, a background of his own choosing. Shneidman recommends using 10 backgrounds (*Living room, Street, Medical, Bathroom, Dream, Bridge, Bedroom, Blank* and two chosen by the subject) for the MAPS administration. Inquiry should be limited to eliciting more story material ("tell me more") and asking for a title for each story. The identity and placement of the figures is recorded on a Figure Location Sheet (FLS). A figure identification card is provided to facilitate the use of the FLS.

The interpretation of the MAPS is done in two ways. A content analysis and formal analysis are carried out. Of the content analysis, Shneidman says that "in general, one interprets a MAPS test protocol in the same way as he would interpret a TAT protocol" (1960, p. 137). It is the formal analysis that is crucial to Shneidman and consists of such things as number of figures used, figure placement, figure selection, figure repetition, figure omission, etc., all which can be gotten from the FLS. Sign and sign pattern frequencies can be calculated for various groups through normative research. An illustration of how fruitful the FLS can be is given by Shneidman (1960, pp. 139-147) in his analysis of the figure placements, selections, etc., of a mute thirteen-year-old girl.

Several normative sign studies of the MAPS have appeared dealing with asthmatic and nonasthmatic children (Fine, 1955), aphasics, suicidal, neurotic and hostile adults (Goldenberg, 1951), disturbed adolescents (Joel, 1948) and schizophrenic and normal hospitalized patients (Shneidman, 1948). Shneidman, Joel and Little (1951), after comparing various scoring systems applied to TAT and MAPS data of a single individual by a number of experts, concluded that the array of TAT scoring systems were applicable to the MAPS. Spiegelman (1956) was able to successfully apply a scoring system developed by Reuben Fine to the MAPS protocols of children referred to a child guidance clinic.

The effectiveness of the MAPS as a clinical instrument has been evaluated in several ways. Hooker (1957) supplied three experts with the Rorschach, MAPS and TAT data of 30 homosexuals and 30 (matched on age, IQ and education) heterosexual men and asked them to identify the sexual proclivities of the subjects from the protocols. The MAPS and the TAT were found to be more useful for this purpose than the Rorschach. The superiority of the TAT and MAPS in this task was due to the appearance of homosexual stories in the protocols. Walker (1951) compared MAPS and Rorschach protocols with clinical manifestations of hostility, as described by therapists, and found a high correlation between the therapists' evaluations and the MAPS protocols in terms of manifest hostility. Bindon (1957) administered the MAPS to rubella-deaf, non-rubella-deaf and normal children. She reported that both groups of deaf children produced fewer normal signs and more schizophrenic signs (as defined by Shneidman's normative MAPS study of schizophrenics and normals published in 1948) than the non-deaf children. Edgar and Shneidman (1958) compared the strength and kind of affective reactions given by psychiatric patients to group discussion sessions, MAPS figures and life-size photographs of people. They report that the photographs elicited more positive reactions than the MAPS figures, which tended to call forth more aggression than the other stimuli. Van Krevelen (1954), working with normals, found no difference in terms of emotional tone, number and kind of figures used, under conditions when the examiner was present and the stories given orally, or when the examiner was absent and the stories written out by the subject. Charen (1954) raised questions about the usefulness of the MAPS backgrounds when he reported the results of a study that suggested that backgrounds were irrelevant in terms of sign productions. He administered two backgrounds with five different sets of characters associated with each background and asked for stories for each of the ten situations from 25 hospitalized normal patients. No sign differences were found between the two backgrounds.

The basic premise that the MAPS is more productive of projective material through construction of a fantasy world has as yet not been tested. This may be due, as Holt (1951) and Zubin, Eron and Schumer (1965) have pointed out, to the paradox that the advantage of stimulus flexibility found on the MAPS is disadvantageous for validating the test. Too many combinations of figures and backgrounds can occur, which makes the task of evaluating the validity of the MAPS one of overwhelming proportions. There is no firm evidence that the MAPS is superior to the TAT as a projective device in terms of eliciting more meaningful fantasy materials. However, it must be pointed out that the clinical and research possibilities of the MAPS are many, the most crucial being that of observing how the subject would populate this world if he could have it so (an advantage which does not occur with the TAT) and the utilization of FLS data for formal-objective interpretation.

THE BLACKY PICTURES TEST

The Blacky Pictures Test was developed by Gerald S. Blum in 1946 as a way of investigating and validating the psychoanalytic theory of psychosexual development. The test (Blum, 1949, 1950, 1960) consists of twelve cartoon drawings chronicling the events in the life of a small dog named Blacky. Blum suggests that the Blacky Pictures "represent an attempt to get at the deeper recesses of personality in a more appropriate setting, geared directly to dynamic interpretation. The pictures themselves are tailored to fit psychoanalytic theory. The psychological variables are specifically delimited, and the subject matter deals with psychosexual development, defense mechanisms, object relationships, and the like" (1950, p. 2). It is further suggested that the usefulness of the test lies in areas other than diagnosis, and that it should be an aid in psychotherapy in that it can help the therapist to a better understanding of the patient. Allowing the patient to respond to the Blacky during therapy will also help him to "work through" many problems. The test's range of applicability is from 5 years of age to adulthood.

The test consists of eleven cartoon drawings in which Blacky is the main character. Three other characters are introduced. They are Blacky's Mama and Papa, and Tippy (a sibling of unspecified sex and age). Each of the Cartoons was designed to depict a stage of psychosexual development. The psychosexual variable measured on each card and a description of that card is as follows:

Card I: *Oral Eroticism*. Blacky is nursing.

Card II: *Oral Sadism*. Blacky, standing alone, is chewing on Mama's dog collar.

Card III: *Anal Sadism*. Blacky covering something with earth.

Card IV: *Oedipal Intensity*. Blacky stands behind a bush watching Mama and Papa holding hands.

Card V: *Masturbation Guilt*. Blacky licking his (her) genitals.

Card VI: *Castration Anxiety for males or Penis Envy for females*. Blacky is watching a knife descending on Tippy's tail.

Card VII: *Positive Identification*. Blacky is "lecturing" a small wooden toy dog.

Card VIII: *Sibling Rivalry*. Blacky is watching Mama and Papa petting Tippy.

Card IX: *Guilt Feelings*. Blacky, in his thoughts, is being assailed by an accusing dog "angel."

Card X: *Positive Ego Ideal for males, and Love Object for females*. Blacky is dreaming of a large "handsome" male dog.

Card XI: *Positive Ego Ideal for females and Love Object for males*. Blacky is dreaming of a large "beautiful" female dog.

When the test is administered to males, Blacky is described as a male, and the introductions to the test, and the specific cards are treated accordingly. The reverse is done for female subjects. Each card is introduced briefly with such comments as "Here is Blacky with Mama" (Card I), "Here is Blacky with Mama's collar" (Card II), "Here Blacky is relieving himself (herself)" (Card III), etc.

The administration of the Blacky is divided in three parts: spontaneous stories, an inquiry, and elicitation of cartoon preferences. The spontaneous stories are elicited in the general test directions and it is not necessary, as it is with most other thematic projective techniques, to probe for antecedents (What led up to this?) or conclusions (How did it turn out?). The Inquiry consists of a series of questions which are asked after the spontaneous stories are given. They pertain to the psychoanalytic dimension measured by that card. (There are different sets of questions for males and females.) Multiple choice items are used mostly for adults.

Each of the multiple choice items has one neutral alternative and two or three alternative answers suggestive of maladjustment.

Card I. "Is Blacky: (a) happy, (b) unhappy, or (c) he doesn't feel one way or the other."

Card I. "Which of the following best describes Blacky? (a) She's a little glutton who never stops eating, (b) She's got a hearty appetite which usually gets satisfied, (c) She sometimes doesn't get enough to replace all the energy she burns up."

There are also opinion questions, for example, Card X. "In Blacky's mind, how does Mama stack up against the dream figure when she compares them?"

The subject is asked to indicate his alternatives on the multiple choice items by letter in case the verbalization of the answer may be too anxiety-provoking.

The Cartoon preference section of the administration consists of asking the subject to stack the cards into stacks of "liked" pictures and "disliked" pictures and to indicate the best liked and most disliked cartoons.

In addition to the administration, information about parents and siblings is elicited.

The spontaneous stories, inquiry, cartoon preference and comments about the cartoons are all used for interpretation. Blum states that all sources of information must be integrated before any inference is to be considered valid. The interpretation of Blacky materials from the four sources is done qualitatively and is dependent upon knowledge of psychoanalysis and projective technique interpretation.

Blum, however, does indicate some guidelines for using the spontaneous stories and Inquiry. Spontaneous story data may be used to rate the intensity of the psychosexual variable being evaluated in terms of "strong" or "not strong." Examples of "strong" and "not strong" stories are given for each card. Unfortunately, these examples are extremely vague and are not very helpful in scoring the stories. The selection of maladjusted alternatives to Inquiry questions are indicative of problems in the psychosexual area. But, unfortunately, Blum also implies that, "selection of neutral alternatives by a patient can mean either true absence of disturbance or attempted denial of existing disturbance" (1950, p. 8). This kind of hypothesis makes the use of inquiry responses difficult to interpret. The same problem arises with cartoon preferences; "The selection of a cartoon as "dislike most" can always be interpreted to indicate strong disturbance in that area. Similarly, the choice of a cartoon as "like best" is also taken to mean disturbance." (Blum, 1950, p. 9). If any related comments are made about cartoons, their presence is also indicative of disturbance in that area of psychosexual development.

Blum (1956) has also developed a Defense Preference Inquiry which is based on the Blacky Test responses and can be used to measure the amounts of avoidance, reaction formation, projection, regression and intellectualization used by subjects.

The vagueness of the scoring system has been criticized by Beck (1959), Lindzey (1961) and Zubin, Eron and Schumer (1965). As a response to such criticisms, Blum (1962) has made an attempt to overhaul the scoring and interpretative hypotheses for the Blacky Pictures. The Blacky Protocols of 210 college males were factor analyzed, card by card, and factors extracted. Blum suggests that each of the variables loading on each factor be given a score of one, so that factor scores may be calculated. Cross-validation of this new scoring system is much needed.

Some questions have been raised about the test as a validation technique of the psychoanalytic theory of psychosexual development. Newton (1959) and Beck (1959) have pointed out that the test is so worded that the subject has to respond in such a way as to fit the psychosexual theory. The scoring system is also such that it does not allow for any response to be scored so as not to confirm the theory (e.g., a neutral alternative on the Inquiry may be interpreted as denial of psychosexual problems). That Blacky data can always be interpreted to fit psychoanalytic theory, and that the use of an unvalidated test to evaluate an unvalidated theory is a dubious procedure has been pointed out by Seward (1950), along with a critique of the Blacky Test development methodology.

Blum and Hunt (1952) have presented an impressive array of validating studies in which construct validity is stressed. Blum and Miller (1952) have pointed out that the construct validation technique uses independent criteria. They illustrated this with data showing that oral eroticism on the Blacky was related to ice cream consumption, leadership ability, boredom and preocupation with gifts (all variables hypothesized to be related to oral dynamics). Rabin (1958) did report that boys raised in a Kibbutz (a communal society) gave fewer Oedipal involvement and sibling rivalry responses than non-Kibbutz (from communities with patriarchal features) raised boys. Pedersen and Marlowe (1960) utilized the Blacky to identify anal retentive and anal expulsive Ohio State University students. They reported that the expulsive subjects could recall more disturbing material than the retentives. On the other hand the retentive subjects remembered more insignificant material than the other subjects. Neuman and Salvatore (1958) factor analyzed the Blacky protocols of males and females. They reported the emergence of factors equivalent to oral, phallic, Oedipal, latency and genital psychosexual areas for the male subjects, but not for the females. Related to this study is one done by Rossi and Solomon (1961) in which they reported that "Blacky" and "Dog" were overwhelmingly rated as masculine on the Semantic Differential by males and females. They suggest that the Blacky Pictures may be more appropriate for males than females. Bernstein and Chase (1955) reviewed the Blacky protocols of ulcer psychosomatic, non-ulcer-psychosomatic and non-ulcer, non-psychosomatic patients and found few significant differences among the scores. These results, they felt, raised questions about the Blacky's validity since oral involvement is an important aspect of the psychoanalytic theory of etiology of psychosomatic ulcers. Margolis (1961) using the Blacky test could find no significant personality differences between the mothers of children with asthma, rheumatic fever and minor cuts and bruises. Carp (1962) did not report finding any more anal retentiveness among stutterers when compared with non-stutterers on their Blacky protocols.

There has been a lively controversy over the reliability of the Blacky scoring system. Granick and Scheflin (1958) working with children between the ages of 6 and 11 reported excellent reliability estimates for the Blacky in terms of judges' ratings of strong and not-strong disturbances in stories, judges' matching of subject's protocols given on a test-retest basis, and, finally, a Rho of .92 between the number of words given to the stories of the odd and even numbered cards. Charen (1956), on the other hand, reported low test-retest reliability for the Blacky pictures given to tubercular patients at the onset of their illness and four months later. Even though information from other tests, such as the Rorschach and various paper and pencil tests, reflected personality changes, the Blacky tended not to reflect such change. Whether Charen's study is more a commentary on the validity of the Blacky pictures or on the stable aspects of personality being measured by the test is not known. But it is doubtful whether Charen's data can be used to criticize Blacky Test reliability. Berger and Everstine (1962) have reported adequate test-retest reliability coefficients for the psychosexual variable scores for fifty male college students, given two administrations of the test four weeks apart. The problem of the test's reliability is still not settled since different techniques have been utilized to measure reliability (judges' estimates, psychosexual variable scores, word counts, etc.) in different ways (test-retest, split-half, inter-judge, etc.). All these methods are not equivalent and do not have identical measurement implications.

The question of validity is also still unsettled. The problem becomes "validity for what?" The test was standardized on college students and norms for other groups have not been systematically gathered. The validity of the test as a "proof" of the psychoanalytic theory of psychosexual development is doubtful. But the validity of the inferences that can be drawn from the test about subjects has the promise of making the Blacky test very useful.

THE OBJECT RELATIONS TEST (ORT)

The Object Relations Test (ORT) was developed by Herbert Phillipson (1955) while at the Tavistock Clinic in England. The ORT was worked on for five years before its publication and represents a close tie between the test materials and certain aspects of psychoanalytic theory.

Phillipson's underlying rationale for the test stems from the object relations theories of Melanie Klein (1948) and W. R. D. Fairbairn (1952) which hold that object relations exist within the personality as well as between the personality and the objects in the external world, and that the inner world of object relations determines the individual's relations with people in the external world. Phillipson states that ". . . in any sequence of behavior in a given stimulus situation . . . an individual will select from the perceptual field, and structure what he selects, to fit with unconscious object relationships which in early life were fantasied in order to satisfy a primitive need. At the same time, he will characterize what he sees in terms of object relationships which have been built up in order to guard against the consequences he fears might result from his unconscious wishes" (1955, p. 13). Basically, the ORT was designed to elicit information about the kinds of object relations sought, the feared consequences of desiring the object relations, and finally the defensive operations used by an individual to avoid the feared consequences.

Phillipson's stated range of interest is confined to the study of object relationships. However, Westby (1959) feels that the ORT is suitable for social research and personnel selection.

The ORT consists of three series (A, B and C) of 4 cards each, on which is to be found either one person, two people, three people or a larger group of individuals. In addition, a blank card is used. The drawings of the people are constructed so as to be ambiguous as to age and sex. The details of the figures are omitted, or indefinite. The A series cards are characterized by light charcoal shading textures. The interpretative rationale for this subset of cards is very much like the usual Rorschach interpretation of surface texture. The A series is expected to elicit responses concerned with early dependency relations, need for affection and security. The B series cards are characterized by heavier shading which gives the feeling of darkness and depth. This characterization is very much like that of achromatic color on the Rorschach and is supposed to highlight fantasy relationships with threatening or uncompromising objects. The C series cards are drawn with clear lines, and details are easily seen. Chromatic color is added to these cards and the stimulus material is supposed to encourage subjects to emit stories emphasizing emotional challenge and involvement. The blank card is like the TAT blank card. A description and rationale for each card may be found in Phillipson (1955, pp. 28-32).

The instructions for administration are as follows:

> I'm going to show you a number of pictures on cards like this. I want you to look at each one and imagine what it might represent. Try to imagine it is some kind of situation and then bring it

to life in your mind so that you can imagine what might be going on in the situation, what the people might be concerned with, what they are doing and what might happen next. We'll do one as an example first of all, then you can do the others yourself. As you look at the picture, make up a brief story about it and try to build it up in this way: Say first of all how you imagine the situation you have in mind came about (do that quite briefly), then tell what you imagine is going on in the situation as fully as you can, and finally (quite briefly) say how you imagine it would turn out or what might happen next. (1955, p. 33).

The examiner may prompt for the temporal material, and if a story is negligible in productivity, may ask the subject to give another story to the same card. Inquiry may be made concerning unusual characterizations and perceptions, lack of story endings, etc., after the administration.

No specific interpretative scheme is given. Phillipson does lean towards a hypothesis-building procedure in which hunches are generated on the first three cards and confirmed or disconfirmed on the basis of the remaining stories. He does suggest a method of organizing the data in terms of 1) the kind of characterizations made; 2) the kind of object relations sought; 3) the consequences attending the seeking of such object relations; 4) the efforts to avoid the consequences; and 5) the story outcomes. No method for organizing the data around the stimulus characteristics (shading, achromatic and chromatic color) or number of persons portrayed in the card is given.

Phillipson reports some extensive normative data from an outpatient clinic sample of 50 patients and for 40 normal adolescent girls in terms of number of characterizations, type of relationship, physical setting, sex of character, etc., for each card (1955, pp. 151-213). In addition Orme (1959) has published typical schizophrenic responses to the ORT.

Validation and reliability studies are rare. Haskell (1961) administered the Rorschach, ORT and eight TAT cards to thirty-eight schizophrenics and found that the ORT was better correlated to therapists' and ward nurses' evaluations of covert and overt hostility than the other tests.

The test has been praised for being derived from a theoretical base, but has been criticized for not detailing the relationship between the cards and the theory, the failure to relate stimulus characteristics of the cards to interpretative hypotheses, and the lack of validity and reliability information (McMahon, 1957; Meyer, 1958). In addition, Kutash (1957) very strongly doubts whether the test can be used for personnel selection in its present form. While the question has been raised by Meyer (1958) as to whether the test has any special features to justify its existence, it could be argued that the stimulus material is so designed as to force the subject into making up stories about people since it curtails avoidance of interpersonal fantasy production.

The Four Picture Test (FPT)

The Four Picture Test (FPT) antedates the introduction of the TAT. D. J. Van Lennep of Holland introduced the test in 1930. Van Lennep (1948, 1951) reports that his test was based on the experimentation with picture materials done by G. A. Roemer. The FPT differs from other thematic tests in that the subject is asked to make one story from four cards which are presented simultaneously.

Van Lennep states that the object of the test is "to discover a subject's general attitude towards life . . . as far as this was determined by his personality structure, by the dynamics of his personality, and above all, as far as these were set in motion in social situations" (1951, p. 158).

The stimulus material consists of four colored but vague drawings of human beings. They are described as follows:

Picture 1: *Being together with another person.* Two people are seen in a room.

Picture 2: *Being personally alone.* A bed in a bedroom is seen and the drawing faintly suggests a figure in the bed.

Picture 3: *Being socially alone.* A man is seen standing alone under a lamppost on an empty street with the rain beating down.

Picture 4: *Being together with many others.* A group of people are seen watching a tennis mach.

The test is administered by placing the four pictures close together in front of the subject. Pictures I and II are on top, with III and IV immediately below. The subject is told that "here you see four totally unrelated pictures. Try to build up a story that combines these four pictures and bring them into relation with one another. You can choose the order in which they are to appear, starting and finishing where you like. You can start here, or here (pointing to the pictures in an arbitrary way)" (1951, p. 161). Subjects may be asked to make up many stories in one sitting or come back at stated intervals for readministration of the FPT.

The FPT data can be interpreted by both a content and formal analysis. Content analysis, Van Lennep states, "depends on experience, knowledge of the psychology of personality and psychopathology . . . and great experience with the FPT itself" (1951, p. 171). Formal analysis has to do with such things as card sequence. Van Lennep reports that the IV-I-III-II sequence is found mostly in normal individuals. The initial use of picture III is reported by Van Lennep as a sign of neurotic disturbance. Formal analysis covers such categories as sequence of social relations, atmosphere, mood, kind of conflict, verbal structure and connection between pictures. A summary form is available (1951, pp. 172-173).

Little is known about the validity status and reliability status of the FPT. This may be due to its low level of popularity in this country.

Many psychologists are only acquainted with the FPT through Van Lennep's article in Anderson and Anderson's *Introduction to Projective Techniques* (1951). This lack of acquaintance and usage has probably lead to a paucity of research on the test. Van Lennep and Houwink (1953) used the FPT to test the hypothesis that emotional adjustment can be measured by flexibility in role taking. They utilized male subjects who had come for industrial vocational guidance tests and told them to make the principal figure a female and to then tell a story. It is reported that well-adjusted males can do this easily, while the poorly adjusted males had difficulty in using a female as a central figure. They either accorded her a secondary role or omitted her completely. However, this is a study of social role behavior, in well- and non-well-adjusted males, using the FPT as a vehicle, and not a study of the validity of the test *per se*.

The Picture Arrangement Test (PAT)

The Picture Arrangement Test (PAT) represents a departure from the usual ways of conceptualizing and utilizing projective techniques. That the test can actually be considered a projective technique is open to question. The test does not meet the criteria described previously in defining a thematic technique. However, because of the underlying theoretical basis and conceptualization of the test, it is of interest because it suggests a future direction for the development of projective testing.

The PAT is a curious mixture of a projective-like test and a psychometric method. It can be group administered and machine scored and was partly designed to ease the burden of administration and interpretation for projective psychologists. The PAT was developed in 1942 at the Harvard Psychological Clinic by Silvan S. Tomkins and David Horn. The idea of using the arrangement of pictures as clues to personality functioning is not new. Van Lennep (1948) and Mayman, Schafer and Rapaport (1951) have utilized the technique. The test is described and various norms detailed in Tomkins (1952), Tomkins and Miner (1955, 1957, 1959).

Tomkins and Miner feel that the typical projective technique is extremely wasteful of the clinician's time because a large bulk of the information gathered does not allow for specific inferences (e.g., the popular bat response on Card I of the Rorscharch or a boy dreaming of being a great violinist theme on Card I of the TAT are very common responses). Many kinds of individuals with many kinds of personalities may give those responses (more as a function of the stimulus pull than that of personality dynamics). It is the rare and exotic percept or story that catches the eye of the clinician and starts him on his train of interpretation. It is these rare responses that have specific inferential power. Common responses are produced by a great number of different individuals and therefore lack any information that can differentiate one from another. Tomkins and Miner developed the PAT in a manner that deals with only rare responses (i.e., that appear about five percent of the time in a normal population). They argue that it is the rare and improbable response that is useful for valid isomorphic inference determination, which is needed for an objective machine-scored projective test. In addition each rare response must be obviously interpretable or else it is not useful to the clinician. The construction and standardization of the PAT represented a search for rare and psychologically meaningful responses.

The test consists of 25 cards or plates with three line drawings on which a person is depicted in different but related activities. It is the same person on all of the 25 plates. The subject is asked to specify a reasonable sequence of the drawings on each of the plates. He is also asked to write a sentence briefly explaining the situation. The plate is arranged so that the pictures are at 120 degree angles from each other. This was done so that there would be no order of presentation bias. The plate can be rotated by the subject. The instructions for the test are rather simple and can be understood by almost everybody. However, the very young, old, dull or under-educated may need help in understanding the instructions.

The drawings are concerned with such things as work, illness, social situations, heterosexuality, public embarrassment, etc. The choice of the plates was made on the basis of hunches that these areas were important ones to most people. The test was standardized on 1500 normal individuals of ten years and over. The sample was gathered by Public Opinion Surveys, Inc. of Princeton, New Jersey and represented a stratified sample, according to the U.S. Census. A modified version of the C.A.V.D. was also administered in order to gather intellectual level data for the sample. Data were also gathered from 755 abnormal individuals in 84 hospitals and clinics across the nation.

On the basis of these data, the authors developed 252 keys, or patterns for scoring. Most of these have to do with rare responses, but some represent validity, age, IQ and education levels. The content keys reflect the rare and interpretable patterns found among five percent of the population (e.g., Key 97 reflects Sociophilia and is constructed from certain patterns among several of the plates.)

The test is scored by searching among the responses for ones that meet the criterion for the key. A subject's responses are transferred to a profile sheet (Tomkins & Miner, 1959, pp. 12-16) and the keys are applied to his responses on the profile sheet. If his responses meet the criterion for any of the keys this is noted. Only those rare keys on which the subject has met the criterion are utilized for interpretation. The other keys are discarded. If a subject does not make any rare responses, then the whole test is discarded.

Interpretation of the PAT depends on rare responses, the contents of the rare responses, and the relationships between rare responses. If, for example, the criteria for the Sociophilia key have been met, then one is alerted to the possibility that the subject has problems in the area of being with people versus being alone. It indicates that this theme has occurred on several different plates. It may also be related to other rare occurrence patterns, or keys. According to Tomkins and Miner, "it is in the interpretation of the profile of scores . . . that the psychologist's training and experience become critical" (p. 32). Also at the time of interpretation, the verbal material (one sentence explanations) may be inspected for whatever clues they yield. Comparison between the rare patterns of the normals and abnormals is also useful, since a rare pattern in normals may be a common pattern among abnormal subjects. The interpretation of the PAT rests, ultimately, on the clinician's skill and not on machine formulas of the kind developed for the MMPI by Marks and Seeman (1963). The method of interpretation and illustrative examples are provided by Tomkins and Miner (1959), which are of great help to the student.

Published research with the PAT is rare. Miner (1960) has reported the PAT has successfully been used to select tabulating machine operators.

The PAT is best described in its authors' terms—as an experiment. The test does have one of the best normative and standardization bases of all instruments described in this chapter. However, the underlying rationale that only rare responses are useful is open to question. Popular and common responses may well reflect that a subject shares common personality traits with others, formulates problems the same way that others do, etc., and could well be useful in predicting behavior in many areas of human functioning. Since our knowledge of the interpretative significance of projective techniques is so inadequate, one cannot make the assumption that this kind of inference can be ignored or taken for granted.

Hand scoring of the test is laborious, and it is best used when machine scoring is available. Its greatest drawback is the limited amount of inferences that can be made because of the limited amount of information admitted for interpretation by the test. In many ways the PAT reminds one of an elephant laboring to pick up a pea. However, the prototypical method of construction of the PAT may well be a sign of the times as far as the future of thematic apperception techniques is concerned, i.e., if the validity status of projective tests is not improved.

OTHER THEMATIC APPERCEPTIVE METHODS

The overwhelming bulk of projective techniques rely on the visual sense modality. A subject is usually exposed to some sort of stimulus material, and after viewing it, is expected to make some sort of response. Because of the heavy utilization of visual perception, most thematic apperceptive techniques are not very useful with sightless or near-sightless individuals. There have been attempts to construct thematic methods which utilize the auditory sense modality. The Auditory Apperception Test is one such test and is discussed below.

Just as most apperceptive techniques rely on the visual sense mechanism as the route for stimulus input, they mostly demand some form of verbal response from the subject. The verbal response is usually either motoric (writing out the story) or vocal (telling the story) behavior. The opportunity to observe 1) a person's bodily attitudes and actions, and 2) his manipulation of objects while telling a story has been given to psychological examiners by Doris Twitchell-Allen's Three Dimensional Apperception test which is also described below.

The Auditory Apperception Test (AAT)

The utilization of the auditory mechanisms in the field of projective evaluation has received less attention and interest than the visual. However, there has been some work done with auditory projective tests. Shakow and Rosenzweig (1940) made use of an apparatus developed by Skinner (1936), which emitted a man's voice making garbled sounds. Subjects were asked to figure out what had been said. Attempts at auditory projective tests were made by Ball and Bernardoni (1953), Davids and Murray (1955) and Wilmer and Husni (1953). Bean and Moore (1964) are constructing, at present, an auditory personality evaluation measure, and information received from the American Foundation for the Blind indicates that they too are developing an auditory projective test for blind individuals (Graham, 1964).

The only auditory projective test that is commercially available is one that utilizes a story telling technique which is given by a subject after he listens to a set of sounds. In the early 1950's David R. Stone developed his Auditory Apperception Test (AAT). The AAT (Stone, 1950, 1953) consists of five 45 r.p.m. records which contain ten sets of three sounds and dialogues. Stone feels that the underlying rationale for the test is similar to that for the TAT. He, however, feels that the AAT may provide richer data than the TAT because, besides using the auditory sensory channels, the imagery aroused by the sounds also makes it a "visual" test, and thus gives rise to rich fantasy productions that are stimulated by two senses instead of one.

Unfortunately, Stone reports no validity or reliability data for his test. Stone goes so far as to deny the usefulness of these for projective testing. He also feels that "norms for the projective field are only of limited value and that the most important element in interpretation is resident in the categories of analysis" (1953, p. 4).

The test is applicable to high school and college students as well as adults and supposedly may be used for diagnostic purposes and for "understanding individual needs and tensions" (1953, p. 6).

The test should be administered in a quiet place since the hearing of the material is quite important. Although, unlike the verbal summator, the sounds are clear and loud enough to be heard distinctly, there is a need for the arrangement of optimal conditions for audition. The subject is asked to listen to three sounds and then use them in a story. The story is to have a beginning, an end and a middle, in which the subject is to describe what is going on now.

Seven of the sets are composed of three sounds.
Example: Set 1
1. a bell ringing
2. a severe wind
3. a horse trotting

Three of the sets have some snatches of conversation.
Example: Set 3
1. Slow music
2. She: "Don't ask me."
   He: "Why shouldn't we?"
   She: "It's not right."
   He: "Just this once."
3. Fast music.

The test may be timed (5 minutes for each set), if the examiner wishes. Stone suggests utilizing time limits because it forces the organization of fantasy productions. However, the choice is up to the examiner. The AAT may be administered to groups and also individually. It is suggested that group testing be done in two sessions with sets 1, 2, 3, 4 and 7 administered first and sets 5, 6, 8, 9 and 10 administered the second time.

No interpretative rules are given beyond Stone's feeling that the AAT may be interpreted in the same way as the TAT. Some norms are presented. There is a tabulation of length of stories, types of characters, description of sounds, types of situations and outcomes of the stories given by 220 college students to each set (1953, pp. 14-23).

It is very difficult to evaluate the AAT since no validity and reliability data are available. The norms (mentioned above) are so few as to be useless. There are no sample interpretations, nor any interpretive suggestions; neither are there any indications that the test is superior (either for sighted or blind individuals) in any way to other tests. However, Bean (1965) in pre-tests with his auditory personality technique has reported that auditory materials do give rise to themes not elicited by visual tests.

There is one critical problem with the test. Two reviewers (Bean, 1959; Swensen, 1959) and the present author who listened to the AAT recordings found many of the sounds poor in auditory quality. The poor quality of the recordings may lead to gross, but justifiable, misperceptions. It is unfortunate that Stone did not pre-test his sounds for clarity. The AAT also has mostly sounds with few human voice materials. Kramer (1962) has found that human auditory content evokes more responsiveness than nonhuman content.

All in all the test does not seem to have anything to recommend it beyond the fact that it is an auditory test.

The Three-Dimensional Apperception Test (3-DAT)

The Three-Dimensional Apperception Test (3-DAT) was developed by Doris Twitchell-Allen (1947, 1948) to fill a need for some inclusion of "gesture" behavior in personality diagnostic testing. She felt that by allowing a subject to handle objects, the probability of the use of bodily movements rises, and the psychologist may then have the opportunity to observe and, later, interpret these gestures. She further felt that the use of three-dimensional forms added another dimension to projective techniques which enriches verbal protocols. In addition, it was also pointed out that a test utilizing gestures may be very useful for persons that are mute or verbally inhibited.

The 3-DAT is composed of 28 baked clay forms. Ten of these are described as geometric forms; three are generalized organic forms; and four represent concrete human and animal forms. The nature of the remaining forms is not described. Caution must be exercised in accepting Twitchell-Allen's description since some of the forms are so shapeless that it is difficult to identify them as representing the designated object.

The subject stands in front of a table on which the pieces are laid out in a prescribed order. He is then asked to choose some of the forms and make up a story about them. He is also instructed to act out the story as it is told. The reaction times, verbalizations and types of gestures made are recorded. The subject is then asked to name the 28 pieces. The examiner may, if he wishes, solicit more stories. The instructions in the manual (Twitchell-Allen, 1948) imply that two stories should be elicited, but the record blank has space for recording eight stories.

No interpretive hypotheses for stories, figure selection or gestures are given. Gesture interpretation, which comprised Twitchell-Allen's basic rationale for the existence of the 3-DAT, receives no comment beyond the note that "gesture is the additional dimension of response which often is decisive in the interpretation of the test data" (1948, p. 15). Neither does she provide normative or reliability and validity data. The validity of the 3-DAT is self-apparent, Twitchell-Allen implies, from the observation of the test behavior. She also feels that the test is a valid projective technique because of the great variety of different names given to the same forms by different subjects. However, such data are not substantiation of validity, but only that the pieces are ambiguously shaped.

Some reliability data for the 3-DAT are reported by Fein (1960). Using a somewhat dubious test-retest method wherein the time interval varied between 15 to 30 minutes, she compared the first and second stories given by normal adults and children. The measures from the two stories that were compared were 1) total time for each story and 2) several indices of story production (number of nouns, verbs, adjectives, etc). She reported coefficients ranging from .30 to .56 which were exceptionally low reliability correlations. Unfortunately, Fein drew a fallacious and presumptuous conclusion from this material when she said that this data "provides statistical evidence of the consistency of the 3-DAT in measuring whatever it purports to measure" (1960, p. 111).

The lack of interpretive hypotheses surrounding the test, the lack of normative materials, the lack of validation and adequate reliability data are unfortunate since the idea behind the 3-DAT is a good one, i.e., information about gesture and body involvement may be useful to the psychologist. Although the idea is not new (it is the basis of all play therapy techniques) it can be of great use, but it is impossible to evaluate the efficacy of the 3-DAT as assessing gesture and body movement in terms of their psychological importance at this time.

Discussion

It is somewhat difficult to draw general conclusions from the existing varieties of thematic methods because of their large numbers, and because they are all somewhat different in aim and scope. The bulk of the methods were developed for specific research problems and were not meant for general usage. They, therefore, need not concern us here. Because the techniques which were reviewed in this chapter are available to psychologists through commercial outlets and are, therefore, in general use, they comprise the locus of the following comments.

Even though each method purports to be somewhat unique, the reader may have been struck with the feeling that there is a great deal of duplication among these tests. Aside from the AAT and 3-DAT (which need more development and improvement) only the MAPS Test uses a format that is different from the TAT. In Shneidman's test the subject has the opportunity to choose how he will construct his own fantasy world through the selection and usage of different figures. The other methods follow the TAT procedure of story telling associated to a set of standard stimuli.[2] It should be noted that the utilization of standard stimuli is superior to the Shneidman procedure in that it more readily allows for the gathering of comparative normative data.

[2] The FPT varies from the other tests only in that the subject needs to tell a story that simultaneously includes all four cards. The PAT also varies from the other tests in that the story telling response is superfluous and all interpretations are based on the arrangements of the stimulus materials made by the subjects.

The rationales for the need for the existence of the various thematic methods needs to be evaluated. The authors of the techniques contend that their tests are unique, either because the stimulus materials are specifically appropriate for certain kinds of subjects (e.g., CAT for children, PST and MPT for adolescents) , or because they are assessing special aspects of personality (e.g., Blacky Pictures for psychosexual development, ORT for interpersonal relationships, FPT for personality-social force interactions) which are not adequately dealt with by other methods. There does not seem to be any substantial evidence to support these contentions. The negative research findings concerning the superiority of animal figures over human stimuli for ease of identification by children has not upheld Bellak's rationale for the construction of the CAT. Symonds drew a conclusion from his standardization study of the PST concerning the identification capacities of adolescents which is extremely pertinent. Although what is to be quoted here has been quoted before, it is worth repeating. He stated that "most adolescents find it possible to identify themselves with babies, with old men and women, with members of the opposite sex, with animals and even inanimate objects" (1949, p. 53) . The contention that special kinds of thematic stimulus materials or tests are necessary for certain groups may well be unfounded.

The proposed superiority of those thematic methods that were developed to evaluate particular aspects of personality also needs to be examined. An adequate evaluation would necessitate comparative validation research which unfortunately does not exist in any appreciable quantity. The MPT, MAPS and Blacky Pictures are well-researched instruments in terms of validity and reliability as well as the gathering of normative data. However, it is possible that other tests (or even a more judicious use of the TAT) could accomplish the same task of specialized evaluations in particular personality areas as well as the methods described in this chapter. The impression lingers that some of these techniques were developed in haste and that the test constructors did not first fully explore the potentialities for special personality evaluations inherent in existing thematic techniques. The array of available thematic methods has outstripped the amount of existing responsible research. The number of available methods is sometimes disconcerting, and when accompanied by meager reliability and validity information, creates a poor impression of the status of projective techniques.

The construction of good thematic methods is arduous. Whatever the rationale for the development of the test may be, the author must pay careful empirical attention to the selection of stimulus materials, develop reliable scoring procedures and provide valid interpretive hypotheses for the measures. He accomplishes this by careful selection of a representative standardizing sample, by conducting validating research of every type, by gathering extensive normative data from various populations, and finally, by constant re-evaluation and replication of the entire test construction procedure. This ideal program has not been followed by the developers of the various thematic methods discussed here.

The lure of thematic techniques is very great. They provide information about a person that has an immediacy unparalleled by any other personality evaluation technique. But their efficacy does depend a great deal on the experience and clinical skills of the examiner. The empirical evaluation procedure represented by the PAT may provide the next direction for the development of projective testing. Such a nomothetic approach has great attractions: examiner influence is curtailed (it can never be eliminated), the psychologist is freed from the testing "chore," and the data that are gathered, while being less globally descriptive, are more precise. Whether these attractions outweigh what can be gained by responsible research with existing thematic techniques depends on the integrity, creativity and industry of projective psychologists.

SUMMARY

After the publication of the TAT, the interest in thematic methods produced a large number of new techniques. Many of the new tests were constructed because of discontent with the potentialities of the TAT stimulus cards. It was felt that the TAT pictures were not suitable for certain subgroups, and that they were either too broad or too confining for evaluation of particular psychological variables. A bewildering number of thematic methods were developed because of these alleged defects. The greater part of them were constructed for specific problems; however, some methods have been published and have come into public usage. This chapter focused on those thematic methods.

From the overview of these thematic methods, is was concluded that 1) there is a great deal of duplication among the tests; 2) that the rationales for the need for the existence of many of these techniques is not empirically supported; and 3) that the sound canons of test construction were not followed in the majority of thematic methods reviewed in this chapter.

REFERENCES

Alexander, T. The Adult-Child Interaction Test. *Monogr. Soc. Res. Child Develpm.*, 1952, *17*, No. 2. (Serial No. 55).

Alexander, T., & Anderson, R. Children in a society under stress. *Behav. Sci.*, 1957, *2*, 46-55.

Amen, E. W. Individual differences in apperceptive reaction: a study of the response of preschool children to pictures. *Genet. Psychol. Monogr.*, 1941, *23*, 319-385.

Anderson, H. H., & Anderson, Gladys L. *An Introduction to Projective Techniques.* Englewood Cliffs, N.J.: Prentice-Hall, 1951.

Andrew, Gwen, Walton, R. E., Hartwell, S. W., & Hutt, M. L. The Michigan Pictures Test: The stimulus value of the cards. *J. consult. Psychol.*, 1951, *15*, 51-54.

Andrew, Gwen, Hartwell, S. W., Hutt, M. L., & Walton, R. E. *The Michigan Pictures Test*. Chicago: Science Research Associates, 1953.

Atkinson, J. W., Heyns, R. W., & Veroff, J. The effect of experimental arousal of the affiliation motive on thematic apperception. *J. abnorm. soc. Psychol.*, 1954, *54*, 1-8.

Ball, T. B., & Bernardoni, L. C. The application of an auditory apperception test to clinical diagnosis. *J. clin. Psychol.*, 1953, *9*, 54-58.

Bean, K. L. The Auditory Apperception Test. In Buros, O. K. (Ed.). *The Fifth Mental Measurements Yearbook*. Highland Park, N.J.: Gryphon Press, 1959. P. 213.

Bean, K. L. Scoring and interpreting responses to semi-structured sound effects. *J. proj. Tech.*, 1965, *29*, 151-160.

Bean, K. L., & Moore, J. R. Music therapy from auditory ink blots. *J. mus. Ther.*, 1964, *1*, 143-147.

Beck, S. J. The Blacky Pictures. In Buros, O. K. (Ed.). *The Fifth Mental Measurements Yearbook*. Highland Park, N.J.: Gryphon Press, 1959. P. 216.

Bellak, L. *The Thematic Apperception Test and the Children's Apperception Test in Clinical Use*. New York: Grune and Stratton, 1954.

Bellak, L. *The Children's Apperception Test*. New York: C.P.S. Co., 1949.

Bellak, L., & Adelman, Crusa. The Children's Apperception Test. In Rabin, A. I. & Haworth, Mary R. (Eds.). *Projective Techniques with Children*. New York: Grune and Stratton, 1960. Pp. 62-94.

Bellak, L., & Bellak, Sonya S. *Manual of Instruction for the Children's Apperception Test*. New York: C.P.S. Co., 1949.

Berger, L., & Everstine, L. Test-retest reliability of the Blacky Pictures Test. *J. proj. Tech.*, 1962, *26*, 225-226.

Bernstein, L., & Chase, P. H. The discriminative ability of the Blacky Pictures with ulcer patients. *J. consult. Psychol.*, 1955, *19*, 377-380.

Biber, Barbara, & Lewis, C. An experimental study of what young children expect from their teachers. *Genet. Psychol. Monogr.*, 1949, *40*, 3-97.

Bills, R. E. Animal pictures for obtaining children's projections. *J. clin. Psychol.*, 1950, *6*, 291-293.

Bindon, D. Marjorie. Make-A-Picture Story Test findings for rubella deaf children. *J. abnorm. soc. Psychol.*, 1957, *55*, 38-42.

Blum, G. S. A study of the psychoanalytic theory of psychosexual development. *Genet. Psychol. Monogr.*, 1949, *39*, 3-99.

Blum, G. S. *The Blacky Pictures: Manual of Instructions*. New York: Psychological Corp., 1950.

Blum, G. S. Defense preferences in four countries. *J. proj. Tech.*, 1956, *20*, 33-41.

Blum, G. S. The Blacky Pictures with children. In Rabin, A. I., & Haworth, Mary R. (Eds.). *Projective Techniques with Children*. New York: Grune and Stratton, 1960. Pp. 95-104.

Blum, G. S. A guide for research use of the Blacky Pictures. *J. proj. Tech.*, 1962, *26*, 3-29.

Blum, G. S., & Hunt, H. F. The validity of the Blacky Pictures. *Psychol. Bull.*, 1952, *49*, 238-250.

Blum, G. S., & Miller, D. R. Exploring the psychoanalytic theory of oral character. *J. Pers.*, 1952, *20*, 287-304.

Briggs, D. L. A modification of the Thematic Apperception Test for Naval enlisted personnel. *J. Psychol.*, 1954, *37*, 233-241.

Brittain, H. W. A study of imagination. *Pedogog. Sem.*, 1907, *14*, 137-207.

Byrd, E., & Witherspoon, R. L. Responses of preschool children to the Children's Apperception Test. *Child Develpm.*, 1954, *25*, 35-44.

Carp, F. M. Psychosexual development of stutterers. *J. proj. Tech.*, 1962, *26*, 388-391.

Cass, W. A. Jr., & McReynolds, P. A contribution to Rorschach norms. *J. consult. Psychol.*, 1951, *15*, 178-184.

Charen, S. The interaction of background and characters in picture test story telling. *J. clin. Psychol.*, 1954, *10*, 290-292.

Charen, S. Reliability of the Blacky Test. *J. consult. Psychol.*, 1956, *20*, 16.

Chowdhury, U. An Indian modification of the Thematic Apperception Test. *J. soc. Psychol.*, 1960, *51*, 245-263.

Cummings, J. D. Family Pictures: a projection test for children. *Brit. J. Psychol.*, 1952, *43*, 53-60.

Davids, A., & Murray, H. A. Preliminary appraisal of an auditory projective technique for studying personality and cognition. *Am. J. Orthopsychiat.*, 1955, *25*, 543-554.

Edgar, Clara L., & Shneidman, E. S. Some relationships among thematic projective tests of various degrees of structuredness and behavior in a group situation. *J. proj. Tech.*, 1958, *22*, 3-12.

Fairbairn, W. R. D. *Psycho-analytic Studies of Personality*. London: Tavistock Publications, 1952.

Fantel, E., & Shneidman, E. S. Psychodrama and the MAPS test. *Rorschach Res. Exch. & J. proj. Tech.*, 1947, *11*, 42-67.

Fein, Leah G. *The Three-Dimensional Personality Test*. New York: International Universities Press, 1960.

Fenz, W. D., & Epstein, S. Measurement of approach-avoidance conflict by a stimulus dimension in a test of thematic apperception. *J. Pers.*, 1962, *30*, 613-632.

Finch, H. M. Young children's concepts of parent roles. *J. Home Econ.*, 1955, *47*, 99-103.

Fine, R. A scoring scheme for the TAT and other verbal projective techniques. *J. proj. Tech.*, 1955, *19*, 306-309.

Goldenberg, H. C. A resume of some Make-A-Picture Story (MAPS) test results. *J. proj. Tech.*, 1951, *15*, 79-86.

Goldstein, A. P. The fakability of the Kuder Preference Record and the Vocational Apperception Test. *J. proj. Tech.*, 1960, *24*, 133-136.

Graham, M. D. *The Braverman-Chevigny Auditory Projection Test. A Provisional Manual.* New York: American Foundation for the Blind, 1964.

Granick, S., & Scheflen, Norma A. Approaches to reliability of projective tests with special reference to the Blacky Pictures Test. *J. consult. Psychol.*, 1958, *22*, 137-141.

Greenbaum, M., Qualtere, T., Carruth, B., & Cruickshank, W. Evaluation of a modification of the Thematic Apperception Test for use with physically handicapped children. *J. clin. Psychol.*, 1953, *9*, 40-44.

Gurevitz, S., & Klapper, Zelda S. Technique for and evaluation of responses of schizophrenic and cerebral palsied children to the Children's Apperception Test (CAT). *Quart. J. Child Behav.*, 1951, *3*, 38-65.

Hartwell, S. W., Hutt, M. L., Andrew, Gwen, & Walton, R. E. The Michigan Pictures Test: diagnostic and therapeutic possibilities of a new projective technique in child guidance. *Amer. J. Orthopsychiat.*, 1951, *21*, 124-137.

Haskell, J. R., Jr. Relationship between aggressive behavior and psychological tests. *J. proj. Tech.*, 1951, *25*, 431-440.

Haworth, Mary R. A schedule for the analysis of CAT responses. *J. proj. Tech.*, 1963, *27*, 181-184.

Henry, W. E. The Thematic Apperception technique in the study of culture-personality relations. *Genet. Psychol. Monogr.*, 1947, *35*, 3-135.

Henry, W. E. The thematic apperception technique in the study of group and cultural problems. In Anderson, H. H. & Anderson, Gladys L. (Eds.). *An Introduction to Projective Techniques*. Englewood Cliffs, N.J.: Prentice-Hall, 1951. Pp. 230-278.

Holt, R. R. The Thematic Apperception Test. In Anderson, H. H. & Anderson, Gladys L. (Eds.). *An Introduction to Projective Techniques*. Englewood Cliffs, N.J.: Prentice-Hall, 1951. Pp. 181-229.

Hooker, Evelyn. The adjustment of the male overt homosexual. *J. proj. Tech.*, 1957, *21*, 18-31.

Howells, J. G., & Lickorish, J. R. The Family Relations Indicator: a projective technique for investigating intra-family relationships designed for use with emotionally disturbed children. *Brit. J. Ed. Psychol.*, 1963, *33*, 286-296.

Jackson, L. Emotional attitudes towards the family of normal, neurotic and delinquent children, Part I. *Brit. J. Psychol.*, 1950, *41*, 35-51.

Joel, W. The use of the Make-A-Picture Story (MAPS) test with disturbed adolescents. *Rorschach Res. Exch.*, 1948, *12*, 155-164.

Johnson, G. B. An experimental projective technique for the analysis of racial attitudes. *J. educ. Psychol.*, 1950, *4*, 257-278.

Kagan, J. Thematic apperception techniques with children. In Rabin, A. I. & Haworth, Mary R. (Eds.). *Projective Techniques with Children*. New York: Grune and Stratton, 1960. Pp. 105-129.

Kass, W. The Symonds Picture Story Test. In Buros, O. K. (Ed.). *The Fifth Mental Measurements Yearbook*. Highland Park, N.J.: Gryphon Press, 1959. Pp. 296-297.

Klein, Melanie. *Contributions to Psycho-analysis 1921-45*. London: Hogarth Press, 1948.

Klopfer, B., & Kelley, D. M. *The Rorschach Technique*. New York: World Book Co., 1942.

Kramer, H. J. Stimulus variables in auditory projective testing. *Amer. Found. Blind Res. Bull.*, 1962, *1*, 33-40.

Krugman, M. The Michigan Pictures Test. In Buros, O. K. (Ed.). *The Fifth Mental Measurements Yearbook*. Highland Park, N.J.: Gryphon Press, 1959. Pp. 250-251.

Kutash, S. The Object Relations Test. *Personnel & Guid. J.*, 1957, *35*, 539-540.

Lasaga y Travieso, J. E., & Martinez-Arrango, C. Some suggestions concerning the administration and interpretation of the TAT. *J. Psychol.*, 1946, *22*, 117-163.

Lebo, D., & Harrigan, Margaret. Visual and verbal presentation of TAT stimuli. *J. consult. Psychol.*, 1957, *21*, 339-343.

Lee, S. G. *Manual for a Thematic Apperception Test for African Subjects*. Pietermaritzburg, South Africa: University of Natal Press, 1953.

Lehman, I. J. Responses of kindergarten children to the Children's Apperception Test. *J. clin. Psychol.*, 1959, *15*, 60-63.

Lessa, W., & Spiegelman, M. Ulithian personality as seen through ethnological materials and thematic test analyses. *Univer. Calif. Publ. Cult. Soc.*, 1954, *2*, 243-301.

Libby, W. The imagination of adolescents. *Amer. J. Psychol.*, 1908, *19*, 249-252.

Libo, L. M. *Measuring Group Cohesiveness*. Ann Arbor, Michigan: Institute for Social Research, University of Michigan, 1953.

Lindzey, G. *Projective Techniques and Cross-cultural Research.* New York: Appleton-Century-Crofts, 1961.

Malpass, L. F. Some relationships between students' perceptions of schools and their achievement. *J. educ. Psychol.,* 1953, *44,* 475-482.

Margolis, M. The mother-child relationship in bronchial asthma. *J. abnorm. soc. Psychol.,* 1961, *63,* 360-367.

Marks, P. A., & Seeman, W. *Actuarial Description of Abnormal Personality.* Baltimore: Williams & Wilkins, 1963.

Mayman, M., Schafer, R., & Rapaport, D. Interpretation of the Wechsler-Bellevue Intelligence Scale in personality appraisal. In Anderson, H. H. & Anderson, Gladys L. (Eds.). *An Introduction to Projective Techniques.* Englewood Cliffs, N.J.: Prentice-Hall, 1951. Pp. 541-580.

McClelland, D. C., Atkinson, J. W., Clark, R. A., & Lowell, E. L. *The Achievement Motive.* New York: Appleton-Century-Crofts, 1953.

McMahon, D. The Object Relations Test. *Occup. Psychol.,* 1957, *31,* 57-58.

Meyer, M. M. The Object Relations Test. *J. proj. Tech.,* 1958, *22,* 250-252.

Miner, J. B. The concurrent validity of the PAT in the selection of tabulating machine operators. *J. proj. Tech.,* 1960, *24,* 409-418.

Moed, G., Wight, B., Feshbach, S., & Sandry, M. A picture story test for use in physical disability. *Percept. Mot. Skills,* 1963, *17,* 483-497.

Morgan, Christina D., & Murray, H. A. A method for investigating fantasies: the Thematic Apperception Test. *Arch. Neurol. Psychiat.,* 1935, *34,* 289-306.

Murray, H. A. *Thematic Apperception Test Manual.* Cambridge, Mass.: Harvard University Press, 1943.

Murstein, B. I. The role of the stimulus in the manifestation of fantasy. In Kagan, J. & Lesser, G. S. (Eds.). *Contemporary Issues in Thematic Apperceptive Methods.* Springfield, Ill.: Charles C Thomas, 1961. Pp. 229-273.

Murstein, B. I. *Theory and Research in Projective Techniques (Emphasizing the TAT).* New York: Wiley, 1963.

Neuman, G., & Salvatore, J. The Blacky Test and psychoanalytic theory: a factor-analytic approach to validity. *J. proj. Tech.,* 1958, *22,* 427-431.

Newton, K. R. The Blacky Pictures. In Buros, O. K., (Ed.). *The Fifth Mental Measurements Yearbook.* Highland Park, N.J.: Gryphon Press, 1959. Pp. 214-216.

Newton, K. R. The Symonds Picture Story Test. In Buros, O. K., (Ed.). *The Fifth Mental Measurements Yearbook.* Highland Park, N.J.: Gryphon Press, 1959. Pp. 298-299.

Orme, J. E. Object Relations Test performance in schizophrenia. *J. ment. Sci.,* 1959, *105,* 1119-1122.

Pedersen, F., & Marlowe, D. Capacity and motivational differences in verbal recall. *J. clin. Psychol.,* 1960, *16,* 219-222.

Phillipson, H. *The Object Relations Technique.* London: Tavistock Publications, 1955.

Rabin, A. I. Some psychosexual differences between Kibbutz and non-Kibbutz Israeli boys. *J. proj. Tech.,* 1958, *22,* 328-332.

Rossi, A. M., & Solomon, P. A. A further note on female Blacky protocols. *J. proj. Tech.,* 1961, *25,* 339-340.

Schwartz, L. A. Social situation pictures in the psychiatric interview. *Amer. J. Orthopsychiat.,* 1932, *2,* 124-133.

Seward, J. P. Psychoanalysis, deductive method and the Blacky Test. *J. abnorm. soc. Psychol.*, 1950, *45*, 529-535.

Shakow, D., & Rosenzweig, S. The use of the tautaphone ("verbal summator") as an auditory test for the study of personality. *Charact. Pers.*, 1940, *8*, 216-226.

Shapiro, Edna, Biber, Barbara, & Minuchin, Patricia. The Cartoon Situations Test: a semi-structured technique for assessing aspects of personality pertinent to the teaching process. *J. proj. Tech.*, 1957, *21*, 172-184.

Sherwood, E. T. On the designing of TAT pictures with special reference to a set for an African people assimilating western culture. *J. soc. Psychol.*, 1957, *45*, 161-190.

Shneidman, E. S. The Make-A-Picture Story (MAPS) projective personality test: a preliminary report. *J. consult. Psychol.*, 1947, *11*, 315-325.

Shneidman, E. S. Schizophrenia and the MAPS test. *Genet. Psychol. Monogr.*, 1948, *38*, 145-223.

Shneidman, E. S. *The Make-A-Picture Story Test.* New York: Psychological Corporation, 1949.

Shneidman, E. S. Manual for the MAPS test. *Proj. Tech. Monogr.*, 1952, *1*, 1-92.

Shneidman, E. S. The MAPS test with children. In Rabin, A. I. & Haworth, Mary R. (Eds.). *Projective Techniques with Children.* New York: Grune and Stratton, 1960. Pp. 130-148.

Shneidman, E. S., Joel, W., & Little, K. B. *Thematic Test Analysis.* New York: Grune and Stratton, 1951.

Skinner, B. F. The verbal summator and a method for the study of latent speech. *J. Psychol.*, 1936, *2*, 71-107.

Spiegelman, M. A. A note on the use of Fine's scoring system with the MAPS tests of children. *J. proj. Tech.*, 1956, *20*, 442-444.

Stone, D. R. A recorded auditory apperception test as a new projective technique. *J. Psychol.*, 1950, *29*, 349-353.

Stone, D. R. *The Auditory Apperception Test (AAT).* Beverly Hills, Calif.: Western Psychological Services, 1953.

Swensen, C. H., Jr. The Auditory Apperception Test. In Buros, O. K. (Ed.). *The Fifth Mental Measurements Yearbook.* Highland Park, N.J.: Gryphon Press, 1959. Pp. 213-214.

Symonds, P. M. Criteria for the selection of pictures for investigation of adolescent fantasies. *J. abnorm. soc. Psychol.*, 1939, *34*, 271-274.

Symonds, P. M. *Manual for Symonds' Picture Story Test.* New York: Bureau of Publications, Columbia University Press, 1948.

Symonds, P. M. *Adolescent Fantasy.* New York: Columbia University Press, 1949.

Symonds, P. M., & Jensen, A. R. *From Adolescent to Adult.* New York: Columbia University Press, 1961.

Thompson, C. E. The Thompson modification of the Thematic Apperception Test. *Rorschach Res. Exch.*, 1949, *13*, 469-478.

Tomkins, S. S. The Tomkins-Horn Picture Arrangement Test. *Trans. N.Y. Acad. Sci.*, 1952, *15*, 46-50.

Tomkins, S. S., & Miner, J. B. Contributions to the standardization of the Tomkins-Horn Picture Arrangement Test: Plate norms. *J. psychol.*, 1955, *39*, 199-214.

Tomkins, S. S., & Miner, J. B. *The Tomkins-Horn Picture Arrangement Test.* New York: Springer, 1957.

Tomkins, S. S., & Miner, J. B. *PAT Interpretation.* New York: Springer, 1959.

Twitchell-Allen, Doris. The Three-Dimensional Test: a new projective technique. *Amer. Psychologist.* 1947, *2*, 271-272.

Twitchell-Allen, Doris. *Three-Dimensional Apperception Test.* New York: Psychological Corporation, 1948.

Van Krevelen, Alice. A study of examiner influence on responses to MAPS test materials. *J. clin. Psychol.,* 1954, *10*, 292-293.

Van Lennep, D. J. *Four Picture Test.* The Hague: Martinus Nijhoff, 1948.

Van Lennep, D. J. The Four Picture Test. In Anderson, H. H. & Anderson, Gladys L. (Eds.). *An Introduction to Projective Techniques.* Englewood Cliffs, N.J.: Prentice-Hall, 1951. Pp. 149-180.

Van Lennep, D. J., & Houwink, R. H. Projection tests and overt behavior. *Acta Psychol.,* 1953, *9*, 240-253.

Veroff, J. Development and validation of a projective measure of power motivation. *J. abnorm. soc. Psychol.,* 1957, *54*, 1-8.

Veroff, J. Thematic apperception in a nationwide sample survey. In Kagan, J. & Lesser, G. (Eds.). *Contemporary Issues in Thematic Apperceptive Methods.* Springfield, Ill.: Charles C Thomas, 1961. Pp. 83-110.

Walker, E. L., Atkinson, J. W., Veroff, J., Birney, R., Dember, W., & Moulton, R. The expression of fear-related motivation in thematic apperception as a function of proximity to an atomic explosion. In Atkinson, J. W. (Ed.). *Motives in Fantasy, Action and Society.* Princeton, N.J.: Van Nostrand, 1958. Pp. 143-159.

Walker, R. G. A comparison of clinical manifestations of hostility with Rorschach and MAPS test performances. *J. proj. Tech.,* 1951, *15*, 444-460.

Walton, R. E., Andrew, Gwen, Hartwell, S. W., & Hutt, M. L. A tension index of adjustment based on picture stories elicited by the Michigan Pictures Test. *J. abnorm. soc. Psychol.,* 1951, *46*, 438-441.

Weisskopf, Edith A., & Dunlevy, G. P. Bodily similarity between subject and central figure in the TAT as an influence on projection. *J. abnorm. soc. Psychol.,* 1952, *47*, 441-445.

Westby, G. The Object Relations Test. In Buros, O.K., (Ed.). *The Fifth Mental Measurements Yearbook.* Highland Park, N.J.: Gryphon Press, 1959. Pp. 251-252.

Wilmer, H. A., & Husni, May. The use of sounds in a projective test. *J. consult. Psychol.,* 1953, *17*, 377-383.

Zubin, J., Eron, L. D., & Schumer, Florence. *An Experimental Approach to Projective Techniques.* New York: Wiley, 1965.

IV

COMPLETION
METHODS

When the subject is asked to respond to an inkblot he is given a great deal of freedom. The unstructured "meaningless" inkblots allow him a wide range (indeed, an infinite number) of responses. The stimulus does not bind the responses greatly. More conformity to the specific reality presented by the TAT-type picture is demanded in the response. The story must incorporate the figures and circumstances portrayed in the picture if it is not to be completely bizarre or autistic. Some methods, such as the ones presented in this section, place even greater constraints upon the productions of the respondent. The respondent must take into account the structure of a sentence stem or the content of part of a story in giving his response—his "completion." The range of freedom of responses is more circumscribed. This alleged limitation, however, has some research advantages to be discussed in Part VII of the book.

The bulk of Dr. Daston's contribution (Chapter 9) is devoted to the Sentence Completion method. Several forms are discussed, and the degree of the subject's awareness of the meaning of his responses is touched upon. (The latter issue is again taken up, in another context, in Dr. Klopfer's chapter in Part VII.) The fruitful application of the Sentence Completion Test in a variety of research projects is also reviewed in this chapter.

A relative newcomer to the field of projective methods is the Story Completion Technique. In Chapter 10, Dr. Lansky gives a thorough historical survey of this method and cites a number of variations on the story completion theme as well as useful illustrations of research applications with it. In recent years the method has stimulated considerable interest. Its potential in the "custom-making" of projective techniques and in further contributing to research methodology is not to be denied.

9

Word Associations and Sentence Completion Techniques

PAUL G. DASTON *

WORD ASSOCIATIONS

Word associations have a long history in psychology. Both Wundt and Galton experimented with the approach (Rotter, 1951; Forer, 1960). Kraepelin and Bleuler were also interested in word associations, primarily as an improved tool for psychiatric description and classification. Jung, who worked with Bleuler at the Burgholzli, recognized it as an efficient means of investigating complexes, i.e., the combination of an idea with its strong affect (Alexander & Selnick, 1966). He carried out a series of investigations using word associations to confirm Freud's theory of repression, and his lectures to American audiences on word associations were well received, perhaps because of the presence of empirical "test" orientation, characteristic of American psychology. It is not without justification that Jung's word association method has been called the oldest of all projective techniques (Peck & McGuire, 1959).

The Kent-Rosanoff Free Association Test was published shortly thereafter, and, although Jung's work is cited as a source (Rosanoff, 1927, p. 371), it appears to have been developed relatively independently. The one hundred words comprising the Kent-Rosanoff list were employed with a sample of 1,000 normal subjects and a tabular classification of responses was developed (Rosanoff, 1927, pp. 546-604).

Word association techniques—the Kent-Rosanoff and many others—flourished during the early years of psychoanalysis. To paraphrase, if dream interpretation provided a royal road to the unconscious, then word associations could be counted on to make the trip easier. Other techniques were seen to serve lesser purposes. For example, Hermann Rorschach writes:

The [Rorschach] test cannot be considered as a means of delving

*Dr. Daston died shortly before the publication of this book.

into the unconscious. At best, it is far inferior to the other more profound psychological methods such as dream interpretation and association experiments [of Jung]. This is not difficult to understand. The test does not induce a "free flow from the subconscious" but requires adaptation to external stimuli, participation of the "fonction du reel" (Rorschach, 1949, p. 123).

He later writes quite the opposite. "[Certain responses] do actually bring unconscious things to the light of day . . . They must stand in the closest relation to what is generally spoken of as the unconscious" (p. 208). Whether this means he had changed his views, in the course of a hundred pages, or had been paying lip service earlier to his more eminent Swiss compatriots cannot be known. The flood of contemporary Rorschach literature and the relative trickle of clinical word association studies attests to the generally greater acceptance of his test. Probably the last high water mark—to continue the metaphor—for word association methods came with Rapaport's studies. He and his associates conducted an intensive study of diagnostic testing and used word associations as one of their techniques (Rapaport, Gill, & Schafer, 1946). This work will be reported, in some detail, later on.

Since then, word associations have been largely supplanted by other techniques. The Kent-Rosanoff is the only one mentioned by Sundberg, and it ranks twenty-ninth in reported clinical usage (Sundberg, 1961). Despite its demonstrated value as a clinical and research instrument, the relatively few current contributions to the applied and clinical research literature make it seem as if word association techniques are falling somewhat into disuse.

Materials

The only materials needed to conduct a word association test are an appropriate list of words, a timing device (e.g., a stopwatch), and paper and pencil to record responses and latencies.

The word list may be obtained from a number of sources. Two are reproduced here (Tables 1 and 2). Examination of the tables reveals the Rapaport list to be composed of nouns only, presumably to minimize selective factors derived from other parts of speech. The Rapaport list also contains many more emotionally-loaded words with direct denotative meanings, whereas the Kent-Rosanoff list contains words less loaded with double meanings, as do the Mental Examiner's Handbook (Wells & Ruesch, 1945) lists (not reproduced here).

Table 1. Kent-Rosanoff Word Association List[1]

1. Table	26. Wish	51. Stem	76. Bitter
2. Dark	27. River	52. Lamb	77. Hammer
3. Music	28. White	53. Dream	78. Thirsty
4. Sickness	29. Beautiful	54. Yellow	79. City
5. Man	30. Window	55. Bread	80. Square
6. Deep	31. Rough	56. Justice	81. Butter
7. Soft	32. Citizen	57. Boy	82. Doctor
8. Eating	33. Foot	58. Light	83. Loud
9. Mountain	34. Spider	59. Health	84. Thief
10. House	35. Needle	60. Bible	85. Lion
11. Black	36. Red	61. Memory	86. Joy
12. Mutton	37. Sleep	62. Sheep	87. Bed
13. Comfort	38. Anger	63. Bath	88. Heavy
14. Hand	39. Carpet	64. Cottage	89. Tobacco
15. Short	40. Girl	65. Swift	90. Baby
16. Fruit	41. High	66. Blue	91. Moon
17. Butterfly	42. Working	67. Hungry	92. Scissors
18. Smooth	43. Sour	68. Priest	93. Quiet
19. Command	44. Earth	69. Ocean	94. Green
20. Chair	45. Trouble	70. Head	95. Salt
21. Sweet	46. Soldier	71. Stove	96. Street
22. Whistle	47. Cabbage	72. Long	97. King
23. Woman	48. Hard	73. Religion	98. Cheese
24. Cold	49. Eagle	74. Whiskey	99. Blossom
25. Slow	50. Stomach	75. Child	100. Afraid

Table 2. Revised Word List from Rapaport et al[2]

1. rat	21. suicide	41. cut
2. lamp	22. mountain	42. movies
3. love	23. smoke	43. cockroach
4. book	24. house	44. bite
5. father	25. vagina	45. dog
6. paper	26. tobacco	46. dance
7. breast	27. mouth	47. gun
8. curtains	28. horse	48. water
9. trunk	29. masturbation	49. husband
10. drink	30. wife	50. mud
11. party	31. table	51. woman
12. spring	32. fight	52. fire
13. bowel movement	33. beef	53. suck
14. rug	34. stomach	54. money
15. boy friend	35. farm	55. mother
16. chair	36. man	56. hospital
17. screen	37. taxes	57. girl friend
18. penis	38. nipple	58. taxi
19. radiator	39. doctor	59. intercourse
20. frame	40. dirt	60. hunger

[1]From Rosanoff, A. J. *Manual of Psychiatry*, Sixth Ed. Rev., N.Y.: Wiley, 1927, pp. 546-604. Reprinted with permission of the publishers.

[2]From Rapaport, Gill and Schafer. *Diagnostic Psychological Testing*, Vol. 2. Chicago: Year Book, 1946, p. 84. Reprinted with permission of the publishers.

The Rapaport list is self-contained, in that the list reproduced in Table 2 is the list to be given. With other lists, the addition of words with personal loadings for the subject is usually recommended; these idiosyncratically-laden words are to be interspersed throughout the regular word list.

Administration

Method of administration is individual. Surrounds should be comfortable and—above all—quiet. Extraneous sounds may interfere with hearing. Word stimuli are almost always presented verbally (Lindzey, 1959), although administration can be visual (Rotter, 1951).

The word association test should be given relatively late in the session. There are two good reasons for delaying. First, this is a threatening procedure, so every effort should have been made to establish a reservoir of good rapport beforehand. Second, if the examiner prefers to follow up clinical hunches by adding words he feels have idiosyncratic loadings to the word list, it stands to reason he will have a better list when he has had more opportunity to obtain information from his client.

Instructions vary somewhat, but all contain statements such as, "I am going to read you a list of words, one at a time. Please answer with the first word that comes into your mind." Rosanoff cautions the client not to repeat the stimulus word itself, nor a different grammatical form of it, and that he respond with one word only, not a compound word, phrase, or sentence. Rapaport, on the other hand, since he uses response modes for evaluation, is not so specific. Wells and Ruesch recommend reluctantly that clients be given illustrations of associations if necessary. Practice trials to help the client understand what is expected of him are usually recommended. Practice words employed are not from the list itself, nor are they recorded.

The examiner reads the words one at a time, slowly and clearly. He records the word response plus the amount of time between audition and verbalization. He may record other behaviors as well, such as fidgeting, flushing, explosive speech, slurring, and the like, but the response word and time required for its emission are critical.

That, in essence, comprises administration of the word association technique, although there are elaborations to this procedure, such as chain associations and homophones. The additions, clinically most interesting, are the Reproduction phase following the first presentation of the list (Rapaport et al, 1946) [3] and a third phase, Response Substitution

---

[3]The Reproduction phase is not really new since Jung employed it in his work (Forer, 1960). The Rapaport classification procedure warrants being called an addition, however.

(Appelbaum, 1960a, 1960b, 1963). The latter two will be discussed in detail later.

Underlying assumptions

Assumptions underlying word associations seem relatively straightforward. Verbalizations reflect ideation, and the study of associative thought under controlled conditions can provide information about personal dynamics and defense systems, as well as being of value in psychiatric labelling. As indicated earlier, the technique became popular in the context of psychoanalytic theory. Assumptions relevant to that theory are probably relevant to word associations, although the technique clearly has no necessary tie to any theory (cf. Kraepelin's work on nosology).

Evaluation and interpretation

The admonition applicable to evaluation and interpretation with other clinical tools certainly ought to apply to their sire, i.e., experience is of critical importance. Lest the neophyte despair, let us hastily add that responses can be categorized in ways which are helpful in labelling, and in clinical interpretation. The four, presented below in brief, are Symonds' summary, Kent and Rosanoff's common vs. individual reactions, Rapaport's outline, and Appelbaum's addition. With the exception of the first indicator (lengthened response time), the Symonds signs are qualitative.

Symonds[4]

1. Long reaction time (any R/T greater than 2.6″).
2. Inability to make any response whatsoever.
3. Extremely short reaction time.
4. Repetition of the stimulus word itself, or perseveration.
5. Apparent misunderstanding of the stimulus word.
6. Defective reproduction of original reaction at second presentation of the stimulus word.
7. Response with the same reaction word to two or more different stimulus words.
8. Strange or apparently senseless reaction.
9. Perseveration of ideas—This is ideational, rather than necessarily the repetition of the same response word.

The Kent-Rosanoff classificatory system is also qualitative, a more or

---

[4] Taken from Rotter, (1951) pp. 282-283.

less "successive elimination" approach, using response content. Each response is evaluated by recourse to tables developed for the hundred words on the list. These norms, based on responses from 1,000 normal subjects, allow estimates of commonness and acceptability to be made for responses. Their categorization follows:

Kent-Rosanoff Response Classificatory Scheme[5]

Common reactions

1. Specific
2. Non-specific (general)
3. Doubtful

Individual reactions

4. Juvenile reactions
5. Sound reactions (neologisms)
6. Neologisms without sound relations
7. Repetition of preceding reaction
8. Reaction repeated five times
9. Repetition of preceding stimulus
10. Derivatives
11. Non-specific reactions (words)
13. Word complements
14. Particles of speech
15. Association to preceding stimulus
16. Association to preceding reaction (by frequency tables)
17. Repetition of previous reaction
18. Repetition of previous stimulus
19. Normal (by tables)
20. Association to preceding reaction (without frequency tables)
21. Unclassified

This general schema resulted in the distribution of responses found in Table 4.

---

[5]Taken from Rosanoff, (1927) pp. 546-604.

Table 4. Association in selected groups of subjects, normal and abnormal[6]

SUBJECTS	Specific (percent)	Non-Specific (percent)	Doubtful Reactions (percent)	Individual Reactions (percent)	Failure of Reaction (percent)
		Common Reactions			
1,000 normal adults	85.5	6.2	1.5	6.8	—
247 insane adults	66.4	4.3	2.5	26.8	—
253 defective children aged over 9 years	75.2	8.2	2.1	13.0	1.5
125 normal white children, 11-15 years	82.0	7.2	1.6	8.6	0.6
175 normal white children, 4-10 years	62.7	4.2	3.2	18.8	11.1
125 normal Negro children, 11-15 years	75.3	7.2	2.5	14.9	0.1
175 normal Negro children, 4-10 years	54.1	3.5	2.5	33.2	6.7

The Rapaport classificatory schema is, like the Kent-Rosanoff, content-based. In addition to the first reading, the examiner reads the list a second time, so there is analysis of reproductions.

Formal Characteristics of Associative Response[7]

1. *Close reaction*

   a. Subject offers S-word as R
   b. Subject offers multi-word definition as R
   c. Subject offers S-word with self-reference (e.g., "house"—"my house")
   d. Subject offers S-word in a word combination or in shortened form
   e. Subject says he didn't get R—only an image of S-word
   f. Subject offers R related in unusual way to S-word
   g. Subject reacts with R which is senseless or distorted in relation to S-word (e.g., "suicide"—"wooicide")
   h. Subject gives slang association or alliteration
   i. Subject names random objects in examiner's office
   j. Miscellaneous close reactions (e.g., all sexual words are reacted to with "embarrassment")

[6]Taken from Rotter, (1951), p. 285.

[7] From Rapaport, D. et al, (1946).

2. *Distant reaction*

   a. Unrelated R's (e.g., "book"—"turkey")
   b. Faint connection, explained by inquiring
   c. Faint connection found by examiner
   d. Idiosyncratic R (e.g., "house"—"empty")
   e. Mildly distant—loosely coordinated R's (e.g., "laugh"—"jaw")

3. *Content disturbances—S or R*

   a. S-word: Subject may profess not to know S-word or the S-word may be misunderstood
   b. R-word: Subject may give proper names or vulgar R's

4. *Reproduction disturbances*[8]

   a. Failure to reproduce original R-word
   b. Delay in reproduction
   c. False reproduction distant from original R-word
   d. False reproduction similar to original reaction word
   e. Variation of original reaction word
   f. False reproduction immediately corrected

Rapaport's evaluation is not based on the usual kind of test scoring. He does, however, list twenty-five types of association disturbance and six reproduction disturbances. Also, in comparing several psychiatric populations (schizophrenics, depressives, neurotics) with normals (state police), he did frequency counts and found differences overall. Specifically, he found differences in:

1. *Popular reactions* (i.e., Subjects giving same or similar words). Normals conform more to instructions and give fewer odd R's.

2. *Close reactions.* More close reactions among clinical groups.

3. *Distant reactions.* These reflect loose thought and were found more in schizophrenic and schizophrenic-like subjects.

4. *Response time.* This was definitely related to clinical groupings, especially delayed response, which was characteristically depressive.

5. *Reproduction.* Those stimuli associated with traumatic ideas gave subjects considerable trouble the second time through.

6. *Traumatic S-words.* Those with sexual, anal, oral, familial, and aggressive connotations gave disturbed subjects most difficulty.

[8]From second reading of word list by examiner, wherein Subject is required to recall verbally his original verbalization to each S-word.

These differences, Rapaport noted, were in *kind* of thought and association as well as *amount*.

Finally, the Appelbaum addition deserves note. He follows the Rapaport free association procedures for Trial 1 and reproduction for Trial 2. He then reads the list a third time, instructing subjects to "Give the first word that comes to mind that is different from the one given before" (Appelbaum, 1963). He has used it primarily with brain-damaged populations, assuming the cognitive functions involved (memory, ability to shift, and word-finding) would be impaired in these groups relative to non brain-damaged. His scoring system for Trial 3 follows:

Appelbaum[9]

1. *Repetitions.* Repetition of the word given on the association trial.
2. *Blocking.* Reaction time of 6″ or more.
3. *Multi-words.*
4. *Unrelated responses.* These do not appear to be associations; they are often given to random objects in sight.
5. *Failure.* The subject does not respond.
6. *Corrected repetitions.* Subject begins to repeat a previous R but corrects it with a new word.
7. *Perseveration.* Subject repeats the same response to successive S-words.
8. *Self-reference.* Subject gives an explicitly personal response.
9. *Proper names.*
10. *Repetitions of the stimulus word.*

Appelbaum has used this general procedure several times (1960, 1963) and finds he can differentiate among brain-damaged, psychiatric, and normal populations, equated roughly on intellectual, educational, and age factors (see Table 5).

Table 5. Results of Trial 3 with three groups: brain-damaged, psychiatric, and normal

	Brain-Damaged (N = 30)	Psychiatric (N = 56)	Normals (N = 37)	P*
Repetitions	11 ($\overline{X}$)	3 ($\overline{X}$)	4 ($\overline{X}$)	.001 ANOVA
Blocking	10 ($\overline{X}$)	7 ($\overline{X}$)	4 ($\overline{X}$)	.001 ANOVA
Unrelated response	11	10	3	.02 x^2
Failure	11	1	1	.001 x^2
Corrected repetition	11	17	13	NS x^2
Multi-words plus repetitions				.001 (discriminant analysis)

[9]From Appelbaum, S. A. (1963), pp. 78-84.

The other factors (Perseveration, Self-Reference, Proper Names, or Repetition of Stimulus Words) did not show up with enough frequency to warrant statistical comparison. Parenthetically, Trial 2 also discriminates the groups, (p <.001), with the brain-damaged failing to recall first associations with greatest frequency. The Trial 3 procedure was a somewhat better predictor.

Research

There seems to be lessening interest in clinical word association research. There is considerable activity in the verbal learning area (cf. Palermo & Jenkins, 1964; Bilodeau & Howell, 1965), but the direct relevance of this work to the clinical enterprise is limited as yet. There is some reported use of the technique in anthropological studies (Lindzey, 1961). He cites the study by DuBois among the Alorese and a study among the Hindu by Carstairs, both of whom found it helpful.

There are a number of problems inherent in the word association method which may limit its research value. One is the problem of response set in general and social desirability in particular. It remains to be demonstrated that responses and response latencies are not highly susceptible to these factors. Another problem is the appropriateness of norms. Language continues to change, and norms become outdated quickly.

A third problem inheres more in the researchers themselves, rather than in the materials. The dynamic, psychoanalytic models in which these techniques flourished are less popular at present. Research psychologists are not as interested in the classes of problems generated by these models; hence, techniques which seem tied to the model are accordingly less favored. The technique can stand by itself, as Appelbaum and others have demonstrated, but its association with the word "psychoanalysis" is an obstacle to be overcome, in the eyes of some people.

INTERMEDIATE TECHNIQUES

Between the word association test and its descendants, the sentence completion methods, there have been several attempts to develop techniques which combine the succinctness of the word association with the freedom of response the sentence completion provides. The Make A Sentence Test (MAST) is a current example of this approach and consists of twenty stimulus words to which the subject is asked to respond with a sentence or a statement using that word in connection with himself. The words were chosen to measure ego-integration and emotional

---

*Where it was warranted, analyses of variance (ANOVA) were carried out. On frequency data, Appelbaum used chi-square.

acceptance of several classes of ideas, thoughts and feelings. The items and area tapped are reproduced in Table 6.

Table 6. MAST items and dynamic areas tapped[10]

Items		Area
1. work	11. earn	productivity
2. angry	12. hate	hostility
3. ask	13. receive	receptivity
4. hit	14. attack	aggression
5. kiss	15. passionate	sexuality
6. free	16. independent	dependency
7. afraid	17. worry	anxiety
8. share	18. join	mutuality
9. dirty	19. soil	anality
10. succeed	20. win	achievement

Responses are scored for Integration (+1), Concern (0), Fantasy (0), and Distortion (−1). The latter also covers repressive mechanisms and evasion, as well as failure to respond. The schema is adequately reliable to score.

The MAST has been used clinically, primarily with psychiatric populations. It has been found helpful as one test in a battery. It has the virtues of being either individually or group administered, is easy to score and has rather broad dynamic categorization.

In one validity study, the MAST was used as a predictor of success in work as a psychiatric aide. It was found, statistically, to be significantly discriminating with two samples. The responses of good aides formed a cohesive cluster around the key concepts of integration, self-awareness, and self-acceptance. It was a powerful demonstration of the effectiveness paper and pencil personality devices can have, even in the face of subjects who were undoubtedly attempting to respond in a socially desirable fashion (Stotsky et al, 1956).

Sacks has continued to work with a modification of the MAST and reports the scores he obtains from his Verb Response Test—a type of written word association measure—predict academic achievement in general psychology classes with greater accuracy than a number of intellective indicators or any of the scales of a well-known forced-choice personal preference measure.[11]

SENTENCE COMPLETION METHODS

Although they have several antecedents, sentence completion methods

---

[10]Reproduced from Stotsky, B. A., Sacks, J. M. & Daston, P. G. 1956. pp. 193-199.
[11]J. M. Sacks, Personal communication, 1966.

are relatively new as projective techniques. In their present form, their history is a short half-century. They represent an extremely flexible and demonstrably useful approach to the assessment of personality and may be adapted easily to the needs of various settings. Sentence completion tests have been used with children, adults, and the aged; with both sexes; with various pathological and non-pathological groups; in institutions and in clinics; for anthropological study; for screening in classrooms and industry; for assessment of marital satisfaction; for management development; and for other purposes. If we examine only reported clinical usage, we find these methods rank second to intellectual evaluations (Sundberg, 1961),[12] which does not nearly cover their spectrum of usage. In sum, wherever we find clinical or personality-oriented questions being asked, we typically find sentence completion tests employed as aids in providing answers.

History

There have been two precursors of the present-day sentence completion technique: word associations as dynamic indicators of complexes, and incomplete sentences as scholastic achievement measures. The former, as we have noted, were popularized by Jung as a means for evoking personally and emotionally meaningful responses to word stimuli. The latter were employed, by both Ebbinghaus and Galton, to study memory (Rohde, 1957). In their familiar academic form, incomplete sentences are recall measures or recognition measures. That is, the subject is given a sentence to complete, and he must fill in the blanks from memory (recall); or, presented with several alternative completions, the subject chooses the one most suitable (recognition). Scoring is necessarily objective, responses are "right" or "wrong," and, in their scholastic achievement guise, incomplete sentences have no particular value as personality measures.

Their first use in clinical work may actually date back to 1910, according to a retrospective statement by F. L. Wells, who at that time ". . . devised and briefly used, in substantial dynamic innocence, a series of phrase-completions that might have passed as an alternate form" of a current series (Wells, 1954). Most reviewers, however, agree that their first systematic use in the area of personality assessment was in the late 1920's and early 1930's, by investigators like Payne and Tendler, who found them of value as indices of response styles and emotional reactions with rather diverse populations (Bell, 1948; Sacks & Levy, 1950; Rotter, 1952; Rohde, 1957; Forer, 1960). There were other uses of the method,

[12]The various intellectual measures have a Total Mention of more than 800. The three sentence completion methods have a Total Mention of 173, followed by Rorschach at 170.

but the sentence completion test developed by Rohde in collaboration with Hildreth warrants special mention as prototypic of current sentence completion tests. It was devised for use with school children, but its rationale and many of its items have found their way into other sentence completion tests (cf. Stein, 1948; Rohde, 1957).

As was the case with so many other devices for personality assessment, demands engendered by the Second World War provided opportunity for spectacular increases in the use of measures as flexible as sentence completions. This was a time for rapid assessment of large groups, a time for quick decisions, for predictions to global and vague criteria. Sentence completions could at one and the same time be made specific and general enough to serve many needs. They were employed in many contexts, of which we shall mention only three: the Office of Strategic Services, aviation cadet selection, and psychiatric screening.

The Office of Strategic Services (OSS) was the "cloak and dagger" arm of the United States Army during the Second World War. It was entrusted with the evaluation and selection of personnel for many roles, ranging from highly secret to clerical. Its selection officers used many tests, including a sentence completion measure ". . . which, though not included in the original program . . . was increasingly valued by the staff. One of a number of projective techniques tried out in the program, it was the only one in use at the end" (OSS Assessment Staff, 1948, p. 71). It was used wherever OSS assessment was carried out. Interviewers found it so helpful that they developed Chinese and Korean versions for work with Oriental OSS counterparts in the Asian theater.

The OSS sentence completion technique covered twelve areas of personality. Gross evaluation was done with two considerations in mind: 1) the rarer the response—on normative, expectancy bases—to a sentence stub, the more significant it was; and 2) the more frequent the same response to different stubs, the more significant. Sentence completion responses were used as a "springboard" for interview questions, and conclusions from interviews were powerful determinants of a candidate's fate. Thus the importance given sentence completions is obvious. Its felt success was so great that Stein developed a one-hundred-item civilian version, still very much in use.

A second source, aviation psychology, also reported positive experiences with sentence completions. The flying officer selection program used a somewhat different version, but complaints centered more about the highly subjective scoring required than about the effectiveness of the technique (Guilford, in Rohde, 1957).

The third context was the more usual—psychiatric screening and evaluation. Following work by Shore, Hutt, and Holtzberg, a forty-item incomplete sentence blank (ISB) was developed by Rotter and Willerman for use in convalescent Army Air Force settings. They attempted to make the items as unstructured as possible and to elicit completions based on personal feelings and attitudes rather than, primarily, associations. Along with the ISB, they devised a three-category scoring system for responses (+ for Conflict, 0 for Neutral, − for Positive), plus a booklet of examples for each item. Their efforts paid off in scoring consistency, with average interscorer reliability being .89. Correlations with a criterion measure were also quite adequate (Rotter, 1951), indicating that, for psychiatric screening purposes, sentence completion methods can be of considerable value. A civilian version of the ISB has been developed and is used primarily in college counseling centers. Like its predecessor, it is carefully designed, responses can be scored reliably, and it distinguishes maladjusted students of both sexes from their adjusted counterparts (Rotter, 1951).

In the past twenty years, there has been a spate of sentence completion devises in addition to those of Rohde, Stein and Rotter. Rather than confuse the reader by sheer enumeration, we will attempt to indicate as many as are appropriate in context. The very fact that psychologists continue to employ these devices, and are creating new ones, indicates their confidence in the sentence completion method.

Underlying assumptions

Common to all sentence completion methods is the assumption that the individual is supplying information about himself when he responds to stimulus stubs. He reveals general personality styles as well as clues about specific conflicts and problem areas. Incomplete sentences are considerably more structured than inkblots and allow greater individual freedom for the test developer in building stubs relevant to his purposes. They also allow greater individual freedom and variability of subject response (i.e., response set) than do such procedures as word associations. This places them in an intermediate position on a dimension of structured-unstructured. As a matter of fact, there is some question as to whether they are tests, methods, or techniques; whether they can properly be called "projective," and whether they do serve an evaluative purpose. However, they are generally classified as projective techniques (Lindzey, 1959).

While there is little doubt that sentence completions are less amorphous than inkblots, there appears to be considerable room left for the projection hypothesis. Sacks and Levy cite ten responses they obtained to the stub, "The way my father treated my mother made me feel. . . ." Five of the responses were positive in tone, five were negative. There were only two repeats. Content ranged from ". . . very happy" through . . . "rather indifferent" to ". . . like killing him" and ". . . he was a sucker." Also, time taken varied from four to 35 seconds (Sacks & Levy, 1950). This is an impressive demonstration of individual differences with personality implications. Rohde puts it well:

Whether the concept of projection is applicable to the sentence completion method appears to depend on the preferred interpretation of projection . . . Thus it does not appear to be especially important whether or not the sentence completion method is classified as a projective technique. What is worthy of consideration is that it yields productions which may be analyzed and by this means be indicative of significant variables and organizations of personality (Rohde, 1957, p. 283) .

A second assumption, an inheritance perhaps from word associations, held that the subject's responses to sentence stubs were not monitored by him and that they were unrelated to situational factors. Rotter and Willerman attempted specifically to minimize associations to the ISB by instructions stressing feelings (Rotter, 1951). Meltzoff attacked the problem experimentally and found responses varied systematically according to conditions of test administration. Subjects responded differently to his sentence completion task under instructions to "fake good" or "fake bad." Ego threat, as compared to anonymity, was also a response determinant. Meltzoff concluded the assumption that responses will be projected without censorship did not hold for sentence completions (Meltzoff, 1952). In other words, response set, and social desirability in particular, is a factor in obtained results.

It may be recalled that assumptions of psychoanalytic theory were basic to word associations. This is not the case with sentence completion methods. Dynamic considerations may well enter into the construction of a sentence completion test, but the areas tapped may be examined independent of psychoanalytic (or other formal) theory. Thus, sentence completion tests can be focused more specifically on criteria, and items with content validity can be developed. For example, on a sentence completion test of work attitudes, Stotsky and Weinberg used items like these:[13]

> When Dick failed in his new job, he . . .
> When they cut his salary, he . . .
> The men under me . . .
> Working for yourself . . .
> As the work became more boring . . .
> My goals . . .
> Dick worked best at . . .

Clinically oriented techniques, like the Sacks Sentence Completion Test (SSCT) or the Stein Sentence Completion Test, contain items specific to personality-relevant areas. The SSCT, for example, has fifteen areas, of which items from three are reproduced here (Sacks & Levy, 1950, 379-382) .

[13]From the Stotsky-Weinberg Sentence Completion Test. Items used with permission.

Attitude toward mother
>   My mother . . .
>   My mother and I . . .
>   I think that most mothers . . .
>   I like my mother, but . . .

Attitude toward friends and acquaintances
>   I feel that a real friend . . .
>   I don't like people who . . .
>   The people I like best . . .
>   When I'm not around, my friends . . .

Fears
>   I know it is silly, but I am afraid of . . .
>   Most of my friends don't know that I am afraid of . . .
>   I wish I could lose the fear of . . .
>   My fears sometimes force me to . . .

Others, like the Michigan Sentence Completion Test and the Forer Structured Sentence Completion Test, provide special check lists and summary sheets for convenience in organizing responses in specific personality areas.

To summarize, it is not necessary to subscribe to the assumptions of any one theory to use sentence completion tests. The method is valuable in obtaining information. The purpose of the investigator determines his dependence on theory and materials he employs.

Materials

By now it should be apparent that while there may be one sentence completion method, there are many sentence completion tests. Materials depend on the focus of inquiry. One can develop one's own test, choosing sentence stubs germane to one's purpose. So long as one exercises appropriate test construction cautions, there is nothing wrong with this procedure. One can also take advantage of existing tests, of which there are many.

Most tests contain between 40 and 100 stubs. The total number is dictated sometimes by rational considerations (e.g., the SSCT covers fifteen areas with four items each), sometimes by area coverage plus "filler" items (e.g., the Stotsky-Weinberg contains 81 items, 69 of which are specifically related to variables they studied, 12 of which were neutral "fillers") (Stotsky & Weinberg, 1956). One is refreshingly direct, its total of 73 sentence stubs dictated by the feelings of the authors (Holsopple & Miale, 1954). Occasionally a total is empirically arrived at, such as the 45 items on the Chillicothe SCT (Cromwell & Lundy, 1954).

Format is relatively consistent across sentence completion tests. They usually run to four pages, with instructions plus demographic information on the first page. Stubs are printed down the left side of the page, with room to the right for the subject's response. Space is limited, which tends to set an upper limit to the amount of response.

Once it is decided which sentence completion test will be used, all that is required is a sufficient supply of pencils and erasers for the subjects, a timing device (a watch is quite sufficient), and adequate work space.

Administration

Administration is perhaps easier for sentence completion tests than for other projective techniques. They can be given individually or to groups of varying size. So long as there is enough room for each subject to be comfortable, neither the surroundings nor the number of persons in the room seems to matter. Usually, administration is written, although there can be oral administration. The subject writes his own sentence completions.

Instructions are printed on the sentence completion blank itself and may be repeated aloud by the examiner. Assuming the subject can read and write adequately, understanding is no problem. (In more than fifteen years of group administration, I do not recall any particular difficulty, other than when subjects have been allowed to complete the test elsewhere than under supervision. A few experiences with "consensus completions" reinforces one's faith in results obtained from supervised settings.)

As test papers are turned in, they can be scanned quickly, names can be checked, and omissions circled. Subjects can be asked to rectify omissions at that time, so one has a complete test record plus some notion of items which might have caused difficulty.

Sentence completions are usually power, rather than speed tests. When time is a factor, completions become shorter (Cromwell & Lundy, 1954; Goldberg, 1965), so the clinician must decide which he wants most: time saving with brevity of response, or longer responses and more time taken for administration. Nonetheless, subjects vary on the temporal dimension. Some work rapidly, others slowly. It is clinically valuable to note the time taken on the test paper itself.

Evaluation and interpretation

What one gets out of a sentence completion test depends considerably on the test, the questions asked, and what one brings to it. There are some who use sentence completion data purely formally. These are in the minority. They concern themselves with spelling and grammatical errors, ratio of various parts of speech to one another, length of completions, and similar frequency counts (Rohde, 1957; Goldberg, 1965). The majority of users are content-oriented and their approaches range from the rather rigorous to the intuitive-impressionistic. Even such a good craftsman and proponent of rigor as Sacks emphasizes ". . . the experience, insight, and understanding of the clinician are of exceptional importance in working with a projective procedure like the sentence completion test" (Sacks & Levy, 1950, p. 361). Rohde puts it more baldly: "It is suggested that too much refinement of scoring be avoided, since it gives the impression that interpretation can be achieved by consulting a handbook of scores without genuine understanding of the theory of personality and psychopathology. To use the test in this manner becomes mechanical and may lead to serious misinterpretations" (1957, p. 64).

The impressionist's view is well put by Holsopple and Miale. They feel our current level of sophistication in personality is limited. As we develop knowledge, we may concurrently be able to develop scoring systems for our sentence completion tests. Scoring is premature at our level of development. Presently, a sentence-by-sentence interpretation seems most appropriate for building global descriptions of personality (Holsopple & Miale, 1954).

It is evident that clinicians evaluate and interpret sentence completions differently. Several representative approaches will be presented briefly to give a flavor of how a sentence completion protocol can be evaluated. The student is referred to the original sources for detailed accounts.

Miale-Holsopple Sentence Completion Test (73 items). These authors suggest the following questions be kept in mind in evaluating sentence completions:

1. Was the completion positive or negative in tone?
2. Was the subject's role active or passive?
3. Was the completion specific or qualified (e.g., "is" vs. "maybe")?
4. Was the response imperative? Declarative?
5. What was the temporal orientation: past, present, or future?
6. Were there differences in subject's identification from one completion to another?
7. Did responses reflect wholehearted commitment or was there hedging?
8. Were there differences in definiteness or vagueness of responses from one completion to another?
9. Was there wide variation in the amount of verbalization to a sentence stem?

The psychologist should read through the entire record to gain a global impression. Following this, he should go through it again, this time getting the feel for sequence, for response clusters, and responses which have little reference to openings. Finally, he should examine individual sentences, after which he should set down hunches and inferences preparatory to outlining the personality picture.

As one proceeds through the sentences, vague structures and outstanding properties begin to emerge. These clarify themselves gradually with full use of the examiner's insight, empathy, and experience, until a personality picture in terms of handling conflict, limitations and defects, as well as positive resources, has developed (Holsopple & Miale, p. 43).

The intuitive approach they espouse epitomizes the art of clinical work and its richness. It also emphasizes the dangers inherent in such subjectivity. Interestingly, the Miale-Holsopple SCT can be used in clinical prediction, as demonstrated by rather good results obtained in predicting community adjustment of delinquent boys (Jenkins & Blodgett, 1960). Somewhat greater structure is provided by the Michigan Sentence Completion Test.

Michigan Sentence Completion Test (100 items). The stubs of the Michigan SCT were developed to provide information about four structured personality areas and some less easily categorizable areas, grouped loosely together. Each area contains twenty items. The areas, with sample stubs, are as follows:

1. *Family and Childhood—Opposite Sex*
   The difference between Mom and Dad was . . .
   Most women are . . .
   She was happiest when I . . .
   As a youth my greatest trouble . . .

2. *Ego Tensions—Self Evaluation—Guilt Feelings*
   It makes me nervous to . . .
   People get upset when . . .
   Sexual lust . . .
   We tend to forget the type of experience which . . .

3. *Goals—Ambitions—Aggression*
   As a youth, I used to daydream about . . .
   My personality would be much better if . . .
   What makes me angry is . . .
   When he struck me in the face . . .

4. *Positive and Negative Interpersonal Relations*
   I like children who are . . .
   When the boss says, "You can do it," I . . .
   The kind of people I like most are . . .
   When the boss says I can't do it, I . . .

5. *Unstructured*
   Freedom . . .
   Sin . . .
   Love . . .
   Death . . .

There is no scoring. Responses are grouped into clusters, and hypotheses are generated from examinations of these.

The MSCT in this rather global form was found helpful in the psychology assessment program sponsored by the Veterans Administration. It gave higher correlations with rated criteria than any of the other projective measures employed (Rohde, 1957).

Hiler developed scoring categories for the items and found fifteen items which differentiated early terminators in psychotherapy from those who remained at least twenty sessions (Hiler, 1959). The same investigator has continued his interest in making the Michigan SCT an objective instrument and has developed a scoring system for each item.[14] A similar approach was employed by Gidynski, using some of Hiler's categorizations. She found that it was highly reliable, and that depressive subjects could be statistically differentiated from controls (Gidynski, 1958).

Forer Sentence Completion Test (100 items). There are several forms of this test, for different groups. Forer has no formal scoring system, preferring to describe rather than quantify. Nonetheless, the evaluatory structure he provides is detailed enough to make quantification a relatively easy next step. He groups responses into four general categories:

A. Interpersonal attitudes
B. Wishes
C. Causes of one's own feeling or action
D. Reactions to external states

He also provides a checklist to aid in formulation of hypotheses and clinical evaluations. Despite his reluctance to quantify, Forer's system is a model of careful development. Parenthetically, at least with the children's version, he recommends the SCT be part of a battery (Forer, 1960).

The last test to be presented is the Stotsky-Weinberg, as an example of sentence completions developed to assess attitudes toward a particular area, in this case—work.

Stotsky-Weinberg Sentence Completion Test (81 items). The authors were interested in a measure of rehabilitative value with chronic psychiatric subjects. They built their test around nine ego-strength dimensions which seemed relevant to adjustment in work settings. Stubs reflected:

1. Reactions to situations of difficulty
2. Need achievement (after Murray)
3. Specificity of goals
4. Reaction to failure

[14]E. Wesley Hiler, personal communication, 1960.

5. Self-reliance
6. Job-persistence
7. Reactions to superiors
8. Reactions to peers
9. Reactions to subordinates
10. Buffer or filler items

Examples of these stubs are found elsewhere in this chapter. Scoring agreement of obtained responses was adequate, responses being categorized as positive $(+1)$, neutral (0), or negative $(-)$. Using success and failure in institutional work assignments as their criterion, the SCT was predictive overall, as were its nine variables. A second set of predictions, this time to a criterion of adjustment six months later, was also highly successful. Again, both the overall SCT score and individual variables were effective in discriminating those who remain on a work program from those who regress (Stotsky & Weinberg, 1956). The same SCT was used by Conners et al with long-term schizophrenic patients. Similar validity coefficients were obtained (Conners, et al, 1961).

Research applications[15]

Much of the clinically relevant research has been interspersed throughout the chapter. No attempt will be made to summarize it here. Instead, two illustrations of research application will be presented, one related more to the method itself, the other to its instrumental use in personality research.

A methodological issue: person reference. The sentence stub dictates to a considerable degree the obtained response. Stub length, its affective tone, and its content are important variables. Also, of importance is the person reference, i.e., first person or third person. Support can be marshalled for stubs which are first person, third person, or both.

Those who prefer first person reference can point to the Sacks study, in which first person stubs came off best. They provided more meaningful information than their third person counterparts and were preferred as a source of data by six of seven psychologists (Sacks, 1949). The same general conclusion was arrived at by Cromwell and Lundy (1954).

Advocates of the third person stub can be heartened by the findings of Getzels and his collaborators. It has been his contention that private attitudes are more easily revealed to third person stubs (Getzels, 1951; Hanfmann & Getzels, 1953; Getzels & Walsh, 1958). In the early study, he found differences among adults between first and third person stubs, the latter being more revelatory. More socially questionable responses were

[15]The reader's attention is directed to Goldberg's excellent and up-to-date review of SCT research (Goldberg, 1965).

provided to SCT third person stubs; and, the disparity between socially unacceptable responses on a direct questionnaire and third person stubs was greater for high-prejudiced than for low-prejudiced subjects (Getzels, 1951). The second study, with Hanfmann, demonstrated that third person stubs are identified often as personally revelatory by subjects (Hanfmann & Getzels, 1953). A somewhat similar procedure was followed by Dorris, et al, using a modification of Getzel's SCT. They found high authoritarian subjects used third person items to deny personal tendencies, particularly the ego threatening and inadequate-passive characteristics they ascribed to third persons. They even speculate that matched first and third person stubs may be measuring distinct, albeit related, variables (Dorris, Levinson, & Hanfmann, 1954).

Getzels and Walsh (1958) carried out two separate investigations, using female college students in one study and heterogeneous groups of school children in the second. For both studies, they employed a direct questionnaire and, independently, a sentence completion test with first and third person stubs. The stubs were built so that responses could be scored reliably as socially acceptable or socially unacceptable, an aim they achieved. Coefficients of inter-judge reliability were all above .90. Stub content dealt with socially-conflicted areas of inquiry (primarily Negroes, parents, personal competence, and religious tolerance) plus neutral and "filler" items.

Results with the college group supported their contention. Significantly more negative responses were obtained in socially-conflicted areas to third person than to first person stubs. The girls could attribute personal incompetence to others much more easily than to themselves (.01-.001); they could express negative attitudes toward parents of either sex (.001); they were much less religiously tolerant in their third person responses (.001); and there were clearly more negative attitudes toward Negroes expressed in all third person responses (.05-.001). In socially non-conflicted areas (e.g., political attitudes), there were no differences between first and third person stubs.

The second study focussed not only on direct (i.e., first person) and indirect sentence stubs (third person) but also on an Index of Differentiation (ID), or the discrepancy between direct and indirect. The postulated ID could meaningfully be looked upon as a measure of socialization in children, a hypothesis that was supported. Younger children had smaller ID's than older children, girls had larger ID's than boys, and children from higher socioeconomic levels had larger ID's than their age and sex equivalents at lower levels (Getzels & Walsh, 1958).

In all, these studies favor third person stubs, and they are discrepant from clinical findings. It may well be that in the population employed lies an answer to the discrepancies. The clinical populations were ostensibly acting as their own agents, seeking help with their problems. It would make sense for them to reveal themselves on first person stubs. All groups whose responses favored third person stubs as revelatory were students, and their private attitudes must be assessed more indirectly. This explanation gains credence in light of Meltzoff's findings. When he asked college students to simulate emotional disturbance, he found self-references in their completions increased markedly (Meltzoff, 1951).

Finally, a caution has been expressed by Stricker and Dawson, who varied first and third person stems of the Rotter ISB. Their subjects were psychiatric patients, who ought to have favored first person stubs. They found, alas, that neither instructions nor stub person had differential effects and concluded that variations along these dimensions may be gratuitous (Stricker & Dawson, 1966).

SCT use in personality research. The kibbutz is an Israeli experiment in community living which entails marked changes in family patterns. Personality development among kibbutz children deserves close study, because of its social and psychological implications. Rabin has conducted a series of cross-sectional comparative studies of kibbutz and non-kibbutz children, using sentence completion techniques as one of his instruments. He modified the Sacks SCT for use with children and adolescents. With young male adults, he used an existing Israeli army SCT. In all cases, he was interested in evaluating possible differences along personality dimensions between these groups from different environments (Rabin, 1965).

He found differences among children, particularly in relation to goals. Kibbutz children tend to define short-term, altruistic goals. Non-kibbutz children are more long-range and personal. Adolescents were reasonably consistent with their child equivalents on these dimensions. In addition, kibbutz children appeared reluctant to admit the experience of fear and were surprisingly moralistic in the sexual area. The young army men from the kibbutz were not much different from their non-kibbutz brethren, except in being more direct (perhaps less defensive) and more dependent on group action.

Reliability and validity

Reliability is pretty much a function of particular sentence completion tests. Most reliability studies have been inter-judge comparisons or matchings, and were reported with their respective test. This author recalls no estimate that was poor and many which were highly satisfactory. Even in one case of split-half reliability, the correlation was .85 (Rotter, 1951). As with other techniques, familiarity of judges with the test is a factor in reliability (Stricker & Dawson, 1966). It seems fair to say that reliability is generally less of a problem with sentence completion tests than it is with most projective techniques.

The same conclusion can be drawn with respect to validity. Concurrent validity is good, and predictive validity is also high. Whether it be global impression, as was the case with assessment of OSS operatives and clinical psychologists, prediction of response to psychotherapy (cf. Morton, in Rotter, 1951), or even remaining in therapy (Hiler, 1959), the method has merit. The author concurs fully with Murstein, who says, "'The Sentence Completion Method is a valid test, generally speaking, and probably the most valid of all the projective techniques reported in the literature" (Murstein, 1965, pp. 777).

Clinical applications

Sentence completion methods are often used as preliminary screening devices and as part of a battery. They are a first measure, hence can serve to generate hypotheses to be followed up in individual testing or interview. Seldom if ever do they stand alone as assessment devices.

The range of situations in which they are employed is vast. Probably their greatest application is in identification of psychopathology; but they have also been used rather successfully in predicting adjustment in marriage (Inselberg, 1964) and in evaluation of prospects for executive management positions.[16] They are used extensively and flexibly. It is quite probable that they will continue to enjoy wide usage.

Research applications

Sentence completions are very much used in research, both in action areas and more basic studies. Probably the fact that there is such a proliferation of different sentence completion tests will make work on the method itself more difficult. However, it is in part the very flexibility of the method, which allows stub content to be developed specifically to criteria, that has led to the profusion. It is hard to fault success, even at cost to methodological questions.

Until recently, one problem in doing large scale research with these devices was mechanical. Responses had to be categorized manually. Now, electronic assistance is at hand. Goldberg reported a study in which sociometric choice was compared with sentence completion content with children (Goldberg, 1966). She had two major hypotheses: 1) that children well-liked by classmates would reveal different structures on the SCT than students not well-liked; and 2) that a computer could perform this analysis. Both hypotheses were confirmed, thus making the computer a clinical and research ally whose potential contribution to method and technique are incalculable.

In brief summary, sentence completion methods are generally assumed to have been developed from word association tests. The latter flourished· in the context of psychoanalytic theories and seem to be used less frequently clinically at present, although there has been continuing interest

16The Frederick Chusid Company. Sidney Barasch, personal communication, 1966.

in word associations by experimental psychologists. Sentence completion methods, on the other hand, continue to perform well. They are versatile and flexible techniques, which can be adapted easily to different settings. Reliability and validity are at least as impressive for these measures as for any projective techniques. Clinical and research workers find sentence completions helpful and productive—this despite lack of consensus regarding some structural characteristics of sentence stubs. Finally, the method seems to be adaptable for analysis by computer, a development which can prove quite valuable, in applied as well as research endeavors.

REFERENCES

Alexander, F. G., & Selsnick, S. T. *The History of Psychiatry*. New York: Harper and Row, 1966.

Appelbaum, S. A. Automatic and selective processes in the word associations of brain-damaged and normal subjects. *J. Pers.*, 1960a, *28*, 64-72.

Appelbaum, S. A. The word association test expanded. *Bull. Menninger Clin.*, 1960b, *24*, 258-264.

Appelbaum, S. A. The expanded word association test as a measure of psychological deficit associated with brain-damage. *J. clin. Psychol.*, 1963, *19*, 78-84.

Bell, J. E. *Projective Techniques*. New York: Longmans, Green, 1948.

Bilodeau, E. A., & Howell, D. C. *Free Association Norms*. Washington, D.C.: Office of Naval Research, 1965.

Conners, J. E., Wolkon, G. H., Haefner, D. P., & Stotsky, B. A. Outcome of post-hospital rehabilitative treatment of mental patients as a function of ego strength. *J. counsel. Psychol.*, 1960, *7*, 278-282.

Cromwell, R. L., & Lundy, R. M. Productivity of clinical hypotheses on a sentence completion test. *J. consult. Psychol.*, 1954, *18*, 421-424.

Dorris, R. J., Levinson, D. J., & Hanfmann, Eugenia. Authoritarian personality studied by a new variation of the sentence completion technique. *J. abn. soc. Psychol.*, 1954, *49*, 99-108.

Forer, B. R. Word association and sentence completion methods. In Rabin, A. I., & Haworth, Mary R. (Eds.) . *Projective Techniques with Children*. New York: Grune and Stratton, 1960.

Getzels, J. W. The assessment of personality and prejudice by the method of paired direct and projective questionnaires. Unpublished doctoral dissertation. Harvard University, 1951.

Getzels, J. W., & Walsh, J. J. The method of paired direct and projective questionnaires in the study of attitude structure and socialization. *Psychol. Monogr.*, 1958, 72, 1, (Whole No. 454) .

Gidynski, Christina B. Quantification of a sentence completion method with depressed patients. Mimeographed report, Duke University Medical Center, 1958.

Goldberg, Janice B. Computer analysis of sentence completions. *J. proj. Techn.*, 1966, *1*, 37-45.

Goldberg, P. A. A review of sentence completion methods in personality assessment. *J. proj. Techn. Pers. Assess.*, 1965, *29*, 12-45.

Hanfmann, Eugenia, & Getzels, J. W. Studies of the sentence completion test. *J. proj. Techn.*, 1953, *17*, 280-294.

Hiler, E. W. The sentence completion test as a predictor of continuation in psychotherapy. *J. consult. Psychol.*, 1959, *23*, 544-549.

Holsopple, J. Q., & Miale, Florence R. *Sentence Completion.* Springfield, Ill.: Charles C Thomas, 1954.

Inselberg, Rachel M. The sentence completion technique in the measurement of marital satisfaction. *J. Marriage Family*, 1965, *26*, 339-341.

Jenkins, R. L., & Blodgett, Eva. Prediction of success or failure of delinquent boys from sentence completion. *Amer. J. Orthopsychiat.*, 1960, *30*, 741-756.

Lindzey, G. On the classification of projective techniques. *Psychol. Bull.*, 1959, *56*, 158-168.

Lindzey, G. *Projective Techniques and Cross-cultural Research.* New York: Appleton-Century-Crofts, 1961.

Meltzoff, J. The effect of mental set and item structure on response to a projective test. *J. abn. soc. Psychol.*, 1951, *46*, 177-189.

Murstein, B. I. *Handbook of Projective Techniques.* New York: Basic Books, 1965.

O. S. S. Assessment Staff. *Assessment of Men.* New York: Rinehart, 1948.

Palermo, D. S., & Jenkins, J. J. *Word Association Norms.* Minneapolis: University of Minnesota Press, 1964.

Peck, R., & McGuire, C. Measuring changes in mental health with the sentence completion technique. *Psych. Rep.*, 1959, *5*, 151-160.

Rabin, A. I. *Growing Up in the Kibbutz.* New York: Springer, 1965.

Rapaport, D., Gill, M., & Schafer, R. *Diagnostic Psychological Testing*, Vol. 2. Chicago: Year Book, 1946.

Rohde, Amanda R. *The Sentence Completion Method.* New York: Ronald Press, 1957.

Rorschach, H. *Psychodiagnostics* (Transl. by Lemkau, P. & Kronenberg, B.) New York: Grune and Stratton, 1949.

Rotter, J. B. Word association and sentence completion methods. In Anderson, H. H., & Anderson, Gladys L. (Eds.). *An Introduction to Projective Techniques.* New York: Prentice-Hall, 1951. Pp. 279-311.

Sacks, J. M. Effect upon projective responses of stimuli referring to the subject and others. *J. consult. Psychol.*, 1949, *13*, 12-20.

Sacks, J. M., & Levy, S. The sentence completion test. In Abt, L., & Bellak, L. (Eds.). *Projective Psychology.* New York: Knopf, 1950. Pp. 357-402.

Stein, M. I. The record and a sentence completion test. *J. consult. Psychol.*, 1949, *13*, 448-449.

Stotsky, B. A., & Weinberg, H. The prediction of the psychiatric patient's work adjustment. *J. counsel. Psychol.*, 1956, *3*, 3-7.

Stotsky, B. A., Sacks, J. M., & Daston, P. G. Predicting the work performance of psychiatric aides by psychological tests. *J. counsel. Psychol.*, 1956, *3*, 193-199.

Stricker, G., & Dawson, D. D. The effect of first person and third person instructions and stems on sentence completion responses. *J. proj. Tech.*, 1966, *30*, 169-171.

Sundberg, N. D. The practice of psychological testing in clinical services in the United States. *Amer. Psychol.*, 1961, *16*, 79-83.

Wells, F. L., & Ruesch, J. *Mental Examiners' Handbook*, Rev. ed. New York: The Psychological Corporation, 1945.

Wells, F. L. Foreword. In Holsopple, J. Q. & Miale, Florence R. *Sentence Completion.* Springfield, Ill.: Charles C Thomas, 1954.

10

Story Completion Methods

LEONARD M. LANSKY

History

1923-1940: Research work and criteria for story completion methods

History should start with beginnings . . . "Once upon a time . .." But in this instance, the beginnings are obscure. Recent writers (Wursten, 1960; Miller, 1960) have presented the Madeline Thomas stories (Thomas, 1937) and the Duess fables (Duess, 1940) as the first story completion tasks. The word "task" is important because clinical tools were not considered tests; rather, they were part of the clinician's armamentarium to be used whole, in part, or even with on-the-spot modifications as aides in working with children.

Yet there were earlier story completion instruments—I dare not use the word "test" yet. Each of those earlier tasks was embedded in a research program. Piaget (1932) asked children to complete stories as part of his study of how children learn to make moral judgments. Before him, Hartshorne and May (1928) used story beginnings in their work on character and deceit. And before them, McGrath (1923) used a story completion instrument in her little-known study of children's moral development.

These research efforts seem to be unrecognized in discussions of story completion methods. Indeed the idea itself (the story completion technique) is still a somewhat illegitimate child in projective testing. Despite its long history—such tasks are certainly older than either the Rorschach or TAT—the justly famous and invaluable compendia by Buros (1961, 1965) contain no references to any story completion method. Furthermore, until recently (Wursten, 1960), story completion tasks have not received a separate chapter in books on projective techniques, a tradition still honored in Murstein's (1965a) volume which pays no attention to the methods to be discussed here.

There is also no mention of story completion methods in two volumes in research methods in anthropology (Hsu, 1961; Lindzey, 1961) despite the cross cultural work of Anderson and Anderson (1954) and Métraux

(1955) with these methods and their particular suitability to work with all societies. It goes without saying that story materials—folk tales, legends, dreams, and the like—have been used extensively by anthropologists. The story completion method, however, is a new tool in that field.

The newness of the techniques to anthropology may explain why they were not mentioned in volumes on projective methods. However, one theme of this chapter may provide a better clue to the seeming illegitimacy of these methods. If you want to use story beginnings, whatever the setting, just go ahead and make up your own stories; tailor-make your instrument to suit your own problems. This cavalier attitude, which has, as we shall see, considerable justification and support from many authorities in the field, has one important consequence: There are few measures which have been *carefully* designed and for which there are data on reliability and validity. Thus the lack of recognition by experts in testing—because such methods are not tests, at least not in the typical use of the term.

But before the reader protests that he knows several published tests which are story completion methods—structured doll play tests, puppetry, TAT's with verbal descriptions, dramatic production tests, and the like— I ought to define "story completion methods." In this discussion there are three criteria for a story completion method: the client or subject is given 1) a *prose stimulus* which is 2) a *story beginning* or *plot outline* which he is 3) *to complete.*

These criteria are quite restrictive but they are dictated by theoretical issues. Prose presentation is different from prose which is accompanied by dolls or doll play (Lynn, 1959; Korner, 1949), puppets (Bender & Woltmann, 1936; Woltmann, 1951; Haworth, 1957), pictures (Raven, 1951) and other stimuli. In these instances the subject is given additional stimulus material beyond his own cognitive, motivational, and affective associations to the words and structure in the story beginning. It seems reasonable to assume that different psychological processes are brought to bear when stimuli are thus added to the prose story beginning.

The second criterion also has a theoretical base. A story beginning or plot is not equivalent to a fraction of a sentence, even when the fraction is "Once upon a time. . . ." One obvious difference is that the sentence stub invites completion of that sentence, whereas, a "What happened next?" after a story beginning asks for a continuation of the plot, a feeling for consequences, and the like. Another story method which is omitted by the second criterion asks the subject to tell a story, favorite or otherwise, or to repeat a story which has just been told to him (Despert & Potter, 1936). Repetition and memory are important psychological processes and are probably related to personality variables. However, these processes are not the same as the personality variables themselves.

The third criterion focuses on the word "completion." The subject or client may complete the story by giving his own responses (Piaget,

1932) or by selecting one or more solutions from a list offered to him (Roody, 1943). Either technique is different from asking the person to explain *why* the hero or heroine did what he did. This question tends to elicit background material including the characters' motives, thoughts, and feelings prior to or during the events depicted in the story beginning (French, 1955; French & Chadwick, 1956). Such responses do not continue or complete the story, however much they may give the clinician or researcher a more complete picture of the client or subject.

In order to look more closely at these criteria, let us examine some items from the three research efforts which we have mentioned. One of McGrath's items was:

> "The four boys had been playing hard all evening and were very hungry by nine o'clock, yet they did not dare go home. Jim proposed that they have a 'lark.' He was game, if the others would back him up to sneak around the corner of old Dominico's fruit stand and roll out a watermelon. If they once got it they could run faster than the old Italian, so there was no danger of being caught.
> "Do you think this was a good thing for the little boys to do? ... Why? ..." (McGrath, 1923, p. 35).

Her questions at the end request a "yes" or "no" and an explanation in terms of moral principles. Indeed, the pointedness of the questions seems to preclude the subject's completing the story; the item looks more like an information or attitude test item than a "projective" one, despite the complex, emotional, and conflictful nature of the story stub and the critical question "why?" In addition, the "why" violates the third criterion; it asks for explanations, not a continuation of the story. But in this instance, the third criterion was not violated because of instructions and the set which McGrath gave to her subjects. She did not ask only for feelings and justification. The subjects were to give more full explanations; to answer the "why," some continued the plot by explaining the consequences of the hero's choices. In some items, additional plot material was requested.

Hartshorne and May's (1938) stories also fit the criteria. In their study of deceit, one measure contained the following instructions:

> "The situations which are described below have actually happened to children. Read the facts given. Then write what you think happened next. Never mind about what ought to have happened. Just guess what actually did happen. Write your answers on the lines" (Hartshorne & May, 1928, p. 292).

Their first item in this instrument is:

1. Mary received a very poor mark in her school work. She took the report card home and showed it to her father. What did her father do? (Hartshorne & May, 1928, p. 292) .

One of Piaget's items is as follows:

"One Thursday afternoon, a mother asked her little girl and boy to help her around the house, because she was tired. The girl was to dry the plates and the boy was to fetch in some wood. But the little boy (or girl) went and played in the street. So the mother asked the other one to do all the work. What did he say?" (Piaget, 1932, p. 276) .

In these examples, the stimulus was a prose story beginning which the subject was to complete. One interesting difference between Hartshorne and May's story and Piaget's is that the former implied that there was a correct answer. They asked "What actually happened?", whereas Piaget did not. He merely asked the child to complete the story.

A fourth research effort belongs with the above three. As part of his pioneering investigation of personality, Murray (1937) devised the story elaboration test. For each of 32 dramatic situations, the subject was to develop a story. For example,

"A man is becoming a burden to his family. They would like to get rid of him." (Murray, 1937, p. 130) .

The obscurity of these beginnings of story completion methods seems to be an historical puzzle. Yet the puzzle can be solved if one looks at the purpose of these stories. Each set was embedded within a relatively obscure complex psychological study: McGrath's study seems to be unknown; Hartshorne and May, while often cited, is rarely examined in detail; for a long time Piaget's work was unrecognized although it has recently been rediscovered in light of the new interest in developmental psychology and cognition (Flavell, 1963) ; and Murray's rich work is immortalized more for the TAT than for his "multimeasure-multitrait" approach to personality, an approach which is gaining recognition anew because it can now be described in such "scientific" measurement terms (Campbell & Fiske, 1959) . In other words, the studies in which the story completion methods appeared were themselves ahead of their time. Or, to put it yet another way, these studies and their methods were left by the wayside after World War II when American psychological research was dominated by statistical techniques and hypothetico-deductive systems.

There is an additionally striking point about the story completion items and the researchers which is critical here. Each method is about morality and moral values. The items refer to conflicts which became, even as an object of study, almost a taboo topic in American psychology. Perhaps in some time to come we shall gain more perspective on this period of American psychology in order to explain these facts. We are certainly seeing, as noted above, a change from the period after World War II. In addition to the new interest in Piaget, there is certainly a new concern about ecological methods (Barker, 1963); Murray's contributions are beginning to be put into a long overdue proper perspective (White, 1963) ; the topic of moral standards occupies many researchers as well as many practitioners. As we shall see later in this chapter, the greatest single use of story completion methods has occurred in the last eight to ten years and has been in studies of guilt and moral values (Kohlberg, 1963, 1964; Hoffman, 1963) .

1923-1940-Clinical work

During the 1930's there was also considerable interest in stories for use with disturbed children. For example, Bender and Woltmann (1936) suggested the value of puppet shows during therapy; Despert and Potter (1936) asked children to tell stories; and several workers reported and theorized about the value of play, with and without dolls, and with and without stories. The interested reader can find a thorough account of such projective techniques in Sargeant's (1945) excellent review article.

These methods, however, do not meet the three criteria of this chapter. So far as I can tell, the first set of prose (only) story beginnings for use in the clinic was published in 1937, in French, by Madeline Thomas (1937) , a Swiss child analyst. In order to open up the child and thus facilitate diagnostic work in a child guidance clinic, she devised a 15-item story completion task, *not a test*. The distinction is important: the Madeline Thomas stories represented for their author, and for Wursten (1960) who translated them into English in 1947, "a clinical method of investigation" (Wursten, 1960, p. 193) . Thus, the instructions are quite vague, the user is advised that he can lengthen or shorten the task, add stories, make them more or less specific, etc. In brief, the stories are to be part of a subtle, complex, clinical diagnostic session and are to be used as the clinician sees fit.

The stories themselves appear in Wursten's (1960) review of story completion methods. The end of the first story resembles the question-answer technique of McGrath:

"A boy (or girl) goes to school. During recess he does not play with the other children, he stays by himself in a corner. Why?" (Wursten, 1960, p. 192) .

The second story, however, asks for a completion:

"A boy fights with his brother. Mother comes. What is going to happen?" (Wursten, 1960, p. 192) .

Another early story completion task also came from work with children in Switzerland. In 1940, Duess (1940) published, in French, the

Duess fables which were later translated into English by Despert (1946) by whose name they are familiarly known in the psychiatric and psychoanalytic clinical literature. Fine revised and extended the set of fables. In his set, the first one is:

> "A daddy and mommy bird and their little birdie are asleep in a nest on the branch of a tree. All of a sudden a big wind blows; it shakes the tree, and the nest falls on the ground. The three birds awaken all of a sudden. The daddy flies quickly to one pine tree, the mommy to another pine tree. The little bird knows how to fly. What is the little bird going to do?" (Fine, 1948, p. 106).

The first story in these two tasks is about independence and dependence, key variables in psychoanalytic thinking about child and adult adjustment and development. In the Madeline Thomas set, the other themes are difficult to classify. Some represent fragments of story beginnings which are connected one to the other. For example, stories 9, 10, and 11 go together.

> "9. It is evening. The boy is in bed, the day is ended, the light turned off. (a) What he does before going to sleep? (b) What is he thinking about? (c) One evening he cries, he is sad. What about?
> "10. Then he goes to sleep. What does he dream about?
> "11. He wakes up in the middle of the night. He is very much afraid. What of?" (Wursten, 1960, p. 193).

The original set of ten Duess fables is also contained in Wursten's chapter on story completion methods (Wursten, 1960) where he discusses these two instruments in considerable detail. For this set, it is easy to identify the themes because Duess labelled each one. The set includes, in part: independence versus fixation to a parent; primal scene and jealousy of the parents' union; weaning complex and sibling rivalry; hostility, death wishes, guilt feelings, self-punishment. Fine doubled the number of fables. In doing so, he did not add any themes so much as he provided more than one item for each. He sees the major variables in the task as dependency, hostility, identification, sibling rivalry, reactions to parental rejection, castration fears, Oedipus complex, and fears and wishes. The theoretical heterogeneity of the list is impressive. The fables are a veritable clinician's grab bag.

Fine's instructions are clear, however. The user is to judge which items to use, in what order, with what supplementary material, and with which additional stories. The coding scheme is also idiosyncratic, based upon themes, defenses, etc., seen by the diagnostician. The key question for both these instruments is, "Who is to be the boss, instrument or clinician?" The answer is unequivocal: the clinician. This theme continues in the clinical work. Furthermore, as we have noted, it also fits the attitude of researchers who use story completions.

1940-49-Clinical work

During this period, nothing was done with McGrath's, Hartshorne and May's, Piaget's, or Murray's use of story techniques for the study of moral standards. There were, however, several new research uses of the methods. (Before looking at these efforts, we shall examine the clinical work.) A number of new story completion methods were devised in the 1940's and considerable work was also done with the Madeline Thomas Stories and the Duess fables. With respect to these latter two tasks, again history is obscure. It is difficult to tell who influenced whom.

For the Madeline Thomas Stories, Wursten (1960), writing in 1960, tells us that he translated them in 1947. The translations were not published, however. Seaton (1949), in presenting background for his own story completion measure, mentioned Anthony's study (1940) of British children's attitudes towards death and notes that Anthony used the Thomas stories. Unfortunately I have not been able to obtain Anthony's book in order to compare his translation to Wursten's. In 1953, Mills (1953) reported that he could find no published account of the stories when he did his master's thesis (Mills, 1949). In addition, he noted that his survey of 50 clinics revealed that only two were familiar with the Thomas stories.

Similar historical confusion reigns with respect to the Duess fables. The most often cited translation is Despert's which was published as part of a clinical research report (Despert, 1946). The data were collected in 1943. However, Mosse (1954), who used the fables in a clinical study, reported that Wertham (1941) had translated them as early as 1941. Again, my data are secondhand; I have not seen Wertham's (1941) paper. We have already noted that Fine (1948) presented a revised and expanded version of the Despert Fables in 1948. He did not mention Wertham.

The point here offers a task for some future historian. How widespread was the use of these two clinical measures during the 1940's? How many clinical psychologists and psychiatrists translated them for local use? Mill's (1953) report only gives a partial answer. Another question is: How many modified versions of the stories or fables were tried out? Or, to ask a parallel question, how many unknown story completion tasks are there? This issue relates, of course, to the clinical attitude which dominates the reports of these methods.

There were other clinical methods produced during the 1940's and they continue this attitude. One is quite obscure (Roody, 1943); the other well known (Sargeant, 1944). As her doctoral dissertation, Roody devised a "plot completion test" for use by high school guidance counselors, school psychiatrists (sic), and teachers of literature. The ten plots, which were not published, dealt with life situations, e.g., parent-child and teacher-pupil relations, and the like.

For our purposes, the issues are: 1) the now-familiar clinical orientation and 2) the innovative use of five carefully chosen endings to each story beginning. These were selected by having judges rate a number of possible alternatives. The five particular solutions were: happy ending; rewarding the likeable and punishing the less amiable response; "a morbid preference for unhappy outcomes"; rejecting the problem and picking an easier problem; and "a superstitious willingness to credit mystical powers and other unscientific beliefs." The subjects' task was interesting. First, for each plot, each S was to rank the five alternatives as to their true-to-life probability. Then he (or she) was to mark the one alternative for each story which made the "best" story, whether true to life or not. Lastly, *if there was time,* the S was to check the most advisable ending for each story. These instructions plus the psychodynamically unsophisticated descriptions of the alternatives may explain the obscurity of Roody's test. There can be little doubt that her intent was not to add to scientific knowledge, but to put a useful tool into the hands of teachers and counselors.

Sargeant's Test of Insight (1944) provides a dramatic contrast to Roody's with respect to theoretical and technical sophistication, but it maintains a strong clinical orientation. For example, the client or subject is to respond to the set of stories in any order he chooses and to omit any stories he wishes. The sophistication occurs in Sargeant's detailed analysis of the requirements of a projective test. The reader who is seriously interested in the topic should study her discussion.

The important issue for this review concerns the ambiguity and neutrality of the stimulus. A useful clinical tool, according to Sargeant, would "meet the requirements of *neutrality, meaninglessness, and disguised purpose,* which at the same time successfully calls forth a response from the subject." (Sargeant, 1944, p. 2.) The italics are mine.

Sargeant's stories are more plot outlines than stories. She called them "armatures," a term she borrowed from art and architecture. She wanted to describe "the bare bones of a situation" which could be "adapted to the creator's purpose." (Sargeant, 1944, p. 4.)

The key points here are: 1) the armature can be adjusted to the creator's usage, i.e., the test user can adapt the procedure as he sees fit; 2) the armatures supposedly are quite neutral and are the bare bones of a situation. Here are two:

1. A young man who is working or studying away from home gets a letter from his mother, after the death of his father, asking him to move back home.
   a. What did he do and why?

b. How did he feel?" (Sargeant, 1944, p. 31)

2. A girl finds that her friends get dates by playing up to the men and taking the initiative. They tell her she is slow.

a. What did she do and why?

b. How did she feel?" (Sargeant, 1944, p. 34)

The questions certainly fit the criteria for a story completion method, but the stories are hardly "neutral." The second is clearly about conflict between sexual needs and other motives. Indeed, the assumptions behind Sargeant's criteria of neutrality, meaninglessness and disguised purpose have recently been questioned in projective testing, especially with regard to the stimulus specificity of TAT pictures (Murstein, 1965b). That instrument is discussed in Chapter 7 of this volume. By questioning these assumptions, later workers with story completion methods (Allinsmith, W., 1960) have also pointed the way towards some particular values of the prose stimulus. By systematically varying the intensity of the conflict, the meaning and the disguise in the story beginning,—to mention but a few variables—the clinician and researcher gain flexibility and great power for testing theoretical and methodological hunches.

Sargeant's items, as well as the other examples already given in this chapter, belie the points of neutrality and meaninglessness. Perhaps this entire attitude—the assumed neutrality of the stimulus—is another manifestation of the unconscious self-deception which Rosenthal (1963) has suggested is operating in much psychological research. The issue of disguised purpose is another matter and will be discussed in a later section of this chapter.

During the 1940's, Fassett (1948) pursued further the scoring and reliability of Sargeant's measure. He created two sets of instructions. One was Sargeant's—do as many items as you wish—the other involved grouping the items and required the subject to do at least one item from each group. The groups were not labelled for the subjects but one group contained items about the family, another about sex, etc. Using 25 college girls for each group of stories, Fassett found that there were more conflictful endings written under the new instruction but more items were done under Sargeant's more permissive one. The reliabilities were "satisfactory" in scoring the new form for the "approaches" and "solutions" to the problem; however, affect could not be scored reliably.

To summarize the clinical work of the 1940's, then, there were three methods used: the Madeline Thomas stories, the Despert fables, and Sargeant's Test of Insight into Human Motives. So far as we can tell, none of these efforts affected clinical work to any considerable degree.

1940-1949-Research work

The research efforts during this period were also meager. The first published study with a story completion method was by Zucker (1943). He studied the differences between delinquent and nondelinquent children's attachments to their parents, their peers, and the effects of parental moralization, using only three stories which he devised. He also discussed what makes an effective story: The author should "keep [it] as unstructured as possible within the limits of one's hypothesis" (Zucker, 1943, p. 38), in order to let each subject's past personality project as much as possible. The author should also create suspense and excitement and minimize hunch factors by whittling the story down to its essentials. This research work was probably done at about the same time as Sargeant's clinical test. It is striking that we find them making similar assumptions about how such a measure should be devised.

His instructions are also interesting: "I have three stories here, but I am going to read only part of each one to you. You're supposed to finish them, put an ending on them. Do you understand?" (Zucker, 1943, p. 33). As I hear these directions, the researcher implies that he knows the ending—he is reading only a part of the story he has in front of him. Perhaps the subjects did not give their own answers but rather gave the answers they thought the researcher already had.

My interpretation of his directions may explain why his 25 delinquents and 25 nondelinquent (they were Boy Scouts) 13-year-old boys differed significantly on two stories but not on all three. The first story was about two accidents, one involving his parents and the other a friend. The friend, however, needs blood. As compared to the Boy Scouts, significantly more delinquents gave blood to their peer. In the third story, the child was caught stealing, was lectured by his father, and then was just walking down the street with a friend. In this story, the delinquents provided more theft stories than the Boy Scouts. The second story yielded no differences between the two groups of Ss. In it, the boy has a winning raffle ticket but has to choose between a red and green box, one of which contains the prize. His parents urge him to take the red box; his peers say the green one.

Let us assume that the Ss were trying to reproduce the story which E said he had written. What guesses might Boy Scouts and delinquents make about a middle-class E? What expectations might they have? The second story beginning, the one on which the two groups of Ss did not differ, is the least "emotionally loaded" of the three. The Ss might, as I see it, have difficulty in working out what E expected in this ambiguous story. There is no *a priori* argument for or against a parental or a peer choice. The boxes differ only in color. Serious accidents (the first story) and theft (the third story) are more serious events than winning a prize by chance. In these two stories, it seems that the expectations are more clear. In the story about the accident, the scouts might expect that E would expect them to be loyal to their parents; the delinquents, on the other hand, might think that E was checking to see if they would give blood to a friend. In the story about theft, the Scouts would get the point at once and so would the delinquents. They would be aware that E expected that they would continue to steal. Thus they might produce endings which fit the expectations of E.

If the reader is disconcerted by the above discussion, the point has been made. As weak as the above arguments are, they are as good—or as bad—as the hypotheses about superego which Zucker brought to the study. There is a tenuous chain of reasoning between the selection of parental responses versus peer responses and feelings about attachments to parents and peers and the effects of parental moral teaching. There are too many alternative explanations of the story responses which do as good or as poor a job of explaining the data. As we shall see in a later section of this chapter, the interpretation of story completion items does tend to go far beyond the data and is especially insensitive to the transactions between subject (client) and experimenter (therapist). This fault is particularly serious in studies which use very few story items and very few measures of each variable.

We have already mentioned Seaton's (1949) study. His title, like Roody's and Sargeant's, called attention to the story completion method, although his major interest was in the children's feelings of being accepted or rejected. His stories, which were selected after extensive pilot study, were about mothers' and children's attitudes towards the same events. For each item, the children first made a free response to the instruction: "Now write what you would expect the person in the story to say or do next." (Seaton, 1949, p. 13). Then each S chose for that story beginning one of three alternative endings which was most like his (her) own. Essentially, the three alternatives described an accepting parent, a rejecting parent, and a neutral parent. His subjects were sixth and seventh grade students, half of whom were under social casework care, the other half serving as controls. The hypothesis that the two groups would respond differently to the stories was not confirmed. The students in treatment were not prone to select the rejecting endings more. Our only explanation for the lack of difference is the reliance on a single behavioral index—rejection or acceptance—to study the complexities of children's reactions to these stories.

In 1946, Despert published a translation of the Duess fables as part of the report of a psychosomatic study of fifty stuttering children. Here, in contrast to Seaton's work, several measures were used. The study is, however, a clinical one; there is no control group and Despert reported only that the fables were useful in understanding the children. The implication, however, is similar to that in a more completely reported clinical study by Schwartz (1950), namely that the fables do add to the total picture of the client.

The final period of this historical review is dominated by research efforts; there are few clinical studies although one development is very important, namely, measures for use with the blind.

The work with the Madeline Thomas stories has already been mentioned. Mills (1953) surveyed 50 clinics and found that the method was virtually unknown. He also devised a version of the stories to be used with college students as an "opening wedge in testing and counseling relationships." (Mills, 1954, p. 2). Mills's stories and his prescriptions for their use fit the clinical model which we have already seen for the Despert fables and Thomas stories. His stories are clinical tools which are useful for augmenting the clinician's judgments.

A similar description applies to the more extensive work since 1950 with the Despert fables. The first item of note is Schwartz's clinical case study of a 10½-year-old Negro boy in which the child was given the Stanford-Binet, H-T-P, Rorschach, and Despert fables (Schwartz, 1950). Schwartz's words summarize the situation: "A test like the Despert fables, devised to elicit material at the more conscious level, supplied more specific information than the more general personality picture gained from the 'major' projective tests." (Schwartz, 1950, p. 172).

We have also mentioned Mosse's (1954) discussion of the fables. Her report merely asserts the usefulness of the stories and the story idea in clinical and psychiatric work. Piexotto (1956, 1957, 1961) provided data on the reliability of the fables for children ages 3 to 8 and also gave a listing of the popular responses for children between 6 and 14. Such normative data is, as we have noted, quite rare and most useful.

Again, as in the 1940's, some impressive work was done with Sargeant's armatures. Sargeant (1953) herself published a volume on the measure; however, so far as the published clinical and research literature is concerned, its use is not widespread. Indeed, the only account which focuses on the test itself is one by Schuman (1952) who demonstrated that inter-scorer reliabilities over .80 could be obtained when detailed scoring rules were given to coders.

Engel extended Sargeant's ideas by devising a parallel test for children, the Children's Insight Test (Engel, 1958; Engel & Rechenberg, 1961). The armatures are barrenly and simply stated; each concerns a possible everyday life situation, e.g., "A boy came home from school and found that his dog ran away. What did he do? How did he feel?" (Engel & Rechenberg, 1961, p. 158). The code is quite formal and concentrates on three categories; affective discharge, management and control, and signs of pathological thinking. According to Engel and Rechenberg, reliabilities between scorers, split-half reliabilities, and test-retest reliability were as satisfactory as those for other projective tests with children.

In 1957, Lebo began a series of investigations (Lebo & Harrington,

1957; Lebo, 1959; Lebo & Sherry, 1959, Lebo 1960; Lebo & Bruce, 1960) using verbal presentations of the TAT. Two major ideas emerge from this work: one, verbal descriptions offer great flexibility which can also be exploited in devising tests for other cultures through translations; two, the verbal TAT can be used as a projective test with sightless persons. The only discouraging point at this writing is that no work has appeared on this idea since 1960; no one has tried other story completion measures with the blind.

Two other efforts need to be mentioned to complete the picture of clinical work. Weisskopf-Joelson and Wich (1961) examined the productivity (the number of words) of introductory psychology students on three successive tasks: 1) tell a story; 2) complete a story in response to an "armature"; and 3) the TAT. The three procedures gave them progressively fewer words. They did not discuss the thematic material which they obtained.

At a workshop on the use of projective techniques with the school-aged child, Brown (1962) reported on the Koppitz or Musterberg Incomplete Stories which are published in the mimeographed report of the conference (Smith, 1962). They fit the pattern we have already described for the Thomas stories and Despert Fables, i.e., they are useful tasks which the clinician may use when he sees fit in any way he wants to draw whatever conclusions he likes. In short, the user is master and the reliability and/or validity of the instrument is almost incidental.

1950-Present-Research work

This review has called attention to three themes in story completion methods: 1) The domination of clinical work and a clinical orientation; 2) a relatively unsophisticated theoretical approach in the research efforts; and 3) an overwhelming stress on looseness of structure as a prerequisite for story beginnings. These three emphases have shifted in the recent past: most work of the last sixteen years has been in research which incorporates sophisticated theoretical analyses which have in turn led to arguments for highly structured and almost manifestly obvious story beginnings. As we shall see, these developments have paralleled, especially in very recent years, growing interests in cognition and phenomenology, interests which suggest that, like the new look in motivation (Dember, 1965), the new look in story completion methods may not be so new after all.

The first two published reports of this period introduced one new feature: an increasing theoretical sophistication with particular emphasis on psychoanalytic thinking. Miller and Stine (1951) devised a set of stories to assess the degree to which 7- to 14-year-old children regress to pregenital modes of thinking under such stresses as castration threat and sibling rivalry. They used these scores to predict the sociometric status of the pupils. Working from a similar theoretical position, Friedman (1952) used some of the Despert fables, as well as some new ones on castration threat, and some TAT-like pictures to test hypotheses about the castration and Oedipal complexes in children.

The results of both studies were promising. Miller and Stine (1951) coded their stories for references to: orality, anality, and magical thinking by counting references to food, olfaction, touch, smearing, cleanliness, mythical characters, etc. The total of these and other pregenital signs correlated, as predicted, with sociometric status of the children, with the more rejected children showing more pregentality. One strikingly unexpected result was that the chosen children had significantly more anal scores than the rejected ones. The authors interpreted this finding as evidence of the value of anal character traits during latency in American culture.

Friedman's results similarly confirmed psychoanalytic hypotheses about conflict. His three fables varied in stimulus strength, i.e., the directness with which the castration threat was expressed. The three stories themselves indicate the shift from a suggested castration of a dog (Fable 1), to a suggested loss to a monkey (Fable 2), to a loss to a child (Fable 3). The second fable was:

> "Once there was a little monkey named Franky (Mary). He had a long curly tail. He liked this tail so much that he looked at it every day and he had all sorts of fun with it. One day, Frankie woke up and saw that something was different. What do you think had happened?" (Friedman, 1952, p. 73).

The important data for this report refer to differences between the stories. The dog's tail was removed least in the stories, the child's finger most. Fable 2 yielded the greatest range of removals; the figure was close to 50 percent. These and other results supported psychoanalytic thinking about conflict.

As we have seen, these researchers got promising results in their attempts to tap particular conflictful areas. However, although they did provide quite specific coding procedures and achieved good reliabilities from their scorers, they were concerned that their projected stimuli not be *too* specific. In comparing his stories to his pictures, Friedman expressed his concern thusly: "The unfinished fable seems to be the less ideal of the two [techniques] for such purposes. This is most probably due to the fact that the story's content must focus attention upon a crucial area to the extent that the child is aware of this focus. In contrast, the picture-card properties are not only more disguised because of their more symbolic nature, but also because the child's attention is not drawn to them through instructions." (Friedman, 1952, p. 126).

The second major shift in story completion methods also reflected the theoretical sophistication of this period. W. Allinsmith (1954, 1960) studied psychoanalytic hypotheses about the relationships between parental child-rearing practises in middle and lower class homes and the reactions to violations of moral standards by young adolescent boys. For the boys, he wanted to focus on the intensity of guilt in response to transgression. Thus he had to distinguish between responses motivated by feelings of guilt and those motivated by fear of being caught and punished. He reasoned that the intensity of guilt would vary for violations of "thou shalt nots" in different content areas: obedience, aggression towards authority, and stealing, to name a few. Thus he had to control content area. He also believed that the intensity of guilt would be affected by the relationship between the hero of the story and the person against whom the violation was committed. For example, aggressive thoughts about a stranger are less taboo than similar thoughts towards a supporting, respected, and close authority such as a coach or parent. These particular variables and others were derived from a theoretical analysis of moral standards.

Because of the theoretical analysis, it became clear that pictures would not serve as projective materials. They would not be precise enough to control several of the relevant variables. While clinical interviews might have been suitable, they would have had to be quite open-ended thus lack the stimulus control of a "test." Such interviews are also difficult to code and time-consuming to administer. Although he entertained the idea, Allinsmith also rejected situational tests. Two particular issues were vexing: 1) controlling the possibility of detection of the violation of standards; 2) varying the relationship to the other persons involved in the situation. Later researchers solved these problems with a number of ingenious designs. (Grinder & McMichael, 1963).

After considerable theoretical struggle, examination of alternative methods, and extensive pilot study, a set of quite long, highly-structured story beginnings was devised. One story was:

> "Charley and his friends have formed a club which meets every Saturday. Each week the club makes up a new secret rule which all the members have to follow for that week. Last Saturday Charley couldn't make the meeting, but one of the members told him that night what the rule for the week was to be. The rule was that every member must wear socks at all times including sleeping, except when taking a bath or at the moment of changing socks. Charley followed the rule carefully. Then on Tuesday morning he wakes up and realizes he didn't wear his socks to bed that night." (Allinsmith, W. 1954, p. 208).

In this story, it is clear that Charley cannot be caught; the reference group is Charley's peers; and the fact that Charley found out what the rule was and then followed it carefully establishes the importance of the rule to Charley. Thus confessions, punishments, and the like could be scored as evidence of Charley's guilt.

Allinsmith's results were promising but complex. He found statistically significant and psychologically meaningful associations between parental reports of child-rearing practices and the intensity of guilt displayed by the children in their story completions. For example, one story was about a son's disobedience to his mother's orders not to take down some boxes in her closet. The children who showed low guilt in response to this story had mothers who reported that they had weaned the boys early and had used rather severe toilet training methods. However, a similar association between guilt and child-rearing practices did not appear for stories about theft. These results fit some hypotheses about the specificity of moral training. According to Allinsmith (1960), it is reasonable to assume that internalization of moral standards follows a different developmental course for different content areas. In addition, there may be different intensities of internalization in the different areas.

The theoretical and methodological implications of these ideas are clear. In order to study moral standards, one must use quite specific methods. This idea, which has been confirmed in other research with story completion methods, points up a methodological weakness in Allinsmith's and similar studies. Insofar as each story beginning contains a unique configuration of moral content area (e.g., theft, disobedience), role relationship between the hero and other persons (e.g., coach, parent, peer), and degree of violation (e.g., temptation only or temptation and violation), the researcher is using a set of one item tests. Thus it is almost impossible to assess the reliability of the measure.

In the literature which follows Allinsmith's study, there is little recognition of this issue. Reliability data are usually confined to the reliability of two or more scorers, not to the reliability of a subject's responses to a subset of stories. To date, no one working with moral standards has produced a carefully matched set of stories in order to test moral responses in any single configuration of variables such as those listed above.

Despite these problems there are several advantages to the structured story completion method. As in the instance cited above, E can carefully create conflict situations designed for specific theoretical issues. In addition, by carefully varying the stimulus elements, E can test the range of any variable in the story: characteristics of the hero or of other persons, the needs and motives of the different persons, etc. Previous workers, especially clinicians, had recognized the flexibility inherent in story methods, but they had not explicitly noticed the potential advantages of making the input direct and highly specific. The concern over giving away the clinician's or researcher's hypotheses had dominated their thinking.

The issue is a real one, especially when the researcher comes to the interpretation of his data. Friedman (1952) expressed the pitfall in the quote above (compare page 303). If the subject is aware of E's hypotheses, will he respond honestly? No one knows, although there is some data in studies with incomplete stories that subjects are not aware of the researcher's intent. One line of evidence focuses on predicting responses under stress. W. Allinsmith's research was part of a broader project (Miller & Swanson, 1960) on moral standards (Aronfreed, 1960), styles of expressing aggression (B. Allinsmith, 1960), and defense mechanisms (Beardslee, 1960; Lansky, 1960). In Aronfreed's (1960) study of moral standards and the two studies of defense mechanisms, each S completed two sets of stories, one prior to and one following an experimental conflict situation. Interviews following these studies revealed that the Ss did not see any connection between the conflict arousal and the story tasks. Furthermore, theoretically meaningful predictions were confirmed. For example, Aronfreed found that college men with conflict about their sex-role identities tended to become more guilty after "accidentally" breaking a piece of apparatus whereas men without such conflict did not.

In these designs, the subjects were tested blind by the Es. Thus the possibilities of experimenter bias as an influence on the subjects seems to have been controlled. However, to date, no one has systematically varied experimenter bias in studies with structured story completion methods. Until such studies are done, the question of experimenter influence on subjects' responses to story completion items must remain open.

Yet there is some evidence that when subjects respond to story completion items, they (the subjects) are not aware of the researcher's hypotheses. If the researcher uses a rather special coding method to classify responses to stories, it is difficult to argue that a subject would be alert to the codes which were intended. A few examples illustrate the point. Bandura and Walters (1959) used some of W. Allinsmith's stories in their study of adolescent aggression. They looked at subjects' reparations following violations. Lansky, et al, (1961) used the W. Allinsmith stories in a study of the correlates of aggression in adolescent boys and girls. They scored the completions for denial of guilt. Rebelsky (Rebelsky, et al, 1963; Rebelsky, 1963) used structured stories to study several aspects of confession; Luria et al, (1963) used similar stories to study confession and other responses to transgression in Israeli children.

Grinder and McMichael (1963) used the task for another cross-cultural comparison, one between American and Samoan children. In this study, story completions were also compared to actual resistance to temptation. The projective measures of guilt which were derived from the story completion task were *not* consistently related to the behavioral indices of resistance to temptation. These findings raise another methodological problem in story completion methods, a problem familiar in projective testing: The responses to the projective test do not correlate consistently with supposedly relevant overt behaviors.

This is, of course, a central issue in all psychological testing. What do the responses tell you? What do they correlate with? What is their predictive validity? Insofar as Allinsmith (1960), Grinder and McMichael (1963) and other recent workers wanted to predict or generalize about overt moral behaviors, the Grinder and McMichael findings were a serious blow. Earlier, the question of predictive validity to overt behavior had not been raised. McGrath (1923) and the other early users of story completion methods were interested in the stories as one index of the *cognitive* components of moral standards. The story responses were seen as indices of these components rather than as stepping stones to the prediction of overt responses.

We shall return to this topic in discussing the underlying hypotheses and interpretations of story completion methods. For the reader who wishes to pursue the literature on moral standards, there are several excellent surveys of the literature (Burton, 1963; Hoffman, 1963; Kohlberg, 1963, 1964). Our concern here, however, is with story completion methods. These reviews include several studies which used another variant of the story completion method, one which is also theoretically sophisticated and which combines the clinical approach with the notion of structured stories. Boehm's (Boehm, 1962a; 1962b; Boehm & Nass, 1962; Boehm, 1964) technique is modeled after Piaget. The purpose of the research is to explore the development of concepts about moral standards. A carefully structured story is followed by a series of questions, some of which lead to further plot material. Boehm used Piaget's "clinical method" and saw each child individually. There were four stories: two about the evaluation of an act as to intent or result, and two about peer reciprocity versus dependence on adult authority. Boehm expected the children to identify with the children in the story and to respond on an affective, as well as on a purely intellectual level. The clinical method requires that E ask questions based upon the subject's responses.

Johnson (1962; Porteus & Johnson, 1965) used a similar method to test Piaget's theory of moral development.

A few examples will illustrate the success of these efforts. Again, as with Miller and Stine (1951) and Friedman (1952), we find that the story completion method is useful in testing theoretical work. Boehm concentrated on the cognitive ability of children to distinguish between right and wrong. The subjects in her studies range in age from 6 to 11 years. Among others, comparisons were made between children of different ages, different socioeconomic levels, and different religious backgrounds. One finding was that "Academically gifted children mature earlier in their moral judgments concerning distinctions between intentions and outcome of an action than children of average intelligence." (Boehm, 1962a, p. 589).

Two issues are important here. 1) Boehm focussed on *cognitive* awareness of right and wrong; however, she also drew inferences from her data about moral behavior of the children or their moral evaluations in everyday life. The inferences need to be tested by future research. 2) She was testing some of Piaget's hypotheses. For example, she reports that "Contrary to Piaget, our data do not show that 'maturity of social judgment' increases as the child becomes independent of adults and achieves peer reciprocity." (Boehm, 1962a, p. 589).

We also mentioned that the structured story technique has been used to study defense mechanisms (Beardslee, 1960; Lansky, 1960). In a recent study Douglas (1965) reported on eight- to sixteen-year-old children's reaction to frustration using two forms of structured stories, one requiring a free response, the other employing alternatives from which the subject chooses. Both sets gave similar results. The older children produced and chose more realistic and less wish-fulfillment solutions than the younger ones. Again the unanswered question is to what extent these results reflected the child's desire to please the experimenter and/or the youngster's awareness, as he gets older, of the "appropriate" response, or something else. The question is especially relevant because of Douglas's instruction. For the free response version of the stories, "S was told that these were stories about real situations that had actually happened to boys (girls) of his age and he was asked to complete the story by telling 'what the hero felt and thought, and how it *really* turned out.' " (Douglas, 1965, p. 166).

In a similar study, Bildfell and Douglas (1965) examined responses to aggression of boys between six and twelve years of age by asking the boys to complete stories and also asking their mothers to tell how they thought their sons would respond to the same stories. The provocations in the stories, in keeping with the idea of carefully designed stories, were intentional:

> "John had quite a big backyard and very often his friends would use it in the afternoon for games and other things. This afternoon they had decided to have races and give a prize to the winner. John was very excited because he was good at running and was sure he had a good chance to win. There were six boys in the race altogether. John ran as fast as he could and was tied with one other boy. Suddenly, just as they were nearing the finish line, John started to go ahead of the other boy. The boy stuck out his foot, John fell flat on the ground, and, of course, the other boy won the race" (Bildfell & Douglas, 1965, p. 174).

The results were encouraging. They fit common sense expectancies with mothers' agreeing with their sons' responses. For example, physical aggression was greatest in the middle of the age range. Younger children were not so physically aggressive nor were the older ones. It is difficult for this writer to argue that children and mothers "know" that the "normal developmental sequence" would have more physical aggression expressed at nine and ten years old rather than at earlier or later ages. In other words the data have strong face validity and thus support the potential in the story completion technique. It appears that experimenter bias is not a problem. Douglas has also progressed towards another of her goals, namely, to establish norms for the story items so that they might serve as diagnostic tools in the clinic.

We must note in passing that in all the studies being reported in this section, the coding-schemes are reported to be specific; intercoder reliabilities are satisfactory for the sample sizes.

Simultaneously with the growth of work on moral standards and defense mechanisms based on careful testing of psychoanalytic theory, Anderson and Anderson developed sets of story completion items for an extensive series of researches on children's perceptions of social conflicts (Anderson & Anderson, 1954), the social values of teachers in three cultures (Anderson & Anderson, 1962), and adolescents' images of teachers in four countries (Anderson, et al, 1959) and in seven countries (Anderson & Anderson, 1961). Anderson's data were also used by Metraux (1955) to study attitudes about wrongdoing in German children. In these studies and in several unpublished researches, many of them master's and doctoral theses by the Andersons' students, they have used structured stories and very carefully worked out coding procedures, in order to separate out the details of responses to conflict. For example, for one story, they used 46 non-overlapping categories of response (Anderson & Anderson, 1954). Rather than examine these details, we produce a story here to give the flavor of the plot and the open-ended, yet controlled, nature of their questions.

> "The mother sends Michael to the butcher. He shall get two pair of fresh liver sausages. On the way home he puts the wrapped-up sausages on the edge of the sidewalk and plays for a short time with his friends. Then a shepherd dog darts forward quickly, claws one pair of liver sausages out of the paper and rushes away with them. Michael wraps up again the remaining sausages and takes them home. What does Michael say to his mother? How does the mother behave? How does Michael then feel about it? Think about these questions, then *finish* this story quickly with a few sentences." (Anderson & Anderson, 1954, p. 248).

The set of six stories in this study was given to over 1200 13-year-old German children. Like Douglas, the Andersons hoped to establish normative data for their story completion method.

Two other sets of studies must be discussed plus a series of individual studies before this history comes to a close. In their work on personality and persuasion, Janis, Hovland, and their associates, (Janis et al, 1955) used an incomplete story measure to assess parental persuasibility. This test was only one of many measures on this dimension. In this sense, it harks back to the early uses of story completion methods with which this chapter began. We also note that, although the topic is persuasibility, the issues in the story can also be described in relation to moral standards. One example is: "Trudy's mother has something she doesn't want Trudy to see. Trudy's mother says, 'Trudy, don't look at it.' Trudy's mother goes outside to hang out the wash. While her mother is out, does Trudy try to look at it?" (Janis et al, 1955, p. 307).

The second set of studies is on an altogether different topic. LeShan (1952) asked eight- to ten-year-old children to tell a story from which the time perspective of the action was assessed in relation to social class. Barndt and Johnson (1955) extended the idea by using incomplete stories; Wallace (1956) similarly studied differences between schizophrenics and normals with an incomplete story task. Lastly, Teahan (1958) examined this variable in relation to optimism and academic achievement. One item is sufficient to indicate the strategy that has been used. "At three o'clock one bright sunny afternoon in May, two men were out walking near the edge of town." (Teahan, 1958, p. 379). This is, of course, a relatively vague stimulus; the code focuses only on the time involved in the action which the subject describes. In general, the items have confirmed the hunches of the researchers: longer time perspectives appear in middle class Ss, normal Ss, and Ss with high need for achievement; shorter time perspectives appear in lower class Ss, schizophrenics, and Ss with low need for achievement. We noted above that no work with story completion techniques with blind subjects has been published since 1960; similarly there have been no recent studies on time perspective using the story completion method.

There are several studies with story completion methods which fall into a miscellaneous category. Some, like Cairns' (1961) study of dependency, are based on a self-designed, four-item "test" for which a relatively simple code is used. Others, like the work of Payne and Mussen (1956) are embedded in a complex theoretical approach to sex-role identification or some other topic. In both these reports, the actual items are not given.

Anastasiow (1965) used one of Friedman's stories about castration anxiety in a study of five- to six-year-old boys' school success and their sexual patterns. The prediction was that, as compared to masculine boys, feminine boys would be less anxious about castration. The prediction was confirmed. In light of the complexity of sex-role identification and the difficulties in measuring this complex concept, this writer is skeptical of Anastasiow's reasoning and the interpretation of the data. Loy and Turnbull (1964) very carefully designed a set of stories with different degrees of frustration of different need systems in order to test some hypotheses about the relations between frustration and aggression. Their work is a direct derivative of the structured story idea we have been discussing. The results tend to confirm their theoretical view; more important, however, they have demonstrated that story beginnings can be scaled. The methodological task, however, is a difficult one, and is not completely solved.

Lastly, Campos (in press) presents a story completion measure of delay of need gratification which provides scores on need acquisition, need affiliation, need aggression, need nurturance, and need achievement. There are two stories for each of the five needs. Campos's report suggests again the value of a carefully designed instrument with a theoretical rationale.

Summary of the history

This history seems to have come full circle. So far as we can tell, the story completion methods began with research efforts, embedded within the context of theoretical concern about complex facets of personality, and with considerable care in designing stories to elicit special types of responses. There is astir in psychology a new interest in cognition, in creativity, and imagination, and in a more phenomenological approach to the study of personality and its development through transactions with the environment. The path seems open for the development of story completion methods to fit the emerging theoretical ideas which strangely enough were anticipated in the beginning. Yet norms are needed. In the remaining sections of this chapter, we shall briefly touch on some specific possible future directions in relation to materials, administration, underlying hypotheses, interpretations, and clinical and research applications.

Materials and Administration

No special materials are needed for any of the story completion methods. Sometimes, as we have seen, stories are administered individually by reading them or reciting them to the client or subject; other times they are presented, one to a page, with room at the bottom for the person to write out his answers. At other times, when older children or adults are being used for research, a booklet is presented to each person in a large group. On these occasions, the administrator may ask all the subjects to do each story together, or each person may be permitted to proceed at his own pace.

There are very few studies which focus on materials and administrative methods. Fassett (1948) used different presentations of materials and directly compared them (see page 298 above). Douglas gave different subjects open-ended and multiple choice versions of the same stories.

These attempts merely scratch the surface of the problems which might be explored. As we have seen, those who describe or prescribe the clinical use of story methods have put few restrictions on the user; however, these same workers do admonish their fellow clinicians to take all factors, including the setting and the administration of the stories, into account when they interpret the data. There is, as one might expect, no information on how this warning is interpreted or used.

In his own research work, this author has only specifically considered the size of the page and the location of the story on it. Larger sheets seem to elicit either longer stories or larger handwriting; but the topic has not been studied in a controlled way.

These administrative matters may be quite important. Certainly a longer protocol does provide a greater opportunity for the subject or client to touch on more scorable themes. Short protocols may reflect difficulty in reading, writing, or speaking as well as the psychodynamic feature being explored with the story completion task. There might also be considerable difference between response patterns when Ss *write* and when they *tell* their completions. One is done more privately, the other is more transactional. The growing interest among psychologists in cognitive styles and creativity are relevant to these methodological issues in story completions in particular and projective testing in general.

Another set of unstudied variables with story completion methods includes the clinician's or researcher's sex, attitude, style, appearance, and the like. Just as there is increasing concern about subtle and unconscious influences which clinicians and researchers exert upon clients and subjects (Rosenthal, 1963), there is a need to look at these rather obvious potential influences on story completion responses. To date, there are no purely methodological laboratory studies on these particular types of variables.

Another interesting variable which we have mentioned several times concerns one particular hypothesis which the subject may have about the endings. Which does the subject believe: that the experimenter has some particular ending in mind or that there really is no right or wrong answer? As we have seen in some instructions, it appears that the experimenter has already completed the story and that the subject's task is to discover that ending. Perhaps most persons respond to such instructions as if any response is acceptable; however, the research needed to establish this point has not been done.

A final set of variables relates to the degree of structure in the story beginning and the questions asked at the end of each story. Since these matters relate most directly to the underlying hypotheses and interpretations of those who use story completion methods, we turn to that section of this chapter.

One's underlying hypotheses about story completion methods affect their design, their use, and the interpretations made of them. All workers agree with some hypotheses; other hypotheses are extremely controversial.

The agreements center around achieving rapport. Clinicians and researchers seem to agree, without any evidence of carefully collected data, that completing stories is fun, especially for children. The "game" is interesting. It is a useful school activity and helps to pass the time on long automobile trips; in the past few years, a successful television show used the idea of a continuing story with different contestants, divided into teams, having to pick up the thread at a given signal.

Among users of story completion tests, the projective hypothesis also seems to be accepted. The subject or client is assumed to "identify with" the hero: male, female, man, beast, third person, first person, or whatever. Because of this identification, the individual then unwittingly reveals areas of his or her personality whether or not he is consciously aware of them. The projective hypothesis carries other implications, however, when the researcher or clinician interprets the responses. Even if the subject or client has identified with the hero of the story, the response repertoire which the subject is using is problematic. Are the completions a reflection of his fantasies, his imagination? The instructions often request an interesting story; sometimes the word "imagination" is used to encourage free responses. Perhaps, the subject or client is telling how he *thinks about* the topic, e.g., moral issues; he is relating what his everyday "cognitive map" is on these matters. If he is presenting either fantasies and wishes or a cognitive map, we already know that these need not coincide in any clear systematic way with his overt behavior. If we look at moral standards, for example, our interest in them as social scientists and helpers stems, in part, from our knowledge that morally relevant situations tap complex admixtures of wish, fantasy, anxiety, defense, and overt action.

The solution to the projective problem can be discussed in several frames of reference. One is relatively concrete: How does the clinician or researcher write and code story completion items? Another, somewhat more abstract view, looks at the worker's underlying hypotheses as he approaches research in personality.

Broadly speaking, the specific concrete decisions about the story beginning, the coding, and the interpretation of the results, reflect rather uncritically accepted goals and theoretical biases. Many such biases are unconscious while others are clear to the clinician or researcher. We have seen several examples. The clinical psychologist who wants to open up a child's fantasy world during an early interview may select any of several sets of story beginnings. Furthermore, the clinician is encouraged to use the stories as he wishes, and to interpret on whatever level suits his theory.

The story task is another clinical tool. The researcher who wants to test a particular model may use relatively open-ended stories but he also has the option of carefully devising special stories for his goals. If he wants to assure, as much as he can, that each subject gets the "same" stimulus and that each respondent's answers can be interpreted in the "same" frame of reference, he will take the approach suggested by Allinsmith (1954).

As we have seen, the clinician's and researcher's goals also affect the language they use to describe their stories, the categories in their codes, the concepts of the interpretation. Indeed, the same material might be described in psychoanalytic language by one worker but in Piaget's terms by another. Regardless of the goals and theory, there is a seemingly uncritical acceptance of a framework. This lack of self-criticism becomes very apparent when we ask a researcher or clinician to relate the story responses to the client's or subject's personality, to his total functioning. Another related question focuses on the uniqueness of the story completion method in comparison to others. Why stories? Surely, not just because they are fun and easy to use.

The first question is an embarrassing one for all of projective testing. Essentially it is a form of the validity issue. What do these instruments measure? For story completion methods, the typical answer draws upon theory. The researcher who believes in habit family hierarchies might connect story responses to potential overt behavior because both are high on the habit family hierarchy. The weakness of the argument is readily apparent. Story telling and action do not belong to the same families for many persons. Indeed, the story may be one place where reality can be ignored.

The same loose thinking about this issue marks other theoretical approaches: the psychoanalytic, the Piagetian, and various eclectic views. The embarrassing question is sidestepped. Implicit assumptions take the place of careful theoretical reasoning and experimental testing. This is not to say that theoretical thinking is omitted in planning the story beginnings. The reasoning does not go far enough.

Lest the reader be too critical at this point, he might attempt his own story completion task. By writing or attempting to write a few story beginnings, by administering them, by attempting to code them, and then by trying to interpret the responses, the severest critic may temper the force of his objections. The clinician and researcher have the same problems. Even when prior decisions have been made about the theoretical framework (psychoanalytic, behavioristic, eclectic), what unit to analyze (sentence, theme, whole story), how specific to make the code (nominal scales, rankings, ratings, some combination, or impressionistic narrative), and to what extent to stick with the manifest content of the responses (completely, partially, not at all, some mixture), the connections between story completions and other behaviors of interest to the reader-researcher may still be obscure. At this point there are several ways out of the discomfort.

One is empirical. Look at the relationship between the story responses and some particular behavior. We have already noted one published study—Grinder and McMichael (1963) got negative results. Similar attempts have also failed, but it is still not clear what researchers and theorists who use story completion methods are going to do with this finding.

Another straightforward solution to the dilemma is to accept the notion that story completions are cognitive responses. Then the worker may focus upon various dimensions of cognition. We have seen examples of this approach in Boehm's (1962a, 1962b, 1964) research, although she too interprets the story responses as if they reflect parallel patterns in overt behavior. Thus, theoretical assumptions, often relatively uncritically examined, are used. The problem of relating stories to other behavior is not solved.

The issue may become clearer if we shift this discussion from the concrete decisions about theory, story specificity, and coding decision to the underlying hypotheses about where one should pursue the study of personality—in the clinic or laboratory. In the clinical use of story methods which we have described above, a holistic view of the client is stressed at the expense of rigor and control. There is a lack of replicability in the methods and their use. In the research work with story methods, however, there is considerable scientific respectability vis à vis reliability, careful procedures and the like, but a relatively sterile view of the person. He is known only by a very limited number of responses to a limited number of "tests."

There is an approach to personality which could exploit the best features of both approaches while eliminating their faults. This research model assumes that rich clinical data and experimental control are both desirable in research on personality. The model itself takes us back to the orientation of the earliest workers with story methods; indeed, it goes back to an earlier era in psychological exploration. McGrath (1923), Hartshorne and May (1928), Piaget (1932), and Murray (1937) were interested in whole persons, in complex psychological processes. They used multiple measurements on each variable they pursued.

One limitation of their multivariate, multimeasurement approach may be avoided by our new technology. It was not possible for McGrath or the other early researchers to pull together all the data in their studies of personality. The studies are "explorations." The computer and new statistical techniques offer the possibility of more systematic and integrated theoretical analyses of multitrait and multivariate studies in which many measures of motivational, cognitive, affective, and behavioral variables are done in a wide variety of settings.

The feasibility of a more phenomenological approach to personality research, including story completion methods, may open up new attacks on several issues raised in this chapter. Indeed, the story may be uniquely suited to such research because it so easily lends itself to controlled variation of its stimulus elements. We have already mentioned one study (Friedman, 1952) in which the similarity of the hero to the child was varied. This manipulation altered the responses to the stories. This type of study could be extended. It seems that some kind of "check list" is needed which would alert the personality researcher to the wide variety of variables which could be systematically varied in the design, coding, and interpretation of stories.[1]

If one previous attempt at a "check list" is any bellwether, such a list would lead to a phenomenological view of the researcher's problem. Erikson (1954), in his analysis of Freud's Irma dream, produced a list for examining the manifest content of the dream. Although he is a psychoanalyst, his categories are not purely psychoanalytic. The list reads more like a social scientific encyclopedia including variables from psychoanalysis, psychology, sociology, history, anthropology, and genetics. It is broadly phenomenological. Indeed, it is so all-inclusive as to be almost unusable. It is clear to Erikson and other workers on dreams that the list is itself a fantasy, the fantasy of a clinician and researcher who wants to achieve "complete" understanding of the person through his behavior, in this instance the report of a dream. In order to do this, Erikson realizes that the interpreter must study more than one or two variables, one or two dreams; and he needs more than one approach to each dimension in the list. Similarly, the story completion methods or any particular set of stories is but one of many measures which can elucidate personality.

In this discussion of underlying hypotheses and of interpretations we have pointed out several flaws in current work with story completion methods. Two recent developments in personality theory must also be mentioned. At the present time, motivation and personality theories are dominated by tension-reduction models: the hydraulic psychoanalytic view; the various modifications of Hullian reinforcement theory; or Skinnerian operant conditioning. But there is another view of motivation and action which is only slowly working its way into the mainstream of psychological thinking: the notion variously called "tension-seeking," "pacing," "competence," "effectance" (White, 1959; Dember, 1965). This view, in my opinion, has more to say about the behaviors which interest the users of story completion methods than the older tension-reduction one. If one begins with a tension-seeking model of motivation, one may design story beginnings which have little resemblance to the present ones. It is also possible that much existing data would be interpreted differently if a tension-seeking model were used.

[1]One glaring omission in current work with stories is any manipulation of the race or the socioeconomic status of heroes.

The second development in personality theory is related to the first one. In previous work with stories, considerable emphasis has been placed on defensive processes for resolving conflict and reducing anxiety. Stories have been used to uncover preferred defensive maneuvers (Lansky, 1960). Kroeber (1964) has suggested that for several defense mechanisms, there are parallel *coping* mechanisms. For example, while projections tend to be rigid, pushed from the past, distortions, and magical reactions to other persons, empathic responses are flexible, look at the present and future, are realistic, and help control feelings in an ordered way.

Just as tension-reducing models tend to see man as pushed towards tension reduction, the defensive processes seem to imply that man is driven by whatever means to avoid or reduce anxiety, often unconscious anxiety. The tension-seeking model on the other hand parallels the idea of coping mechanisms. Both imply that man is more in control of himself and his interactions with his environment.

These theoretical developments are raised here because these views of personality functioning have not been used in the planning of story completion methods. A forerunner of the coping ideas may be seen in Beardslee's (1960) and Lansky's (1960) coding of "realistic problem solving" as responses to conflicts about aggressive feelings towards loved and respected authorities. They did not see the possibility of other coping mechanisms in their stories. Perhaps they were there, however. Again there is work for the future.

In summary then, underlying hypotheses and interpretations of story completion methods reflect the clinician's and researcher's theories and biases, conscious and unconscious. Throughout the work on story completion methods, one finds a condition similar to that with most personality testing. There is too little attention paid to careful theoretical analysis, too many unexamined assumptions rather than careful experimental investigation and theorizing, and a reluctance to abandon the confines of a clinical looseness (*intuition*) or a rigid experimental approach (*science*) in favor of what this writer sees as a needed phenomenological research-oriented view.

Despite the difficulties noted in this section, story completions are being used. We turn now to applications.

CLINICAL APPLICATIONS

We have already examined the clinical use of story completion methods. Several techniques are available and in use as aides to rapport and diagnosis. However, it is clear that there are no measures available today with proved value for differential diagnosis or even for unique identification of deviations from the norm. Normative studies are sorely needed. The difficulties are enormous; but such work is long overdue if story completion methods are to be maximally useful in the clinic. Loevinger has stated the problem most succinctly:

> "Persons without extensive training in the area of test and measurements are prone to believe that a test, as every schoolboy knows, is a more or less clever set of items. Professional workers in the field, however, tend to borrow one another's items rather freely, on the grounds that the items alone do not constitute a test, but only the items together with a scoring key and appropriate norms. The number of cases needed even for a modest normative study is now recognized as being so great that for some types of test not only expertise but also commercial backing is necessary. To construct a scoring manual for a projective test, even larger numbers are required to get adequate empirical validation. We may conclude that for short-term (say, less than three years) or small-scale (less than about one thousand cases) research, tests that other investigators have studied empirically, however fallible they may be, are almost necessarily better than ad hoc tests. To say this, however, is not to condone taking the claims implied in the title or in the promotional literature at face value" (Loevinger, 1965, p. 91).

RESEARCH APPLICATIONS

The research opportunities for work with story completion methods are broad, but as we have noted, beset with difficulties. How does one decide whether or not to devise one's own measure, with the risks entailed, in order to gain the specificity which is required to test one's hypotheses? I do not know the answer. Each researcher must decide for himself. Loevinger has offered an important warning: "The psychologist or psychiatrist initiating a research project in the clinical field may be tempted to think that since no well-established test exists for exactly the trait he wants to measure, his best course is to make his own test. This view is particularly tempting to those who do not know a great deal about the effort that has been expended on many more or less unsuccessful tests." (Loevinger, 1965, p. 91).

The story completion methods can be useful, especially when they are preceded by careful theoretical analysis. Again, Loevinger, while discussing clinical research, has put her finger on the central issue:

> "There are no easy or magical formulas for overcoming these dilemmas. In meeting the problems, the standard paraphernalia of the statistical consultant—his factor analysis, analysis of variance, and computer search for patterns—are of as little avail as the unbridled intuition of the clinician. To meet such problems requires evolving a mature science in which measurement, theory, and

empirical verification are integral parts of a single enterprise. What the methodologist should bring into the clinical field is not a bag of statistical tricks, but the habit of rigorous and precise thought and a sense of where to look for errors that bias the result. The clinician must bring to the research area his problems and concerns as they impinge on him, his sense of the relative importance of different questions and of the genuineness or spuriousness of proposed approaches.

"To be truly scientific requires more investment in constructs and theories than many psychologists find congenial; yet the great sciences of modern times are shaped in terms of theory. The basic observations on which measurement rests should be as little inferential as possible, but meaningful scores must correspond to and be arrived at by reference to constructs" (Loevinger, 1966, p. 92).

SUMMARY

This chapter has primarily traced the history of story completion methods. The beginnings are obscure. They are found in large scale, more or less phenomenologically oriented, studies of complex personality processes by such famous persons as Hartshorne and May (1928) and Piaget (1932). Then, a predominantly clinical projective testing orientation held sway with strong emphasis on the task as servant to the clinician's judgment and intuition. Lastly, we have seen a swing back to research interest in story completion methods and a new emphasis on structured stimuli, stimuli which pinpoint and control certain variables in order to test specific theoretical hypotheses. Today, the subject matter tends to be specific: defense mechanisms, moral standards, responses to moral situations, complex motives, and the like, not so much from a phenomenological view however, as from a careful analysis of some particular theory. These new studies have pointed up both the promise and the problems for the future of story completion methods—methods which are still not well enough developed to deserve the name "tests." One critical point is common to all projective techniques. What do the responses measure? How do they relate to the total functioning of the person? Much theory, much research, and new approaches are needed to answer these questions.

The beginnings of these methods are obscure. So is the future. Perhaps the reader can finish the story. What happens next?

REFERENCES

Allinsmith, B. B. Expressive styles: II. Directness with which anger is expressed. In D. R. Miller & G. E. Swanson (Eds.). *Inner Conflict and Defense*. New York: Holt-Dryden, 1960, Pp. 315-336.

CHAPTER 10 · Lansky

Allinsmith, W. The learning of moral standards. Unpublished doctoral dissertation, University of Michigan, 1954.

Allinsmith, W. Moral standards: II. The learning of moral standards. In D. R. Miller & G. E. Swanson (Eds.). *Inner Conflict and Defense.* New York: Holt, 1960, Pp. 141-176.

Anastasiow, N. J. Success in school and boys' sex-role patterns. *Child Develpm.,* 1965, *36,* 1053-1066.

Anderson, H. H., & Anderson, G. L. Children's perceptions of social conflict situations: A study of adolescent children in Germany. *Amer. J. Orthopsychiat.,* 1954, *24,* 246-257.

Anderson, H. H., & Anderson, G. L. Image of the teacher by adolescent children in seven countries. *Amer. J. Orthopsychiat.,* 1961, *31,* 481-492.

Anderson, H. H., & Anderson, G. L. Social values of teachers in Rio de Janeiro, Mexico City, and Los Angeles County California: A comparative study of teachers and children. *J. soc. Psychol.,* 1962, *58,* 207-226.

Anderson, H. H., Anderson, G. L., Cohen, I. H., & Nutt, F. D. Image of the teacher by adolescent children in four countries: Germany, England, Mexico, and United States. *J. soc. Psychol.,* 1959, *50,* 47-55.

Anthony, S. *The Child's Discovery of Death.* New York: Harcourt, Brace, 1940.

Aronfreed, J. Moral standards and sex identity. In D. R. Miller & G. E. Swanson (Eds.). *Inner Conflict and Defense.* New York: Holt, 1960. Pp. 177-193.

Bandura, A., & Walters, R. H. *Adolescent Aggression.* New York: Ronald Press, 1959.

Barker, R. (Ed.), *The Stream of Behavior.* New York: Appleton-Century-Crofts, 1963.

Barndt, R. J., & Johnson, D. M. Time orientation in delinquents. *J. abn. soc. Psychol.,* 1955, *51,* 343-345.

Bender, L., & Woltmann, A. G. The use of puppet shows as a psychotherapeutic method for behavior problems in children. *Amer. J. Orthopsychiat.,* 1936, *6,* 341-354.

Beardslee, B. J. Mechanisms of defense: IV. Aggression and the second family of defenses. In D. R. Miller & G. E. Swanson (Eds.). *Inner Conflict and Defense.* New York: Holt, 1960. Pp. 256-271.

Bildfell, G., & Douglas, V. I. Children's responses to aggression: A developmental study. *Canad. Psychol.,* 1965, *6a,* 173-178.

Boehm, L. The development of conscience: A comparison of American children of different mental and socioeconomic levels. *Child Developm.,* 1962a, *33,* 575-602.

Boehm, L. The development of conscience: A comparison of students in Catholic parochial schools and in public school. *Child Developm.,* 1962b, *33,* 591-602.

Boehm, L. The development of conscience: A comparison of upper-middle class academically gifted children attending Catholic and Jewish parochial schools. *J. soc. Psychol.,* 1964, *59,* 101-110.

Boehm, L., & Nass, M. L. Social class differences in conscience development. *Child Developm.,* 1962, *33,* 565-575.

Brown, J. Verbal projective methods. In D. C. Smith (Ed.). *The Use of Projective Methods with the School-aged Child.* Unpublished manuscript, Ohio State University, 1962.

Buros, O. K. (Ed.), *Tests in Print: A Comprehensive Bibliography of Tests for Use in Education, Psychology, and Industry.* Highland Park, New Jersey: Gryphon, 1961.

Buros, O. K. (Ed.), *The Sixth Mental Measurements Yearbook.* Highland Park, New Jersey: The Gryphon Press, 1965.

Burton, R. V. The generality of honesty reconsidered. *Psychol. Rev.*, 1963, *70*, 481-500.

Cairns, R. B. The influence of dependency inhibition on the effectiveness of social reinforcement. *J. Pers.*, 1961, *29*, 466-488.

Campbell, D. T., & Fiske, D. W. Convergent and discriminant validation by the multitrait-multimethod matrix. *Psychol. Bull.*, 1959, *56*, 81-105.

Campos, L. P. The development and use of a story-completion measure of delay of need gratification. *J. proj. Tech. Pers. Assess.* (in press).

Dember, W. N. The new look in motivation. *Amer. Scientist*, 1965, *53*, 409-427.

Despert, J. L., & Potter, H. W. Technical approaches used in the study and treatment of emotional problems of children. Part I: The story, a form of directed fantasy. *Psychiat. Quart.*, 1936, *10*, 619-638.

Despert, J. L. Psychosomatic study of fifty stuttering children. *Amer. J. Orthopsychiat.*, 1946, *16*, 100-113.

Douglas, V. I. Children's responses to frustration: A developmental study. *Canad. J. Psychol./Rev. Canad. Psychol.*, 1965, *19*, 161-171.

Duess, L. La methode des fables en psychoanalyse. *Arch. Psychol., Geneve*, 1940, *28*, 1-51.

Engel, M. The development and applications of the Children's Insight Test. *J. proj. Tech.*, 1958, *22*, 13-25.

Engel, M., & Rechenberg, W. Studies in the reliability of the Children's Insight Test. *J. proj. Tech.*, 1961, *25*, 158-163.

Erikson, E. H. The dream specimen of psychoanalysis. *J. Amer. psychoan. Assoc.*, 1954, *2*, 5-56.

Fassett, K. K. A preliminary investigation of the Sargeant Insight Test. *J. clin. Psychol.*, 1948, *4*, 45-55.

Fine, R. Use of the Despert Fables (Revised Form) in diagnostic work with children. *Rorschach Res. Exch. J. proj. Tech.*, 1948, *12*, 106-118.

Flavell, J. H. *The Developmental Psychology of Jean Piaget*. Princeton, N.J.: Van Nostrand, 1963.

Friedman, S. M. An empirical study of the castration and oedipus complexes. *Genet. Psychol. Monogr.*, 1952, *46*, 61-130.

French, E. G. Some characteristics of achievement motivation. *J. exp. Psychol.*, 1955, *50*, 232-236.

French, E. G., & Chadwick, I. Some characteristics of affiliation motivation. *J. abn. soc. Psychol.*, 1956, *52*, 296-300.

Grinder, R., & McMichael, R. Cultural influences on conscience development: Resistance to temptation and guilt among Samoans and American Caucasians. *J. abn. soc. Psychol.*, 1963, *66*, 503-507.

Hartshorne, H., & May, M. A. *Studies in the Nature of Character*: *Vol. I. Studies in Deceit*. New York: Macmillan, 1928.

Haworth, M. R. The use of a filmed puppet show as a group projective technique for children. *Genet. Psychol. Monogr.*, 1957, *56*, 257-296.

Hoffman, M. L. Childrearing practices and moral development: Generalizations from empirical research. *Child Developm.*, 1963, *34*, 295-318.

Hsu, F. L. (Ed.), *Psychological Anthropology*: *Approaches to Culture and Personality*. Homewood, Ill.: Dorsey Press, 1961.

Janis, I. L., et al. *Personality and Persuasibility*. New Haven; Yale University Press, 1955.

Johnson, R. A study of children's moral judgment. *Child Developm.*, 1962, *33*, 327-354.

Kohlberg, L. Moral development and identification. In H. Stevenson (Ed.). *Child Psychology. 62nd Yearbook National Society for the Study of Education.* Chicago: University of Chicago Press, 1963. Pp. 177-332.

Kohlberg, L. Development of moral character and moral ideology. In M. L. Hoffman & L. W. Hoffman (Eds.). *Review of Child Development Research: Vol. I.* New York: Russell Sage Foundation, 1964. Pp. 383-432.

Korner, A. F. *Some aspects of hostility in young children.* New York: Grune and Stratton, 1949.

Kroeber, T. C. The coping functions of the ego mechanisms. In R. W. White (Ed.). *The Study of Lives.* New York: Atherton, 1964. Pp. 178-199.

Lansky, L. M. Mechanisms of defense: V. Sex identity and defenses against aggression. In D. R. Miller & G. E. Swanson (Eds.). *Inner Conflict and Defense.* New York: Holt, 1960. Pp. 272-288.

Lansky, L. M., Crandall, V. J., Kagan, J., & Baker, C. T. Sex differences in aggression and its correlates in middle-class adolescents. *Child Developm.,* 1961, *32,* 45-58.

Lebo, D. An empirical approach to problems concerning the diagnostic value of a pictureless TAT. *J. proj. Tech.,* 1959, *23,* 107.

Lebo, D. The development and employment of VTAT's or pictureless TAT's. *J. Psychol.,* 1960, *50,* 197-204.

Lebo, D., & Bruce, R. . Projective techniques recommended for use with the blind. *J. Psychol.,* 1960, *50,* 15-38.

Lebo, D., & Harrigan, M. Visual and verbal presentation of TAT stimuli. *J. consult. Psychol.,* 1957, *21,* 339-342.

Lebo, D., & Sherry, J. P. Visual and vocal presentation of the TAT descriptions. *J. proj. Tech.,* 1959, *23,* 59-63.

LeShan, L. L. Time orientation and social class. *J. abn. soc. Psychol.,* 1952, *47,* 589-592.

Lindzey, G. *Projective Techniques and Cross-cultural Research.* New York: Appleton-Century-Crofts, 1961.

Loevinger, J. Measurement in clinical research. In B. B. Wolman (Ed.). *Handbook of Clinical Psychology.* New York: McGraw-Hill, 1965, Pp. 78-94.

Loy, D. L., & Turnbull, J. W. Indirect assessment of anger dispositions. *J. proj. Tech. Pers. Assess.,* 1964, *28,* 314-321.

Lynn, D. B. *Structured Doll Play Test (SDP): A Projective Test for Use with Children.* Denver, Colorado: Test Developments, 1959.

Luria, Z., Goldwasser, M., & Goldwasser, A. Response to transgression in stories by Israeli children. *Child Developm.,* 1963, *34,* 271-281.

McGrath, M. C. A study of the moral development of children. *Psychol. Monogr.,* 1923, *32,* No. 2. (Whole No. 144) 1-190.

Métraux, R. The consequences of wrongdoing: An analysis of story completions by German children. In Margaret Mead & Martha Wolfenstein (Eds.). *Childhood in Contemporary Cultures.* Chicago: University of Chicago Press, 1955. Pp. 306-327.

Miller, D. R., & Stine, M. E. The prediction of social acceptance by means of psychoanalytic concepts. *J. Pers.,* 1951, *20,* 162-174.

Miller, D. R. Motivation and affect. In P. H. Mussen (Ed.). *Handbook of Research Methods in Child Development.* New York: Wiley, 1960. Pp. 688-769.

Miller, D. R., & Swanson, G. E. (Eds.). *Inner Conflict and Defense.* New York: Holt, 1960.

PART IV

Mills, E. S. A study of the Madeleine Thomas Completion Stories Test with fifty elementary school children. Unpublished master's thesis, Claremont College, 1949.

Mills, E. S. The Madeleine Thomas Completion Stories Test. *J. consult. Psychol.*, 1953, *17*, 139-141.

Mills, E. S. A story completion test for college students. *J. clin. Psychol.*, 1954, *10*, 18-22.

Mosse, H. L. The Duess Test. *Amer. J. Psychother.*, 1954, *8*, 251-264.

Murray, H. A. Techniques for a systematic investigation of fantasy. *J. Psychol.*, 1937, *8*, 115-143.

Murstein, B. I. (Ed.), *Handbook of Projective Techniques.* New York: Basic Books, 1965a.

Murstein, B. I. The projection of hostility on the TAT as a function of stimulus, background and personality variables. *J. consult. Psychol.*, 1965b, *29*, 47-48.

Payne, D. E., & Mussen, P. H. Parent-child relations and father identification among adolescent boys. *J. abn. soc. Psychol.*, 1956, *52*, 358-362.

Peixotto, H. E. Reliability of the Despert Fables, a story completion projective test for children. *J. clin. Psychol.*, 1956, *12*, 75-78.

Peixotto, H. E. Popular responses for the Despert Fables. *J. clin. Psychol.*, 1957, *13*, 73-79.

Peixotto, H. E. Personality dynamics of American children as revealed by Despert Fables. *Vita Humana*, 1961, *4*, 242-248.

Piaget, J. *The Moral Judgment of the Child.* Harcourt, Brace, 1932.

Porteus, B. D., & Johnson, R. C. Children's responses to two measures of conscience development and their relation to sociometric nomination. *Child Developm.*, 1965, *36*, 703-711.

Raven, J. C. *Controlled Projection for Children,* (2nd ed.). London: H. K. Lewis, 1951.

Rebelsky, F. G., Allinsmith, W., & Grinder, R. E. Resistance to temptation and sex differences in children's use of fantasy confession. *Child Developm.*, 1963, *34*, 955-962.

Rebelsky, F. G. An inquiry into the meanings of confession. *Merrill-Palmer Quart.*, 1963, *9*, 287-294.

Roody, S. I. The plot completion test. *J. experim. Educ.*, 1943, *12*, 45-47.

Rosenthal, R. On the social psychology of the psychological experiment. *Amer. Scientist*, 1963, *51*, 268-283.

Sargeant, H. An experimental application of projective principles to a paper and pencil personality test. *Psychol. Monogr.*, 1944, *57*, (Whole No. 265) 1-57.

Sargeant, H. Projective methods: Their origins, theory, and application in personality research. *Psychol. Bull.*, 1945, *42*, 257-293.

Sargeant, H. *The Insight Test: A Verbal Projective Test for Personality Study.* New York: Grune and Stratton, 1955.

Schuman, E. P. A scoring rationale for the Sargent Test of Insight into Human Motives. *J. proj. Tech.*, 1962, *26* (4), 462-468.

Schwartz, A. A. Some interrelationships among four tests comprising a test battery: A comparative study. *J. proj. Tech.*, 1950, *14*, 153-172.

Seaton, J. K. A projective experiment using incomplete stories with multiple-choice endings. *Genet. Psychol. Monogr.*, 1949, *40*, 149-228.

Smith, D. C. (Ed.), *The Use of Projective Methods with the School-aged Child.* Unpublished manuscript, Ohio State University, 1962.

Teahan, J. E. Future time perspective, optimism, and academic achievement. *J. abn. soc. Psychol.*, 1958, *57*, 379-380.

Thomas, M. Méthode des histories a completer pour le dépistage des complexes et des conflits affectifs enfantins. *Arch. Psychol., Genève*, 1937, *26*, 209-284.

Wallace, M. Future time perspective in schizophrenia. *J. abn. soc. Psychol.*, 1956, *52*, 240-245.

Weisskopf-Joelson, E., & Wich, R. An experiment concerning the value of a "pictureless TAT." *J. proj. Tech.*, 1961, *25*, 360-362.

Wertham, F. The matricidal impulse. *J. crimin. Psychopath.*, 1941, *2*, (no. 4) (April).

White, R. W. (Ed.), *The Study of Lives: Essays on Personality in Honor of Henry A. Murray*. New York: Atherton Press, 1963.

Woltmann, K. G. The use of puppetry as a projective method in therapy. In H. H. Anderson & G. L. Anderson (Eds.). *An Introduction to Projective Techniques*. New York: Prentice-Hall, 1951. p. 606-638.

Wursten, H. Story Completions: Madeline Thomas stories and similar methods. In A. I. Rabin & M. R. Haworth (Eds.), *Projective Techniques with Children*. New York: Grune and Stratton, 1960. Pp. 192-209.

Zucker, H. The emotional attachment of children to their parents as related to standards of behavior and delinquency. *J. Psychol.*, 1943, *15*, 31-40.

V

EXPRESSIVE
METHODS

As Lawrence Frank pointed out, there are a large variety of methods involving the cathectic element. Some of these methods border on the therapeutic domain. Representative samples of this category—bearing in mind the applicability of the methods to the assessment process and the availability of research literature—are included in this section. (Methods in which the therapeutic, rather than the diagnostic, function is stressed, such as psychodrama, are not included in this volume.)

The doll play technique is applicable to both assessment and therapy. Dr. Haworth, in the first part of her chapter, presents a clear and succinct statement of this method and its widespread applications in assessment and child development research. She points out some areas still to be explored by means of this technique, especially those that can utilize its diagnostic and idiographic potential.

Puppetry is the subject of the second part of Dr. Haworth's chapter. Studies with this method have been, by and large, more clinical in orientation and more concerned with dynamic intrafamilial processes than with individual parameters of personality structure. These methods are especially applicable to young children, for whom play is the accustomed means of communication and, according to some, "the royal road to the unconscious."

Another cluster of expressive methods, in which "expressive movement," as well as content, plays an important role, is represented by the projective drawings. The Draw-A-Person (DAP), the House-Tree-Person (HTP), drawings of the family, animals, etc., are some of the variations on the expressive drawing theme. After a brief discussion of the various methods, Dr. Hammer, in his chapter on "projective drawings," concentrates on the DAP as the representative method. His rich illustrations and corresponding clinical material, as well as interpretive comments, make the subject alive and give the reader a glimpse into the clinician's operations in the interpretive process. In addition, the author comes to grips with some of the controversial issues involved in the process of validation of clinical hypotheses and interpretations underlying these methods.

The particular advantages of these primarily non-verbal methods in cross-cultural research, as well as with highly non-communicative subjects or patients in our own culture, need to be stressed. Recent reports of investigations in the culture and personality area readily attest to the applicability of the techniques and to the fruitfulness of the results obtained.

11

Doll Play and Puppetry

MARY R. HAWORTH

Dolls have had a universal appeal for young children in all countries and for many centuries, from early antiquity to the present day. The earliest doll-like figures very likely were constructed as representatives of various gods or idols, as totems to be appeased, as funeral figures, or as symbols of supernatural powers for use in festivals or as good luck charms. Puppets have traditionally replicated many adult characters in addition to the usually playful and carefree Kasper, Guignol or Punch. Portrayals of complete doll families originated with religious figures, such as the Holy Family. Fashion dolls were made in France as long as 600 years ago and doll houses, with dolls, have been known to date back at least 300 years. Childlike and baby-dolls, so universally regarded as appropriate toys for children today, did not appear on the scene until the nineteenth century (World Book, 1950).

DOLL PLAY

While both doll play and puppetry would appear to be excellent media for eliciting fantasies from young children, their actual clinical use has been rather limited. Levy (1933), in his classical sibling rivalry experiments, was perhaps the first to systematically explore psychological phenomena with the use of dolls. Conn (1938) extended Levy's structured procedures into "planned play-situations" whereby the child is helped to re-enact, through doll actions, his own past traumas or conflicts. Lowenfeld (1939) elaborated on these early concepts of doll play in her World Test which included a large variety of "people" and accessory materials, such as animals, cars, small houses, trees and fences. No initial "situations" were presented; the child was free to construct whatever he wished with the materials at hand. Despert (1940) reports extensive observations on the use of four large family dolls by normal nursery school children.

Lerner and Murphy (1941) used unstructured doll play as one of several media in an early, comprehensive study of personality in young children. Murphy (1956) has subsequently described their Miniature

Life Toys in more detail. Her procedures are probably those most used by clinicians today, i.e., an assortment of family-life materials, furniture, dolls and objects (cars, trains, tame and wild animals, soldiers, Indians) are presented to the child with relatively little structure. The clinician's role is to observe, evaluate, and interpret the child's activities and verbalizations for clues to personality patterns, attitudes, conflicts, anxieties, and relationships with parents and siblings.

Doll play techniques have been utilized most frequently with young preschool children and are a particularly suitable means of eliciting projective responses from this age group. The materials have a "natural" appeal and can be manipulated without the need for speech; consequently, they are especially useful for children who cannot tell elaborate stories to pictures, give scorable Rorschach responses, or draw beyond a scribble. Doll play is also effective with deaf children, those with language and speech problems, and with retarded subjects. A few doll play studies have been reported with latency and early adolescent subjects and with psychotic adults.

The projective rationale for all doll play techniques is based on the premise that the child will recreate situations, with the doll figures, which he has experienced in his own home and with respect to his own family members. Fears, anxieties, rivalries and aggressive impulses will also be revealed. Information should be forthcoming with respect to the objects and agents of aggression, to dependence-independence strivings, and to identifications and attachments. The basic underlying assumption, therefore, would be that the child's constructions will reproduce his reality situations. But, as Levin and Wardwell (1961) point out, the child's products may also represent fantasy and wish-fulfillment; consequently, interpretations of content must take this possibility into account.

Murphy (1956, p. 29) speaks of doll play as ". . . a technique for recording the life space of children." She also points out that the *content* of the child's doll play reveals *what* he is disturbed about and the *structure* of his play and fantasy reveals *how* disturbed he may be. Structural aspects include such dimensions as rigidity, disorganization, stereotypy, flexibility, spontaneity, and are as important as the specific doll activities when analyzing and interpreting the child's play patterns.

Materials

The most commonly used materials include a low, unroofed, one-story doll house filled with appropriate furniture and a family of doll figures, either a "standard" family (mother, father, boy, girl and baby) or a "duplicate" family whose composition is similar to that of the child subject. (Peixotto and Hill, 1964-65, have provided two complete sets of families so that the child can discard a "bad" family and substitute a "good" family in its place.) Accessory materials may vary widely, including animals, cars, and any variety of small details, lamps, tiny dishes, toy foods, baby carriage, bed clothes. It is generally felt that projection is impeded when too many minutiae are presented, or where the furnishings are too realistic, e.g., drawers that open, doors on hinges, knobs that turn, since the child becomes so intrigued with manipulations that play content is reduced (Phillips, 1945; Driscoll, 1959). When prior information is available relative to possible conflict areas, special "props" can be included, such as a miniature dog if the child has a dog phobia.

The Driscoll Play Kit (Driscoll, 1959) has been produced to provide standard materials for research and clinical use. Included are five family figures, durable and well-proportioned furniture and a carrying case which unfolds to form five rooms and bath. Lynn's (1959) Structured Doll Play Test (SDP) uses no real furniture; instead there are 8½" x 11" cardboard pictures of different rooms, showing: 1) a crib and a bed; 2) a hospital bed and table; 3) a bathroom with potty chair, toilet and tub; 4) a double bed and a single bed. There are a few die-cut eating utensils and eight black-and-white family figures: mother, father, boys and girls (two clothed and one nude of each sex.) There is no explanation given for the omission of a baby figure. Identical family figures are also available with Oriental and with Negroid features. The manual presents specific problem situations and standard procedures are followed throughout the test administration. Lynn sees the test as appropriate for children from three to eleven years of age, and points out that the highly structured aspects should facilitate research. He also feels that the structuring helps to focus the subject's attention on the presented problem situations and discourages the tangential and exploratory play found so frequently with the use of more realistic materials.

Administration

Methods of doll play administration have varied from a completely "free field" to the use of highly structured situations which describe a problem and require the child subject to "act out" the solution.

Unstructured presentations. The usual procedure for the unstructured situation is to invite the child to play with the materials in any way he likes. If he hesitates, the examiner may need to offer encouragement, or make a first demonstration of possibilities. If the child does not accompany his play with verbalizations, Murphy (1956) suggests statements such as: "Tell me more about it"; "What does the mother say when the children don't eat?"; "Why did the mother spank the baby?"

Methods of administration, even in the free field, need to be suited to the age level of the subject. When working with children from eight to thirteen years of age, both Erikson (1951) and Witkin et al (1954) asked the children to construct a scene from an imaginary story, play or motion picture.

Structured presentations. The more highly structured procedures clearly specify, and limit, the number and kinds of materials available. Specific verbal instructions are given and clearly defined problem situations are presented for the child's solution.

Levy (1933) used only three dolls (mother, baby and same-sex child doll) in his sibling rivalry experiments. The child watched while the examiner affixed clay breasts to the mother doll who was then seated in a chair holding the baby. The child doll was introduced and the subject was asked to tell what the child would do if this were the first time he had seen the baby at the breast.

Conn (1938, 1940, 1948) devised "planned play-situations" which were tailormade to the individual child's presenting symptoms (enuresis, car sickness, phobias) or specific difficulties in real-life situations (acceptance of the new baby, death of a family member, etc.) Conn sees the child as both the objective observer (as the therapist outlines the problem situation using the doll characters) and as a participant (as the doll's attitudes, concerns and feelings are discussed).

Another variation, for very young children, might involve presenting the furnishings for only one room at a time, along with the doll family, and asking the child to show what happens in that room. For instance, oral attitudes and needs should be revealed in a dining room-kitchen arrangement, anal concerns in the bathroom, and parental and/or sibling rivalries in bedroom sequences. Theoretically, at least, it would seem that more specific dynamic material in each of the psychosexual areas might be elicited when the child's attention is thus focused on only one room at a time, than when the whole house is available for free exploration. In the latter instance, one room may become so intriguing that the entire time is spent there, yet there would be no justification for assuming that this was where the child's "problems" were necessarily centered.

The highest structuring involves the use of pre-determined problem situations which are presented via the dolls. Such problem statements resemble sentence- or story-completion tasks. In fact, Mosse (1954) has suggested using small dolls and animals to dramatize the presentation of the Duess (Despert) Fables when administering these story-completions to very young children. With careful planning, a variety of areas and situations can be covered in a brief play session.

Perhaps the first investigator to prepare a structured series of incomplete doll-play situations was Korner (1949) in her study of hostility in young children. Using a set of ten everyday situations, the examiner outlined the problem and enacted it with the appropriate parent and child dolls, with the instruction for the child to show (and tell) how the child figure reacts or how he arrives at a solution.

Moore and Ucko (1961) devised an imaginative and well-planned series of eight scenes for use in a longitudinal study of the fantasy life of young children. For example, in the first situation, only four chairs and four plates are set out for a family of five dolls, to test for readiness to share. The next situation involves a spilled bowl of food to see if the child regards this as an accident or as a punishable offense.

The Structured Doll Play Test (Lynn, 1959) represents the most recent adaptation of doll play procedures. The test consists of cardboard background pictures of rooms and furnishings and die-cut doll family figures. The accompanying manual gives specific instructions for the presentation of 18 structured situations in which the subject must usually make a choice between immature and mature behaviors, between the parents as gratifiers or as punishers, or between same- or opposite-sex agemates. Moore (1965) questions this choice procedure in that the child may want to use both parents in the initially presented situations, or carry over the same parent in the alternate situations (in which the examiner introduces the previously non-chosen parent as the only available figure). Moore also doubts that an adequate measure of "maturity" can be derived from only three items as used in this test.

In reviewing the various structured story situations used by different researchers and clinicians (Ammons & Ammons, 1949; Korner, 1949; Lynn, 1959; Moore & Ucko, 1961; Stamp, 1954; Stolz et al, 1954; Winstel, 1951) there were enough similarities between items to warrant the following overall compilation of areas included and types of incomplete problems presented:

Food and eating situations: Choice of bottle or cup; dislike of foods; preferred parent to sit beside or to be fed by.

Toileting: Choice of toilet or potty chair; bed wetting, soiling or wetting on the floor; attention or punishment from which parent.

Messing: Spilled food; messy room or floor; clothes dirty.

Bathing and dressing: Help from which parent.

Sleeping: Choice of crib or bed; not wanting to go to bed; who puts to bed; who sleep with; night fears and who comforts; dreams and nightmares.

Parent preferences: For routines (see above); who helps child most; who does the child like to help; who does child sit next to in car or hold hands with on walks; who reads to the child or fixes his toys.

Parent rivalries: Situations where parents are talking alone and exclude the child; parents leave child alone for short time.

Misbehavior and punishment: Nature of disobedience or wrong-doing; nature of the punishment; agent of scolding or punishment.

Reactions to siblings and new baby: Child's reactions when told of new baby and when seeing mother feed the baby; sharing and taking turns with siblings; smaller siblings get into older child's toys.

Peer relationships: Sex choice of playmates; peer fighting; parental interventions; no one to play with.

Injuries and illnesses: Nature and cause of; reactions to doctors and hospitalization.

Parental restrictions: Cannot go outside because it's raining; cannot have candy.

Child's moods: Happy; unhappy; angry; upset; disappointed; afraid.

It is important to consider the overall sequence of story presentations and to give careful attention to the possible impact on the child. Most of the story sets examined used a final story which was pleasant or at least non-threatening, except for Lynn's (1959) Structured Doll Play Test in which the last two stories both relate to night fears and bad dreams. This seems a most unfortunate oversight.

Finally, Ammons and Ammons (1952) make some practical suggestions for securing the maximum amount of information when asking specific structured questions. They met with fewer refusals if questions were stated in terms of "What are the dolls doing?" rather than "What are the dolls saying?" They also found fewer refusals with affect-laden questions. They strongly advise careful planning of the questions before the actual interview takes place, and if specific information is desired, the situation to be presented should be pre-arranged. They also recommend starting with content which has interest appeal to the child, and gradually introducing known aspects about the specific child's background to make the situation familiar to him.

Recording and interpretation

Lynn (1959) provides a detailed test manual with recording form and tally sheet. Diagrams indicate the figures to be used and their correct placement with respect to each other and the background cards. Space is also provided for recording the child's responses to each play situation. The tally sheet is somewhat ambiguous, does not include seven of the 18 test situations, and suffers from the lack of descriptive titles for several of the tabulations. Nevertheless, accurate completion of the sheet will give a record of parental choices in several situations, choice of peers, and immature versus mature choices in the feeding, toileting and sleep sequences. Standardization data are presented in the manual for 240 children from ages two through six, drawn from private schools, from higher than average socioeconomic levels, and with a large proportion of broken homes. Data are presented in fragmented fashion with 12 tables of isolated information at each age level and no overall summary material. No data are given for subjects beyond age six, although Lynn recommends the test's use through 11 years. As Ross (1965) points out, items such as the one concerning which parent will take the child to the toilet are obviously not suitable for latency-age children.

The play situations in the Moore and Ucko (1961) study lend themselves to categorization and ratings on the following dimensions: constructive, punitive, aggressive, anxious, and passive. The authors present tables showing the percentages of each sex giving type of response at ages four and six. They also analyze the play productions for the roles assigned to the various doll characters; signs of dependence or independence; degree of socialization; concepts of transgression and punishment; and constructiveness of solutions.

Obviously, the interpretation of the content of doll play should be handled in the same way as any other verbal and/or symbolic response in a projective test situation. Such methods need not be spelled out in detail here. Several of the investigators have also emphasized the wealth of adjunct information which can be secured, such as: observations of the child himself, his attitude toward the task, his method of approach, the use of his body, voice quality, meticulousness or need for order. These and other items are elaborated more fully by Murphy (1956, pp. 382-386) in a detailed outline for the analysis of records of Miniature Life Toy situations. Headings include items such as: initial approach; relationship to the examiner; chief activities; level of organization and structure; level of fantasy; process or sequences; level of emotional expression; motor and manipulative behaviors; cognitive activity; perceptual behavior; sensory responses; verbal expression; use of space, toys and objects; and evidences of the child's feelings about himself, his parents and siblings, home and community.

Murphy (1956, p. 98) also points to the ". . . need for a sensitive weighing of nuances of the child's behavior, which must go into every appraisal of a play session. A furtive glance at the experimenter after an abortive gesture toward a toy subsequently ignored may be more revealing than fifteen minutes of representative 'safe' play which uses conventionality to prevent expression of real feelings. A record of 'aggression' is incomplete if we have no indication whether it is for excitement, or a means to an end, or a reaction to a frustration, and whether it is followed by satisfaction, more aggression, anxiety, restorative behavior, or constructiveness."

Witkin et al (1954), in a study of the doll play of children eight to thirteen years of age, conclude that the configurational or formal characteristics of doll play are more meaningful than the content of the play itself. They mention such elements as: organizational patterns; spatial relationships; number of themes; motor expressive behavior; mode of handling and placing of objects; tightness or looseness of groupings; open versus closed productions; symmetrical versus assymmetrical formations; special attention to door and window openings. They further state: ". . . the play situation by its very nature invites the child to experiment with concrete formulations and syntheses for his impulses and ideas, and accords such experiments unusual permissiveness. Yet, nonetheless, no player is completely free to formulate at the whim of his impulses or of his field forces. To a specific opportunity to play he, as a whole person, comes with personality institutions and equipment which have evolved out of his past attempts at regulation and control of these same dynamic sources of play with which he has had long and intimate association. The ensuing interaction between the contents of play and his efforts at mastery of them can be presumed to be as much a part of the player as his play life itself . . . His behavior in the face of the conflicts inherent in the choices imposed, his modes of dealing in thought and action with anxiety, the confidence with which he deals with himself and the field, and his quality of awareness of self and objective realities are all factors that can be seen to mold the form of play, but also are all factors that must enter into other life operations" (Witkin et al, 1954, p. 378).

Doll Play Research

There is quite an accumulated body of research literature relating to methodological aspects of doll play (the influence of age, sex, materials, antecedent experiences) as well as some exploration of personality variables (such as aggression, identification, parent-child relationships). A sampling of these studies will be briefly reviewed along with some consideration of the reliability and validity aspects of this technique.

Methodological studies

The early methodological studies of Sears and his group have been reviewed elsewhere by Sears (1947) and, more recently, by Levin and Wardwell (1962). Such studies have been concerned with the establishment of standardized procedures which could be replicated by other investigators, and with the investigation of the effects of various stimulus variables which might affect the child's responses irrespective of his personality structure *per se*. The goal in these early studies was largely one of developing quantitative measures by means of which norms could be established, groups could be compared, and the reliability of recording techniques could be determined.

Materials. Phillips (1945) found that preschool children exposed to dolls and furniture which were highly realistic engaged in more exploratory play (manipulation of small parts), and showed more continuity of thematic content with fewer theme changes, while children presented with toys low in realism, e.g., ambiguously shaped wooden blocks, spent more time in tangential play and play involving attempts to organize the items. Pintler (1945) found that where materials were initially presented in an "unorganized" arrangement (with no room dividers and the furniture laid out in two rows), more time was spent in first organizing the materials. Bremer (1947) explored the relative effectiveness of household and playground furnishings and found more frustration with the play-yard. Bach (1945) utilized a school setting to control for social-environmental factors, since all the subjects were attending preschool. The furniture was all glued to the floor to prevent undue preoccupation with the materials as such and so forced the child to progress toward more involvement with the dolls themselves. Dolls used were a teacher, a boy and a girl doll, an another doll of the same sex as the subject.

Doll family constellations. The number of dolls available, their age and sex, can be expected to influence the kind of play patterns, fantasies and themes which the child will produce. Isch (1952) used only two dolls, a mother and a child, and obtained only one-third to one-half as much thematic material as reported by other investigators. Robinson (1946) compared the use of a standard doll family (mother, father, boy, girl and baby figures) with a selection of dolls which duplicated each subject's actual family. These were presented indirectly as "a mother, the little girl, her baby brother," etc. She found that children relate themselves more to the dolls and doll situations with the duplicated family and also direct somewhat more aggression toward the mother doll.

In contrast to Robinson's technique, Baruch (1941) made obvious efforts to encourage identification of the duplicate dolls with members of the child's family. Bach (1945) also urged the child to identify with one of the child dolls in the preschool set-up by saying, "I wonder where (child's name) is," or "We should have a boy like you in the preschool, shouldn't we?" Bach found that children who refused to identify under the examiner's instigation gave fewer aggressive responses and seemed less emotionally involved in the procedures than those who accepted the direct identification. Bach speculates that such adult pressure for the child to identify may serve to remove the whole doll play situation from the realm of relative safety to confrontation with the real world and the real people in it, leading to a generalization of inhibition from social experiences to thematic play behavior.

Number and length of sessions. The majority of the studies referred to above employed three or four sessions which were 20 to 30 minutes in length. Usually more exploratory, investigative, and organizational activity took place in the first portions of each doll play session. Phillips (1945) specifically studied the length of session as an independent variable, comparing three 20-minute sessions with one single session of 60 minutes. She found the same proportion of exploratory activity in the first 20 minutes of the hour-period as in the first of the three shorter session, but there was much less of this type of behavior in the remainder of the hour session than in the other two short sessions. On the other hand, toward the end of the one-hour session there were evidences of more frustration, more tangential behavior, and tangential-aggressive behavior than at the end of each shorter session.

Age levels. Most of the experimental and projective studies utilizing doll play have been employed with very young, preschool subjects. Nevertheless, latency children have also been studied. Bookbinder (1955) used six- to ten-year-olds in a study of punishment fantasies; Krall (1953) studied accident repeaters between the ages of five and eight years; Bach and Bremer's (1947) sample was composed of eight- to ten-year-old pre-delinquents. Latency children were the subjects of two studies of chronic illnesses: Lynn and Glazer (1962) with rheumatic fever subjects, and Peixotto and Hill (1964-65) with asthmatics. Witkin et al (1954) studied aspects of field-dependence as related to the doll play responses of children eight, ten and 13 years of age.

Honzik (1951) and Erikson (1951) both report results when pre-adolescents (ages 11 to 13) were presented with a variety of blocks and toys as well as a full complement of dolls and furniture. Rosenzweig and Shakow (1937) used doll play with adult schizophrenics.

Studies of age differences have largely concentrated on the younger age levels. For children from two to six years of age, Ammons and Ammons (1952) found a decrease in responses of direct aggression and an increase in the use of verbal techniques, displacement of aggression onto objects, and denial or inhibition of aggression, with age. In contrast, P. Sears (1951) found a marked increase in aggressive responses between the three- and four-year levels, and a leveling off by five years of age. Lynn and Lynn (1959), in comparing four- and six-year-olds, found more dependency and more immaturity in the four-year-olds and more same-sex parent choices in the six-year-olds. Using the same two age groups, Moore and Ucko (1962) found age differences in reasons for parental punishments (for toilet lapses at age four, and for fighting at age six). Anxiety was associated, at age four, with spilled food, fighting, mealtime, and the baby being fed, while at age six, anxiety was most often shown in situations depicting naughtiness, or the child wakening in the night.

Sex differences. Most doll play studies report more aggressive responses for boys than for girls at the younger ages, with this differential disappearing with increasing age. Bach (1945) also found that girls produced more doll actions, used more verbal commands, more themes of affection and more socially-approved themes than did boys. Pintler, Phillips and Sears (1946), as well as Bach (1945), found girls gave more stereotyped responses than boys. They explain the observed differences in terms of divergent cultural expectations for the two sexes in that doll play is a socially-approved pastime for little girls and they bring to the play session much previous, stereotyped experience with these materials. Boys may find doll materials an unfamiliar medium and so will not be hampered by awareness of the traditionally expected types of doll-play;

consequently, they will produce more non-stereotyped, i.e., more "projective," responses.

Moore and Ucko (1962) found more sex differences at age four than at six. Boys, at age four, gave many refusals, and few constructive responses while four-year-old girls gave more punitive responses than did the boys. Both sexes made equal use of punishment responses by age six.

In pre-adolescence, Honzik (1951) found that girls show more interest in family figures and home furnishings, while boys made greater use of blocks, vehicles, and doll figures in occupational uniforms. Erikson (1951) also found that girls tend to spread the furniture out over a broad table-top area and include many family people, while boys build tall, compact buildings to accommodate their person figures. Witkin et al (1954) found no remarkable sex differences at any of their pre-adolescent age levels, but there was more variability within each group of boys.

Quantification of observations. Bach (1945) developed a system of "behavior unit recording" whereby content categories were defined and quantified to yield normative data. Time sampling techniques were employed, with occurrence of activities being checked in each two-minute segment. His notational system included 26 response categories which could be recorded while observing the play session. Each action or unit of response could then be classified as stereotyped (reproducing routine actions appropriate to the setting) ; non-stereotyped (aggressive, affectionate, commanding, escape) ; thematic (concerned with a story) ; and non-thematic. A record was also made as to whether the dolls were instigators or recipients of actions. Reliabilities of two observers ranged from 71 to 97 percent for the different categories.

Both Pintler (1945) and Phillips (1945) also used time sampling techniques (15-second segments) , making judgments as to the dominant behavior occurring in each interval. Categories used included such items as: exploratory behavior, appropriate or inappropriate organization, use of self doll, stereotyped or non-stereotyped thematic behavior, tangential behavior, aggression.

The results obtained from quantification studies will depend on the number of categories originally selected for observation. There is always the danger that some portions of the observable "pie" will be cut into smaller pieces than others, thus yielding distorted results when comparisons are made between the segments of behavior within a single study. Levin and Wardwell (1962, p. 41) also show concern for this issue with respect to cross-study comparisons when they state: "The tendency to proliferate basic categories and to recombine them into various indices presents a difficult problem for comparing and evaluating studies. Since a larger number of combinatorial indices are possible from a few basic variables and since experimenters choose for theoretical or other reasons to form different combinations, studies which should be comparable are not."

In none of these early quantification studies was any consideration given to projectively meaningful content or sequential aspects of the doll activities. Consequently, these methods provide a means of securing very structured, sterile normative data, but they do not yield projective information. Indeed, they were not designed with projective purposes in mind.

Reliability. Observer reliabilities have generally been quite satisfactory, ranging from the .70s to .90s (Ammons and Ammons, 1952; Bach, 1945; Phillips, 1946; Robinson, 1947; P. Sears, 1951). Since several of the earlier doll play studies utilized more than one play session, it is interesting to note that test-retest findings suggest that a single session may give as reliable a picture as the multiple ones. P. Sears (1951) found session-to-session correlations of .73 for boys and .49 for girls. Ammons and Ammons (1952) found a correlation from one session to the next of .61, and odd-even reliabilities of .77 and .75 for each of two sessions. Stamp (1954), using the Driscoll Play Kit, studied percent of aggressive responses in each of three sessions and found correlations of .75 from first to second session; .86 from second to third; and .61 from first to third. The average percentages of each of four sub-types of aggression were similar for all three sessions.

Emmerich (1959) used a rating scale for evaluating the nurturance-control dimension with respect to the child doll's attitudes toward parents and toward a younger figure. He reports test-retest reliability coefficients of .69 for mother-child items; .50 for father-child items; and .73 for child-baby items, and concludes that the scale was reflecting stable concepts of parental nurturance and control.

Validity. In a comprehensive review of doll play research, Levin and Wardwell (1962) view the problems of establishing validity as stemming from the conceptual difficulties of determining whether doll play represents a replication of real-life experiences or a means of wish fulfillment. After reviewing numerous studies employing criteria ranging from observations of real-life behavior, teacher ratings, and questioning of the child, to relationships with other assessment techniques, they conclude that the findings generally are conflicting and contradictory.

Only a few examples of validation procedures will be presented here. Bach (1945) found little relationship between teacher ratings of overt behavior and doll-play fantasy behaviors. An examination of groups at the extremes of the fantasy variables did reveal some association between high stereotypy and high compliance, and between low stereotypy and high emotional involvement. Subjects who identified strongly with one of the dolls showed a significantly higher proportion of thematic content related to preschool activities (a preschool setting was used) while those who resisted identifying were generally less emotionally involved with the entire process.

Korner (1949) found that hostile behaviors reported by parents correlated only .21 with fantasy expressions of aggression in doll play. Half the children were hostile in one situation and not in the other. She advises caution in making projective interpretations of doll play responses but points out that we are still getting information as to how the child feels about his life experiences. She also suggests that inconsistencies indicate differential adaptations to hostility in real life and in fantasy.

Isch (1952) compared measures of mother-child interaction in an interview situation with subsequent doll play fantasies and found low, but positive correlations between the two. Children whose mothers were high on rejection and aggression portrayed mother dolls as highly aggressive, with both child and mother dolls the recipients of a large number of aggressive acts.

Manipulation of environmental variables

Sex of examiner. Caron and Gewirtz (1951) found that boys tend to give a higher percentage of aggressive responses with male examiners than with females, while girls give the same percentages of aggressive responses with examiners of either sex. Hartup and Himeno (1959) found similar results for boys with male examiners and for each of two sessions with varying antecedent conditions: isolation or verbal interaction with the examiner. Girls gave somewhat more aggressive responses with female than with male examiners, but only during the first session, irrespective of the antecedent condition.

Experimenter-child interaction. The role played by the clinician in a projective activity such as doll play could be a very crucial variable in assessing the results. Is he passive or does he actively initiate play sequences? Does he demonstrate warmth and interest or is his manner detached and impersonal? Is there much or little verbal structuring or verbal commentary on the dolls' activities? Does he pressure the child to "produce"? Does he ask innumerable questions about the doll figures and their activities?

Pintler (1945) attempted to answer some of these questions by manipulating the amount and kind of experimenter interaction. Her low level of interaction consisted of no more than five interventions (suggestions, elaborations, interpretations, interested attention) in any five-minute period; high level interaction involved 15-20 interactions in each similar time period. She found that high levels of interaction yielded more individualized thematic play, a greater variety of themes, more thematic aggression, and aggression appearing earlier in the sessions, indicating a greater lessening of inhibitions. There was more tangential behavior (unrelated to the doll house set-up), and more tangential play, in the groups receiving low levels of interaction from the examiner.

Bach (1945) made provision in his scoring schema for assessing the effect on the child's fantasy responses of differing amounts of verbal stimulation from the examiner. He found little relationship between the two variables, e.g., the examiner's comments suggesting aggression correlated —.20 with the subject's aggressive fantasies.

Baldwin and Levin (1964) were interested in the effect of verbal conditioning in shaping specific doll-play responses, i.e., whether an increase in the use of specific dolls would result if reinforcement was given to the prior use of these same dolls. Three groups were studied in which different reinforcements were used: the adult doll, the child doll, or random reinforcement. Reinforcements included repeating what the child said, verbalizing what the child did, or smiling at the child. When the use of the adult dolls was reinforced, the use of such dolls was increased over the three experimental sessions. Reinforcement of the child dolls was not clearcut, while random reinforcement yielded only the expected chance effects.

Stolz et al (1954) found that results from one section of their doll play data were not consistent with the rest of their findings in a study of the effects of father-absence. It was subsequently discovered that one of the examiners had altered the administration techniques midway through the story-completion sequences of doll play in such a way that the subjects were being encouraged to continue after "completing" the presented stories; also, no consistent limits were set on the termination of the play sessions. Such findings serve to emphasize the necessity for specifying and controlling the examiner's behavior in the potentially "open field" of a doll play session, not only for research purposes but also for the sake of consistency in interpretations in projective situations as well.

Antecedent and concurrent experimental conditions. Levin and Turgeon (1957) predicted that the mother's presence in the doll play session would reduce the number of aggressive responses. In the second of two sessions the mother was present in the experimental condition, and a neutral strange adult was present in the control group. Contrary to expectations, the mother-present group showed a significant increase in aggression in the second session for both sexes, while the decrease in aggression for the control group was non-significant.

The effects of immediately prior conditions have been explored in several studies. Yarrow (1948) reasoned that if a child's play could be sufficiently influenced by preceding events, then the resulting fantasy responses would not be truly representative of deeper motivational systems. He presented one group of preschoolers with a frustration situation (tinker toy construction beyond their ability) and a second group with a satiation task (peg boards to be monotonously filled in), immediately before their second doll session. He found a lack of consistent differences in behaviors following frustration, but frustration did result in an increase of aggressive play, tangential behavior, and regressive and withdrawn behaviors. Boys from the satiation group exhibited an increase in aggression directed toward the equipment.

Hartup and Himeno (1959) found a ten-minute period of non-punitive isolation (waiting for the examiner to return) led to an increase in aggressive responses as compared to doll play behavior following a ten-minute period of verbal interaction between the child and the examiner. Gordon and Cohn (1963) predicted a slower rate of increase of aggressive responses from first to second session if the affiliative drive could be aroused. (Previous doll play studies uniformly report an increase in aggression from session to session.) They divided the sample into High and Low Aggressives on the basis of aggressive responses secured during the first doll play session. Before the second session, children were randomly assigned to an experimental group in which a story with an affiliative theme was read, and a control group hearing a neutral story. Arousal of the affiliative drive yielded a clear decrease in aggressive behavior relative to the control group.

Bach (1945) reasoned that the frustration of a prior rest period (which presumably interferes with the child's desire to play) should result in more aggression in subsequent doll play. Using a preschool doll play set-up, he compared responses of children in a preschool group taking a short rest period with a group required to take a long nap. The long-nap group gave significantly more rest themes, a greater proportion of non-stereotyped responses, a greater proportion of doll act aggressions, and a greater amount of thematic aggression which involved the teacher doll.

Hollenberg and Sperry (1951) found the usual increase in aggressive responses over four highly permissive sessions with a control group. When the experimental group was given verbal disapproval of each aggressive response in the second session, there was no increase in aggressive responses during that session and there was a significant decrease in the following session. By the fourth session, aggressive responses were approaching the level of the control group. Presumably the introduction of punishment served to increase aggression anxiety with the subsequent temporary reduction of aggressive responses.

Personality assessment

Research reports on the projective uses of doll play are spotty in coverage, with overemphasis in some areas and very meager treatment in others. Some attention has been directed to the assessment of identification patterns and to parent-child interactions, particularly with respect to punishment, and to superego and guilt indicators. Expressions of aggression have received the most extensive study, possibly because aggression is frequently displayed in the play of young children.

Identification and parent preference. The Sears group of studies has tended to make the assumption that the doll most frequently used as the agent of action represents the child's identification figure (see Levin and Sears, 1956) . Emmerich (1959) questions this assumption and calls attention to the fact that a specific doll's actions may merely represent activities commonly associated with the parent represented by that doll and not necessarily mean that the child himself is identifying with the role which he is having the doll perform. Further complications involved in the Sears hypothesis concern the inability of an observer to actually determine whether the child's use, for instance, of the mother doll, is always in the role of "mother." Particularly, in a non-verbal child's doll play, this same doll figure may become successively mother, sister, baby, self-doll or even brother or father without the examiner's being aware of any shift. Young children are not rigidly bound to the adult stereotypes with respect to appearances, sex characteristics, or sex-typed attire. A further difficulty in determining identification is the fact that many different dolls become action agents in the course of a doll play session; which of these agents then becomes the identification representative? Or, are we to assume the child's identification is "fragmented" if he portrays several different figures in various action roles? .

The studies of parental preferences and/or identification can be grouped into three types: 1) asking for specific preferences in dolls or toys, or arranging story situations in such a way that the subject must make a choice between two parents; 2) presenting stories which will tap perceived attitudes toward each parent; 3) using an outside measure of identification (most often the IT Scale) and then assessing doll play characteristics of extreme groups.

In an early study of parent preferences, Rabban (1950) presented an array of dolls and toys commonly associated with girls' or boys' activities and observed children's masculine or feminine choices. He also asked the child which of the family dolls looked most like himself. Boys were found to be more clearly aware of sex-appropriate behaviors than were girls, and both sexes, from the lower socioeconomic groups, were aware of these differences at an earlier age than were the middle-class children. Ammons and Ammons (1949) asked which parent doll the same-sex child doll liked best, and then presented a series of structured situations to determine the preferred parent to participate in toileting, dressing, eating, playing, and so forth. They found a definite father preference in three- and four-year-old boys and a definite preference for mothers in four- and five-year-old girls.

In a study requiring choices of parents, Lynn and Sawrey (1962) found girls chose the mother doll significantly more often than boys chose the father doll. When the choices involved child dolls, girls chose the boy doll more often than the girls, while boys' peer choices were fairly evenly distributed. P. Sears (1953) reports more use of the same-sex parent doll (than of the opposite-sex parent doll) as agents of "good" behavior by both girls and boys, but this difference was only significant for girls.

Emmerich (1959) used an ingenious method of assessing identification with parental roles. The subject's perceptions of nurturance and control on the part of the parent dolls toward the child doll were compared with the nurturance and control displayed by the child doll toward the smaller baby doll. Children identified more with the same-sex parent than with the opposite-sex parent and both sexes saw the mother as the more nurturant (and less controlling). In both instances the differences were significant only for boys.

Several studies (Hartup, 1962; R. Lynn, 1961; Mussen & Distler, 1959; Mussen & Rutherford, 1963) have used responses to the IT Scale (Brown, 1956) as a measure of sex-role identification and then explored differences in responses to parent figures by the groups scoring at the extremes of the scale. Studying the dimension of perceived nurturance-control, Mussen and Distler (1959) with boys, and Mussen and Rutherford (1963) with both sexes, found that subjects with high sex typing scores saw their same-sex parents as exhibiting more nurturance and more control, and consequently as being the more "powerful" parent. There were no differences in the high- and low-masculine boys in their perceptions of mothers, but there was some evidence, in the Mussen and Rutherford data, that the father has more effect on the girls' femininity, than the mother has on the boys' masculinity. Lynn (1961) found that girls with high femininity scores viewed mothers as displaying more warmth than did low-feminine girls; while the low-feminine girls attributed more hostility and less warmth to the mother doll than to the father doll. Hartup (1962) also found femininity in girls (as measured by the IT Scale) to be associated with imitation of the mother, but he found no clear differences in boys associated with sex-typing.

In summary, both sexes demonstrate a preference for the same-sex parent, and these preferences tend to become more pronounced with increasing age. In some studies, girls identified with their mothers more strongly than boys with their fathers, while in others studies boys showed the stronger identification. Much of the ambiguity doubtless reflects small samples, different procedures, and interpretations at different levels.

Parent-child interactions. Child transgressions, parental punishments, and superego dimensions have been studied to a certain extent with doll play procedures. (Studies of the relationship between actual parental punishment and fantasy doll play aggression will be discussed in the next section). Bach and Bremer (1947) hypothesized that there would not be a strong anticipation of punishment when identification with the father is incomplete or impossible. They examined only doll play fantasies involving the father figure in two groups of children aged seven to ten years. The experimental group were all from broken homes, had experienced prolonged periods of parental hostility and neglect, and were currently committed to a home for "pre-psychopathic" children. The control group was comprised of presumably normal youngsters from intact homes. The disturbed group gave significantly fewer fantasies involving the father. More of this group gave stories of the father leaving home, while there was only a trend for them to direct more aggression toward the father figures. In fact, more of the control group portrayed the father as aggressing against the children. The investigators interpret their findings as suggesting that the experimental child's aggressive feelings toward the father may have been reduced as a result of his aggressive acting-out which necessitated institutionalization. They see the emotional indifference toward the father and the weak anticipation of punishment as reflecting the lack of a strong identification with the real father and ineffectual superego development.

Bookbinder (1955) used the Driscoll Play Kit to study class differences in punishment themes in the doll play of children six to eight years of age. Although more middle-class children used punishment themes, the only significant difference was in the greater use of severe physical punishment by the lower socioeconomic groups. There were no class differences in terms of the agent of punishment, with the mother portrayed as agent in 75 percent of all play sequences, and being assigned to this role more often by girls than by boys.

Carroll and Levin (1956) describe their methodology, presenting doll play situations in which the child doll does something wrong, in an attempt to develop a measure of superego development along a continuum ranging from demonstrations of fear (escaping from the external punisher) to guilt (self-punishment). For boys, guilt indicators were found, such as the mother acting as the agent of punishment toward the boy doll, and attempts at retribution on the part of the child dolls. At the opposite pole, no "fear" indices were discernible but some of the findings suggested an equally (or perhaps more) logical dimension of "nonguilt" including variables such as counter-aggression and avoidance of punishment. Findings for girls were similar but not as conclusive.

Fantasy aggression. The personality dimension most widely studied in doll play research has been aggression. The earliest studies of Levy (1933, 1936, 1951) were specifically concerned with the deliberate instigation of aggressive responses in sibling rivalry experiments. Later explorations have been more concerned with the measurement of aggressive responses, under varying conditions, as they occur in the course of the usual doll play sessions with normal children. Recently, Cohn (1962) has published a comprehensive review and evaluation of doll play research on aggression, while Levin and Wardwell's (1962) general review of doll play has, of necessity, emphasized the aggression studies since these constitute the major portion of doll play research.

Findings which appear in the majority of studies of fantasy aggression include:

1. A predominance of aggressive responses, with greater prevalence at the younger ages (Ammons & Ammons, 1953; Bach, 1945; Baruch, 1941; Korner, 1949).

2. An increase in aggressive responses from the first to subsequent sessions (Ammons & Ammons, 1953; Bach, 1945; Gewirtz, 1950; Hollenberg & Sperry, 1951; Isch, 1952; Levin & Sears, 1956; Phillips, 1945; P. Sears, 1951).

3. A decrease in the latency for the first aggressive response from the first to subsequent sessions (Pintler, 1945; Yarrow, 1946) and especially for boys (P. Sears, 1951).

4. Sex differences, with more aggressive responses from boys (Bach, 1945; Caron & Gewirtz, 1950; Hartup & Himeno, 1959; Levin & Turgeon, 1957; Phillips & Sears, 1946; P. Sears, 1951; Sears, Pintler & Sears, 1946). Differences in the content of aggressive acts, with boys using bodily injury, violence and catastrophe themes while girls use more verbal aggression or mischievous behavior (P. Sears, 1951). Boys show more aggression toward the father doll than do girls, but there are no sex differences with respect to the amount of aggression directed toward the mother (P. Sears, 1951).

5. Differences related to sibling status, with "only" children (Levin and Sears, 1956; P. Sears, 1951), and younger (P. Sears, 1951), showing more aggression than "oldest" siblings.

6. Several studies have explored the possible relationships between child-rearing practices and fantasy doll play aggression. Korner (1949) compared expressions of hostility in doll play with the extent of parental acceptance or rejection and found no clear relationships. Isch (1952) found that children whose mothers were the most aggressive in observed mother-child play situations also reproduced this mother-to-child aggression in their doll play. Hollenberg and Sperry (1951) found a trend for children whose mothers were either highly frustrating or highly punishing to show more aggression in doll play; those whose mothers were both highly punishing and frustrating were more aggressive than those whose mothers were least punishing and least frustrating. Similar effects of severe punishment were noted by Sears, Whiting, Nowlis and Sears (1953). Levin and Sears (1956) found the level of punishment-aggression of the same-sex parent to be the most effective in determining the frequency of aggressive doll play acts. Furthermore, boys who were highly identified with their fathers, and usually punished by him, showed the highest frequency of aggressive fantasy, while the degree of severity of the punishments had no effect on boys' doll play aggression. For girls, severe punishment from the mother led to the most fantasy aggression, while the least aggression was produced by girls whose mothers administered mild punishments.

Levin and Wardwell (1962) call attention to the many inconsistencies between different research studies with respect to findings on aggression.

They suggest that we first need more evidence as to whether doll fantasies in young children are reflecting wish fulfillment or are 'replications of real-life situations. It may be equally valid to interpret the dolls chosen as agents and as objects of aggressive acts, as representing projections and reversals of real-life roles, as to assume that actual experienced relationships are being revealed. Doll play findings on aggression may well be reflecting displacement, drive conflict, and/or anxiety over the expression of aggression. Consequently, great caution must be observed when interpreting the findings.

Personality traits. Witkin et al (1954) used doll play as one of their procedures in the study of field dependence as related to personality functioning in children 8, 10 and 13 years of age. It was predicted that children who had demonstrated marked field resistance in the previously administered perceptual tests would take an active approach to the doll play task of setting a "stage" for an imaginary story or play, while field-dependent subjects would be non-assertive, passive, and less able to maintain control of their unconscious processes. When doll play productions were rated for their organizational patterning, it was found that ability to impose a logically organized structure in the doll play was associated with the ability to resist field influences in the perceptual tasks. The relation between the pattern of play organization and perceptual performance was also more clear-cut for boys than for girls.

Stamp (1954) administered incomplete stories with the Driscoll Kit to two groups of latency age children who were judged by their teachers to be very submissive or rebellious. There were no significant group differences in the overall number of aggresive responses, but, when four subcategories of aggression were examined, more of the submissive group used indirect aggression, and more of the rebellious group used displaced aggression.

Differences in self-concepts of under-achieving and adequately-achieving boys (all of high intelligence) were studied by Walsh (1956), again using the Driscoll materials. Judges rated each of ten story-completions for: freedom of action, freedom of emotional expression, belongingness, response to environmental stimuli, and sex identification. All but the latter category differentiated between groups, with the greatest difference appearing in the category relating to freedom of action.

Commoss (1962) administered incomplete stories with the Driscoll Kit to children rated as "accepted" and as "isolates" on a sociometric test. She found the social isolates were more uncertain of the reactions of others and were less able to supply definite outcomes to the problem situations. No differences were found in the learning of same-sex roles as measured by the use of the same-sex dolls.

Emotional disturbance. Only two studies have made an attempt to contrast behaviors of normal subjects with those who are emotionally disturbed. Hartley, Frank and Goldenson (1952) observed that preschool children with emotional difficulties engaged in endless repetitive play or rearrangement of objects; tended to use items in inappropriate ways; played out numerous themes of violence, catastrophe and attack. Well-adjusted children were more consistent, placid and casual in their approach, and reproduced scenes of everyday events.

In a doll play study with schizophrenic adults, Rosenzweig and Shakow (1937) found that hebephrenics exhibited little planning or organization, engaged in much nonessential and incidental activity which often became bizarre, and used the various objects randomly and indiscriminately. Paranoid schizophrenics showed more planning but this was obsessive in character, and there was much vacillation, indecision and "fussiness" in carrying out their plans. They were rigid and formalistic, concerned about the eventual disposition of their productions, and tended to incorporate their personalized experiences and preoccupations. In contrast, normal adults showed the most foresight and planning, and produced well organized, meaningful structures with a logical sequence of events.

For some unaccountable reason no doll play studies have been carried out with specific clinical groups of children, such as childhood schizophrenics and other psychoses of childhood, behavior problems, the brain damaged, or the mentally retarded. For the diagnosis of young children in each of the above categories, it would seem that doll play procedures would provide a fruitful projective medium. Obviously, we first need data on large samples in each of these groupings to establish guidelines for comparative purposes.

Influence of situational factors

Absence of the father. Several studies have attempted to assess the specific effects of the father's absence on identification, aggression, and personality development as revealed through doll play responses. Time-limited absences due to military service have been studied as well as the effects of parental occupations necessitating prolonged absences from home.

Sears, Pintler and Sears (1946) and P. Sears (1951) compared a group of preschool boys and girls whose fathers were in the armed forces with a group whose fathers were still at home. Father absence had very little effect on girls' aggressive responses, but father-absent boys showed significantly less aggression than boys whose fathers were at home. These differences were particularly evident at age four. Father-present boys demonstrated the most aggression toward father and boy dolls (presumably indicating clear sex-typing) while father-absent boys showed less aggression toward each doll figure so that their responses resembled those of both girls' groups. The investigators interpret these findings as suggesting an inhibition of aggression in young boys as a result of living in predominantly female environments.

Bach (1946) carried out a similar study with older children (ages six to ten years). While both father-present and father-absent children produced about equal amounts of fantasy related to family life, the father-present group gave significantly more fantasies involving the father. With respect to specific types of father fantasies, the father-absent group emphasized stereotyped representations of family life, with more affection and less authoritative behaviors on the part of the father figures. The father-separated children appeared to have created a fantasy of an ideal father in an ideal home setting, in contrast to the more realistic situations portrayed by the father-present children who showed the father as punitive, authoritarian and aggressive.

Stolz et al (1954) report some doll play data as part of a very intensive study of 19 families in which the first child was born while the father was away on military duty and the second child was born after the father's return. The father-separated subjects showed significantly higher ratings of aggressive feelings than did control subjects from continuously intact families. There were also more inhibitions against aggressive behavior and a greater number of aggressive acts in the separated children. In a second series of doll play experiments involving story completions, no differences were found between the two groups.

Scott (1954) compared five-year-old children living in intact families with children who had been separated from their parents and placed in institutions for at least one year. The children living with their families made significantly more use of all doll family figures, gave more stereotyped responses, and more responses reflecting affection, hostility, and intrafamilial interactions. The institutionalized children significantly more often took the part of the parent or authority figure directly, rather than mediating this role through a parent doll. There was no real interaction between parent dolls and child dolls and the child dolls were portrayed as passive, compliant and submissive to the demands of authority.

The effects of prolonged vocational absences of the father have been studied by Lynn and Sawrey (1959, 1962). The Structured Doll Play Test was administered to latency age children whose sailor-fathers were often absent for periods of two years at a time. Father-absent boys gave more immature responses than father-present boys, but they also chose the father doll more often in the choice situations. More of the father-absent girls chose the mother doll in separation situations and gave more dependency responses. So, for both sexes, father absence was associated with more dependency and immaturity and more choices of the same-sex parent dolls.

Illness and physical handicaps. Miller and Baruch (1950) found that young allergic (mostly asthmatic) children expressed significantly less direct and indirect hostility in doll play than did a group of controls. The allergic subjects did direct significantly more hostility against themselves or against the self-figures in doll play. Sandler (1964-65), using the Structured Doll Play Test, found that asthmatic children saw the mother as less warm and more hostile than either of the control groups of chronically ill or well children. Peixotto and Hill (1964-65) report that administration of the Driscoll Kit to asthmatic girls yielded fantasies of the ideal family with emphasis on orderliness, routines, and no fighting or quarreling. Mothers were seen as satisfying dependency and oral needs and fathers as passive breadwinners. The investigators felt that other tests, such as figure drawings, revealed the more realistic aspects of the actual home situations.

Lynn, Glaser and Harrison (1962) studied rheumatic fever cases with the use of the Structured Doll Play Test, which contains items relating to illness and hospitals. When compared to children with minor illnesses, the rheumatic fever patients portrayed the dolls as being more seriously ill, as having the same illness as the subject, and as receiving much additional attention.

Mayhew (1963) used the London Doll Play Technique in studying the emotional development of six-year-old spastic children (mean IQ's in the low 80's), comparing them with the normal data of Moore and Ucko (1961). The spastics resembled the normal four-year-olds more than the sixes, which probably reflects the greater similarity in mental levels. Spastic girls gave more constructive and more punitive responses while the boys gave more aggressive responses and more refusals.

Erickson (1958) was interested in assessing four-year-olds' reactions to intrusive medical procedures. She presented clinical equipment (thermometer, hypoderic needle, enema, tongue blades) and doctor and nurse dolls, along with the traditional doll family, to children when hospitalized and also upon their return home. In contrast to the control group of nursery school children who reacted very little to these materials, most of the hospitalized children were able to dramatize and verbalize their feelings about hospitalization, played out hostile behavior toward the doctor and nurse, and used the clinical equipment for intrusive procedures.

Krall (1953) used doll play with chronic accident-prone children. When compared to a control group, the accident repeaters showed significantly more aggression in their doll play, less delay in the expression of this aggression, more verbal aggression and more of the non-stereotyped (projective) thematic play. Results suggested more lability for this group with less conscious control of impulsive behaviors.

Racial awareness and racial differences. Racial awareness of three- to seven-year-old Negro children was studied by Clark and Clark (1947) by presenting two white and two colored dolls and asking which doll the child preferred, which looked like a white child and a colored child, and which looked like himself. No significant differences were found between subjects from racially mixed Northern schools and segregated Southern schools. A first knowledge of racial differences appears to be present by three to four years of age, but such awareness does not necessarily lead to accurate self-identification. (Only 66% chose the Negro doll as most like themselves.) A clear majority chose the white doll as the "nicest" and the one they would like to play with, and conversely, saw the colored doll as "bad." The preference for the white doll did decrease with age.

In a somewhat parallel study of white boys (two to six years of age), Ammons (1950) also found recognitions of differences increased with age, with the older children expressing more negative feelings toward Negro dolls and using them as scapegoats. Goodman (1952) made a comparative study of Negro and white four-year-olds, using Negro and white families of dolls and incomplete story presentations. She found racial patterns reflecting cultural stereotypes, with the white children being "in-group" oriented, while the Negro children already sensed their "difference" and expressed a preference to be white.

Doll play studies have been carried out with other races. For instance, Levy (1939) administered his sibling rivalry experiments to children in Guatemala and Argentina, and found reactions of jealousy, regression, self-punishment and guilt similar to results with American children. Gewirtz (1950) compared Indian children of Sac and Fox settlements with data from white children, finding less aggression with the Indian subjects. Ritchie (1957) used doll play, and play with clay, in a normative study of personality development in Maori children of Rakau.

Socioeconomic status. Very few studies have attempted to assess differences in doll play responses which might be attributable to socioeconomic factors. In fact, most of the doll play data have been secured in university preschools which generally serve highly intelligent children whose parents are engaged in professional occupations. Some of the later Sears data have been gathered as part of the larger pattern study of Sears, Maccoby and Levin (1957) which used upper lower and upper middle socioeconomic groups, but very little of the results from the doll play are reported in terms of social class variables. Levin and Sears (1956) do report no differences in the percent of aggressive responses when comparing these large samples of middle class and working class children.

Rabban (1950) was specifically interested in sex-typed responses as related to class status. He found that both boys and girls from working class backgrounds are aware of sex roles more clearly and at earlier ages than are children from upper middle class families. Bookbinder (1955) studied the relationship of social status to different types of punishments as revealed in doll play. Children from low socioeconomic groups made more use of severe physical punishments, while more middle class children used themes of deprivation. There were no class differences in the doll used as agent of punishment.

Murphy (1956) calls attention to the fact that certain symbols may have different meanings when used in different subcultures, and that the extent of organization or disorganization in structures may be reflecting actual living conditions rather than deeper personality deviations. Rural and urban children can also be expected to react to doll play situations in different ways, in terms of the freedom to use space, and extent of autonomy. She also states: "Each subculture provides its own patterns of greater or less rigidity—the child's visual experience of streets, trees and flowers, yards, and houses; his day's design of more, or less, systematically scheduled routines; the rich or meager, pleasant or unpleasant sounds, smells, looks of the people around him all fuse into personal concepts of what the world looks like . . . Not only the texture and the pattern of the culture, but the child's sense of his place in it, can emerge if we watch closely to see just what is going on. Play tells us then about the child's own feelings about his perception of his culture, and his inner feeling of relationship to it, in other words his 'idiosyncratice life space' " (Murphy, 1956, pp. 12-13).

Conclusions

It seems remarkable that a technique that has been studied to such an extent as doll play should have yielded so little in the way of projective information. There has been much attention to methodological details which lend themselves to easy categorization and measurement, and too little study of the projective aspects relating to such dimensions as drives, defenses, conflicts and anxieties.

Perhaps the materials themselves tend to inhibit fantasy due to their close resemblance to real-life persons and objects. As Bach (1945) ascertained, about 75 percent of doll play responses are of the stereotyped variety, i.e., concerned with everyday aspects and routines. Only 25 percent of responses depart from a reality base and depict feelings and fantasies. The theory underlying the more traditional projective techniques (such as the Rorschach, TAT, CAT) emphasizes the ambiguous aspects of the stimuli, an element which is certainly not present in the doll play materials.

In the analysis and interpretation of the meager projective material that has been elicited, little mention is made, for instance, of defense mechanisms. It is difficult to tell, from the published reports, whether such defenses were in fact absent, or were merely not being assessed. Certainly, at the preschool ages, one would not expect highly organized defensive structures to be present, but the more primitive defense mechanisms, such as regression, denial, introjection and projection, should be revealed if this medium is truly "projective" in nature.

Much of the reported research has been concerned with the tabulation of isolated variables which were selected for specific study purposes. Consequently, activities of the various doll figures have been reduced, in the analyses, to their simplest surface manifestations. If meaningful information is to be derived from doll play procedures, more attention must be paid to the sequences of behavior throughout the play session and to the various interrelationships developed over time between the different doll figures.

PUPPETRY

Puppets have been used for entertainment purposes for centuries, but only in the last few decades have they been adopted in clinical settings as media for diagnosis and therapy. Drama had been recognized as a means of facilitating identification and projection long before psychologists became interested in these processes and gave labels to them. Puppet dramas provide a usable technique for eliciting projective material from children, as they readily identify with the puppet characters and project their conflicts and emotions as the action progresses. Cassell (1965, p. 2) points out some of the advantages of puppetry over doll play in ". . . the more ready transference of the child's feelings to his puppet, the greater identity with the puppet, more easily maintained anonymity for himself, and the diversity of movement possible for the puppet. Puppet play also has its advantages in the use with older boys, who may feel that doll play is a 'sissy' activity but are more willing to engage in puppet play."

Puppets can be used with individuals or with groups of children; story themes can be "invented" spontaneously by the child or children, or specially selected scripts can be performed by a skilled clinician-puppeteer. Throughout this discussion, hand or finger puppets are intended, rather than the marionette. In the former types, the puppeteer is in direct contact with the puppets, resulting in spontaneity of action, an aspect which is particularly important if the child is manipulating the figures. The marionette, on the other hand, requires a more formalized script, much prior practice of movements and maneuvers, and more attention to a finished product at the expense of warmth and projection.

Much of the clinical work with puppets has been carried out on the Children's Ward of Bellevue Hospital and reported by Bender and Woltmann (1936, 1941-42) and Woltmann (1940, 1951). These were structured shows presented to groups of children. Bender and Woltmann (1936, p. 352) state their purpose and rationale as follows: "The puppet shows lend themselves readily to these identification processes with all sorts of characters, and permit the children to project problems into the characters and live them out freely and come to a happy solution. By the impersonal nature of the characters with whom they identify themselves, and the fact that they are puppets and cannot really be hurt, the children are able to express their emotions freely and without guilt, anxiety or apprehension . . . It is undoubtedly one of the greatest therapeutic factors that the child learns that other children about him are experiencing the same feelings that he is, and he is aided and abetted in the expression of his aggressive tendencies by the fact that all the others about him are loudly acclaiming his own feelings . . . It is particularly important to realize that it is not enough for the children to be allowed a free expression of their aggressive tendencies but that there should always be a solution of the problem with equally free expressions of love."

Woltmann (1951) traces the development of Casper, his main puppet character, back to an East Indian shadow puppet in 5000 B.C. Fond of eating and drinking, beating and being beaten, this was the first real comedian. He has since fought, outwitted, clowned and connived his way through history from ancient Greece to modern Germany. He has gone under various names—Vidusaka in East India, Karagöz in Turkey, Petrushka in Russia, Harlequin in Italy, Guignol in France, Punch and Falstaff in England, and Hanswurst or Casper in the Germanic countries. He appears sometimes as a servant, sometimes as a farmer or a court jester, but always as a rollicking and boisterous character, immune to all danger. He has endeared himself to the common man, and symbolizes his feelings, appetites and emotions. He does on the stage what his audience feels but dares not do in reality. In introducing Casper to children's groups, Woltmann maintained the essential spirit of the adult Casper but without his lewdness or coarseness. His appearance remains the same, with his fool's cap and "ageless" garb and he could be *any* boy between the ages of six and twelve.

A unique feature of puppet characters is their unrealistic, symbolic, fantasy nature. Woltmann (1951) feels this unreality is an aid in identification and that real human figures would be too threatening. Inasmuch as puppets have been universally accepted as the prototypes of *all* people they would seem to fulfill the same projective purpose as the generalized types of ambiguous characters used in standard picture-story tests. In addition, puppets have the added features of movement and speech, which add to the ease of eliciting responses from children.

Puppet characters and scripts

Children's reactions to the Bender and Woltmann puppet plays have revealed that each character portrays certain attitudes, emotions or aspects of personality. Casper is seen as a hero who is able to defend himself and harms others only in self-defense. He symbolically expresses strong infantile drives which demand satisfaction, yet he can also adapt to the demands of reality. Casper's stick, bequeathed to him by generations of previous puppets, has a phallic significance and also serves as a symbol of power. It is the weapon of aggression and defense that has been used by all primitives and children.

The witch personifies the bad mother on whom the child can project all that is harsh, demanding, refusing and unloving in his own mother. It is safe and acceptable to hate and destroy this symbolic figure. Woltmann points out that the witch never actually hits, harms or kills another character on the puppet stage, yet the children consistently endow her with all her traditional attributes of hatred, evil and cruelty. On the other hand, it is only the truly fantasy characters who are killed in the plays: the witch, crocodile, ghost or giant. These killing sequences employ the use of countless repetitions which seem to have a cathartic effect that would be missed, for instance, if the witch died just one sudden death. In this respect the puppets can go beyond the limits of real-life situations.

The bad father is represented variously by the giant, with his powerful physical threat, and by the magician, who maintains his superiority through magic and scheming. The good parents become superego representatives, e.g., the father-detective is a symbol of authority and the representative of law and order.

Several animal figures are used. The monkey represents id impulses with its mischievousness, impishness, and lack of guilt. The crocodile personifies insatiable oral cravings and dangerous oral aggression and elicits fears of retaliation and punishment for unacceptable oral impulses.

"A puppet show in which only realistic characters appear is too logical and does not allow for fantasy digressions. A puppet show in which only fantasy characters act is too unreal and fantastic and does not allow for identifications on a reality level. A good puppet show, like a good fairy tale, should therefore combine both realistic and fantasy factors. This mixture of reality and fantasy makes it easier for the child to enter into the spirit of the problem presented, and aids in the identification. Since parts of the show or some of the puppets (witch, devil, giant, and so on) are symbolic expressions of attitudes, the child himself feels free to project his own attitudes into the show" (Woltmann, 1951, pp. 616-617).

Synopses and scripts for several puppet plays are presented by Bender and Woltmann (1936), Woltmann (1951), and Hartley, Frank and Goldenson (1952). Woltmann (1951) also lists some of the characteristics of a good puppet play: the use of ordinary language familiar to the child audience; much action and repetition of actions and solutions (especially traumatic and aggressive sequences); a plot or theme which is easily understood; combinations of realistic and fantasy elements; provision for close interaction between the audience and the puppets which is achieved by improvization and free discussion.

Administration

Puppet plays can be presented to individuals or to groups; they can be performed by the child or by the clinician. Previously prepared scripts can be used or the play can proceed spontaneously as determined by the ad-libbed interaction between the selected characters. Throughout a performance the puppeteer endeavors to elicit as much spontaneous response and reaction as possible from the child audience. Such interaction between audience and puppets greatly enhances the value of the show, contributes to projection and provides a means of insight into the dynamic mechanisms of the children who are responding.

Woltmann also made use of the "half-show" procedure whereby the puppeteer stops midway through the performance, at a crucial dramatic point, and asks the children what they think will happen next. If, as is assumed, the child has identified with the puppet characters, and if his emotions have been strongly aroused, his spontaneous, unpremeditated responses in the half-show constitute a very meaningful type of projection. As Woltmann (1951, p. 619) states: "The various solutions made are colored by the child's own problems and his ability to understand intellectually and emotionally the implications contained in a particular problem. Although each child tries to unravel the conflict in terms of his own involvement, background, family constellation, and general level of maturity, he is not aware of the fact that he talks about himself. By discussing the puppets and their problems, he is spared the embarrassment of talking about himself. In this fashion, relevant material, disclosing the child's own dynamics and attempts to work through his own conflicts, is brought to the surface in an easy fashion." After the half-show discussion, the play is continued to its logical conclusion. It is extremely important, from the therapeutic standpoint, that the child audience have the opportunity, at the completion of the play, to ask questions, express their feelings and discuss the action and the solution.

As a projective technique, the child's comments during the show and half-show, and his discussion following the play, provide the data for projective analysis. Further follow-up procedures suggested by Woltmann (1951) include drawing pictures or modeling clay scenes suggested by the show; telling or re-enacting the story to other groups of children. The material selected for emphasis, the additions made or portions omitted all yield projective data.

In contrast to the literature on doll play where experimental and research studies far outnumber clinical reports, most of the puppet literature describes clinical uses, while research coverage is quite meager.

Clinical use of puppets

Lerner and Murphy (1941), as part of a comprehensive study of various methods for the projective study of very young children, used puppets of a horse, clown, mother, father, teacher and child. They presented structured situations and asked specific questions as to what the puppets did and felt.

Most of the work reported by Woltmann (1940, 1951, 1960) and Bender and Woltmann (1936, 1941-42) involved the presentation of plays written by adults and presented to groups of children. In true puppeteer fashion, the themes and plots were continually revised and adapted to meet the needs of each particular group of children. Woltmann (1960) also presents illustrative protocols of the projective use of puppets in small spontaneous group interactions among several children.

Hartley, Frank and Goldenson (1952) used puppets with groups of normal nursery school and kindergarten subjects. They use a "standard family" of puppets—mother, father, boy, girl, baby—plus a monkey and one nondescript character, "Mr. Everybody." Brief scripts were developed around the following themes: arrival of a new baby, peer aggression, harsh or unjust treatment from parents, separation from a parent, fears of getting dirty, and sibling rivalry. These shows were presented to groups of five or six children at a time. Examples are presented of different children's reactions to illustrate the effectiveness of puppet plays in releasing aggressive feelings, facilitating identification, and throwing light on individual problem areas.

Rambert (1949) used puppets with individual children as a means of diagnosis and of therapy. On initial presentation, the child was encouraged to make up his own plays. Later, in therapeutic sessions, and as resistance set in, the therapist would initiate themes along the lines which the child had previously employed. Once the play was started, the child would be asked to tell what the character would do next, and how he felt, with the child being encouraged to take the part of at least one of the characters. When indicated, the therapist would introduce specific characters to work through situations related to the child's current conflicts. Rambert feels that there are age differences in the use made of puppets, with younger children (ages five and six) identifying with the puppet characters and representing conflicts directly through the interactions of family members. At later ages, more puppet "types" are employed, such as the witch and devil, which are used dynamically as symbolic representatives of feelings and attitudes.

In discussing his puppet work with individual children, Woltmann (1960, p. 308) states: "The emphasis is on spontaneity . . . the puppet, the stage, the actions and the spoken word are only a means to an end. They are the media through which the child expresses and brings to a tangible level some of his ideas, concepts, modes of action, perceptions and levels of understanding, as well as his fears, his anxieties and his reaching out for love and acceptance . . . It does not matter whether or not the child follows a carefully constructed dramatic build-up that leads to a climax. Important is the fact that the child feels free enough to let the puppets act for him what he thinks, how he would like to handle situations, or how he would meet and overcome obstacles."

Lyle and Holly (1941) have encouraged adult psychiatric patients to make their own puppets, write and perform the plays. They point to the sense of mastery experienced by the performer as a therapeutic value and also call attention to the fact that a puppet play necessarily involves an audience of at least one other person. Jenkins and Beckh (1942) prefer finger puppets to full-sized ones for individual work. They view puppets as an avenue for the child to portray his conflicts through the impersonal "third person"; aggression or tabooed activities can be projected onto the puppets and the child can express, through the puppet's actions, feelings which are difficult to put into words.

Research with puppets

Puppets were presented by Stern and Asherman (1955) to children from eight different ethnic groups in a study of children's reactions to various aspects of discipline and family expectations as affected by the presence of grandparents in the home. In each play sequence, the experimenters used the mother and father puppets to outline a specific problem situation. The subject then used the child and grandparent puppets to work through a solution. Results indicated perceptions of less concern on the part of the grandparents than of the parents toward the child and ascription of more negative than positive traits to the grandparents. There was a high incidence of conflictual material, with the children showing resentment of the contradictory aspects of the grandparents and awareness of the distortions and conflicts in the value judgments of the three generations.

Cassell (1965) was interested in studying the effect of brief puppet plays on children's ability to tolerate cardiac catheterization procedures. Criteria of success were ratings of less disturbance during the medical procedures, less emotional disturbance on the ward and subsequently at home, and more willingness to return for further treatment on the part of the group receiving puppet sessions as compared to a control group who did not see the shows. The puppets used included a doctor, nurse, boy, girl, mother and father. Miniature medical equipment similar to that actually used in the catheterization process was also introduced. The medical procedures were first enacted with the therapist taking the doctor's role and then the child subject played the doctor's part. One session was given on the day before the catheterization and a second session on the day following the procedure. The puppet-exposed group showed significantly less disturbance than the control group during the catheterization and expressed more willingness to return for further treatments. No differences were observed with respect to the extent of emotional disturbance on the ward or subsequently at home. In fact, both groups showed less disturbance after the procedure than before.

The puppet play, *Rock-A-Bye, Baby,* written and performed by A. G. Woltmann has been recorded on film (Haworth & Woltmann, 1959) in an effort to make the show more readily available for clinical use. The filmed version can be shown to groups of children and would appear to be a useful instrument for screening large numbers of children in a relatively short period of time. Previous research with projective films in France and Italy (see Haworth, 1960) suggested that children would respond at earlier ages to the pictorial animation of a film than to still pictures, such as are used in the traditional picture-story tests. Furthermore, the child-subject is not required to "make up" a complete story in the film situation, but responds spontaneously to the ongoing activities and to the characters with which he more readily identifies since they speak and act. The filmed version of *Rock-A-Bye, Baby* is a 35 minute, 16mm, black and white film with sound. It is suitable for children from five to ten years of age.

Administration. The film is administered, as is the "live" puppet show, up to a climactic incident, at which point a length of blank film has been inserted as a signal to the projectionist to stop the show, turn on the lights and initiate the half-show discussion. The remaining portion of the film is then shown to its completion and followed by individual questioning of each child. A standard set of questions is provided in the test manual and covers areas such as preferences for various characters, perceptions of Casper's attitudes toward his parents and toward the baby sister, and indications of the subject's reactions to Casper's misdeeds.

The film can be shown to groups of 10 to 15 children at one time. Three or four adults then need to be available for the final individual inquiries, so that no child needs to wait more than 10 or 15 minutes.

Evaluation of responses. An analysis sheet has been constructed for use in personality assessment. Indices of Identification, Jealousy, Aggression to Parents, Guilt (masturbatory), Anxiety (castration), and Obsessive Trends have been based on specific types of responses to the various interview questions. Sample protocols are presented by Haworth (1957, 1960) to illustrate high "scores" on the different indices. Interscorer reliabilities for three judges scoring the protocols ranged from .83 to .94.

Norms of expected responses were obtained on the basis of an initial sample of approximately 250 children and substantiated on a subsequent sample of equal size. If an individual child's responses deviate markedly from these norms, then further testing with individual projective measures would be indicated.

Research. The initial sample (Haworth, 1957) of 244 children was taken from nursery school, first, third and fifth grades. In a repeat study

(Haworth, 1961) of 257 children in kindergarten, first and second grades, findings for both first grade samples were markedly similar with respect to the proportions of deviant responses in specific areas. Consistent developmental progressions were also observed, with the incidence of high scores on Aggression to Parents, Guilt and Anxiety being quite high at the early grades and showing a marked drop between the second and third grades to a lower level which was maintained through fifth grade. These indices reflect conflict problems generally regarded as characteristic of the pre-latency period and their pattern of occurrence could be explained on this basis. In contrast, three other indices (Identification, Jealousy and Obsessive Trends) remained at fairly constant levels throughout the age span under study, suggesting that these measures are tapping more enduring aspects of personality.

One further validation study reported by Haworth (1962) involved the administration of individual projectives to children who had previously seen the film. Fifteen children were selected on the basis of high scores either on the Obsessive Index or on both the Guilt and Anxiety dimensions. A matched control group was selected from the pool of cases who had given no deviant film responses. A battery of individual projective techniques, consisting of the Rorschach, CAT, Despert Fables and Draw-a-Person Test, was administered to each child 8 to 12 months after the film test. Each subject was also asked to recall as much of the film story as he could. Judges evaluated the protocols for evidences of disturbance with particular reference to the same dimensions (Obsessive, Guilt and Anxiety) for which the experimental group was chosen originally.

Comparative findings indicated generally consistent results, with the obsessive responders to the group film test scoring in similar fashion on "obsessive" measures used in evaluating the Rorschach and CAT. In addition, these subjects were the only ones to recall those scenes from the film which were concerned with obedience, parental punitiveness and Casper's "naughtiness." Similarly the Guilt-Anxiety group, who were initially chosen on the basis of responses reflecting concerns with the witch and her aggression and symbolism relating to castration fears, gave responses, on the individual tests, which emphasized bodily injury and fears of attack. They also only recalled those film sequences which were related to the witch. Haworth (1962, p. 60) concludes: "It would appear that children do tend to respond in dynamically consistent fashion on individual and group tests and over extensive periods of time. Since evaluations comparable to those secured from individual projectives can be obtained in a group situation with the film test, the latter instrument has demonstrated its usefulness as a quick screening device in the school situation."

Conclusions

The facility with which puppets elicit projective responses is probably due to their speech and actions and the ease with which they can be used symbolically to recreate situations and re-enact conflicts. Puppets can be presented "live" or on film by the examiner or therapist, or children can create their own play sequences spontaneously. Puppets appeal to a greater range of ages than do family dolls and capture the interest of boys as well as of girls. Very little research has been reported, either with real puppets or the filmed shows but, theoretically at least, the use of puppets for projective purposes should yield promising results.

SUMMARY

Both doll play and puppetry techniques are designed to facilitate children's identifications by the use of miniature human figures, and to encourage the projection of emotional aspects and interpersonal relationships through the activities of the characters. It is surprising that these materials have not been used more extensively in diagnostic, projective testing in view of the appeal of dolls and miniature objects to young children (as well as to retarded and nonverbal youngsters) at age ranges where more clearly verbal and reasoning types of tasks are beyond their ability levels.

Perhaps the sterility of research findings in doll play studies has discouraged more imaginative uses and interpretations of these materials. Certainly there is a need for more attention to the global aspects of an individual child's responses, and to the sequence of activities and various role relationships portrayed. For assessment purposes we also need information concerning expected responses of various clinical groups rather than piecemeal, atomistic analyses of the effects of isolated environmental variables.

The highly realistic nature of dolls and household objects violates one of the major characteristics generally deemed important in a projective instrument. In contrast, the ambiguity, universality, and possibilities for symbolic representation which characterize puppet figures suggest that more fruitful results might be secured by further exploration of various methods for utilizing puppetry as a projective medium.

REFERENCES

Ammons, Carol H., & Ammons, R. B. Research and clinical applications of the doll-play interview. *J. Pers.*, 1952, *21*, 85-90.

Ammons, Carol H., & Ammons, R. B. Aggression in doll-play: interviews of two- to six-year-old white males. *J. genet. Psychol.*, 1953, *82*, 205-213.

Ammons, R. B. Reactions in a projective doll-play interview of white males two to six years of age to differences in skin color and facial features. *J. genet. Psychol.*, 1950, *76*, 323-341.

Ammons, R. B., & Ammons, H. S. Parent preferences in young children's doll-play interviews. *J. abnorm. soc. Psychol.*, 1949, *44*, 490-505.

Bach, G. R. Young children's play fantasies. *Psychol. Monogr.*, 1945, *59*, No. 2 (Whole No. 272).

Bach, G. R. Father-fantasies and father-typing in father-separated children. *Child Develpm.*, 1946, *17*, 63-80.

Bach, G. R., & Bremer, Gloria. Projective father fantasies of preadolescent, delinquent children. *J. Psychol.*, 1947, *24*, 3-17.

Baldwin, Clara P., & Levin, H. Reinforcement of agents of action in doll play. *J. abnorm. soc. Psychol.*, 1964, *68*, 328-330.

Baruch, Dorothy W. Aggression during doll play in a preschool. *Amer. J. Orthopsychiat.*, 1941, *11*, 252-259.

Bender, Lauretta, & Woltmann, A. G. The use of puppet shows as a psychotherapeutic method for behavior problems in children. *Amer. J. Orthopsychiat.*, 1936, *6*, 341-354.

Bender, Lauretta, & Woltmann, A. G. Play and psychotherapy. *Nerv. Child*, 1941-42, *1*, 17-42.

Bookbinder, Kathryn F. The relation of social status and punishment as observed in stories obtained with the Driscoll Play Kit. *Dissert. Abst.*, 1955, *15*, 1252-53.

Bremer, G. The effect of two fantasy environments on children's doll play responses. Unpublished master's thesis, State University of Iowa, 1947.

Brown, D. G. Sex-role preference in young children. *Psychol. Monogr.*, 1956, *70*, No. 14 (Whole No. 421).

Caron, A. J., & Gewirtz, J. L. An investigation of the effects of the sex category of the interacting adult, chronological age (6, 8 and 10), and sex of child, on aggressive (hostile) behavior in doll play. *Amer. Psychologist*, 1951, *6*, 307. (Abstract)

Carroll, J. B., & Levin, H. A method for determining the polarity of behavior items. *Child Develpm.*, 1956, *27*, 427-438.

Cassell, Sylvia. Effect of brief puppet therapy upon the emotional responses of children undergoing cardiac catheterization. *J. consult. Psychol.*, 1965, *29*, 1-8.

Clark, K. B., & Clark, Mamie P. Racial identification and preference in Negro children. In T. M. Newcomb & E. L. Hartley (Eds.), *Readings in Social Psychology*. New York: Holt, 1947. Pp. 169-178.

Cohn, Fay S. Fantasy aggression in children as studied by the doll play technique. *Child Develpm.*, 1962, *33*, 235-250.

Commoss, Harriet H. Some characteristics related to social isolation in second grade children. *J. educ. Psychol.*, 1962, *53*, 38-42.

Conn, J. H. A psychiatric study of car sickness in children. *Amer. J. Orthopsychiat.*, 1938, *8*, 130-141.

Conn, J. H. Children's reactions to the discovery of genital differences. *Amer. J. Orthopsychiat.*, 1940, *10*, 747-754.

Conn, J. H. The play-interview as an investigative and therapeutic procedure. *Nerv. Child*, 1948, *7*, 257-286.

Despert, J. Louise. A method for the study of personality reactions in pre-school age children by means of analysis of their play. *J. Psychol.*, 1940, *9*, 17-29.

Driscoll, Gertrude P. *The Driscoll Play Kit.* New York: Psychological Corporation, 1959.

Emmerich, W. Parental identification in young children. *Genet. Psychol. Monogr.,* 1959, *60,* 257-308.

Erickson, Florence H. Play interviews for four-year-old hospitalized children. *Monogr. Soc. Res. Child Develpm.,* 1958, *23,* No. 3 (Serial No. 69) .

Erikson, E. H. Sex differences in the play configurations of preadolescents. *Amer. J. Orthopsychiat.,* 1951, *21,* 667-692.

Gewirtz, J. L. An investigation of aggressive behavior in the doll play of young Sac and Fox Indian children, and a comparison to the aggression of Midwestern white preschool children. *Amer. Psychologist,* 1950, *5,* 294-295. (Abstract) .

Goodman, Mary E. *Race Awareness in Young Children.* Cambridge, Mass.: Addison-Wesley, 1952.

Gordon, J. E., & Cohn, Faye. Effect of fantasy arousal of affiliation drive on doll play aggression. *J. abnorm. soc. Psychol.,* 1963, *66,* 301-307.

Hartley, Ruth E., Frank, L. K., & Goldenson, R. M. *New Play Experiences for Children.* New York: Columbia University Press, 1952.

Hartup, W. W., & Himeno, Yayoi. Social isolation versus interaction with adults in relation to aggression in preschool children. *J. abnorm. soc. Psychol.,* 1959, *59,* 17-22.

Hartup, W. W. Some correlates of parental imitation in young children. *Child Develpm.,* 1962, *33,* 85-96.

Haworth, Mary R. The use of a filmed puppet show as a group projective technique for children. *Genet. Psychol. Monogr.,* 1957, *56,* 257-296.

Haworth, Mary R. Films as a group technique. In A. I. Rabin & Mary R. Haworth (Eds.) , *Projective Techniques with Children.* New York: Grune and Stratton, 1960. Pp. 177-190.

Haworth, Mary R. Repeat study with a projective film for children. *J. consult. Psychol.,* 1961, *25,* 78-83.

Haworth, Mary R. Responses of children to a group projective film and to the Rorschach, CAT, Despert Fables and D-A-P. *J. proj. Tech.,* 1962, *26,* 47-60.

Haworth, Mary R., & Woltmann, A. G. *Rock-A-Bye, Baby: A Group Projective Test for Children.* (Manual and film) . University Park, Pa.: Psychological Cinema Register, 1959.

Henry, J., & Henry, Zunia. Doll play of Pilagá Indian children. In C. Kluckhohn & H. A. Murray (Eds.) , *Personality in Nature, Society, and Culture* (2nd ed.) . New York: Knopf, 1953. Pp. 292-307.

Hollenberg, Eleanor, & Sperry, Margaret. Some antecedents of aggression and effects of frustration in doll play. *Personality,* 1951, *1,* 32-43.

Honzik, Marjorie P. Sex differences in the occurrence of materials in the play constructions of preadolescents. *Child Develpm.,* 1951, *22,* 15-35.

Isch, Maria J. Fantasied mother-child interaction in doll play. *J. genet. Psychol.,* 1952, *81,* 233-258.

Jenkins, R. L., & Beckh, Erica. Finger puppets and mask making as media for work with children. *Amer. J. Orthopsychiat.,* 1942, *12,* 294-300.

Korner, Anneliese F. *Some Aspects of Hostility in Young Children.* New York: Grune and Stratton, 1949.

Krall, Vita. Personality characteristics of accident repeating children. *J. abnorm. soc. Psychol.,* 1953, *48,* 99-107.

Lerner, E., & Murphy, Lois B. Methods for the study of personality in young children. *Monogr. Soc. Res. Child Develpm.*, 1941, *6*, No. 4 (Whole No. 30).

Levin, H., & Sears, R. R. Identification with parents as a determinant of doll play aggression. *Child Develpm.*, 1956, *27*, 135-153.

Levin, H., & Turgeon, Valerie P. The influence of the mother's presence on children's doll play aggression. *J. abnorm. soc. Psychol.*, 1957, *55*, 304-308.

Levin, H., & Wardwell, Elinor. The research uses of doll play. *Psychol. Bull.*, 1962, *59*, 27-56.

Levy, D. M. Use of play technique as experimental procedure. *Amer. J. Orthopsychiat.*, 1933, *3*, 266-277.

Levy, D. M. Hostility patterns in sibling rivalry experiments. *Amer. J. Orthopsychiat.*, 1936, *6*, 183-257.

Levy, D. M. Sibling rivalry studies in children of primitive groups. *Amer. J. Orthopsychiat.*, 1939, *9*, 205-214.

Levy, D. M. The use of projective techniques in the interpretation of hostility patterns. In H. H. Anderson & Gladys L. Anderson (Eds.), *An Introduction to Projective Techniques*. New York: Prentice-Hall, 1951. Pp. 676-704.

Lowenfeld, Margaret. The World Pictures of Children: a method of recording and studying them. *Brit. J. med. Psychol.*, 1939, *18*, 65-101.

Lyle, Jeanetta, & Holly, Sophie B. The therapeutic value of puppets. *Bull. Menninger Clin.*, 1941, *5*, 223-226.

Lynn, D. B. *Structured Doll Play Test (SDP): A Projective Test for Use with Children*. Burlingame, Calif.: Test Developments, 1959.

Lynn, D. B., Glaser, Helen H., & Harrison, Grace S. Comprehensive medical care for handicapped children: III. Concepts of illness in children with rheumatic fever. *Amer. J. Dis. Child.*, 1962, *103*, 120-128.

Lynn, D. B., & Lynn, Rosalie. The Structured Doll Play Test as a projective technique for use with children. *J. proj. Tech.*, 1959, *23*, 335-344.

Lynn, D. B., & Sawrey, W. L. The effects of father-absence on Norwegian boys and girls. *J. abnorm. soc. Psychol.*, 1959, *59*, 258-262.

Lynn, D. B., & Sawrey, W. L. Sex differences in the personality development of Norwegian children. *J. genet. Psychol.*, 1962, *101*, 367-374.

Lynn, Rosalie. Sex role preference and mother-daughter fantasies in young girls. Unpublished doctoral dissertation, University of Denver, 1961.

Mayhew, P. First findings on doll play with spastic hemiplegic children. *Develpm. Med. Child Neurol.*, 1963, *5*, 483-490.

McElvoney, Muriel B. Four types of fantasy aggression in the response of "rebellious" and "submissive" children to the Driscoll Play Kit, structured by parental-demand and neutral stimulus stories. *Dissert. Abstr.*, 1958, *19*, 364.

Miller, H., & Baruch, Dorothy W. A study of hostility in allergic children. *Amer. J. Orthopsychiat.*, 1950, *20*, 506-519.

Moore, T. Structured Doll Play Test. In O. Buros (Ed.) *The Sixth Mental Measurements Yearbook*. Highland Park, N. J.: Gryphon Press, 1965. Pp. 520-522.

Moore, T., & Ucko, L. E. Four to six: constructiveness and conflict in meeting doll play problems. *J. child Psychol. Psychiat.*, 1961, *2*, 21-47.

Mosse, Hilda L. The Duess Test. *Amer. J. Psychother.*, 1954, *8*, 251-264.

Murphy, Lois B., & collaborators. *Personality in Young Children*, Vol. 1. *Methods for the Study of Personality in Young Children*. New York: Basic Books, 1956.

Mussen, P., & Distler, L. Masculinity, identification, and father-son relationships. *J. abnorm. soc. Psychol.*, 1959, *59*, 350-356.

Mussen, P., & Rutherford, E. Parent-child relations and parental personality in relation to young children's sex-role preferences. *Child Develpm.*, 1963, *34*, 589-607.

Peixotto, Helen E., & Hill, Evelyn F. Phantasy in asthmatic children with special reference to Driscoll Doll Play. *J. asthma Res.*, 1964-65, *2*, 199-204.

Pintler, Margaret H. Doll play as a function of experimenter-child interaction and initial organization of materials. *Child Develpm.*, 1945, *16*, 145-166.

Pintler, Margaret H., Phillips, Ruth, & Sears, R. R. Sex differences in the projective doll play of preschool children. *J. Psychol.*, 1946, *21*, 73-80.

Phillips, Ruth. Doll play as a function of the realism of the materials and the length of the experimental session. *Child Develpm.*, 1945, *16*, 123-143.

Rabban, M. Sex-role identification in young children in two diverse social groups. *Genet. Psychol. Monogr.*, 1950, *42*, 81-158.

Rambert, Madeleine. *Children in Conflict*. New York: International Universities Press, 1949.

Ritchie, Jane. *Childhood in Rakau*. Wellington, New Zealand: Victoria Univer. Publ. Psychol., No. 10, 1957 (Monographs on Maori Social Life and Personality).

Robinson, Elizabeth F. Doll play as a function of the doll family constellation. *Child Develpm.*, 1946, *17*, 99-119.

Rosenzweig, S., & Shakow, D. Play technique in schizophrenia and other psychoses. *Amer. J. Orthopsychiat.*, 1937, *7*, 36-47.

Ross, A. O. Structured Doll Play Test. In O. Buros (Ed.), *The Sixth Mental Measurements Yearbook*. Highland Park, N.J.: Gryphon Press, 1965. Pp. 522-523.

Sandler, Louise. Child-rearing practices of mothers of asthmatic children. *J. asthma Res.*, 1964-65, *2*, 109-142; 215-256.

Scott, R. G. Projective parental fantasies of parent-separated children and children in families. Unpublished Ed. D. project report, Teachers College, Columbia University, 1954.

Sears, Pauline S. Doll play aggression in normal young children: influence of sex, age, sibling status, father's absence. *Psychol. Monogr.*, 1951, *65*, No. 6 (Whole No. 323).

Sears, Pauline S. Child-rearing factors related to playing of sex-typed roles. *Amer. Psychologist*, 1953, *8*, 431. (Abstract)

Sears, R. R. Influence of methodological factors on doll play performance. *Child Develpm.*, 1947, *18*, 190-197.

Sears, R. R., Maccoby, Eleanor E., & Levin, H. *Patterns of Child Rearing*. Evanston, Ill.: Row, Peterson, 1957.

Sears, R. R., Pintler, Margaret H., & Sears, Pauline S. Effect of father separation on preschool children's doll-play aggression. *Child Develpm.*, 1946, *17*, 219-243.

Sears, R. R., Whiting, J., Nowlis, V., & Sears, Pauline S. Some child-rearing antecedents of aggression and dependency in young children. *Genet. Psychol. Monogr.*, 1953, *47*, 135-234.

Stamp, Isla M. An evaluation of the Driscoll Play Kit used with incomplete stories as an instrument for the diagnosis of personality. Unpublished Ed. D. project report, Teachers College, Columbia University, 1954.

Stern, E. M., & Asherman, N. Grandparent behavior and attitudes as perceived by children. Unpublished Ed. D. project report, Teachers College, Columbia University, 1955.

Stolz, Lois M. et al. *Father Relations of War-born Children.* Stanford, Calif.: Stanford University Press, 1954.

Walsh, Ann M. *Self-concepts of Bright Boys with Learning Difficulties.* New York: Bur. Public., Teachers College, Columbia University, 1956.

Winstel, Beulah. The use of a controlled play situation in determining certain effects of maternal attitudes on children. *Child Develpm.,* 1951, *22,* 299-311.

Witkin, H. A., Lewis, H. B., Hertzman, M., Machover, Karen, Meissner, Pearl B., & Wapner, S. *Personality Through Perception.* New York: Harper, 1954.

Woltmann, A. G. The use of puppets in understanding children. *Ment. Hyg.,* 1940, *24,* 445-458.

Woltmann, A. G. The use of puppetry as a projective method in therapy. In H. H. Anderson & Gladys L. Anderson (Eds.), *An Introduction to Projective Techniques.* New York: Prentice-Hall, 1951. Pp. 606-638.

Woltmann, A. G. Spontaneous puppetry by children as a projective method. In A. I. Rabin & Mary R. Haworth (Eds.), *Projective Techniques with Children.* New York: Grune and Stratton, 1960. Pp. 305-312.

World Book Encyclopedia, Vol. 4. Chicago: Field Enterprises, 1950.

Yarrow, L. J. The effect of antecedent frustration on projective play. *Psychol. Monogr.* 1948, *62,* No. 6 (Whole No. 293).

12

Projective Drawings

EMANUEL F. HAMMER

Anthropologists have demonstrated how a past world may be imaginatively reconstructed from one of its products, even if it be only a fragment of a tool, a pot, or some drawings left on walls. Similarly, an individual's inner world may be understood through a sensitive reading of a series of his projective drawings—free renditions of a House, a Tree, a Person, a Family, an Animal, his favorite doodles, and so on.

Since their birth almost two decades ago, projective drawings as a clinical tool have moved relatively rapidly into a secure niche in the projective battery. By virtue of their time economy, ease of administration, and rich clinical yield, projective drawings appear to be the most frequent supplement, along with the TAT, to the Rorschach in the clinician's work-a-day projective armamentarium. In addition to Buck's House-Tree-Person and Machover's Figure Drawing techniques, various clinicians employ one or more of the following: the Draw-A-Person-in-the-Rain modification of Abrams, which attempts to elicit clues to the self-concept under conditions symbolizing environmental stress, Schwartz's Draw-An-Animal approach (useful for disclosing the biological side of the bio-social coin), the Draw-A-Family procedure, Harrower's Unpleasant Concept Test, Kinget's Drawing Completion Test, and free doodles.

In projective drawings, the subject's psychomotor activities are caught on paper. The line employed may be firm or timid, uncertain, hesitant or bold, or it may consist of a savage digging at the paper. In addition, as we shall later see, the subject's conscious and unconscious perception of himself and significant people in his environment determine the content of his drawing. In such expression, the unconscious levels of the subject tend to utilize symbols—symbols whose meanings can be unraveled through study and understanding of dreams, myths, folklore, psychotic productions, and so on. The illustrations that follow will support and elaborate the thesis that drawing productions are employed by a subject as one of the many forms of symbolic speech.

THE CLINICAL BEGINNINGS

Florence Goodenough, having devised an intelligence scale based mainly on the number of details put into the drawing of a man, became aware, along with other clinicians, that her test was tapping personality factors in addition to intellectual capabilities of her child subjects. The present writer, for example, in using the Goodenough "Draw-a-Man Test" also became aware of the fact that emotional factors, more so than intellectual ones, were constantly pressing into view. In checking a drawing for credit for the inclusion of a hand, it soon became apparent that whereas the same quantitative IQ credit was given for a balled-up, clenched fist, or a delicate and open hand in a feminine gesture patting the cheek, produced by a male subject in his drawing of a male, more important qualitative clues to the functioning of the total personality were being ignored. The subject was granted identical quantitative credit whether he drew his person with the arms crossed defiantly over the chest, hanging flexibly at the sides, or placed timidly behind the back, but the fact that these several arm positions had vastly different qualitative implications was not taken into account, and much valuable diagnostic, and even prognostic, material was overlooked. Similarly, the large range of facial expressions, size, placement on the page, and so on, seemed to offer more information about non-intellectual components than about the intellectual capabilities.

Many clinicians have had similar experience with drawings, experience expressed in the rule so often quoted: "Children draw what they know, not what they see."

Both the House-Tree-Person Drawing device (H-T-P) and the Figure-Drawing procedure, as personality tools, were an outcropping of intelligence scales. Machover's (1949) Figure-Drawing technique grew from her experience with the Goodenough tool for appraising children's intelligence. Similarly, Buck's (1948) H-T-P procedure grew out of an intelligence scale upon which he was working at the time Wechsler came out with his Intelligence Scale. Buck, having had the same experience observing the flooding of the drawings with non-intellectual personality factors, salvaged the H-T-P drawing test from his other intellect-tapping subtests, and developed it into the productive projective technique it has, by now, become.

MATERIALS AND ADMINISTRATION

A No. 2 pencil and a sheet of paper are handed the subject. His drawing of a House is requested with the longer axis of the sheet placed horizontally before the subject. His drawings of a Tree and Person, in turn, are then obtained on separate sheets of paper with the longer axis placed vertically. The subject is asked to draw as well as he can, but he is not told what kind of House, Tree and Person to draw. If the subject protests that he is not an artist, he is assured that the H-T-P is not a test of artistic ability at all but that we are interested, rather, in how he does things. Any questions he asks are reflected back to him in such a way as to indicate that there is no right or wrong method of proceeding but that he may do the drawing in any manner he wishes.

After he draws the Person, the subject is then handed another sheet of paper and this time asked to draw a Person of the sex opposite to that of the first Person drawn. The pencil and the pencil drawings are then taken away, crayons (a fifteen-cent box of eight *Crayola* crayons obtained at any five-and-ten-cent store) are substituted, and a chromatic set of drawings of a House, Tree and Person of each sex obtained. The subject is allowed to use the crayons in any way he wishes, as few or as many as he chooses, to shade in or draw only the outline as he elects to, and all questions are handled non-directly. In addition, in pencil again, the subject may be asked to draw the most unpleasant thing he can think of, to draw a person in the rain, or to complete or make a drawing from certain lines which serve as stimuli (The Drawing Completion Test). With children, we may occasionally also ask for a drawing of a family and/or a drawing of an animal (Hammer, 1958).

UNDERLYING HYPOTHESES

Projective drawings tap the stream of personality needs as they flood the area of graphic creativity. Certain concessions must, however, be made to psychology's demand for standardization: hence, the same concepts (House, Tree, Person, Animal) are asked for from the subject, on the same size paper with standard material.

Armed with the knowledge that man's deeper needs 1) color his creative efforts and 2) show an affinity for "speaking" in pictorial images, the clinician and/or experimenter has at his disposal a rapidly- and easily administered technique for eliciting submerged levels of human feelings. Basically, the subject's relative emphasis on different elements within his drawings, in addition to his global drawing performance, tells us a good deal of what matters to him, what it does to him, and what he does about it.

In the field of projective drawing, interpretation empirically rests upon the following foundation stones: 1) The use of common psychoanalytic and folklore meanings of symbols, derived from study of dreams, myth, art, fantasy and other such activities steeped in unconscious determination. 2) Clinical experience with the mechanisms of displacement and substitution as well as a wide range of pathological phenomena, especially the conversion symptoms, obsessions, compulsions, and phobias—all of which become understandable only within the framework of the concept of symbolism. 3) Unraveling of the symbolization employed in drawings by inviting the patient's associations. 4) Empirical evidence with previous patients' drawings. 5) Following the lead provided by the flooding of symbolization onto the drawing page, from the unconscious of psychotics, we can then detect more subtle murmurings in the same tongue of symbolism in the drawings of non-psychotics. 6) The correlation between projective drawings made at intervals during the course of therapy and the clinical picture at the times the drawings were produced.

7) Internal consistency between one drawing and another, between the drawings and the other techniques in the projective battery, between drawings and dreams, between drawings and the behavioral picture, and between drawings and the case history. 8) And lastly, but most importantly, experimental studies.

The field of projective drawing interpretation also rests upon several theoretical postulates: (a) There is a tendency in man to view the world in an anthropomorphic manner; that is, in his own image. (b) The core of the anthropomorphic view of the environment is the mechanism of projection. (c) Distortions enter into the process of projection to the extent to which the projection has a defensive function; that is, the projection is in the service of ascribing to the outer world that which the subject denies in himself.

Distortions in the mechanisms of projection are very much like the situation of a man who, according to the analogy of Gondor (1959), "has only a limited number of slides for a projection machine, and, no matter what the situation or the type of screen, can project only his available pictures" (p. 11).

The emotionally disturbed person's perception of the world is not always accurate. It may give him distorted views—and one's characteristic distortions of the world are sampled by projective drawings.

How It Works: Some Illustrations

While it is beyond the space allotted to this chapter to attempt to illustrate in any meaningful way the array of various projective drawings commonly used, perhaps the operant flavoring and "feel" of one aspect of it can be conveyed by focusing on the drawing of a Person. But even the use of just the drawing of a Person as a projective technique can be presented, within the space limitations, only in a most introductory way. For deeper treatment of the Draw-A-Person and for an extension of the presentation to include the other related drawings, the reader is referred to *The Clinical Application of Projective Drawings* (Hammer, 1958).

One woman, a 25-year-old school teacher, had entered therapy because she had a problem relating to men and a block against getting married.

Figure 1. Drawing by a 25-year-old school teacher after becoming engaged, suggesting sexual panic at impending marriage

She sensed that her moderate obesity might be a defense against males. After approximately a year-and-a-half of treatment, she was able to reduce, had begun going out, and had established a "going steady" relationship with one young man. One day, she came to the therapy session, proudly showed an engagement ring, and announced jubilantly that she was to be married.

Feeling that she had accomplished her goals in therapy, but also having some marginal doubts, she asked if she might re-take the H-T-P to compare it with the one she had initially taken upon entering treatment: to thus assess what the test revealed and to see if it matched her subjective feeling of how far she had come and where she now was. The drawing of a female she now produced (Figure 1) was better integrated, prettier, more feminine and certainly no longer the representation of the obese woman it had been. The figure, like the earlier one, still stood on phallic feet, however, and the hands now were drawn into a position of "pelvic defense." Both hands, in spite of the ring now conspicuous on the third finger of one of them, were drawn to a position of guarding the genital area. Whereas noteworthy gains in self-image were apparent, the projective drawing cried out with the problem of fear of intercourse and some underlying masculine identification still unresolved.

In support of the implications of the fear of sexuality which the impending marriage was now crystallizing, there were two parataxic slips made by the patient during that session. When I had asked her when she was getting married, she answered, "I'm getting *engaged* in June" instead of "married" then; thus revealing her inner desire to put the marriage further off. Relating the slip to the drawing, it was not difficult to help her to sense that her treatment was not yet complete.

As the session ended and we walked to the door, I happened to have asked her how much Christmas vacation, which she was then on, she had. She replied, "My vacation ends June 3rd, I mean January 3rd!" Our eyes smiled, she then burst into laughter, and in the sesssions which followed, we settled down to the work remaining to be done.

The reader might find it instructive to be able to view drawings, side by side, made by individuals suffering from the same symptom. In this manner, common denominators may become apparent. Figures 2 and 3 were both offered by male alcoholics, one in his early forties and one in his late forties. Both had a long history of drinking finally producing the chronic alcoholic pattern, which now assumed the center of their existence. In their perception of women, we note strikingly threatening, repellent aspects which may have contributed—among the other motives—to their initial need to retreat into the all-male atmosphere of bars, and there to dilute their fear of females and to quiet the inner voice of doubt regarding their masculinity.

The awareness of these two men's perception of women as overwhelmingly hostile, powerful, scary and even ghoulish, suggests that their turning to drink may be in the service, among the other needs, of achiev-

Figures 2 and 3. Drawings by two male alcoholics reflecting their view of women

ing a pleasant plateau from which to survey the world of men-and-women with some equanimity, to handle their harsh perceptions so that the edges are blurred and threatening figures made softer. Emboldening themselves with whiskey, their problems may diffuse, and the world of females which they cannot handle (both men are married) fades, leaving them in a solitary haze.

Figure 4 was drawn by an overt homosexual and labeled by him a man. In spite of the man's hat, the rest of the figure conveys an impression of a female in slacks, with feminine hip curve, a hint of a breast delineation, lipsticked mouth, delicate nose and emphasized eyebrows. His feminine identification—of being a woman merely dressed in male clothing—is compellingly conveyed in the projective drawing.

Figure 5, in contrast, was drawn by an overtly heterosexual, even Don Juan, individual who was rather frantically pursuing one affair after another. Following one such affair in which, to his amazement, he suddenly found himself impotent, he then exhibited his penis on a subway on his way home—an offense for which he was referred for psychological examination. Among other things, we particularly note the high heel he gives the shoe, the shading around the buttocks area indicating anxiety, and the hint of a phallic protrusion showing at the genital area. The fear of attack from the rear, conveyed by the excessive and inappropriate shading at the buttocks, is supported by the heavy collar pulled up around the back of his neck, as if to protect a vulnerable rear, up and down.

CHAPTER 12 · Hammer   371

Figures 4 and 5. Drawing by an overt homosexual (left); drawing by a latent homosexual male using Don Juanism as a defense (right)

Figure 6. Drawing by an adolescent boy with conspicuous compensatory defenses and also symptoms of exhibitionism. On the original drawing, the figure crowded the margins and the shoes extended beyond the lower edge of the page

The demonstrative efforts at masculinity which unwittingly escape him as he draws the front of the trousers (as they did in his recent offense) thus suggest that compensatory efforts at proving himself more of a male than he inwardly feels serve as a defensive maneuver to handle and subdue his covert homosexual panic.

Profiting from the understanding of the communication of the previous drawing, we can now more readily decipher the next one (Figure 6). This was drawn by a seventeen-year old adolescent boy who, on the surface, was a wincingly self-conscious young man. Shy and retiring, his was a cautious and hampered adaptation as he related to peers at school and at home. Yet on paper he draws a large male crowding the edges of the page, one with over-expanded shoulders, the suggestion of a mustache, and simultaneously carrying not one, but two, symbols of athletic prowess, a tennis racket in one hand and a baseball bat in the other—this in spite of their incongruity for simultaneous use. What is perhaps even more noteworthy, against this backdrop, is that the baseball bat appears to emanate directly from the fly of the trousers, and then at the other end has a hint of a urethral-like indentation or opening. The entire rendition could not be more phallic if such an attempt had been deliberately and consciously made. His loud protesting on paper that "I am indeed a man!" and the directly phallic direction these efforts took were later confirmed. This youngster, having entered therapy for problems of incapacitating shyness, within several weeks confided to the writer that he also wished help for his exhibitionistic behavior, for a tendency he had to wait for young girls to pass outside his window, for him then to drop his pants and knock on the window to attract their attention.

To illustrate the way projective drawings may mirror affective states, note Figure 7, drawn by a narcotic addict suffering a depressive reaction. The subject is a twenty-one-year-old male, a withdrawn individual feeling unhappily alone, isolated from others, and panicky and fearful in his efforts to escape from human advances of even a gentle and friendly kind. His whole life pattern demonstrated a weakly adaptive style of interpersonal relationships. The withdrawn quality reflected in the almost back view, the regressive aspects connoted by the figure all but curled up, the abject feelings of despondency, despair, and hopelessness are conveyed in every line. The figure drawing suggests a crushed self-esteem and the agonized state of a self beaten down. (The drawing was supported by his TAT performance where futility ran through all the stories to embrace one protagonist after another in failure.)

Figure 7. Drawing by a narcotics addict with depressive reaction

The figure drawing thus reflects his need, behind his use of narcotics, to withdraw into a silent, cushioned solitude. The absence of clothing mirrors his tendency to remove himself from the conventions of the jarring social world he experiences around him.

The next illustration was offered by a twenty-eight-year-old female, a concert pianist who had begun to develop a feeling of awkwardness and lack of flexibility in her hands which was currently interfering disasterously, with her performances. Numerous neurological examinations had all yielded consistently negative findings, and hence she was referred for a psychological examination.

On the Rorschach, the writer found her as he described in the following excerpts:

> Intense feelings of anger, struggle and competition define her inner psychological state. The perception of people on the Rorschach as "resisting each other, working against each other, rather than together," the perception of animals as "angry, struggling, fighting," and the projection, "two people pulling against each other" all combine to convey the flavoring of her inner competitive struggle and hostility. Her major defense at this time is to attempt to employ repression to manage and contain these unacceptable feelings underground. The "blood" and "fire" images in her Rorschach further imply that intense, primitive affects are associated with major tensions. She responds to one of the chromatic cards (Card IX) by offering the following: "Fire . . . two witches . . . smoke . . . conflict . . . eruption . . . volcano . . . hatred . . . and hell . . . and here is the Greek God of Wrath." The sequence from fire to hell and the God of Wrath illustrate the strong sense of guilt which caps off the feeling of aggression symbolized by the initial association of fire. The "conflict" in the middle of this stream of associations, which then goes on to "eruption" and "volcano," further emphasizes the strong struggle she is attempting in order to keep her anger from breaking forward into overt behavior. The inference of aggression pressing forward becomes considerably less speculative when she adds "hatred" to the more symbolic "eruption" which preceded it.

In keeping with the above, her projective drawing provides a rather important clue to the block and inhibition in performing as a pianist from which she is suffering. The patient draws someone (Figure 8), essentially well-rendered and effectively presented except for one glaring exception. The hands are drawn in such a way that they don't look like human hands at all, but much more like an animal's paws—with the claws extended. She had commented, while drawing, "I just couldn't draw the hands." The subject then describes the drawn Person as "She wants to move, but doesn't know how."

Figure 8. Drawing by a concert pianist suffering a performance block

The freezing of her movement—out of the pervading fear that angry,

savage, animalistic, hostile impulses may be released in these movements
—the drawing suggests, may be what interferes with the smooth and fluid
execution of hand motions so necessary to her as a pianist. It is in the
area of angry feelings, hence, that the therapeutic focus will be most rewarding, in the interests of helping her to face, and then resolve, her
secret rage behind her block as a pianist. We may also note the flowing
skirt presented as if thrown into motion by stirred up, churning feelings
beneath it, which may suggest the impulses of sexuality as an attendant
problem.

Figures 9 and 10. Drawings by an 18-year-old male showing surface and sub-surface
personality levels respectively

The nuanced language of drawing projection is particularly suited
for stating the complexities and human contradictions as they balance
and interrelate within a single personality. At such times, the apparent
contradictions can be seen to possess an inner harmony, as in the musical
statement and counterstatement of a fugue. Figure 9, drawn by an
eighteen-year-old male caught stealing a TV set, constitutes such a pictorial statement. Beneath the obvious attempts at an impressive figure of
masculine prowess, there are more subtle trends of the opposite: of inadequacy and inconsequentiality. The muscles of the drawn figure have
been inflated, beyond the hard and sinewy, into a puffy softness as if it is
a figure made of balloons; the legs taper down to insubstantiality and,
finally, absent feet, and an incongruous hat is placed on the boxer making comical his lifting of one gloved hand in victory.

The same dichotomy can be seen in his projections onto Rorschach
Card V: "looks like a wasp." The popular response to this card is a bat
or a butterfly. The subject, instead, projects an index of felt smallness,

while at the same time attempting to make up for this by aggressiveness. Thus he is saying, in effect, "I may be small, but I'll show you I can be something to be reckoned with."

His passive-aggressive strategy become all the more dramatically apparent in the comparison of his pencil and later crayon-drawn persons.

On the one hand, emblematic of his defenses, his drawn achromatic person is the "twenty-year-old" boxer with muscles flexed and a weight-lifter's build. Beneath this inflated image, however, on the crayon drawing of a person (which, due to the impact of color, tends to tap the relatively deeper levels of personality (Hammer, 1958) he offers now only a "six-year-old boy" who then looks even more like an infant than a child: with one curlicue hair sticking up and the suggestion of diapers on (Figure 10, shown here in black-and-white). The ears are rather ludicrous in their standing away from the head and, all in all, the total projection in this drawing is that of an infantile, laughable entity, rather than the impressive he-man he overstated on the achromatic version of a person. Beneath his attempts to demonstrate rugged masculinity (which may have culminated into the offense with which he is charged), the patient experiences himself as actually a little child, dependent and needing care, protection and affection.

Figure 11. Drawing in which masochism, homosexuality and exhibitionism are evident

Projective drawings may, we see from this and the next drawing, sometimes provide a highly personal statement. I don't believe I have ever seen a Rorschach response which can match a drawing, such as Figure 11, for communicativeness of intimate expression. This is because a subject, while drawing, can, in a relative sense, exclude the examiner —can immerse himself more deeply, and become more absorbed, in the unfolding graphic projection, than he ever can in directly relating to the examiner and telling him what he sees in one response after another on Rorschach stimuli.

Intertwined in this drawing of a person are masochistic, homosexual, and exhibitionistic needs, in that order of dominance. The exhibiting of the buttock area combines the last two mentioned trends. The manacling of the hands and the tying of the feet apparently expressed and, in cyclic fashion, further produced so much masochistic involvement and excitement, that in an orgiastic-like mood he wanted more. He then provided this for himself in the blown-up addition of the large foot to the side of the drawing proper, with (one is tempted to say) loving care emphasis upon the enslaving chains and encasing metal bands.

For contrast, Figure 12 presents the sadistic side of the sado-masochistic coin. The subject offering this drawing had been Head Disciplinarian of a boys' reformatory for some years until he was suspended for uncontrollably striking the youngsters. He described himself as having, bootstrap-fashion, mastered his early difficulties as a youth. As to his description of his drawn person, he said it "looked like a Prussian or a Nazi General." (Consistent with this identification, his TAT themes were smeared with gore and strident with sadism.)

To illustrate, at this point, the range along the continuum—from schizoid to schizophrenic conditions —on which the clinical psychologist is most often asked to make his diagnostic contribution, Figures 13 to 19 are presented.

Figure 12. Drawing by an authoritarian and sadistic male

Figures 13 and 14. Drawings by a schizoid individual

Figures 13 and 14 represent the drawing of a male and female by a schizoid patient. The drawn male (Figure 13) is more mannequin-like than human and actually suggests a store dummy. Figure 14 was described as, "She looks like a paper doll." His projections thus are not of flesh and blood beings, but of derealized humans who cannot engage in emotional give-and-take. Within the patient, the sap of affect has grown thin. He feels himself to be a somewhat synthetic being, rather than a full, or living person. This is an individual who does not appear to be buoyed by any connection he feels with the human environment. He appears to have lost the sensations of spontaneity, play, warmth, autonomy, or even of emotional authenticity. The "bloodless" man and woman drawn suggest the feelings of alienation within the subject. A sense of isolation, of distance, aloneness and separateness from the human environment appears central to his portrait of himself. He lives beside life more than in it.

Consistent with his drawings, on the TAT he demonstrated a failure to include much about the relationship between the people shown in the stimuli. On the Rorschach, the number of his movement responses was diminished, and when they were given, the forms were static. The humans or animals did not act, but were only about to act or were acted upon. Color was also absent, vitality low, and zest for living muted. Emphasis was almost exclusively on Form as a determinant, again implying minimal feelings of emotional life within.

The implications for therapy are that his sterility and restriction of personality, and his markedly schizoid structure will limit and define his behavior in the therapeutic situation. A long period of treatment would be necessary to achieve a gradual melting through the wall of his detachment by human warmth and interest; and it would have to be extended with care to avoid stimulating further protective withdrawal.

To move further along the continuum, we may next observe Figure 15.

The patient who drew this person is a well-built, immaculately dressed, thirty-seven-year-old Negro man. He had served in the Navy and received an honorable discharge, having attained the rank of an officer. He then attended college and received his B.A. After this, he was an assistant preacher in a Southern church for several years, and then came to the North. He was referred for examination because he was convicted on three counts of assault, involving two men and a women. The police officer had found a straight razor, a packing knife and a pen knife on the defendant's person. The complainants had never seen the defendant before. The men and woman were standing near a candy booth when the defendant pushed his way between them, knocking the woman off balance and causing her to fall. One man—according to his story—shouted, "Are you crazy or something?" which enraged the defendant who then struck the man on the side of the head and the woman about the mouth. At that point, the second man appeared, came to their assistance, and the defendant pummelled him with his fists.

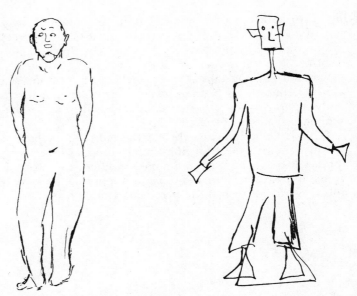

Figures 15 and 16. Drawing by a man suffering from a borderline schizophrenic condition (left) ; drawing by a schizophrenic patient (right)

The defendant's version was that the man who had exclaimed, "Are you crazy or something?" had added, "you black nut!" Thus the referring probation officer raised some question concerning a racial issue having inflamed the defendant's reaction. The diagnostic query which accompanied the referral for an examination was, "Is this man emotionally sick, is there any presence of significant pathology, and is he capable of peculiar reactivity?"

On the Rorschach, the patient emerged as a borderline schizophrenic individual. Primary thinking processes seeped through to color his perception of the world in raw, primitive terms. His drawings of people were both of nudes, his drawn female a massive, threatening figure, whereas his drawn male (Figure 15) stands timidly with hands behind his back, eyes suspiciously and paranoidally alerted, and chin exaggerated in a demonstration of compensatory needs to prove himself assertive. What is more important, however, is the reality-testing impairment. He describes his drawn male as "standing there and talking . . . talking to a neighbor or someone he sees passing on the street." Here, the strikingly inappropriate description of a nude male standing and talking to a neighbor or passer-by on the street conveys the impaired reality testing and dissociative capacities of the subject. The Form Minus responses, which accumulate on his Rorschach, (responses where the percepts do not fit the outline of the blot) further convey the level of diminished reality-testing on which this man operates.

Past the borderline range and well into the schizophrenic domain,

Figure 16 stands as a reflection of frank pathology. The geometric rendition of hands, feet, and ears suggest an arbitrary perceptual tendency (to over-abstract and possibly also to rely upon magical signs). The robot-like head and neck add to the autistic quality, while the absence of a mouth and the pupil-less eyes reflect the communication difficulties schizophrenics so agonizingly experience. The line for the ground suddenly comes up in a rather peculiar way as if to add some stability to his footing, no matter how artificially.

This is an individual who, at the most, has a pseudo-integration of personality, with the frail links barely keeping him together. His illness appears to serve, at best, as a mere expedient for survival amid the contradictions within him. The patient appears to have constructed an unreal world into which he is retiring from sanity.

Figure 17. Drawing by a highly depersonalized schizophrenic individual

Figure 17 carried the reflection of the depersonalization process still further. This patient's identification is with a fluid and formless being; a truly tragic conception of personal identity. Ego boundaries fade and the figure melts away. Haunted by a picture of himself as a creature whose outlines blur, he has eventually given in, and by now, a back ward patient of a mental hospital, has lost sight of who and what—and if—he is.

A search through the hospital folder revealed a Draw-A-Person projection done, upon admission, many years earlier. His Person was standing rigidly at attention, body and head very stiff, legs pressed closely together, arms straight and held to the body. The kinesthetic emphasis was on the rigid posture and on the tension with which the posture was held, keeping the self closed off against the world around. The over-all impression was of a person frozen into a posture, unable to move over the threshold of action.

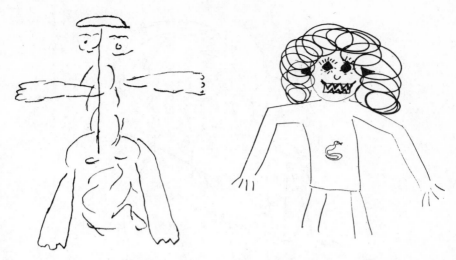

PART V

Figures 18 and 19. Drawing by an extremely deteriorated back ward patient (left); drawing by an acutely paranoid, psychotic man (right)

Still further along the continuum to massive deterioration, Figure 18 reflects an individual with body image totally gone, with peripheral lines no longer present around the face, and a body wall through which the intestines have spilled.

Figure 19 stands as an extreme example of one particular type of schizophrenic reaction, the paranoid sub-type. The savage mouth expresses the rage-filled projections loose within him. The emphasized eyes and ears with the eyes almost emanating magical rays reflect the visual and auditory hallucinations the patient actually experiences. The snake in the stomach points up his delusion of a reptile within, eating away and generating venom and evil.

At times, issues of life-and-death import themselves may be picked up by the projective drawings. Figure 20 was drawn by a man suffering from an involutional depression. He drew the large figure first; then when he saw that he could not complete the entire figure on the page, he drew the smaller figure. He momentarily paused, looked at both figures, said that the larger figure lacked a collar, picked up the pencil he had laid down, and drew the "collar" by slashing the pencil across the throat of the drawn male. It was almost as if, the writer got the eerie feeling, the patient were committing suicide on paper. Along with this, the patient offered a story to TAT Card 1 which consisted of the boy picking up and smashing the violin. We recall Bellak's theory of the violin's representing the body image and here find consistency with the suicidal impulses acted out on the drawing page. The witnessing of this man slashing his drawn throat on paper was too vivid a demonstration to take lightly. Conferring with his psychiatrist resulted in the patient being

Figure 20. Drawing prophesizing a suicide attempt

institutionalized. Some time later the patient actually made a suicidal attempt, but fortunately, owing to the protective surroundings of the institution, this was detected, and the bathrobe belt with which he attempted to hang himself was cut down in time.

Generally, regarding acting-out, we may state that *the stronger, the more frank, the more direct (and hence unsublimated) the expression of impulses which break through in the projective drawings, the more the defensive and adaptive operations of the ego may be presumed to be insufficient in their assimilative function, and the more the likelihood of acting-out.*

A word of caution: although the previous examples were presented as graphic illustrations of projection in drawing, they were meant to be exercises only. In actual clinical practice, the dangers of basing interpretative deductions on isolated bits of data are obvious. In practice, confirmation of interpretative speculation on the basis of one drawing must be checked against not only the other drawings, but the entire projective battery, the case history, the clinical impression gleaned during the interview with the subject and all other available information. If, for example, a subject for his Most Unpleasant Concept draws someone having run over someone else in an automobile, for his house drawing sketches a picture of a cathedral, and for his animal drawing offers a lamb, the sequence suggests a common denominator that one might *speculatively* read as follows: I attempt to conquer the anger and hostility within me by denial and reaction-formation (that is, I say that the most unpleasant thing for me would be to aggressively harm someone else), by restricting myself to what is pure, innocent, good and holy (the drawing of a cathedral) and gentle (the choice of a lamb for an animal drawing) in interpersonal exchange. Rage will not erupt (the most unpleasant thing I can think of, as reflected in the Most Unpleasant Concept Test) if I cling to a saintly ideal (the cathedral drawing and to a lesser degree, the lamb drawing) to see me through crises which may, at times, arise.

This tentative formulation must then be checked against the Rorschach and the clinical impression. On the behavioral level, the subject may assume a self-effacing, Pollyanna role in which he attempts to present himself as being good, sweet and noble. The projective drawing induction may be offered further support by the Rorschach content of aggressive hostility. Thus, if the drawings fit in, persuasively, with the overt behavior and the Rorschach content to make a continuous pattern of the reaction-formation variable within the subject's personality, we may, with greater confidence, accept their implications.

Interpretations should ordinarily represent the convergence of several sources of data. This *principle of convergence* is essentially no different from that which guides dream analysis, psychoanalytically-oriented therapy, Rorschach interpretation, and thema analysis of Thematic Apperception Test data. In fact, it is a basic principle of all scientific methodology.

RESEARCH: STUDIES AND CHALLENGES

The research studies in the field of projective drawings are, by and large, so contradictory that the writer finds himself taking a deep breath as he settles down to try to make sense of the mosaic. On the one hand, a number of studies have failed to demonstrate that psychologists are able to make accurate diagnoses on the basis of figure drawings (Sherman, 1958a, 1958b; Sipprelle & Swensen, 1956; Swensen, 1957; Whitmyre, 1953). Some of Machover's (1949) interpretive hypothesis, when put to the experimental test, have emerged lacking in validity (Blum, 1954; Fisher & Fisher, 1950; Grams & Rinder, 1958; Hammer, 1954; Reznikoff & Nicholas, 1958; Ribler, 1957).

On the borderline, yielding both negative and positive results, Hammer and Piotrowski (1953) found 1) a relatively high degree of both reliability in the judgments of the degree of aggression and its validity as manifested in a subject's free-hand drawings of a House-Tree-Person; 2) in spite of this high degree of reliability and validity, on a secondary level the clinicians' interpretations appear to have been also influenced by their own projections and areas of sensitivity. Perhaps the second finding raises the question of the possibility of a personal psychotherapeutic experience for the clinician serving as diagnostician, as it has long since been advocated, by many, for the clinician serving as therapist.

On the positive side, numerous studies have demonstrated clear-cut differences between "normal" (or random selections of people) and various pathological groups (Anastasi & Foley, 1941; Berrien, 1935; Eigenbode, 1951; Goldworth, 1950; Gunzberg, 1954; Holzberg & Wexler, 1950; Hozier, 1959; Plaut & Grannell, 1955; Reznikoff & Tomblen, 1956; Schmidl-Waehner, 1942; Singer, 1950; Springer, 1941; Wexler & Holzberg, 1952). Substantiating correlations have been found between ratings of personality traits based on figure drawings and ratings based on case histories, other tests, and interviews (Katz, 1951; Mott, 1936; Richy & Spotts, 1959; Singer, 1957; Spoerl, 1940; Tolor & Tolor, 1955; Witkin, Lewis, Hertzman, Machover, Meissner & Wapner, 1954). Steinmann, (1952) devised a scoring system which was found by Graham (1955) to correlate quite highly ($r = .70$) with degree of pathology in psychosis. Hiler and Nesvig (1965), using adolescent subjects, showed that normals and psychiatric patients could be differentiated on the basis of their drawings. The valid criteria of pathology which were substantiated were drawings revealing the following characteristics: "bizarre," "distorted," "incomplete," and "transparent." The most valid of the four criteria was "bizarreness," under which heading were subsumed: "schizy," "grotesque," "inhuman," "sinister," "sick," "ghoulish," "wierd" and "gnome-like." In the cross-validation sample, 46 percent of the patients and only 2 percent of the controls produced a drawing which was by independent judgment described as "bizarre."

Goldworth (1950) found 32 percent of his sample of schizophrenics and 58 percent of his sample of people with organic brain damage drew heads which were characterized by the judges as "bizarre," or "grotesque." In contrast, none of his sample of 50 normals and only four of his group of 50 neurotics drew heads so characterized.

Waehner's (1946) results support small size and insufficient pressure as typifying anxious, constricted children. Alschuler and Hattwick (1947) demonstrate that small figures are associated with withdrawn or emotionally dependent behavior; light strokes with low energy level, inhibitions, and depression; and heavy strokes with more self-assertive tendencies. Lack of restraint revealing itself in an over-expanding drawing size, was correlated with aggressiveness and a tendency toward release of it into the environment (Zimmerman & Garfinkle, 1942).

Albee and Hamlin (1950), having devised a scale for the ratings of drawings which correlated .62 with the patient's case history, applied this scale to three groups: normals (a group of dental patients), anxiety cases in treatment, and schizophrenics in treatment. It was found that the scale did not differentiate between the two sub-types of patient groups, the schizophrenics and the anxiety cases, but that it did reliably differentiate between the normals and each of the groups of patients.

Whereas this study by Albee and Hamlin did not find differences between anxiety neurotics and schizophrenics, Griffith and Peyman (1965) did find support for the hypothesis that eye and ear emphasis in the drawing of a person is associated with ideas of reference. This study is noteworthy in drawing to our attention the superiority of actual overt behavior to official psychiatric classification in attempts to validate projective techniques. The authors point out that Swensen's judgment (1957) that figure drawings are of use in clinical work only "as a rough screening device" was based on studies with certain defects of design. Most of the studies Swensen reviewed used psychiatric diagnoses as the criteria. The reliability of psychiatric diagnoses, however, has been more and more questioned of late. Had psychiatric diagnosis been the criterion in the Griffith and Peyman study, non-significant, rather than significant, results would have been the yield.

Also avoiding psychiatric diagnosis as the criterion, Schmidt and McGowan (1965) demonstrated the relationship between drawn Persons and the traits of the subject offering the drawing: figure drawings by physically disabled persons could be distinguished by judges from figure drawings by physically normal persons.

Perhaps the most jolting marshalling of negative results was provided by Swensen in his *Empirical Evaluations of Human Figure Drawings* (1957) alluded to above. How then are we to explain the striking inconsistencies and contradictions in the research findings on projective drawings? The fallacy of employing psychiatric diagnoses as the criteria has already been mentioned as one explanation among several.

In a study of the psychologists themselves, Schmidt and McGowan (1965) found that the clinician-judges they employed to evaluate the drawings tended to fall into two categories: 1) those whose orientation might be considered "affective," who employed an impressionistic or "feeling" approach to the drawings, and 2) a "cognitive" group who displayed a tendency to evaluate the drawings more in terms of specific signs. The first group, the one using a more artistic, intuitive approach, they found could diagnostically sort the drawings into the correct group successfully. The more "scientific" and "intellectualized" group of judges could not. Those who relied on their feelings apparently could receive the subtle kinesthetic communication embedded in the figure drawing; those who attempted to merely use their heads were, we might deduce, on a different wave length. It may be, then, that the contradictory findings in the field of figure drawings are as much dependent upon what type of judge is used in the study as they are upon errors in criteria employed, research design, or matching of samples from one experiment to the next.

My own experience, derived from teaching the Annual Summer Workshop in Projective Drawings, is that in the hands of some students projective drawings are an exquisitely sensitive tool, and in the hands of others, those employing a wooden, stilted approach, they are like disconnected phones. It may be because of this that, in spite of the contradictory research findings, clinicians who can use drawings with some artistry—those whose every day clinical experience demonstrates the frequently remarkable and compelling congruence between the dynamics of patients and their figure drawings—continue to use them in the projective battery. In fact, a recent survey (Sundberg, 1961) indicates that projective drawings have risen to become the second most frequently used projective tool, preceded only by the Rorschach. The remarkable staying power of the projective drawing tool attests to the unshakeable conviction of clinicians that this technique has within it the capacity to provide them with useful information about clients.

To return to Swensen's (1957) review: Several fallacies are expressed which invite correction before other research workers fall into the use of the same misconceptions. In the face of so comprehensive and integrated a review of the literature, criticism of Swensen's article is perhaps super-derogatory, but because his paper has become so pivotal a survey in the field, several points of clarification must be made.

Swensen reports that Holzberg and Wexler (1950) found no significant difference between normals and schizophrenics in drawing naked feet with the toes delineated, in drawing feet with the toenails indicated, or in a tendency to begin a drawing on one part of the page and then start some place else on the page, turning the page over, or showing other signs of disorganized sequence. Also, no significant differences were found between normals and schizophrenics in the frequency of drawing internal organs which showed through a transparent body wall. Swensen interprets these findings as contraindicating Machover's hypotheses concerning these signs' suggestion of schizophrenic processes in the subject.

The occurrence of naked feet with toenails delineated, the occurrence of disorganized and bizarre sequence in the order of the various parts of the human figure drawn, and the representation of internal organs almost invariably, in my experience, are associated with schizophrenia. In view of this experience, I can not help suspecting that the responsibility for the lack of statistical support for these clinical findings lies with the experimental approach rather than with the hypotheses: All of these three "schizophrenic signs" are relatively infrequent in projective drawings of the human figure, but where they do occur, they occur in the drawings of schizophrenics. Thus, to test these hypotheses adequately, only instances where the sign occurs should be included. For example, to wait to accumulate twenty such drawings and then determine the incidence of schizophrenia in the subjects who submitted these drawings, would be the only way to assess fairly the validity of the sign. If one had to wait until two hundred drawings were accumulated in order to obtain twenty in which these signs occurred, and then one found that in eighteen of the twenty the subject was actually schizophrenic, this would then constitute an investigation of the meaning of such a sign. However, to investigate a relatively infrequent occurrence by comparing fifty "normals" with fifty schizophrenics and deducing from the respective instance of zero and two frequencies of such signs that there is "no statistically significant difference" between the two groups does violence to the actual clinical use of such signs and to the statistically sophisticated investigation of their meaning.

The next point of clarification concerns those studies investigating hypotheses which are formulated on a not-too-careful reading of Machover's contribution. Swensen states that Machover reports that the drawing of knee joints suggests a faulty and uncertain sense of body integrity, and occurs chiefly in schizoid and schizophrenic individuals. Swensen then interprets Holzberg and Wexler's (1950) finding, that normal women show the knee joint significantly more often than hebephrenic schizophrenic women, as a direct contraindication of Machover's hypothesis.

Actually, a reading of the section of Machover's book in which the meaning of "joints" is discussed (and it is only one paragraph) will find the following sentences: "The schizoid, the frankly schizophrenic individual, and the body narcissist in decline, will lean on joint *emphasis* (my italics) in order to stave off feelings of body disorganization," and "Most drawings that involve joint *emphasis* (my italics) . . ." Thus, the flavor of the hypothesis concerns over-emphasis on detailing of joints in the drawings. The mere *inclusion* of the knee joints in the drawings, without over-emphasis, is consistent with the better reality contact and assessment of the normal women as compared with the hebephrenic schizophrenic women, and is not research data opposing the hypothesis as clinically employed.

Elsewhere Swensen points out that "erasures are considered an expression of anxiety" but that Goldwirth (1950) found that, in general, normals employed more erasures than other groups. Swensen concludes that, "These results appear to contradict Machover."

This type of research reasoning embodies a popular fallacy in which groups of subjects are compared with other groups of subjects, and extremes in each group tend to cancel each other out, thus yielding a more benign Mean for the group. But clinicians find that neurotic and psychotic groups tend to deviate from the norm in either direction. Thus, sick individuals will draw a figure much too large (at the grandiose end of the continuum) or much too small (reflecting direct feelings of inferiority and inadequacy); they will either draw with too light a line (reflecting anxiety, hesitancy and uncertainty) or too heavy a line (reflecting aggression and inner tension); similarly they will erase too much or not erase at all. As with all areas of behavior, it is the deviation in either direction from the mean which is clinically noteworthy. Group comparisons, then, on any variable, tend to obscure the extreme emphasis, in both directions, of that group and to cancel out the noteworthy occurrences.

In regard to the specific hypothesis about erasures, some erasure, with subsequent improvement, is a sign of adaptiveness and flexibility. Over-emphasis upon erasure, particularly in the absence of subsequent improvement in the drawing, is the correlate of excessive self-doubt, self-disapproval, and conflicts which result from perfectionistic demands upon one's self. A total absence of erasures, on the other hand, may denote a lack of adaptive flexibility.

In cases such as this, a comparison of Means has no valid meaning. The only research design that is applicable would involve employing a three-point (or five-point) rating scale: 1) over-emphasis, 2) "normal" emphasis, and 3) under-emphasis and absence. Then the comparison between groups which is appropriate would be in regard to percentages falling in the extreme categories, not with the obscured picture of the Means.

Cronbach, in his American Psychological Association Presidential Address, took researchers to task for treating individual differences as a merely bothersome variation—to be reduced by adequate controls or treated as mere error variance. Such assumptions cannot help but lead to an oversimplified set of results, because the simplification is built into the experiment before it gets off the ground. Schafer (1954) has expressed a similar criticism: "Recognizing and specifying complexity (in a projective record) is objectionable only to those clinicians who cling to mechanical 'sign' interpretation and to those score-oriented researchers who naively expect that dumping all patients described as 'paranoid' (or 'anxious,' 'schizophrenic,' 'well adjusted,' etc.) into one group will consistently yield highly instructive means, variances, or correlations, and whose conception of test theory and research stops right there."

In a charming and lively paper, Dunnette (1966) refers to some of the sterile exercises which sometimes pass as research, as "methodologically our favorite *pets*." Naming the game "Tennis Anyone?" he defines it as "the compulsion to forget the problem—in essence, to forget what we are really doing—because of the fun we may be enjoying with our apparatus, our computers, our models or the simple act of testing statistical hypotheses. Often, in our zest for this particular game, we forget not only the problem, but we may even literally forget to look at the data!"

As David Campbell (Dunnette, 1966) has remarked, "We seem to believe that *truth* will be discovered somehow through using more and more esoteric techniques of data manipulation rather than by looking for it in the real world."

It is my own feeling that projective drawings, resting on repeated clinical verification, will survive to eventually stimulate more knowledgeable experimental approaches and the devising of less crude nets through which the elusive complexities of clinical data will slip less easily.

The fact that present correlations are low between ratings of traits reflected in drawings, on the one hand, and personality characteristics of the subject, on the other, should not be surprising. A drawing of a man and a drawing of a woman are, after all, a pretty small sample of an individual's expressiveness. The use of a *battery* of drawings therefore is suggested for research approaches, as it is used clinically by those who employ the H-T-P, rather than only the Draw-A-Person. In fact, the drawing of a House, Tree, and Person of each sex, and then four crayon drawings, a House, Tree, male and female Person, provide eight drawings, which when rounded out with the Draw-A-Family procedure, the Draw-An-Animal, the drawing of the Most Unpleasant Concept a subject can think of, and the other miscellaneous drawings would *only then* actually provide a pool of data sufficient to more validly "test" projective drawings. Otherwise, it is much like testing the validity of a Rorschach examination by employing only the first two cards.

To take the implication in the other direction, the shaky results of research studies based merely on the Draw-A-Person test suggest that clinicians, in their everyday work, should employ a wider projective drawing net than just the two drawings of the human figure. Caligor (1962) found that paranoid trends could be detected in only 25 percent of a group of paranoid schizophrenics when only one drawing was used, but could be detected in 85 percent of the cases when a series of eight drawings was employed.

In terms of experimental design, what we need currently are more multivariate statistical methods which incorporate the uniqueness of the pattern of the individual's behavior, as it is the pattern rather than individual elements which are really what emerge in projective technique assessment. It is the harmony or lack of harmony between various elements which form the essence of personality, not the individual traits *per se*. Swensen (1957) himself points out that studies which attempt to evaluate the significance of *patterns* of signs on the Draw-A-Person test appear to be more promising than attempts to evaluate the significance of *individual* signs. This, of course, has also been maintained by Buck (1948) and by Machover (1949).

The last point that requires clarification in Swensen's review concerns the very *basic premise* of projective drawings as a reflection of the self. Swensen reports Berman and Laffal's (1953) comparison of figure drawings with the body type of the subjects offering the drawings. A Pearson r of .35, significant at the .05 level of confidence, was yielded on the basis of Sheldon's body types. In inspecting Berman and Laffal's data, Swensen points out that "only" 18 of their 39 subjects drew figures that were judged to be of the same body types as the subject's body type, and concludes that for some subjects, the figure drawn represents the subject's own body, but for the majority of subjects, the figure drawn represents something else. Swensen deduces, "Since in clinical work the reliable diagnosis of the clinical case is of paramount importance, this lack of consistent evidence supporting Machover, . . . suggests that the DAP is of doubtful value in clinical work."

Here Swensen is entangled in a relatively unsophisticated notion of the concept of the self. Some subjects tend to project themselves as they experience themselves to be, while other subjects tend to project themselves as they wish to be. The idealized version of the self is an integral component of the self-concept and is necessary in describing personality. In actual clinical context, most drawings are neither one nor the other, but represent a fusion of both the realistic perceptions of one's self and the ego ideal. In addition, the picture is further complicated by the fact that the perceptions of one's self *as one fears one might be* also color the total picture. Since the *self* actually includes what we are, what we wish to be, and what we fear we might sink to, we must expect all three to appear in projective drawings and not regard any deviation from perfect correlation on any one of these variables between the drawing and the subject, as a contraindication of the basic hypothesis.

The trouble with Swensen's interpretation of the results of Berman and Laffal's study is that he too narrowly defines the self as both experienced by the subject and as projected in his drawing. As the present writer points out elsewhere (1958), an additional facet that must be reckoned with in the understanding, and investigation of, projective drawings, involves a perception of significant figures in one's early developmental years. Thus, the projective drawing interpreter and/or research worker must grapple with the problem of disentangling the influences of four different projections on the drawing page: What one *feels* oneself to be, *fears* oneself to be, *wishes* to be, and perceives *others* to be.

For example, a subject who suffers from "castration anxiety" will reveal *the fear of what he may become,* in his drawing. A subject who feels himself to be obese may draw a fat person (*what he feels himself to be*); another subject who suffers from obesity but who has not yet lost the capacity to yearn for, and strive for, an ideal figure, will draw a very shapely person (*what he wishes to be*). A child who experiences his father as threatening may, as one subject recently did, draw a male with teeth bared, a dagger in one hand, and scissors in the other, with a generally menacing facial tone and violent look in the eyes (*his perception of others*).

In the face of a complex world, the research worker is obliged to recognize the complexity of the variables he attempts to come to grips with in his investigations, and steer vigorously away from the dangers of atomistic studies, naively conceived, and dogmatically interpreted.

REFERENCES

Albee, G. W., & Hamlin, R. M. An investigation of the reliability and validity of judgments inferred from drawings. *J. clin. Psychol.*, 1949, *5*, 389-392.

Albee, G. W., & Hamlin, R. M. Judgment of adjustment from drawings: The applicability of rating scale methods. *J. clin. Psychol.*, 1950, *6*, 363-365.

Alschuler, A., & Hattwick, W. *Painting and Personality*. Chicago: University of Chicago Press, 1947.

Anastasi, Anne, & Foley, J. P., Jr. A survey of literature on artistic behavior in the abnormal: Experimental investigations. *J. gen. Psychol.*, 1941, *23*, 187-237.

Berman, S., & Laffal, J. Body type and figure drawing. *J. clin. Psychol.*, 1953, *9*, 368-370.

Berrien, F. K. A. A study of the drawings of abnormal children. *J. educ. Psychol.*, 1935, *26*, 143-150.

Blum, R. H. The validity of the Machover DAP technique. *J. clin. Psychol.*, 1954, *10*, 120-125.

Buck, J. N. The H-T-P technique, a qualitative and quantitative scoring method. *J. clin. Psychol. Monogr.*, 1948, no. 5, 1-120.

Caligor, L. The detection of paranoid trends by the 8 Card Redrawing Test. (8 CRT). *J. clin. Psychol.*, 1952, *8*, 397-401.

Dunnette, M. Fads, fashions, and folderol. *Amer. Psychol.*, *21*, 1966, 343-352.

Eigenbode, C. R. Effectiveness of the Machover signs and others in differentiating between a normal group and a schizophrenic group by use of the projective drawing test. Unpublished master's thesis. George Washington University, 1951.

Fisher, S., & Fisher, Rhoda. Test of certain assumptions regarding figure drawing analysis. *J. abn. soc. Psychol.*, 1950, *45*, 727-732.

Goldworth, S. A. A comparative study of the drawings of a man and a woman done by normal, neurotic, schizophrenic, and brain damaged individuals. Doctoral dissertation, University of Pittsburgh, 1950.

Gonder, E. *Art and Play Therapy*. New York: Doubleday, 1954.

Graham, S. Relation between histamine tolerance, visual autokinesis, Rorschach human movement, and figure drawing. *J. clin. Psychol.*, 1955, *11*, 370-373.

Grams, A., & Rinder, L. Signs of homosexuality in human figure drawings. *J. consult. Psychol.*, 1958, *22*, 394.

Griffith, A., & Peyman, D.: Eye-ear emphasis in the DAP Test as indicating ideas of reference. In Murstein, *Handbook of Projective Techniques*, New York: Basic Books, 1965.

Gunzburg, H. C. Scope and limitations of the Goodenough drawing test method in clinical work with mental defectives. *J. clin. Psychol.*, 1954, *10*, 8-15.

Hammer, E., & Piotrowski, Z. Hostility as a factor in the clinician's personality as it affects his interpretation of projective drawings. *J. proj. Tech.*, 1953, *17*, 210-216.

Hammer, E. Relationship between diagnosis of psychosexual pathology and the sex of the first drawn person. *J. clin. Psychol.*, 1954, *10*, 168-170.

Hammer, E. F., (Ed.). *The Clinical Application of Projective Drawings*. Springfield, Ill.: Charles C Thomas, 1958.

Hiler, E., & Nesvig, D. Evaluation of criteria used by clinicians to infer pathology from figure drawings. *J. consult. Psychol.*, 1965, *29*, 520-529.

Holzberg, J. D., & Wexler, M. The validity of human form drawings as a measure of personality deviation. *J. proj. Tech.*, 1950, *14*, 343-361.

Hozier, Ann. On the breakdown of the sense of reality: A study of spatial perception in schizophrenia. *J. consult., Psychol.*, 1959, *23*, 185-194.

Katz, J. The projection of assaultive aggression in the human figure drawings of adult male Negro offenders. Unpublished doctoral dissertation, New York University, 1951.

Machover, Karen. *Personality Projection In the Drawing of the Human Figure.* Springfield, Ill.: Charles C Thomas, 1949.

Mott, S. M. The development of concepts: A study of children's drawings. *J. genet. Psychol.*, 1936, *48*, 199-214.

Plaut, Erika, & Crannell, C. W. The ability of clinical psychologists to discriminate between drawings by deteriorated schizophrenics and drawings by normal subjects. *Psychol. Rep.*, 1955, *1*, 153-158.

Reznikoff, M., & Tomblen, D. The use of human figure drawings in the diagnosis of organic pathology. *J. consult. Psychol.*, 1956, *20*, 467-470.

Reznikoff, M., & Nicholas, A. An evaluation of human figure drawing indicators of paranoid pathology. *J. consult. Psychol.*, 1958, *22*, 395-397.

Ribler, R. I. Diagnostic prediction from emphasis on the eye and the ear in human figure drawings. *J. consult. Psychol.*, 1957, *21*, 223-225.

Richey, M. H., & Spotts, J. V. The relationship of popularity to performance on the Goodenough Draw-A-Man test. *J. consult. Psychol.*, 1959, *23*, 147-150.

Schafer, R. *Psychoanalytic Interpretation in Rorschach Testing.* New York: Grune and Stratton, 1954.

Schmidl-Waehner. Formal criteria for the analysis of children's drawings. *Amer. J. Orthopsychiat.*, 1942, *17*, 95-104.

Schmidt, L. D., & McGowan, J. F. The differentiation of human figure drawings. *J. consult. Psychol.*, 1959, *23*, 129-133.

Sherman, L. J. Sexual differentiation or artistic ability? *J. clin. Psychol.*, 1958a, *14*, 170-171.

Sherman, L. J. The influence of artistic quality on judgments of patient and non-patient status from human figure drawings. *J. proj. Tech.*, 1958b, *22*, 338-340.

Singer, R. H. A study of drawings produced by a group of college students and a group of hospitalized schizophrenics. Master's thesis, Pennsylvania State University, 1950.

Singer, R. H. Various aspects of human figure drawings as a personality measure with hospitalized psychiatric patients. Unpublished doctoral dissertation, Pennsylvania State University, 1957.

Siprelle, C. N., & Swensen, C. H. Relationships of sexual adjustment to certain sexual characteristics of human figure drawings. *J. consult. Psychol.*, 1956, *20*, 197-198.

Spoerl, D. T. Personality drawing in retarded children. *Character Pers.*, 1940, *8*, 227-239.

Springer, N. N. A study of the drawings of maladjusted and adjusted children. *J. genet. Psychol.*, 1941, *58*, 131-138.

Steinmann, K. The validity of projective technique in the determination of relative intensity in psychosis. Unpublished doctoral dissertation, School of Education, New York University, 1952.

Swensen, C. H. Empirical evaluations of human figure drawings. *Psychol. Bull.*, 1957, *54*, 431-466.

Sundberg, N. I. The practice of psychological testing in clinical services in the United States. *Amer. Psychol.*, 1961, *16*, 79-83.

Tolor, A., & Tolor, B.: Judgments of children's popularity from their human figure drawings. *J. proj. Tech.*, 1955, *19*, 170-176.

Waehner, T. S. Interpretation of spontaneous drawings and paintings. *Genet. Psychol. Monogr.*, 1946, *33*, 3-70.

Wexler, M., & Holzberg, J. D. A further study of the validity of human form drawings in personality evaluation. *J. proj. Tech.*, 1952, *16*, 249-251.

Whitmyre, J. W. The significance of artistic excellence in the judgment of adjustment inferred from human figure drawings. *J. consult. Psychol.*, 1953, *17*, 421-424.

Witkin, H. A., Lewis, H. B., Hertzman, M., Machover, K., Meissner, P. B., & Wapner, S. *Personality Through Perception*. New York: Harper, 1954.

Zimmerman, J., & Garfinkle, L.: Preliminary study of the art productions of the adult psychotic. *Psychiat. Quart.*, 1942, *16*, 313-318.

VI

EXTENSIONS OF THE
PROJECTIVE HYPOTHESIS

Almost any kind of standardized testing situation, even the type that employs standard and structured stimuli, may offer the clinician an opportunity for projective interpretation. In such instances the examiner does not focus solely upon the "correctness" of the response to, let us say, an intelligence test question. He is more concerned with the subtler aspects of the response that are beyond formal correctness or incorrectness. The subject's "cognitive style," manner of reasoning, idiosyncratic content, and patterns of successes and failures become grist for the interpretive mill. The subject projects of himself in addition to offering objectively correct or incorrect answers or responses.

This "extension" of the projective hypothesis to tests which were not originally designed as projective techniques is the focus of the present section. The Bender-Gestalt was originally devised to assess "perceptual-motor abnormalities." The author (Hutt) in the context of his chapter utilizes and interprets the reproductions of the Bender-Gestalt figures in a dynamic, personality-relevant fashion. In his keen and sensitive analysis of what may appear to the untrained eye to be meaningless lines and curlicues, the author illustrates the clinician's intuitive art. However, he does not stop there. Some quantitative systematic data are available in support of the clinical hunches. The clinician's judgment is not a "wild analysis" but is buttressed by a good deal of experience and some hard data which he has assimilated. Both types of interpretive evaluation of the Bender-Gestalt—the clinical-intuitive and objective scoring method are included in Chapter 13.

Extension of the projective hypothesis to intelligence testing is illustrated by the next chapter (Blatt and Allison). Here the relevance of intelligence test results to personality assessment becomes manifest. The authors have built upon the early pioneering work of Rapaport and his associates. The rationale of the subtests of Wechsler's Adult Intelligence

Scales (WAIS) is analyzed, and the differential effects of various personality dynamisms upon the effective performance of the subject is treated in detail. The illustrative case material brings out the salient principles underlying the interpretive analysis based on the projective hypothesis —broadly defined.

Finally, in the last chapter of this section and in the longest of the book, Dr. Campos covers a wide array of methods which could not be discussed in separate chapters because of space limitations. Each of these methods—the Szondi, the Hand Test, the Lowenfeld Mosaic Test, the Kahn Symbol Arrangement Test, and the Drawing Completion Techniques—is described in some detail. They represent different stimulus materials and belong to the several classes of projective methods; for example, the Hand Test could be classified in the expressive methods category, the drawings in the completion category, etc.

In addition to describing the test materials and procedures, the author has succeeded in presenting critical comments and research data concerning the several methods in the relatively limited space at his disposal. Some of these methods have not been developed or used as extensively as the major time-honored tests. However, there is some evidence for their potential usefulness in clinical work as well as in research.

13

The Projective Use of the Bender-Gestalt Test

MAX L. HUTT

As currently employed, the Bender-Gestalt Test consists of nine geometric figures, each of which is presented on a card about the size of the usual index card. Although there have been a number of modifications of these figures, two sets of cards, one prepared by Bender and the other by Hutt (see below), are the ones currently in widest use. These simple materials, the ease and rapidity of their administration, and the increasingly rich clinical and research evidence which have become available, have made this instrument very popular among clinicians. In general, two different, but complementary, approaches have been employed in the use of the test: 1) as a device to assess disturbance in the perceptual-motoric aspects of behavior, usually with some objective measure of the severity of this disturbance; and 2) as a projective technique to assess various aspects of personality functioning, sometimes with objective scores, sometimes with single or configurational indices, and sometimes with careful, clinical evaluation of all aspects of test behavior as well as test performance.

In the present discussion, we shall focus our attention on the projective uses of this instrument.

HISTORICAL PERSPECTIVE

The test figures which are employed in this instrument were *adapted* from those employed by Wertheimer in his studies of Gestalt principles involved in visual perception. Bender selected nine of these figures and modified them for use, originally, in her study of "regressed and defective schizophrenics." As she states, "Only test figures A, 3, 7 and 8 closely resemble the designs used by Wertheimer. The others have been modified usually to simplify them or to accentuate some basic Gestalt feature" (Bender, 1963). As Bender's work continued she shared her drawings with some co-workers and others closely associated with her—often the drawings were reproduced free-hand, and somewhat later they were available in mimeographed form. The drawings contained the imperfections (and even distortions in size) that resulted from free-hand drawings. These drawings, on cards that did not always have a consistent size, were still being utilized when Bender published her monograph summarizing her postulates about the "test" and her richly incisive clinical observations in 1938 (Bender, 1938). At this time the Bender cards were not easily available, and they were frequently copied from those which others had in their possession or from the designs published in the 1938 monograph.

One of those who had been impressed by the potential clinical value of this technique was Hutt, who also utilized the relatively make-shift stimuli then available. In 1944 and later in 1945, when this writer was senior instructor in the Officers' Clinical Psychology Program at the Adjutant General's School in the U. S. Army, he was asked to teach projective theory and methods. For various reasons, he thought it best to secure more accurate reproductions of the Wertheimer figures and to make it possible to have consistent stimuli that were available on test cards that were constant in size. Among these reasons were: 1) the advisability of adhering as closely as possible to stimuli that met Wertheimer's Gestalt criteria; 2) the need to eliminate irregularities in the drawings (such as uneven lines, and inopportune angles of crossing in some of the figures); and 3) the need for easy and consistent reproducibility. In cooperation with F. L. Wells, of Harvard University, such a set of cards was produced and distributed to clinical psychologists throughout the U. S. Army. At the same time, this writer prepared a tentative guide for use by such psychologists in which he presented his clinical and early research findings on possible projective uses of the "test" (Hutt, 1945).

It is interesting to note that there soon followed a very rapid increase in the use of this test. Prior to 1945 the Bender-Gestalt test was not even mentioned in the rankings in popularity of psychological tests employed by clinical psychologists (Sundberg, 1961). According to the same survey, by 1946 it ranked 54th in popularity, and in 1960 it ranked 3rd. In their study, Schulberg and Tolor found that among experienced clinicians, 95 percent utilized the test, and four out of five of these clinicians believed it had value for clinical purposes (Tolor & Schulberg, 1963). It is also significant that there were only a handful of publications dealing with the test before 1945, and that there had been no systematic research studies to evaluate its possible validity. There were a number of clinical investigations, chief among which were those by Bender, and these served to highlight the kinds of phenomena which occurred on test performance associated with certain of these clinical pathologies. Between 1946 and 1966 almost 300 publications appeared; these included—in addition to clinical papers—research studies on scoring; research on methods of administration; validation studies utilizing a wide variety of criteria; systematic reviews of the technique; and, clinical demonstrations of "blind" interpretations of the test protocol.

In 1946, as a result of the new interest in the procedure, Bender published a brief manual for the clinical use of her test (Bender, 1946). At the same time, her forms of the test cards became commercially available through the American Orthopsychiatric Association. Just one year before this, this author had published his *Tentative Guide for the Administration and Interpretation of the Bender-Gestalt Test* (Hutt, 1945). However, the set of cards which he and Wells had prepared became unavailable with the conclusion of the War in 1946. These cards became available again in 1960 through the publishers, Grune and Stratton, when Hutt and Briskin published the first clinical handbook devoted expressly to the projective use of the test (Hutt & Briskin, 1960).

The first attempt to develop and test an objective scoring approach to evaluate the test appeared in 1948 (Billingslea, 1948). This approach was characterized by atomistic analysis of specific aspects of test performance and, on the whole, yielded negative results. A few years later, another of the officers who had attended the Clinical Psychology course in the Army, with the cooperation of a colleague, published a different type of scoring method which was based on the assumption that the greater the total amount of distortion in test performance, the more severe the underlying psychopathology (Pascal & Suttell, 1951). Despite its relative crudity, this method yielded promising results and demonstrated the scoring method's potential in differentiating psychosis from normality as well as its possibilities in differentiating neurotic conditions from normal adjustment. This method of scoring has been widely used and is most applicable for adults.

A number of other workers devised methods of scoring and norms for the evaluation of children's records. Perhaps the most useful of these, in terms of single objective scores, is that by Koppitz (Koppitz, 1964). This work includes norms for children between the ages of 5 and 10 years. It will probably supersede the tentative norms for children 6 to 8 included in Pascal and Suttell's earlier work. Norms for children between 6 and 12 years of age have been presented by Armstrong and Hauck (1960).

We shall not attempt to summarize or describe the variety of methods of administration or the many kinds of clinical and predictive uses which have been proposed. An excellent summary and evaluation of the many ways in which this "test" has been administered, evaluated, and "validated" is available in the work by Tolor and Schulberg, already cited. And Billingslea has also prepared a summary and perspective which merits careful reading (Billingslea, 1963). Many of the claims for various methods of evaluating the test have not been confirmed, but others have withstood critical assault, sometimes even arbitrary and excessively critical evaluation. The technique is certainly very useful in detecting some types of organic pathology, psychotic conditions—especially schizophrenic reactions—readiness for reading, mental retardation, and perceptual-motoric immaturity. It has been less useful in differentiating psychoneurotic from normal and psychotic reactions. There is considerable dispute concerning its validity in assessing specific personality variables, although when analyzed as a projective technique and utilizing clinical rather than atomistic and mechanical methods of evaluating the protocol, highly significant predictions about personality dynamics and even about therapeutic outcomes have been demonstrated, as our later evaluation of these studies will attest.

For want of a better term, the Bender-Gestalt has usually been referred to as a "test." In the strict meaning of this term, it is not a test. Rather it is many tests, it is a projective approach to assessment, and it is no test at all. It is many tests in the sense that responses to the stimuli have been analyzed in many and quite different ways. Each of these attempts to make the procedure into a test requires the use of standard stimuli (the test cards), and tries to provide: a method of scoring or evaluating the responses; norms for evaluation; and, validating evidence. However, since test cards have differed, methods of administration have varied, and above all, the rationale and methods of scoring have differed greatly, there are, in fact, many Bender-Gestalt tests. Careful evaluation requires that these differing approaches be considered separately, and that generalizations about "the test" be severely limited.

It is a projective approach to assessment when the projective properties of the testing situation and the protocol are maximized. Sometimes this has been done on a fairly straightforward clinical-intuitive basis; sometimes it has been done using objective scoring schema. The values and limitations of such approaches need to be examined on the basis of the kinds of results which have been achieved with them, as well as on the basis of the theory or rationale underlying them. We shall devote most of the remainder of this chapter to such approaches.

It is not a test at all when neither of the sets of conditions noted above has been satisfied. A set of test cards no more constitutes a test than does a set of random stimuli casually assembled by some "parlor clinician." When, however, test materials are selected on the basis of psychological principles, experimental evidence, or clinical experience, and when methods of administration and evaluation are carefully spelled out and "controlled" in some appropriate manner, and finally when test responses are evaluated in terms of basic principles or empirical evidence, we may then have a test indeed.

The Test Materials

As we noted above, the test stimuli consist of nine relatively simple geometric designs, developed by Wertheimer, and adapted by Hutt to conform as closely as possible to the Gestalt principles elaborated by Wertheimer. Each design is presented in black line drawing on a 3 x 5 inch card. Because of previous usage and notation, the first one was called design A, and the remainder were numbered from 1 to 8. Figure 1 shows these designs.

(Reduced approximately 45% from the card size)

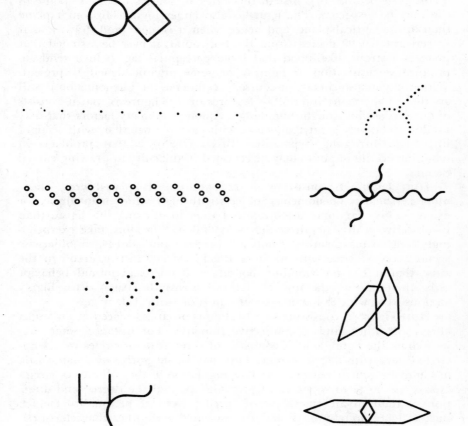

Figure 1. The Bender-Gestalt figures as adapted by Hutt. Reprinted by permission of Grune and Stratton, Inc., Publishers

A few comments about the major characteristics of each design may be helpful in understanding the subsequent projective analysis of test protocols. Hutt Figure A, consisting of a circle and a square, tangential to each other, is the simplest of the nine figures, requiring a maturational level of approximately seven years for accurate perception and reproduction. Hence, it is a useful buffer design with which to introduce the test. It is also useful to compare performance on other designs with performance on this one. For example, if S has more difficulty with this design than with the others, some disturbance in perceptual-motoric development, some unusual reaction to this design because of its particular qualities or because it is first in the series, or some symbolic response to this may be suspected. The figure is also larger in the horizontal plane than in the vertical plane, and hence when it is seen (and drawn) as if it were rotated 90 degrees from the horizontal, it may be assumed that there is a strong likelihood that some perceptual lag (which tends to produce verticalization of figures) or some organic deficit is present. (Other explanations may, of course, account for the phenomenon.) Still another of the many interesting features of this figure is that it consists of a curved and a straight-line design. Among the many factors that may produce relatively greater difficulty with curved lines than with straight lines, one intriguing hypothesis (Breen, 1953) is that problems in handling hostile impulses may be reflected in difficulty in drawing curved designs.

Hutt Figure 1, consisting of 12 equidistantly placed dots, elicits other personality phenomena. Subjects with high achievement drive, for example, give far more attention and time to drawing this figure than its objective reality requires; they may "fill in" the dots, take excruciatingly long to make sure the dots are placed equidistantly, or otherwise spend excessive time with it. Since the figure is "unstructured" in the sense that it has no confining boundary, it elicits abnormal behavior (like perseverating the line of dots all across the page) with highly anxious Ss or with Ss having certain kinds of cortical damage.

Hutt Figure 2, consisting of 10 columns of circles placed at an angle, elicits still other kinds of projective responses. For instance, some subjects draw the figure as if it consisted of three rows of circles in a semicircle drawn with S as its center. This may be suggestive of a narcissistic or highly egocentric personality. The angulation of the columns of circles "forces" some Ss to rotate the figure slightly, and the degree and direction of rotation are suggestive of specific types of personality factors, such as depression, hostility, and (if associated with other characteristics) organic brain damage.

Hutt Figure 3, the arrowhead, presents other projective possibilities. To some Ss this figure is highly threatening, and it is therefore perceived in distorted form. The lack of a definitive boundary around the figure seems to increase its projective properties. Some subjects "simplify" the figure (see below for discussion of test factors) and destroy its Gestalt properties.

Hutt Figure 4 has some of the same properties as Hutt Figure A, but it is a much more difficult figure. It tends to elicit projections in the sexual area as well as in the authoritarian area, and as with Figure A, the relative distortions in the curved as compared with the straight-line portions can be quite revealing.

Hutt Figure 5 presents still other projective possibilities. The compulsive individual cannot tolerate the "imbalance" of this figure and tries to correct it, usually making it more symmetrical. Paranoid subjects quite frequently see this figure as threatening and may distort it considerably, usually making it less "aggressive-looking."

Hutt Figure 6, the intersecting sinusoidal curves, often reveals problems in emotional or impulse control. Both the curvature and the intersecting characteristics tend to elicit marked distortions when such problems are present.

Hutt Figures 7 and 8 often elicit projections in the area of sexual conflict, and particularly in the area of phallic competency or striving (Suczek & Klopfer, 1952).

It should not be expected that the kinds of personality manifestations often elicited by the stimuli, as noted above, have a simple, high, linear relationship to the stimuli. The sample of findings reflect both extensive clinical experience with these test stimuli and research results obtained in relevant studies. They are therefore to be regarded as either *possible or probable hypotheses* about a particular S, rather than as conclusive, to be confirmed or rejected by concurrent evidence from this test or from other sources of data. It should be emphasized that in all likelihood no stimulus has equivalent meaning for all Ss, even if its symbolism is quite common in a given subculture; rather, each subject responds to a given stimulus in terms that are necessarily idiosyncratic for him. The clinician's task, therefore, is to utilize probable hypotheses as a means of exploring a given Ss unique, personal world.

ADMINISTRATION AS A PROJECTIVE TEST

We have noted before that these figures have been administered in a great variety of ways. It has been found, for example, that some methods of group administration, even with children, are about as effective as individual administration (Keogh & Smith, 1961). The tachistoscopic method of presentation of the test cards, as Hutt suggested, can improve the differentiation of organic from non-organic conditions (Hutt, 1960; Snortum, 1965). The method of recall (i.e., reproduction from memory) has been studied extensively, and found useful in improving the diagnosis of organicity and of evaluating intellectual efficiency (Olin & Reznikoff, 1957; Peek & Olson, 1955). Each method of administration may have unique advantages; some methods may be generally more useful in clinical work than other methods.

The method which we are about to describe is believed to have the greatest utility when the purpose of the procedure is to highlight under-lying personality characteristics of S. It can be modified or supplemented if some other, specific objective of the testing is at issue. The method is based on extensive experience with a variety of methods, on careful clinical appraisal of results, and on empirical evidence obtained (mainly with male adults) with 130 adults who were diagnosed as psychoneurotic, 38 adults diagnosed as schizophrenic, 119 adults with a variety of organic damage, and 25 hospitalized patients for whom there was no suspicion of psychiatric disturbance. Findings during the *copy phase* of the testing (earlier called the *basic method*) were compared with findings obtained with the elaboration (and association) method. A comparison of the percentage of diagnostically accurate predictions (in terms of nosological category) made on the basis of the copy phase protocol with those made on the basis of protocols based on *both* the copy phase and the elabora-tion phase showed that the latter procedure gave better predictions; the difference was significant at the .05 level of confidence. This experience has led to a rationale for the present method which will be discussed below.

The method consists of three phases: the *copy phase;* the *elaboration phase;* and the *association phase.* Time for administration for the adult S varies considerably, depending on many features of Ss condition, but generally takes from 25 to 35 minutes.

The copy phase. A pile of papers, $8\frac{1}{2}$ x 11 inches, unlined, is placed before S (slightly to one side), with the long axis of the papers perpen-dicular to S. E then takes out the test cards, upside down, and says in effect (the words can be altered so long as the intent covers the following features) :

> I am going to show you some cards, one at a time. Each card has some simple drawing on it. I want you to copy the design *as well as you can* (emphasizing the last phrase) . Work in any way that is best for you. This is not a test of artistic ability, but try to copy the drawings *as accurately as possible.* Work as fast or as slowly as you wish.

The subject is given a medium-soft pencil and an eraser is also made available. E takes one sheet of paper off the pile and places it directly before S. He then exposes card A, placing it before S and slightly to one side so as not to interfere with the subject's drawing. The additional instruction is then given: "Copy this as well as you can."

All questions by S concerning how to proceed are dealt with by the same general comment, indicating "That's up to you," or "Do it the way you think is best." The only restriction is that S is not to use any mechan-ical guide (such as a ruler or a coin) to assist him.

The subject is left entirely free to use a single sheet of paper, a sheet of paper for each design, or two or more sheets for the reproduction of all of the designs.

The rationale for this procedure is that it tends to leave the situation undefined, so that S is compelled to define or structure it for himself. Should he use a single sheet of paper for each drawing or one sheet for all the drawings? Should he increase or decrease the size of the figures? Should he line the figures up on one side of the page? Should he use the eraser or cross out a drawing with which he is dissatisfied? Can he return to a previous figure and correct or modify it? All of these and similar considerations are purposefully left undefined. The intent is to promote the maximum projective interpretation of the whole test situation by the subject.

After the subject has completed design A, the next design is placed before him as design A is taken away and covered, and again the subject is told, without further comment, "Now copy this drawing as well as you can." The rest of the cards are presented in similar fashion. Only one further restriction is added to the testing situation. If S tries to change the position of the test card which has been placed in front of him he is discouraged with some comment as, "The card has to be in this position." Reasons: 1) The orientation of the card for S must remain constant if he is to deal with the same objective stimulus that is given to others. Reversal of the card, for example, in some instances drastically changes its Gestalt qualities. 2) If a card is reversed and drawn in that position, the phenomenon of *perceptual reversal* (see below) cannot be assessed readily.

In actual clinical practice many intriguing, and sometimes frustrating, situations arise which are not dealt with adequately by the instructions given above. Space does not permit us to discuss these, but sometimes even the most ingenious E, trying to maintain the proposed set, will have unusual difficulties. When serious deviation from "standard" administration occurs, E will, of course, have to take these into consideration in evaluating the results.

The elaboration phase. In order to increase the projective properties of the testing situation, this phase attempts to increase the degree of the "unstructuredness" of the test.

The drawings made by the subject in the copy phase are removed as E commends S for his cooperation and effort with this phase of the procedure. Then he states:

> Now I'm going to ask you to do something else with these figures. This time I'd like you to modify the figure in any way you wish so as to make them more pleasing to you. Feel free to change them in any way you like. You can change the drawings as little or as much as you please. Just make them more pleasing to yourself.

Any questions by E are responded to in terms of this framework. If the subject states that he likes the figure as is, he is, nevertheless, asked to draw it again, for he may modify it even if he does not intend to.

The cards, or a sampling of them,[1] are again presented as in the copy phase, one at a time. Again, S is left free to use as much or as little paper as he wishes. Any spontaneous comments made by S are recorded for later analysis.

The rationale for this phase includes the assumption, which clinical experience seems to bear out, that when confronted with the requirement to "modify" the figures, more of Ss unconscious determinants of behavior will emerge. Although some Ss are obviously threatened by this new task and so may attempt to defend themselves in one of a number of different ways, whatever modifications are made can be quite revealing of aspects of the personality not hitherto revealed on the test. Thus, the sample of projective behavior tends to become enlarged, or perhaps more accurately, it tends to be more sharply etched. Another aspect of the rationale is that the elaboration phase reveals which aspects of the performance are more stable than others. It permits inspection of a possible answer to the question: "Under increased stress, which aspects of perceptual-motoric behavior remain relatively constant and which are modified?"

The association phase. This last part of test administration requires that S offer associations to *both* the original test stimuli and his elaborations of these stimuli when *both* are presented together. E re-presents each stimulus card, in turn, placing it alongside Ss elaboration of that same figure, and in each case asks:

> Now look at the drawing on the card *and* at the modification you made of it. What does *each of them* remind you of? What *could* each be or look like?

E notes Ss association (s) to both the original and modified figures. If the subject offers an association only to one of the pair, he is urged to find an association to the other figure as well. Note is made of the figure that is associated to first.

The reason for presenting the subject with both the original stimulus and the modification simultaneously should be explained. It is believed that since unconscious determinants are more likely to be operative in the elaboration than the copy phase, requiring S to examine and compare both figures tends to focus his conscious attention on the differences, if any, and so is more likely to trigger off more significant associations. Again, clinical experience has frequently shown that this is exactly what appears to happen. It would be most helpful if we had research evidence to test this conclusion and to demonstrate what increments in prediction, if any, do emerge.

The data available as a result of this projective approach to utilizing these Gestalt figures fall into the following categories:

---

[1]In practice, an adequate sample of behavior can usually be obtained by using cards A, 2, 4, 6, 7, and 8.

1. The drawings produced during the copy phase together with the use of space (space on the page and number of pages utilized for all of the drawings).

2. The drawings produced during the elaboration phase together with the use of space.

3. The associations produced in connection with the original stimuli and the modifications of them.

4. Ss behavior (postural, motoric, verbal, etc.) during each of these phases.

METHODS OF INTERPRETATION

Any armchair analyst can make "wild analyses" of the data available. The role of the clinician-scientist is much more difficult and much more responsible. Although it may be popular to utilize some objective scoring scheme which others have developed without any particular concern for its rationale, such usage may lead to serious abuse of the "test's" potentialities. Even when some scoring method has been carefully validated, the serious clinician will wish to know the limitations of such validity studies and the hypotheses which generated them. Only then can he properly apply the method to a particular case, for only then will he be aware of the degree to which generalizations about the "scale" have meaning in a given case. The use of objective scoring methods has many advantages, but they also have serious limitations. Our purpose should be to develop replicable methods which can stand the close scrutiny of research analysis, but the best methods are not necessarily easily replicable. In such cases, they should rest on clearly formulated rationale or theory (construct validity), and they should be constantly evaluated on the basis of meaningful criteria in clinical experience or real-life situations.

The present discussion cannot possibly do full justice to even the limited area of analysis of projective use of test protocols. For a more complete discussion, the reader is referred to the clinical manuals and the references cited in them (Hutt, 1968; Hutt & Briskin, 1960). We shall, however, highlight one of the clinical-intuitive methods of analysis, one of the configurational methods of analysis, and a promising objective method of scoring based on a projective hypothesis.

A clinical-intuitive method of analysis. The writer believes that, at the present time, one of the most rewarding methods of analysis is that of the clinical-intuitive approach. It is an intricate, complex, and time-consuming method—it requires considerable effort in generating appropriate hypotheses and in testing them—and it has serious limitations since each analysis is like doing research with a single case. A method such as this should rest on extensive clinical, research, and theoretical findings with which the clinician is himself thoroughly familiar.

This type of analysis, previously also called "inferential analysis" (Hutt & Briskin, 1960), "goes beyond the simple statement of a correlational relationship between each phenomenon and each 'trait.' It assumes, on the contrary, that the successive productions of a given sequence of events are uniquely determined by the interaction of multi-determined events over a span of time so that the final product on the test represents the idiosyncratic resultant of the *given constellation of events operating over time*" (p. 75).

In this method, E examines each aspect of test behavior, utilizing the kinds of data referred to previously, and *follows S through his successive behaviors*, first on the copy phase, then on the elaboration phase, and finally on the association phase, meanwhile attempting to formulate relevant hypotheses to help explain the behavior (sometimes a number of such hypotheses for a given sample of behavior). These successively developed hypotheses (sequential hypotheses) are critically examined in the light of all of the evidence, and are increasingly confirmed, altered, or rejected. Finally, these inferences about the meaning of the behavior on the test are integrated in order to offer the most succinct explanation, and when other kinds of data are available (from other tests, life history, clinical manifestations, etc.) these inferences are checked against such data.

In order to utilize this approach effectively, the clinician should understand the meaning of perceptual-motoric behavior in general, and should be familiar with the probable meanings of specific test factors and test behavior. We shall consider each of these now, in brief, and then offer a concrete illustration of the application of this approach.

The development of perceptual behavior in the human animal has been extensively studied, as has also the development of perceptual-motoric behavior (Solley & Murphy, 1960; Tagiuri & Petrullo, 1958; Bruner & Krech, 1950). Gradually it has become clearer how basic perceptual-motoric processes influence personality development and mediate other behaviors. The young infant seems to rely greatly upon perceptual defenses in trying to deal with the impinging world and the impact of stress upon his organism. Visual perception, together with the motoric adjustments of which he is capable, probably afford the most effective method of coping and defending. When input of stimulation is threatening he can close his eyes, or turn them. He can also turn his head, and later turn his whole body away from the threatening stimulation—even if he still cannot remove his body, *in toto*, from the threatening situation. Thus, his perceptual-motoric behavior can be conceptualized as falling into the general continuum of *adience-abience* (or *approach-avoidance*) behavior. It is possible that the early style of such adient-abient behaviors rapidly becomes structured and influences the general style of personality adaptation. The style of avoidance may be developed as a response to excessive stress, just as the style of approach may be developed in a relatively benign environment for the organism. This perceptual-motoric style may manifest itself, in perceptual responses, by defensive reactions to the size of objects (such as seeing them "smaller" or "larger" or as altering their veridical characteristics in some other way). Similarly, as Mira has shown (Mira, 1939-1940), defensive reactions to authoritative objects in the world may produce alterations in both perception and movement in the vertical plane.

Together with the development of adient-abient perceptual styles, the infant, and later the child, may associate other psychological defenses, such as denial, repression, and projection. These, in turn, tend to become associated with motoric and postural styles, so that the abient child may be slow in motoric response, may stand and move in a less-than-normal upright position, and so on. Further differentiation of the perceptual style, during the early stages of perceptual development, may produce concomitant affective-perceptual modes of behavior, so that, for example, flattened affect is associated with perceptually reduced awareness of curved figures and surfaces, and distorted perception of visual phenomena involving angulation.

Thus, perceptual-motoric behavior is affected by the nature of the individual's psychological experience (along with genetic and maturational factors). Such behavior seems, therefore, to offer important clues to possible personality variables. More than this, when an individual is asked to "elaborate" visual designs—as during the elaboration phase of the test we are discussing—he may respond with perceptual-motoric behaviors whose origins he is unaware of. Unconscious determinants, or preconscious determinants, may have produced these seemingly "accidental" responses. Then, when S is confronted with both the original and the elaborated drawings, and is made more consciously aware through such presentation that there are discrepancies, he may either produce associations of which he was unaware or, in fact, whose significance may still partially escape him. In fact, as a later illustration will indicate, the motoric response *plus* the perceptual response may facilitate "connections" which might otherwise not have been readily available.

Thus, the clinician has at his disposal a number of rich sources of data for evaluation. The fact that this procedure is primarily non-verbal, and that only the association phase is essentially verbal may have two kinds of consequences which differ from the more common verbal projective techniques. The non-verbal features of the response may uncover different areas of personality functioning than verbal methods reveal. In this sense this technique is supplementary to other methods. In the second place, associations and behaviors that are elicited primarily by non-verbal methods may tap deeper or earlier modes of personality development.

As we noted, the clinician should also be familiar with specific test factors and their possible interpretative significance. Hutt has proposed

25 such factors, grouped into five categories (Hutt & Briskin, 1960). Undoubtedly, further clinical experience and research will produce significant modification in the number of factors, their definition and measurement, and their clinical values. For example, in a very careful study of the factor of curvilinearity with adult psychiatric patients, using factor analytic methods, Guertin was able to extract five relatively discrete factors to account for the distortions (Guertin, 1954). In another study, in an attempt to select and weigh factors that would differentiate brain damaged cases from psychiatric cases without brain damage and from "normal" cases, 31 possible test indicators were evaluated, and 15 of these showed considerable promise in differentiating the experimental population (Hain, 1964). Of these, 8 test indicators accounted for most of the variance. Findings such as these suggest that it may be possible to reduce the total number of factors and to combine them in ways that are more effective than present usage indicates.

We shall offer an example or two of each of the five categories of factors proposed by Hutt. The first category is that of *Organization*. One of the factors included in this category is that of *Sequence* which refers "to the successive positions of the drawings as they are reproduced by the patient on the page." Sequence is subdivided into four subtypes: *overly methodical, methodical, irregular,* and *confused or symbolic.* Each of these is defined and precise methods of measuring and identifying them are given. It is contended that the style of sequence is related to ego functions and to methods of intellectual control. Compulsive individuals usually demonstrate overly methodical sequence, while anxious schizophrenics show confused or symbolic sequence. Also of interest is the point in the test at which unusual disturbances in sequence occur. Such points are triggered by Ss traumatic reaction to the idiosyncratic symbolic meaning of a particular test figure.

The second category is that of *Size*. Size may be generally increased or decreased, it may be progressively increased or decreased, or it may be modified in connection with only one or special types of figures (isolated changes in size). A number of studies have indicated that significant change in the size of a figure is an indicator of overt or covert anxiety. Highly anxious Ss tend to decrease the size of all or most figures. It should be noted that modification in the size of drawings may have other than emotional determinants, such as socioeconomic status, cultural conditioning, and the like. Hence, in clinical-intuitive analyses, this possible indicator of anxiety and the method of dealing with it are evaluated in terms of other test and non-test indicators of anxiety.

The third category is that of *Change in the Form of the Gestalt*. Such factors as *closure difficulty, curvature difficulty,* and *change in angulation* are included in this group. As with each of the other factors, definitions, criteria for measurement, and interpretative significance are given. As an example of factors in this category, the factor of *closure difficulty* will be discussed briefly. This phenomenon has been studied extensively not only on the Bender-Gestalt but in many studies of drawing and perceptual behavior. It refers to difficulty in joining parts of figures or adjoining figures when the stimulus shows an actual joining of these parts or figures. Such difficulty may be manifested by actual separation of the adjoining parts, by erasures at the point of joining, by re-drawing or over-drawing at such points, and the like. Both clinical and experimental evidence indicate that this kind of phenomenon is related to problems in interpersonal relationship, or, in more technical terms, represents difficulty in maintaining appropriate cathexes (Clawson, 1959). Again, this indicator together with other indices make the possible interpretation more incisive. For instance, closure difficulty for an adult male, on the "phallic" figures 7 and 8, together with evidence of high anxiety, and distortion on the Gestalt qualities of these figures is presumptive of severe conflict over latent homosexual tendencies.

The next category is *Distortion of the Gestalt,* and represents distortions of such severity that the original Gestalt qualities of the figures are entirely destroyed. They generally occur in severely disturbed adults, and especially in cases with brain pathology or with certain forms of psychosis. Occasionally they may occur when some figure has a traumatic impact upon an otherwise well-compensated or moderately well-functioning adult. This category includes the factors of *rotation, retrogression, simplification, fragmentation, perseveration,* and the like. To illustrate this category, we may examine the factor of *fragmentation* which refers to the reproduction of a Gestalt by breaking it up into parts or reproducing only part of it. It represents a severe loss in the capacities of organization and abstraction. Typically, it is found in the records of brain damaged and psychotic patients. It sometimes appears in cases of acute anxiety. Another factor in this category is that of *perseveration.* Two types of perseveration are distinguished. One type consists of the repetition of a response elicited in a previous figure on the subsequent figures, as when S continues to use dots (instead of circles) for figure 2 because dots were used in figure 1. The other type consists of continuation of the features of the design well beyond the limits called for by the stimulus, as when S reproduces figure 1 which contains 12 dots by drawing a line of 18 dots all across the page, stopping only when he reaches the margin. Both types of perseveration usually represent loss in ego control so that inhibitory process, critical judgment and attention behavior are disturbed.

The last category is that of *Movement and Drawing.* The direction of movement when S reproduces the drawings tells us something of how he perceives himself in relationship to the world. Mira has studied this phenomenon extensively (Mira, 1943); so has Werner (1957). We have learned that counter-clockwise direction of movement suggests oppositional trends in the personality, that drawing from the inside of a figure to the outside similarly represents such attitudes, and that difficulties in the area of movement in the vertical field represent conflict with authority figures. Inconsistencies in direction of movement also have demonstrable personality correlates—so does the line quality of the drawing. Each of these and other features of movement and drawing quality are useful in personality appraisal. However, it is probably true that factors in this category are susceptible to specific learning and general cultural conditions, and that caution in interpretation is especially needed.

The following selected materials from an intensive case study may help to concretize the previous discussion. Of course, the reader may not be familiar with all of the test factors that are discussed, nor with the specific sources for the interpretive remarks.

This young man, 26 years old, was a patient in a psychiatric hospital and was regarded as "highly refractory" to treatment. He had been picked up by the police for exhibitionistic behavior on the front steps of a church, became very violent when apprehended, and was later placed in the hospital for psychiatric observation and possible treatment at the request of his father. In his relations with both the psychiatrist and the psychologist he was usually quite oppositional, often refused to talk, and was unwilling to tell much about his background or about the circumstances leading to his apprehension by the police. The complexities of his case history are many, and only a few of these, as they relate to the evaluation of the test protocol, will be discussed. At the time of testing, he was still quite negativistic. On the Rorschach he had given a single response to each card, and all but one of these responses was popular or near-popular, given quite rapidly and without elaboration.

On the Hutt Adaptation of the Bender-Gestalt he worked quite rapidly, but said almost nothing, only occasionally making some grunt-like noise. It was only during the association phase of the test that he seemed to become involved and offered a number of important associations. The reproductions do not adequately represent all of Ss test behavior; for example, the use of space and the sequence in which the drawings were placed on the two pages of his drawings are not indicated. Nevertheless, we can capture a few of the aspects of a clinical-intuitive analysis of this material (see Figure 2).

Design A was placed near the center of the page, drawn rapidly, and no corrections or erasures were made. *Inferences*: egocentric in orientation, impulsive tendencies in behavior, little critical control or superego factors operative. It is noted further that the circle is significantly larger than in the original, while the square is both in comparative and absolute terms, smaller. *Inferences*: possible identification with the female role, possible fear of and/or hostility toward male symbols, possible deprecatory attitudes toward males. Closure difficulty is noted on both

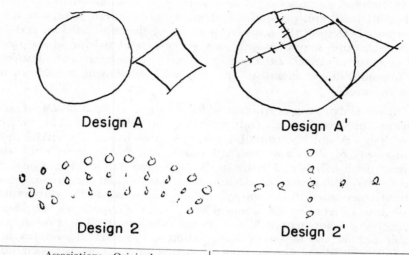

Associations—Original	Associations—Elaboration
A. Oh, just a circle and a box. That's all. Nothing to it.	A'. I don't know. I put a cross in there (circle). Oh, it's a college hat on a bald pate. Yeah! It reminds me of a bridge table in a fish pond.
2. A picket fence or some round pegs.	2'. Just a fence. And, oh yeah, I guess it could be a cross, damn it.

Figure 2. Sample reproductions of two original designs, their elaborations, and the associations to each

parts of design A, due apparently to impulsivity as well as to perceptual factors. *Inferences*: difficulty in maintaining close interpersonal relations, and corroboration of trends toward impulsive behavior. The square shows concave curvature of the sides. *Inference*: impulsivity accompanied by hypomanic trends. The line quality of the drawings shows slight tendencies toward irregularities. *Inference*: internal tension level is high. (There is no evidence thus far for an organic basis for this manifestation.)

Design 2 reveals a number of outstanding features, only some of which will be commented on. Most outstanding is the distortion of the Gestalt so that it resembles an arc composed of circles and drawn as if S were the center of the arc. *Inference*: highly egocentric personality structure. (Confirms egocentric inference on design A.) There is no initial difficulty in the angulation of the rows of circles, but the angulation is changed as the arc-like configuration is developed. *Inference*: emotional needs interfere with critical judgment and reality testing. Not only is closure difficulty shown on most of the circles, but some circles are reproduced as dashes or as dots. *Inferences*: ego boundaries are not well-maintained, and psychotic-like regressions or severe acting-out may be expected. Despite the unusual qualities of the reproduction, certain obsessive features may be noted, such as the careful spacing of the rows and columns of circles. *Inference*: probable over-development of super-ego functions due to moralistic training, with subsequent breakdown of these defenses.

On the elaborations, certain new features appear in addition to con-firmation of some of the trends noted on the copy phase. The subject drew design A quickly, initially making a cross within the circle, then erasing part of the cross (hatched lines), and finally completing the "square" with half of this figure in the circle and half outside. Again, as in the original drawing, the circle is made larger than the square. Most of the factors noted in the copy phase are also noted on the elaboration phase, thus offering confirmation of some of those hypotheses. The most interesting development is found in the associations. The subject was unable to offer any meaningful association to the original stimulus, but simply described the figures (named them), whereas in his associations to his elaborations, after some denial, he offered two, highly idiosyncratic associations! The first of these was apparently evoked in his reaction to the examiner (a college professor!) and may have indicated his hostile feelings (a parataxic reaction), but the second suggested some highly personal meaning. The initial explanation of his elaboration ("I put a cross in there.") is also highly suggestive of personal meaning. In dis-cussing these associations with S (which, surprisingly, he did with ani-mation and involvement), he said the bridge table and fish pond which "he had drawn" reminded him of an incident in his early childhood which he had forgotten about. His father, who was highly moral and very severe in his training orientation toward the two children (there was also a younger brother) had caught him playing cards in the house. Such behavior was, according to the father, sinful and unforgivable. The father was enraged, rushed into the room, grabbed the bridge table on which S was playing cards with two friends, and in a fit of anger threw it through the glass doors and into a little pond just outside the house. This memory, apparently elicited by Ss perceptual-motoric elaboration, told a great deal about the subject and the nature of his psychopathology. It also strongly confirmed some of the inferences already made about S from his protocol on the copy phase of the test.

The associations to design 2, as well as the elaboration of design 2 are also exceptionally revealing. The elaboration of this figure reveals the same general features as does the copy phase, but the arrangement of the circles in the form of a cross is unique. The association to the original stimulus as a picket fence suggests that S may feel "hemmed in" and, taken together with other findings, may explain his defensive withdrawal into narcissistic preoccupation. The second association to the elaboration ("I guess it could be a cross, damn it.") suggests that concern over the cross (and religion and/or morality) has a high valence for this individual. As further discussion with the subject about his associations revealed, his younger brother was a priest, his exhibitionistic act on the church steps was a phase in his acting out behavior toward this feared-hated brother (and his identification in Ss eyes with his father), and simultaneously an attempt to deny his own homosexual strivings by "showing off" his physical potency.

This fragment of the test material and the case record cannot convey fully all of the inferences derived from the test nor all of the leads that were furnished and that could then be dealt with clinically. It is, however, suggestive of the clinical-intuitive method and of the kinds of findings it makes possible. What we have not illustrated is also important; namely, how the various inferences and hypotheses which are derived are checked, modified, or discarded. Examples of these ramifications of the method may be found in Hutt's analyses of Bender-Gestalt records in the volume edited by Rosenthal (1963).

A configurational method of analysis. This method takes advantage of the well-known fact that clusters of signs, scores, or traits, especially if they are appropriately weighted, tend to predict more accurately than a score based on a single variable or scale, some kinds of psychiatric conditions or personality constellations. A number of workers have attempted to develop such configurations for the Bender-Gestalt, often with good empirical results. Hain's study, noted previously, is an example of this kind of approach to test evaluation. The example we shall offer is not based, however, on refined statistical analysis. It is based on empirical findings with a large population of clinical and non-clinical cases, but it remains for future research to validate or to modify the proposed configurations.

In the volume by Hutt and Briskin (1960), noted above, configurations are presented for: essential psychoneurosis, intracranial damage, schizophrenia, mental retardation, and manic states. Cross validation, generally confirming the configuration's predictive capacity has been obtained for three of these categories: schizophrenia, intracranial damage, and mental retardation. In each configuration, the indicators are divided into two groups: essential discriminators and associated discriminators. The clinician evaluates the record for the presence of each of these indicators. The rule of thumb which is proposed is that the presence in a record (copy phase) of *"five or more* of the phenomena in the *essential* group is sufficient to merit the diagnostic categorization of that group" (Hutt & Briskin, 1960). When a record presents five or more indicators from more than one psychiatric category, the record should be labelled as that of a mixed condition. The configurations apply to adult records only.

One example of the configuration for schizophrenia is given so that its make-up may be noted. This group contains 12 essential discriminators and 7 associated discriminators. The essential discriminators are: 1) confused or symbolic sequence; 2) placement of first figure in abnormal position; 3) very uneven use of space; 4) collision tendency; 5) pronounced shift in position of stimulus cards; 6) severe angulation; 7) severe rotation; 8) retrogression on 2 or more figures; 9) fragmentation; 10) simplification; 11) cohesion; 12) doodling, usually marked. The associated discriminators are: 1) perseveration, especially type A; 2) marked decrease in curvature; 3) crossing difficulty; 4) marked inconsistencies in direction of movement; 5) marked and progressive increase in size; 6) excessive hugging of margin; 7) frank elaboration of sexual symbols.

It should be remembered that any attempt to predict the nosological category of a patient is fraught with difficulties. For one thing, the nosological category is simply the result of many, possibly different, underlying dynamic processes; correlated with the above, any nosological group is really a heterogeneous population even though there is some degree of commonality of clinical symptoms. Nevertheless, the configurational method, or some derivative of it, is a useful clinical tool for some purposes. The final diagnostic categorization of a patient should, of course, rest upon much more than this one source of evidence.

An objective scoring method based on a projective hypothesis. Based upon the considerations discussed previously, we became interested in developing a scale for measuring degree of *adience-abience*. It was assumed that such a measure would relate to some underlying and basic perceptual style: the tendency to shut out or the tendency to receive and accept visual stimulation of a meaningful kind. Hence it was *not* expected that such a measure would correlate highly with *overt* manifestations of approach-avoidance behavior which, in turn, was presumed to be the end product of many intervening processes. Rather, it was hypothesized that this basic perceptual style would be related to some complex, real-life indicators which would themselves be related to the capacity of the individual to "take in" various forms of stimulation. A scale was developed and was tested out against three quite different types of populations: 1) a large group of deaf mental retardates; 2) a relatively small group of patients undergoing psychotherapy; and 3) two groups of schizophrenics, one process and the other reactive. The scale was significantly predictive in all three types of populations, thereby suggesting that it had considerable promise.

We shall illustrate the scale and its application to the deaf-retarded population. The scale consists of 12 factors, each of which is given a weight from +2 to −2. The score is obtained by the algebraic addition of the 12 weights. The higher the total score the more perceptually adient S is presumed to be; the lower the score the more perceptually abient he is presumed to be. The categories of factors are: space, height of figures, amount of space used, sequence, placement of the first figure, closure difficulty, crossing difficulty, change in angulation, rotation, fragmentation, simplification, and elaboration. As an example of the type of definitions and scale values, we may take the factor of *fragmentation*. For purposes of this scale, this factor is defined as: "breaking the Gestalt into component parts, or gross separation of the 2 parts of the figures A, 4, and 7." A score of +2 is given if no fragmentation is present, whereas a score of −2 is given if fragmentation is present on 2 or more of the figures.

In the study on the deaf-retarded population[2] two separate analyses were undertaken. In the first phase, out of a population of about 200 adult patients, 30 were selected at random from the extremes on a preliminary measure of perceptual adience-abience. As part of a larger study, each patient had been given a battery of psychological tests, which included the Hutt Adaptation of the Bender-Gestalt. The two extreme groups were then compared statistically on 6 measures: a score of degree of psychopathology; a clinical rating of psychopathology; the Goodenough IQ score; a clinical rating of degree of intellectual impairment; age of admission to the hospital (or institution); total length of hospitalization. It was predicted that the group high in adience would show less psychopathology, obtain higher scores and ratings in intelligence, be older at the time of hospitalization, and have shorter length of hospitalization. All of the differences were in the expected direction and five of them attained statistical significance (at the .01 level or better). The remaining difference was significant at the .05 level and was thought to be significant in view of the restricted nature of the population.

In the second, cross-validation phase of the study, all of the remaining members of the population were utilized. Four of the criterion variables used in the pretest were utilized again, and three new criteria were added: Wechsler Adult Scale of Intelligence IQ, rating of overt hostility, rating of aggression. This time differences in adience-abience scores were obtained between groups that were high or low on each of the seven measures used in this portion of the study. Separate tests of statistical significance were made for males and females.

All of the differences were in the expected direction and all but two attained statistical significance. Only in the case of males was there a less significant difference between the extreme groups on impairment in intelligence, and even this difference—with a population of males who

[2]Hutt, M. L., and Feuerfile, D. The clinical meanings and predictions of a measure of perceptual adience-abience for a deaf-retarded group. Paper presented at Amer. Psychol. Assoc., Philadelphia., Sept., 1963.

were less impaired intellectually than females—was significant at the .25 level—clearly not statistically acceptable, but probably still meaningful in view of the circumstances. The other variable that generated only a moderately significant difference (at about the .05 level) was the rating on aggression. Taken together, these findings are consistent with the general hypothesis that individuals who are high on adience are more likely to function comparatively better and to be able to profit more (take in more) than those who are high in abience.

Thus we have evidence for the utility of an objective measure, based on a projective hypothesis, that seems to tap a fundamental personality characteristic.

Concluding Statement

It seems reasonable to conclude that the projective use of the Bender-Gestalt has promising possibilities and that its popularity with clinicians is not without merit. It is one of the few non-verbal projective instruments currently available. It has wide use as a buffer test. It seems to tap some aspects of the personality not readily tapped by other measures, and can therefore supply rewarding supplementary clinical evidence. It is especially useful in differentiating suspected cases of brain damage. It has a wide range of applicability: from young children through the adult levels, and with populations varying greatly in cultural, linguistic, and experiential background. It can be used in a great variety of ways: with objective score or as a sensitive clinical instrument; as a measure of perceptual-motoric maturity, or as a technique for the projective evaluation of the personality.

As with any technique, long and extended use and research are needed both to refine the method and to validate its possible uses. This technique is quite far from the objective of a well-established and validated measure or instrument. Refinement, further testing of the technique, and careful and critical evaluation of the findings will finally supply a more adequate evaluation of its utility.

REFERENCES

Armstrong, R. G., & Hauck, P. A. Correlates of the Bender-Gestalt scores in children. *J. clin. Psychol.*, 1960, *11*, 153-158.

Bender, L. *A Visual Motor Gestalt Test and its Clinical Use.* New York: American Orthopsychiatric Association, Research Monographs, No. 3, 1938.

Bender, L. *Instructions for Use of the Visual Motor Gestalt Test.* New York: American Orthopsychiatric Association, 1946.

Bender, L. Foreword. In A. Tolor & H. C. Schulberg. *An Evaluation of the Bender Gestalt Test.* Springfield, Ill.: Charles C Thomas, 1963.

Billingslea, F. Y. The Bender-Gestalt: an objective scoring method and validating data. *J. clin. Psychol.*, 1948, *4*, 1-27.

Billingslea, F. Y. The Bender-Gestalt: a review and a perspective. *Psychol. Bull.*, 1963, *60*, 233-251.

Breen, H. The differential diagnostic technique as a measure of hostility. Unpublished doctoral dissertation, University of Western Ontario, 1953.

Bruner, J. S., & Krech, D. *Perception and Personality: A Symposium*. Durham: Duke University Press, 1950.

Clawson, A. The Bender Visual Motor Gestalt Test as an index of emotional disturbance in children. *J. proj. Tech.*, 1959, *23*, 198-206.

Guertin, W. H. A factor analysis of curvilinear distortions on the Bender-Gestalt. *J. clin. Psychol.*, 1954, *10*, 12-17.

Hain, J. D. The Bender Gestalt test: a scoring method for identifying brain damage. *J. consult. Psychol.*, 1964, *28*, 34-40.

Hutt, M. L. A tentative guide for the administration and interpretation of the Bender-Gestalt Test. U.S. Army Adjutant General's School, 1945 (Restricted).

Hutt, M. L. The Bender-Gestalt Test. In D. Rosenthal (Ed.). *The Genain Quadruplets*. New York: Basic Books, 1963.

Hutt, M. L., & Briskin, G. J. *The Hutt Adaptation of the Bender-Gestalt Test*. New York: Grune and Stratton, 1960.

Hutt, M. L., & Feuerfile, D. The clinical meanings and predictions of a measure of perceptual adience-abience for a deaf-retarded group. Paper presented at American Psychological Association, Philadelphia, 1963.

Hutt, M. L. *The Hutt Adaptation of the Bender-Gestalt Test: Revised*. New York: Grune and Stratton, 1968.

Keogh, B. K., & Smith, C. E. Group techniques and proposed scoring system for the Bender-Gestalt test with children. *J. clin. Psychol.*, 1961, *17*, 172-175.

Koppitz, E. M. *The Bender Gestalt Test for Young Children*. New York: Grune and Stratton, 1964.

Mira, E. Myokinetic psychodiagnosis: a new technique for exploring the cognitive trends of the personality. *Proc. roy. Soc. Med.*, 1939-1940, November-April.

Mira, E. *Psychiatry in War*. New York: Norton, 1943.

Olin, T. D., & Rezinkoff, M. Quantification of the Bender-Gestalt recall: a pilot study. *J. proj. Tech.*, 1957, *21*, 265-277.

Pascal, G. R., & Suttell, B. J. *The Bender-Gestalt Test: Quantification and Validity for Adults*. New York: Grune and Stratton, 1951.

Peek, R. M., & Olson, G. W. The Bender-Gestalt recall as an index of intellectual functioning. *J. clin. Psychol.*, 1955, *11*, 185-188.

Rosenthal, D. *The Genain Quadruplets*. New York: Basic Books, 1963.

Solley, C. M., & Murphy, G. *Development of the Perceptual World*. New York: Basic Books, 1960.

Snortum, J. R. Performance of different diagnostic groups on the tachistoscopic and copy phases of the Bender-Gestalt. *J. consult. Psychol.*, 1965, *29*, 345-351.

Suczek, R. F., & Klopfer, W. G. Interpretation of the Bender-Gestalt Test: the associative values of the figures. *Amer. J. Orthopsychiat.*, 1952, *22*, 62-75.

Sundberg, N. D. The practice of psychological testing in clinical services in the United States. *Amer. Psychol.*, 1961, *16*, 79-83.

Tagiuri, R., & Petrullo, L. *Person, Perception and Interpersonal Behavior*. Stanford: Stanford University Press, 1958.

Tolor, A., & Schulberg, H. *An Evaluation of the Bender-Gestalt Test*. Springfield, Ill.: Charles C Thomas, 1963.

Werner, H. *Comparative Psychology of Mental Development*, Revised Edition. New York: International Universities Press, 1957.

14

The Intelligence Test in Personality Assessment

SIDNEY J. BLATT AND JOEL ALLISON

The conceptualization and application of the intelligence test has gradually but persistently evolved and expanded in scope. This has been reflected in part in a shift away from a limited preoccupation with the global IQ score to a broader focus on the diverse tasks of an intelligence test as an assessment of ego functions. Increased interest has also been shown in the principles and patterns in which these various ego functions are organized and integrated into various types or modes of adaptation. Thus, while the purpose of early intelligence testing was to evaluate an individual's general intellectual capacity by comparing it to appropriate norms and standardization groups more recent conceptualization and utilization of intelligence tests have increasingly questioned the arbitrary separation of intelligence, as a functional concept, and personality. To some extent the interrelationship of intelligence and personality was recognized at the outset, but in the somewhat static concept that personality factors could influence and interfere with test efficiency. For example, it was noted relatively early that many patients showed a decline or deterioration as well as marked variability in their intellectual functioning, and interest was focused on the relationship between the range of the scores and various psychopathological conditions. This conceptualization of the relationship of psychopathology to gross scatter of test scores was then refined to include the hypothesis that the variability (or scatter) reflected selective impairments that were specific to various psychopathological states. The development of the Wechsler-Bellevue in the mid-1940's with its subtests, each of which was administered to all subjects, was an important stimulus to this revised, more refined concept of test scatter because the Wechsler scales permitted more specific and

This chapter was written with the support of the Cooperative Research Program of the Office of Education, United States Department of Health Education and Welfare, Project No. 1931, "Non-Intellectual Factors in Cognitive Efficiency." We are endebted to Roy Schafer, Cynthia Wild and Alan Feirstein for their comments on drafts of this chapter.

consistent comparisons (Rabin, 1965). It was also with the development of the Wechsler scales that some of the guideposts were established for clarifying the inseparability of intelligence and total personality functioning. The addition of a theoretical analysis of the various psychological functions assessed by the different subtests (Rapaport, Gill & Schafer, 1945; Wechsler, 1944) supplied an interpretive rationale for viewing the interrelationship of the various psychological functions reflected in subtest scores with personality organization. In large measure, this new approach reflected the systematic application to intelligence tests of the hypothesis that each act of the individual bears the imprint of his unique personality organization (the projective hypothesis). This more dynamic conception of intelligence as an integral aspect of personality organization has been re-emphasized, expanded and extended in more recent years (Fromm, Erika, 1954, 1955, 1957, 1960; Mayman, Schafer & Rapaport, 1951; Waite, 1961).

This chapter will also deal with the integral relatedness of intelligence and personality, primarily as seen on the Wechsler scales. First, the role of the intelligence test in personality assessment and how the projective hypothesis applies to intelligence testing will be considered. Then an analysis of the psychological functions assessed by the individual Wechsler subtests and how scores, and the patterns of scores, can be interpreted, will be presented. This will be followed by a detailed discussion of the WAIS of one individual to demonstrate how various sources of test data —the scores on the subtests, attitudes toward one's responses and being tested, and the content of the responses and of asides and gestures during testing—interweave to give insight into the complexities of unified psychological functioning. Last, there will be a review of recent research on the relevance of the WAIS to personality assessment.

THE WAIS AND PERSONALITY ASSESSMENT

There are essentially three ways in which the projective hypothesis can be applied to intelligence tests.

1. *The content of responses* can contain personalized concerns and idiosyncratic preoccupations.

2. *The style of responses,* and the quality and nature of the clinical transaction represent aspects of personality organization.

3. *The structure or organization of psychological functions* as indicated in the patterning of diverse abilities, both between and within subtests, is an integral aspect of personality organization.

1. *The content* of specific test responses including asides and comments can reflect important areas of concern and preoccupation. Unlike the Rorschach and the TAT, the intelligence test assesses adaptive potential in situations that involve relatively habituated, routine functions and

past achievements. A number of tasks are presented with the demand and expectation that responses be organized and realistic, and that they remain relatively free of personal issues and of primitive wishes and fantasies. In contrast to the Rorschach and TAT which permit less logical thought organization and encourage the embellishment and enrichment of responses by fantasies, the intelligence test requires functioning which is logical, organized and relatively attuned to reality.

In general, personalized concerns tend to interfere with efficient functioning on the intelligence test and their presence invariably serves as a harbinger of their prominence as situations become less restrictive and less structured and require the individual to organize his responses according to his inner world. Thus, minor content variations on the WAIS often appear in major proportions on the TAT and Rorschach. The intelligence test, therefore, is not a test of central importance if one is primarily interested in learning about various content concerns of an individual. Content in the intelligence test is more relevant to assessing the degree to which such concerns enter into and interfere with cognitive efficiency in relatively routine, impersonal situations. Psychological functions such as perception, memory and visual-motor organization play important roles in adaptation (Hartmann, 1958) and for these processes to be effective they must remain relatively free and undisturbed by the various pressing concerns of the individual (Rapaport, 1958). When these cognitive functions are infused by drives and personalized preoccupations and organized by less logical principles (as in psychosis), efficiency is sharply curtailed. It is primarily in the severely neurotic and particularly in psychotic conditions that psychological functioning in the routine and relatively neutral situation of the intelligence test is undermined by personal preoccupations or autistic elaborations. For example, a girl with intense depressive concerns received only partial credit on the sixth Picture Arrangement of the WAIS (the flirt sequence) by arranging her cards in the order of JNAET. She explained her sequence by stating that the King has gotten out of his car because of his interest in the "hat" rather than in the girl, thereby revealing her feelings that any interest on the part of men does not reflect recognition of her essential worth. This same patient in relating a fly and a tree on Similarities revealed another aspect of her depression—her oral neediness—by seeing the similarity in the fact that "both require food to live." A more severe intrusion of a personal nature occurred in the WAIS of a chronic schizophrenic young man beset by feelings of unreality. When asked why we should keep away from bad company, he responded, "because from Confucius on down it is bad to associate with people more confused than yourself." Not only do the concerns expressed about confusion suggest the possibility of impaired reality testing, but the clang association and the symbolic and non-relevant thinking in the blending of "confusion" and "Confucius" indicates that thinking can be alogical and governed by rather primitive principles.[1]

Though effective functioning on the WAIS generally requires a minimal intrusion of irrelevant material into responses, this does not mean that a well-intact WAIS protocol should contain only perfect "textbook" responses. Such records can be banal, trite and uninteresting, and reflect a highly conventional individual who may find difficulty in expressing personal feelings, interests, and needs. Highly organized skills and psychological functions should have a degree of autonomy from drives but it is equally important that a degree of autonomy be maintained from the environment as well (Rapaport, 1951, 1958). Though the degree of autonomy from the environment can be assessed most readily in an individual's capacity to give imaginative and creative responses to the Rorschach and TAT, the degree of autonomy from environmental demands can also be considered to some extent on the WAIS. The structure of the WAIS tends to limit the range of cognitive strategies that can be employed, but the subtests differ in the limitations and restrictions they place in defining an acceptable response. Subtests such as Information require circumscribed, precise responses while subtests like Comprehension and Vocabulary require more verbalization and have a wider latitude of acceptable responses. The content of responses on these subtests may reflect unique aspects of personality without necessarily indicating a disruption of functioning or pathology.[2] For example, in defining travesty, both "a mocking imitation" and "burlesque" receive full credit but it is of some interest when "burlesque" (a less usual response) is

[1]Although the relationship between "Confucius" and "confusing" might well appear in humor, this response was not presented as humor but rather as a serious attempt to cope with demands of the question. The attitude and mood tone which accompany a response are an important aspect of the response process. A somewhat alogical answer could be offered as a humorous alternative or it can represent more pathological thinking when it has a forced quality or where the individual is unable to establish distance and juxtapose the humor with a more appropriate response.

Attitudes taken toward responses can aid in the differentiation of momentary playful and controlled regression from less voluntary and more persistent regressed modes of functioning (Holt & Havel, 1960; Kris, 1952; Schafer, 1958; Wild, 1965).

[2]Assessing the individual's relative position in reference to conventional environmental demands is important in at least one other respect. The reality presented by the WAIS involves procedures and ways of perceiving and organizing experiences which are crucial for success in the "usual" tasks of our culture. Some members of our society live essentially in subcultures which are somewhat removed from the mainstream of middle class experience and from conventionally learned approaches to cognitive tasks. The WAIS (and most intelligence tests) presents a more novel situation to such people than it does to people schooled in the types of procedures and tasks presented by the tests. It is important to remember that though the WAIS is generally considered to be more structured than most other psychological procedures, it can also be experienced in very different ways depending upon earlier educational experiences.

offered by a young man whose father is an accomplished actor whom he feels able to imitate only weakly but angrily in the caricatured style of an old, decrepit vaudevillian. Another example: in response to the question, "What is the Vatican?" subjects often allude only to its being the home of the Pope. It is less common to have included in the response—still accurate however—the fact that the Vatican is an enclosed city, as in the following response: "The Vatican is a city enclosed . . . which is within the confines of Rome and in which the Papacy of the Catholic Church has its seat." In this instance the reference to enclosure raises specific questions as to the relevance for this subject of issues of protection, and a felt need to maintain an internally imposed barrier against certain aspects of experience.

Generally, however, the WAIS tells us more about autonomy from drives than from the environment since it places such a high premium on habituated, logical thinking. Successful, efficient WAIS functioning occurs within a structured and organized context and we must look to the results of a battery of tests which include a diversity of types of thinking, some of which permit relatively little variation in cognitive approach and discourage any embellishment of responses by drives, and others which permit and even encourage more variation in style of approach and enrichment by drives. In this way we can observe a broader spectrum of a subject's adaptive efforts and note the degree to which he is equally at home with thinking which is based on more primitive principles of organization and contains drive content (primary process thinking) as he is with a more rigorous, logical, and drive-free approach (secondary process thought).

2. *The subject's style of responding* to the WAIS items is also relevant for personality assessment. Are the verbalizations, for example, pedantic, overdetailed, and marked by incessant qualification (obsessive style); or hesitant, blocked and interspersed with self-depreciatory remarks (depressive style); querulous, distrustful and legalistic (paranoid style); or expansive, outpouring and excited (hypomanic style)? More subtle aspects of stylistic differences are also apparent in consistent approaches to the solution of a problem, e.g., when a subject routinely relies on trial and error behavior to solve certain Performance subtests, or shows a tendency to be inflexible in trying new alternatives when an initial effort at solution is found to be incorrect.

There is often no clear distinction between style of responding and the content of a subject's responses and comments. Content features interact with functioning and often reflect not only the concerns of a subject but also the specific and habitual modes or styles of response to internal and environmental stimulation. Relevant in this regard are statements to the tester which can reveal a variety of interpersonal styles. Schafer (1954) has discussed at length the varied styles of interpersonal relatedness which can occur in the Rorschach testing situation—styles which he has classified as involving projection, isolation, intellectualization, compulsive perfectionism, repression, denial, reaction formation against hostility or dependent needs, passive demandingness, counterphobic defenses, or masochistic, ingratiating or rebellious attitudes.

It is revealing to assess such stylistic variations in the WAIS situation as well. A subject confronted with the Picture Completion item (a woman looking in the mirror) states, ". . . the front leg on the left hand side is too short. Also, though the woman is powdering her nose you can't see the reflection of her hand or the powder puff in the mirror. Nor can you see her right arm which should be visible in the perspective as it is." (What was intended to be missing?) "The reflection in the mirror. As I look at the leg now its just a crude drawing." By shifting the locus of his difficulty from his own indecisiveness to the deficiency of the drawing, this subject is, through his emphasis on orderliness, implicitly blaming the tester for confronting him with a crude, i.e., primitive, and possibly, messy stimulus. We can hypothesize further that it may be the "too short" leg and its suggestion of body deficit and castration which is disturbing to the subject. Instead of acknowledging to himself his upset in this regard or his indecisiveness when faced with this stimulus, he devalues the external stimulus and the tester. With this subject we would be alert to other indications of a similar style of response, namely becoming indecisive and meticulous and blaming others when faced with his own felt shortcomings or deficiencies.

3. *The organization of specific cognitive functions,* as measured by the subtests, is another source of data for understanding personality organization. The patterns of diverse abilities (intersubtest scatter) and the patterning of success and failure within a single subtest reflect the organization of a number of ego functions which are important aspects of the capacity for adaptation. Recent research on cognitive styles and cognitive control principles has indicated that the organization of these ego functions reflects consistent modes of adaptation which include general cognitive abilities as well as the styles of mediating, filtering and controlling drive and impulse expression in a wide variety of situations (Gardner, et al, 1959, 1960; Kroeber, 1963; Witkin, et al, 1962) . Cognitive variables, like those involved in the WAIS (e.g., anticipation, planning, attention and concentration) are believed to represent the basic functions which are integrated into the broad principles of organization that appear early in development and are involved in psychological defenses as well as the processes which cope realistically with external reality.

It is important to stress that the various aspects of psychological functioning do not exist in isolation; rather, one is always observing and assessing the balance among affects, drives, defenses and cognitive controls.

If the pattern of scores on the WAIS subtests reflects general modes of adaptation, then there should be close concordance between the principles which account for the organization of these various psychological functions and other aspects of the WAIS protocol, such as the content of the responses and the style of the clinical transaction. Such consistency has been found between style of response, content of personal concerns and their psychosexual emphasis, symptom formation, psychological defenses, and cognitive abilities. These consistencies have been called character styles (e.g., Fenichel, 1945; Reich, 1949; Shapiro, 1965) and they are based in part on diagnostic concepts, but in an expanded sense. The concept of character is an attempt to differentiate general modes of adaptation on the basis of the styles of thinking, perceiving and experiencing rather than solely on the basis of manifest behavior, such as symptom formation. For example, a paranoid style will reflect a style of response that is cautious, rigid and legalistic; the content of concerns will tend to focus on insulation and protection and comments to the tester will often involve suspiciousness regarding the verbatim recording, feelings of being tricked and efforts to externalize and project blame for difficulty onto the tester and/or the test; the content of concerns moreover is likely to revolve around power (who is in control). As for the specific cognitive abilities, scores related to functions involving hyperalertness to details (Picture Completion and/or Picture Arrangement) and a heightened emphasis on bringing together and relating disparate things (Similarities) are usually intact and somewhat elevated compared to other functions in a paranoid character structure although not necessarily in a paranoid psychosis. The unique contribution of the WAIS in this evaluation, however, is the understanding of the organization of the psychological functions assessed by the various subtests.

"By using the WAIS to study organization of cognitive processes and the relative balance of primary and secondary process thinking, intellectual processes are considered to be a more integral part of personality. A great deal of understanding about the organization of ego functions can be achieved through an analysis of the patterns of subtest scores. Inasmuch as the scaled scores reflect an individual's standing on a number of specific abilities and psychological functions, variations between and within the different functions do occur as a result of the individual's uniqueness, whether the variations in adaptive capacity are because of strengths or because of weaknesses due to pathological impairment of certain processes. Each of these sources can contribute to variations in the subtest scatter and in each case they reflect the organization of psychological functions we call personality. The weighted subtest score, however, becomes meaningful only in the context of the total score pattern, for it is in the variation among scores that the particular organization of psychological processes is expressed and not in the absolute level of the scores. Thus, two people may have identical scores on a subtest, but for one it may be his highest subtest score, and for the other it may be his lowest subtest score. In interpreting a WAIS profile, then, a baseline must be established from which the variation in subtest scores can be viewed.

This baseline assesses the general intellectual level of the individual and variations in subtest scores are considered in relation to it.

"There are several baseline measures. The one most widely used is the Vocabulary subtest, since it is usually the single best estimate of intelligence and is relatively impervious to the effect of functional and organic conditions and to the overall decline in functioning which accompanies age. The subtests may be viewed as having positive or negative deviation from the Vocabulary score.

"In order to fully utilize the concept of scatter, one must understand the particular psychological processes tapped by each of the subtests. In the section to follow, the psychological functions assessed by the subtests will be discussed. These interpretive rationales have been greatly influenced by the theoretical ego psychological formulations of David Rapaport and his colleagues (1945, 1951)" (Allison, Blatt, & Zimet, 1967). It should be stressed that these interpretive rationales represent assumptions derived from extensive clinical experience. As yet, many of these assumptions have not been adequately evaluated in research. Research on these hypotheses will be more fully discussed in a later section of this chapter.

INTERPRETATIVE RATIONALE FOR WAIS SUBTESTS[3]

Verbal subtests

Vocabulary. As indicated previously, this scale correlates most highly with the Total IQ. This is so primarily because it represents the breadth of concepts, ideas and experience gained during one's lifetime. The acquisition of these concepts and their availability to memory is contingent both on innate ability and on an enriched early life experience. Although emotional conflicts as well as characterological features may affect the acquisition of an adequate vocabulary, it is, in general, still the single best estimate of intellectual capacity, being stable over time and relatively resistant to neurological deficit and psychological disturbance. Because of its relative invulnerability, reliability and predictive capacity, the Vocabulary subtest offers an excellent baseline to which other tests can be compared.[4] It is in relation to the Vocabulary score that one may

---

[3]From "The Scatter of Subtest Scores." Copyright © 1967 by Joel Allison, Sidney J. Blatt, and Carl N. Zimet. From the forthcoming book, *The Interpretation of Psychological Tests.* Reprinted by permission of (the authors and) Harper & Row, Publishers.

[4]An exception to this general rule occurs when early life experiences have been intellectually impoverished in some way, where intellectual stimulation has been minimal, as in many economically and socially deprived families, and where very early school experience has been irregular and disrupted. With such people one must look to scores other than Vocabulary such as the mean of all the subtests, to establish a baseline for comparison.

consider positive or negative scatter, the elevation and heightened investment in certain ego functions, or the disruption of ego functions due
either to temporary inefficiencies or to more marked and permanent
organic or psychogenic problems.

Information. This subtest is seen as measuring the wealth of available
information which, like Vocabulary, is acquired largely as a result of
native ability and early cultural experiences, but which, unlike Vocabulary, is more alterable by defensive processes or by schooling or persistent
efforts at academic achievement. Self-made men, for example, often show
a level of Information that exceeds their Vocabulary scores. Rapaport
et al (1945) indicated that the effort to acquire a general fund of information is frequently an indicator of "intellectual ambitiousness."
Inasmuch as repression is geared toward blocking out memories from
awareness, the acquisition of general knowledge is especially hindered by
repression when it is a primary mode of defense (Rapaport, et al, 1945).
Repression may interfere with the fund of information either in the initial
learning process in which the material is acquired or in later attempts to
recall the material. This concept of memory further implies that experiences are delivered into consciousness when a situation again appeals to
the same needs, strivings, interests or affects with which the experience
is linked in the subject's frame of reference. Repressive people, with their
marked degree of memory blockage, therefore, are likely to show disruptions, inefficiency, and variability on a task like Information which concerns long range memory, relates to active intellectual strivings, and deals
with piecemeal, sharply defined bits of experience. The obsessive compulsive, on the other hand, with his characteristic pedantic emphasis on
detail and his intellectual strivings, will tend to obtain a relatively high
score.

Comprehension. This subtest presents a subject with a series of more
or less conventional social situations and asks about appropriate behavior
and its rationale. Comprehension, therefore, measures a subject's grasp
of social conventionality and social judgment (Rapaport, et al, 1945).
This subtest is frequently a very sensitive indicator of maladaptation;
low scores may represent a need to defy or ignore social conventionality,
or they may indicate an impairment of judgment or a diminished interest
in social interaction, as in schizophrenic conditions. Frequently the Comprehension subtest, because it deals with social situations and judgments
appropriate to these situations, may yield material related to issues of
morality and superego organization. Antisocial trends are frequently expressed in the content of the subtest via such comments as "check to see
whether there's any money in it," in response to the envelop item. There
are some psychopaths, however, who tend to score very high on this subtest; they are the more glib and socially facile individuals. However, high
Comprehension may also represent a push toward hyperconventionality or
conformity and reflect the naivete, conventional thinking and moral

strivings of individuals with hysterical features. High Comprehension, especially coupled with lower Information, therefore, is characteristic for hysterics. The reverse pattern, high Information and lower Comprehension is generally seen in the obsessive-compulsive, largely because of the obsessive's uncertainty and excessive qualification but excellent fund of information. It is important to note that three items on the WAIS Comprehension subtest require the interpretation of proverbs. These items assess primarily the capacity for abstract thought rather than social judgment. In drawing inferences from this subtest one must consider the extent to which the score is affected by these three items.

Similarities. This subtest is essentially a measure of verbal concept formation (Rapaport, et al, 1945; Wechsler, 1958). Conceptual abstraction can be carried out on one of three general levels of cognitive development. The concrete similarity between two objects, a specific common feature of the objects (e.g., a table and a chair both have legs or a dog and a lion both have fur) represents the lowest level of cognitive development. This type of concept formation, which is correct in a limited sense, acknowledges a most direct and obvious feature of the objects without attempting to reach for broader and more abstract generalizations. The thinking is unusually specific, direct, limited in focus, and generally constitutes a rather poorly articulated concept which at best receives only a partial score. A second type of concept formation is the functional definition which defines a utilitarian purpose as the basis for the conceptual category (e.g., piano and violin, play them both). Though this type of abstraction of concept formation is more sophisticated than a concrete conceptualization, it still falls short of a high level abstraction. In terms of personality functioning, the extensive use of functional categories may indicate an inability on the part of the ideational processes to serve as a buffer against impulsive action. Rather than ideation serving as a form of delay and planning, a general move toward activity and acting out may be indicated. The third type of concept formation is the abstract level, which captures the essential common characteristic of the objects. This is the highest level of thought and stands in marked contrast to the prior two forms of more concrete thought processes (Rapaport, et al, 1945). From the general level of abstraction on the Similarities subtest, and also from its relationship to the Vocabulary baseline, and the qualitative features of the derived concepts, valuable clues can be derived concerning the level, flexibility, and appropriateness of conceptual thinking and the role of abstract ideational processes in the subject's total psychological organization.[5] When Similarities fall exceptionally low within the scatter, one may suspect central nervous system

[5]Concrete and functional responses may also be a function of impoverished educational experiences rather than a reflection of psychopathology or intellectual limitations.

impairment. In acute schizophrenic states, impaired thought processes would not be limited to Similarities, but, as will be discussed shortly, would also affect such other scales as Comprehension (judgment) and possibly Arithmetic (concentration). Similarities, because of its demand for abstraction, tends to be elevated in character styles such as the obsessive and the paranoid where there is an emphasis on abstract and symbolic modes of thought.

Digit Span. In presenting a subject with increasing lengths of rote material for immediate memory and recall, this subtest generally taps passive reception of stimuli and the automatic effortless process called attention (Rapaport, et al, 1945). Attention functions best when it is not disrupted by preoccupations, anxiety, or the intrusion of drive derivatives. A Digit Span score which is markedly below the Vocabulary level tends to indicate the presence of anxiety whereas a Digit Span score which is high in relation to Vocabulary indicates blandness of affect and is frequently found in detached, schizoid people. In schizoid records the blandness usually represents a lack of conscious anxiety, chronicity and an acceptance of pathology. High Digit Span, which indicates a lack of anxiety, may also be seen in psychopathic protocols and in hysterics characterized by "la belle indifference." Conversely, a low Digit Span may suggest a more positive prognosis, since it reflects an acute state of subjective distress in which the disorder has not become ego-syntonic or the person comfortable with it and unmotivated to change. A one- to three-point difference may be expected in favor of digits forward over digits backward. If this pattern is reversed, one should also be alerted to blandness or negativism.

In other contexts, low Digit Span may have yet another meaning. One of the primary features of central nervous system damage is a severe distractability which accompanies diminished cortical control. The capacity to attend is adversely affected by distractability, and, therefore, an impoverished Digit Span with added indications of concrete concept formation and unusual motor impairments frequently is seen in brain damaged patients.

Arithmetic. Complex arithmetical reasoning requires extensive concentration and attention (Rapaport, et al, 1945). Concentration is foremost in this task, since the subject has to actively focus his attention in order to acquire the information within the problem and to manipulate meaningfully its complex dimensions. The subject must attend to the specific numbers of the problem, maintain an overview so that various elements are seen in their relative positions in the problem matrix and the interrelationship between the various elements must be manipulated in order to arrive at a solution. The tasks on the Arithmetic subtest require the subject to utilize skills that have been attained comparatively early in development and during the educational process. In this sense the subject has to turn back to prior skills and apply them to a particular task. The test also introduces time pressures for the first time, and the subject is forced to apply himself actively to the problem while reducing distracting elements from within the problem or from the total environment. Arithmetic is like Vocabulary and Information in that it depends upon memory and prior learning, but it differs markedly in the fact that it requires concentration and active application of select skills to cope with a new and unique situation.

By comparing functioning on the Digit Span and Arithmetic subtest, the relative balance between attention and concentration can be ascertained. Attention is the relatively passive and automatic reception of stimuli without effortful attempts to organize the material or to establish mnemonic devices. It is usually a one-step assimilation of a stimulus field which can be disrupted by internal preoccupations. Concentration is a more active, effortful process, and, though it depends on attention to some degree, it goes beyond it in organizing and manipulating a complex series of events. The relative balance and interweaving of these two psychological functions have important implications for understanding psychological organization (Rapaport, et al, 1945). Efforts to compensate for disruptions in attention, for example, often involve extensive efforts at concentration to bolster processes which should occur in a relatively automatic way. Lapses in attention usually occur as a function of anxiety, whereas difficulties in concentration indicate more serious thought disorder. This interpretation of possible thought disorder, however, may be made only when Arithmetic and Digit Span are widely disparate. A low score solely on Arithmetic relative to Vocabulary for example is typically found in hysterical and narcissistic individuals who avoid active, effortful ideation and the elaboration of internal experience. The diagnostic implication of an Arithmetic score lower than Digit Span becomes all the more critical when Digit Span is higher than Vocabulary, for then it indicates a lack of anxiety and a blandness when there are difficulties in concentration (Rapaport, et al, 1945). Should both Arithmetic and Digit Span be low, as frequently occurs in anxious, unreflective hysterics (or in brain damage), impairments both in active concentration and attention are present. The differential relationship between Arithmetic and Digit Span and their relationship to the Vocabulary baseline, therefore, are most important diagnostic considerations.

Performance subtests

Picture Arrangement. In arranging a series of sketches into a sequence which creates a meaningful story, the subject is required to understand the inner relationships of a series of events and to grasp the essential message of a social interaction. The skill necessary for seeing the inner connections between sequences of enduring, continuing, and causally related events, is really a capacity to recognize what effects one event has on the next. Meaningful continuity in everyday experiences is largely dependent on the capacity to anticipate, to judge and understand the possible antecedents and consequences of any event. Poor performance on this subtest frequently reflects an impaired capacity to anticipate events and their consequences and to plan effective courses of action (Rapaport, et al, 1945). On the other hand, subjects with cautious, guarded, hyper-alert paranoid features are frequently extremely sensitive to social events and consequent behavior and are highly involved in an attempt to anticipate the future. Their psychological orientation may be reflected in an elevation of the Picture Arrangement subtest score.

The Picture Arrangement subtest also reflects, as does the Comprehension subtest, the response to stimuli that are concerned with social interactions. These two subtests allow comparison of well-learned social conventionalities (Comprehension) with the capacity to anticipate and plan in a social context (Picture Arrangement). A profile containing high Picture Arrangement but low Comprehension scores may be seen in a character disorder where there is sensitivity to interpersonal nuances, but a disregard for social conventionality. The glib psychopath with a social facade may receive high scores on both the Comprehension and Picture Arrangement subtests. It should also be noted that Picture Arrangement is the only subtest that contains an element of humor. Frequently the inability to see the humorous aspects of life interferes with an optimum capacity to function on this subtest.

Picture Completion. This subtest requires visual organization and the capacity to attend to and observe the inconsistencies and incongruities within a picture. One must focus attention on the details of the picture and actively examine and check the drawing, either in terms of its symmetry or in terms of an internalized image of the object. In this sense the major function seems to be, again, concentration, but in contradistinction to Arithmetic, the concentration is directed towards an externalized form and there is only minimal demand for the more internalized processes required in the Arithmetic subtest (Rapaport, et al, 1945). As in Arithmetic, the time limit is of considerable importance in placing additional demands upon the subject. The instructions of this subtest ask the subject to appraise critically and look for defects within the stimuli. Occasionally this subtest may be affected by a subject's reluctance to criticize, to assert himself, to attack actively or find fault with an aspect of his environment. The Picture Completion score will be high and frequently have positive Vocabulary scatter in paranoid subjects for whom hyper-alertness and hyper-vigilance is a prime mode of functioning. Obsessive compulsives may also have inflated scores because of their pedantic, meticulous examination of every aspect of the picture. Since the objects or people are shown in an incomplete state, a low score may reflect concerns over bodily intactness with a possible emphasis on castration concerns; a low score may also be seen as a function of passivity. Specific conflictual issues may be reflected in long delays, failures on relatively easy items, or failures involving particular content. This latter type of failure often takes the form of an emphasis on "supports" missing, e.g., someone holding a pitcher, or the flag, or else in an emphasis on people missing, e.g., no one in the rowboat. Depending on the context, missing supports may reflect feelings of helplessness and passivity and missing people may reflect feelings of estrangement from people and a need for contact.

Object Assembly. In dealing with jigsaw puzzles, subjects are required to grasp a whole pattern by anticipating the inner relationship of the individual sections. On some items and for some subjects, anticipation of the final pattern is immediate and the task is one of simple visual-motor coordination (Wechsler, 1958). On more difficult items within the sub-test, some subjects may not have immediate insight into the final pattern, in which case the subject frequently resorts to trial and error behavior. Bringing subparts together often furthers the progressive emergence of the total pattern, and in this press toward solution one can observe the subject's capacities for trying new leads, for shifting set, and for functioning on minimal cues. Equally important is observing the smoothness, accuracy and rapidity of a subject's visual-motor coordination which may express habituated and stereotyped motor actions. Also, in presenting an object which has been broken apart, we implicitly confront the subject with something dismembered. Performance on this test, therefore, is adversely and particularly affected by intense concerns over bodily integration and intactness and/or inadquate defenses against these concerns. It should be noted that on occasion blocking occurs on specific items which may also be related to conflictual issues (e.g., on the hand in subjects with concerns over aggression or masturbation).

Block Design. In this test of visual-motor organization (Wechsler, 1958), the subject is presented with a pattern which he is asked to reconstruct out of blocks that are identical to each other in size and design. Block Design differs markedly from Object Assembly: in Object Assembly the end product must be anticipated from the part objects; in Block Design the final pattern is presented and must be broken down and then reconstructed in block size units (Rapaport, et al, 1945; Wechsler, 1958). The differentiation of a part of a design and the specification of its inter-relationships with other parts is essentially a concept formation task involving both analysis and synthesis. The visual organization demanded to differentiate partially a total design and the motor action needed to integrate the blocks is frequently interfered with by central nervous system damage. Since anxiety interferes with attention to small details, performance is facilitated by the blandness and lack of anxiety frequently seen in schizoid personalities. It is important to note the procedure which the subject uses to duplicate the pattern, i.e., whether it is orderly and follows along the outline of the blocks or is haphazard and goes from one

434

section of the design to the other in a random pursuit to find the "magical" clue.

Digit Symbol. In comparison to the other performance tests, Digit Symbol is generally a measure of the capacity for imitative behavior (Rapaport, et al, 1945). It requires relatively little learning, concept formation, anticipation planning or analytic-synthetic functioning; rather, it involves the simple utilization of energy for a smooth and unhesitating duplication of simple patterns (Wechsler, 1958). In the past the Digit Symbol subtest was thought to be a measure of learning ability. Recent research, however, has indicated that a minimal degree of learning takes place during this task and also that few subjects rely on memory; therefore, we see the test primarily as a measure of the capacity to utilize energy in a simple task. Inasmuch as the subject is required to muster up energy and to apply it, this task reflects the amount of energy output a subject can generally bring to his work and his activities. Thus, a low Digit Symbol, markedly below Vocabulary, is frequently a sign of a depressive lack of energy output, whereas Digit Symbol above Vocabulary may be evidence of an overcompliant striving and a desire for achievement going beyond one's intellectual capacities. It is also noteworthy that this is the first subtest in which subjects are asked to write, to use a pencil. Particularly for school-age subjects this test may arouse feelings about classroom demands. Digit Symbol, when it is elevated above other Performance tests, indicates that reduced functioning in the other Performance tests may not be due to a lack of speed and low energy output, but rather to specific problems related to the unique functions tapped by these other subtests.

The relationship of Digit Symbol to Digit Span is often of particular diagnostic import. We have observed a frequent pattern in which Digit Span is relatively low and suggests considerable anxiety and Digit Symbol is relatively high and reflects a marked energy output. In these cases, the individual seems to be controlling strong and pressing anxiety by excessive activity. This activity may represent an attempt to conform and win approval and acceptance. Such passivity, conformity and even ingratiation could be in the service of reducing the level of anxiety by minimizing the possibility of attack and criticism.

When we find the reverse pattern, a high Digit Span and a low Digit Symbol, we are usually confronted with an essentially depressed person who is attempting to ward off recognition of depressive affect perhaps in a hypomanic way, usually via denial, but not necessarily through activity and acting out behavior.

Digit Symbol, also, like Digit Span and Block Design, deals with essentially neutral, content-less material and it may be for this reason that some people, e.g., schizophrenics, at times do especially well on these subtests despite the fact that these patients clinically may show highly anxious behavior and despite the finding that performance on these subtests is particularly vulnerable to the effects of anxiety. With such schizophrenics it is their basic blandness, their isolation from, and lack of relatedness to, their seemingly intense affects and also their heightened powers of attention and passive receptivity in contrast to their impaired concentration that is revealed through their high scores on these subtests.

Differences in Verbal and Performance IQ

In addition to evaluating the specific subtests, inferences can be obtained from the comparison of the Verbal and Performance IQ's. In the Bright Normal and Superior ranges, the Verbal IQ usually tends to be a little higher than the Performance IQ, and the difference increases as the Full Scale IQ rises because marked abilities and accomplishments in one area lead to a relative de-emphasis on the development of other functions. Thus, for the highly ideational person, efficiency in motor activities will often lag behind verbal efficiency. An eight- to ten point difference between Verbal and Performance IQ's where there is, for instance, a Total IQ of 135 (e.g., Verbal IQ, 138, Performance IQ, 127, Full Scale IQ, 135) is of limited diagnostic significance and indicates only a highly verbal subject with possible obsessive-compulsive tendencies. When the Verbal IQ begins to show a marked imbalance over the Performance IQ (by greater than 15 points), more serious pathological trends may be considered. A markedly obsessive concentration on words and thoughts or an extreme variability in functioning such as might result from a psychotic condition may be apparent. Usually, however, and depending on the subtests scores, two additional possible inferences are suggested by a marked elevation of the Verbal over the Performance IQ: depression and/or central nervous system pathology. Depression often involves psychomotor retardation, and tasks with time limits and those subtests which require active manipulation tend to reflect this retardation. On the Performance scale, Digit Symbol in particular but also Object Assembly and Block Design, are generally lowered. The Performance IQ is also lowered in brain damaged patients, but rather than solely affecting subtests on which speed is an issue, brain damage involving visual-motor deficits is reflected on those Performance subtests which require planning, organization, concept formation, concentration and attention. Block Design in particular is a difficult task for these patients, and the score on this test is usually lower than any of the other Performance subtests. Several Verbal subtests, Vocabulary and Information, are often unaffected in brain damaged patients, since much of the material is explicitly contingent upon prior experience and has been overlearned. Thus, while there may be some decrements in the Verbal IQ of organic patients because of low scores on Digit Span, Arithmetic and Similarities, the Verbal IQ is maintained at a level closer to the premorbid intellectual level than is the Performance IQ.

In the lower intelligence ranges, the Performance IQ tends to be a little higher than its Verbal counterpart, largely because the emphasis on motor functioning tends to be associated with a reduced investment in ideational modes. But a Performance IQ greater than a Verbal IQ in individuals of at least average intelligence is atypical. Three major diagnostic trends, all of which have acting out as a primary feature, are suggested by such a pattern: hysteric, narcissistic and psychopathic character disorders. In the hysteric, the repression of impulses and impulse derivatives usually results in restriction of intellectual and cultural interests and pursuits. Functioning on the Verbal scales of the WAIS is often strikingly influenced by repression, naivete, and inability to remember, and although hysterical women from rich cultural backgrounds may acquire a superficial cultural and intellectual veneer that can lead to an elevated Verbal IQ, this "modern" hysterical pattern still maintains much of the subtest scatter seen in the more classic hysterical states (especially the Comprehension above Information). Performance IQ is also often higher in narcissistic character disorders and in individuals with psychopathic trends (Wechsler, 1958), since these are generally "action oriented" people who are unable to establish the delay necessary for dealing with questions requiring thought and concentration and internal elaboration. They are much more comfortable with tasks which require external manipulation and action, and thus function better on the Performance subtests. The comparison of the Verbal IQ and Performance IQ and the examination of the pattern of the subtests of the WAIS is an important step in the diagnostic process. It allows the clinician to describe the individual's unique organization of psychological functions and from this to infer the defenses, the nature and quality of the drives and impulses, the degree and type of pathology, as well as his assets and capacities for adaptation and coping.

Intra-subtest scatter

Since each subtest of the WAIS presents items of increasing difficulty, there should be a tapering off of efficiency and accuracy. However, some test records, particularly of patients, show a certain degree of variability of passes and failures within some subtests. Occasionally this takes the form of missing easy items initially but at other times the pattern is more one of intermittent fluctuation. In general, marked intra-subtest variability indicates a considerable degree of psychological disruption due to temporary inefficiencies or to a permanent loss of capacities, such as in organic brain damage. On occasion, variability also can occur in a person with consistently disturbed school experiences where information and ways of coping with the various tasks of an intelligence test will have been acquired in a sporadic and uneven way. In hysterical patients it is usual to find variability primarily on the Information subtest since in these patients repression often serves as a general defensive orientation and serves to block out access to information even distantly associated with particular areas of conflict. Variability and disruption on Blocks and Similarities likely reflects an organically based problem as does recurrent variability throughout the tests. Epileptics, for instance, have a typical pattern of alternation of passes and fails with a waxing and waning quality usually regardless of the subtest or of the specific content of the items. An important rule of thumb in assessing the degree to which organicity is suggested by intra-subtest variability is whether the test disruptions seem unrelated to specific preoccupations of the individual. Disruptions which are unrelated to specific concerns but are more associated with general cognitive functioning occur in organically based interference with ego functioning. In schizophrenia the fluctuation is likely to be due more to areas of preoccupation, although in more chronic longstanding patients, ego efficiency may be affected in a more global way and result in poorer efficiency with some easier items. In such instances other test data may be crucial for ruling out organic brain damage.

CASE PRESENTATION

In order to illustrate the contribution of the WAIS to diagnostic assessment, sections of a WAIS protocol will be presented and discussed in terms of an analysis of the organization expressed in the subtest scores and in the content and style of the responses.[6] The patient is a 33-year-old housewife, with a history of a possible psychotic episode 13 years previously. In the year preceding her current hospitalization she is described as having gradually diminished her activity outside the house, having increased feelings of inadequacy and crying spells, showing aggression toward her husband and two children, and eating compulsively.

Her WAIS scaled scores follow:

Comprehension	16	Picture Arrangement	9
Information	14	Picture Completion	9
Digit Span	15	Block Design	9
Arithmetic	9	Object Assembly	7
Similarities	13	Digit Symbol	9
Vocabulary	15		

Verbal IQ: 121; Performance IQ: 91; Total IQ: 109

[6] Brief summaries of Wechsler protocols for a variety of psychological disorders are available in Allison, Blatt and Zimet, 1967; Mayman, Schafer and Rapaport, 1951; Schafer, 1948; Wechsler, 1958.

Among the outstanding aspects of these scores is the striking variability: the large discrepancy between Verbal and Performance IQ's and the wide range of subtest scores (from 7 to 16). Considering her Vocabulary and other high Verbal subtest scores as a baseline, her intellectual potential would be estimated to be in the high Superior range (estimated Verbal IQ of 129). Since she obtains an overall IQ of only 109, and such low Performance subtest scores, there is obviously a marked degree of inefficiency in this woman's psychological functioning which is of at least severe neurotic degree.

A more detailed consideration of the test variability suggests specific hypotheses regarding the nature of the disturbed functioning. The discrepancy that exists between her Verbal and Performance IQ's reflects a marked impairment of visual organization and visual-motor efficiency that is unlikely to occur outside of an organic condition or one of depressive retardation. Some of the test scores, however, tend to contradict the hypothesis of an organic condition: her verbal abstract thinking on Similarities and her attention span on Digit Span, as well as an independent assessment of her memory efficiency do not suggest organicity. If such a Verbal-Performance discrepancy were due to organicity then it would be likely that there would be disruption of abstract thinking and attention. Inasmuch as her abstract reasoning and attention are not impaired and by qualitative observation her motor execution is not inefficient in the sense of being tremulous or uneven, the only remaining organic possibility is some visual impairment. This possibility could be evaluated further as we proceed through the WAIS and with other tests.

Because of the extent of the deficit on Performance tests there is also a strong possibility of marked depressive features. The scatter suggests, however, that the picture is not simply one of depressive energy depletion and psychomotor retardation. For the high Digit Span with its suggestion of blandness and lack of anxiety contrasts with the Performance subtests scores and indicates thereby that the depressive features may be masked and superficially defended against, probably by denial. Unlike a person who is consciously beset by anxious and depressive thoughts and feelings (as would be apparent when Digit Symbol—a test of energy output—and/or other Performance subtests are low, as well as Digit Span), this person's scatter suggests efforts to defend against pressing dysphoric concerns.

A further hypothesis which can be derived from the scatter involves the discrepancy between a high Comprehension score and the low Picture Arrangement score. This suggests an adequate adherence to conventional social judgment (high Comprehension) but an inability to act on this judgment through planning, anticipation and organization of experience. One would hypothesize that her ability to control her experience and to set future goals is limited in comparison with her verbal judgment and that her verbal social capacities may obscure to some extent her deficiency in this regard. One would wonder therefore about an underlying psychotic process which may not be readily apparent because of her heightened awareness of appropriate versus inappropriate behavior as indicated in the high Comprehension score. The low score on Arithmetic is also conspicuous and reflects an interference with concentration which could also suggest either a psychotic process or a more narcissistic or hysterical avoidance of active, effortful ideation.

The relationship between her Comprehension and Information scores (Comprehension > Information) is consistent with the hypothesis of hysterical trends in that conventional, moral and social knowledge takes precedence over factual information (which is more dependent on memory functioning and more subject to repression [forgetting]). Because her Information score is relatively high and is at her Vocabulary level we would argue that this function is not disrupted and therefore the imbalance of several points in favor of Comprehension over Information suggests only minor hysterical trends.

To recapitulate: it is possible that some of the lowered Performance scores could be due to an organic visual disturbance but the primary issue is probably a depressive picture with noteworthy efforts to defend against dysphoric feelings and thoughts. A disturbance of concentration and planning ability and a marked variability of psychological functioning raises the possibility of a psychotic condition which is accompanied by a considerable preservation of verbal reality adherence and social conventionality. Hysterical trends are also suggested. Clearly intellectual efficiency is interfered with markedly.

At this point we will turn to the individual subtests with these hypotheses in mind in an attempt to glean further material from the more qualitative features of the test responses and from the scatter within each subtest. Because of space limitations, the entire record will not be presented but only those responses with interpretive import will be discussed.

Information. She misses 18, 20, 22, 23, 26, 29, reflecting a fair amount of variability which could be due to the effect of repression on overall memory efficiency. Asked the height of the average American woman she responds correctly, "about 5'5" to 5'6"," then adds, "she's getting taller all the time, that's for sure." This response with its specific emphasis on the process of continuous growth suggests a cognitive conception that things (and one's experience) exist in a marked state of flux and transition; it also suggests in its content the conception that women—starting from a possibly smaller and inferior position—are rapidly increasing their stature. This latter conception may be an attempt to contain and ward off depression. It is stressed further by the expression "that's for sure," introducing an attempt to establish a sense of certainty into a situation of rapid changes. These hypotheses will be checked and elaborated as we proceed.

Also noteworthy in the patient's responses to the Information items is a degree of childlike, infantile expressiveness. Her responses are accompanied by mouth noises and coupled with egocentric comments ("geography is my downfall"), and expressions like "pish posh." Usually she does not recklessly guess when she is unsure of an answer; neither is she notably critical of herself or self-disparaging when she is incorrect.

Comprehension. On the item "Why should people pay taxes?" her response is "In order to maintain what we have and improve what we have, and in order to pay for all the things within the bounds of the country we supposedly need." Though this response is scored 1, it is of interest because of its emphasis on maintenance and on the setting of a clear, somewhat constricted boundary to which taxes apply. This response contrasts with her response to the Information item about woman's height in which the body boundary seemed rather fluid and changeable. Here the attempt rather is to set clear and even narrow limits. These two responses which are both at least partially correct are nevertheless suggestive of a certain degree of tension between two opposing modes of experience, expansive alteration versus narrow containment. Her reference to things "we supposedly need" also suggests that she is in conflict about, and is attempting to distance herself from, the intensity of her needs. Some effort at containment, in this case of impulsive action, is also apparent in her response to the "movies" item. "What I would do, I would quietly go to the manager and tell him to do something fast." Although this response receives full credit, the special emphasis on control indicated by the word "quietly," contrasts with the final appearance of the urgent action.

Her response to child labor is also of interest. "Many of us, many people might put children to work when mentally and physically they're not ready for it and could be doing far better things in their formative years." Her subtle shift from the more personal "us" to "people" more generally bespeaks of an attempt to whitewash herself belatedly of some felt injustices toward children. This may directly reflect some self-criticism in regard to the treatment of her children. It demonstrates what we hypothesized from the scatter, namely that there will be efforts to defend against pressing depressive concerns.

Another response on which she receives full credit but which contains personalized content is on the "Forest" question, "Well, if the sun sets in the west and I know I could be helped in the west, I would go, I would use the sun as a guide. I hope it is a sunny day. Or, a river can be used, follow it." Her opening remark of "Well, if the sun sets in the west . . .", suggests some uncertainty regarding the trustworthiness and regularity of her experience. At her level of intellectual capacity there can be little doubt that she knows where the sun rises and sets and that the inavailability of this information reflects her feeling in a "lost" situation of being unsure about where the rising and setting of the sun occurs. She adds that she would go to the west if she knew help could be forthcoming there which suggests her needfulness, dependency, and confusion when faced with interpersonal isolation. This emphasis on going in the direction of the setting sun also carries the suggestion of a focus on the experiences of setting, getting low, and of depressive mood. Later in the response she hopes "it is a sunny day," thereby repeating the hypothesized relationship between a depressive orientation and her efforts at defense by trying to see things as sunny and optimistic.

Her final response of note on Comprehension is to the "swallow" item. "I've never heard it before. It doesn't mean anything to me (what might it mean?). It might mean a person swimming during summer might swallow a gulp of water but he has yet to anticipate more swallows because he has lots more swimming." On the preceding question she also was initially unsure of its meaning, guessed and closely approximated the answer. Here however she personalizes her answer entirely. She construes the swallow as an oral intake and the orality is essentially of a disturbing nature. Thus, despite the fact that the context is a potentially pleasant summer scene a noteworthy dysphoric oral theme intrudes. Once again, as suggested in the scatter, we see a coupling of a depressive theme with an attempt to defend against it by denial (emphasizing the positive, pleasant, hopeful, abundant). Implicitly there is a suggestion of death (suicide?) by drowning. Her defensive efforts at denial are unsuccessful in that she is unable to sustain a pleasant image without letting the depressive theme intrude. The peculiar and somewhat illogical quality of her answer suggests the possibility of psychotic thinking which she is attempting to contain as suggested by her initial attempts to avoid responding.

Arithmetic. She misses the 10th, 12th, 13th, and 14th questions. She gets 10 when asked to check her response and gets 13 overtime. During the harder questions she immediately and consistently protests her inability to figure out the problems stating that she gives up; but with outside pressure she relents and attempts to solve the problems. Her failures on this subtest thus seem compounded by avoidance of effortful application and hastiness.

Similarities. Several responses are of special interest. To the question, how are air and water alike, she replies, "Free, no that's not the way. Nature's elements. (What did you mean by free?) There are boundless quantities of air and water, salt water anyway . . . yeah, fresh water too." This response recalls earlier concerns with expansive, limitless activity (the growing women, the continuous swimmer). Here the expansive quality is especially prominent; the "boundless quantities" smack of unlimited supplies and are consistent with the defense by denial this patient is employing against her depressive ideas and feelings seen previously, especially in the Swallow item of Comprehension. The effort to present experience as pleasurable, full and satisfying was noted previously. It is a constellation typically found in a hypomanic patient; that is, an emphasis, usually driven, on those qualities of experience directly in opposition to depression: fullness versus emptiness, energy versus apathy, feeding versus needing to be fed, happy versus sad, innocent versus guilty.

The next response of interest is an incorrect answer and is to poem and statue. "I guess durability, no . . . a beautiful poem and a beautiful statue, enduring; a tribute to, it might be." It is noteworthy that she introduces the concept of durability, of lasting and not wearing out. It reflects a personalized depressive preoccupation with fantasies of death and with what is fleeting or lasting, transient or permanent both regarding her experience of outer reality and her inner resources. On the "taxes" item in Comprehension it will be recalled that she emphasized maintenance and improvement of "what we have," which suggested a similar concern. Consider that there has been an equivalent highlighting of the theme of freedom, boundlessness, and flux which seems an aspect of her hypomanic strivings. The instability of her defenses is again indicated in this case in the expressed depressive fear of wearing out (possibly as regards her age, energy and attractiveness). Again it is of note that her depressive concerns are juxtaposed with the beauty and attractiveness of the poem and statue and that the sequence of defensive efforts is to deny the initial depressive statement by the emphasis on beauty.

Also noteworthy is her response to fly and tree. "They're nature's, nature's that's all. (What do you mean?) They're something man isn't responsible for, something nature created, not man created." Her intent is to say they are not created by man but her statement about man's responsibility introduces a theme of moral responsibility. In an earlier response she seemed to show concern with injustice toward children. This is an additional reflection of guilty concerns which are verbalized, then modified and backed away from. Her defense, therefore, is shaky in that these concerns are not totally blocked out and instead they break through and only secondarily are defended against.

Picture Completion. Her failures consist of two responses which she correctly got overtime, several on which she sees supports missing (e.g., no hand holding the pitcher), and some on which she does not see anything missing. Her functioning therefore is made up of ideational retardation, avoidance and a thematic trend emphasizing need for support. Thus there is again some suggestion of a breakthrough of depressive feelings.

Block Design. Her asides are of interest here. Early in this subtest she states, "Oh, this would be great for the kids." A little later she appears very excited and very childlike, and finally after the last design, the third in a series of failures because of a too bold approach (using full color blocks to make stripes instead of red-white ones), she ends by stating, "I'm exhausted, truly . . ." Her aside about the meaning of this subtest for children suggests that she may use the maternal posture as part of the denial of needfulness and depression. Her comment about energy depletion is in contrast to her excited, energetic behavior during much of the test and it reveals the driven quality of her energy output and the underlying depression. It is of further interest that she is able to do all ten Block Designs correctly but the last three were completed after she had considerably exceeded the time limits.

Picture Arrangement. She has some mild difficulty on the 5th item and feels she "must be awfully thick." This aside is another bit of evidence suggesting self-depreciation and depression. Later on the 7th item her interpretation about the story of the king fishing includes the notion that "someone was stocking the pond." The help to the king is seen by her therefore as indirect.

Her interpretation of the last story—her order is incorrect but close—is that the man brings the bust close to him because of a "sense of propriety" rather than a desire to protect the bust. The emphasis therefore as previously in the WAIS, is holding on to what one has and of concern with proper behavior.

As for the rest of the test, her behavior remains consistently excited, jovial, yet complaining and externalizing blame for difficulties. Expressions like "pish posh," "crazy, man, crazy," and "come on fellows, this is silly," are characteristic. Her externalization of blame is an alternate to clearly stated self-blame in other instances and to the concerns with guilt (injustices and responsibility). We would add to her defensive maneuvers the use of projection; but as with most of her current defenses it is unstable and does not ward off a sense of inner disturbance.

Vocabulary. At one point in this subtest she asks, "Where's Webster?" and when defining "tangible," she demonstrates with her hands and adds, "what would I do without hands?" The need of support and a concern with loss suggested in Picture Completion is reiterated and the explicit theme of body damage (castration) is added, which in retrospect is supported by the fact that Object Assembly was her lowest subtest.

An additional feature of her test performance involves the question of whether a visual disturbance affects her functioning on Performance subtests. There is little in the qualitative features of the tests to indicate a particular visual disturbance. Instead there is often a slowing down of her visual-motor efficiency which is consistent with the depressive orientation. Fluctuations of mood are probable in the clinical picture because of the unstable appearance of both defense against depression and the occasional emergence of dysphoric ideation. Hypomanic trends appear to be prominent but mild projective trends are also noted. The marked disruption of functioning along with disturbances in concentration (Arithmetic) and anticipation and planning (Picture Arrangement), and the peculiar verbalization to the Swallow item of Comprehension suggests that the patient is probably functioning at best at a borderline psychotic level but this would have to be clarified by material from other sources.

This case illustrates how a systematic analysis of the cognitive processes assessed in the relatively neutral and well structured context of the

WAIS can make a significant contribution to the process of clinical assessment. Rather than being concerned with whether the profile of scores were most similar to the pattern of one diagnostic group or another, an attempt was made to understand the relative efficiency of a number of psychological functions and how these were integrated into unified and organized modes of functioning. The organization of the various psychological functions could have been highly congruent with a standard diagnostic category or it could have involved several types or levels of organization indicating either a complex interaction of several levels of defense and impulse or that the patient is in the process of transition to a higher or lower level of functioning.[7] The full contribution of the WAIS to clinical assessment, however, depends on careful observation of the processes through which the individual copes with the various tasks and upon a careful analysis of the content and organization of the individual's verbatim responses.[8]

REVIEW OF RECENT RESEARCH

The preceding analysis of the WAIS protocol also highlights some of the difficulties encountered in attempting to test the process of clinical inference. Though independent clinical material, including additional test data, supports many of the inferences and formulations made from the WAIS, there still remains the critical question of the validity of the conclusions drawn. Disagreement between judges (lack of reliability) can be a function of differences in level of training or orientation. If nosological categories are used as the validating criteria in a research design, should this patient be considered severely neurotic, psychotic or borderline with both neurotic and psychotic features? Should she be considered a hypomanic patient, and if so, is it clearly understood and accounted for in the research design that this also implies strong underlying depressive features? The suggestion in the material of subtle hysterical and projective trends adds yet another complication in classifying this patient and in defining adequate control groups.

Various tests in the clinical battery evaluate, at least in part, different levels of functioning, and a lack of agreement could represent variations in functioning at different levels of organization as well as suggesting inconsistencies. In the latter case, the question remains: Which segment of the clinical data (interviews or which of the various tests) does one use as the validating criterion?

[7]The differentiation of whether a patient is in the process of reintegration or is in danger of potential regression is a complex clinical problem which requires utilizing data from the entire battery of psychological tests.

[8]Extended recording forms and memorization of the instructions for the entire test can enable the clinician to be more available in the clinical transaction.

Rather than attempting to test the final diagnostic formulations of the total clinical protocol, research can be directed at testing individual assumptions made about the various segments of the protocol. This testing of individual assumptions can be made either in a clinical or in an experimental setting. For example, one of the bits of evidence for the formulation of hypomania in the preceding case was the marked imbalance between Digit Span and Digit Symbol. Clinically this has been observed in other cases where denial was a predominant defense mechanism, and denial is theoretically expected to be a major defense in hypomania. The hypothesis about the relationship of the Digit Span to Digit Symbol and about denial as a defense mechanism can be evaluated independently by selecting Ss with this Digit Span—Digit Symbol pattern from the general population or from clinical files. Major difficulties, however, will be the selection and definition of an acceptable independent criterion measure of denial and of adequate control groups.

Despite these and other methodological problems, a great deal of research has been conducted on the role of the intelligence test in clinical settings.[9] Research has included comparisons of the extent of scatter in various pathological groups, attempts to identify specific responses or patterns characteristic of types of psychopathology, and attempts to test underlying assumptions of the various subtests in a variety of ways, including the use of experimentally induced affect states such as anxiety or depression. Generally the research on the subtest scatter has offered little support for the assumption that the simple range or extent of scores is a consistent aid in differential diagnosis. Attempts have also been made to study the concept of differential scatter as presented by Wechsler (1944) and elaborated extensively by Rapaport, Gill and Schafer (1945), but the results have been mostly contradictory and inconclusive.

As pointed out by Rabin (1965), one of the major stumbling blocks in attempting to evaluate the hypotheses about selective impairment and scatter may be the persistent use of nosological or diagnostic categories as validating criteria. Many problems exist in the use of nosological concepts in clinical research. Studies often use these classifications as if there is a universal agreement about the conceptual definition of the categories. Rarely do investigators indicate their criteria; schizophrenia, for example, is rarely defined or differentiated from other psychotic states. The frequent wide variation in the definition of diagnostic categories is highlighted by the fact that there can be sharp disagreement about definitions and criteria within a single clinical facility.

[9]Reviews of the research literature on the Wechsler scales are available in many sources (e.g., Anastasi, 1961; Cronbach, 1960; Guertin, Rabin, Frank & Ladd, 1962; Littell, 1960; Rabin, 1965). Therefore this review will present primarily recent studies (since 1960) not covered in earlier reviews. There is also extensive literature on the Wechsler scales and central nervous system damage (e.g., Reitan, Heilbrun), but this will not be included in the present paper.

Even if there were essential agreement about the conceptual basis, these criteria are frequently applied with varying degrees of precision. It is unusual for a research paper to specify the degree of reliability between judges or even to simply indicate how the diagnostic classifications were established. One rarely has a basis for knowing whether a diagnostic classification was established as an admitting diagnosis by a first-year trainee or resident after a brief twenty-minute interview or whether it was the considered and joint opinion of a diagnostic council after weeks of intensive study of the patient. With such poorly defined criteria, frequently applied in imprecise ways, there is little surprise that the research with diagnostic categories has lead to ambiguous findings. The number of studies attempting to compare organics, schizophrenics, character disorders, neurotics, hospital attendants or nurses and college students are by now legion. These studies continue despite the fact that there is increasing disillusionment with current diagnostic categories which are, at best, a gross classification system. Usually in clinical work, diagnostic assessment involves a dynamic formulation which includes several levels of psychological organization which transcend any single category. Rather than searching for specific patterns for diagnostic categories, a more productive line of research may be to test systematically the assumptions about the processes assessed by individual subtests and how they are organized into consistent modes of functioning. Specification of the individual processes assessed by the subtests and their interrelationships and organization may in turn lead to more meaningful and precise conceptualizations of psychopathology. This approach does not have to be limited to test scores—it can also include qualitative aspects, such as the style of verbalization, content of responses, the tone of the clinical transaction and the individual's attitudes towards his performance.

There is a trend in recent research to move away from a comparison of diagnostic groups and instead, to study the processes assessed by each of the subtests and their relationships to more general psychological organizations. Typical of this trend is the research on measures of anxiety on the Wechsler scales. Much research has been devoted to examining the hypothesis that Digit Span, as a measure of attention, is disrupted by anxiety. One group of studies includes research on patients with varying diagnoses such as anxiety neurosis, anxiety state, or anxiety reaction (e.g., Gilhooly, 1950; Lewinski, 1945; Rashkis & Welch, 1946; Warner, 1950) and these studies have offered little support for the hypothesis that Digit Span is impaired by anxiety. Another group of studies attempted to evaluate this hypothesis by correlating Digit Span performance with traditional anxiety scales and the results have been contradictory. Many studies have found no consistent relationship between the Taylor Scale and Wechsler scores (e.g., Dana, 1957; Goodstein & Farber, 1957; Matarazzo, 1955) while others report positive findings (e.g., Siegman, 1956; Jurjevich, 1963). A recent and interesting approach has been the attempt to evaluate the hypothesis that Digit Span measures attention as defined as the "effortless, passive, unhampered contact with outside reality . . . a free receptivity" (Rapaport, et al, 1945). Guertin (1959) and Craddick and Grossman (1962) studied the effects of distraction upon Digit Span and neither auditory nor visual distraction seems to affect significantly Digit Span performance. But as pointed out by Allen (1962), both these studies used "external distractors" which may not be the same as internal distraction and anxiety. Maupin and Hunter (1966) attempted, in several ways, to test the hypothesis that Digit Span measures attention, including studying the relationship of Digit Span to subliminal receptivity. Their findings, however, have not supported the hypothesis that Digit Span is related to attention. These studies (Craddick & Grossman, 1962; Guertin, 1959; Maupin & Hunter, 1966) represent an attempt to approach the problem more systematically, first by investigating the assumption that Digit Span assesses attention and if this is supported, then proceeding to investigate the relationship between attention and anxiety.

Another group of studies represents the attempt to induce anxiety experimentally and to study its effects on performance. Though the studies in this approach also present discrepant findings, a number of studies offer some support for the hypothesis that Digit Span is disrupted by anxiety (e.g., Capretta & Berkun, 1962; Griffiths, 1958; Moldowsky & Moldowsky, 1952; Walker & Spence, 1964; Wright 1954). A recent experiment (Sherman & Blatt, 1966) studied Digit Span, Digit Symbol and Vocabulary performance after experiences of success or failure were induced by presenting anagrams at two levels of difficulty and by initially misinforming Ss as to peer group norms. Consistent with the findings of a pilot study, Digit Span was comparatively elevated after the experience with difficult anagrams. Vocabulary seemed to be relatively unaffected by the experimental manipulation, but Digit Symbol, like Digit Span, was elevated after the failure experience. The result with Digit Symbol, a measure of speed and energy output, could indicate that the experience of the failure increased Ss' involvement in the experiment; that is, both Digit Span and Digit Symbol were elevated because of increased effort and investment in performance. A failure manipulation may cause varying degrees of distress and/or anxiety. Depending upon the meaning of failure for the individual, it may either disrupt or facilitate performance. In this regard, the study by Walker and Janet Spence (1964) found reduction in Digit Span only in those Ss who reported being distressed by the experimental manipulation. (They were told that they had been selected because of questionable academic performance.) In subsequent research on Digit Span and experimentally induced anxiety, it seems important to assess the predisposition for becoming anxious, to differentiate which Ss are made anxious by the procedures, and to differentiate Ss who may be able to manage anxiety and improve their performance from Ss who may be disrupted by the experience.

Within the Digit Span subtest, Ss usually remember one or two more digits forward than they remember digits backward. A secondary hypothesis about Digit Span is that digits-backward equal to, or greater than, digits-forward, reflects negativism. In a recent study (Fox & Blatt, 1965) three groups of Ss were selected from clinical files: 1) a group which had digits-forward one or two greater than digits-backward; 2) a group in which digits-forward were equal to digits-backward; and 3) a group in which digits-forward were two less than digits-backward. Ss were also selected so that the three groups were matched on age, sex, and Total IQ, and they included in- and outpatients ranging in diagnosis from neurotic to psychotic but did not include any Ss in whom there were questions of organicity or mental retardation. A significant relationship was found between the extent to which digits-backward exceeded digits-forward and two Rorschach expressions of negativism: the number of white space responses (S) and the number of responses with rare detail (Dr). This significant relationship between independent and assumed expressions of negativism on the Wechsler and Rorschach lends support to the hypothesis that digits-backward superior to digits-forward is a possible indication of negativism; this aspect of Digit Span needs more study.

There have been two lines of research which support the hypothesis that Digit Symbol primarily assesses psychomotor speed. Several studies report that Digit Symbol production is unrelated to the extent to which the symbols are learned (Burik, 1950; Luchins & Luchins, 1953). Recently, Murstein and Leipold (1964) found that Digit Symbol performance did not correlate with group tests of intelligence and achievement but did correlate significantly with tests of motor ability. A second line of investigation with Digit Symbol has been based on the assumption that psychomotor speed reflects Ss'. willingness to exert energy on a simple imitative task and that, as such it can reflect a degree of motivation for achievement. Several studies report an elevation of Digit Symbol subsequent to failure experience (Gallahar, 1964; Sherman & Blatt, 1966). Wachtel and Blatt (1965) found significantly greater Digit Symbol production in Ss who were in the upper third of their college class, but equal in overall intelligence (as measured by WAIS Vocabulary and by College Boards) to Ss in the lower third of the class. In contrast to the positive relationship of Digit Symbol to achievement motivation, several studies (Matarazzo & Phillips, 1955; Goodstein & Farber, 1957; Wachtel & Blatt, 1965) report no relationship between Digit Symbol and anxiety. Sarason and Minard (1962) also found no relationship between Test Anxiety and Digit Symbol production. They did find, however, that "achievement orienting instructions" (threat of failure) elevated Digit Symbol production in Test Anxious women but lowered it in Test Anxious men. This is consistent with the other studies (Gallahar, 1964; Sherman & Blatt, 1966) which also found an elevation in Digit Symbol after failure instructions.

In addition to the few studies which suggest that Digit Symbol assesses energy output and a motivation for achievement, several studies have been conducted on some qualitative aspects of Digit Symbol performance. Levine, Glass and Meltzoff (1957), found that the number of "N" reversals on the Digit Symbol was significantly related to intelligence and to the capacity to delay a response. This is consistent with the findings of Wolfson and Weltman (1963) who found that short term planners (students who applied very late for admission to nursing school) made more errors on Digit Symbol than students who applied early for admission. The study by Wachtel and Blatt (1965), which found a positive relationship between academic performance and Digit Symbol performance, also attempted to examine whether differences between high- and low achieving Ss was a function of differences in psychomotor speed on Digit Symbol or whether there were also differences in the deployment of energy. Manifold carbon papers, placed under the Digit Symbol form, made it possible to measure the pressure which a subject exerted while writing the symbols. Low achieving Ss not only completed fewer symbols but they also pressed harder. Thus, the difference in the Digit Symbol was not only a function of speed but also seemed to be a difference in the capacity to direct energy into adaptive endeavors and to restrict relatively undefined and poorly directed efforts (Wachtel & Blatt, 1965).

The Picture Completion subtest requires concentration on a stimulus with careful noting of subtle details and a willingness to comment on inconsistencies and defects in the picture. A factor analysis of the WAIS Picture Completion items (Saunders, 1960) reports three major factors in Picture Completion performance: a maintenance of contact, a maintenance of perspective, and the effect of uncertainty. Saunders concludes that these three factors support the distinction made by Rapaport, et al (1945) that failures can result from "increased distance from the picture," "a loss of distance," and where uncertainty causes seeking of information rather than concentration on the item. There has also been a study of the types of errors made on Picture Completion items (Wolfson & Weltman, 1960) which found that patients, particularly psychotic patients, made more unique errors. Wiener (1957) found a positive relationship between a distrustful attitude and the response of "nothing missing" to the Picture Completion items. The total scores for Picture Completion and Vocabulary, however, were not significantly lower for the distrustful group. The fact that distrustful Ss did no worse on Picture Completion is consistent with Rapaport's formulation (1945) that distrustful or suspicious Ss may function effectively on Picture Completion because of their tendency to be hyper-alert to subtle cues and details.

Both Wechsler (1944) and Rapaport, et al (1945) agree that the Object Assembly test is essentially a test of visual motor organization. Rapaport, et al (1945) reports that Object Assembly can be impaired by depression and/or anxiety. Studies have examined the relationship of

Object Assembly to anxiety (Griffiths, 1958; Hafner, Pollie & Wapner, 1960; Matarazzo, 1955) or to brain damage (Balthazar, 1963; Fisher, 1958; Penfield & Milner, 1958) and the findings are inconsistent. A recent study (Blatt, Allison & Baker, 1966), however, indicates that Object Assembly can be disrupted by intense body concerns. Object Assembly scores were significantly lower in children with intense body concerns than in a control group, and there were no significant differences between these two groups on any other WISC subtest. In addition, a group of adult patients with Object Assembly as the highest or second highest subtest were compared with a group comparable in age, sex and Total IQ, but whose Object Assembly was the lowest or second lowest Wechsler subtest. The group with low Object Assembly had a significantly greater percentage of Rorschach responses indicating intense body concerns (e.g., anatomical, blood, sex, X ray responses). These findings suggest that Object Assembly may be affected by anxiety which is centered around the particular issue of body intactness. Considering that the objects presented in the Wechsler Object Assembly are primarily dismembered parts involving a specific content, that is, whole bodies and parts of bodies, it seems likely that the items stimulate preconscious thought about body concerns. In subsequent research it would be of interest to examine whether the relationship between Object Assembly and body concerns is a function of the content of the items or whether the relationship exists with dismembered objects of a more neutral content.

The major contribution in the study of the relationship of Block Design to personality has been the work of Witkin and his colleagues on field independence. Witkin (1965) has found the Block Design, with its demand for analytic thinking, to be highly correlated with measures of field independence. The wide range of variables related to field independence are consistent with clinical assumptions that Block Design assesses the capacity for abstract thought. Field independence has been found to relate to a preference for the ideational and conceptual rather than for the sensory, to a tendency to use isolation as a defense as compared to repression and denial, and for a tendency to be less influenced by and less aware of people (Witkin, 1965). Thus, an elevation in Block Design, as compared to other Performance subtests, might be expected in over-ideational individuals and clinically in patients with obsessive and/or paranoid features. Conversely, hysterical features (e.g., use of repression and denial, a heightened social conventionality, memory inefficiencies) would be one alternative suggested by a relatively low Block Design. Sarason and Minard (1962) report a significant negative relationship between Test Anxiety and Block Design scores.

The Picture Arrangement subtest is considered by Wechsler (1944) and Rapaport, et al (1945) to assess social judgment, and Rapaport, et al thought that it also requires the capacity for anticipation and planning. Several tests of the hypothesis that Picture Arrangement requires a capacity for anticipation and planning have been conducted with findings which consistently support this assumption. In one study (Dickstein & Blatt, 1966) Picture Arrangement was used to investigate the relationship between the degree of conscious concern and preoccupation with death and temporal experience. It was assumed that when death is not a predominant concern, an individual will percieve himself as a participant in life and his temporal experience would extend further into the future. College males, equal in overall intelligence (Vocabulary) but in the upper or lower quartile on a questionnaire about degree of conscious concern about death, were compared on the WAIS Picture Arrangement and on a story completion technique. Low death-concern subjects had significantly higher Picture Arrangement scores and their story completions had greater future time perspective than did the high death-concern group. An alternative explanation for the significant relationship between death-concern and lower Picture Arrangement could be that a depressive psychomotor retardation in the high death-concern Ss caused them to lose time bonus points on the Picture Arrangement. This was not the case, however, for low death-concern Ss gained only a total of 11 time bonus points as compared to 10 time bonus points gained by the high death-concern group and no points were lost in either group for exceeding time limits. The lower Picture Arrangement scores of high death-concern Ss, therefore, seems to be a function of a restriction in their capacity for anticipation and planning.

In a second study (Dickstein & Blatt, 1967), a significant and positive relationship was found between Picture Arrangement performance and future time perspective in stories told to TAT cards and to the stems of a story completion technique. A third study (Blatt & Quinlan, 1967) studied punctual and procrastinating students, selected on the basis of when in the semester they met course requirements. The two groups of students did not differ on measures of general intelligence (Vocabulary and College Board Scores), college grades and the number of extracurricular activities. The procrastinating students, however, were significantly different on a number of temporal parameters. They had lower Picture Arrangement scores, less future time perspective in stories told to story stems and they reported greater concern and preoccupation with death than did the punctual group. The significant differences between punctual and procrastinating subjects as well as the findings in the prior two studies support the hypothesis that the Picture Arrangement, at least in part, assesses the degree to which the capacity for anticipation and planning is impeded.

Another aspect of the Picture Arrangement is the fact that the items all deal with social interactions. The performance on this subtest therefore can reflect the degree of involvement in and appreciation for issues in social situations. A study by Schill (1966) offers some support for this assumption. High and low introverts were selected on the basis of the

MMPI Social Isolation scale and Ss who were considered social introverts had significantly lower Picture Arrangement scores.

Differences between Verbal and Performance IQ have been examined in a number of studies of individuals with a history of antisocial behavior. Though earlier studies (e.g., Fields, 1960; Foster, 1959) failed to confirm the significant elevation of Performance IQ reported by Diller (1955) and by Wiens, Matarazzo and Gavor (1959), more recent studies (e.g., Corotto, 1961; Craddick, 1961; Fisher, 1961; Frost & Frost, 1962; Kaiser, 1964; Manne, Kandel & Rosenthal, 1962) have all found significant elevation of Performance IQ over the Verbal IQ in antisocial disorders. These later studies, which found Performance IQ greater than Verbal IQ in acting out individuals, were conducted primarily with adolescents while the earlier studies which did not support the hypothesis (e.g., Fields, 1960), were conducted with adults. The findings that Performance IQ is greater than Verbal IQ in acting out seem to be very consistent in adolescents, while with adults, the findings are more equivocal (Kingsley, 1960). Some of the inconsistency in the findings with adults may be a function of the attempt to differentiate psychopaths from non-psychopaths (e.g., Clark & Moore, 1950; Craddick, 1961; Gurvitz, 1950). In these studies, psychopathic prisoners did not differ significantly from non-psychopathic prisoners in the extent to which Performance IQ exceeded Verbal IQ. But in most of these studies, the prisoners as a total group had a Performance IQ which was significantly higher than their Verbal IQ. It may be more appropriate to consider Performance IQ greater than the Verbal IQ as indicating a tendency toward acting out and antisocial behavior which can occur in several types of patients, not just in psychopaths.

A Verbal IQ significantly greater than Performance IQ on the other hand, has been reported in Yeshiva University students (Levinson, 1959) who, as a group, were considered to be somewhat over-ideational with little tendency for impulsive action.

Though there has been considerable research on the Performance subtests, relatively little research has been conducted on the Verbal Scales other than Digit Span. Several recent studies (e.g., Kaspar, 1958; Ginnett & Moran, 1964) offer further support for the relative stability of the Vocabulary subtest as compared to the other Wechsler scales. Though Vocabulary may decline somewhat with test anxiety (Sarason & Minard, 1962) and in severe organic and functional disturbances (e.g., Blatt, 1959; Rabin, King & Ehrmann, 1955), possibly in part because of the demand for precise verbalization, Vocabulary remains relatively stable as compared with other WAIS subtests. As such, it offers, in most cases, a reasonable estimate of general intelligence which can serve as a baseline when considering the relative efficiency of the other subtests.

An item analysis of the Information subtest (Norman & Wilensky, 1961) found that schizophrenics, as compared to a large sample of normals, had significantly greater difficulty on eight Information items which seemed to require reasoning rather than pure recall. This suggests support for the assumption (Rapaport, et al, 1945) that schizophrenics have relatively greater difficulty with complex cognitive tasks which require concentration and reasoning.

There has been little research, however, which has investigated the assumption that the Information scale reflects intellectual strivings and ambition. This hypothesis could be studied systematically if the Information subtest were compared in subjects equal to one another in Total IQ (and other control variables) but who varied on independent measures of their emphasis on intellectual achievement and academic strivings.

Two recent studies offer some support for the assumption that the Comprehension subtest assesses social competence and responsibility. Kippner (1964) reported a significant positive correlation between Comprehension and the Vineland Social Age. The sample in this study was limited and this relationship should be examined further in other samples and with other criteria of social competence. Another study (Hunt, Quay & Walker, 1966) reported a significant negative correlation between judgments, by clinicians, of an individual's antisocial tendencies and their performance on the Comprehension subtest.

Janet Spence (1963) studied patterns of response to the WAIS Similarities. Brain damaged patients made fewer conceptual responses, while schizophrenics were more likely to try to respond or to deny that the items were similar than to admit that they did not know. Contradictory findings in one respect, however, have been reported by Watson (1965), who found that schizophrenics, compared to organics, tended not to attempt to respond when uncertain.

Arithmetic seems to have been relatively neglected in terms of recent research, despite Rapaport's (1945) observation that the capacity for concentration demanded by this test can be disrupted by thought disorder. In clinical practice and research with the Arithmetic subtest, it is useful to distinguish between types of errors which occur. Errors can be simple careless computational mistakes (such as multiplying rather than dividing) or the errors can reflect more extensive confusion and an inability to maintain an adequate focus while transforming and manipulating numbers during the various operations of the problem. These two errors can frequently be identified by asking the individual how he arrived at his answer. A factor analysis of the Information and Arithmetic subtests (Saunders, 1960) offers support for differentiating these two groups of errors in the Arithmetic subtest. Saunders found two major factors: a "numerical information" factor and a factor of "numerical operations." It is the latter factor which Saunders interprets as possibly assessing "ideational discipline" or "concentration."

In conclusion, the recent research on the WAIS has shifted away from an interest in signs and patterns associated with particular diagnostic groups to an investigation of the psychological processes assessed by the subtests. Though a few studies using nosological categories as a research criterion have offered interesting and consistent findings, there has been a move toward considering the Wechsler scales in a broader context and toward using more reliable and more precisely defined criteria.

Much of the recent research has evolved from the conceptualization that the WAIS assesses a variety of ego functions, all of which play important roles in adaptation. This ego psychological model has not only contributed to a redefinition and a redirection in research, but as discussed earlier in this chapter, it has made an extensive contribution to clinical practice as well. Rather than viewing psychopathology in terms of discrete and mutually exclusive categories, psychologists can consider individuals according to the variations in the level of efficiency of a number of ego functions. This assessment of ego functions on the WAIS must be integrated with assessment on other procedures which study these and other functions under different conditions and varying degrees of external structure. By assessing the efficiency of ego functions in a variety of conditions, the relative efficiency of each function can be specified; that is, the conditions under which particular ego functions are likely to have a predominant role in adaptation and how and when inefficiencies of specific ego functions might be most manifest. Thus, the organization of psychological processes is conceptualized in a hierarchical fashion with a primary level of organization having secondary features which may be expressed and utilized in different contexts and under different conditions. This type of evaluation and psychological assessment is no longer based primarily upon manifest behavior such as symptom formation, but stems from a consideration of dynamic issues and of the structural organization of psychological functions of the individual. The organization of psychological functions may be congruent with classic diagnostic categories such as obsessive-compulsive neurosis or hysteria, but more likely, it will be a blend of several levels of organization which transcend any specific diagnostic category.

The enumeration of the relative efficiency of the various ego functions from the scatter of subtest scores may seem to be done in a somewhat mechanical fashion, but this is only a preliminary step in clinical assessment. In order to specify how the ego functions are organized into consistent modes of adaptation, the analysis of the variations in ego functions must be integrated with an understanding of the concerns and preoccupations expressed in the content of the responses and in the quality and nature of the clinical transaction. It is the specification of the principles which organize these various facets of the consistent modes of adaptation which requires extensive clinical experience.

Though there is extensive theory and clinical experience with the WAIS, there is a marked discontinuity between the level of clinical experience and theory with the WAIS and much of the research. Earlier research has generally offered little support for the clinical application of the WAIS and for the basic assumptions about the relationships between cognitive processes and personality. More recent research has been somewhat more encouraging but there are still many basic assumptions that are made in clinical practice which need systematic investigation. There are also many important clinical observations with the WAIS which should contribute to the further clarification of the integral role that cognitive processes have in personality organization. Research with the WAIS should not only contribute to a refinement of clinical practice but it should also add understanding and knowledge about cognitive processes and how the various ego functions such as memory, perception, concept formation, visual-motor organization, anticipation and planning, are integrated into a variety of modes of adaptation, some limiting and distorting and others allowing for growth and for creative and constructive expression.

REFERENCES

Allen, R. M. The real question in Digit Span performance. *Psychol. Rep.*, 1962, *11*, 218.

Allison, J., Blatt, S. J., & Zimet, C. N. *The Interpretation of Psychological Tests.* New York: Harper and Row, 1967.

Anastasi, Anne. *Psychological Testing*, 2nd ed. New York: Macmillan, 1961.

Balthazar, E. E. Cerebral unilateralization in chronic epileptic cases: The Wechsler Object Assembly subtest. *J. clin. Psychol.*, 1963, *19*, 169-171.

Blatt, S. J. Recall and recognition vocabulary: implications for intellectual deterioration. *AMA Arch. gen. Psychiat.*, 1959, *1*, 473-476.

Blatt, S. J., Allison, J., & Baker, B. L. The Wechsler Object Assembly subtest and bodily concerns. *J. consult. Psychol.*, 1965, *29*, 223-230.

Blatt, S. J., & Quinlan, P. Punctual and procrastinating students: a study of temporal parameters. *J. consult. Psychol.*, 1967, *31*, 169-174.

Burik, T. E. Relative roles of the learning and motor factors in the Digit Symbol subtest. *J. Psychol.*, 1950, *30*, 33-42.

Capretta, P. J. & Berkun, M. M. Validity and reliability of certain measures of psychological stress. *Psychol. Rep.*, 1962, *10*, 875-878.

Clark, J. H., & Moore, J. H. The relationship of Wechsler-Bellevue patterns of psychiatric diagnosis of Army and Air Force prisoners. *J. consult. Psychol.*, 1950, *14*, 493-495.

Corotto, L. V. The relation of performance to verbal IQ in acting out juveniles. *J. psychol. Stud.*, 1961, *21*, 162-164.

Craddick, R. A. Wechsler-Bellevue IQ scores of psychopathic and non-psychopathic prisoners. *J. psychol. Stud.*, 1961, *12*, 167-172.

Craddick, R. A., & Grossman, K. Effects of visual distraction upon the WAIS Digit Span. *Psychol. Rep.*, 1962, *10*, 642.

Cronbach, L. J. *Essentials of Psychological Testing*, 2nd ed. New York: Harper, 1960.

Dana, R. H. Manifest anxiety, intelligence and psychopathology. *J. consult. Psychol.*, 1957, *21*, 38-40.

Dickstein, L. S., & Blatt, S. J. Death concern, futurity, and anticipation. *J. consult. Psychol.*, 1966, *30*, 11-17.

Dickstein, L. S., & Blatt, S. J. The WAIS Picture Arrangement subtest as a measure of anticipation. *J. proj. Tech. Pers. Assess.*, 1967, *31*, 32-38.

Diller, Judith C. A comparison of the test performances of male and female juvenile delinquents. *J. genet. Psychol.*, 1955, *86*, 217-236.

Fenichel, O. *The Psychoanalytic Theory of Neurosis.* New York: Norton, 1945.

Fields, J. G. The Performance-Verbal IQ discrepance in a group of sociopaths. *J. clin. Psychol.*, 1960, *16*, 321-322.

Fisher, G. C. Selective and differentially accelerated intellectual dysfunction in specific brain damage. *J. clin. Psychol.*, 1958, *14*, 395-398.

Fisher, G. M. Discrepancy in Verbal and Performance IQ in adolescent sociopaths. *J. clin. Psychol.*, 1961, *17*, 60.

Foster, A. L. A note concerning the intelligence of delinquents. *J. clin. Psychol.*, 1959, *15*, 78-79.

Fox, Elizabeth, & Blatt, S. J. WAIS Digits backwards and forwards and Rorschach white space responses. Unpublished manuscript, 1965.

Fromm, Erika. Projective aspects of intelligence testing. In A. I. Rabin & Mary R. Haworth (Eds.). *Projective Techniques with Children.* New York: Grune and Stratton, 1960.

Fromm, Erika, & Hartman, Lenore, D. *Intelligence: A Dynamic Approach.* Garden City, N.Y.: Doubleday, 1955.

Fromm, Erika, Hartman, Lenore, D. & Marschak, Marian. A contribution to a dynamic theory of intelligence testing of children. *J. clin. experim. Psychopath.*, 1954, *15*, 73-95.

Fromm, Erika, Hartman, Lenore, D., & Marschak, Marian. Children's intelligence tests as a measure of dynamic personality functioning. *Amer. J. Orthopsychiat.*, 1957, *27*, 134-144.

Frost, B. P., & Frost, R. The pattern of WISC scores in a group of juvenile sociopaths. *J. clin. Psychol.*, 1962, *18*, 354-355.

Gallahar, P. Effects of increased verbal scale difficulty and failure on WAIS digit symbol performance. *Dissert. Abstr.*, 1964, *24*, 179.

Gardner, R., Holzman, P. S., Klein, G. S., Linton, Harriet B., & Spence, D. P. Cognitive control: a study of individual consistencies. *Psychol. Iss.*, 1959, *1*, no. 4.

Gardner, R. W., Jackson, D. N., & Messick, S. J. Personality organization in cognitive controls and intellectual abilities. *Psychol. Iss.*, 1960, *2*, no. 4.

Gilhooly, F. M. Wechsler-Bellevue reliability and the validity of certain diagnostic signs of the neuroses. *J. consult. Psychol.*, 1950, *14*, 82-87.

Ginnett, L. E., & Moran, L. J. Stability of vocabulary performance by schizophrenics. *J. consult. Psychol.*, 1964, *28*, 178-179.

Goodstein, L. D., & Farber, I. E. On the relation between A-scale scores and Digit Symbol performance. *J. consult. Psychol.*, 1957, *21*, 152-154.

Griffiths, J. S. The effects of experimentally induced anxiety on certain subtests of the Wechsler-Bellevue. *Dissert. Abstr.*, 1958, *18*, 655-656.

Guertin, W. H. Auditory interference with Digit Span performance. *J. clin. Psychol.*, 1959, *15*, 349.

Guertin, W. H., Rabin, A. I., Frank, G., & Ladd, C. Research with the Wechsler Intelligence scales for Adults. *Psychol. Bull.*, 1962, *59*, 1-25.

Gurvitz, M. S. The Wechsler-Bellevue Test and the diagnosis of psychopathic personality. *J. clin. Psychol.,* 1950, *6,* 397-401.

Hafner, A. J., Pollie, D. M., & Wapner, I. The relationship between the CMAS and WISC functioning. *J. clin. Psychol.,* 1960, *16,* 322-323.

Hartmann, H. *Ego Psychology and the Problem of Adaptation.* New York: International Universities Press, 1958.

Holt, R. R., & Havel, J. A method for assessing primary and secondary process in the Rorschach. In M. Rickers-Ovsiankina (Ed.). *Rorschach Psychology.* New York: Wiley, 1960. Pp. 263-319.

Hunt, W., Quay, H., & Walker, R. The validity of clinical judgment of asocial tendencies. *J. clin. Psychol.,* 1966, *22,* 116-118.

Jurjevichk, R. M. Inter-relationship of anxiety indices on Wechsler intelligence scales and MMPI scales. *J. gen. Psychol.,* 1963, *69,* 135-142.

Kaiser, M. The WISC as an instrument for diagnosing sociopathy. *Dissert. Abstr.,* 1964, *25,* 2612.

Kasper, S. Progressive matrices (1938) and emotional disturbance. *J. consult. Psychol.,* 1958, *22,* 24.

Kingsley, L. Wechsler-Bellevue patterns of psychopaths. *J. consult. Psychol.,* 1960, *24,* 373.

Kippner, S. WISC Comprehension and Picture Arrangement subtests as measures of social competence. *J. clin. Psychol.,* 1964, *20,* 366-367.

Kris, E. *Psychoanalytic Explorations in Art.* New York: International Universities Press, 1952.

Kroeber, T. C. The coping functions of the ego mechanisms. In R. W. White (Ed.). *The Study of Lives.* New York: Atherton Press, 1963.

Levine, M., Glass, H., & Meltzoff, I. The inhibition process, Rorschach human movement responses, and intelligence. *J. consult. Psychol.,* 1957, *21,* 41-45.

Levinson, B. M. Traditional Jewish cultural values and performance on the Wechsler tests. *J. educ. Psychol.,* 1959, *50,* 177-181.

Lewinski, R. J. The psychometric pattern: I. Anxiety and neurosis. *J. clin. Psychol.,* 1945, *1,* 214-221.

Littell, W. M. The Wechsler Intelligence Scale for Children: Review of a decade of research. *Psychol. Bull.,* 1960, *57,* 132-156.

Luchins, A., & Luchins, E. Effect of varying administration of the Digit Symbol subtest of the Wechsler-Bellevue Intelligence Scale. *J. gen. Psychol.,* 1953, *43,* 125-142.

Manne, S. H., Kandel, A., & Rosenthal, D. Difference between Performance IQ and Verbal IQ in a severely psychopathic population. *J. clin. Psychol.,* 1962, *18,* 73-77.

Matarazzo, Ruth D. The relationship of manifest anxiety to Wechsler-Bellevue subtest performance. *J. consult. Psychol.,* 1955, *19,* 218.

Matarazzo, J. D., & Phillips, Jeanne I. Digit Symbol performance as a function of increasing levels of anxiety. *J. consult. Psychol.,* 1955, *19,* 131-134.

Maupin, E., & Hunter, Diane. Digit Span as a measure of attention: attempted validation studies. *Psychol. Rep.,* 1966, *18,* 457-458.

Mayman, M., Schafer, R., & Rapaport, D. Interpretation of the Wechsler-Bellevue Intelligence Scale and personality appraisal. In H. H. Anderson & G. L. Anderson (Eds.). *An Introduction to Projective Techniques.* New York: Prentice-Hall, 1951.

Moldowsky, S., & Moldowsky, Patricia C. Digit Span as an anxiety indicator. *J. consult. Psychol.,* 1952, *16,* 115-118.

Murstein, B. I., & Leipold, W. D. The role of learning and motor abilities in the Wechsler-Bellevue Digit Symbol Subtest. *Educ. Psychol. Meas.*, 1961, *21*, 103-112.

Norman, R. P., & Wilensky, H. Item difficulty of the WAIS Information subtest for a chronic schizophrenic sample. *J. clin. Psychol.*, 1961, *17*, 56-57.

Penfield, W., & Milner, Brenda. Memory deficit produced by bilateral lesions in the hippocampal zone. *AMA Arch. Neur. Psychiat.*, 1958, *79*, 475-497.

Rabin, A. I. Diagnostic use of intelligence tests. In Wolman, B. B. (Ed.). *Handbook of Clinical Psychology*. New York: McGraw-Hill, 1965.

Rabin, A. I., King, G. F., & Ehrmann, J. C. Vocabulary performance of short-term and long-term schizophrenics. *J. abn. soc. Psychol.*, 1955, *50*, 255-258.

Rapaport, D. The autonomy of the ego. *Bull. Menninger Clin.*, 1951, *15*, 113-124.

Rapaport, D. The theory of ego autonomy: a generalization. *Bull. Menninger Clin.*, 1958, *22*, 13-35.

Rapaport, D., Gill, M., & Schafer, R. *Diagnostic Psychological Testing*, Vol. I. Chicago: Yearbook Publishers, 1945.

Rashkis, H. A., & Welch, G. S. Detection of anxiety by use of the Wechsler scale. *J. clin. Psychol.*, 1946, *2*, 354-357.

Reich, W. *Character Analyses*. New York: Noonday Press, 1949.

Sarason, I. G., & Minard, J. Test anxiety, experimental instructions, and the Wechsler Arithmetic, Information, and Similarities. *J. educ. Psychol.*, 1962, *6*, 299-302.

Saunders, D. A. A factor analysis of the Picture Completion items on the WAIS. *J. clin. Psychol.*, 1960, *16*, 146-149.

Saunders, D. A. A factor analysis of the Information and Arithmetic items of the WAIS. *Psychol. Rep.*, 1960, *6*, 367-383.

Schafer, R. *The Clinical Application of Psychological Tests*. New York: International Universities Press, 1948.

Schafer, R. *Psychoanalytic Interpretation in Rorschach Testing: Theory and Application*. New York: Grune and Stratton, 1954.

Schafer, R. Regression in the service of the ego: Relevance of a psychoanalytic concept for personality assessment. In Gardner Lindzey (Ed.). *Assessment of Human Motives*. New York: Rinehart, 1958.

Schill, T. The effects of MMPI social introversion on WAIS Picture Arrangement performance. *J. clin. Psychol.*, 1966, *22*, 72-74.

Shapiro, D. *Neurotic Styles*. New York: Basic Books, 1965.

Sherman, A. R., & Blatt, S. J. The effects of success vs. failure experiences on Digit Span, Digit Symbol and Vocabulary performance. Unpublished manuscript, 1966.

Siegman, A. W. The effort of manifest anxiety on a concept formation task, a non-directed learning task and timed and untimed intelligence tests. *J. consult. Psychol.*, 1956, *20*, 176-178.

Spence, Janet T. Patterns of performance on WAIS Similarities in schizophrenia, brain damage and normal Ss. *Psychol. Rep.*, 1963, *13*, 431-436.

Wachtel, P. L., & Blatt, S. J. Energy deployment and achievement. *J. consult. Psychol.*, 1965, *29*, 302-308.

Waite, R. R. The intelligence test as a psychodiagnostic instrument. *J. proj. Tech.*, 1961, *25*, 90-102.

Walker, R. E., & Spence, Janet T. Relationship between Digit Span and anxiety. *J. consult. Psychol.*, 1964, *28*, 220-223.

Warner, S. J. The Wechsler-Bellevue psychometric pattern in anxiety neurosis. *J. consult., Psychol.,* 1950, *14,* 297-304.

Watson, C. G. WAIS error types in schizophrenics and organics. *Psychol. Rep.,* 1965, *16,* 523-530.

Wechsler, D. *The Measurement of Adult Intelligence.* Baltimore: Williams & Wilkins, 1944.

Wechsler, D. *The Measurement and Appraisal of Adult Intelligence,* 4th ed. Baltimore: Williams & Wilkins, 1958.

Wiener, G. The effect of distrust on some aspects of intelligence test behavior. *J. consult. Psychol.,* 1957, *21,* 127-130.

Wiens, A. N., Matarazzo, J. D., & Gavor, K. D. Performance and Verbal IQ in a group of sociopaths. *J. clin. Psychol.,* 1959, *15,* 191-193.

Wild, Cynthia. Creativity and adaptive regression. *J. pers. soc. Psychol.,* 1965, *2,* 161-168.

Witkin, H. A. Psychological differentiation and forms of pathology. *J. abn. Psychol.,* 1965, *70,* 317-336.

Witkin, H. A., Dyk, R. B., Faterson, H. F., Goodenough, D. R., & Karp, S. A. *Psychological Differentiation: Studies of Development.* New York: Wiley, 1962.

Wolfson, W., & Weltman, R. E. Implications of specific WAIS Picture Completion errors. *J. clin. Psychol.,* 1960, *16,* 9-11.

Wolfson, W., & Weltman, R. E. Visual-motor proficiency of long and short term planners. *Percept. Mot. Skills,* 1963, *17,* 908.

Wright, M. W. A study of anxiety in a general hospital setting. *Canad. J. Psychol.,* 1954, *8,* 195-203.

15

Other Projective Techniques

LEONARD P. CAMPOS

Introduction

A modern introduction to projective techniques does not merely concentrate its attention on the "tried and true" method. Techniques must be included which reflect outstanding promise for the future and which serve as new and creative variations of the Old.

If we agree that any stimulus can be formed to elicit a projective R, the task of evaluating experimentally and clinically useful methods of projection becomes formidable. The projective hypothesis has been extended to materials which encompass a wide range of stimuli not covered elsewhere in this book: diverse objects, lines, forms, designs, patterns, expressions, words, pictures, cartoons, films, shadows, reflections, ideas, movements, toys, blocks, animals, paint, clay, drama, sounds, colors, clouds, symbols, dreams, memories, and pain. Indeed, the existence of various "World" techniques (Bolgar & Fischer, 1947; Bühler, Lumry & Carrol, 1951; Lowenfeld, 1960) attests to the limitless applicability and logical extension of the projective hypothesis. Many stimuli have such projective "pull" that the proliferation of projective "methods" is an inevitable consequence. Projection potential in perception and so-called objective techniques complicate the picture (Levy, 1963).

At first it was the intent of this writer to include many techniques; however, limitations of space demanded a selective rather than an exhaustive treatment of extension of the projective hypothesis to five classes of stimulus materials: 1) the human face; 2) the human hand; 3) symbols; 4) mosaics; and 5) incomplete drawings. The techniques discussed exemplify how the projective hypothesis may be tested with selected interpersonal, behavioral performance, and motor-expressive stimuli.

THE HUMAN FACE

History and Theory

Interest in the human face, of course, has a long history. Long before the face was used as a medium for personality projection by psychologists, anatomists such as Bell (1806) and Piderit (1859), in their desire to make anatomy useful to the painter and sculptor, emphasized the importance of knowing facial muscles for representation of emotional expression. Darwin (1872) was one of the first investigators to employ facial photographs for obtaining judgments of emotions. Since his early studies there have been many series of photographs designed to elicit such judgments (Woodworth & Schlosberg, 1954). The face as a stimulus has also proved popular in experiments on "expressive movement" (Wolff, 1943). Perhaps Murray's (1933) use of photographs to measure the effect of a fear situation on projected "maliciousness" of facial stimuli marks the first projective technique of this kind.

The Szondi Test

Perhaps of all the projective techniques using faces as stimuli now available, the Szondi test (ST) originated by Lipot Szondi, an Hungarian psychiatrist, has received the most research attention. In a recent text, Horrocks (1964) stated that this test is "in the unique position of being a widely known test in America with practically no support in American psychology. Most who write about it take it upon themselves to warn prospective users against its clinical use" (p. 651). Up to 1950, research publications mushroomed from one publication in 1939 to a maximum of 50 in 1950 (David, 1954). In 1949 the *Szondi Newsletter* was born. Its subsequent decline in America was as dramatic as its earlier rise. In the five years between 1951 and 1955, *Psychological Abstracts* listed a total of 118 publications; in the five years between 1961 and 1965, there was a total of six publications. The last issue of the *Szondi Newsletter* was published in 1958. The ST is included in this book because of its highly important heuristic value for understanding a modern approach to projective personality assessment.

Starting with an initial publication of the test in 1937 Szondi (Szondi, 1937) presented a theory of *Schicksalanalyse* (fate analysis). He hypothesized that a person's "Schicksal" or fate is largely directed by the action of latent hereditary factors (recessive genes) or instinctive drives in the "familial" or "lineal unconscious." He wished to bridge the gap between Freud's personal or ontogenetic unconscious and Jung's collective unconscious. These latent hereditary drives guide an individual's life choices, such as the choice of love objects, friendships, occupation, and form of mental illness. A detailed treatment of Szondi's gene theory cannot be given here. Its first systematic presentation was published in a 1947 treatise, translated by Aull for a 1952 English edition (Szondi, 1952). Later refinement of theory and method appeared in his two volumes on *Triebpathologie* (Szondi, 1952, 1956) which at the time of this writing had not appeared in English translations. The most up-to-date presentation of Szondi theory is found in Szondi, Moser and Webb (1959).

Szondi stipulated four independent hereditary systems of mental disorders representing four basic drive vectors which consisted of four genetically definable clinical reaction types (cf. Table 1). For each drive *vector,* two drive *factors* were identified for a total of 8 instinctive *drives.* On the assumption of a basic ambitendency of such drives, two opposing drive tendencies (genetically smallest drive unit) are differentiated from the eight drives. One of these tendencies is repressed or socialized and sublimated, so that only one of the two tendencies will be lived out in its original form. Hence, 16 drive tendencies, 8 drive factors, and 4 vectors comprise the drive system of Szondi's "experimental diagnostics of drives" (Szondi, 1952).

If latent genetic factors direct instinctive choice reactions, then by presenting an individual with facial photographs of mental patients of varying diagnosis, this "genotropism" will operate to direct the S's responses to the photographs congruent with his own drive system. In this manner, the genetic theory generates a method for its measurement.

Deri's (1949) text has served as the primary reference for the Szondi test in the U.S. In that same year, the *Szondi Newsletter* was born. Deri "Americanized," so to speak, Szondi genetic theory, by more parsimoniously assuming that the eight drive factors represented by Szondi's pictures corresponded to eight *need systems* which need not be genetic in origin. Following Lewinian theory, briefly stated, personality is conceived as consisting of a number of need-systems and can be measured by determining the quantitative distribution of tension in these needs and the way the person handles these need tensions. If a S's need system is in a state of tension, the pictures are assumed to acquire valence character and the S selects pictures corresponding to his own tension system. It is important to note that in spite of the modification of *theory,* Deri continued to employ Szondi's *method,* a method which was generated by a genetic theory more congenial to earlier European currents of thought.

Materials and Instructions

The stimulus materials consist of 6 sets of pictures (approx. 2" x 3"), each set containing 8 photographs of the various types of mental patients corresponding to the drive factors as summarized in Table 1. Hence there are six pictures for each of the diagnostic categories for a total of 48 pictures.[1]

[1]For the interested reader, all 48 pictures of the Szondi test are illustrated in Szondi, Moser, & Webb (1959, p. 17ff.)

Figure 1. Set of Szondi pictures. Reproduced by permission; see p. 520.

464

PART VI

Briefly stated, the standard procedure for administration requires that the S select the two pictures of each set (presented in two rows of four pictures each) he likes best (or most) and the two he likes least (or dislikes most). This is repeated for the remaining five sets. Administration time will vary from as little as 10 minutes to a half hour or longer, depending on the S. The test administration is to be repeated at least six, preferably 10 times, with at least one day intervals between administrations for valid interpretation, and accompanied by instructions designed to discourage the operation of memory.

There are other modifications in instructions which will not be covered here. A group form has also been used.

Recording and Scoring System

On the basis of this procedure, 12 pictures will be considered to have a "like" (L) positive affective values (+) and 12 a "dislike" (DL) negative affective value (−). For the recording of these R's, a profile record sheet is used. The upper half of the profile sheet with 8 squared columns, corresponding to the 8 diagnostic categories or factors, is used for graphically representing the L R's; the lower half is used for recording DLR's (in contrasting color).

Six major scoring principles for analyzing the factorial choice reactions will be briefly covered here:

1. The first major category of choice for any given factor reaction may be designated as *positive* or *negative*. It is positive (+) if two or more choices in any one factor fall in the "likes" category and like choices are at least twice as numerous as the dislike choices in the same factor; it is negative (−) if two or more choices fall in the dislike category and the dislike choices are at least twice as numerous as the like choices. A positive R for pictures of a given factor indicates conscious or unconscious identification with the needs depicted by the photograph of the respective factor; a negative R indicates counter-identification or nonacceptance of the particular need represented by the picture. If after repeated administrations, plus and/or minus reactions are stable, for any given factor, such factors are assumed to serve as "root" factors, i.e., most likely to act as unconscious driving forces underlying actual behavior.

2. *Ambivalent* reactions (±) to any given factor are those in which there is a minimum of four selected pictures, evenly or almost evenly divided between likes and dislikes. Here identification and counter-identification are present simultaneously to the same need represented in any given factor. Such a reaction is "loaded," i.e., it creates a state of tension within the personality, in which the S is faced with the task of self-imposed control against direct need gratification. They are also referred to as "subjective symptom factors," or factors reflecting this

control of need tension discharged in observable behavior.

3. *Open* reactions (o), in which there is a maximum of two choices, either as like or dislike, one choice, or none at all. Here there is absence of tension in the need represented by its factor. Need tension associated with the need is discharged. Such factors are "objective symptom factors," since they can be observed in manifest behavior.

4. *Ratio of sum of open to sum of ambivalent reactions (tendenz-spannungs-quotient)* within the complete series is assumed to measure acting out tendencies. It measures the relative proportion of the amount of available channels for discharging tensions as against the amount of self-control to restrain needs from overt manifestation. When the ratio is smaller than 1, behavior is over-controlled; if larger than 5, the S exercises too little control over need-gratification.

5. *Profile series,* obtained by repeated administration of the test, yields an overall picture of changes or variability of the need-systems represented by the factors. This will range from little essential change in normal subjects to changes such as that found in factors in which there is frequent complete reversal of direction (plus to minus and vice versa) and assumed indicative of pathology or very unstable need-system.

6. General *vectorial* configurations or similarities and differences of R to the two factors of the same vector are also evaluated.

Table 1. Szondi Test content and simplified rationale

Vector	Picture Content (psychiatric diagnosis) and Factor (category)	Interpretation*
Sexual (S)	Homosexuals (h)	Need for "passive" tenderness, yielding, femininity
	Sadists (murderers) (s)	Need for physical activity, aggression, masculinity
Paroxysmal or Control (P)	Epileptics (e)	Need for control over anger, hatred; reflects way S handles aggressive, hostile emotion
	Hysterics (hy)	Need for exhibitionism, self-assertion; reflects way S handles tender emotion
Schizophrenic or Ego (Sch)	Catatonics (k)	Need for self-sufficiency, maintenance of ego's separateness from environmental objects
	Paranoid schizophrenics (p)	Need for self-expansion; tendency to fuse into objects of environment
Circular or Contact (C)	Depressives (d)	Need for acquisition, "anal" type of object relationship
	Manics (m)	Need for dependency, "oral" type of object relationship

*Adapted from Deri, 1949; Szondi, 1952

Technical Adequacy

No systematic tabulation of normative data is given in Deri's text (Deri, 1949). There are many studies, such as those of Harrower (1949), with a sample of 1300 profiles of clinical and non-clinical groups, which may be considered "normative" data; however, what is sorely needed is an integration of data in an appropriate manual.

Since variability across Szondi profiles with successive administrations has been considered to reflect true subject variance rather than error variance (unreliability), statistical indices of stability have been considered inapplicable. Nevertheless, even though test-retest coefficients have been low (Borstelman & Klopfer, 1953) across sets, the important findings of Guertin (1950) that Ss' selections from a single *set* were highly reliable, indicated that with a different method of presentation, high test-retest reliability could be demonstrated. This is confirmed in a doublecross validation study of Lingoes (1957). By presenting the ST pictures as a *Q-sort* task, to samples of 200 patients and controls, highly significant test-retest reliability of Rs to individual Szondi pictures was found and cross-validated.

MAJOR RESEARCH AND CLINICAL APPLICATIONS

Szondi Test Assumptions

The vast majority of research studies seem to have been addressed to a critical evaluation of Szondi test assumptions (Schafer, 1950, succinctly lists these).

One line of research addressed itself to genetic assumptions. If R's are determined by genetic factors (recessive genes) then significant differences in factorial choice or direction would be expected to occur between a population of monozygotic and dizygotic twins. From the study of Rabin (1952) to the study of Nolan (1961), this expectation has not been confirmed. With respect to Szondi's "genotropism," sociometric studies have lent some support to the expectation that some mutual preference will exist among persons of similar personality structure (Terstenjak, 1956; Shipman, 1957) but not necessarily because of genes.

Another research question was related to the extent to which the distribution of choice reactions of any factor for any group of subjects was a function of the stimulus values of the six photographs representing the factor rather than a function of *chance*. The research answer to this question was unequivocal: choice patterns do differ significantly from chance (Fosberg, 1951; Hill, 1951; Guertin, 1950a). It had to be pointed out, however, that the Szondi or Deri theory of need-tensions is neither confirmed nor disconfirmed since failure of chance to account for S's responses does not spell out the mediational processes that may be operating between the S's responses and the stimulus material.

A second research question was addressed to the nature of Szondi test stimulus values. One approach was to demonstrate that different groups of Ss could identify the diagnostic categories of the Szondi pictures at better than chance expectancy. (Rabin, 1950; Fosberg, 1961; Dudek & Patterson, 1952; Steinberg, 1953; Silverstein, 1957). As Sappenfield (1965) points out, these researchers merely cross-validated Szondi's original exhaustive efforts in selecting the pictures. This was one way to demonstrate that the Szondi test stimuli were "meaningful." Most correct matching of pictures with diagnosis it should be noted, were obtained for the h, m, and p factors.

Another line of research was to have the pictures matched with personality descriptions (Davis & Raimy, 1952; Richardson, 1952) ; another was factor analysis (Gordon, 1953). Thus, Richardson (1952) had 10 Ss match each set of 8 pictured patients with successive sets. Each picture matched with the others so that "the same dominant emotion, attitude, or way of feeling" was expressed. The purpose was to find out to what extent Szondi pictures having the same diagnostic classification would be judged to express the same "drive factor." Chance expectancy of matching any diagnostic category with any other category would be 12.5 percent. The correct matchings for the m, h, s, and p pictures were 34, 32, 22, and 24 percent respectively (p<.01) . The hy, d, k, and e categories were 16, 16, 15, and 12 percent, respectively which fell at below the P .05 level. Again, the h, m, s, and p pictures seem to be the most meaningful. Since no relationship was found between like-dislike choice and success in matching the categories, the author concluded that the basis of choice must be other than the diagnostic classification, possibly facial expressions. In Gordon's (1953) factor analysis, 13 factors were extracted from Rs of 118 university Ss. Most of the factors cut across all categories with the like-dislike Rs related to identifiable characteristics of the pictured patients such as age, sex, conventionality of appearance, etc. Little similarity of factor content was found between sets and there was a wide range of preference value within sets. The most unambiguously extracted factor ("clean-cut") was defined predominantly by the h pictures.

Several studies have tested the assumption that the selection of pictures of the same category would show more positive relationship than pictures from different categories (factors) (Lubin & Malloy, 1951; Szollosi, Lamphiear, & Best, 1951; Borstelman & Klopfer, 1953) , with negative results. Cohen and Feigenbaum (1954) determined the number of significant positive associations among Rs to photographs representing the same factor for 200 male psychiatric patients. Of 120 pairs of associations studied, only 25 were found to be significantly related, and only

16 of these significantly positive. Again it will be noted that most of the latter came from the m, h, and s factors.

Since the majority of Szondi factors contain items sharing little variance in common with others in the same factor, many investigators have proposed that the Szondi pictures be redesignated in accordance with the empirically demonstrated association values, or that the stimulus materials be used for measuring Rs to *individual* pictures (Szollosi, Lamphiear, & Best, 1951; Borstelman & Klopfer, 1953; Gordon, 1953). In this respect, Borstelman and Klopfer (1953) conclude that although the mediational process was unknown, two groups of pictures, out of the eight factors, appear to have stimulus values appropriate to Deri's rationale: the *h* and the *m* pictures. With respect to all 48 pictures, however, the Szondi test did not provide any better stimuli for evaluating differences than control "pseudo-Szondi" sets of pictured normal Ss. Thus, Guertin (1951) has found that in ranking picture preferences deviations from chance selection were no more significant for Szondi pictures among a sample of 32 college-age Ss than they were with nonclinical pictures. Indeed it was the viewpoint of the author, shared by others, that the Szondi was not a very *efficient* way of testing Deri's need theory. A more efficient method was that employed by Hamilton (1959). He administered the test to a group of 40 psychiatric cases and a group of 40 normals, equally divided as to sex and not significantly different in age, in two ways: the regular manner and in a procedure in which Ss *rank ordered* the photographs in each of eight factors according to his or her preference. A factorial design was used to test the hypothesis that control of incidental stimulus values (age, sex, grooming, etc.) by the rank order procedure would result in a confinement of choices to a few factors. Analysis of variance showed a significant increase in confinement of both L and DL choices and significantly more so in this respect for the L choices; inspection of loaded Rs showed that the confinement was variable. The author concluded that incidental stimulus values, associated with social desirability, do not completely account for total R variance; that a portion of the R variance was attributable to underlying *need-tensions*. This conclusion is as gratuitous, of course, as earlier conclusions which negated the theory of need tension since no independent external criterion of need tension was employed. Aumack (1957) described this lack of external validation in Szondi research.

It would seem, then, that modified methods of Szondi test administration are a more efficient approach to testing Deri need theory. To cite one example of this point, any attempt to confirm Deri's theory that positive Rs to a factor measure conscious or unconscious "identification" with the factor is rendered infirm by studies of the following kind: A sample of 48 college-age Ss were given the test with instructions to give their L and DL responses according to usual test procedure (conforming profile) and then in terms of their *real feeling* of L and DL (honest profile). It was found that the DL responses were relatively genuine but that the L responses merely reflected conformity to the Szondi test instructions (Barraclough, Cole, & Reeb, 1952). A most promising method which efficiently utilizes the *individual* pictures is the Q-sort method (Lingoes, 1957).

Two other assumptions which have been given research attention will be briefly mentioned here. Comparisons of normals and six clinical groups yielded no significant differences on the quotient of tendency tension (Fleishman, 1954). As for Szondi profile series variability, it will be recalled that it was assumed that any excessive interseries changes reflected pathology. When investigators compared normals with pathological groups on this scoring category (Whiteman, 1951; Hurley, 1957) little significant differentiation was found. Patients may have greater variability but not for any specific factor (David & Rabinowitz, 1951), and not because of any unique characteristic of the Szondi test. Thus, Fleishman (1956) hypothesized that differences between normals and disturbed Ss in directional changes from test to retest could exist as a result either of a) unique "pull" of the Szondi, or b) generalized response differences between normals and disturbed Ss to a wide variety of stimuli. The Ss were given two administrations of the Szondi test and a control set of photographs (of normals). Parallel response differences occurred on both sets of photographs, supporting the latter view.

Differential Diagnosis

Borstelman and Klopfer's (1953) review of the Szondi test research literature to 1953 concluded that a significant indication of a favorable prognosis for this test is the *absence* of studies of differential diagnosis! The inadequacies of using nosological groups as external criteria for instruments not designed primarily to make such differentiations are stressed. Early, and more recent, studies (Fosberg, 1951; Ramfalk & Rudhe, 1961) designed to test Szondi test diagnostic discriminability yielded negative results. To cite a critical study, David, Orne, and Rabinowitz (1953) demonstrated that of 25 "signs" purportedly differentiating a group of epileptics and homosexuals, only 3 signs for epilepsy and 3 signs for homosexuality were statistically significant in the predicted direction. When, however, the profile sheets were given to Szondi experts, of 139 attempted "blind" diagnoses (73 homosexuals, 66 epileptics), 93 were correctly diagnosed: 75 percent of the homosexuals (P<.01) and 58 percent of the epileptics (N.S.). Hence, qualitative diagnosis of homosexuality may yield significant data. Several German investigators (Moser, 1954; Walder, 1955; Laszlo, 1958) have supported the utility of the Szondi pictures for assessing masculinity-feminity or homosexuality. In Walder's (1955) study of 15 sex offenders, the h factor was found to be particularly meaningful.

In addition to its clinical utility in the area of sex-role identification, the diagnostic discriminability of some of the Szondi pictures is highlighted by research studies of antisocial or delinquent behavior. Deri's (1954) clinical study of 88 antisocial Ss reported high frequency of +h and −m Rs, indicative of "a basic infantile character and oral frustration." Also high +s and −e suggested a tendency to react with unsublimated aggression. Scott (1955) attempted to verify Deri's assumptions of the delinquent personality by comparing 600 delinquents with a control group of 600 non-delinquents matched on sex and age. Of 26 comparisons, 14 were inconsistent with Deri expectations. The delinquent pattern was characterized by +h, −p, and open m. Particularly notable was the significantly higher frequency of +m in the non-delinquency group, especially in girls. Hence, the pictures measuring the m factor seem useful for differential diagnosis of delinquency in an adolescent. Guerrier's (1954) factor analysis of Rs to the m factor in a group of maladjusted adolescents found it to be related to family rejection.

Coulter (1959) analyzed Scott's data in order to test Deri's (1949) nine supposed "indicators" of antisocial behavior and five "counterindicators." In comparing the normal and delinquent groups on all 14 indicators, a chi-square test of significance only approached significance ($p<.10$). Hence all the signs could not be relied on, as a group, for identification of delinquency. For this sample, only the +s and +h were statistically significant in the expected direction. When this finding is added to the importance of the +m responses as a counterindicator of delinquency (Scott, 1955) it can be safely concluded that pictures in the h, s, and m factors can be used for predicting delinquency. To further support this conclusion is the study of Harrower (1958); 83 delinquents were compared to 77 controls yielding a significantly different typical profile of +h, +s, and −m for the delinquent sample.

There have been other applications of the ST which can not be reviewed adequately here. It has been amenable to experimental manipulation of various kinds (Deri, 1950; Simpson & Hill, 1953; Logan, 1961) and there is some evidence demonstrating the effect of demographic variables, e.g., socioeconomic factors (Rainwater, 1956) and of subject-examiner interaction (Scherer, 1952; Van Krevelen, 1954).

A review of research applications with the ST indicates that Deri's need theory has been neither confirmed nor disconfirmed. The reason for this should be clear to the reader: with the exception of pictures classified into h, m, s, and possibly p factors, the ST has proven to be, in its present form, an ill-chosen method for testing need theory. Need theory has proven clinically fruitful in personality research (Eriksen, 1954) and, more specifically, has helped to explain why we choose to "like" and "dislike" other persons (Horwitz, 1958). As noted earlier, if modifications of the Szondi test are utilized for more efficiently testing need theory, as suggested by the many investigations discussed in this report, then the ST should rightfully resume its position in the mainstream of American research. Indeed, there is sufficient research evidence to indicate that it may be highly useful for assessment of sex-role identification and sociopathy.

Other Facial Photographs

There are many other facial photographs of research use. Several investigators have used series of photographs to measure individual differences in trait attribution. Some use line drawings of faces (Warshaw & Bailey, 1961); others, posed photographs showing different emotional expression (Glad & Shearn, 1956). Underlying theoretical rationale may differ. Thus, Drombose and Slobin's (1958) psychoanalytically oriented Id-Ego-Superego test employs a "photo-analysis" subtest which consists of 9 photographs of men for whom three descriptions are given corresponding to assumed id trait, ego trait, and superego trait scores. An alternative approach to Szondi's method for testing need theory is Chamber's Picture Identification Test (Chambers & Lieberman, 1965). The PIT consists of 10 sets of 8 pictures taken from a college annual. Subjects are instructed to match photographs with need descriptions based on Murray's 21 needs. They are also instructed to make affective "like" and "dislike" selections. The relationships between matchings and affective values of the photographs have yielded scores which measure significant differences in "need-attitudes" of diverse nosological groups.

THE HAND TEST

History and Theory

Like the human face, the human hand is singularly suitable for eliciting projective responses. The use of the hand as a medium for making inferences about human behavior has a long history. The symbolic use of hands can be found in primitive religions and Christianity. About 3500 B.C. Egyptian and other cultures employed the hand as a symbol of life, "ka," the vital principle. Philosophers and physicians of antiquity were interested in the hand as a "diagnostic" aid for assessing a person's "temperament." The age-old prescientific pursuit of palmistry reflects an abiding interest in the use of the hand's palm lines for reading "character" or predicting future behavior. Charles Bell (1834) discussed the expressive value of the hand in art, particularly in portraits.

The first groping, scientific attempts in relating the hand to personality developed out of the study of body types. In discussing the theory of somatotypes, Kretchmer (1931) reported that the "pyknic" type of man with a disposition to manic-depressive states, has a large and rather short hand with stout fingers; the "asthenic" man, with a pre-disposition to schizophrenia, possesses a long and slender hand.

An important contributor to the study of the hand was Charlotte Wolff (1943). She introduced a theory of "chirology" based on the early typological work of Carus (1848) and Vaschide (1909). Recognizing adaptive functions of the hand, such as prehension and touch, she emphasized the relationship between the hand and brain via motoric and tactile representation of the hand in the brain. As stated by Wolff (1943): "The hand is the seismograph of emotional reactions . . . The pale hand of the melancholic, the red hands of the choleric, the moist hands of the inhibited adolescent, the cold hands of the terrified—all show the repercussion of emotion, produced by the functioning of the autonomic nervous system." She studied certain selected characteristics of the hand such as its form, nails, parts, lines, and handedness and derived a "practical method of hand interpretation" based on these characteristics.

Perhaps the first empirical research was a report by Carmichael, Roberts, and Wessell (1937). As was the case with the human face, most of the initial interest in the hand focused on "expressive movement" or the judgment of manual *expression*. Picture of hands as posed by actors represented by 35 titles were presented to several hundred students with the task of judging the emotional expression portrayed by still or motion pictures of the hands. In the former situation, most easily judged were attitudes of prayer, pleading, thoughtfulness, surprise, and fear. With the former method, in addition to these, determination, anxiety, warning, and satisfaction were also well portrayed. No difference was found between the sexes and between Ss with or without training. The authors suggested the possible research use of cinematographic technique in studying manual expression.

Werner Wolff's (1943) work in expressive movement should also be mentioned as an historical antecedent to the hand test. Photos of the subjects' hands were taken without their knowledge; they were then asked to characterize the hand. As on other forms of expression (voice, silhouettes, gait, etc.) Ss seldom recognize their own expression consciously. Thus, the percentage of non-recognition of self-expression, for the hands, was found to be 73 percent.

The Hand Test (HT), which is of interest in this chapter, was originated by E. Wagner, in 1959. It sprung from Wagner's abiding interest in the projection of aggression Rs (Wagner, 1961a). In his search for a medium which would reflect some important action tendencies found in Rorschach M (human movement) responses, related to interpersonal responses, Wagner chose pictures of hands.

After putting together the test material, Wagner published the first initial exploratory study (Wagner, 1961b) in which the drawings of hands were used to differentiate normals from schizophrenics. In 1962, Bricklin, Piotrowski and Wagner (1962) published a monograph with an initial rationale and scoring system for the HT in an application of the test to assessment of aggressive behavior in diverse nosological groups. A manual by Wagner (1962) appeared, in the same year, with a slightly modified and expanded scoring system.

By way of theoretical rationale, it was assumed that "prototypal action tendencies" would be projected into pictures of hands since the hand is considered important for interacting and relating to the external world; the hands supply kinesthetic feedback and, in coordination with our brain, enables us to organize our perceptions of reality (Wagner, 1962, p. 1). It is particularly likely to reflect action tendencies close to the motor system action tendencies that are readily activated and which are therefore likely to be apparent in overt behavior (Bricklin, Piotrowski, & Wagner, 1962; Wagner, 1962).

The theoretical rationale generated a classification system for Hand test Rs upon which the scoring system is based (cf. below). Thus, since the human organism interacts with 1) other living things and 2) inanimate objects, Rs to the hands yield two major scoring categories: *Interpersonal* and *Environmental*. These generic categories can be further subdivided according to the more differentiated modes in which interpersonal and environmental relations are handled. Projected failure in carrying through prototypal action tendencies, because of internal weakness in the protagonist, yields a *maladjustment* score. A more severe pathological reaction to the environment, accompanied by disintegration of adaptation, would yield a scoring category of *Withdrawal* and be expressed by the S's inability to project an appropriate action onto the drawn hands.

Unlike Szondi genetic theory, the theoretical rationale which guided Wagner's choice of stimulus materials is an excellent example of a theoretical system which is economical, close to the data, adequately comprehensive, and verifiable. Some of the later psychoanalytic interpretations of HT responses, however, are further removed from the data and accompanied by little empirical verification. In the monograph, clinical inference of a S's defensive system is indicated by the following Rs: "a hand holding a poison pellet" (obsessional anal sadistic); "a fearful hand protecting itself" (phobic reaction); "a performing hand that wants to be admired" (hysterical trends), etc. Verification through research and not clinical inference is needed here.

Materials and Instructions

The technique consists of 10 cards (approx. 3" x 5"), 9 of which contain india ink drawings of hands, and one of which is blank.

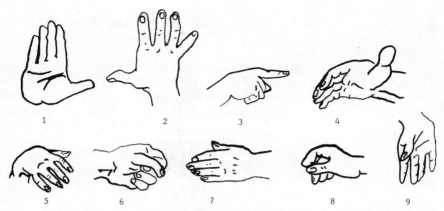

Figure 2. Hand Test stimulus materials. Reproduced by permission from Bricklin, B., Piotrowski, Z., and Wagner, E. *The Hand Test,* Charles C Thomas, Inc., 1962

Instructions for administering the HT are relatively simple. In administering the HT the examiner shows the S the cards, one at a time. The subject then tells what the pictured hand "might be doing." When the last card is reached, the examiner says: "This card is blank. I would like you to imagine a hand, and tell me what it might be doing."

The S is permitted and encouraged to take the cards and examine the drawings but nothing is said to encourage or discourage R productivity. Cards are presented right side up, but the S may turn the card as he wishes.

Other administrative details include prompting on the first card; also, for some Rs describing hand activity, the E can establish the object, e.g. the object of the "reaching" hand—providing the original R can't be unambiguously scored.

Recording and Scoring System

Rs are recorded verbatim together with initial reaction time per card. Card turning and other characteristics of the test behavior are recorded and coded with standard scoring symbols.

Average administration time is about 10 minutes. A group form of the test is also being used for research purposes (Wagner, 1966; Wenk, 1966).

Subjects' responses to the hand test, as given in the manual, are essentially classified into 15 formal "count" scoring categories which are grouped into four major classes:

1. *Interpersonal* (INT), or sum of the following Rs: Affection (AFF), Dependence (DEP), Communication (COM), Exhibition (EXH), Direction (DIR), and Aggression (AGG). INT responses are those scored by

the examiner as involving relations with other people. AFF, DEP, and COM are considered socially positive or cooperative; DIR and AGG are considered socially negative.

2. *Environmental* (ENV), or sum of responses scored as Acquisition (ACQ), Active (ACT), and Passive (PAS). ENV response reflect a generalized attitude toward the impersonal, a readiness to respond or to handle the environment. Such responses may be acquisitive, active or passive.

3. *Maladjustive* (MAL) or sum of responses scored as Tension (TEN), Crippled (CRIP), and Fear (FEAR). These reflect impotent expenditure of energy, physical incapacitation, and concern with self-injury, respectively.

4. *Withdrawal* (WITH), or sum of Rs scored as Description (DES), Bizarre (BIZ), and Failure (FAIL) —or unscorable R.

In addition to these four major categories, a *pathological* (PATH) score is derived equal to the sum of MAL + 2 (WITH), considered as a "convenient approximation of amount of psychopathology in a record." Included in the formal scoring is the number of responses (R), average initial time to each picture (AIRT), range of reaction time to pictures (High-low or H-L), and two ratios: an acting out ratio or ratio of the sum of AFF, DEP, and COM to the sum of DIR and AGG scores. Since the former are considered socially positive or cooperative, and the latter socially negative or undesirable, this ratio is an "approximate measure of the probability of behaving in an overt, hostile, anti-social manner." In the monograph, the acting out score is expressed as the arithmetical difference between the sum of the DIR and AGG responses and FEAR, AFF, COM, and DEP responses. An experience ratio (ER) is also recorded as a function of the ratio: INT: ENV: MAL: WITH. It provides a "useful overall estimate of basic, gross personality structure."

In addition to these formal scoring categories, the manual describes nine content areas for "qualitative" analysis: sexual (SEX), immature (IM), inanimate (INAN), hiding (HID) —hands perceived as concealing something, sensual (SEN) —responses emphasizing tactual sensitivity, internalization (IN) —a turning inward of a feeling or action, homosexual (HOM), denial (DEN), and movement (MOV).

In evaluating HT procedure, it is hoped that the use of Rorschach and TAT models may not actually serve as a retarding influence on the development of the HT. Controls on S differences in productivity and increase in number of stimuli paralleling the Holtzman modification of Rorschach inkblots, will help reduce sources of error in interpretation. Identification of "populars" will be needed and difficulty values of the cards established before clinical interpretation of RT to the cards is rendered unambiguous.

Because the HT is relatively un-threatening, easy to administer, and has wide applicability to a variety of population, it should prove very popular in the years to come.

Technical Adequacy

Two main sources of "normative" data are the monograph by Bricklin, Piotrowski, and Wagner (1962) and the *Hand Test Manual* (Wagner, 1962). Essentially, with the exception of some supplementary data, it is derived from circumscribed geographical areas (mainly Akron, Ohio and vicinity—in the manual; Philadelphia, Pennsylvania—in the monograph).

In the monograph, mean number and percentage of responses in each scoring category is given for several nosological groups (32 normals, 30 neurotics, 30 schizophrenics, 59 inmates, 10 organics, and 10 epileptics), the data of which is used in an analysis of clinical case studies and as establishing expected performance levels for adults.

In the manual more adequate normative data are provided for a total of 1,020 Ss (200 normal adults, 250 students, 160 schizophrenics, 100 organics, 220 sociopathic personalities, 40 neurotics, 25 depressives, 25 mental retardates, and 50 children). As noted in the manual, the data were collected from known diagnostic groups, tested subsequent to the formal adoption of the 15 scoring categories. Hence, these data presumably do not include cases from the monograph. The author acknowledges some shortcomings of the data, i.e., most of the Ss were residing in Ohio at the time of data collection, that the size of some of the samples is small, and that there is a need for inclusion of other groups.

In contrast to the monograph, the data—with the exception of AIRT and H-L scores—are more appropriately expressed in centile measures. Supplementary "normative" data for individual scoring categories have been appended to the manual for an Illinois sample of 50 institutionalized retardates and an Ohio sample of 205 children, aged 7 to 15. The data are reported in the form of means which creates some difficulty in comparing it with the centile data in the manual.

Because of the initial concern with diagnostic validation, no reliability data were reported for Hand test scoring until the appearance of the manual in 1962. One hundred protocols were randomly selected from the pool of norm groups and independently scored by 3 scorers (A, B, C) using the manual as a guide. Since the PATH score distributed itself continuously over the 100 protocols and served as a meaningful summary score, it was used for establishing split-half (odd-even) and interscorer reliabilities. Percentage agreement between pairs of scorers over all 15 formal scoring categories was also computed. For the PATH score, split-half reliabilities were .85, .84, and .85, for scorer A, B, and C respectively. Interscorer reliabilities between A and B, A and C, and B and C were .86, .96 and .92, respectively. Percentage agreement over all 15 scoring categories for between A and B, A and C, and B and C: 80, 78, and 83 percent, respectively. No data are presented for specific scoring categories. It is stated that disagreements were not serious, mostly within rather than between the major scoring categories. Most frequent disagreements were between ACT and ACQ and between DIR and COM. None of the research applications, to be reported on below, present any data on reliability of scoring. It would seem, then, that further reliability data are needed, particularly test-retest or stability indices. As a new test, major research applications of the HT have been addressed to its validation.

MAJOR RESEARCH AND CLINICAL APPLICATIONS

Differential Diagnosis

In Wagner's (1961) first attempt in using the Hand test as a projective medium for differential diagnosis, protocols were scored for the following classes of Rs: interpersonal, inactive (passive), active, maladjustive, and withdrawal Rs. A comparison of 50 male schizophrenics and an unmatched sample of 50 college students on these 5 scoring categories, differentiated the two groups at less than the P<.001 level on all but the inactive category. Maximum differentiation was obtained from the WITH category. A Phi coefficient of .81 was found between presence of WITH responses and schizophrenia.

In a second study, Wagner (1962) compared a sample of 60 schizophrenics and 40 neurotics, matched on age, on four scoring categories: INT, ENV (combining inactive and active responses), MAL, and WITH responses. The INT category significantly differentiated the two groups at the P<.01 level and the WITH category beyond the P<.001 level.

The Bricklin, et al (1962) monograph describes and compares differences in number and percentage of Rs as well as other scoring categories for groups of 32 adult normals, 30 neurotics, 30 schizophrenics, 59 inmates, 10 organics, and 10 epileptics. Some findings which may be briefly reported are as follows: normals have the highest R, inmates the lowest; epileptic patients give the greatest number and percentage of aggressive Rs; schizophrenic patients have the greatest number and percentage of Fear Rs. According to the authors, absolute number of Rs (R) in the categories give us some idea of the amount of psychological activity, or total action tendency potential, while the percentage terms indicate the importance of the particular area, or action tendency, in the total psychic life of the individual. The proportions determine overt behavior. The monograph also presents several clinical cases for demonstrating the clinical use of the HT.

The HT manual also presents complete protocols and short case histories for a total of 40 Ss of different nosological groups, independently diagnosed. For purposes of differential diagnosis, the manual supplies "signs" to watch for in diagnosis of schizophrenia, organic psychosis, depression, mental retardation, and sociopathy which would be beyond the scope of this chapter to discuss.

Aggressive Behavior

By far the greatest number of studies with the HT has been devoted to validating the acting out score (AOS). In the monograph, Bricklin, et al (1962) state the rationale that the probability of overt aggression increases as dominant, aggressive attitudes outweigh attitudes indicative of cooperation. They derived a score expressed as the aritthmetical difference between the sum of DIR and AGG, on the one hand, and the sum of non-aggressive attitudes, or Fear (F), AFF, COM, and DEP responses, on the other.

It was expected that in persons who act out, the combined AGG and DIR scores would outweigh the combined F, AFF, COM, and DEP scores. It was also expected that in the normal adult there would be a numerical balance between the two areas, or that the latter would outweigh the former. Four major investigations were carried out to test this expectation. In the first study, groups representing acting out cases (59 inmates, 17 acting out psychiatric patients) were compared on AOS with Ss representing non-acting persons (32 normal adults, 20 indigents, and 20 non-acting out psychiatric patients). The expectation was confirmed, an X^2 test of significance yielding significant differences at $P<.001$ level. An interesting finding was that in absolute numbers, normals had more AGG responses (1.80) than inmates (1.42). When, however, the relative distribution of total number of responses (R) among scoring categories is given in percentages, AGG responses account for only 7 percent of R in the normals and 15 percent of R in the inmates. The authors conclude that sociopaths differ from normals not in what they possess to a great extent (i.e. aggressive attitudes) but rather in what they *lack* (i.e. socially cooperative attitudes).

In a second study, the expectation that the AOS is related to chronological age or developmental level was confirmed. A sample of 49 normal children with a mean age of 12 years achieved a significantly higher AOS than the sample of 32 normal adults. A third expectation, based on the clinical literature, that a sample of 23 children with reading problems would have more difficulty expressing overt aggressive responses on the HT than the group of normal children and a matched (on age) group of 13 children without reading problems, was also confirmed. The expectation was based on the clinical rationale that such children have "passive-aggressive" personalities. A *t*-test of significance yielded differences between the groups at the $P<.01$ level.

A fourth study compared a group of 37 recidivist criminals with an unmatched group of 37 non-recidivist criminals to test the hypothesis that the former group would have a significantly higher AOS. A *t*-test of significance yielded differences significant at the P<.05 level, confirming the expectation. The data were analyzed in terms of different categories of crime. Highest mean AOS was attained by rapists and men who committed armed burglary; lowest scores were achieved by alcoholics and vagrants.

The HT has also been used in studies of teenage juvenile delinquents. Wagner (1962) in an initial study compared a sample of 30 convicted delinquents with 30 normal teenagers matched for sex and age on AOR and R (productivity). Since Bricklin, et al (1962) had found productivity to be significantly lower in inmates as compared to normals, Wagner predicted the same for the delinquents. An X^2 test of significance confirmed the expectation. As expected, the AOR was significantly higher in the delinquent sample (P<.02). Some qualitative differences in content of Rs was also found.

In a later, better controlled, study (Wagner, 1964), a sample of 30 "assaultive" and 30 "non-assaultive" delinquents, matched on sex, age, number of convictions, IQ, social class, and racial characteristics, were compared on the AOS. Assaultive delinquents had a higher AOS than the non-assaultive group, significant at the P<.001 level. The AOS successfully differentiated 47 out of 60 Ss (78 percent). Again, no base rate data are given, nor are the findings cross-validated.

Selg (1965) has also reported on the discriminative power of the acting out index in differentiating between aggressive and non-aggressive children. Wenk (1966) has included a custom-made series of hands designed specifically for tapping aggressive tendencies, presented on slides for group presentation. Wagner (1966)[2] reports, in a yet unpublished study, that the HT successfully predicted recidivism among a group of first-time juvenile offenders.

The HT has also been used to differentiate aggressive from non-aggressive Ss in other populations. Wagner and Medvedeff (1963) compared two samples of 35 undifferentiated schizophrenics matched on sex and age judged as "aggressive" or "non-aggressive" by a ward psychiatrist and nurse using 10 criteria of aggressive and unaggressive behavior on two HT scores, the AOS and WITH responses. It was assumed that WITH responses were a counterindication of aggression because they represent withdrawal from reality contact, aggressive or otherwise. Comparing the two groups in terms of whether they had AOS scores of none or one or more, or WITH of none or one or more, their expectation that aggressive patients would give significantly more acting out Rs and less WITH responses was confirmed at P<.01 and P<.001 levels, respectively. The AOS permitted correct classification of 67 percent of the cases;

2Personal communication.

WITH score permitted correct classification in 71 percent of the cases.

The HT has undoubtedly proven itself useful in assessing acting out tendencies and a beginning has been made to demonstrate predictive validation which would be requisite for establishing its clinical utility. As pointed out by Loevinger (1959) a common error found in research with a new method is to confuse significance levels of differences between groups *with expected proportion of errors in diagnosis* or other *clinical decisions*. Without comparisons of enumeration data with base expectancy rates and cross validation, the clinical use of the HT remains subject to errors of decision.

Other Applications

Other research applications include the use of the ACT score for evaluating employee work performance (Wagner & Copper, 1963; Huberman, 1964; Wagner & Hawver, 1965), the study of SEX content indicators for differentiating Ss with and without sexual problems (Wagner, 1963), and validation of hypnotically induced emotional states (Hodge & Wagner, 1964).

LOWENFELD MOSAIC TEST

History and Theory

There do not seem to be any historical predecessors of the Lowenfeld Mosaic Test. Margaret Lowenfeld became interested in this method sometime before 1930, between the Wars, during which time she was a child psychiatrist and founder of the Institute of Child Psychology in London. She observed that individual European communities had their own distinct folk costume patterns and designs. Different arrangements or patterns of form and color in dress embroidery seemed to be reliable clues as to a person's community or village of origin. The test originator's initial interest centered about the question of whether one could predict a S's community by an investigation of these basic patterns of form and color. Noting a predominance of geometric forms in the embroideries of Southeastern Europe, she took advantage of the fact that a manufacturing firm was producing collections of light wooden pieces of different geometric shapes, range of colors, and thickness. She gave these chance assortments to Ss of various nationalities and recorded their designs. Since she found some interesting differences, in 1929 she decided to standardize the composition of the materials.

Lowenfeld considered four aspects of the materials: shape, color, thickness and number of pieces. After some trial and pilot work she finally came up with, essentially, the present form of the test. Thinner plastic material was employed in 1948 when the supply of wooden material became exhausted. For some 20 years the test was used mainly in Great Britain until it caught the attention of American testers during World War II. In a 1950 conference held in Washington, D.C. the test author noted definite differences between American and British mosaic productions which led subsequently to speculations about personality differences. It was not until 1954 (Lowenfeld, 1954) that Lowenfeld systematized 25 years of work into a text or manual.

There is no indication that any personality theory guided the test author's choice of stimulus materials used in the test. Rather, it appears that her initial interest in inter-cultural differences guided its origin. As discussed by Lowenfeld (1954, p. 15), the test requires "direct action" by the subject and global analysis by the examiner. The test registers a person's "power to perceive and manipulate accurately objects of defined shape." Her emphasis has been on perception and disturbances of perception.

Although never fully elaborated by the test originator, one basic principle underlying the test was expounded by others. Early workers (Diamond & Schmale, 1944; Wertham, 1950; Reiman, 1950; Zucker, 1950; Pascal, 1952) stated that as a performance test it measured the ability to organize elements of the visual-motor perceptual field into "Gestalten."

Materials and Instructions

In its final form, Lowenfeld's selection of materials consisted of two sets of 228 mosaic pieces, for a total of 456 pieces, "a sufficient number of each shape in each color to make possible the construction, in each color, of the most characteristic fundamental patterns for that shape." The shapes occur in six colors considered common to European folk patterns: white, green, black, yellow, blue, and red, and arranged in that order in the standard wooden box provided by the present test distributor. It contains two plastic containers of 228 tiles each having the following "fundamental" form characteristics:

24 squares	$1\frac{7}{16}$"
48 half-squares (isosceles, right-angled triangles)	$1\frac{7}{16}$", $1\frac{7}{16}$", $1\frac{7}{16}$"
48 diamonds	$1\frac{7}{16}$"; angles 45° and 135°
36 equilateral triangles	(3) $1\frac{7}{16}$"
72 scalene triangles	$1\frac{7}{16}$", $1\frac{5}{16}$", $\frac{13}{8}$"

This standard set is provided with a wooden framed tray (12 3/8" x 10 1/4") in which the subject must construct his mosaic.

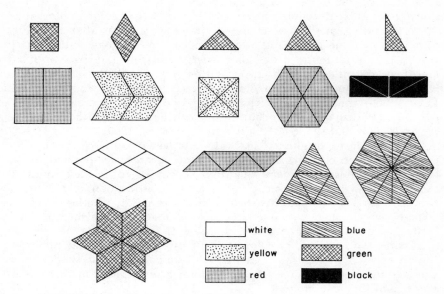

Figure 3. Fundamental Mosaic patterns. Reproduced by permission of Margaret Lowenfeld, Badger Tests Co., Ltd., London, England. (See p. 520.)

Some investigators have made minor modifications of this standard set, in the number, size, shape, or color of the mosaic tiles (Wertham & Golden, 1941; Diamond & Schmale, 1944; Bowen, 1954; Wideman, 1955; Metz, 1961). These will not be described here.

The instructions accompanying the materials are in four languages—English, French, German, and Spanish. There have been minor variations in the wording of instructions stated in different investigations. Essentially, however, the subject is shown a sample of each shape and of each color and informed that all the five shapes come in all the six colors.. He is asked to make anything he wishes except that the pattern be assembled on the tray provided. Upon completion the subject is asked to tell what it represents. Slight variations are adapted to age and intelligence characteristics of the Ss. Before 1951, Lowenfeld had demonstrated the interrelation of the tiles to the Ss, but because this constituted an element of suggestion, this procedure was dropped. Modification of administration for non-Western cultures is also reported in the manual. The E is to observe the testing situation and note S's attitude, approach to the task, etc.

Recording and Scoring System

Following the administration (which averages about 20 minutes, with 1 hour as the allowable maximum time), the Mosaic is recorded by the

E. S produces his mosaic on a white sheet of paper fitted to the dimensions of the tray. Recognizing the prohibitive costs of color photography —the recording method of choice—Lowenfeld suggests that recording of designs be done by tracing around each piece of mosaic with a sharp pencil; the initial letter of the color is written within the space outlined and then later filled in with crayon. Other investigators have used other recording methods: color photography (Diamond & Schmale, 1944; Levin, 1956) gummed paper shapes of proportionate size and color to the tiles (Wideman, 1955); colored ink rubber stamps, with one stamp for each color and shape (McCullough & Girdner, 1949).

A record form, originated in 1951, is provided with the manual for the examiner, to evaluate about 30 qualitative categories phrased in the form of questions: six general questions pertaining to the description of the design, tray placement, attitude, time, and classification; sixteen questions for the abstract patterns such as description, i.e., whether single or several, overall shape, symmetry ("super-symmetry"), asymmetry, successful vs. unsuccessful, structure, coverage of tray, whether the pattern is a frame, slab, and use of color (s); four categories of similar questions for all types of designs such as the kind and number of shapes used, whether any pieces are superimposed; whether any attempt made to stand pieces, and further comment.

Lowenfeld (1949) and other early workers have stated that since the Mosaic test measures "Gestalten," an exact numerical scoring system was of limited value. Mosaic results "are capable neither of statistical assessment nor of verbal evaluation in current terms" (1954, p. 27). Because of this configurational approach, the "scoring system" employed in the manual consists solely of classifying or enumerating descriptive characteristics of the mosaic productions.

Lowenfeld's classification of mosaic productions falls into three main groups:

1. *Representational*—designs in which the mosaic represents an external object or set of objects, or imagined or fantasied idea or concept. These are classified into five subcategories ranging from highly concrete representations such as the "kite" reaction, to bizarre representational designs. These designs are analyzed for projected movement, use of color, and degree of skill shown by the S.

2. *Conceptual*—designs which represent an idea or concept subclassified into three types: a) abstract ideas, e.g. "harmony and disharmony"; b) emotional or mental concepts, e.g. "blood"; and c) concepts of general significance.

3. *Abstract patterns* or non-representational designs—consisting of two major categories: 1) *with recurring form* and 2) *without recurring form*. The former consists of six kinds: a) single patterns placed free within the area of the tray; b) patterns with a relation to the edge of the tray: edge, frame, and corner patterns; c) patterns essentially related

to edge and making use of the whole area of the tray; d) collective patterns (several small patterns not considered by maker as composing a single design) ; e) symmetrical patterns; f) three-dimensional, in which the pieces may be layered or superimposed. The second major category (*without recurring form*) considers the intentions of the S as essential and consists of 4 kinds: a) patterns related to whole area of tray; b) "slab" patterns in which pieces are placed closely or loosely in juxtaposition without creation of an overall shape; c) incoherent patterns; d) three-dimensional, such as piling of pieces.

All of these patterns can be analyzed in terms of the questions used in the record sheet discussed above.

Several users of the test have employed a variety of descriptive categories which overlap Lowenfeld's basic classification (Diamond & Schmale, 1944; Himmelweit & Eysenck, 1945; Wertham, 1950; Walker, 1957; Ames & Ilg, 1962). The first major attempt to devise an objective "scoring" system is usually attributed to Wideman (1955). He presented, basically, another system of 39 categories or scoring "signs" addressed to the use of color, shape, characteristic of total design, design location on tray, and time. It will be noted that in all these so-called scoring systems the nominal ("count") level of measurement is employed.

Technical Adequacy

Except for mosaic characteristics of children, no normative data, as we understand that term, is presented in the manual. Mosaic productions are described, for the most part, according to the classification system discussed above and applied to an analysis of mosaics of mental retardates, the normal personality, neurosis, "mental disorders," and subjects with different cultural backgrounds.

Age norms are now available for an intellectually and socioeconomically homogeneous population thanks to the extensive developmental analysis of Ames and her associates (cf. below).

Because of the affinity for a configurational approach, early studies addressed themselves to the consistency of the "whole" mosaic design or pattern. Early workers (Diamond & Schmale, 1944; Himmelweit & Eysenck, 1945; Lowenfeld, 1949; Zucker, 1950) reported retention of the original "Gestalt" upon retesting, although constitutent parts of the whole may be altered. Thus, Himmelweit and Eysenck (1945) reported test-retest reliability after a 30-minute interval for a group of 100 male neurotics of .65 and .49, on number of pieces and colors used, respectively.

In the manual (Lowenfeld, 1954) no systematic presentation of reliability data is given. Wideman (1955) checked the test-retest consistency of 37 mosaic scores or "signs" for a group of 32 psychiatric patients and 36 undergraduate students. Of 37 scoring categories, for both groups, 7 categories were consistent at the P<.01 level; 9 at the P<.05

level. Six other categories were significantly consistent for the patient group only; 2 others significant for the control group only. Thirteen categories were not consistent at all; only 15 were sufficiently consistent for any reliable analysis of group tendencies.

Judging from the literature, on the whole, subjects' consistency in the use of particular categories from test to retest, is, at best, at a moderate level. To cite one study, Horne and Lane (1960) tested 2 matched groups of 28 college students at two different intervals, 1 week and 3 months. Very few significant relationships obtained. On any single criterion, men were more consistent than women; there was somewhat more consistency after the 1 week interval. Johnson (1957) has asserted that little statistical reliability can be expected for the Mosaic test. Horne and Lane suggested that this instability of the mosaic productions may be due to "creativity" in the Ss. Be that as it may, the following discussion on research applications must bear in mind the lack of stability from test to retest.

In Wideman's (1955) study, scorer reliability for a group of 34 patients was found to be satisfactory; all correlations reached or exceeded .59. Levin (1956) and Walker (1957) confirmed the finding that interjudge agreement in scoring a variety of mosaic descriptive categories is adequate.

In Walker's (1957) study, all Ss were administered the LMT and immediately retested. For a sample of 28 Ss, the test was readministered twice, a month later. Consistency was analyzed for 3 kinds of scores: 1) "count" scores, e.g., total time, total number of pieces, etc.; 2) classification and ratings, e.g., class, form level, color class, and compactness; and 3) blind matching of first and second mosaic productions. Walker concluded that the more global the method for assessing reliability, the higher the consistency. For some specific "count" scoring categories, such as total time and number of pieces used, reliability was substantial; for others, such as number of colors used, moderate consistency was found. The use of the month interval revealed that increased sampling of mosaic products yielded consistency where a single pair of products failed to do so. When the mosaic products of the Ss are pooled (in effect, doubling the test length), greater reliability is obtained. A second mosaic tends to be more coherent, and tends to be more colorful. Ss' behavior is typically exploratory. As stated by Walker, "A mosaic design should not be considered *the* mosaic product of a child but only one of a potential series" (p. 144).

Major Research and Clinical Applications

Differential Diagnosis

Certainly, as with many of the tests treated in the present chapter, concurrent validation of the Mosaic test for differential purposes constitutes the largest share of its research application and claims of clinical utility. Here we can only highlight major points and gain some perspective on the vast literature, at times contradictory and inconclusive, that exists.

Bell (1948) and Dorken (1952) summarize findings of the early studies which compare the mosaic products in different clinical groups. There are few well-controlled studies employing satisfactory research designs (Dorken, 1956). Comparison groups have not usually been equated on relevant demographic variables. Early studies, such as that of Wertham and Golden (1941) established characteristics of clinical groups by blind interpretation and later comparison with clinical records. Since this writer can only be selective, findings for a few diagnostic groups will be covered here.

Hansen (1954) summarized and integrated the characteristics for schizophrenics and normals from the literature up to that date: 1) super-symmetry, 2) repetition or stereotypy, 3) design is abstract rather than representational, 4) attempt to make concrete object is unrealistic or excessively schematized, 5) disregard of color, 6) simple agglutination (compact mass of a few closely placed pieces without discernible organization, which according to Wertham (1950) "are as pathognomic for severe chronic functional psychoses as the Wasserman test is for syphilis"), 7) condensations (excessively abbreviated designs which appear inappropriate), 8) literality (pieces stood on edge, rather than flatly), 9) bizarre choice of subject, 10) tendency towards construction of unrelated patterns, 11) incoherence of design, and 12) definition of a border. As for the "normal" mosaic production, the criteria are: 1) clear, distinct configuration, 2) free usage of shape, 3) free use of color, 4) successful achievement of intended end, 5) total number of pieces used is relatively large, 6) abstract designs are symmetrical, 7) use of common subject matter. As Hansen states, schizophrenic designs "look crazy."

Wideman (1955) in his development and initial "validation" of an objective scoring method for the LMT, using X^2 tests of significance of differences, compared a group of 107 normal Ss with an unmatched group of 70 schizophrenics, 48 neurotics, and 20 organics, on 39 categories. Of these, he found 32 which showed significant differences between the normal and one or more of the patient groups. Since only 15 of the scoring categories were sufficiently reliable for intergroup comparisons, these differences must be evaluated with this fact in mind. With respect to the differentiation of schizophrenics from the other groups, differentiation from normals was best (26 significant differences) and differentiation from organics worst (8 significant differences). With respect to the former, only about 15 categories were reliable for both groups. Normals showed significantly higher frequency on the following consistent mosaic characteristics: percent yellow, number colors, total color percentage, percent use of isosceles triangle, form symmetry, concrete representation (seascape scenes) , completeness, complexity, and aesthetic quality. Without better controls, refinement by selection of only reliable items, and cross-validation, the findings remain ambiguous. It was found that the older Ss used more chromatic color, the more highly educated used all six shapes more often, and gave more complex designs. Verbal IQ estimate was found related to ratings of complexity and aesthetic quality.

Other studies have not been as successful in demonstrating diagnostic discriminative value for the mosaic. Neither Rioch (1954) nor Levin (1956) were able to support claims of previous investigators. Rioch (1954) found no significant differences among a variety of clinical groups on frequency of concrete, abstract or symbolic designs.

Levin (1956) compared 52 normals, 14 maladjusted Ss, 14 neurotics, 34 mentally retarded, 29 paretics, and 35 schizophrenics with no control on relevant demographic variables and came up with very few significant differences among the groups. The Mosaic, on the whole was no better than chance in identifying Ss on the basis of absence or presence of behavioral correlates of pathology as measured by the Wittenborn rating scale. Levin concludes that clinicians probably use cues in the testing situation to identify Ss, erroneously attributed to the Mosaic test. On the whole, neurotics are difficult to differentiate from normals (Dorken, 1952, 1956) .

The literature is less contradictory and more consistent in its claims for the validity of the mosaic in identifying the organically impaired. Wertham and Golden (1941) and Wertham (1950) offered the most extensive data on the organically impaired. Two kinds of mosaic impairment are described: a "cortical pattern" (inability to achieve a good configuration, use of a few pieces, use of shapes inappropriate for their goal, indiscriminate use of color, and simplicity of design) found in patients such as those with severe cerebral arteriosclerosis, Korsakov psychosis, and severe encephalopathy following trauma. And a "subcortical pattern," primarily characterized by "stone bound" designs in which the subject fixates his response to the stimulus (color and form) values of the mosaic tiles. This was noted in patients with cerebral arteriosclerosis, postencephalitic parkinsonism, congenital spastic paraplegia, and Jacksonian epilepsy. Earlier, Colm (1948) had reported finding this "stimulus bondage" in brain-damaged children. However, as noted in our discussion of mental retardation, later, Shotwell and Lawrence (1951) found only 2 out of 22 brain-injured *retarded* children giving such a performance.

Wideman's (1955) chi-square analysis of intergroup differences yielded the following organic picture for 20 patients: significantly less number and use of colors and color patterning than normals; significantly less total tray area, more small simple compact designs, poorer symmetry, and lower aesthetic quality than normals and neurotics; significantly less number of pieces used, less use of oblong pieces than normals, neurotics, and schizophrenics. For the most part, the findings are consistent with those of previous investigators. Rioch's (1954) report, although negative with respect to other diagnostic groups, observed an inability of the sample of organics to integrate mosaic tiles into an organized "whole."

Maher and Martin (1954) presented a modified list of Wertham's criteria of organic signs to a group of five judges who were to classify blindly the mosaics of 20 elderly arteriosclerotics and a control group of 20 Ss, matched on age. For both Wertham's cortical and subcortical criteria, the organics and controls were significantly differentiated. These organic signs were: 1) designs of one or more lines; 2) unsuccessful design as reported by the subject; 3) homogeneous relationship of separate pieces to design, i.e., a square made of squares; 4) side-by-side placement of pieces with no discernible overall pattern, 5) absence of successfully executed representational designs.

Ascough (1962), in an attempt to validate and cross validate the Wertham and Maher-Martin signs and the Wideman signs in two studies of 29 organics and 14 controls, was able to validate and cross-validate the Maher-Martin criteria; only one of Wideman's signs—color patterning—held up with cross-validation.

In spite of some inconsistencies, the research literature confirms that certain signs of mosaic performance may be used for the differential diagnosis of organicity. Further research will be needed before the findings can be accepted for predictive purposes, however. Thus, Ascough (1962) found that even with the use of the Maher-Martin signs, percentage of false positives was 33 percent in the validation study and 20 percent in the cross-validation study.

Mental Retardation

Several early workers concluded from their studies that mental age had no relationship to mosaic productions above an MA of 8 years. Whatever the exact cutting-off point may be, there is sufficient evidence to indicate that mosaic Rs are related to intelligence in children. With respect to adults, the research is contradictory (Dorken, 1956).

There is a large literature devoted to mosaic correlates of mental retardation. Early studies of mosaic patterns reported "characteristic" performance among samples of mental retardates. Wertham's (Wertham, 1950; Wertham and Golden, 1941) studies listed the following as typical of the mosaic product of retardates: small, simple, compact and completed designs; pieces used are of one shape; one piece of each available color used. At very low MA levels, however, this simple organization does not occur; rather, products are incoherent, scattered, and fragmentary. McCulloch and Girdner's (1949) study of a sample of 200 retardates with CA ranging from 7 to 50 and MA from 5 to 12, also noted, besides this, simplicity of organization, low use of number of pieces, shapes, poor color harmony, and concreteness, with poorer performance by the lower grade Ss. Upon sorting the Ss into different levels of MA, a significant correlation of .43 (P<.01) was found between ratings of "overall goodness" of mosaics and MA level.

Shotwell and Lawrence's (1951) study of institutionalized retardates, in a more sophisticated design, compared a sample of 30 "familial" retardates with a sample of "brain-injured" retardates matched on CA, (mean age, 14) MA, (mean MA, 7), and IQ on formal aspects of mosaic design, as well as organization and content or feeling tone. Tests of significance yielded the following significant differences: brain-injured Ss used significantly greater number of pieces (P<.05), showed significantly shorter reaction time (P<.05), and took twice as long to make their products (P<.05). No significant differences were found between the groups on use of shape and color. Organizationally, the brain injured showed poorer organization, but it improved with increase in MA. Wertham's signs mentioned above seemed best to describe the products of the lower grade familial retardate. Above an MA of 8-5 overall organization was good. The brain injured tended to make complicated "unsuccessful" designs. In spite of expressing satisfaction with their products, 41 percent of the brain injured wanted to change their designs, as compared to only 20 percent of the familial retardates. Contrary to expectations, only 2 out of the 22 brain-injured Ss showed "stone-bound" designs.

Carr (1958) tried to cross-validate Shotwell and Lawrence's findings on a group of non-institutionalized retardates. A sample of 27 brain-injured (BI) subjects, consisting of mostly Ss with cerebral palsy was paired with 27 non-braindamaged (NBI) subjects, with a mean CA of 10 years and MA of 6 years. Contrary to previous findings, the BI subjects gave significantly fewer incoherent and scattered designs and more compact, additive groupings than the NBI subjects. BI subjects preferred significantly more corner and edge locations, while NBI subjects preferred to center their designs on the tray. The BI subjects also produced more single direction patterns than the NBI subjects. No significant difference was found on a number of pieces, contrary to previous research. With respect to other formal features, found by previous investigators, no significant differences were found in color and shape use. Also, consistent with previous research was the finding of a significantly longer time taken to complete the mosaic design, and significantly shorter reaction time (P<.05) of the BI subjects.

The research does partially confirm the diagnostic use of the LMT in assessing retardation but it also indicates the fruitfulness of making finer distinctions among the population of retardates rather than to assume that they constitute an homogeneous sample.

490

Developmental Studies

The mosaic productions of children have been found to be distinctly different from those of adults. Early studies (Dorken, 1952) noted that, with age, incoherent designs decreased, symmetry of form and color increased, designs became more abstract; by adolescence little difference from adult mosaics is found. The test manual reports 10 stages of development of the mosaic for the child under 6 and mosaic characteristics of children in general between 7and 14 years of age. Limitations of space preclude a detailed analysis. Stewart and Leland's (1955) findings with 100 five- to seven-year-old first graders were compared with mosaic patterns of 125 11- to 5-year-old eighth graders (Stewart, et al, 1957) showing significant changes in the direction of increased number of abstract patterns, appearance of cruciform and winged patterns, and almost complete disappearance of the earlier concrete "kite" reaction.

By far the most extensive developmental analysis of mosaic productions is provided by Ames and her colleagues (Ames & Ilg, 1962; Ames and Ilg, 1964; Ames, Ilg, & August, 1964) . Ames and Ilg's initial publication (1962) described mosaic changes for a New Haven, Connecticut sample of 1500 children between 2 and 16 years of age (25 boys, 25 girls at age 2; 50 boys, 50 girls at each year level thereafter) . For each year, and for each sex, children's mosaics are described quantitatively as to classification in terms of type of structure, form level, color, naming, and other formal properties, and analyzed qualitatively. On the basis of the data, developmental tables are derived showing mosaic characteristics which would be below, at, or above age. In addition, sex differences are fully described for each age group, and accompanying characteristic behavior and verbalization is given, plus many illustrative plates.

In two other studies of 5- to 10-year-olds, Mosaic records of 301 children sampled in North Haven, Connecticut (Ames, et al, 1964) , and 132 from Weston, Connecticut (Ames & Ilg, 1964) are compared with the earlier study group in order to check on the consistency of developmental trends from one sample to another. Differences in measured intelligence and socioeconomic status created some minor differences between the three groups but, on the whole, developmental trends were remarkably consistent. The group representing the highest intelligence and socioeconomic status attained developmental levels sooner than the other two groups; type of product was most advanced; they arrived sooner at achievement of non-representational products; they gave larger products, and the fewest slabs. Shape and color use was the same among all three groups. Representational designs led for both sexes at all ages, and increased with age. All three groups used the large triangle shape most at 5 years, and the square most after that age. Except for nine-year-old girls in one group, blue was the color used most often by all Ss; yellow was used the least at all ages. Number of pieces used increased with age for all Ss. Specific age trends are also described for naming of products. Perhaps the most striking finding was the consistent sex differences found, which will be discussed presently. The authors conclude that it is possible, in general, to assign a developmental level for any given subject in terms of age, particularly between five and ten years of age. Also worthy of note is the fact that in a sample of 87 Ss of the Weston study, 62 percent showed "improvement" in their mosaics with age, i.e., "matured."

The developmental studies discussed above had shown that as a subject matures, mosaic Rs "improve" from non-representational products without pattern, through non-representational products with pattern, to representational objects and scenes. A study by Pelz, Pike, and Ames (1962) found that with increasing levels of deterioration, elderly Ss reverse the order. Furthermore, only 15 percent of the Rs of a "deteriorated presenile" group were considered "successful," 40 percent for a "medium presenile" group, 50 percent for the "intact presenile" group, and 71 percent for the normal group. The authors concluded that the LMT could be used for predicting presenility. Again, however, without larger samples, better control for demographic variables, and cross-validation, there is no justification for generalizing to predictive validity from concurrent validation studies.

Perhaps one of the most significant findings of the developmental studies was the occurrence, in normal children, of mosaic Rs considered by some investigators to be abnormal in *adults*. As stated by Ames and Ilg (1962), "an understanding of age factors can help us distinguish 1) mere immaturity; 2) behavior normal and characteristic of a given childhood age, though perhaps not 'normal' for adults; and 3) behavior which, even in the very young child, may be considered abnormal." After examining supposed "danger" signals in childhood mosaics, the authors conclude that the Mosaic test "may give its clearest indication of danger not so much by the specific pattern *per se* as when it identifies the pattern made by any given child as being conspicuously immature for the age in question . . ." (p. 201).

Personality Factors

The findings of cultural differences in mosaic productions (Lowenfeld, 1954; Stuart & Leland, 1952) suggests the utility of the LMT in cross-cultural personality research. Of greater clinical utility is the considerable evidence indicating consistent sex differences in productions of children (Kerr, 1939; Reiman, 1959, to recent studies of Ames & Ilg, 1964; Ames, Ilg, & August, 1964). To briefly summarize: in boys, representational patterns lead at every age; at every age but 5½ and 6, girls make more central designs than boys; at every age from six on, boys make more scenes; for girls "flowers" occur more often; for boys more often are vehicles, guns, arrows, and rockets. The startling parallel performance of the sexes to that found in the Franck test—to be discussed shortly—should be noted. This suggests that the Mosaic test may be useful in assessment of masculinity-femininity.

As a *performance* projective technique the LMT can enhance the utility of the standard battery of projectives. However, Lowenfeld's preference for a "theory-less" descriptive analysis of mosaic characteristics has underscored the need for identifying mediating personality constructs. Several studies have begun in this direction. Walker (1957) relates specific mosaic characteristics to personality variables of stability, surgency, aggression, and creativity in children. Others also suggest the use of mosaics for studying creativity (Barron, 1958; Horne & Lane, 1960). The recent factor analytic study of Metz (1961), in which 96 children were administered a modification of the LMT devised specifically to elicit realistic productions, yielded six factors related to creativeness which the author labeled "ego strength": freedom of emotional and behavioral involvement, freedom of ideational flow, duration of involvement, precision and complexity of ideas, imaginative enrichment of ideas, and self-restraining autonomy.

THE KAHN TEST OF SYMBOL ARRANGEMENT (KTSA)

History and Theory

It is generally agreed that the process of man's development beyond mere animal existence has been achieved largely by his ability to use and invent symbols (Whittick, 1960). "Symbol" is a generic term which includes all that is meant by a sign, mark, or token, i.e., that which stands for something else. It can be an object that stands for another object, or an object that stands for an idea. We are all familiar with a host of traditional symbols: the crown, symbol of glory; the hourglass, symbol of time; the ring, symbol of marriage; the owl, symbol of wisdom; the swastika, symbol of revival, and many more. For the interested reader, Whittick (1960) is an excellently illustrative account of symbols in the history of mankind.

Although many psychologists have been interested in symbols, it was not until 1949 that three-dimensional symbol objects were used projectively by Kahn. Kahn, who had been interested in symbols since 1939, observed, by "chance" during 1949, the behavior of purchasers of small plastic objects in a Los Angeles hobby shop. Of these objects, which apparently had symbolic appeal, he selected those "common symbols found in our culture."

Initially the underlying theoretical rationale was not spelled out beyond that of the significance of symbols in human behavior. The only apparent criterion that guided the choice of stimulus materials was that the objects to be used in the test "represent in symbolic form, a cross-section of human experience in cultural relationships" (Kahn, 1957, p. 103).

By observing how a person handles symbol objects, Kahn discerned four "symbol-apperceptive personality" reaction types: two types found in severe pathology in which the subject either 1) regards all, or almost all, new experience as a total symbolic equivalent of old experience, or 2) shows a blocked or defective capacity for symbol formation and therefore cannot interpret a new experience symbolically; 3) a neurotic type for whom new experience is regarded as "semi-symbolic," showing an unawareness of the symbolic component which colors reality and hence leads him to misperceive; finally 4) that type manifested by the well-adjusted subject who approaches new experiences objectively and employs a flexible, selective use of symbols from past experience (Kahn, 1957, p. 100).

Aside from this typology, the test was not actually designed through the use of an explicitly spelled out personality theory as we understand it. In Kahn's own words, "a psychological test does not come into being because it is designed but because it is used" (Kahn, 1957, p. i). L'Abate and Craddick (1965) extend the rationale of this new symbol approach to cognitive theory. Since the role symbols play in adjustment and psychopathology refers to the concrete-abstract dimension of behavior, i.e., cognition, they offer this theory as possibly providing the necessary mediating process between the test stimuli and subject's response. The cognitive theoretical system of Harvey, Hunt, and Schroder (1961) is suggested as being particularly congenial to explaining KTSA behavior.

The first manual of the test appeared in 1949 (Kahn, 1949). Kahn's doctoral dissertation (1950), the following year, marked its entrance into the scientific literature. Early work on demonstrating differences between normals and psychotics (Kahn, 1950; Fils, 1950) preceded the appearance of a revised manual in 1953 which, in addition to minor modifications, added a sorting task. This revised manual (which will serve as the basis of our discussion), was later published in 1956 (Kahn, 1956) followed by a clinical manual in 1957 (Kahn, 1957), in which the number of scoring categories is considerably reduced. An unpublished manual in 1962 (Hill & Latham, 1962) provided some changes in instructional materials and made some minor changes in scoring principles in order to clarify and enhance consistency of scoring.

Materials and Instructions

The KTSA is actually an omnibus performance projective technique consisting of several subtests. The subject is instructed to repeat arranging 15 symbol objects as described in Table 2 on a felt strip composed of 15 equally spaced segments consecutively numbered from 1 to 15. The subject is first asked to arrange the objects on the strip any way he pleases, to give the reason (s) for doing so, and then to name the objects. On this, as well as on successive arrangements, the E records on a record sheet the S's responses and the direction of object placement, time, and position of objects. On the second trial, (II) the subject is asked again to arrange the objects anyway he pleases and in addition to giving the reason for doing so, to tell what the objects represent or symbolize. It is in this arrangement that a sixteenth object is used called the Y piece, consisting of a segment of a circle which the subject is instructed to place over any object he wishes. Again, the reason for arrangement, the S's symbolization, and the object chosen with the Y piece is recorded. The third trial (III) is a recall arrangement task in which the subject is asked to estimate the number of arranged objects, the order of which he thinks he can recall correctly; the subject then arranges the objects and is again asked to guess the number of correctly placed objects. During this trial the subject is also asked to place the four transparent objects (cf. Table 2) over any of the objects he wishes. All of the subject's responses are recorded as usual. In the fourth arrangement (IV) required of the sub-ject, he is asked to arrange the objects on a continuum of most- to least-liked and then give the reason for most liking the first three objects and least liking the last three objects. In a final arrangement (V) the subject again arranges the objects any way he wishes, with an additional instruction to sort the objects on the back of the record sheet which is marked off into 8 rectangles and in large print labeled LOVE, HATE, BAD, GOOD, LIVING, DEAD, SMALL, LARGE, akin to a novel object "semantic differential" approach. An additional "testing of limits" arrangement (VI) is used if the subject fails to give reasons for earlier arrangements or if the reasons given then were of the "No Reason," no symbolizing, category.

Average administration time is estimated to be about a half an hour.

Recording and Scoring

A record sheet is provided for recording S's responses, as noted above. Abbreviations of the test objects are used; a coding system is used to indicate sequence of placing objects; the way the subject handles objects in the naming of symbolizing tasks, position of the objects on the strip, overlapping, and results of the "objects over" tasks of the second and third arrangements are noted.

Two major scoring systems are used, an "objective" and a "semi-objective" system. In the former, the E can "count" score 11 variables: recall estimates in arrangement III, direction of placement, arrangement time, position of objects on strip, degree of contact of objects in naming and symbolizing tasks, degree of contiguity of similarly shaped objects on strip, chosen objects in "objects over" task, object preference in the arrangement IV, reaction time to symbolization task of arrangement II, sorting ratios in terms of number of objects placed in "emotional" vs. "unemotional" categories, "positive" vs. "negative" categories, and large vs. small categories, and frequency of agreement of the subject's naming Rs in arrangement I with established naming norms (cf. Table 2). The record sheet does not provide recording of assigned numerical values for these objective scoring categories.

Table 2. Selected KTSA Characteristics. Adapted from Kahn, 1956, 1957. Used by permission of Psychological Test Specialists, Missoula, Montana, and the author.

Test objects	Naming norms*	Popular responses	Unconscious meanings
Anchor (A)	Anchor	Pertaining to ships, boats, harbors, cities, travel or adventure. To a lesser extent, security and safety, as, a ship in the harbor.	Security, faith, travel, escape
Butterfly (B) large, brown Butterfly (b) trin, transparent	Butterfly, moth "	That which flies or has wings, phylogenetic relationship to other objects, flight, aviation, summer or spring, beauty, freedom, escape.	Life, flight, freedom, fragility
Circle (C) transparent	Circle, disc, eyeglass, any type of lens, round piece of plastic	Pertaining to seeing, the heavenly bodies, earth, geometry, eternity.	Femininity, women, status
Cross (+)	Cross, plus, sign "x" (letter of alphabet)	Pertaining to the Christian religion or to other groups which have a cross as a symbol, such as the Red Cross Organization. Also, concepts based on the plus sign or crossroads.	Authority, father figure, death
Dog (D) large, black Dog (d) small, black Dog (w) small, white	Dog, a particular breed of dog, puppy " "	Any common attribute of the dog, pet, home, family, loyalty, companionship, man's best friend.	Parental figure, mother, older sibling Sibling, wife, companion Self, or an aspect of self

(continued on following page)

PART VI

(continued from preceding page)

Test objects	Naming norms*	Popular responses	Unconscious meanings
Heart (H) large, transparent Heart (h) blue " Heart (R) red "	Heart 	The tender emotions. Less frequently ideas relating to the heart as an organ, occasionally also as the "Ace of hearts" in card games or as a symbol for an organization such as the Heart Foundation.	Superficial affections, shallowness Past emotional trauma, sadness Tender emotions, love of mother or spouse, normally sorted on "love"
Parrot (P)	Any kind of bird, gun, man, lizard, alligator, "I don't know"	"I don't know what it is"; anything related to birds or animals. If this object is seen as a gun, related ideas are given.	Phallic symbol, male sexuality
Star (S) large, transparent Star (1) (2)	Star Star	a star of the stage or High achievement such as screen; or success, hope, ambition in the abstract. Anything relating to the heavenly bodies or organizations which have stars as emblems; materials in which stars appear, such as "Star in our flag," "Stars in the sky," also, "My lucky star"; astronomy, astrology, and derivatives.	Superficial ambitions, shadow or shell of real ambitions or hopes Ambitions, hopes, the future

*For children and adults.

Semi-objective scoring consists of deriving a letter and a number element for a "symbol pattern." With respect to the former, 42 items (reasons for arrangement in I, II, V and VI if limits tested; levels of symbolizing in II; and reasons for liking and disliking objects in IV) are assigned a letter category corresponding to the response criteria listed in Table 3. The frequency of occurrence of each of these categories is considered a "raw score" which is then multiplied by weights derived from t-test values found in earlier studies of differences between normals and organic and non-organic psychotics. Table 3 gives the scoring weights (from 0 to 8) for each of the scoring categories. It will be noted that except for the initial A, "bizarre" category, this letter element score measures degrees of abstraction, from the most concrete to the most

Code Letter (with weight)	Table 3. KTSA Letter-Element Categories (Adapted from Kahn, 1956, pp. 314-315; 1960, p. 8)
A (0)	Autistic, bizarre, overvalent responses, description which can not take place in nature such as: "Hearts that bark" ("dogs that bark" would be acceptable as an X, since it occurs in nature.
B (1)	Failure to respond (no reason) or evasion of responses, includes "I don't know," non-pertinent responses: "This is difficult."
C (1)	Repeat of previously given response ("same as before") but only if the previous response was scored X, Y, or Z, and only if similar shapes are involved. For example, the red star is symbolized "hope" and later the transparent star is symbolized "hope" or "same as the other star" or "same as before." If the star is liked most (in Ar. IV) because it symbolizes "hope," it is given a C because Reasons for Arrangement, Symbolizing, and Reasons for Liking/Disliking are considered to be separate units without a scoring carry-over.
D (1)	Simple defining, describing, or naming the test object instead of saying what it represents (e.g., reason for arrangement; "a dog runs").
E (3)	Exterior emphasis, i.e., appearance, attractiveness, looks, likeness of shapes, symmetry, workmanship (e.g., reason liking/disliking: "I like its looks. It's thin").
F (3)	As E, except that color or absence of color is specifically mentioned. *Note*: F and E are scored in addition to all other scores so that a subject can obtain E, F, X or F, E, D for any one response. However, F and E are never scored in Symbolizing. E- and F-type responses in symbolizing are usually scored D (e.g., "I like the color").
X, Y, Z	These are the higher-level responses requiring capacity for the integration of stimuli.
X (4)	Is scored when the response represents something outside of the actual test object which has the same general shape as the test object or is essentially predicated on shape similarity with the test object (concrete association, e.g., "the heart is an important organ").
Y (6)	Is scored when the response represents something outside of the actual test object, which has substance, is tangible, or has finite boundaries in time or space and has a different shape from that of the test object. Y is given to "Z level" concepts that are not expressed as nouns, such as "having hope," "studying the stars" (tangible abstraction).
Z (8)	Is scored when the response represents something that has no finite boundaries and is not tangible. It is always a noun and is independent of anything in the life of any specific individual or group of individuals. Z qualities can theoretically persist as long as the human race exists, even if they are represented by only one surviving individual. Examples: "love" and "mother's love" (meaning the generalized idea of mother's love) is scored Z (intangible abstraction).

abstract. "Popular" associations to the KTSA objects are presented in Table 2; for qualitative analysis, assumed "unconscious symbolization" of the objects is suggested for clinical interpretation of protocols and is also given in Table 2.

The sum of the weighted scores for each letter element category yields the number element of the symbol pattern. To obtain the symbol pattern, the letter element categories are listed in a row behind the number element in order of descending frequency of occurrence. Almost all of the research applications of the KTSA have focused on these "semi-objective" scores.

Technical Adequacy

The standardization data for adults as reported in the 1957 and 1962 manuals are based on data of previous studies collected over a seven-year period, of 453 men and 47 women, aged 17-87 years, with a mean educational level of 10 years, and IQ of 103. Occupationally, 10 percent were unskilled, 46 percent semi-skilled, 21 percent skilled, and 13 percent professional or semi-professional (Kahn, 1956). The symbol pattern yielded by these data served as the norm in deriving a psychogram of the nine semi-objective categories against which Ss could be evaluated. Although Kahn states that this psychogram should be used tentatively and for research purposes only, it is still being used in essentially the same form at the present time.

Normative data are reported in the form of diagnostic tables giving letter and number element scores for normals and a variety of clinical groups (Kahn, 1957, p. 154-155). These data are based on experiments demonstrating that the formulas derived from the symbol patterns of known groups could be used relatively effectively in classifying unknown groups (Kahn, et al, 1956). Also, when unknown groups were classified, using the diagnostic formulas derived from the previous studies, and then compared with actual psychiatric diagnoses, the symbol pattern formulas correctly identified the majority of each group. Pooled data from this and previous studies yielded the normative diagnostic formulas given in the manual. Norm data for objective scoring criteria are also given in the manuals.

The normative data reported in the manual are limited primarily to adult men. A much-needed modification of norms is the inclusion of more women and children with, perhaps, separated sex and age norms. Abidin (1965, 1966) has provided initial sorting and symbolization norms for children. Certain descrepancies between his data and that of Kahn's auxiliary evaluation guide (Kahn, 1960) either point up a possible need for local norms or caution in generalizing from the latter.

For the most part, two kinds of KTSA reliability are reported in the literature. Test-retest correlations reported range from .66 (Kahn, et al,

1957) to .95 (Kahn, 1950) indicating adequate stability of KTSA performance. As an idiographic technique which employs variability of performance across trials as a source of true variance, the test-retest procedure might be considered inapplicable, however.

Most of the research is devoted to interscorer reliability for overall symbol pattern (or number element) scores or individual letter element categories. Kahn's studies (Kahn, 1950; Kahn, et al, 1957) reported extremely high overall scorer reliability (.97-.99). Later studies did not find such high agreement, however. For different pairs of judges varying in experience, correlations on overall performance range from a low of .59 (Anderson & Clack, 1966) to a high of .94 (Craddick & Stern, 1965). For overall scoring, interscorer reliability is adequate.

With respect to individual letter categories, the literature is consistent in the finding that categories A, D, and X are the most unreliable or yield the lowest scorer agreement (from a low of .41 to high of .81). Summarizing the studies, scorer reliability from least to most is as follows: A, D, X, E, Y, C, B, Z, and F. Excluding the first three letter scores, scorer reliability is quite adequate. The lack of consistency for the A, D, and X categories indicates the need for discarding or clarifying these scoring criteria.

RESEARCH AND CLINICAL APPLICATIONS

Differential Diagnosis

Almost all of the research applications of the KTSA have been devoted to demonstrating its utility for differential diagnosis. Over two dozen studies exist, clearly confirming its discriminative value in differentiating groups of less disturbed Ss (normals, neurotics and character disorders) from schizophrenics and organics (L'Abate & Craddick, 1965). To cite a good representative study, Kahn, et al, (1956) applied KTSA diagnostic formulas to the symbol pattern scores of an unknown group of 175 subjects for classification of Ss as normal, neurotic, character disorder, borderline schizophrenic, and psychotic. As was expected from previous studies, comparison with actual psychiatric diagnoses showed considerable overlapping of neurotics and normals, of neurotics and character disorders. In the character disorder group, only 15 percent were misclassified as borderline schizophrenics. Also, 48 percent of the borderline schizophrenic group were misclassified, but of these, 20 percent were called "psychotic." In the psychotic group, 94 percent were classified as either psychotic or borderline schizophrenic.

Other recent studies have found successful diagnostic classification to be somewhat lower. Thus, White and McLeod (1963) using multiple discriminant analysis for comparing 50 psychotics, 50 neurotics, and 50 character disorders, found that the 150 subjects were correctly classified only 49 percent of the time. Hedlund and Mills (1964) were unable to corroborate the clinical usefulness of the KTSA in differential diagnosis when used by itself, independent of other information. They found that the percentage of concordance between symbol pattern diagnosis and final psychiatric diagnosis over a total of 129 cases was only 29 percent for one author, and 30 percent for the other.

Many of these studies are vitiated by lack of base rates, unreliability of psychiatric diagnosis and errors of measurement. Not only is it essential for predictive validation to estimate the probability of misclassification on an independent criterion of behavior, but a modern approach to projective personality assessment would require data on the "payoff" function of the KTSA, i.e., what gain in information does the KTSA provide over life-history data or other sources of personality diagnosis? Even when no significant relationship between KTSA diagnosis and psychiatric diagnosis is found, as was the case in the Hedlund and Mills studies, conclusions cannot be validly drawn because of criterion unreliability.

When Murphy, et al, (1957) used the KTSA as an independent instrument for blindly classifying 48 patients into four categories (neurotic, character and behavior disorder, organic, and schizophrenic) 79 percent of the patients were correctly identified. All of the four organics in their sample were identified correctly—the chance expectancy of this occurring is one in eighty million. From the early work of Kahn (1951, 1955) to more recent work of L'Abate (L'Abate, et al, 1962; L'Abate, et al, 1963) , the KTSA has proved to be diagnostically useful for assessment of "brain damage." L'Abate, et al (1962) compared 30 organics and 30 schizophrenics matched by pairs on age, education, and length of hospitalization in performance on the Welsh figure preference test, Reitan's trail making test, the Benton Visual Retention test (BVRT) and the KTSA. Both the BVRT and KTSA yielded significant differences between the two groups; however, KTSA differentiation was successful only with male subjects. The authors concluded that new validity data is needed for women. Since L'Abate, et al (1963) found no significant correlations between the BVRT and KTSA, both useful for identifying organicity, they suggest that these two tests can be used in a battery for more efficient prediction. Summarizing from these studies: organics can be identified by use of the symbol pattern; organics show more concrete associations to KTSA objects while schizophrenics give more bizarre Rs; also organics perform more slowly and misplace more objects on the felt strip than do normals.

Differential diagnosis, however, is only a first step in personality assessment. The KTSA is a unique and versatile instrument which may be useful for understanding normal as well as clinical personalities. It may generate other symbol-object performance projective techniques in the future. Particularly promising is the use of the sorting task which could be expanded into a highly useful symbol-object semantic differential approach! For a more efficient use of the technique, a briefer form may prove profitable, especially for use with children. Deletion of unvalidated procedures (e.g. "objects over" task) may aid considerably in its refinement.

Other Applications

The research evidences some sex differences in KTSA performance. Theiner (1965) and Wyman (1963) found certain differences of performance between college-age men and women. In Theiner's study, women gave significantly more Z and B responses and men more Y and X responses; in Wyman's study, a significant difference in NE score in favor of the women was found. Kenny's (1963) study of children showed that boys tended to give more D and B responses; girls more C and Z scores. Other differences were also found.

Kahn (1966) [3] has referred to his technique as a "projective psychoanthropological technique," and thus suggests its wider application to the study of cultural differences. An initial study in this direction, carried out by Theiner and Giffen (1963), found some cultural variation but, on the whole, a high level of similarity in symbol pattern for three unmatched samples of 35 Vietnamese, 40 Germans, and 50 American adults was obtained.

Although the evidence of a relationship of the KTSA to intelligence in adults is not consistent (L'Abate & Craddick, 1965), it appears to be established for children. Fink and Kahn (1959) found, for a sample of 77 normal children, a significantly positive correlation between NE scores and MA of .46 (P<.01). In 1960, Kahn also originated an experimental intelligence test (KIT) for use with children using KTSA stimulus materials.

DRAWING COMPLETION TECHNIQUE (DCT)

History and Theory

The unique contribution of the DCT for personality assessment lies in the projective use of expressive motor activity. It requires the subject to project his personality by expressing himself in the activity of completing incomplete drawing tasks.

According to Bell (1948), the earliest use of the DCT was for estimating intelligence, e.g., the work of Pintner and Toops (1918). The first use of the DCT for personality appraisal is usually attributed to Sander (1928). Sander developed a "Phantasie Test" in which a variety of lines were to be organized by the subject. The theoretical rationale

---

[3]Personal communication.

rested on Gestalt principles in which it was assumed that the subject projected "structural" characteristics that govern tendencies to form or "organize" line stimuli. Others employed lines to demonstrate graphic expression in which Ss were instructed to represent emotions, ideas, etc. in line structure, e.g., the work of Hippius (1936). Wartegg (1939) standardized these line stimuli as presently used by Kinget (1952, 1958). Kinget adapted Sander's typology describing different modes of "organization"; she analyzed the graphic elements of the DCT in terms of a fourfold classification or "schema" of personality: emotion (outgoing vs. seclusive), imagination (combining-reality oriented vs. creative), intellect (practical vs. speculative), and activity (dynamic vs. controlled). Kinget (1952) freely admitted that this rationale is "an eclectic compound that meets the necessities of practice more than the requirements of theory" (p. 8).

Sanford developed a completion test (1943) which was used by Murray (1938) in his investigation of fantasy. In 1939, Hellersberg adapted the "Imagery Scale" of the Horn Art Aptitude Scale for measuring an individual's "relation to reality" (1945). The results of her use of the test were reported in a monograph (Hellersberg, 1950). The theoretical rationale postulated two factors involved in "normal functioning": 1) degree of *objectivity*, defined in terms of our culture, and 2) quality and quantity of *subjectivity* available in the individual. The test situation is assumed to parallel the S's adaptation to reality or everyday life.

Other forms of the DCT range from the "Symbol Elaboration Test" of Krout (1950) to the "Graphoscopic scale" of Pikunas (Pikunas & Carberry, 1961). Franck's (1946) interest in so-called sexual symbols generated a DCT measure of masculinity-feminity (M-F) which has proved to have the widest range of research and clinical applications. Briefly stated, its underlying rationale asserts that the line stimuli elicit a S's expression of his body image, both in structure and impulses, and that it can be used as a measure of degree of acceptance of one's sex role (Franck & Rosen, 1949).

In this chapter, our discussion will be limited to the stimulus materials devised by Wartegg—as used by Kinget (1958), Horn and Hellersberg, and Franck.

Technical Adequacy

Kinget's (1952) study of 383 "normal" adults, aged 18 to 50, heterogeneous with respect to occupation and education, does not provide any objective norms or statistical analysis of score frequencies. However, Takala (1953, 1964) has standardized the Wartegg data on several hundred Finnish children and adults; Scarpellini (1962) has done the same for samples of Italian subjects.

Hellersberg (1950) did not report any objective normative data either. From experience she reports that the normally functioning adult shows 36 percent or more of his drawing completion to fall in the objective zone, while 29 percent is the criterion for the adolescent. In the third edition of the manual (Hellersberg, 1961), developmental norm data are given for 28 American preschool children, 116 primary school children, and 143 Japanese primary school children based on a developmental scale derived from drawing performance. Preliminary age norms were also reported earlier for 225 children (Ames & Hellersberg, 1949).

With respect to the Franck test, there exist two manuals, a "California" (about 1952) and an "Australian" (undated) manual. In the former, standardization data in terms of raw scores and standard scores are reported, based on approximately 600 college-age subjects (Franck & Rosen, 1949). The Australian manual presents percentile norms based on data obtained from 267 male and 132 female students, over 18 years of age, from 8 countries. Initial norm data are also reported for 133 boys and 177 girls, aged 6 to 14. The need for standardization data is great.

Since little quantification of data is attempted by Kinget (1952) or Hellersberg (1950, 1961), no reliability data are reported. The modern reader must not confuse lack of quantification however, with *unquantifiability*. These investigators merely prefer a configurational approach to the data based on clinical experience. Olson (1955) reported a median score-rescore (rho) reliability value of .87 and a median test-retest reliability of .54 for a sample of 100 subjects on 35 scoring variables of the Kinget test. Perhaps, as may be the case with other instruments discussed in this chapter, repeat reliability indices are inapplicable.

Kinget (1952) "validated" the Wartegg test blank by comparing the results of DCT completions with data from three sources (a self-report inventory, paired-word forced-choice test, and rating scale), the Rs to which were classified into the fourfold diagnostic schema mentioned earlier. Percentages of agreement were, for men and women, respectively, 58 and 70 percent on emotion, 70 and 74 percent on intellect, 59 and 70 percent on activity, with no data reported for imagination. On the basis of these data and cluster analysis of the criteria, new variables were introduced and graphic variables redesignated to the diagnostic schema. Hence, the final scoring system is essentially unvalidated (Gleser, 1959).

In agreement with Kinget, Hellersberg feels that internal consistency among various sources of data, as defined by the clinician, is preferable to quantification. Hellersberg's method is to interrelate test behavior, drawing performance and verbal expression in order to arrive at a "consistent" picture of the S. As stated by Hellersberg (1950), "validity, therefore, depends on inner and qualitative consistency, a concept which more and more displaces that of proof by mere quantitative measures" (p. 52). The idea of criterion contamination is either overlooked or ignored.

In contrast to the "wideband" techniques of Kinget and Hellersberg, the Franck test yields a narrower band of information (masculinity-femininity) at a higher level of dependability. Although the two manuals do not report reliability data, a large and growing literature indicates highly satisfactory interscorer reliability. Franck and Rosen's (1949) original study reported scorer reliability between .84 and .90 with little difference between trained and untrained scorers. Averaging the coefficients reported in several studies (Jaskar, 1962; McCaulley, 1964; Reed, 1957), a value of .84 is obtained. Reliability indices of equivalence, internal consistency, and stability are needed. Lansky's (1962) data suggested that the Franck test was stable but also susceptible to experimental manipulation. Shepler (1951) found that, despite high scorer reliability, the manuals were in need of refinement: some items are relatively easy to score, while others are very difficult owing to lack of clarity of directions. Some stimuli lacked discriminability, indicating a need for item analysis.

Materials and Instructions

The variety of stimuli presented to the subject is suggested by a glance at Figure 4 which gives the first four incomplete drawing stimuli for two DCT methods.

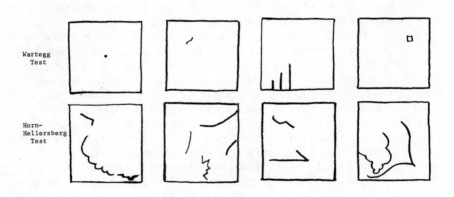

Figure 4. First four stimuli of selected DCT Methods. Reprinted by permission; see p. 520.

Wartegg's blank is composed of eight squares on a black background; the Horn-Hellersberg (HH) test blank consists of 12 squares, four to a page; and Franck's test consists of a total of 36 items, 12 to a page. Instructions are essentially the same in that the subject is instructed to complete the line stimuli anyway he wishes, and in no set order. In the Wartegg and HH test, the subject numbers his drawings and either tells what it represents or titles it. Kinget establishes no time limit but reports that the average completion time is about 20 minutes; average administration time for the HH test takes up to an hour; Franck gave Ss up to an hour to complete the drawings, but for group administration, Lansky discourages Ss from taking more than 15 minutes. After the 12 pictures are completed by the subject on the HH test, a 13th blank one is presented for obtaining a free drawing. A handwriting sample is also recorded based on instructions to describe one of the pictures drawn. Hellersberg (1961) states that the sample helps to "check the interpretation of the drawing" (p. 4). Observation of test behavior is also recorded.

Recording and Scoring Systems

Kinget's system of evaluating the S's responses to the stimuli consists of three approaches: 1) consideration of the drawings in relation to a given stimulus or to qualities symbolized by the stimulus,—organic "feminine" versus mechanical "masculine" stimuli, dynamic vs. static stimuli, complex vs. simple, etc.; 2) content of drawings in terms of degree of "representational value," from scribblings, through abstractions, to pictures (realistic to fantasied); and 3) formal characteristics such as form level, line characteristics, shading, composition, etc.

For 36 formal and content elements, a "count" score is given on a scoring blank for each of the 8 stimuli, ranging from a coded half point to three points, corresponding to intensity or magnitude of occurrence. There are several items for which no quantitative scoring is provided, such as continuity of line stroke, degree of clarity, popularity, etc. It is not clear why these items should present any more difficulty for scoring than the other criteria. A profile blank is also employed for graphically plotting scores against the fourfold personality schema. Since, as Kinget (1952) states, its value is essentially typological, and since it is of dubious validity, it would have to be placed on a sounder empirical footing.

For each scoring element Kinget evaluates subject's protocols in terms of the criterion data. To select one graphic element, line intensity, she writes, "a constant fact about strong lines is that they always reveal the presence of a strong vital drive . . ." (p. 79) "Weak intensity is always unfavorable, whatever the context in which it appears" (p. 83). Since we do not know what specific relation line quality has to the criterion data it is difficult to properly evaluate the validity of her analysis. According to Kinget, "the significance of the single variable is largely dependent on the *configuration* variables into which it appears. Consequently, a quantitative presentation would offer precision, not scientific validity" (p. 24).

A prerequisite for refining the scoring system is to discriminate valid from invalid criteria. A review of experimental research in graphology to 1960 (Fluckiger, et al, 1961) provides sufficient evidence, e.g., of a significant, relationship between line *pressure* and differences in body type, sex, and psychiatric diagnosis. Graphic elements associated with motor release and control (expansion-constriction, contraction-release) also appear to have high discriminative value (Hammer, 1958; Fluckiger, et al, 1961).

Hellersberg (1950) also employs a method of global assessment of content and formal elements in evaluating Ss' responses to the line stimuli. Forty frequently occurring themes or topics are listed on a chart corresponding to each of nine columns (I-IX) indicating from which "zone" of reality the S has chosen these themes. Tallied in coded form on the chart are four kinds: 1) main topic, valued at five points; 2) secondary meaning of a topic, valued at two points; 3) each single object, one point; and 4) intended objects, one point. In charting these topics, the E places them in the appropriate column or reality zone. The chart is divided into two main zones: 1) *objective zone,* corresponding to the first 10 themes when they are related to the S's own life experience, direct observation, and present day events or learned about in some way (I, II, III); 2) the *subjective zone* (remaining area) consisting of topics the subject experiences in a more personal subjective manner and divided into 4 major subzones ranging from the normal *emotional-expressive* zone to a *loss of reality* zone indicative of extreme subjectivity and escape from reality challenges.

The scoring system is essentially a topographical map indicating the frequency with which the S's drawing completions fall into objective and subjective categories. The percentage of items that fall into the zones is computed. Scoring in the objective zone is assumed to indicate to what degree the individual shares the experiences of reality with other people of the culture. A broad scattering over the subjective zone is assumed to reveal a capacity for varied and rich reality experiences; a conspicuous clustering in single areas shows an inability to deal with reality in a flexible way.

In addition, to content, formal elements are recorded on a separate chart into seven main areas, for example, type of title and drawing sequence, selected characteristics of composition, etc. In evaluating the scoring system it should be noted that the author's attitude toward quantification overlooks the promising weighted score system assigned to the different classes of themes. As with the Kinget test, this test is amenable to more precise quantification.

In the Franck test, the subjects' drawing elaborations are scored according to certain criterion categories as listed in Table 4. The scoring procedure is simply to count those items completed in a "feminine" direction. This is aided by a scoring key for each item in which scoring for "male" and "female" are amply illustrated. The Australian manual gives a scoring key that is somewhat more elaborate than the California manual. For purposes of clinical interpretation, some unvalidated qualitative principles are discussed for evaluating extreme cases, e.g., man with a high feminine score or women with high masculine score. Lansky (1966)[4] reports working on a new scoring method in which every code category (and some new ones) is applied to every drawing completion.

MAJOR RESEARCH AND CLINICAL APPLICATIONS

Table 4. Criterion categories of the Franck Drawing Completion Test

Criteria	Men tend to	Women tend to
Closure	close off stimulus area	leave area open
Expansion	expand outward, mainly upward—this expansion is sometimes specified as "protrusion" or "upward expansion" or "building up."	limit themselves to the area circumscribed by the stimulus itself.
Internal elaboration	(infrequent)	add one or more lines within the stimulus area.
Angularity	use sharp angles in their own drawing, leave unmodified or else exaggerate those given in stimulus.	use few angles in their own drawings, blunt or disguise those given in stimulus.
Unity	unite or connect two unconnected parts of stimulus.	treat as two separate units the unconnected parts of stimulus.
Reliance upon single line	"trust" a single horizontal or slanting line to carry "weight."	reinforce by doubling or similar measures single horizontal or slanting lines.
Content	draw self-propelling objects; profiles; tools; steeples, towers, skyscrapers.	"static" objects; frontal faces; flowers; "stick figures"; houses.

4Personal communication.

In 1959, Kass stated, in writing about the Kinget test, that "the ingenuity . . . the brevity of its format, and the richness of the productions it elicits, presage a popularity for this test as a research instrument applicable to clinical populations" (p. 130). Because of its lack of quantification, this prediction has not born fruit in American research literature. In Europe, however, where global assessment techniques find a more congenial soil, there are some reports of its research use.

Bauer (1952) and Takala (1964) employed the Wartegg stimuli for differentiating various clinical groups. Bauer reports finding "distinctive" characteristics among a clinical sample of 100 children of varying diagnoses. Takala, on the other hand, reports finding no significant difference in performance on a variety of scoring criteria between a sample of normal and neurotic Ss.

With respect to certain relevant background experiences, the evidence indicates a significant relationship between the Wartegg test performance and art ability, sex differences, and occupational differences (Olson, 1955; Takala & Hakkarainen 1953). Takala also reports low but significant relationships with intelligence (Takala & Hakkarainen 1953; Takala 1964).

For use in projective personality assessment, then, the proportion of test variance attributable to these factors must be identified and accounted for. Although there are a few reports demonstrating its amenability to experimental manipulations (Bochnik, 1954; Pikunas, 1966), hardly any research since Kinget's (1952) publication has addressed itself to identifying valid scoring criteria for personality assessment.

Even less personality research use has been made of the Horn-Hellersberg test. Except for a few scattered references to its use in clinical case studies, such as that of Bell (1949), it appears to have been used mainly for evaluating developmental changes in children and adolescents. Ames and Hellersberg (1949) reported data on HH test responses of three- to eleven-year-old boys and girls and identified 17 tentative states of development in drawing completions ranging from mere scribbling to abstract designs. It will be recalled that developmental norm data are also reported in the manual (Hellersberg, 1961). In a research project on personality development in adolescent girls, Hellersberg (1953) describes some differences in drawing completions of 100 prepuberal, 100 puberal, and 100 adolescent girls, with little presentation of statistical data.

Other research applications include Hellersberg's (1950) report of cultural differences, and on the basis of her clinical experience with clinical groups, a description of five major indications of a disturbed relation to reality: forming of closures, compulsive use of meaningless lines, morbid and horror images, delusional images, and bizarre forms together with unrestrained productivity.

DCT methods, such as those of the Kinget and HH techniques, cannot be used efficiently to complement other projective techniques until relevant graphic variables are related to clinically significant personality traits. The HH test of the subject's "relation to reality" should be construct-validated against other measures of ego strength. As mentioned earlier, since the DCT method may measure motor control, we can expect that its clinical utility will be enhanced by relating it to behavioral motor activity. Personality traits such as behavioral undercontrol and overcontrol, or more specifically, acting out tendencies, seem particularly relevant.

The utility of this approach has been confirmed by the Franck test, the stimulus materials of which have been primarily related to the personality variable of sex identity or "masculinity-femininity." Lansky (1965) reports a Franck test bibliography of 58 references since Franck's original publication (Franck & Rosen, 1949). In Franck and Rosen's original study, 60 stimuli were selected and presented to a group of 250 students. Of these, 36 stimuli yielded significant sex differences and provided an initial formulation of scoring criteria. The scoring criteria were cross-validated on a new group of 150 men and 150 women. Since the publication of this study, a considerable number of studies have confirmed its ability to differentiate the sexes of subjects of college-age or above. Interestingly, some of the scoring criteria, presented in Table 4, which on the whole appear to validly differentiate the sexes, have been noted in the play constructions of preadolescents (Erikson, 1951) and mosaic productions of children (Ames & Ilg, 1962).

Several correlational or factor analytic studies (Shepler, 1951; Engel, 1962; McCaulley, 1964), have reported low to negligible correlations between the non-verbal Franck test and other verbal measures of "manifest" masculinity-femininity (Strong Mf scale, Gough Brief Fe Scale, Terman-Merrill Attitude-Interest scale, MMPI Mf scale). In the light of the fact that the Franck test discriminates between the sexes at a highly significant level, the consensus of opinion is that it must be measuring a latent, covert, or unconscious level of sex identity.

The research utility of this distinction is reflected in several studies comparing Ss of differing combinations of conscious-unconscious sex identity as measured by the Gough Brief Femininity (Fe) Scale (Gough, 1952) and the Franck test. Thus, for males, three different sex identity groups are usually identified: unconsciously and consciously masculine (MM); unconsciously feminine and consciously masculine (FM); and unconsciously and consciously feminine (FF). To cite two studies, Aronfreed (1960) and Lansky (1960) compared MM, FM, and FF subjects on a story completion measure before and after experimental conflict arousal. With the interpolation of a guilt arousal condition, it was found that FM and FF men were more inclined than MM to complete story endings which expressed very severe moral standards and references to guilt, guilt-defense, and loss of control (Aronfreed, 1960). Under a condition of sexual conflict arousal, FF men were found to favor denial and withdrawal defenses in an aggression-associated situation. FM men become intropunitive and passive; they are more emotionally contricted but not significantly so. MM men use more realistic attempts to resolve conflict.

Very few studies are directed to comparisons of clinical groups. Reed (1957) found significant differences between psychotic and normal women, the former showing significantly lower femininity scores than the latter. Jaskar (1962) however, did not find any significant differences on the Franck test between a sample of 30 hospitalized and 30 non-hospitalized subjects. Other studies include attempts to relate Franck test femininity scores to anxiety (Kooser, 1955) and hypnotic susceptibility (Weitzenhoffer, 1957).

Another area of research application is the attempt to relate sex identity with certain characteristics of family structure (Lansky, 1964). Greenstein (1961) reported no significant differences in Franck test scores between 25 boys of father-absent homes and 50 boys from father-present homes, nor was Winer (1962) able to demonstrate any significant relationship between this measure of sex identity and satisfaction with mother in a sample of 164 adolescents. Teepen (1963), on the other hand, found that in two-child families, adolescent boys with older sisters were on the average significantly more feminine on the Franck test than were boys with older brothers. Many of these studies have not been cross-validated. Nevertheless, they demonstrate some of the interesting research uses of the Franck test.

REFERENCES

Introduction

Bolgar, Hedda, & Fischer, Liselotte K. Personality projection in the world test. *Amer. J. Orthopsychiat.*, 1947, *17*, 117-128.

Bühler, Charlotte, Lumry, Gayle, K., & Carrol, Helen, S. World test standardization studies. *J. Child Psychiat.*, 1951, *2*, 1-81.

Levy, L. H. *Psychological Interpretation*. N.Y.: Holt, Rinehard, & Winston, 1963.

Lowenfeld, Margaret. The world technique. *Top. Probl. Psychother.*, 1960, *3*, 248-263.

The Human Face: The Szondi Test

Aumack, L. The Szondi: internal or external validation? *Percept. mot. Skills*, 1957, 7, 7-15.

Barraclough, Patricia, Cole, D., & Reeb, Mildred. The influence of test instructions on Szondi results. *J. clin. Psychol.*, 1952, *8*, 165-167.

Bell, C. *Essays on the Anatomy of Expression in Painting*. London: Longmans, Green, 1806.

Borstelman, L. J., & Klopfer, W. G. The Szondi test: a review and critical evaluation. *Psychol. Bull.*, 1953, *50*, 112-132.

Chambers, J. L., & Lieberman, L. Differences between normal and clinical groups in judging, evaluating, and associating needs. *J. clin. Psychol.*, 1965, *21*, 145-149.

Cohen, J., & Feigenbaum, L. The assumption of additivity on the Szondi test. *J. proj. Tech.*, 1954, *18*, 11-16.

Coulter, W. M. The Szondi test and the prediction of antisocial behavior. *J. proj. Tech.*, 1959, *23*, 24-29.

Darwin, C. *Expression of the Emotions in Man and Animals.* London: Murray Publishers, 1872.

David, H. P. A Szondi test bibliography, 1939-1953. *J. proj. Tech.*, 1954, *18*, 17-32.

David, H. P., Orne, M., & Rabinowitz, W. Qualitative and quantitative Szondi diagnosis. *J. proj. Tech.*, 1953, *17*, 75-78.

David, H. P., & Rabinowitz, W. The development of a Szondi instability score. *J. consult. Psychol.*, 1951, *15*, 334-336.

David, H. P., & Rabinowitz, W. Szondi patterns in epileptic and homosexual males. *J. consult. Psychol.*, 1952, *16*, 247-250.

Davis, N. E., & Raimy, V. Stimulus functions of the Szondi cards. *J. clin. Psychol.*, 1952, *8*, 155-160.

Deri, Susan. *Introduction to the Szondi Test.* New York: Grune and Stratton, 1949.

Deri, Susan. The Szondi test. In Abt, L. E. & Bellak, L. *Projective Psychology.* New York: Knopf, 1950. Pp. 298-321.

Deri, Susan. Differential diagnosis of delinquents with the Szondi test. *J. proj. Tech.*, 1954 *18*, 33-41.

Drombose, L. A., & Slobin, M. S. The IES test. *Percept. mot. Skills*, 1958, *8*, 347-389.

Dudek, F., & Patterson, H. Relationship among the Szondi test items. *J. consult. Psychol.*, 1952, *16*, 389-394.

Eriksen, C. W. Needs in perception and projective techniques. *J. proj. Tech.*, 1954, *18*, 425-440.

Fleishman, M. The discriminative power of Szondi's quotient of tendency tension. *J. proj. Tech.*, 1954, *18*, 42-46.

Fleishman, M. The investigation of changes in directional reactions on the Szondi test. *J. gen. Psychol.*, 1956, *54*, 197-202.

Fosberg, I. A. Four experiments with the Szondi test. *J. consult. Psychol.*, 1951, *15*, 39-44.

Glad, D. D., & Shearn, C. R. An emotional projection test. *Percept. mot. Skills*, 1956, *6*, 1-12 (Monogr. suppl. no. 1).

Gordon, L. V. A factor analysis of the 48 Szondi pictures. *J. Psychol.*, 1953, *36*, 387-392.

Guerrier, R. La signification du facteur "m" de Szondi. *Psyché Paris*, 1954, *9*, 255-258.

Guertin, W. H. A consideration of factor loadings on the Szondi test. *J. clin. Psychol.*, 1950a, *6*, 262-266.

Guertin, W. H. A test of the basic assumption of the Szondi. *J. consult. Psychol.*, 1950b, *14*, 404-407.

Guertin, W. H. A comparison of the stimulus values of the Szondi pictures with those of normal Americans. *J. clin. Psychol.*, 1951, *7*, 163-166.

Hamilton, J. T. A study of incidental stimulus values in the Szondi test. *J. clin. Psychol.*, 1959, *15*, 322-324.

Harrower, Molly. Experimental studies with the Szondi test. *Szondi Newsltr.*, 1949, *1*, (suppl.).

Harrower, Molly. The first offender: a study of juvenile delinquents by the Szondi test. *Szondi Newsltr.*, 1958, *6* (3), 1-16.

Hill, V. T. The Szondi test and chance. *Szondi Newsltr.*, 1951, *3*, 1-16.

Horrocks, J. E. *Assessment of Behavior.* Columbus, Ohio: C. E. Merrill Books, 1964. Pp. 66-74.

Horwitz, M. The veridicality of liking and disliking. In Taguiri, R. & Petrullo, L. (Eds.). *Person Perception and Interpersonal Behavior.* Stanford University Press, 1958. Pp. 191-209.

Hurley, J. R. Psychodiagnostic limitations of Szondi interseries changes. *J. clin. Psychol.*, 1957, *13*, 396-399.

Laszlo, C. Die homosexualität des mannes im Szondi test. *Beitr. Sexual. Forsch.*, 1958, *8*, 112.

Lingoes, J. C. Minnesota multiphasic personality test correlates of Szondi picture preferences. *Szondi Newsltr.*, 1957, *6*, 1-12.

Logan, J. C. Szondi profile changes from sorrow arousal. *J. proj. Tech.*, 1961, *25*, 184-192.

Lubin, A., & Malloy, M. An empirical test of some assumptions underlying the Szondi test. *J. abnorm. soc. Psychol.*, 1951, *46*, 480-484.

Moser, U. The determination of the relative strength of masculine-feminine drives by means of the Szondi procedure. *J. proj. Tech.*, 1954, 75-88.

Murray, H. A. The effect of fear upon estimates of the maliciousness of other personalities. *J. soc. Psychol.*, 1933, *4*, 310-329.

Nolan, E. G. Szondi test protocols of monozygotic and dizygotic twin populations. *J. proj. Tech.*, 1961, *25*, 471-476.

Piderit, T. *Mimik und Physiognomik,* (4th ed.) Detmold & Meyers, 1925.

Rabin, A. I. Szondi's pictures: identification of diagnosis. *J. abnorm. soc. Psychol.*, 1950, *45*, 392-395.

Rabin, A. I. Genetic factors in the selection and rejection of Szondi's pictures: a study of twins. *Amer. J. Orthopsychiat.* 1952, *22*, 551-556.

Rainwater, L. A study of personality deficiencies between middle and lower class adolescents: the Szondi test in culture-personality research. *Genet. Psychol. Monogr.*, 1956, *54*, 3-86.

Ramfalk, C. W., & Rudhe, L. A contradicted hypothesis related to Szondi's theory: the Szondi test used on alcoholics. *Scand. J. Psychol.*, 1961, *2*, 100-104.

Richardson, H. The discriminability of the "drive factors" represented in the Szondi pictures. *J. clin. Psychol.*, 1952, *8*, 384-390.

Sappenfield, B. R. Test of a Szondi assumption by means of M-F photographs. *J. Pers.*, 1965, *33*, 409-417.

Schafer, R. Review of Deri, Susan, *Introduction to the Szondi Test. J. abnorm. soc. Psychol.*, 1950, *45*, 184-188.

Scherer, I. W., Winne, J. F., Page, H. A., & Lipton, H. An analysis of patient-examiner interaction with the Szondi pictures. *J. proj. Tech.*, 1952, *16*, 225-237.

Scott, E. An investigation of juvenile profiles on the Szondi test. *J. clin. Psychol.,* 1955, *11*, 46-50.

Shipman, W. G. Similarity of personality in the sociometric preference of mental patients. *J. clin. Psychol.*, 1957, *13*, 292-294.

Silverstein, A. B. "Diagnosing" Szondi's pictures. *J. proj. Tech.*, 1957, *21*, 396-398.

CHAPTER 15 · Campos   513

Simpson, W. H., & Hill, V. T. The effects of verbal reward and punishment upon picture selection on the Szondi test. *Szondi Newsltr.*, 1953, *4*, 2-15.

Steinberg, A. Szondi's pictures: discrimination of diagnosis as a function of psychiatric experience and of internal consistency. *J. proj. Tech.*, 1953, *17*, 340-348.

Szollosi, E., Lamphiear, D. E., & Best, H. L. The stimulus values of the Szondi pictures. *J. consult. Psychol.*, 1951, *15*, 419-424.

Szondi, L. Contributions to fate analysis: analysis of marriage. *Acta Psychol.*, 1937, *3*, 1-80.

Szondi, L. (Tr. by Aull, G.) *Experimental Diagnostics of Drives*. New York: Grune and Stratton, 1952, *18*.

Szondi, L. *Triebpathologie, Vol. I. Elemente der exakten Triebpsychologie und Triebpsychiatrie*. Bern: Hans Huber, 1952.

Szondi, L. *Triebpathologie, Vol. II. Ich analyse*. Bern: Hans Huber, 1956.

Szondi, L., Moser, U., & Webb, M. W. *The Szondi Test in Diagnosis, Prognosis, and Treatment*. Philadelphia, Penn.: Lippincott, 1959.

Terstenjak, A. A critical study of the hypothesis of the affinity of instincts and sympathetic facial expression. *Arch. Psicol. neur. Psich.*, 1956, *17*, 1063-1092.

VanKrevelen, Alice. Some effects of subject-examiner interaction on projective test performance. *J. proj. Tech.*, 1954, *18*, 107-109.

Walder, H. Die h-Bedürfnisse und ihre krimogene Bedeutung. *Beih. Schweiz. Z. Psychol. Anwend.*, 1955, *26*, 112-128.

Warshaw, L., & Bailey, M. Person perception in relation to personality projection. *J. proj. Tech.*, 1961, *25*, 216-220.

Whiteman, P. H. An experimental investigation of interseries changes as a diagnostic factor in the Szondi test. *Amer. Psychol.*, 1951, *6*, 342 (Abstract).

Woodworth, R. S., & Schlosberg, H. *Experimental Psychology*. New York: Henry Holt, 1954. Pp. 111-120.

The Hand Test

Bell, C. *The Hand. Bridgewater Treatise*, Vol. IV. London: William Pickering, 1834.

Bricklin, B., Piotrowski, Z., & Wagner, E. *The Hand Test: A New Projective Test with Special Reference to the Prediction of Overt Aggressive Behavior*. Springfield, Ill.: Charles C Thomas, 1962.

Carmichael, L., Roberts, S., & Wessell, N. A study of the judgment of manual expression as presented in still and motion pictures. *J. soc. Psychol.*, 1937, *8*, 115-142.

Carus, C. G. Über Grund und Bedeutung der verschiedenen Formen der Hand. *Verschied. Personen.*, Stuttgart, 1848.

Hodge, J. R., & Wagner, E., The validity of hypnotically induced emotional states. *Amer. J. Hyp.*, 1964, *7*, 37-41.

Huberman, J. A failure of the Wagner Hand Test to discriminate among workers rated high, average, low on activity level and general acceptability. *J. proj. Tech. Pers. Assess.*, 1964, *28*, 280-283.

Kretchmer, E. *Körperbau und Charakter*. Berlin, 1931.

Loevinger, Jane. Theory and techniques of assessment. *Ann. Rev. Psychol.*, 1959, *10*, 287-316.

Selg, H. Der Hand Test. *Diagnostica*, 1965, *11*, 134-137.

Vaschide, N. *Essai sur la psychologie de la main*. Paris: Rivière Marcel, 1909.

Wagner, E. E. The interaction of aggressive movement responses and anatomy responses on the Rorschach in producing anxiety. *J. proj. Tech.*, 1961a, *25*, 212-215.

Wagner, E. E. The use of drawings of hands as a projective medium for differentiating normals and schizophrenics. *J. clin. Psychol.*, 1961b, *17*, 279-280.

Wagner, E. E. *The Hand Test. Manual for Administration, Scoring, and Interpretation.* Akron, Ohio: Mark James, 1962a.

Wagner, E. E. The use of drawings of hands as a projective medium for differentiating neurotics and schizophrenics. *J. clin. Psychol.*, 1962b, *18*, 208-209.

Wagner, E. E. Application of the Hand test indicators of antisocial action tendencies in adults to teenage juvenile delinquents. Paper read at Eastern Psychological Association, April, 1962c.

Wagner, E. E. Hand test content indicators of overt psychosexual maladjustment in neurotic males. *J. proj. Tech. Pers. Assess.*, 1963, *27*, 357-358.

Wagner, E. E., & Copper, J. Differentiation of satisfactory and unsatisfactory employees at Goodwill Industries with the Hand Test. *J. proj. Tech. Pers. Assess.*, 1963, *27*, 354-355.

Wagner, E. E., & Hawkins, R. Differentiation of assaultive delinquents with the Hand Test. *J. proj. Tech. Pers. Assess.*, 1964, *28*, 363-365.

Wagner, E. E., & Hawver, D. A. Correlations between psychological tests and sheltered workshop performance for severely retarded adults. *Amer. J. ment. Def.*, 1965, *69*, 685-691.

Wagner, E. E., & Medvedeff, E. Differentiation of aggressive behavior of institutionalized schizophrenics with the Hand Test. *J. proj. Tech. Pers. Assess.*, 1963, *27*, 111-113.

Wenk, E. Perceptual differences between aggressive and nonaggressive CYA wards. Unpublished manuscript, 1966.

Wolff, Charlotte. *The Human Hand.* New York: Knopf, 1943.

Wolff, W. *The Expression of Personality.* New York: Harper, 1943.

Mosaics: The Lowenfeld Mosaic Test (LMT)

Ames, Louise, B., & Ilg, Frances, L. *Mosaic Patterns of American Children.* New York: Harper & Row, 1962.

Ames, Louise B., & Ilg, Frances, L. Age changes in children's mosaic responses from five to ten years. *Genet. Psychol. Monogr.*, 1964, *69*, 195-245.

Ames, Louise B., Ilg, Frances, L., & August, Judith. The Lowenfeld Mosaic Test: norms for five to ten year old American public school children and comparative study of 3 groups. *Genet. Psychol. Monogr.*, 1964, *70*, 57-95.

Ascough, J. C., & Dana, R. H. Concurrent validation of the mosaic and Bender-Gestalt tests. *J. consult. Psychol.*, 1962, *26*, 430-434.

Barron, F. The psychology of imagination. *Scient. Amer.*, 1958, *199* (3), 150-166.

Bell, J. E. *Projective Techniques* New York: Longman, Green, 1948.

Bowen, Barbara. An extension of the Mosaic test designed to increase its prognostic value. *J. proj. Tech.*, 1954, *18*, 5-16.

Carr, Gwen, L. Mosaic differences in non-institutionalized retarded children. *Amer. J. ment. Def.*, 1958, *62*, 908-911.

Colm, Hanna. The value of projective methods in the psychological examination of children: the Mosaic test in conjunction with the Rorschach and Binet tests. *Rorschach Res. Exch., J. proj. Tech.*, 1948, *12*, 216-233.

Diamond, B. L., & Schmale, H. The Mosaic test. An evaluation of its clinical application. *Amer. J. Orthopsychiat.*, 1944, *14*, 237-250.

Dorken, H., Jr. The Mosaic test: review. *J. proj. Tech.*, 1952, *16*, 287-296.

Dorken, H., Jr. The Mosaic test: a second review. *J. proj. Tech.*, 1956, *20*, 164-171.

Hansen, I. The Mosaic test as a diagnostic indicator of schizophrenia. Unpublished master's thesis, University of the Pacific, 1954.

Himmelweit, H. T., & Eysenck, H. J. An experimental analysis of the Mosaic projection test. *Brit. J. Med. Psychol.*, 1945, *20*, 283-294.

Horne, E. P., & Lane, W. P. Constancy or creativity in patterning Mosaic test performance. *J. genet. Psychol.*, 1960, *63*, 165-170.

Johnson, T. F. The function of the Mosaic test in clinical practice. *J. gen. Psychol.*, 1957, *56*, 51-58.

Kerr, M. The validity of the mosaic test. *Amer. J. Orthopsychiat.*, 1939, *9*, 232-236.

Levin, M. L. Validation of the Lowenfeld Mosaic Test. *J. consult. Psychol.*, 1956, *20*, 239-248.

Lowenfeld, Margaret. The mosaic test. *Amer. J. Orthopsychiat.*, 1949, *19*, 537-550.

Lowenfeld, Margaret. *The Lowenfeld Mosaic Test.* London: Newman Neame, 1954.

Maher, B., & Martin, A. Mosaic productions in cerebro-arteriosclerosis. *J. consult. Psychol.*, 1954, *18*, 40-42.

McCullough, T., & Girdner, J. Use of the Lowenfeld Mosaic test with mental defectives. *Amer. J. ment. Def.*, 1949, *53*, 486-496.

Metz, J. R. A method for measuring aspects of ego strength. *J. proj. Tech.*, 1961, *25*, 457-470.

Pascal, G. R. Gestalt functions: the Bender-Gestalt, Mosaic, and World tests. In Brower, B. & Abt, L. (Eds.). *Progress in Clinical Psychology,* Vol. I. New York: Grune and Stratton, 1952, chapt. 11.

Pelz, K., Pike, F., & Ames, Louise B. A proposed battery of childhood tests for discriminating between different levels of intactness of functions in elderly subjects. *J. genet. Psychol.*, 1962, *100*, 23-40.

Reiman, Gertrude, M. The Mosaic test: its applicability and validity. *Amer. J. Orthopsychiat.*, 1950, *20*, 600-616.

Rioch, Margaret, J. The mosaic test as a diagnostic instrument and as a technique for illustrating intellectual disorganization. *J. proj. Tech.*, 1954, *18*, 89-94.

Shotwell, Anna, M., & Lawrence, E. S. Mosaic patterns of institutionalized mental defectives. *Amer. J. ment. Def.*, 1951, *56*, 161-168.

Stewart, Ursula, & Leland, Lorraine, A. American versus English mosaics. *J. proj. Tech.*, 1952, *16*, 246-248.

Stewart, Ursula, & Leland, Lorraine, A. Lowenfeld mosaics made by first grade children. *J. proj. Tech.*, 1955, *19*, 62-66.

Stewart, Ursula, Leland, Lorraine, & Strieter, Edith. Mosaic patterns of eighth grade children. *J. proj. Tech.*, 1957, *21*, 73-79.

Walker, R. N. Children's mosaic designs: a normative and validating study of the Lowenfeld mosaic test. Unpublished doctoral dissertation, University of Minnesota, 1957.

Wertham, F. The mosaic test: technique and psychopathological deductions. In Abt, L. E., & Bellak, L. (Eds.). *Projective Psychology: Clinical Approaches to the Total Personality.* New York: Knopf, 1950.

Wertham, F., & Golden, Lili. A differential diagnostic method of integrating Mosaics and colored block designs. *Amer. J. Psychiat.*, 1941, *98*, 124-131.

Wideman, H. Development and initial validation of an objective scoring method for the Lowenfeld Mosaic Test. *J. proj. Tech.*, 1955, *19*, 177-191.

Zucker, Louise. The clinical significance of the Mosaic and Rorschach methods. *Amer. J. Psychother.*, 1950, *4*, 473-474.

Symbols: *Kahn Test of Symbol Arrangement (KTSA)*

Abidin, R. R. KTSA sorting norms for school age children. *J. clin. Psychol.*, 1966, *22*, 85-90.

Abidin, R. R. KTSA symbolization norms for school age children: interpretive notes. Unpublished manuscript, Lackland AFB, 1965.

Anderson, L., & Clack, G. S. Interscorer reliability and the KTSA. Unpublished manuscript, Lackland AFB, 1966.

Craddick, R., & Stern, M. Note on the scorer reliability of the KTSA. *J. clin. Psychol.*, 1965, *21*, 197.

Fils, D. H. Comparative performance of schizophrenics and normals on an object symbol arrangement test. Unpublished doctoral dissertation, University of Southern California, 1950.

Fink, H. H., & Kahn, T. C. A comparison of normal and emotionally ill children on the KTSA. *J. educ. Res.*, 1959, *53*, 35-36.

Hammer, E. F. Expressive aspects of projective drawings. In Hammer, E. F. (Ed.). *The Clinical Application of Projective Drawings*. Springfield, Ill.: Charles C Thomas, 1958.

Harvey, O. J., Hunt, D. E., & Schroder, H. G. *Conceptual Systems and Personality Organization*. New York: Wiley, 1961.

Hedlund, J. L., & Mills, D. H. Cross validation of the KTSA with a psychiatric population. *J. clin. Psychol.*, 1964, *20*, 100-103.

Hill, L. K., & Latham, W. R., (Eds.). *Kahn Test of Symbol Arrangement*. Revised edition (mimeo). Lackland AFB, Texas, 1962.

Kahn, T. C. Manual for the Kahn test of symbol arrangement. Beverly Hills: Western Psychological Service, 1949 (revised, 1953).

Kahn, T. C. Comparative performance of psychotics with brain damage and non-psychotics on an original symbol arrangement test. Unpublished doctoral dissertation. University of Southern California, 1950.

Kahn, T. C. An original test of symbol arrangement validated on organic psychotics. *J. consult. Psychol.*, 1951, *5*, 439-444.

Kahn, T. C. Cross validation of the organic brain pathology scale for a test of symbol arrangement. *J. consult. Psychol.*, 1955, *19*, 130.

Kahn, T. C. Kahn test of symbol arrangement: administration and scoring. *Percept. mot. Skills*, 1956, *6*, 299-334 (suppl. no. 4).

Kahn, T. C. The Kahn test of symbol arrangement: clinical manual. *Percept. mot. Skills.*, 1957, *7*, 97-168 (suppl. no. 1).

Kahn, T. C. Auxiliary Evaluation Guide for use with Kahn test of symbol arrangement. Psychological test specialists, 1960.

Kahn, T. C., & Giffen, M. B. *Psychological Techniques in Diagnosis and Evaluation*. New York: Pergamon Press, 1960.

Kahn, T. C., Ferriman, M., & Ferraro, C. The use of the KTSA in differentiating between normals, neurotics, character disorders, borderline schizophrenics, and psychotics. Unpublished manuscript, Wright-Patterson AFB, 1956.

Kahn, T. C., Harter, H., Rider, P., & Lum, M. D. Reliability and validity of the KTSA as a technique in screening schizophrenics, psychotics with brain damage, and non-psychotics. Unpublished manuscript, Wright-Patterson AFB, 1957.

Kenny, J. A. Maladjusted children: a comparison of 216 normal and maladjusted children on the basis of their performance on psychological tests. Unpublished doctoral dissertation, Johannes Guttenberg University, Mainz, Germany, 1962.

L'Abate, L., Boelling, G. M., Hutton, R., & Mathews, D. L., Jr. The diagnostic usefulness of four potential tests of brain damage. *J. consult. Psychol.*, 1962, *26*, 479.

L'Abate, L., & Craddick, R. A. The Kahn test of symbol arrangement (KTSA): a critical review. *J. clin. Psychol.*, 1965, *21*, 115-135.

L'Abate, L., Vogler, R. E., Friedman, W. H., & Chused, T. The diagnostic usefulness of two tests of brain damage. *J. clin. Psychol.*, 1963, *19*, 87-91.

Murphy, P. D., Ferriman, M. R., & Bolinger, R. W. The Kahn test of symbol arrangement as an aid to psychodiagnosis. *J. consult. Psychol.*, 1957, *21*, 503-505.

Theiner, E. C. Differences on abstract thought processes as a function of sex. *J. gen. Psychol.*, 1965, *73*, 285-290.

Theiner, E. C., & Giffen, M. B. A comparison of abstract thought processes among three cultures. In McKenzie, R. E. (Ed.). *Proceedings of the 4th Annual Conference of AF Clinical Psychologists.* Brooks AFB, Texas: USAF SAM, 1963.

White, P. O., & McLeod, H. W. A multiple discriminant analysis comparing psychotic, neurotic, and character disorder patients on the Kahn test of symbol arrangement. *Ontario Psychol. Assoc. Quart.*, 1963, *26*, 1-5.

Whittick, A. *Symbols, Signs, and Their Meaning.* Massachusetts: C. T. Branford, 1960.

Wyman, B. A. The effect of sex differences, masculine-feminine interests, and opposite sex roles on performance on the Kahn test of symbol arrangement. Unpublished master's thesis, New Mexico State University, New Mexico, 1963.

Expressive Motor Activity: Drawing Completion Techniques

Ames, Louise, B., & Hellersberg, E. G. The Horn-Hellersberg test: responses of three to eleven year old children. *Rorschach Res. Exch. J. proj. Tech.*, 1949, *13*, 415-432.

Ames, Louise, B., & Ilg, Frances. *Mosaic Patterns of American Children.* New York: Harper & Row, 1962.

Aronfreed, J. M. Moral behavior and sex identity. In Miller, D. R. & Swanson, G. E. (Eds.). *Inner Conflict and Defense.* New York: Holt, 1960. Pp. 177-193.

Bauer, L. Erfahrungen mit dem Warteggtest auf unserer Kinderstation. *Nervenarzt.*, 1952, *23*, 52-55.

Bell, J. E. *Projective Techniques.* New York: Longman, Green, 1948. Pp. 406-409.

Bell, J. E. The case of Gregor-psychological test data. *Rorschach Res. Exch. J. proj. Tech.*, 1949, *13*, 155-205.

Bochnik, H. J. Tests unter alkoholbelastung. II. Wartegg-Zeichentest und psychiatrische Diagnostik. *Z. diagnost. Psychol.*, 1954, *2*, 33-55.

Engel, Illona, M. A factor analytic study of items from five masculinity-femininity tests. *Dissert. Abstr.*, 1962, 307-308.

Erikson, E. H. Sex differences in the play configuration of preadolescents. *Amer. J. Orthopsychiat.*, 1951, *21*, 667-692.

Franck, Kate. Preference for sex symbols and their personality correlates. *Genet. Psychol. Monogr.*, 1946, *33*, 73-123.

Franck, Kate. Franck Drawing completion test: preliminary manual. Melborne, Australia: Australian Counsel for Educational Research (undated, about 1952).

Franck, Kate. Manual for completion test (masculinity-femininity scale). Berkeley, Calif.: E. S. Mimopolous, 1949 (mimeo). Reproduced by Lansky, L., 1958.

Franck, Kate, & Rosen, E. A projective test of masculinity-femininity. *J. consult. Psychol.*, 1949, *13*, 247-256.

Fluckiger, F., Tripp, C., & Weinberg, G. A review of experimental research in graphology, 1933-1960. *Psychol. Rep. Percept. mot. Skills*, 1961, *12*, 67-90.

Gough, H. G. Identifying psychological femininity. *Educ. psychol. Measmt.*, 1952, *12*, 427-439.

Gleser, Goldine, C. Review of Kinget drawing completion test. In Buros, O. K. (Ed.). *Fifth Mental Measurements Yearbook*. New Jersey: Gryphon Press, 1959. Pp. 130.

Greenstein, J. Father characteristics and sex-role identification in a delinquent group. *Dissert. Abstr.*, 1961, *22*, 1716.

Hellersberg, Elizabeth, F. The Horn-Hellersberg Test and adjustment to reality. *Amer. J. Orthopsychiat.*, 1945, *15*, 690-710.

Hellersberg, Elizabeth, F. *The Individual's Relation to Reality in Our Culture*. Springfield, Ill.: Charles C Thomas, 1950.

Hellersberg, Elizabeth, F. The Horn-Hellersberg Test. *Monogr. Soc. Res. Child Developm.*, 1953, *16*, 138-170, 214-316.

Hellersberg, Elizabeth, F. The Horn-Hellersberg Test. Manual (mimeo), 1961, (3rd edition).

Hippius, M. Graphischer Ausdruck von Gefühlen. Z. *Psychol.*, 1936, *51*, 257.

Jaskar, J. O. Levels of body image assessment of hospitalized and non-hospitalized subjects. Unpublished doctoral dissertation, University of Portland, 1962.

Kass, W. Review of Kinget drawing completion test. In Buros, O. K. (Ed.). *Fifth Mental Measurements Yearbook*. New Jersey: Gryphon Press, 1959.

Kooser, E. de T. The relation of masculinity-femininity orientation to self-report anxiety. Unpublished master's thesis, University of North Carolina, 1955.

Kinget, G. Marian. *The Drawing Completion Test*. New York: Grune and Stratton, 1952.

Kinget, G. Marian. The drawing completion test. In Hammer, E. F. (Ed.). *The Clinical Application of Projective Techniques*. Springfield, Ill.: Charles C Thomas, 1958. Pp. 344-364.

Krout, Johanna. Symbol Elaboration Test (SET): the reliability and validity of a new projective technique. *Psychol. Monogr.*, 1950, *64*, 1-67.

Lansky, L. Mechanisms of defense: sex identity and defenses against aggression. In Miller, D. & Swanson, G. E. (Eds.). *Inner Conflict and Defense*. New York: Holt, 1960. Pp. 272-288.

Lansky, L. The stability over time and under stress of conscious and unconscious masculinity-femininity. *Amer. Psychol.*, 1962, *17*, 302-303.

Lansky, L. The family structure also affects the model: sex-role identification in parents of preschool children. *Merrill-Palmer Quart.*, 1964, *10*, 39-50.

Lansky, L. References to the Franck drawing completion test. Unpublished manuscript, 1965.

McCaulley, Mary, H. Dimensions of masculinity-femininity in relation to field dependence, dogmatism, and other estimates of perceptual-cognitive differentiation. Unpublished doctoral dissertation, Temple University, 1964.

Murray, H. A. *Explorations in Personality*. New York: Oxford University Press, 1938.

Olson, J. T. The test-retest reliability of the Kinget drawing completion test. Unpublished master's thesis, Fresno State College, Fresno, California, 1955.

Pikunas, J. Operant conditioning effects upon drawing content. *J. proj. Tech. Pers. Assess.*, 1966, *30*, 172-176.

Pikunas, J., & Carberry, H. Standardization of the graphoscopic scale: the content of children's drawings. *J. clin. Psychol.*, 1961, *17*, 297-301.

Pintner, R., & Toops, H. A. A drawing completion test. *J. applied Psychol.*, 1918, *2*, 164-173.

Reed, M. R. The masculinity-femininity dimension in normal and psychotic subjects. *J. abnorm. soc. Psychol.*, 1957, *55*, 289-294.

Sander, F. Experimentelle Ergebnisse der Gestaltpsychologie. *Berlin Kongr. Exp. Psychol.*, 1928, 23-38.

Sanford, R. N., & others. *Physique, Personality, and Scholarship*. Wash., D. C. National Res. Council, *Soc. Res. Child Develpm.*, 1943.

Scarpellini, C. Diagnosis della personalitá col reattivo di realizzazione grafica—dal reattivo di disegno di E. Wartegg (WZT). *Contrib. Inst. Psicol.*, 1962, *26*, 1-83.

Shepler, B. F. A comparison of masculinity-feminity measures. *J. consult. Psychol.*, 1951, *15*, 484-486.

Takala, M. Studies of the Wartegg drawing completion test. *Ann. Acad. Scient. Finl.*, 1964, *131*, 1-112.

Takala, M., & Hakkarainen. M. Über Faktorenstruktur und Validität des Wartegg-Zeichentests. *Ann. Acad. Scient. Finl.*, 1953, *81* (ser. B), 1-95.

Teepen, Nancy. Sibling relationships in sex-role identification. Unpublished master's thesis, Ohio State University, 1963.

Wartegg, E. Gestaltung und Charakter. *Z. angew. Psychol. Beih.*, 1939, *84*.

Weitzenhoffer, A. M. Hypnotic susceptibility as related to masculinity-femininity. *Dissert. Abstr.*, 1957, *17*, 1397.

Winer, F. The relationship of certain attitudes toward the mother to sex-role identity. *Dissert. Abstr.*, 1962, *22*, 4416.

Acknowledgments

Hellersberg, Elizabeth, F. The Horn-Hellersberg Test and adjustment to reality, *Amer. J. Orthopsychiat.*, 1945, *15*.

Lowenfeld, Margaret. In Stern, E. *Handbuch der Klinischen Psychologie, Band I. Die Tests in der Klinischen Psychologie* Abteilung II. Rashen, Switzerland, Fig. 1, 665.

Szondi, Lipot. *Experimentelle Diagnose der Triebe*, 6th ed. Berne, Switzerland: Hans Huber Publishers, 1966.

Wartegg, E. In Kinget, G. Marian. *The Drawing Completion Test*. New York: Grune and Stratton, 1952, ii.

APPLICATIONS

This seventh, and concluding, part of the book consists of four chapters. Two of them are concerned with issues involved in the employment of projective methods in the clinical setting, while the other two chapters focus on research applications of the various techniques.

Dr. Klopfer's contribution (Chapter 16) deals with the issue of multi-level interpretation via projective methods and how it can be interlaced with data available from other, non-test sources. He is concerned with appropriate communication of test results and makes a plea for the avoidance of high-order abstractions in interpretation. Prediction should be close to the behavioral level and not excessively speculative; i.e., close to the data from which it is evolved. Particularly valuable is the analysis of the combinations of the several levels of awareness with respect to specific behavioral qualities. Illustrative material is also offered.

Although not specifically concerned with projective methods, Dr. Levine's chapter is concerned with a fundamental question in a variety of clinical settings: to test or not to test. From the vantage point of decision theory the author attempts to give some answers to the crucial question. Related is the implication of the irrelevance of conventional tests of reliability to projectives, and the criterion of the additional information given by the test, which would not be otherwise obtained, emerges.

Research applications are the main focus of Dr. Singer's critical but constructive chapter. In the first part of the chapter, the author surveys a wide range of studies—those reporting research on the projective methods themselves, those concerned with disturbance and personality change, and the research involved in testing personality theories. In the second part of the chapter, the author presents a critical examination of projective methods as research tools and discusses the use of these methods in the study of imagination and in the study of the psychoanalytic theory of thought and delay of gratification. The chapter concludes with some interesting "projections" concerning new directions in the use of these techniques in research settings.

Finally, a related chapter (by Rabin) is concerned with the issue of "custom-making" projective techniques for special research and clinical purposes. Following a discussion of the types of innovation employed by various workers who have been able to vary the projective theme, the research literature is examined in an effort to elicit some clues and, possibly, some principles underlying the process of devising and adapting projective methods for special or specific purposes. There is a degree of convergence between this and the preceding chapter in the direction of more useful and extensive utilization of projectives in the research endeavor concerned with personality in all its complexity.

16

Integration Of Projective Techniques in the Clinical Case Study

WALTER G. KLOPFER

The Purpose of the Clinical Case Study

It is regrettable that as clinical psychologists, so many of us acquire consummate skill in detecting the fine points of interpretation of psychological tests, reading between every line in an interview, and splitting every diagnostic hair without having any clear guidelines as to what to do with this information and what the purpose of the evaluation should really be. As scientist-clinicians, we have a nagging curiosity which generates an interest in doing the case study for its own sake, because we hope that it will help us to gain a broader and deeper understanding of any given personality and build up our apperceptive reservoir. However, in looking at the matter somewhat more practically, we see that there are really three parties involved in the clinical case study whose needs must be considered and somewhat met if the whole project is to be worthwhile. These are the examiner, the patient, and the reader of the clinical case study. Each one of these has a stake in the enterprise although each may perceive his interests in a somewhat different manner. In addition to his rational goals, the examiner, for instance, may want to use the clinical case study as a way of communicating a certain impression to the reader: he might like the reader to consider him erudite, sophisticated, agreeable, gregarious, or intellectually stimulating. It may be that the clinical case study will serve as a political instrument, designed to sell a particular point of view to anyone who may come across it. It is possible that interprofessional or intraprofessional relationships which are currently tense will be attacked indirectly through a description of certain kinds of causality and the prediction of certain outcomes on the basis of the case study.

The reader of the report, too, may have his understanding of the matter obscured by irrelevant considerations. For him, the examiner

The writer is indebted to William Singer, Vincent Glaudin and Gordon Filmer-Bennett for their suggestions regarding this chapter.

and/or the techniques employed may be on trial; the theory implicit in the report may be either consonant with the reader's point of view or it may not; he may want to use the study as a way of confirming his own views and defending them to some higher authority.

Often lost in the shuffle is the third party, the patient. Both the reader and the examiner may get so interested in their own intellectual byplay and their power struggle that the real question of contributing something tangible and significant to the patient's welfare may be partially lost. The patient has extremely ambivalent feelings about whether he wants to be understood or not. On the one hand, it would seem that the more that is known about him by the professional people involved in his case, the more efficiently they will be able to bring about some happy resolution of his problems. On the other hand, the patient is far from sure that these people will be able to make the kind of use of the information that will enable them to constructively help him in ways in which he is willing to be helped. There is an unresolved question of whether they can be trusted. Perhaps he is enamored of his defenses and loathe to discard them in favor of some unknown, frightening vulnerability. This applies particulary to that part of the case study which is based upon projective techniques. By their very nature, projective methods elicit material that the individual might not be willing to reveal about himself if he had more complete conscious control over what he was communicating; therefore, we are deliberately attempting to get under his guard, reach inside of his character armor, and tease out aspects of his personality. Sometimes we may be pitting ourselves against his conscious will. In order to justify this procedure, we must be very sure that our purpose is genuinely constructive and that the information given will be truly used for the patient's benefit. This implies consideration of the impact of the report upon the primary and the secondary readers. Just as there is little reason to cast pearls before swine, there is no point in presenting information concerning a patient's unconscious life to people who are uninterested or unsympathetic to this view of personality; neither should we supply such information to those who would use it to make unjustified administrative decisions or who would subject the patient to confrontations that might shame and humiliate him.

A clinical study should be a document designed to enable the examiner to use his skill to integrate the results of projective and other methods of personality assessment and to communicate them in a way which is correct not only scientifically, but tactically and politically as well. This requires the use of proper language, the censoring of some material, and the enhancing of those points which are most pertinent to the administrative or clinical problems under consideration. The clinical case study should be made available only to those persons who can make proper use of it in the light of the above considerations. If some part of this material or all of it is to be presented to the patient, this consideration should certainly influence the format of the report. Since it is not customary to give patients written copies of their own case study, however, this point will not ordinarily be an issue.

The next question that might be raised is that of the purpose of the case study in terms of the explicit content, irrespective of what is involved from the viewpoints of the various interested parties. It would seem that there are three different purposes:

1. The understanding of the patient. This is, of course, the most common purpose of the psychological report and the one that most readily comes to mind. The understanding must originate from the examiner, who is thus enabled to communicate something about the person which is meaningful. Obviously if this understanding is to be transmitted to the readers of the clinical case study, there must be a common frame of reference, which must manifest itself not only in such obvious tools as words and technical terms, but also in the basic assumptions made, the theory assumed, and the connecting links alluded to.

One might make the further assumption that the ultimate purpose of the clinical case study is to give the understanding of the patient back to him. The understanding that is gained from interviews and objective personality inventories is often already available to the patient, since he ordinarily has conscious control of the material he provides by the use of these techniques. Thus the conscious material already present in the patient which is transmitted to the examiner and subsequently back to the patient will come as no great surprise. The reader will gain little more information from these sources than is already apparent to the patient. In contrast, the understanding of the patient which comes from the examiner's use of projective methods is often not consciously evident to the patient himself. It might be ultimately of use to the patient if it could be communicated back to him in more rational (consciously acceptable) form during the course of feedback or subsequent psychotherapy. This presumes that making the patient aware of those motives of which he is unaware will give him more rational choices to make and enhance his mastery of reality. Thus, the potential therapist can gain information of direct use.

2. The next important purpose of the report is the prediction of future behavior. As the art and science of clinical psychology continue to develop, more and more agencies, institutions, industrial firms, and individuals are looking to the clinical psychologist for concrete help in making decisions. For example, Matarazzo et al (1964) report the use of projective and other techniques of personality assessment as a way of predicting high or low risk of a psychiatric sort for applicants for a metropolitan police force. Obviously this is a very important prediction. Other clinical psychologists are taking chances every day predicting that somebody will or will not be able to function outside of a hospital, be a prospect for surgery, be a good candidate for parole, commit suicide, make

good managerial material, be a good candidate for graduate work in clinical psychology, etc. Previous research with psychological reports (Ullmann, Berkman & Hammister, 1958) has indicated that the value of the clinical case study for prediction is limited by the ambiguity and universality of many of the statements made, implying a lack of courage on the part of examiners in using their data to make forthright predictions. The predictive value of the clinical case study has also been limited by the reluctance of many examiners to give feedback to the patient himself. This reluctance has not been displayed in the field of vocational counseling, wherein test scores regarding interests, aptitudes, achievements, and personality traits are regularly supplied to the counselee as a way of helping him to set more realistic goals for himself and to be aware of some of the forces within him that are likely to sabotage or enhance his efforts. Presumably, the examiner who uses projective tests and who thus possesses a greater range of information that he can help the patient with, can share at least some of it with the party most involved. It seems that sometimes clinical psychologists have a tendency to take over inappropriate medical customs which dictate that a cloak of mystery surrounds the findings of the (witch-doctor) examiner. Much of the information contained in the clinical case study could be of great value to the patient, not necessarily in profoundly changing his personality or immediately producing a shift in his behavior, but at least showing him a map so that he can find his way to his own motives if he wishes and thus make decisions somewhat more clear-sightedly than otherwise.

3. The third purpose of the clinical case study is to serve as a record of the patient's psychological state at a given time. The problem of baseline is an annoying one in clinical research, to say nothing of its being an insurmountable problem in many tasks of clinical evaluation. For example, how can a psychologist accurately answer the question of whether someone has been brain damaged by an accident if there is no baseline data with which to compare the tests given to him following the accident? How can the psychologist judge that a given individual has undergone a change in the direction of abnormality or greater pathology, for the purpose of testifying at a trial when he can say nothing about the patient in his premorbid state? Many diagnostic concepts involve the assumption of "change" and yet our measures are usually cross-sectional. One of the regrettable customs within the mental health professions is that information is frequently not shared and that each examiner feels that only he, because of his allegedly superior diagnostic skill, has any understanding of the patient. Thus, he does not take the trouble to study data painstakingly acquired by other professionals and the patient is not as well understood in terms of the sequence of events that have taken place in his life. Crude baselines such as number of jobs, previous marriages or years of school may be as misleading as they may be helpful. Just as a physician should have a record of previous medical

examinations, and the dentist ought to familiarize himself with a patient's dental history, so should the psychologist consider the patient's history in constructing a clinical case study that can serve as a valuable record of the person's psychological state at a given time and place, and under a given set of circumstances.

The Extent of the Clinical Case Study

One of the basic fallacies in clinical evaluation and clinical research is that there is such a thing as a "basic" or "true" personality. Frequently, one can see the spectacle of a clinician comparing the results of various tests from various modalities together with the patient's life history and the results of interviews, trying to decide which of these is "correct." It is almost as though he were saying "Will the real personality of patient X please stand up!" This is a shallow and dangerous game to play. In contrast, the present author would like to make the assumption that behavior is always basically consistent and that every piece of behavior that we collect during the process of acquiring data for the clinical case study must be integrated into a conceptual framework concerning the patient if we are to come up with anything resembling the truth. The only way that the three blind men can tell what the elephant looks like is to compare notes and see whether they can arrive at a superordinate hypothesis concerning the nature of the beast. Within this chapter, an attempt will be made to specify levels of personality by using the multilevel framework first presented by Leary in his book, *The Interpersonal Diagnosis of Personality* (1957). One slight modification will be made in Leary's system based upon research which has been carried out since that time. The levels to be alluded to are the following:

Level I. The level which Leary called the level of "public communication." It is operationally defined as the level at which an individual is perceived by significant others using ranking techniques. Other ways of measuring it include having persons well known to the patient fill out adjective check lists on him, describe him, be interviewed about him, or be observed in interaction with him and then questioned. This may seem to be a strange level to discuss in a chapter focusing upon the use of projective techniques in a clinical case study; however, some of the research reviewed in this book indicates quite clearly that projective methods may sometimes lead to correct prediction of Level I behavior. Conscious self-report on the part of the patient is, of course, distorted by social desirability factors, but since the interpretation of projective tests is done by others, the relationship between projective tests predictions and predictions based upon direct Level I measures is often higher than might be expected. An example of this is given in the study by McGreevey (1962).

Level Ia. The level of public image perceived by the patient himself. This is a level not mentioned by Leary; it has been discovered by research carried on by the present author. Previously it has been assumed that the best estimate that a given patient could make of his public image was his perception of himself. Thus, when he describes his own traits as being radically different from those described by significant others it was assumed that he was lacking in social awareness and consequently likely to elicit inappropriate and confusing feedback from other people. However, it was felt that perhaps an individual might make a better prediction of his public image if asked to do so directly. In an ongoing research program by Warren and Klopfer (1965) it was discovered that small groups of subjects who knew each other well were able to predict their own Level I image quite correctly when asked specifically to do so and that this prediction of Level I (herein called Level Ia) was not significantly different from their true Level I; whereas, their conscious self-concept (Level II) was significantly different from Level I.

Level II. The level of conscious self-concept. This is the level, of course, at which people perceive themselves and is operationally defined as their performance on the Interpersonal Adjective Checklist. It can also be measured by objective personality inventories, by direct interviews, and as will be demonstrated below, by certain so-called projective techniques, such as the Sentence Completion Test. This level has to serve as a reference point within which one can study the degree of distance from awareness of those thoughts and feelings revealed under projective conditions. Since the controversy concerning the level of awareness of the material elicited by projective techniques rages to this day, (witness for example Murstein's contention that the TAT measures nothing but what can be elicited in an interview [1963]), it is well to be able to specify this level for the purpose of making a comparison between it and others more public or private.

Level III. The level of "private symbolization," operationally defined by Leary as the level measured by projective tests. This is a rather broad concept, but he narrows it down somewhat. For example, in the case of the TAT he distinguishes the TAT "hero" and the TAT "other" levels. The assumption here is that even though both of these are slightly distant from awareness, the feelings and thoughts attributed to the "other" figures in the TAT are somewhat more distant from the conscious feelings of the patient than those feelings attributed to the central or "hero" figure. This is somewhat akin to Tomkins' (1947) "distanciation theory" first enunciated in his book some years ago. Within fantasy there may be further distinction between that which is manifest and that which is inferred (latent).

The contention which will be elaborated upon in the present chapter is that the clinical case study can only be considered complete, can only be of value in terms of the objectives enunciated above, if some attempt is made to measure each of the above levels and to integrate the total picture into something coherent, with clearly defined predictive qualities. In order to illustrate the importance of the multi-level schema, the following illustration is given:

First, take a single personality trait—aggression. Let us further crudely dichotomize aggression by calling the overt presence or manifestation of aggression plus (+), and calling the absence of overt or manifest aggression, minus (−). This violates the actual measuring technique, since we think of a continuum, but this kind of dichotomy will serve for present purposes. Let us further assume that we have only three levels that we want to measure, namely Level I, the trait as viewed by significant others; Level II, the trait as viewed by the individual himself; and Level III, the trait as judged from projective tests. This then leads to eight different combinations. In each case, the first symbol will be that measured by Level I, the second measured by Level II, and the third measured by Level III. These eight combinations will be briefly discussed in terms of the interpretation that would be assigned to each in connection with this one trait.

A. +++ This is a patient who demonstrates overt aggression as viewed by other people, as admitted to by himself, and as revealed by projective tests. We may assume that he is an unusually aggressive person, that this aggression is not alien to him, that he may perhaps even possess more of it than is overtly expressed, and that there is no particularly severe conflict about its expression. He may make others uncomfortable.

B. ++− In this instance the aggression is perceived by others as well as the individual himself but is not manifest by judgments based or projective tests. Here we may assume that since aggression is not present at the fantasy level that either the individual expresses all the aggression he needs to and gets it out of his system, or else that he may perhaps be demonstrating more aggression than is needed by him in terms of his own value system. It may be that he is part of a subculture in which the presence of aggression is socially sanctioned and even strongly desired, and that therefore he has trained himself to behave and think of himself in this manner.

C. +−+ This is an individual whose aggression is manifest at the behavioral or public level as well as at the fantasy level, but he himself does not admit it. This is the fairly typical picture of a neurotic individual who has been trained to consider aggression as an evil act, so that taking it into awareness would arouse giult. However, the fact that he still possesses it and that it influences his behavior is quite evident to others behaviorally and projectively even though it may be obscure to the individual himself.

D. +−− In this case the aggression is behaviorly manifest although denied by the individual and absent in fantasy. This may mean that the individual, in terms of pecking order, is the most aggressive person in a generally passive group. It may mean that he is in a situation where he has learned to behave in a pseudo-aggressive manner to conform to the "rules," either explicit or tacit. Perhaps he is a member of the Marines or some other group in which this kind of behavior is absolutely essential. However, he does not find it necessary to deceive himself and his projective tests also reveal the lack of genuine motivation for his behavior.

E. −++ This is an individual who does not show behavioral aggression that other people can see, but he deems himself aggressive and also has shown aggression at the fantasy level. Here we may be dealing with an instance of consciously controlled aggression in which the individual realizes that the unrestrained expression of aggression may alienate and antagonize other people, and has chosen to inhibit or control these tendencies. However, they continue to seethe within him and he is very much aware of them, not finding it necessary to delude himself.

F. −+− This is a case of an individual who shows very limited fantasy aggression but still deems himself aggressive. This may be because he is in a situation where being aggressive is socially sanctioned and desired, and so, in wanting to be an accepted member of the group, he has managed to convince himself that he is aggressive; however, his basic lack of aggression as demonstrated by fantasy is transmitted into behavior, and he is no more able to delude other people than he is to delude the judge of the projective material.

G. −−+ This is a fairly standard picture of the neurotically repressed individual who is unable to express aggression or to even permit it full access to awareness, but who turbulently bubbles with it underneath the surface as revealed by the material in the projective tests. The aggression may rise close to the surface but is systematically excluded from self-concept.

H. −−− Here we have an individual who shows no manifest aggression behaviorly, consciously, or projectively. One may well ask what happened to his aggression. Fortunately, Leary has another level to account for this kind of behavior which he calls Level IV. It is alluded to here only parenthetically because no operational definition of it has been provided. Level IV is the level of the "unexpressed unaware" which is described as material which is systematically excluded at all other levels. Whether the patient with a picture like this is really lacking in aggression or whether the aggression is so intensely ego-alien that it has to be excluded even from projective material is, of course, hard to say.

From the above illustration it can be seen that projective material is most meaningful when looked at within the context of the other sources of information. When projective material is used alone, and when the question of whether we are predicting overt behavior, conscious self-concept or merely fantasy, is left unanswered, the reader may legitimately feel that we are confounding him with our ambiguity. Of what earthly use is it to talk about "latent homosexuality" or "masturbatory anxiety" or "confusion about sexual role" when it is completely unclear whether we are talking about one or the other of these different levels? Take for example the matter of "latent homosexuality." Are we talking about a person who is extremely effeminate and makes readily discernible passes at other men and whose latency consists only in the fact that he does not actually engage in anal coitus? Or are we talking about someone who has never engaged in homosexual contacts but who is very much preoccupied with fantasies and ideas and wishes concerning homosexuality which cause him excruciating anxiety? Or are we talking about someone who merely gets confused about the sex of the figures in the Rorschach and TAT, and who has never had a conscious thought or feeling concerning homosexuality in his life? It may be that some clinical psychologists feel that this is a trivial question and that latent homosexuality is latent homosexuality, no matter at what level you find it. However, with this point of view the present author would take violent exception. Much of the difficulty that clinical psychologists have gotten themselves into with communities and governmental agencies is due to this very kind of slovenliness in making predictions. I surely would not want to be evaluated for an important government job or denied access to classified information solely because of someone's interpretation of my projective material. Not enough is known at this point concerning the predictive efficiency of symbolic material to make such use of projective data warranted. However, if the fantasy material is integrated with the objective and behavioral material, we may then be able to come up with an interpretation and prediction which has considerably more justification and reliability.

This argument also applies to the question of whether we should use "blind" interpretations of projective material as part of the case study. I think this would be a legitimate procedure for training purposes, for research purposes, or perhaps for the purpose of playing some kind of power game. However, if our purpose involves recommendations concerning the fate of human beings and of groups of human beings, it would seem that a less risky approach would be indicated. As illustrated by the above example, a given piece of projective behavior may be interpreted differentially, depending on the context within which it is found in comparison to other levels. If we consider that in the above illustration only one trait is employed, and even that trait is crudely dichotomized, the number of combinations and permutations that are possible when we compare projective with other materials, becomes extremely large.

Thus, it seems that the scope of the clinical case study should be fairly broad, although not necessarily long. The personality assessor should take it as his task to say something concerning the individual's interpersonal behavior and his perception thereof (Levels I and Ia), his conscious view of himself and how similar or different it is from the above (Level II), and his fantasies (Level III). Every single aspect of his personality can be discussed at all three levels. His relationship with each one of the significant people in his life can be described in a multi-level fashion. For example, it would be possible to say that he behaves timidly towards his wife, considers himself on good terms with her, but has fantasies in which he behaves quite aggressively towards her. Thus we are comparing the same relationship at three different levels. Similarly, we can talk about his attitude towards his work. It may be that he behaves as though he did not care whether he did well in college, that he says he wants to do well in college, and his fantasies reveal his basic alienation from intellectual pursuits. Any given point of interpretation made in the clinical case study and specifically, any contribution made to the clinical study by projective material can be presented in a sophisticated and integrated manner as illustrated above. Thus it is bound to be of much greater value than the usual naive presentation of projective data as either fantasy or reality, with the reader left to choose and to integrate it with other data as best he can.

What Level Do Projective Techniques Measure?

Leary (1957) makes the bland assumption that projective techniques measure a single level which he referred to as Level III, or the level of "private symbolization"; however, it is the judgment of the present writer that this assumption will not bear close scrutiny and that in fact, projective techniques are extremely complex in terms of the levels that they measure and the kind of prediction that can be made from their data. In order to illustrate the complexity involved, two projective tests will be discussed in detail and some allusion will be made to others. The first that will be taken up is the Rorschach test.

The Rorschach. The Rorschach consists of two kinds of stimulus elements which lead to different sorts of predictions. First, there are those stimulus elements that can be verified by common consent. These include color, shading, and form. Unless the subject perceiving the blots is color-blind, he will know that some blots are black and white, others contain red, and still others contain many different colors. Consequently, whatever the significance of color reactions may be, the prediction made from such reactions will be in terms of an individual's reaction to commonly experienced aspects of the external environment. Thus, the hypotheses regarding color made in the Rorschach literature are all at Level I; in other words, predictions of publicly observable behavior. This is a reasonable hypothesis and if color reactions cannot lead to experimentally verifiable Level I hypotheses, the experimenter is justified in considering this as evidence questioning the validity of that aspect of the Rorschach test.

The matter is somewhat different in regards to shading. Although shading nuances are a commonly perceived aspect of the Rorschach stimulus situation, the stimulus involved is sufficiently subtle so that not all subjects perceive them. It may be that some people looking at the blots are not sufficiently perceptive, sensitive or keen-sighted; hence, they will not be aware of this particular stimulus property of the blot and not respond accordingly. As a result, the clinician tends to be less explicit in talking about what responses to shading stimuli mean. Even though they sound at first blush like Level I hypotheses, (the individual is "sensitive" or "sensuous" or "aware of the nuances of the environment") yet there is a careful avoidance of translating such interpretations into directly observable behavior. There are other kinds of shading reactions (k, K, FK), placed on the left side of the psychogram (Klopfer et al, 1954), to which no behavioral significance whatever is attached—for example, FK. Here the common interpretation in terms of an "introspective inclination on the part of the perceiving subject" certainly is not something that can be clearly translated into behavior or for which Level I criteria can be explicitly formulated. The same thing is true of the KF response commonly alluded to as "free floating undifferentiated anxiety." This term is rather vague and is not operationalized. No one has claimed that factor analytic studies failing to find a relationship between this kind of determinant and something like the Taylor Manifest Anxiety Scale (TMAS) necessarily invalidate either measure. This is because this is not a measure of manifest anxiety, so it is therefore not at all clear what it *is* a measure of. Thus we are forced to conclude that shading is quite unclear in terms of its level significance and this is probably one of the reasons why its interpretation in Rorschach research has always been somewhat obscure.

The measure of perceptual accuracy (or form level) on the other hand, has been a solid basis for making behavioral predictions. For example, the work of McReynolds (1951) indicates that form accuracy can distinguish between people with greater and lesser reality ties. When a subject says that the side large Ds on card VIII look like animals or that the whole of card V looks like a bat or a butterfly, we consider him as having dealt with his world in a realistic manner. It is essentially a question of whether someone calls a table a table or a chair a chair, according to our common agreement on how we label such objects. If an individual were to refer to a table as a chair, or a chair as a table, we would, by means of our democratic system of consensual validation, rule him psychotic and send him to the state hospital, (especially if he hit us with the chair). However, he might have memorized the name "table" for the object usually designated in this manner, and the term "chair" for the object usually designated as such without really believing it privately. This is why it is particularly useful to show him a Rorschach inkblot to which he has had no previously conditioned verbal response. If he looks at the side details on card VIII and calls them "fish," or if he looks at the whole of card V and labels it a "frog," we know that he does not perceive objects, or label them, in a way which is common, and is likely therefore to get himself into difficulty in our society and end up making other people sufficiently uncomfortable so that they will feel that intervention is warranted. We may therefore conclude that form accuracy is an extremely significant aspect of Rorschach interpretation and one from which clear-cut Level I predictions are made. Very few clinical psychologists would make a diagnosis of psychosis on the basis of deviant content alone, unless there were some tangible evidence of the subject's inability to perceive the way others in his society commonly do.

An entirely different frame of reference is involved in connection with movement responses. None of the inkblots typically has been known to move; they do not kiss; they do not kick; they do not have sexual intercourse nor do they fly about the room; and yet all of these actions are commonly attributed to them by perceiving subjects. When these attributes are imputed to the cards we do not regard this as pathological; rather, we talk about the individual using his inner resources in a way that creatively modifies his perception of the environment. Thus it would appear that movement responses are clearly Level III responses since they are measures only of the inner world of the subject, and at best can be labeled fantasy; thus, we might validate the interpretive significance of movement responses by correlating them with TAT material (if the latter is indeed a Level III measure), or with manifest dream content. However, even here the evidence is contradictory. For example, a recent study by Bendick and Klopfer (1964) indicates that both sensory deprivation and motor inhibition, when imposed upon subjects, tend to artificially increase the number of movement responses given to standard Rorschach cards under standard methods of administration. This seems to imply that the external environment does influence the projection of movement onto the blots and thus casts some doubt on the interpretation of movement responses as a reaction to internal stimuli alone. In the past it has been common for theorists to poke fun at the idea of Rorschach movement being related to general movement of a motoric sort. A typical caricature of a paradigm that might be thought up is that a pedometer is to be attached to a subject during the day, and that the amount of walking around he does might be correlated to the amount of movement response he produces on the Rorschach. This kind of design was thought up to ridicule the idea that movement might have a literal kind of significance rather than an attributive significance due to the reaction of the individual to an external stimulus on the basis of his inner creative life. However, after obtaining results such as those of Bendick and Klopfer (1964), this design might not appear quite as ludicrous. It appear that as more and more research with the Rorschach test progresses, the number of areas that are strictly Level III diminish.

Certainly the whole area of "manner of approach" is one which has always been presented in a Level I manner. The hypotheses regarding whole and details that have been presented in standard textbooks such as those of Klopfer, Ainsworth, Klopfer, and Holt (1954), and Beck (1945), are all couched pretty much in Level I terms. When the clinician says that the subject is likely (with an overemphasis on whole responses) to "look upon the situation as a whole," or "deal with life problems in their entirety," or "attack problem-solving in a global, undifferentiated manner," these certainly sound like statements that can be translated into directly observable Level I behavior. Similar statements have been made concerning usual and unusual details and white space (S) responses. In the old days of Rorschach theorizing, when a great deal of attention was paid to Jung's introversion-extratension dichotomy, all sorts of hedging went on in connection with such interpretations. For example, it was assumed that a preponderance of figure-ground reversal in an introversive context would have a meaning different from a similar preponderance in an extratensive context. The oppositionalism was assumed in the former case to be directed "against the self." Whatever was meant by that seems to have been dropped from the current literature and most recent works emphasize figure-ground reversal as having direct behavioral significance and being an analogue to other kinds of figure-ground reversal or oppositional ways of perceiving the world.

When it comes to the area of conventionality or originality, the interpretations are likely to be fairly directly analogous to observable behavior. We refer to people looking at the world the way others do, or having an unusual approach to situations, and we talk about their thought content either as being like that of the average person in their culture, or as being very much unlike it; thus, it would appear that we are not dealing with any mysterious Level III area here, but rather a fairly concrete Level I or II area. The area of content analysis on the other hand is one in which there may be some legitimate doubt. Certainly, it is in the area of symbolization that the interpretations made would seem rather obscure from the viewpoint of either conscious self-concept of public image. The kind of statements that one often finds in reports that are based upon the analysis of content are such as these: "The individual has difficulty with his basic sex identification," "there are indications of latent homosexuality," "there seems to be a basic fear of castration on the part of the perceiving subject," or again, "there is a good deal of bodily preoccupation on the part of the subject." The key word in many of these interpretations seems to be the word "basic." The word "basic" is kind of a weasel word in personality evaluation. It is referred to here as such because it clouds the issue of the level at which we are doing assessment and making predictions. If we say "basic" and somebody says that they cannot see this behavior taking place publicly, then we have a way out and say that of course we did not mean that. If we use this same word "basic" and the subject subsequently denies having this feeling or experience in an interview situation, then we say that we did not mean that either. So by a process of elimination it would appear that what we mean is that this is a Level III phenomenon of which the individual may not be consciously aware. This gets us into our usual bind—we use psychoanalytic kinds of concepts where we can neither really prove nor disprove our allegations. However, even the area of content analysis has become somewhat less mysterious lately. The research in the area of the prediction of aggression on the basis of content analysis carried on by such authors as Elizur (1949), Finney (1955) and Murstein (1956), indicates that frequently aggressive content is the best single predictor of aggressive behavior. This is another shattering blow to those who assumed there was no obvious, tangible connection between projective data and actual behavior. It also tends to cast some doubt on the assumption made over many years that we could only predict behavior from the Rorschach on the basis of such consensually validatable aspects of the blot environment as color, form accuracy, and manner of approach. It appears that the veil of mystery is about to be lifted from the area of content and that here, too, we have a reasonably direct bridge between projective data, public behavior, and possibly conscious thought content.

What shall we then conclude about the Rorschach? The Rorschach seems to be a very multi-level kind of instrument. Probably the one level we allude to the least in connection with Rorschach interpretation is Level II, and this is probably why the Rorschach is a particularly useful instrument. There are many aspects of behavior that an individual hesitates to reveal about himself. As we have said, traditionally, a projective test is a test which reveals data which the individual either will not or cannot bear to reveal about himself. Probably most of the confusion arises because of socially desirable traits that the individual has in less abundance than he would like to, or socially undesirable traits that he possesses but that he wishes that he did not. The amazing part of the foregoing analysis is that so much of Rorschach data is transmitted in Level I form. This, however, is not particularly surprising in view of some of the results of research. Take for instance the study by McGreevey (1962). Even though McGreevey's study did not deal with the Rorschach but with other projective tests, it nevertheless has some bearing on the present argument. McGreevey had groups of subjects who were ranked by their peers on four personality traits, two desirable and two undesirable. They also ranked themselves on these same traits. Discrepancies were found in the expected direction; that is, they over-evaluated themselves on desirable traits and under-evaluated themselves on undesirable traits. Judgments based upon projective tests in this study indicated that even in the case of high discrepancy groups (large Level I-II discrepancy), the judges using the projective data were able to predict the ranking of the individual on the trait by the peer group (Level I) with greater accuracy than the individual himself was able to (Level II). We have always known that people, because of their own ego defenses, were unable to predict public image aspects of behavior of which they were ashamed or which for some reason or another, have been excluded from awareness. The news is that projective tests enable us to cut through this ego-defensiveness and to make predictions close to the level of public image. Thus, the bridge between projective tests and the kind of administrative predictions that we are often asked to make may be at least halfway built.

The Sentence Completion Test. Another so-called projective test which nicely illustrates some of these points is the Sentence Completion Test (SCT). The SCT has been variously assumed to measure each one of the levels described above. Sometimes it is assumed that the completed sentences reflect behaviors which are publicly observable and which would then be consistently rated by significant others. Sometimes the SCT is assumed to measure the level of conscious perception, in which case the examiner uses it as a structured interview, assuming that all of the statements, including both the stem and the ending are consciously acceptable, ego-syntonic, and would have been elicited by direct questioning as well. Sometimes the SCT is treated as a Level III instrument. Under the latter conditions, it would be assumed that measures tapping other levels of behavior should not be correlated with it and that it measures only unacceptable, nonobservable aspects of personality functioning. In clinical practice the test is often used without any direct references to level of behavior, making it possible to rationalize any given inference at whatever level it happens to fit the best. Therefore, if the individual is described in a certain way by significant others, but does not necessarily admit it, the SCT can be assumed to be a Level I test. If the individual admits the trait in himself, the SCT is a Level II test, and if neither of the above situations exist, then the test may still be considered a valuable projective tool. This kind of fuzziness in demarcating the level of behavior predicted by the SCT can only lead to a lack of precision in the clinical use of the test.

Many early authors of SCT studies, such as Rhode (1946), use ways of validating their instruments which seem rather naive in the light of our present framework. She, for example, validated her test by scoring it on the basis of Murray's needs, and then "corroborating" the results by an interview with the subject, which seems to beg the question of levels. A more conscious attempt to deal with the problems of levels is indicated by the study by Meltzoff (1951). The author states certain basic assumptions, such as, that time pressure leads to uncensored data, that a complicated task will produce more specifically individual responses, and that an individual will reveal himself in describing others. He used third person stems on the SCT and had 20 socially desirable, 20 socially undesirable, and 20 neutral items, the sequence of which was random. He employed four test conditions which were: "faking good," "faking sick," producing threat, and anonymous. The author's conclusion, based on his system of classification, was that the mental set of the subject determines the tone of his completions. The conditions of ego threat and the set of faking good produce similar results. The question of levels is pertinent insofar as conscious set does seem to change the responses, even when they are given in the third person. This would perhaps not be true if the completions were not conscious; that is, if they were truly Level III phenomena.

An example of really begging the question is the study by Lindgren (1954), who used the SCT before and after a course, to review attitudinal changes. He received an average interjudge agreement of 75 percent, classifying the scores as accepting, projecting, and neither. Since the papers were anonymous, he matched them by handwriting. The changes were treated as though they were conscious attitudinal changes (II), even though the SCT was selected as the instrument of choice because of its supposedly indirect and projective nature (III).

An example of a study which used the SCT to predict future Level I behavior is one by Stotsky and Weinberg (1956), who wanted to use the test to predict work adjustment. They developed appropriate stems dealing with ego strength and its various vocational manifestations. Eighty psychiatric inpatients took the test, and their responses were scored as positive, neutral, and negative. The criterion in this study was work performance, the group being dichotomized into high and low performance. Attempts to have SCT scores predict work adjustment after six months proved successful 71 percent of the time.

An example of a study which used SCT to measure Level II was one by Burwen, Campbell, and Kidd (1956). They used a multiple choice form of the SCT to measure attitudes towards superiors and subordinates. Because the interjudge reliability was only .12, the authors had to strain the data somewhat; however, they did conclude that the test was a measure of Level II.

An example of the study which demonstrated that the SCT is a Level III instrument is the one by Gray and Klaus (1956). Herein the SCT was one of several used in a parental identification study, where items concerned father and mother, the responses being scaled on a five point continuum of affection. The two writers agreed on 84 percent of the judgments, and were satisfied in judging differences with one-tailed tests and a 5 percent level of significance. The focus was on "identification," which was defined operationally as a similarity between self and perceived same-sex parents. The results seem generally encouraging. If one assumes that the identification with a parent is deemed to be unconscious, this would seem to demonstrate Level III utility for the instrument. Unfortunately, however, there is another possible interpretation, namely that the subject's verbalized similarity between himself and the same-sex parent is due to social stereotypy, in which case it might demonstrate more of a Level II relationship.

One of the most puzzling studies ever published in terms of the Levels hypothesis is the one by Stone and Dellis (1960), which used as subjects a group of "pseudo-neurotic schizophrenics." Apparently, the operational definition of such a person is one who looks more confused on the Rorschach than he does behaviorally, although the authors claim to have had independent criteria for making this diagnosis. The authors hypothesize a sort of movement towards greater depth (unconsciousness) from the Wechsler-Bellevue to the SCT to the TAT to the Rorschach, and all the way down to the Draw-A-Person Test. There were 20 persons in this group, and each test was judged on a 100-point scale of health-sickness. The reliability of the judgments was .72 on the SCT. The results indicated that on the basis of these ratings, the Wechsler and SCT were indistinguishable, as were the SCT and TAT. The Rorschach and the DAP test were in a class by themselves in that they were indistinguishable from one another, but cut off sharply from the rest. It is difficult to know what to make of these results. There are those who would argue that this indicates that the Rorschach and DAP test were the most sensitive in that they picked up the "true" pathology of these individuals which had been precluded by the rest. But this begs the whole question as to what we are using tests for and what we are really trying to predict. Do we really want to have people condemned to existence in a state hospital situation because they are having difficulty maintaining our version of reality in tests like the DAP and the Rorschach? This raises the question of why people generally end up in state hospitals in the first place. It is the contention of the present writer that hospitalization most frequently occurs not because of distorted thinking processes but because of disturbed behavior which makes the individual objectionable to other people and produce a desire on the part of society to cast them out. If we assume that the Case History, the Wechsler, and the SCT are more directly related to observable behavior than the Rorschach and the DAP tests, then it would seem that the more direct instruments are more relevant in determining clinically whether someone is in need of hospitalization or not. Thus, it may be that we are hoisting a patient by the petard of our own double-binding way of instructing him on tests.

How many readers of this book have sometimes experienced guilt because of the dishonest instructions they give on tests like the Rorschach? We say to a patient that we are going to show him ten cards with ink-blots on them and that what he sees on these blots in an entirely individual matter. We tell him there are no right and wrong answers and that different people see different things. This is all very well, except that it does not happen to be the truth. The fact of the matter is, that there *are* right and wrong answers, and that an individual who takes us literally and gives his imagination full play and says whatever he would like to and whatever occurs to him spontaneously, is likely to end up as one of the subjects in a study such as the one by Stone and Dellis. It is even possible that some psychologists or psychiatrists will make up a diagnosis like "pseudo-neurotic schizophrenia" to account for the fact that the patient has really given a psychotic-appearing Rorschach but does not look that way on other tests or on the basis of his observable behavior. So the present writer is inclined to form quite different conclusions from those of Stone and Dellis. Not necessarily assuming that some tests are more accurate than others (more "real"), he is likely to assume that the SCT, the Wechsler-Bellevue, and the TAT predict *judged* behavior better than the Rorschach and the DAP.

Struggling in the direction of determining a level for the SCT is the study by Arnold and Walter (1957). In this study a first and third person form of the SCT was used; one being a standardized version, and the other a presumed equivalent. For the third person form, the subjects were instructed to express the "real feelings of the average person your own sex and age." Scoring reliability was .87; the correlation of the two forms was only .55, from which the authors deduced that the two forms were not interchangeable. This may be very important in that it implies that the first and third person forms indeed do measure different levels. If we assume that the first person form is a measure of Level II, than perhaps the third person is more distant in the direction toward Level III. A more refined study along the same line is the one by Dorris, Levinson, and Hanfmann (1954). They investigated the percentage of self-references in items, which seem to be rather high (70 percent) except in instances where threat is in play. Fifty SCT items were employed, half of which were in the first person and half in the third; the content was matched. The subjects were asked to evaluate self-references for each item. Scores developed were ego threat scores as well as others.

Results show that the first person form demonstrates less self-reference for ego threatened items, that this is not the case for the third person form. Also, the third person form tends to discriminate the authoritarian and egalitarian subjects in regard to ego threat, whereas the first person form does not. It does seem that the level of awareness is highest for ego syntonic first person items, next for ego threatened first person items, then ego syntonic third person items that involve ego threat. It seems that the level of awareness going from the conscious to the unconscious can be partly determined by, and structured by, the nature of the stem and partly by the personal and social desirability attributes of the stem. A study by Davids and Pildner (1958) gives further information as to when the SCT can be a Level II instrument and when it cannot: The authors raise the question of whether direct and projective measures are likely to be more congruent under the condition of an "honest" approach as opposed to a "fake good" approach. The "fake good" set was assumedly present in a group of subjects who were applicants for a position. A special 100-item sentence completion test was used and scored for variables of interest to the authors. This study again involved a comparison of first person and third person items. A simple maladjustment score called an index of alienation was the measure used, and this correlated .83 for the control (honest) subjects and .44 for the experimental (applicant) subjects between the two forms of this test. This study demonstrates that conscious control is exercised more easily for first person items. It is interesting to note that by just changing the pronoun in the stem we can make such progress away from Level II to Level III. In a study by Getzels and Walsh (1958) the matter of levels was attacked by using the sentence completion test and a direct inquiry. The SCT stems were third person items disguised as a speed test. The first person form was used as a measure of direct expression of attitudes and opinions. The items were worded so as to facilitate dichotomous classification, to be free of affect-laden words, and to present a behavioral situation that would have differential value for various subsections of the population. The basic score was the number of responses. The experimenters discovered that socially conflicted areas showed interlevel disparity, that socially neutral areas showed low interlevel disparity; that if one level is in conflict with social norms, the other will be different, but if one level is in accord with social norms, the other is likely to be the same or different and that reactions to conflicted areas are J-shaped for Level II and normal for Level III.

Thus it can be seen that hope exists for distinguishing levels in connection with the SCT. The preceding studies imply that the first or third person stem distinction has potentially great value in nailing down the level at which we are measuring behavior. It seems fairly obvious that the first person stem makes the SCT very much like a structured interview. When we ask a subject to end a sentence with the first thing that comes to his mind, and the stem is in the first person, it seems likely that he would answer it as he would an interview question. It seems ludicrous to expect him to do anything else. It seems more surprising that we can fool people so easily by simply making it into a third person pronoun or name; however, there does seem to be some evidence of this. The question of whether we can use the SCT as a way of predicting behavior is the same question that is always involved when we use a paper and pencil test for that purpose.

There are also other projective tests about which the question of levels has been raised. Murstein devotes an entire book (1963) to the question of what the TAT measures. Obviously he has some very definite ideas along this line and documents them with great care. He believes that the TAT is basically a Level II instrument. What level is measured by the Draw-A-Person Test is very difficult to say. However, the reader is referred to other chapters in this book in the hope that he can draw appropriate inference concerning each instrument and find its proper place in the clinical case study in terms of the level schema described herein.

THE COMMUNICATION OF FINDINGS FROM PROJECTIVE TECHNIQUES AS PART OF THE CLINICAL REPORT

One of the most crucial problems in integrating projective techniques into the clinical case study is communicating hypotheses culled from projective tests in a report which is also based on other sources of information. These other sources may be interviews with the patient himself and significant others, as well as the interpretation of data based on objective personality inventories, intelligence tests, and direct observations. This question will be broken down in several sub-sections and an attempt will be made to make some suggestions in each category.

How to avoid vagueness and universality

A classic study by Forer (1949) indicates that universality presents a great temptation to the clinical investigator. In his study Forer presented what was described as a projective test to a class of students and subsequently presented them with "reports" ostensibly based on this material. In actuality, the interpretations were identical, each subject receiving the same one. They were asked to specify the degree to which the interpretations were accurate in each one of their cases, and how much confidence they had in them. These "psychological reports" were received with great enthusiasm by the class and they were amazed at the specific accuracy of the allegations made concerning their personalities. This study bears a startling and frightening resemblance to many studies actually dealing with the validation of projective tests. The statements made in Forer's standard report were, of course, of a very universal nature. They got by, just as statements of astrologers, crystal-ball gazers, and the makers of Chinese fortune cookies get by. They also got by in the same way that the statements of many clinical psychologists, psychiatrists, psychiatric social workers, vocational counselors, and other legitimate practitioners get by. Regrettably, much of our behavior in communicating psychological findings consists of a kind of weasel-wording and psychological razzle-dazzle which precludes the dissemination of any specific information. Just recently the present author began working as a consultant to a school system in his home town. After sending his first reports to the teacher in charge of the guidance program, she wrote back saying that she was certainly glad to get some reports that said something about the children instead of the usual standard stereotypes that she has come to know and ignore. It is probably true of most of the people that we test: that they have intelligence beyond that which they are currently employing, that they have difficulty in their relationships with their fellow men and women, that they have some tendency to be immature and do not clearly identify themselves with their appropriate sex role, and that they are sometimes partially immobilized by tension and emotional distress. Surely these interpretations are correct in most instances, and they are undoubtedly appropriate to most of the readers of this book; however, their very universality makes them of very dubious value in a psychological report. Excessive generality as well as universality tends to make communication infinitely less valuable. The classic study is the one by Ullmann, Berkman and Hammister (1958), in which psychological reports are used in an effort to predict adjustment in an adult nursing home. The findings were most humiliating to the unknown and unspecified authors of these psychological reports. Number of years of hospitalization was found to be a better predictor of adjustment in an adult nursing home than judgments based upon the entire psychological report. Psychologists have frequently been criticized for the universality and ambiguity of their statements, as for instance in the study by Garfield, Heine, and Leventhal (1954). One of the reasons why psychologists have often felt forced to be universal and ambiguous is because they have not taken into account the possibility of breaking down their data into levels, as has been promulgated in this chapter. It is our contention that a breaking down of projective data into levels will fortify the clinician with courage and enable him to make specific statements for which he is willing to be responsible. This hopefully means that he will be more willing to focus his report in some specific manner, either in terms of a diagnostic classification, an administrative decision, or whatever focus is desired by those requesting the report.

How best to join the findings of projective tests and other methods

The contention in this chapter has been that many of our psychological tests have properties which enable the clinician to make predictions on one or another level, and that sometimes a given test has within it characteristics that lead to predictions at various levels. However, the most refined and sophisticated kind of personality analysis comes from the integration of projective techniques with other methods of personality assessment. The procedure for organizing psychological reports described by the present author (Klopfer, 1960) enables the clinician to make maximal use of all of this data. It has always seemed to the present author that not only can an individual make legitimate inferences from a single modality which he may not want to make on the basis of the over-all evidence as it accumulates, but more importantly, he may often be able to make superordinate hypotheses on the basis of various types of data which cannot legitimately follow from any single source of information. Thus, a patient with organic brain damage may have a

Bender more distorted than his Rorschach, whereas a schizophrenic may have a Rorschach more distorted than his Bender. A schizophrenic who is primarily paranoid may show a much higher level of efficiency in an intelligence test than he does in a test like the Rorschach. A person who shows one kind of test-taking aptitude as revealed by the validity scales on the MMPI, may have his projective instruments interpreted quite differently from a person who shows another kind of test-taking aptitude. A protocol from the MMPI characterized by gross pathology and a plethora of symptoms may be interpreted quite differently in the light of a basically solid Rorschach from a protocol in which the reaction to inkblots is as haphazard and peculiar as the reaction to true and false items. Also, the patient's work history, the reactions to him on the part of significant others, and the observations made of him directly by nurses, social workers, and other professional people, may have quite a different meaning in the light of one kind of projective performance as opposed to another. Thus, for example, spontaneous, extroverted behavior may be interpreted as genuine interest and liking for people on the one hand, whereas on the other hand it may be regarded as a frantic attempt to maintain some thin hold on reality, with the alternative being a complete schizophrenic withdrawal.

It seems a great mistake to use projective data and other data as equivalent to one another and to be interested only in similarities rather than disparities. Most people will tend to demonstrate interlevel disparity no matter how well adjusted they are. People who are emotionally disturbed are almost bound to show some differences between their behavior at one level and at another. Therefore, the differences between results of projective tests and other sources of information are likely to be one of the most crucial sources of information upon which a clinical study can be based. Any psychologist who ignores this point and obscures the differences by focusing upon similarities will soon tire of the use of projective techniques, since it is obvious that they are not as useful in securing Level II data and sometimes Level I data, as other techniques are. The best way to find out what a patient thinks is to ask him. The best way to find out what he does is to observe him. To get the latter kind of information indirectly and tortuously, by showing him inkblots and having him make up stories is certainly doing it the hard way; only if the projective information will lead to a more refined and sophisticated interpretation of that which is directly observed, and only if the directly observed behavior is used to refine and produce a more sophisticated interpretation of the projective data, is it worthwhile to engage in both types of clinical detective work. If the latter course of action is followed, the result is likely to be an extremely sensitive, penetrating and insightful analysis of the patient's personality which will be of value to all persons concerned with the case. If, in turn, the clinician manages to communicate his findings in some reasonable way which can be generally understood and appreciated by other workers, he will have rendered a great service to all concerned, and more specifically, to the patient, who will be understood beyond the usual superficial way in which people regard and judge one another.

The desirability of avoiding statements which imply a level other than the one upon which the inference is based

One of the greatest sources of error in communicating projective findings as part of a clinical case study is statements that set up a false criterion. Let us say, for example, that the individual shows passivity, tenderness, and a generally "feminine" orientation on the basis of his style and content in the Rorschach test. Let us say further that his performance on the TAT implies that he tends to be dependent on other men, emphasizing affiliation, softness, and giving in, rather than virility, independence, and possessiveness. Let us assume further that his overt behavior as judged by the examiner during the progress of the evaluation is more like that of a woman, culturally speaking, than like that of a man. It seems justified to many examiners under these conditions, to say in the psychological report that this patient has "strong homosexual tendencies." However, the statement, "strong homosexual tendencies" may well be interpreted at a level not intended by the examiner and not justified by the data. It is quite possible for all of the above factors to have been correctly and reliably observed and yet for the patient to not have any demonstrable homosexual tendencies. For example, he may never have been erotically stimulated by members of the same sex, may never have had fantasies about sexual activities involving members of the same sex, and there may be no reason to assume that he has been a problem to other men by being seductive in his relationship to them. Yet all of the latter possibilities would be implied by the statement, "strong homosexual tendencies." How much better it would be for the psychological report under the above conditions, to speak of the individual's softness, tenderness, and passivity directly rather than extrapolating in a manner which can so easily be misinterpreted and misunderstood!

This raises the whole question of whether there is any particular value in shorthand symbolization based upon some particular theory. It is always tempting to the psychological evaluator to conceptualize at a high level of abstraction. For example, he may have a patient who cuts off inconsequential parts of the blot on the Rorschach test, draws a person on the DAP with his hand in his pocket, tells stories on the TAT in which the hero is unable to provide an adequate solution to the dilemma posed, and reacts with panic and fear to failure to answer questions on the WAIS. The examiner may then try to integrate all of this material in the phrase, "castration anxiety." Seemingly, this would be very desirable in that it promotes the discourse to a very high level of inference from which presumably, the primary and secondary readers of the report could draw all sorts of appropriate conclusions in a wide variety of areas. Unfortunately, this is not as self-evident as it would appear at first blush. The phrase, "castration anxiety" may lead to any one of the following kinds of predictions:

1) The individual feels powerless in situations that are intellectually beyond him, and reacts by being critical and picayune; 2) the individual is afraid of other people and tends to behave in a placating and subservient manner, constantly abasing himself before they have a chance to injure him; 3) the individual masturbates excessively and is concerned about this because he feels it will injure him either mentally or physically; or 4) he suffers from the psychotic delusion that some person or persons either known or unknown, are going to take a knife and cut off his genitalia.

It would make it much easier for the reader of the clinical case study if the person preparing the report would specify which of these possibilities he had in mind rather than leaving it to the imagination of the reader to determine the choice. By going directly from the test data to the prediction, and by making the prediction at a specific and verifiable level of interpersonal functioning, much of the above confusion could be obviated. Thus, the subject who cuts off pieces of the Rorschach blots could be described directly as being critical and behaving in a way which wastes time and does not further the purpose, out of fear of being caught short. The person not resolving problems on the TAT could be described as not being able to plan ahead to the solution of dilemmas in which he can conceive himself to be; the person reacting to failure with panic on the WAIS could be described as having a great deal of difficulty maintaining his sense of self-esteem under conditions of apparent failure, and the person with his hands in his pockets could be described by the DAP in some manner congruent with the theory of the examiner. Unfortunately, the present writer has no hypothesis to offer in the latter instance in view of the lack of evidence that this kind of phenomenon is related to any other kind of behavior.

Using projective statements to imply a behavioral condition which can be directly checked is the most common error made in clinical case studies involving confusion among levels. However, it is by no means the only error that is made. As implied earlier in this chapter, it may be possible to make behavioral predictions from projective data which the examiner would be reluctant to make because of his feeling that projective tests can never measure anything except fantasy. For example, the evidence concerning the relationship between aggressive Rorschach content and aggressive behavior would certainly lead the examiner of the patient with aggressive content on the Rorschach to appropriately make the prediction that this patient is likely to behave in an aggressive manner. Thus, if he were to restrict himself in the report to merely pointing out that this patient has aggressive fantasies he would be depriving the reader of some important predictive information which might possibly be of administrative and clinical value. Similarly, there may be Level II information which can be derived from projective tests, or so-called projective tests, which the reader would benefit from if he were made aware of it. For example, the SCT obviously could give information about a patient's conscious feelings and ideas, especially when a form using first person stems has been employed. Yet the report will often obscure the significance of this data by referring to it as fantasy data or projective data exclusively. Also, the individual may make personal references during the Rorschach test or the TAT which make it quite clear that he is referring to conscious experiences, feelings, and thought which would be important Level II data, and yet are not described as such in the report. There are times when it would be much more accurate and helpful to say "the patient feels that," or "the patient claims that," rather than to say "projective material reveals that," or "the patient's fantasies imply that."

Thus, the communication of findings from projective tests should always deal with the appropriate levels, and a statement should not hint at or imply a level other than the one that is justified by the evidence. This will greatly enhance the possibility of using data derived from projective techniques in an appropriate manner and integrating it properly with data derived from other sources.

The importance of clarity of style and language in statements derived from projective techniques

Interpretations of material based upon projective tests can often be recognized in the clinical case study by the peculiar shift in style of language which seems to occur. The style of the report up until a certain point may have been precise, factual, and clear. The reader has probably been told that the individual has a particular level of intelligence, that his behavior during the examination was thus and so, that his relationships with significant others in his life have been of a particular sort, and that he displays the following symptoms. Now we come to the part of the report based upon projective tests. All of a sudden we are in a kind of never-never land in which we hear about "basic regressive goal mechanisms" or "unresolved Oedipal problems which interfere with current heterosexual relationships," or "obsessive fantasies which have a defeatist flavor." Also, instead of hearing about the subject's or patient's relationship with real people, we are now bombarded by information concerning his attitudes and feelings towards "father figures" and "mother figures." Even though the conservatism of the interpreter in referring to these as "figures" rather than actual parents is commendable, the whole style of the report shifts from talking about an individual to talking about mechanisms and symbols which have no clear-cut connection with what has preceded this section.

Particularly difficult is the kind of esoteric language which sometimes creeps into the report when it deals with material derived from projective techniques. Take for example the use of pithy symbols like letters. We may talk about K—now which are we talking about? Are we talking about MMPI K? Are we talking about Szondi K? Are we talking about Rorschach K, or what? Obviously this is a kind of private language which requires more elaboration than it is worth in a clinical case study. Part of the difficulty arises from a basically incompetent examiner who uses projective techniques in a cookbook manner without really understanding their relationship to personality or to behavior. Thus he may take statements directly from a standard textbook dealing with interpretations of the psychogram, the various percentages and ratios, the card-by-card analysis and put them together in an undigestible hodge-podge. Many such questions of organization and language have been discussed in the book on report writing (Klopfer, 1960). The recommendation the present author would make in this instance is that the statements derived from projective techniques should become indistinguishable from other parts of the report in terms of style and language. That is to say, they should be integrated and become part of a description of personality based upon all the material derived by the clinical psychologist.

By using the multilevel framework, information obtained from observation, objective tests, intelligence tests, and projective tests can all become part of a single description of personality and behavior which is organized along more rational lines than that of sources of information. I would say that anyone incapable of translating projective material into everyday language has an inadequate understanding of it and of its relationship to personality.

Why Clinical Case Studies Are Not Complete Without Projective Tests

The concluding section of this chapter will deal with the whole question of whether projective instruments should be included in a comprehensive case study. The present author feels that no case study is complete without projective tests, for the following reasons:

1. It would be very unsafe, unwise, and incorrect to assume that a patient either can or wants to present all aspects of his personality fully to the examiner at the time he presents himself for personality evaluation. One possible reason for this is that he may have been precipitated into the examination through circumstances which make him feel ashamed and defensive. He may have been referred by a law enforcement agency, by a dissatisfied marital partner, or by a disgruntled parent.

He may distrust the examiner or the examining situation and want to hold back his full confidence until he feels more assured that the matters he reveals will be adequately received and properly and constructively used for his benefit. Even if he consciously feels totally cooperative and trusting, there may still be matters which he is unable to communicate because he himself is unaware of them. Thus, the present writer would argue that ego-defensiveness precludes the presentation of complete information through interviews or questionnaires. The projective situation is uniquely suited to getting beneath the patient's character armor and discovering where his vital organs are. This is not to say that this information cannot be gotten in other ways; however, getting it through premature direct confrontation with the patient may pose dangers to the patient's mental health which can be reduced through the use of projective tests. The projective tests enable one to get inside and out again quickly before the patient is aware of the fact that he is being so searchingly investigated.

The relationship between the examiner and the person being examined is likely to be one which will not outlast the examination itself. Sometimes the psychologist doing the evaluation acts as a consultant and reports the result to someone else, such as an agency or a potential therapist. Sometimes the evaluation might be part of a teaching procedure and the feedback will go to trainees rather than to the patient himself. It seems rather irresponsible to expect the patient to become very trusting and involved with the examiner under conditions like this since something will be begun and there will be no opportunity to continue. This makes the evaluation of hidden personality traits through indirect means such as projective techniques a much more attractive proposition than the exposure of the patient prior to his readiness to assimilate the information.

2. One of the reasons given for the possible exclusion of projective techniques from the clinical case study is that the observations of others will suffice, assuming that these others are sufficiently skilled and professionally competent, and that not enough is added to the total clinical case study by the use of projective instruments to deserve the added expense and trouble. This places a good deal of responsibility upon the judgment of clinicians which does not seem to be warranted by the evidence concerning the reliability of clinical judgments. All too often, research projects which hinge upon the reliability of clinical judgments end up in chaos. A good example is the study by Filmer-Bennett and Klopfer (1962), which was an attempt to place the SCT and the TAT in a hierarchical continuum in terms of the levels frame of reference. The study included 20 college students who were asked to rank themselves on four continua which had been pretested in such a way as to assure relative normality of distribution of the self-ratings once they were made. A group of judges, who were considered experts in the two tests men-

tioned above, were used to provide criterion measures. The hypothesis was that the self-ratings would be predicted with greater accuracy on the basis of the SCT than on the basis of the TAT, the rationale being that the SCT would have greater face validity for use as a comparison with self-ratings than the TAT. However, the study demonstrated that neither the TAT judges nor the SCT judges were able to approximate the self-ratings, and furthermore, that they disagreed with one another. It seems that clinicians have great difficulty in making straightforward judgments such as predicting self-ratings. Reports from the judges indicated that they were unable, for example, to predict whether somebody would deem themselves as being overtly aggressive or not. Even when the projective evidence seemed to indicate that the individual was not possessed of aggression, the clinician would say to himself, "I wonder why this patient is assiduously avoiding the expression of aggression. Probably he is seething with aggression which is threatening him to the extent that he is unable to face the possible onslaught of such an ominous and overwhelming amount of aggression. This is the reason he is deceiving himself, but not me. I will not be fooled and I will rank him high in aggression." The trouble with this reasoning, of course, is that the judge is not sticking to the level of interpersonal functioning at which he has been asked to make predictions. Now there may be some clinicians who can make straightforward predictions at a level which has been specified by the experimenter, but they have not been clearly identified thus far.

Another problem that arises when one relies upon the observation of the patient by others, is that no matter how skilled an observer may be, his judgment is likely to be clouded by subjective influences due to his own psychological blind spots and by dyadic interactional influences. To substantiate this point, one need only refer to some of the work of Masling (1959), who demonstrated to the chagrin of a good many people that patients could influence the judgment of examiners in any one of a variety of ways. For example, he demonstrated that such a seemingly objective matter as a WAIS score could be influenced by a female subject's seductive or nasty attitude towards a male examiner. If even this kind of ostensibly objective datum can be influenced by dyadic interactional influences it would seem very likely that straight observation or the clinical interview could be similarly influenced. The above is not, of course, an argument solely for the inclusion of projective tests, but for the use of multiple measurements from a variety of modalities. Certainly it would appear that projective tests, even though they are capable of being influenced by transient and situational factors, are harder for the patient to manipulate by means of a set than some other kinds of situations in which he might be observed. Surely we have enough questions about the adequacy and completeness of our methods of personality assessment generally to discourage us from discarding a tool with potential value as great as that of a projective test.

3. One of the most frequent reasons given for not including projective tests in a clinical case study is that they are not standardized instruments and consequently they are more subject to examiner misinterpretation than others. This criticism is justified if the projective instrument is used in a non-standard manner. Unfortunately, those clinicians likely to be most critical of projective tests are the ones most likely to use them in a haphazard, inappropriate , and slovenly manner. For example, they will give some of the Rorschach cards and not others, they will use only the free association part of the procedure and not conduct a proper inquiry. They will give the entire test, but merely subject it to a kind of sign approach for specific purposes such as the detection of schizophrenia, which hardly exploits the potentialities of the instrument. Similarly, the TAT may be used to get information about the patient's attitudes toward significant others without taking into account the stylistic possibilities of the performance and the possibility of forming superordinate hypotheses from comparing TAT material with interview material and the observations made of the patient directly. The worst offenders are those who use some kind of an esoteric system of scoring and classification culled from various sources, and then claim that there are no standards available. Certainly there are no norms available for a system which is original with the particular clinician. However, a test like the Rorschach has definitely been standardized according to certain major systems like those of Beck and Klopfer. Also, there are developmental norms available to compare the performance of children at various ages with their peers. It is only when the projective test is used in a standardized manner that its scientific as well as artistic contribution to the clinical case study is fully exploited.

REFERENCES

Arnold, F., & Walter, V. A. The relationship between a self-and-other reference sentence completion test. *J. counsel. Psychol.*, 1957, *4*, 65-70.

Beck, S. J. *Rorschach's Test. Vol. II*. New York: Grune & Stratton, 1945.

Bendick, Maureen, & Klopfer, W. G. The effects of sensory deprivation and motor inhibition on Rorschach movement responses. *J. proj. Tech. Pers. Assess.*, 1964, *28*, 261-264.

Burwen, L. S., Campbell, D., & Kidd, J. The use of a sentence completion test in measuring attitudes toward superiors and subordinates. *J. appl. Psychol.*, 1956, *40*, 248-250.

Davids, A., & Pildner, H. Jr. Comparison of direct and projective methods of personality assessment under different conditions of motivation. *Psychol. Monogr.*, 1958, *72*, No. 11 (Whole No. 464) .

Dorris, R. J., Levinson, D. J., & Hanfmann, Eugenia. Authoritarian personality studied by a new variation of the sentence completion test. *J. abnorm. soc. Psychol.*, 1954, *49*, 99-108.

Elizur, A. Content analysis of the Rorschach with regard to anxiety and hostility. *Ror. Res. Exch.*, 1949, *13*, 247-284.

Filmer-Bennett, G., & Klopfer, W. G. Levels of awareness in projective tests. *J. proj. Tech.*, 1962, *26*, 34-35.

Finney, B. C. Rorschach test correlates of assaultive behavior. *J. proj. Tech.*, 1955, *19*, 6-17.

Forer, B. The fallacy of personal validation; a classroom demonstration of gullibility. *J. abnorm. soc. Psychol.*, 1949, *44*, 118-123.

Garfield, S. L., Heine, R. W., & Leventhal, M. An evaluation of psychological reports in a clinical setting. *J. consult. Psychol.*, 1954, *18*, 281-286.

Getzels, J. W., & Walsh, J. J. The method of paired direct and projective question-naires in the study of attitude structure and socialization. *Psychol. Monogr.*, 1958, *72* (1).

Gray, S. W., & Klaus, R. The assessment of parental identification. *Genet. Psychol. Monogr.*, 1956, *54*, 87-109.

Klopfer, B., Ainsworth, Mary D., Klopfer, W. G., & Holt, R. R. *Developments in the Rorschach Technique.* Vol. I. New York: World Book, 1954.

Klopfer, W. G. *The Psychological Report: Use and Communication of Psychological Findings.* New York: Grune & Stratton, 1960.

Leary, T. F. *The Interpersonal Diagnosis of Personality.* New York: Ronald, 1957.

Lindgren, H. The use of SCT in measuring attitudes among college freshmen. *J. soc. Psychol.*, 1954, *40*, 79-92.

McGreevey, J. C. Interlevel disparity and predictive efficiency. *J. proj. Tech.*, 1962, *26*, 80-87.

McReynolds, P. Perception of Rorschach concepts as related to personality deviations. *J. abnorm. soc. Psychol.*, 1951, *46*, 131-141.

Masling, J. The effects of warm and cold interaction on the administration and scor-ing of an intelligence test. *J. consult. Psychol.*, 1959, *23*, 336-341.

Matarazzo, J. D., Allen, Bernadene, Saslow, G., & Wiens, A. N. Characteristics of successful policemen and firemen applicants. *J. appl. Psychol.*, 1964, *48*, 123-133.

Meltzoff, J. The effect of mental set and item structure upon response to a projective test. *J. abnorm. soc. Psychol.*, 1951, *46*, 177-189.

Murstein, B. I. The projection of hostility on the Rorschach and as a result of ego threat. *J. proj. Tech.*, 1956, *20*, 418-428.

Murstein, B. I. *Theory and Research in Projective Techniques.* New York: Wiley, 1963.

Rhode, Amanda, R. Explorations in personality by the sentence completion method. *J. appl. Psychol.*, 1946, *30*, 169-181.

Stone, H. K., & Dellis, N. P. An exploratory investigation into the levels hypothesis. *J. proj. Tech.*, 1960, *24*, 333-340.

Stotsky, B. A., & Weinberg, H. The prediction of the psychiatric patients' work adjust-ment. *J. counsel. Psychol.*, 1956, *3*, 140-144.

Tomkins, S. *Thematic Apperception Test.* New York: Grune & Stratton, 1947.

Ullmann, L. P., Berkman, V. C., & Hammister, R. C. Psychological reports related to behavior and benefit of placement in home care. *J. clin. Psych.*, 1958, *14*, 254-259.

Warren, Sue, & Klopfer, W. G. *Prediction of Public Image by Means of Self-report.* (unpublished study).

17

Why and When to Test: The Social Context of Psychological Testing

DAVID LEVINE

The major contention of this chapter is that errors in the interpretation of psychological test results occur frequently because the psychologist has not concerned himself sufficiently with the general purpose of the psychological evaluation—because he has underestimated the importance of a clear comprehension of the referral question in its broadest possible context. Although I shall be able to present some clinical and theoretical material to support this idea, I am not familiar with any controlled research which is relevant to it.

It is well known, however, that most requests for psychological testing are not presented to psychologists in terms of a question to be answered or a decision to be made. Too many referrals come from anxious psychiatric residents who are not sure how to manage a patient, from school administrators who feel they need test evidence to support a decision they have already made, from teachers who want test data to convince a recalcitrant parent of the seriousness of a child's problem, from parole board members who want to make use of "every available resource" before committing themselves to a final decision, from social workers "because we have always done it this way"—all these referrals illustrate the kinds of non-test considerations which tend to confuse the referral context and to put the psychologist in an ambiguous position.

In this chapter I plan to analyze and to clarify some of the more typical situations in which psychological testing has been employed. If the major contention is correct, such a clarification will lead to fewer errors in psychological test interpretation, to more meaningful psychological test reports, and ultimately to more effective social use of psychological test results. I shall present an analysis of five institutional settings within which psychological tests are used: the psychiatric setting; the general medical setting; the legal setting; the educational setting; and the setting of the psychological clinic. A clear understanding of these social contexts will not obviate the need for continued care in the selection of appropriate tests, in the administration and scoring of these tests, and in the interpretation of these test results in accord with the most recent information about the tests and about personality theory in general, but it should avoid some unnecessary confusion and—especially among younger psychologists—it may help direct energies toward important considerations, rather than toward irrelevant issues.

THE PROBLEM

Recently—especially during the past five years—attacks on psychological tests have increased in frequency and scope. Moreover, these attacks come not only from extremist groups or crusading journalists (Gross, 1962; Hoffman, 1962) ; they have come also from well-meaning, thoughtful people in positions of high social responsibility.

On Friday, June 4, 1965 during the hearings of a House Special Subcommittee on Invasion of Privacy of the Committee on Government Operations, Representative Benjamin S. Rosenthal said: ". . . I am so impressed [by the evidence I have heard today that] I am prepared to offer a bill on Monday to prohibit the giving of psychological tests by any Federal agency, under any circumstances, at any place, and to make it a Federal crime for any Federal official to do it." (Testimony before House Special Subcommittee on Invasion of Privacy of the Committee on Government Operations, 1965, p. 982.)

This point of view was shared by other senators and congressmen during the two weeks of hearings conducted in June of 1965 on the question: Do psychological tests constitute an invasion of privacy?

On April 5, 1966, Representative Rosenthal introduced a bill in Congress (HR 14288) "to prohibit, except in certain circumstances, the expenditure of funds by any department for the acquisition or use of personality inventory tests. . . ."

On February 26, 1964, an Illinois Fair Employment Practices Commission hearing examiner issued a "decision and order directing Motorola to cease the use of Test 10 (a low level test of intellectual ability) because it did not reflect and equate inequalities and environmental factors among the disadvantaged and culturally deprived group." (Motorola's Employment Test Procedure, 1964.) Motorola claimed that the applicant scored below the cutoff point on a screening test which all their applicants must take. The Negro applicant did not argue this point, but he claimed that the test was so constructed as to be unfair to Negroes.

At about the same time, in response to the criticism that group intelligence tests were unfair to Negroes and Puerto Ricans, the Board of Education of the City of New York outlawed the use of group tests of intelligence in its public school system. In a small town in Texas, the same end was achieved by burning psychological tests. Although these are attacks on intelligence tests, projective tests are also open to the criticism that the responses are interpreted in terms of white middle class norms (Auld, 1952). Thus, although some people may have accepted the social contribution of psychological testing, many are becoming concerned about the possible harm which psychological testing can do as a result of invasion of privacy and because of the possibility of discrimination.

Testing procedures are also criticized on theoretical grounds. As the result of a careful analysis of measurement and decision making, Churchman (1961) concludes:

> "In this sense, of measurement taken as a decision-making activity designed to accomplish an objective, we have as yet no theory of measurement. We do not know why we do what we do. We do not even know why we measure at all. It is costly to obtain measurements. Is the effort worth the cost?" (p. 102).

There is also a problem, however, of an excessive reliance on psychological tests. Although psychological tests are under attack by lay people, an increasing number of social workers, psychiatrists, physicians, judges, educators, and businessmen seem to be placing more faith in psychological testing than many psychologists feel is justified, or using psychological testing for a host of inappropriate reasons, rather than for information about a patient or client. This problem will be discussed in greater detail when we analyze the five institutional contexts.

Attacks on psychological testing come not only from outside psychology; they come from psychologists as well. Meehl (1960), during the course of the clinical-actuarial controversy, wrote:

> "My advice to fledgling clinical psychologists is to construct their self concept mainly around 'I am a researcher' or 'I am a psychotherapist,' because one whose self concept is mainly 'I am a (test oriented) psychodiagnostician' may have to maintain his professional security over the next few years by not reading the research literature, a maneuver which has apparently proved quite successful already for some clinicians. Personally, I find the cultural lag between what the published research shows and what clinicians persist in claiming to do with their favorite devices even more disheartening than the adverse evidence itself" (p. 26).

Although Meehl (1965) has pointed out that "commentators have tended to polarize and oversimplify my . . . views," his writings have left many young psychologists and graduate students much bewildered. They were taught in graduate school to give tests; they are hired to give tests; they spend much time testing; they try to arrive at meaningful conclusions about their patients or clients; and their reports are considered seriously as part of the decision making process. Yet Meehl's data and arguments that personality tests are invalid seem extremely persuasive (Meehl, 1954, 1960).

It is interesting to observe the kinds of reactions which psychologists adopt in response to this conflict and to the threat to their professional self-esteem.

Holzberg (1961) in an analysis of "defensive reactions to research role conflicts" among young psychologists describes several kinds of adjustments which are analogous to what is experienced by psychologists confronted with this threat to their psychodiagnostic self-esteem. Holzberg describes the defenses of withdrawal, projection, denial, identification, and intellectualization.

The psychologist who "withdraws" decides to abandon the function of psychological testing completely, declaring that society will benefit more by the therapy and research that will be done. The psychologist who falls back on "clinical intuition" to the extent that he feels he has a special talent and does not need to concern himself with research being done in assessment, generally combines *identification with a psychologist* whom he tries to emulate and *projection*—"no other tests or psychologists can do the job as well as we can."

The *intellectualizer* takes full responsibility for very few psychological referrals, but is always available to consult on someone else's case. He can shift ground very easily depending on the particular situation in which he finds himself.

The reactions to this conflict by psychologists are not difficult to understand; the implications for the larger social good are, however, difficult to determine. Would society be better off if psychological testing were abandoned? This question will be raised again in terms of the specific social institutions we will explore.

Thus many psychologists, through ignorance, apathy, insecurity, or rigidity approach their patient or client with little concern for the purpose of the evaluation. The following incident illustrates how futile a psychological examination can be when the psychologist is oblivious of the purpose of his task.

During a consulting visit to a hospital, I agreed to observe a psychology student administer a WAIS. Since the student was ready to begin, I went into his office, followed almost immediately by the supervising psychologist and the patient. The supervising psychologist introduced the patient and the student and then left. The following is a description (as nearly as I can recall it) of what took place:

T (trainee) : Name?
P (patient) : Joseph Burns.
T: Birthdate?
P: August 6, 1923.

T: Age?
P: Forty-three.
T: Married?
P: No, single.
T: Nationality?
P: American.
T: Occupation?
P: Truck driver.
T: Education?
P: One year of high school.
T: What does rubber come from?
P: Trees.
T: Name four men who've been President of the United States since 1900.
P: Truman, Kennedy, Eisenhower, Johnson.
T: Who was Longfellow?

. . . and so on through the entire WAIS.

This exchange took place in a formal atmosphere, the trainee asking the questions in a precise, businesslike manner and the patient giving his responses laconically. As I recall, the patient was not especially tense at the start of the testing; he was cooperative and his affect was flat. The trainee went through the 11 WAIS subtests in order, generally reading the instructions, and as the examination progressed, the patient became increasingly terse in his responses. He didn't talk at all during the performance tests, started smoking in an agitated manner, and, by the time he was doing the Block Design Test, was obviously making no serious attempt to solve the more difficult items. After the last item on the Object Assembly was completed, the trainee said, "Thank you, we're finished," and the patient got up and walked out without a word.

The trainee had received instructions at the university concerning "establishing rapport" and "understanding the referral." He had been told by his supervisor at the hospital that he would be assigned a patient to test and that he was to give a WAIS because it was the only test he had learned, but he had not been told why this patient was to be tested —nor did he ask. He had previously been told by the supervising psychologist that he should interview patients he would test. The student was highly recommended by his undergraduate instructors and is expected to do well in graduate school. He will learn. He had apparently not yet learned, however, that psychological testing is an interaction between human beings.

It should be clear that on the basis of his hour and a half with the patient, this student is in no position to make much of a contribution. It is my contention that he doesn't even know how intelligent the patient is, let alone know how to begin to formulate a "working image" (Sundberg & Tyler, 1962) of him. Furthermore, I suspect the patient distrusts him and that the trainee would have a very difficult time gaining the patient's confidence in the future. This kind of situation occurs more often than we would like to admit. The bulk of this chapter is devoted to an attempt to analyze how this kind of situation has come about and what can be done to change it. The analysis of the five social contexts will be simplified if we first review some recent developments in "decision theory."

DECISION THEORY AS A THEORY OF MEASUREMENT

What has been called "classical measurement theory" considers the psychological test as a measuring instrument, analogous to a ruler or a thermometer, with test theory "directed primarily toward the study of accuracy of measurement on a continuous scale" (Cronbach & Gleser, 1965). This kind of measurement theory necessarily centers on the classical problems of reliability and validity—with the ultimate criterion of a good test being its use as an accurate predictor. The philosophical position in which this approach is rooted is logical positivism and operationism and the accomplishments of this school of measurement have been great.

Within the past decade, however, there has been an important new development in test theory. Cronbach and Gleser (1965) describe this new approach:

> "The value of a test depends on many qualities in addition to its [predictive] accuracy. Especially to be considered are the relevance of the measurement to the particular decision being made, and the loss resulting from an erroneous decision. Recommendations regarding the design, selection and interpretation of a test must take into account the characteristics of the decisions for which the test will be used, since the test that is maximally effective for one decision will not necessarily be most effective elsewhere.
>
> "An appropriate test theory can evolve from a general and systematic examination of the decision problems for which tests are used and of the demands these problems placed upon the test" (pp. 1-2).

The present chapter may be considered a part of such an examination.

Cronbach and Gleser's point of view is shared by many psychologists (Sundberg & Tyler, 1962; Levy, 1963). Although no attempt will be made to review in detail the history or mathematics of decision theory, some landmarks should be mentioned.

The modern history of decision theory begins with the publication of von Neumann and Morgenstern's *Theory of Games and Economic Be-*

havior in 1944. A game is conceived of as "any situation in which money (or some valuable equivalent) may be gained as the result of a proper choice of strategy" (Edwards, 1954, p. 406). Edwards summarizes von Neumann and Morgenstern's contribution as follows:

"It is of course impossible to condense a tremendous and difficult book into one page. The major points to be emphasized are these: the theory of games is not a model of how people actually play games (some game theorists will disagree with this), nor is it likely to be of any practical use in telling you how to play a complicated game; the crux of the theory of games is the principle of choosing the strategy which minimizes the maximum expected financial loss; and the theory defines a solution of a game as a set of imputations (a set of payments made as a result of a game, one to each player) which satisfies the principle for all players" (p. 408).

Although the theory of games seems to have no immediate relevance to our problem, Wald's extension of game theory to the problem of decision making has. Decision making is defined as deciding . . .

". . . on the basis of observations which cost something to make, between policies, each of which has a possible gain or loss. In some cases, all of these gains and losses and the cost of observing can be exactly calculated, as in industrial quality control. In other cases, as in theoretical research, it is necessary to make some assumption about the cost of being wrong and the gain of being right" (Edwards, 1954, p. 409).

The emphasis in decision theory has been on attempts to specify utilities or payoff functions which will enable the decision maker to make the decision which minimizes loss, maximizes gain or minimizes regret, where "regret is defined as the difference between the maximum which can be gained under any strategy given a certain state of the world and the amount gained under the strategy adopted" (Edwards, 1954, p. 409).

In 1957, the first edition of Cronbach and Gleser's *Psychological Tests and Personal Decisions* appeared, presenting an analysis of decision theory and psychological testing. The revised edition, which appeared in 1965, includes a chapter which covers the intervening years. We are now beginning to see a way in which decision theory may be of some value to decisions based on psychological tests. The "observations which cost something to make" may be viewed as the psychological tests while the "policies each of which has a possible gain or loss" are the alternatives open to the decision maker.

To facilitate the later discussion, let us briefly define some terms which have been developed in decision theory and re-define some other concepts in terms of decision theory.

Tests: Any "information-gathering procedures including interviews, biographical inquiries, and physical measurement" (Cronbach & Gleser, 1965, p. 7).

Institutional vs. Individual Decision: An institutional decision is one in which one person (or group of persons) makes many comparable decisions. An individual decision "is one in which the choice confronting the decision maker will rarely or never recur" (Cronbach & Gleser, 1965, p. 7). Institutional decisions are made in regard to many people and the decision maker will make decisions which will—in the long run—be best for the institution, be it a large corporation, mental hospital, penal complex, or large community.

In an individual decision, the best choice "depends on the individual's value system and varies from one individual to another" (Cronbach & Gleser, 1965, p. 8).

Values: Since decisions are good or bad depending on the outcome of the decision, much of decision theory has been concerned with the study of outcomes or, as they are called in decision theory, *payoffs* or *utilities*. For almost all kinds of payoffs, however, the nature of the payoff functions is difficult to specify and the study of values becomes—for the first time in measurement theory—a crucial problem. It may be that the greatest contribution of decision theory will be that it forces the decision maker to be explicit about his value system.

Girshick (1954) writes:

> "... decision theory demands a great deal of the decision maker. It demands that he be in a position to evaluate numerically for every possible state of nature in the situation under consideration the consequences of any of the actions he might take . . . The inability of the decision maker to formulate clearly the loss function is, in fact, a stumbling block in determining what a rational mode of behavior is for him . . . It is impossible to tell a person what is an optimal way for him to behave if he is unable to formulate clearly what he is after. . . ." (p. 463).

To paraphrase Girshick: Decision theory is a gadfly for the psychodiagnostician. It says to him: You cannot be of any service to the person making the referral unless you can specify what decision he is facing, what alternatives are available to him, what the utility or value of these alternatives is, and finally, what relevance test data and observations have in terms of specifying outcomes for each of the alternatives once they are adopted.

The problem of values is especially difficult because the values of one decision maker may differ from the values of another decision maker. As Bross (1953) writes:

"I have already noted that the various rules for action reflect various attitudes that might be taken toward the real world— optimism, pessimism, and the like. So presumably we should select the rule which comes closest to expressing the outlook of the customer, the person who has come for advice on decision. While this procedure is plausible, it is not very practical. The statistician would have to find some device for measuring the customer's general outlook on life. Things are complicated enough with predicting systems and value systems without having to take this further step—although it may come about someday" (p. 110).

Maximization: The strategy of maximizing the average gain (or minimizing the average loss) over many similar decisions. According to Cronbach and Gleser (1965, pp. 8-9) this strategy is not generally relevant for individual decisions. Ward Edwards (1963, 1966) disagrees, emphasizing that our opinions about (our probabilities for) various possible events may be relatively clear or relatively vague, but are never utterly clear or utterly vague and that individual decisions should be made on the same basis as institutional decisions.

Sequential Strategy: Classical test theory generally assumed that a final decision was made on all individuals at one time on the basis of a single test battery. Sequential strategy involves several stages of information-gathering at each of which some decisions are reached, but other decisions put off.

Bandwidth: This term—taken from information theory—refers to the scope of information which the test is designed to obtain. Achievement tests have narrow bandwidth; projective tests are wideband procedures. Generally, greater bandwidth is achieved by sacrificing accuracy of measurement.

Incremental Validity: The extent to which a test improves decisions over the strategy which would have been employed without the test. This should be contrasted with comparing the test-based strategy with a random strategy.

Bounded vs. Unbounded Problems: The distinction between bounded and unbounded problems is described by Levy (1963):

The bounded problem is one involving a discrete prediction or decision, usually circumscribed in time and most often concerned with the classification or disposition of a case, whereas the unbounded case involves problems of case management such as in psychotherapy, where the therapist requires of psychodiagnosis a formulation that will serve as a continuing guide in his moment-to-moment and day-to-day decision making. While in the bounded case we know in advance the conditions under which the psycho-diagnostic product will be used, in the unbounded case such information is generally lacking or of the most diffuse sort. Considering the distinctive characteristics of each, the formal approach to psychodiagnosis, of which the actuarial method of prediction is one example, is found most appropriate and efficient when dealing with bounded problems, while the interpretive approach offers distinct advantages in the case of unbounded problems" (p. 194).

Conclusion vs. Decisions: Tukey (1960) has formulated a distinction between decisions and conclusions. Decisions involve acting "for the present as if" the outcomes of different alternatives are known because a decision between alternatives is necessary at the time. The decision maker weighs . . .

"... both the *evidence* concerning the relative merits of *A* and *B* and also *the probable consequences in the present situation* of various actions (actions, not decisions!). Finally, we have decided that the particular course of action which would be appropriate if *A* were truly greater than *B* is the most reasonable one to adopt in the specific situation that faces us.

"A conclusion is a statement which is to be accepted as applicable to the conditions of an experiment or observation unless and until unusually strong evidence to the contrary arises . . . These characteristics are very different from those of a decision-theorist's decision" (pp. 2-4).

Decision to Do Nothing: The decision to do nothing has received little attention in decision theory, but Tukey quotes Barnard as saying:

"The fine art of executive decision consists in not deciding questions that are now not pertinent, in not deciding prematurely, in not making decisions that cannot be made effective, and in not making decisions that others should make" (p. 5).

The decision to do nothing occupies a special place in decision theory.

The model of testing which I have adopted, then, is based on a decision theory which requires that 1) a decision must be made; 2) psychological tests can be expected to contribute information which will enable the decision maker to maximize his strategy; and 3) the decision maker will actually alter his strategy to coincide with this new information.[1]

It should be noted that some psychologists hold that testing not be limited in this way. Sundberg and Tyler (1962) cite "twin functional goals of clinical assessment as the process used for decision making and for developing a working image or model of the person-situation." They write:

> "The making of decisions is not all there is to clinical assessment . . . To some degree the clinician always builds up a *picture* of the person with whom he is dealing . . . This function of assessment is what we have called the development of a working image or model. By the working image or model we mean the *clinician's set of hypotheses about the person and the situations in which he presently or potentially operates* . . . The working image is the best approximation a clinician can achieve of a representation of the other human being" (pp. 84-85).

Levy's concept of "unbounded psychodiagnostic problems" seems to be dealing with the same kind of approach and seems to fall logically outside a formal decision theory model as presented here. His "interpretive approach"—which he says is appropriate for unbounded problems— ". . . is found to culminate in a set of assertions (not decisions) based upon the clinician's experience, observations, theories, and beliefs. . . ."

The logic and mathematics of decision theory are intriguing in their own right and the implications are likely to be of value to psychology in a way that far transcends test theory. Good starting points for the reader who is interested in exploring this material further are Cronbach and Gleser (1965), Bross (1953), or Churchman (1961).

THE PSYCHIATRIC SETTING

"We regard the human brain as the *chef d'oeuvre,* or masterpiece of creation . . . Insanity is but a disease of this organ, and when so regarded, it will often be prevented, and generally cured, by the early adoption of proper methods of treatment" (American Journal of Insanity, 1844, back cover).

This point of view—the manifesto of the officers of the New York State Lunatic Asylum—was probably shared by the majority of physicians who met in 1844 to establish the American Association of Mental Hospital Superintendents—later the American Psychiatric Association. However,

---

[1]It has been suggested that, since the criterion problem remains, decision theory does not represent a conceptual advance over classical measurement theory. Even if this turns out to be the case, our analysis of the social context of psychological testing has been facilitated by conceiving of it in terms of decision theory.

the cure of syphilis (and subsequent decline of paresis), the advent of psychoanalysis, the introduction of the tranquilizers, and recent developments in psychology, sociology, and anthropology have led most psychiatrists to adopt a much broader perspective to their work. The establishment within the past few years of community mental health centers illustrates this broadening of perspective in psychiatry from the study of the brain to the study of the individual in transaction with family, society, and culture.

These multiple developments make it difficult to speak of a single psychiatric setting and, for purposes of our discussion, we will speak of the psychologist in relation to the psychiatrist as ward administrator; the psychiatrist as psychotherapist; and the psychiatrist as physician.

Psychiatrist as ward administrator

The psychiatrist as hospital administrator or ward administrator is a clear example of a decision maker. He is responsible for the health and well-being of his patients; he has the authority to administer a wide variety of medical procedures; he has the authority to say whether a patient will be free or locked up. Shall I discharge the patient? Shall he be transferred to an open ward? Is he a suicide risk? And so on. As with most people in positions of authority, the hospital administrator will utilize help to assist in making these decisions. Why then is the psychologist in the mental hospital so often the one most frustrated in his role as psychodiagnostician?

There seem to be several reasons. First, these decisions are difficult ones in the sense that the base rates are not well established. We don't know how many patients who attempt suicide will eventually be successful. We don't know how many patients who have threatened to kill somebody will actually commit murder. But we do know that these are rare occurrences and the prediction of rare occurrences is an extremely difficult task.

Second, when evaluated in terms of classical measurement theory, our projective tests have often been found wanting. Psychologists have been taught in graduate schools that the goal of measurement is prediction, but find that in practice the procedures they employ are not accurate predictors.

Third, many psychiatrists ignore at times the results of psychological examinations without discontinuing the practice of asking that these examinations be made.

Why do hospital administrators continue to hire psychologists as psychodiagnosticians? Most often the psychologist is seen as filling a technician's role—much like an X-ray technician or laboratory technician. The possible seeds for the growth of tension and dissatisfaction for the Ph.D. psychologist in this kind of situation are obvious.

From the point of view of the physician, biochemical analyses are done by laboratory technicians, not by Ph.D.'s in biochemistry. Why then should he not expect that psychological tests be done by psychological technicians with the integration of all findings being left up to the physician? He has learned what a 10,000 white blood cell count means, why can't he learn what an M:C ratio of 1:4 means? Why does the psychologist insist on long-winded descriptions when all he wants is a diagnosis?

But is that really all he wants? As Szasz (1963) has pointed out, the psychiatrist as ward administrator has altered his major professional responsibility from treatment to custody and his major decisions involve not diagnosis and treatment, but questions of the freedom of the patient and the safety of society. To the extent that psychiatric diagnosis is helpful in making these social decisions, diagnosis is an important step. But classical psychiatric nosology has been found to be irrelevant to these decisions. Whether or not a patient is schizophrenic is not helpful in deciding whether he is dangerous to himself or others.

If the decision is made to keep the patient in the institution, a host of subsequent decisions must be faced: To what kind of ward shall he be assigned? To what kind of activities? Which of the available "therapies" is likely to be of benefit to him?

The psychologist working in a mental hospital who receives a referral for "psychologicals" with no further information may respond in accordance with his own needs, the defensive reactions I described earlier in this chapter—withdrawal, rationalization, projection, etc. Or he can attempt to determine what the relevant and important decisions are which will have to be made with respect to the patient and then try to obtain information relevant to these decisions. The first step in finding answers is to determine the appropriate questions.

But, to the extent that the psychologist is unwilling to accept the fact that the psychiatrist as hospital administrator has been charged by society with the legal responsibility for decisions about patients—to that extent the psychologist will be unable to use psychological testing procedures to help the psychiatrist. In a decision making model of testing, the importance of knowing the decision maker's values has been clearly demonstrated.

Psychiatrist as psychotherapist

Much difficulty develops when the psychiatrist confuses his own roles. When a psychiatrist attempts to function as both therapist and caretaker or when he shifts haphazardly from one role to another, the nature of his relationship with the patient—and with the psychologist—is likely to become ambiguous at best and tense and distorted at worst. Many psychological referrals are outcomes of difficult situations which psychiatrists have gotten into because of their attempt to play several conflicting roles in relation to their patients.

However, let us try to explore the situation in which a psychotherapist refers a patient for testing at some point during psychotherapy. A referral *before* psychotherapy asks the question "Is this patient suitable for psychotherapy?" and has been one of the traditional functions of psychological assessment. This kind of referral is clear-cut and, to the extent that the psychologist is willing to accept it, generally presents few problems.

A referral made during the course of psychotherapy is generally more complex because it frequently reflects anxiety on the part of the therapist, whose expectations about what the patient should be doing are not being fulfilled. Frequently, if the psychologist is to make an honest evaluation of the situation, he must communicate to the psychotherapist that the therapist's expectations are unreasonable, rather than that the patient is not being a "good patient." This "diagnostic triad" is the kind of situation which Towbin (1960) has analyzed so lucidly.

Psychiatrist as physician

Special problems ensue from the basically different frames of reference which psychiatrists and psychologists bring to understanding the patient. Although there is clearly much overlap between the two frames of reference, most psychiatrists view their patient's problems in terms of a disease model while most psychologists see the patient's problems as arising from his difficulties in living with people and in society. The psychologist—as tester—needs to be able to communicate with the psychiatrist. If the psychiatrist asks the question "Is this patient schizophrenic?" of a psychologist who feels that the concept "schizophrenia" is vague, confused, oversimplified, and stupid, the psychologist will have difficulty answering the question. The question, "Is the patient schizophrenic?" may, however, be one of several different questions. The psychiatrist may be saying:

"This new patient must be classified because of legal statutes and hospital regulations. I know as well as you do that 'schizophrenia' is a philosophically embarrassing concept, but we have a job to do, so let's do it."

Or, "This patient can only give vague explanations for coming to the hospital. I suspect he has a lot of very peculiar ideas which he is not talking about and I'm worried that he might behave in a way to hurt himself or someone else on the basis of these peculiar ideas. On the basis of a psychological evaluation, what is your opinion of the nature and quality of his thinking processes?"

Or, "I know the scientific research on this is very poor, but I have to decide whether to give this patient tranquilizing medication, electric convulsive therapy, or psychotherapy and it is my best opinion that patients diagnosed schizophrenic, rather than neurotic or brain damaged, can be treated most efficiently (in decision theory terms, the payoff is best) by tranquilizers. What is your opinion about the best classification of this patient?"

A psychologist who views his role in psychological assessment as a "technician" rather than as a "consultant" (Towbin, 1960) will not be able to distinguish among these three possibilities. The psychologist *qua* psychologist, i.e., a person trained and experienced in the scientific study of behavior, will make a serious attempt to understand the psychiatrist's frame of reference and is likely to formulate his contribution in terms of the psychiatrist's constructs—not because he feels they are most heuristic, but because he realizes that the job at hand requires the maximum communication. He may have to translate the psychiatrist's concepts into terms which he feels are scientifically meaningful and then retranslate them so as to communicate his findings to the psychiatrist; this may be difficult—certainly more difficult than finding a recipe for a cake which doesn't exist.

GENERAL MEDICAL SETTING

This discussion of theoretical models and formal language is important for the effective functioning of the psychologist as psychodiagnostician in a general medical setting. The medical psychologist not only needs to learn a complex and extensive medical vocabulary, but he needs also to appreciate that a medical decision is different from a scientific decision (or conclusion); the loss function of not rejecting a null hypothesis because of insufficient data is different from the loss function of not performing an operation because of insufficient data. Furthermore, the loss function of not performing one kind of operation is likely to be different from the loss function connected with not performing another kind of operation, or with not performing an operation when the patient is showing one set of symptoms as compared with not performing the operation when the patient is showing a different set of symptoms. Rarely in medicine are these loss functions specifically stated. How then are medical decisions arrived at?

I am familiar with no systematic study of this question. But it is well known that physicians are trained to make these decisions, to use all possible resources to aid in making these decisions, but to assume final responsibility for them. The fact that the physician is the person who is licensed under the Medical Practices Act and who therefore has the legal responsibility for these decisions is a social factor that the psychologist must be prepared to accept if he is to function as efficiently and constructively in the medical setting as in the psychiatric setting. The responsibility and authority for the decision rests with the physician, not with the psychologist. When we are reminded, however, of the estimate that two-thirds of the patients a physician sees in his regular medical practice have a significant emotional component in their illness, the potential contribution of a clinical psychodiagnostician to medical decision making is obvious. Good medical practice is based on an awareness of the psychosomatic factors, the unity of mind and body.

The kind of referral from a physician that is likely to present most difficulties for the psychologist is the one which asks him to "evaluate the emotional factors" in a patient who complains of low back pain, or stomach distress, or headaches but for whose symptoms the medical examination has failed to reveal any organic etiology. The physician is faced with the problem of recommending some kind of treatment, but in the absence of positive signs of mental disorder is hesitant to recommend psychotherapy. If the psychologist could find a psychological disorder, the medical decision would be simplified. Can a psychologist ever fail to find some sign of emotional upset? Especially in someone who is physically ill? On the other hand, can psychological tests rule out organic factors? It appear as if—in this kind of referral situation at least—the professional roles are reversed. Instead of having the psychologist diagnose and the physician do the treatment, it would seem more logical for the physician to diagnose, i.e., rule out organic factors, and for the psychologist to treat those patients for whom no organic etiology can be established.

A common referral in the medical context which makes more sense is the one which asks the psychologist to evaluate the possibility of neurological involvement. Here the psychologist is able to supplement the information obtained in the neurological examination. Whereas the neurological examination focusses primarily on the peripheral nervous system, the psychological examination is concerned with determining if the higher mental processes are intact. However, even this referral is relevant primarily when the physician has a decision to make. If the presence or absence of neurological involvement would not alter the treatment program, there seems little point in the referral. At times, however, signs of deterioration of the higher mental processes may point toward the need for more refined and risky evaluative procedures, such as a ventriculogram or explorative surgery. Here psychological tests may be seen as one stage in sequential decision making, a common kind of decision making in medical practice.

Increasingly, psychologists have become involved in psychological testing prior to surgery. Here the surgeon is interested in evaluating the risk of a stress reaction consequent to the operation. Although the research in this area is at a preliminary stage (Janis, 1958) this kind of question appears to be a logically appropriate one for a clinical psychologist.

A final illustration of the kind of referral which psychologists receive from physicians is the one from the pediatrician, whose contacts with a family have led him to suspect the beginnings of a serious psychological disorder, and who wants to have this hypothesis explored. This kind of referral stems from the widely accepted emphasis on preventive medicine. In this case, it is often helpful—if not essential—to evaluate the difficulty which the pediatrician may face in confronting the parents with the psychologist's findings and with their resistance to the psychologist's recommendations. Thus, it is not of much help merely to confirm or disconfirm the pediatrician's hypotheses; rather it is necessary to go beyond confirmation and assist in planning for the next step in intervention. Often this next step is the one which requires the greater clinical judgment and psychological wisdom.

THE LEGAL CONTEXT

Of the two disciplines—law and psychology—law has the grander tradition and the more awesome stature. Yet, within the past ten years, psychologists have entered legal chambers with increasing frequency and, even if at times psychologists have appeared inept or stupid, the courts in general afford psychologists much respect.

Law is a system of regulating man's relations in society and it "aims at the just resolution of human conflict" (Cowan, 1963). As such, the study and practice of law by attorneys and jurists encompasses a wide range of human knowledge, not only in the scientific sense, but also in the broader humanistic tradition. Modern legal philosophers are much concerned, for example, with the results of historical studies, sociological research, philosophy, and cultural anthropology (Northrop, 1959).

The law evolves as society evolves. Hence the law is generally cognizant of the contributions to knowledge which are made by other disciplines. But law is also conservative and changes in legal procedure will be slow. We may expect, therefore, that the psychologist's contribution to the legal process will be marked with difficulties and will be characterized by ups and downs.

Probably the most striking advance in the stature of psychologists in the court came in connection with the Jenkins case (Hoch & Darley, 1962) during which the "acceptibility of testimony by properly qualified psychologists in cases involving the determination and meaning of mental disease or defect as productive of criminal acts" was sustained by a 7-2 vote of the United States Court of Appeals for the District of Columbia (p. 626).

A low point—the lowest with which I am familiar—took place in the District Court of the District of Columbia during which

> ". . . the witness [a psychologist] testified that a psychologist could diagnose illness by the pictures a subject selected as those he liked or disliked [the Szondi test]. At this point the judge threw the cards down. At a Bench conference the defense attorney asked:

'May the record reflect that after the last question the Court slammed the cards down?'

Court: 'The record may reflect it but the record may show I am throwing it all out. That will take care of that session' (Jeffery, 1964, p. 843).

The role of the judge in a jury trial and in legal decision making in general is a controversial one in legal philosophy and jurisprudence (Wasserstrom, 1961). What is not controversial, however, is that legal decisions, whether they are made by judge, jury, or attorney, are not made in the same way that scientific decisions or medical decisions are made and the psychologist who expects the court or the jury to make use of his contribution to the decision making process will need to be familiar with the legal system and to have a clear understanding of the specific contribution he is being called upon to make.

Cowan (1963) has presented a most careful analysis of decision making in the legal context and writes:

> "The scientist *generalizes;* the lawyer *individuates.* It would take a lifetime to substantiate this bald assertion, but since none of us has a lifetime to give to it, I shall confine myself to a summary statement: *Litigation aims to individuate, and the judicial process is most at home when it disposes of a unique conflict situation uniquely* . . . I believe that the law will warp and twist the facts, sometimes in an apparently shameless manner, if necessary, to obtain what it thinks of as the *just* result . . . True equality in law might almost be said to consist in the maxim: *no two cases are ever really alike"* (pp. 1065-66).

If no two cases are ever alike what we need is a theory of individual decisions, not institutional decision. Cowan's conclusions are relatively pessimistic in this regard:

> ". . . there is nothing in present technology or theory, or even in the minds of the investigators of decision making, that suggests that the *individual decision* will ever become the object of scientific investigation. I should like to be able to report that some scientific interest in this matter does exist. But if it does I have not come upon it . . . Among the 'homely truths' to be borne in mind are the following:
>
> 1. No general theory of social action exists that has received widespread acceptance even among social scientists. . . .
>
> 2. No general theory of human motivation in the individual exists . . ." (p. 1072).

It may be that Cowan is unfamiliar with the psychological and social-psychological literature or that his standards for a "general theory" are more stringent than the standards of most psychologists. Theories of individual motivation do exist; scientific validation of these theories may not reach the standards Cowan has set up. Nevertheless, the psychologist who is aware of these theories and who is aware, at the same time, of the nature of the evidence which is available to support aspects of these theories is in a position to serve society by furnishing an expert opinion to the courts.

What is expert testimony?

"To warrant the use of expert testimony, then, two elements are required. First, the subject of the inference must be so distinctively related to some science, profession, business or occupation as to be beyond the ken of the average layman, and second, the the witness must have such skill, knowledge or experience in that field or calling as to make it appear that his opinion or inference will probably aid the trier in his search for truth. The knowledge may in some fields be derived from reading alone, in some from practice alone, or as is more commonly the case from both" [McCormick, Evidence (1954)].

"The trial judge should make a finding in respect to the individual qualifications of each challenged expert. Qualifications to express an opinion on a given topic are to be decided by the judge alone. The weight to be given any expert opinion admitted in evidence by the judge is exclusively for the jury" (United States Court of Appeals. No. 16306, cited by Hoch and Darley, 1962, pp. 648-650).

Many psychologists express the opinion that the psychologist will make his contribution most efficiently if he is used as a "friend of the court." He can thus avoid being involved in legal tangles or appearing foolish when a colleague employed by the "other side" presents an opposing opinion.

Much as the psychologist may prefer to be called into a case as a "friend of the court," our system of jurisprudence is based on the advocacy principle—that truth and justice are most likely to emerge when opposing attorneys engage in a legal contest.

In terms of criminal law, the psychologist may be called in at almost any stage of the proceedings: During the investigatory stage by the police (though rarely); by the prosecuting attorney to assist in determining what crime has been committed (e.g., manslaughter or first degree murder); by the defense attorney (often as a last resort); by the judge to contribute to the presentation of evidence; by the judge after the trial to assist in determining the sentence; by the penal officer to plan for the criminal's prison term; by the parole board to assist in their decision; or by the parole officer to assist in rehabilitation planning.

Frequently the psychologist is called into a case by a defense attorney who is trying to establish an innocent verdict by reason of insanity. The many discussions of the M'Naughten rule, irresistable impulse, and the Durham decision are controversies with which legal psychologists must be familiar (Leifer, 1964). Whether or not a psychologist is willing to give an opinion about these issues in any particular case is up to his individual conscience. But he must be prepared to be cross-examined: that is the nature of our legal system. As Harry S. Truman said, "If you can't stand the heat, get out of the kitchen." But if a psychologist believes that our legal system is of value, he will probably feel that there is a legitimate place in it for his expert opinion.

THE EDUCATIONAL CONTEXT

The role of education—especially public education—in our society has been expanding, not only since Sputnik, but for hundreds of years. President Johnson's Great Society, with programs such as the Job Corps, Project Head Start, and the Elementary and Secondary Education Act of 1965, has given an added impetus to this development. In a social institution which is changing rapidly, the role of psychological testing can be expected to be changing as well.

The nature of psychological testing in schools is much less uniform than it is in hospitals, but many of the issues are the same. There is the need for the psychologist to be able to understand the educator's decision problems and the language in which he formulates his alternatives. When a teacher refers a child to find out if he has a "learning block," he is probably trying to get more information so that he can decide whether this child should be retained in grade, transferred to a slower educational program, or advanced in grade but recommended for psychotherapy. The school psychologist needs to know what alternatives are available to the educator and what non-test considerations may be involved in the decision making process.

The recent policy statement made by the senior staff specialist of Project Head Start describing the psychologist's function in the program de-emphasizes the role of psychologist as tester and places much more emphasis on the psychologist's functioning as a consultant to the teacher (Spickler, 1966).

It is unfortunate that so many educators have adopted a medical model of human behavior without fully comprehending the implications of such a model. By so doing, they have made the assumption that "early identification" (which is seen as analogous to early medical diagnosis) is always a desirable goal—that early identification of problem children will lead to the early institution of treatment procedures and that early treatment will lead to early "cure." But there are dangers associated with labelling a potential "problem" too early. The Society for the Psychological Study of Social Issues (SPSSI) Council statement issued in connection with the use of the Glueck Prediction tables for the early identification of potential juvenile delinquents points out that

> ". . . unless the utmost caution and care are taken, children who are 'identified' and labelled as probable future delinquents are likely to be treated and isolated as 'bad' children by teachers and others who are now subjected to the virtually hysterical climate of opinion concerning juvenile delinquency. Such treatment is likely to increase the child's sense of social alienation and thereby, increase the probability of his becoming delinquent or of developing other forms of psychological maladjustment" (SPSSI Newsletter, 1960).

This is an example of the self-fulfilling prophecy which makes it difficult to assess scientifically the validity of psychological test procedures. The SPSSI statement also pointed out that the predictive claims associated with the Glueck tables were based primarily on extreme base rates.

The analogy of "early identification" of behavior problems with the "early diagnosis" of medical illness is, moreover, what Oppenheimer (1956) calls a "disanalogy." Except for some cases of mental retardation and organic brain damage (and probably fewer of these than we believe), the problem of diagnosing educational problems is not analogous to medical diagnosis. Among other differences, a medical problem involves a single individual while an educational problem generally involves a family constellation. Further, an educational problem can be understood only in terms of a complex of variables within the individual, while a medical diagnosis may hinge on a single factor. Oppenheimer has pointed out that when a model has more disanalogous elements than analogous elements, a new theoretical model is generally found. A theory is available to educators, i.e., that educational problems are part of a more global failure of the child to create a socially effective life style because of disturbed interpersonal relations in the family. This model is not as simple and straightforward as a disease model, but it does seem generally more consistent with observations.

The adoption of this model, however, would introduce some difficulty for the psychological tester in the school system: no longer would it be desirable simply to test the "slow learner" and make a diagnosis. It would now be necessary to evaluate the total family picture for a clear understanding of the factors involved in the learning problem. Whether or not the family was willing to cooperate in such an enterprise would become an important consideration.

An especially difficult situation exists when a disruptive family is combined with an emotionally disturbed teacher. Towbin's diagnostic triad of psychiatrist, patient, and psychologist presents problems for the psychologist, but the configuration of people involved in most school referrals is much more complex and involves many more possible sources of tension and misunderstanding. Besides the child, his parents, and the teacher, also involved may be the principal, a guidance counselor, and, in a small community, members of the school board. Each of these people represents a possible source of conflict and every combination of forces may need to be understood. In addition, the hierarchical and authoritarian structure of most school systems makes the nature of these tensions especially difficult to uncover and—if uncovered—to deal with.

A related problem for the school psychologist which does not exist to any great extent as yet in the medical or legal setting is the question of group testing. The question then becomes "When and Why to give Group Tests." If it is good to identify disturbed youngsters as early as possible, why not "institute a large scale group testing program and really handle the problem."

The evidence presently available does not support the notion that early identification leads to more effective treatment (Levitt, 1957, 1963). Most theories of psychotherapy, especially recent ones developed in the framework of community mental health programs, stress the importance of timing in therapeutic intervention. Although the timing of intervention needs to be studied further, the idea that therapeutic effectiveness is based to a considerable extent on motivation for change and that motivation for change exists at times of crisis, is gaining wide acceptance.

One implication of this discussion is clear: the question for the psychologist is not simply "How disturbed is this youngster?" or even "What is the nature of his disturbance?" The additional question "Is there sufficient motivation in this family at this time so that therapeutic intervention should be recommended?" must be considered. As Cole and Magnussen (1966) have suggested, evaluation must be geared to action.

THE PSYCHOLOGICAL CLINIC

In the medical, legal, and educational institutions, the psychologist functions as a consultant to the decision maker; in the psychological clinic, the psychologist is himself often the decision maker. Although he must operate under legal restraints, it is primarily *his* value system which will effect the decisions. What are the implications of this for the question of "Why and When to Test?" What kinds of decisions does the psychologist in a psychological clinic make? What kinds of questions is he asked? What kinds of clients does he see?

First, there is the sizeable group of "self-referrals," people who are uncomfortable or dissatisfied and who have heard about psychotherapy.

They come to the clinic hoping to be relieved of their misery. In most of these situations, psychological testing is irrelevant; it is necessary to agree on a workable psychotherapeutic relationship and to start the treatment process. Generally the client is in some kind of a crisis and is well-motivated so that the time is propitious for starting psychotherapy.

There will be some self-referrals, however, which the psychologist feels —for one reason or another—are not suitable cases for a psychological clinic: either the medical factors are too prominent; there are legal implications which must be clarified first; or the nature of the client's psychological disturbance is such that institutionalization may be necessary during the course of the treatment. In these cases, the psychologist may feel the need for more information before making a decision about psychotherapy: psychological testing is an appropriate way to get this information. It is important that the client realize that the tests are being given to help the psychologist decide how to proceed. The tests are not being given to help the patient directly.

A second category of psychological clinic cases are children brought to the clinic by parents, either because the youngster is not doing well in school, has gotten into trouble with the police, or is in some way not living up to parental expectations. These cases require special precautions before testing is begun. As indicated in the discussion of the educational setting, this kind of referral needs to be understood in the broadest terms. What other agencies has the family worked with? What relationship exists between the school and the family? The court and the family? More often than not, the specific incident which finally led the parents to seek professional help is only one event in a long pattern of social disturbance. If the psychologist were to take a parent's request at face value, he might test the child, give a diagnostic interpretation to the parents and make a recommendation. This procedure would be the one followed in a narrowly conceived medical model, although now even physicians and psychiatrists realize that a narrow disease model is inappropriate for problems of this kind. What is needed is a global evaluation of the family dynamics: the family's relation to the community and the relations of members of the family to one another.

To illustrate this kind of situation: I received a call from a woman who asked if the Psychological Clinic gave aptitude tests; she said she wanted to have her sixteen-year-old son receive aptitude tests because he couldn't make up his mind about what kind of work he wanted to do. I replied that we did give aptitude tests if we felt that they would help answer a relevant question, but that I would first want to discuss with her in more detail what aptitude testing might be expected to accomplish. An appointment was set up with her for the following week.

At the interview I learned that her son did not attend the regular public school, but was in a private home for boys in a nearby town; apparently he had been having trouble in school and with the police.

Her lawyer and the juvenile judge had reached an agreement that he be sent to this Boys' Home. Why couldn't he profitably remain at home with his family and receive professional help? She then told me that she had three younger children and was working full-time because she was in the process of getting a divorce from her husband who was in the state hospital where he had been for about a year. During the preceding year the boy had been in individual therapy at the local Child Guidance Clinic; she had attended several group therapy sessions for parents, but had stopped going because she didn't feel she could benefit from *group* therapy.

I decided that vocational aptitude testing was irrelevant to the problems which this mother was presenting and discussed with her the possibility of trying to get a better understanding of the total family situation. She agreed to such a plan and a case conference was arranged. Attending this conference were the therapist from the Child Guidance Clinic, the probation officer from the Juvenile Court, the social worker from the Boys' Home, the guidance counselor from the public schools, the mother's attorney, the State Hospital psychiatrist working with the boy's father, and a representative of the Psychological Clinic. At the conference it became clear that there were important decisions to be made: Should the father be released from the State Hospital? Should he be allowed to visit his son at the Boys' Home? What kind of educational program was appropriate for the boy? Should he be allowed home visits? Should the mother be encouraged to resume psychotherapy?

Psychological evaluations of the boy, the mother and the father were carried out and were part of the information available for discussion at a follow-up conference—at which tentative decisions were reached—but the final decisions generally rested with agencies other than the Psychological Clinic. Does this procedure make more sense than giving the younger aptitude tests and handing out some test scores? I think so, but I'm not sure how one would proceed to study this issue scientifically.

In a psychological clinic, a psychologist will also receive referrals from other decision makers, especially when these decision makers do not employ their psychologists. It is sometimes possible in the clinic to consider the problem in a broader perspective than when one is closely involved with an agency. We received a referral from the local Sanity Board—a Board consisting of a psychiatrist, lawyer, and Clerk of the District Court—which has the legal responsibility for committing patients to the state mental hospital. The Board wanted us to test a man whose wife had filed a sanity complaint against him; they questioned his sanity but found the decision a difficult one to make. Although the results of psychological testing revealed no clear evidence of psychosis, they were difficult to interpret with much confidence until we decided to ask the wife to come in for an evaluation. As a result of this evaluation the entire situation became clearer. Although not overtly psychotic, the wife's projective test performance reflected a profoundly disturbed woman who had very meager psychological resources. In this case, by the way, a follow-up is available. The couple were seen jointly in psychotherapy, but after about six or seven sessions, the wife started complaining that the therapy sessions were too upsetting; soon after, she stopped coming. The husband continued for about ten more sessions, which he seemed to use in a moderately productive way.

IMPLICATIONS

We have sampled the kinds of institutional settings in which psychologists work in an attempt to understand under what conditions psychological testing will improve decision making. Although I might have discussed other settings, such as industry, university counseling centers, welfare departments, prisons, and so on, I have decided to stay close to my own experience. This excursion has led me to arrive at several judgments about the process of psychological evaluation—judgments which I think can be generalized to other work settings and to other social institutions.

First, a decision making model for psychological testing is a heuristic one. It will often assist the psychologist in dealing with the individual case in a more constructive way than would otherwise be possible. It will help him focus on the essential aspects of the problem and avoid digressions and irrelevancies.

Second, the complex context of most psychological testing requires careful analysis to determine the essential referral question and the nature of the available alternatives. It is an essential—perhaps crucial—part of the psychologist's job to understand this complex situation. It is unrealistic to expect that the decision maker will always be able to formulate the referral question in a clear and concise manner. In fact, psychologists are called upon generally only in the most difficult or complex cases. If a patient is obviously psychotic, no referral may be made. If, however, there are serious doubts about the patient, the psychologist is expected to contribute to the decision making process. The person who views his role simply as a tester will be unable to make this analysis. But a psychologist, a person trained in the study of behavior and skilled in the understanding of interpersonal factors in a complex social setting, will be equipped to analyze the total referral context.

Third, the clinical psychodiagnostician must consider himself responsible for learning the theories and the language of the institutional setting in which he works. He must be more than a psychologist; he must also be knowledgeable about the realistic alternatives available to the decision maker. Emphasis should be given to the great responsibility which the clinical psychologist assumes when he undertakes to provide "service" of any kind, even to the extent of admitting that his efforts provided no answers to the question. This responsibility is primary to the referred patient, child, or whoever it is, *not* to his favorite tests, his professional status, or the field of clinical psychology.

Fourth, new measurement techniques emphasizing interpersonal interactions rather than individual dynamics need to be developed. At the University of Nebraska Psychological Clinic we have found the Family Relations Test (Elias, 1949) and the family diagnostic interview (Tyler, 1962) useful, but these kinds of techniques are at too early a stage of development.

Fifth, the training of clinical psychologists should continue to be broad in scope, consistent with the Boulder scientist-professional model, and we should resist suggestions that we train psychodiagnosticians at a technicians' level. Although it is possible to teach a person to administer tests, to score them accurately, and to "interpret" them according to some cookbook principles, this use of psychological tests is not flexible enough to assist in individual decisions nor sophisticated enough to develop tests which will be useful in institutional decisions. Further, this kind of tester is insufficiently knowledgeable about general and social psychological theory and principles to comprehend the subtleties of complex referrals and to formulate meaningful alternatives.

Sixth, much of the research on test validity is not immediately relevant to the practical use of psychological tests. The question of the value of tests becomes not "Does the test correlate with a criterion?" or "Does the test accord with a nomological net?" but rather "Does the use of the test improve the success of the decision making process?" either by making it more efficient, less costly, more accurate, more rational, or more relevant. The clinical-actuarial controversy becomes academic since most of the research in that area is irrelevant in decision making. For example, Lindzey's (1965) demonstration that clinical psychologists can identify homosexuals from the TAT has no decision making relevance. Furthermore, all the demonstrations that psychological tests do not agree with psychiatric diagnoses fall into the "so what?" category.

Seventh, values held strongly by the psychologist may conflict with the values of the decision maker, e.g., sterilization procedures for the mentally retarded, capital punishment for first degree murder. If this conflict is irreconcilable, the psychologist may have to admit that he cannot function effectively as a psychological consultant in this context. More serious difficulties may ensue if the psychologist is unaware of this conflict in values or insists on arguing that the decision maker change his values. In the latter case he is not functioning as a psychological consultant even though he may be accomplishing a more important social purpose.

Finally, the problems we face in connection with the use of psychological tests will not all be solved by the suggestions made in this chapter. Rather, we face new and perhaps more difficult problems. Attempts to understand the values of the decision maker will present enormous theoretical and practical problems; decision makers generally do not like to be studied. We will probably have difficulty developing psychological tests which measure complex social-psychological variables. Research on the question of whether testing improves the payoff function is difficult because of the impact which the psychological report has on the attitudes of people working with the patient, i.e., the self-fulfilling prophecy. I am personally more excited about these challenges than I was about the clinical-statistical controversy or the argument about construct validity.

REFERENCES

American Journal of Insanity. 1844, back cover.

Auld, F., Jr. Influence of social class on personality test responses. *Psychol. Bull.,* 1952, *49,* 318-332.

Bross, I. D. J. *Design for Decision.* New York: Macmillan, 1953.

Churchman, C. W. *Prediction and Optimal Decision: Philosophical Issues of a Science of Values.* Englewood Cliffs, N.J.: Prentice-Hall, 1961.

Cole, J. K., & Magnussen, M. G. Where the action is. *J. consult. Psychol.,* 1966, *30,* 539-543.

Cowan, T. A. Decision theory in law, science, and technology. *Science,* 1963, *140,* 1065-1075.

Cronbach, L. J., & Gleser, G. C. *Psychological Tests and Personnel Decisions.* Urbana, Ill.: University of Illinois Press, 1965.

Edwards, W. The theory of decision making. *Psychol. Bull.,* 1954, *51,* 380-417.

Edwards, W., Lindman, H., & Savage, L. J. Bayesian statistical inference for psychological research. *Psychol. Rev.,* 1963, *70,* 193-242.

Edwards, W. Personal communication, 1966.

Elias, G. Construction of a test of non-homeyness and related variables. Unpublished doctoral dissertation, Purdue University, 1949.

Girshick, M. A. An elementary survey of statistical decision theory. *Rev. educ. Res.,* 1954, *24,* 448-466.

Gross, M. L. *The Brain Watchers.* New York: The New American Library of World Literature, Inc., 1963.

Hoch, E. L., & Darley, J. G. A case at law. *Amer. Psychol.,* 1962, *17,* 623-654.

Hoffman, B. *The Tyranny of Testing.* Riverside, N.J.: Macmillan, 1962.

Holzberg, J. D. The role of the internship in the research training of the clinical psychologist. *J. consult. Psychol.,* 1961, *25,* 185-191.

Janis, I. L. *Psychological Stress.* New York: Wiley, 1958.

Jeffery, R. The psychologist as an expert witness on the issue of insanity. *Amer. Psychol.,* 1964, *19,* 838-843.

Leifer, R. The psychiatrist and tests of criminal responsibility. *Amer. Psychol.,* 1964, *19,* 825-830.

Levitt, E. E. Results of psychotherapy with children: an evaluation. *J. consult. Psychol.,* 1957, *21,* 189-196.

Levitt, E. E. Psychotherapy with children: a further evaluation. *Behav. Res. Ther.,* 1963, *1,* 45-51.

Levy, L. H. *Psychological Interpretation.* Chicago: Holt, Rinehart, Winston, 1963.

Lindzey, G. Seer versus sign. *J. experim. Res. Pers.*, 1965, *1*, 17-26.

Meehl, P. E. *Clinical Versus Statistical Prediction*: *A Theoretical Analysis and a Review of the Evidence*. Minneapolis: University of Minnesota Press, 1954.

Meehl, P. E. The cognitive activity of the clinician. *Amer. Psychol.*, 1960, *15*, 19-27.

Meehl, P. E. Seer over sign: the first good example. *J. experim. Res. Pers.*, 1965, *1*, 27-33.

Motorola's Employment Test Procedure, 1964.

Northrop, F. S. C. *The Complexity of Legal and Ethical Experience*. Toronto: Little-Brown, 1959.

Oppenheimer, R. Analogy in science. *Amer. Psychol.*, 1956, *11*, 127-135.

Society for the Psychological Study of Social Issues Council statement dated January 31, 1960 on the New York City Youth Board Report: An experiment in predicting juvenile delinquency. SPSSI Newsletter, April, 1960.

Spickler, M. W. Psychological services in a child development center: a guide for teachers and teacher-aides. Project Head Start 382-8544, mimeographed final draft, January 28, 1966.

Sundberg, N. D., & Tyler, Leona E. *Clinical Psychology*. New York: Appleton-Century-Crofts, 1962.

Szasz, T. *Law, Liberty, and Psychiatry*. New York: Macmillan, 1963.

Testimony Before House Special Subcommittee on Invasion of Privacy of the Committee on Government Operations. *Amer. Psychol.*, 1965, *20*, 955-988.

Towbin, A. P. When are cookbooks useful? *Amer. Psychol.*, 1960, *15*, 119-123.

Tukey, J. W. Conclusions versus decisions. *Technometrics*, 1960, *2*, 423-433.

Tyler, E. A., Truumaa, A., & Henshaw, Patricia. Family group intake by a child guidance team. *Arch. gen. Psychiat.*, 1962, *6*, 214-218.

Wasserstrom, R. A. *The Judicial Decision*. Stanford: Stanford University Press, 1961.

18

Research Applications of
Projective Methods

JEROME L. SINGER

In addressing oneself to a review of the research applications of the projective methods one must confront a curious dilemma of cultural lag and the sociology of professional practice. The widespread practical application of projective techniques continues almost unabated in mental hospitals and clinics. Indeed Sundberg's (1961) survey indicated that the Rorschach, Thematic Apperception Test, Draw-a-Person and Bender Visual-Motor Gestalt Test (often used projectively) head the list of frequently used assessment techniques in 185 hospitals, counseling centers and clinics. Even today the situation seems relatively unchanged despite increasing doubts about the validity and practical utility of many of these procedures (Zubin et al, 1965). If the research literature on projective techniques tells us anything (and I think it tells a great deal) it clearly suggests that the current clinical uses of those war horses like the Rorschach, TAT, and Figure-Drawing are old-fashioned and unsophisticated either psychometrically or in relation to personality theory. Indeed, the literature on research with the projective methods provides ample evidence that many ingenious modifications and variations of these methods exist and could be better applied in dealing with specific questions such as the prediction of aggressive behavior. Nevertheless, faced with a live patient across the desk, we clinicians cling to our battered original set of inkblots like a three-year-old to his tattered old blanket. Did not Rorschach himself claim he had alternate series of blots? Are we oblivious still to the existence of alternate forms such as the Behn or Holtzman or Harrower series and of the many experimental uses of alternate series for special purposes such as Siipola and Taylor's (1952) or Barron's (1955) blots, to mention just a few? The present chapter represents an effort by one who has long loved his fingerprint-bedecked, somewhat battered old "bat" blots and that pathetic "boy with the violin" picture (will he or

Some of the research and bibliographical work described in this paper was supported by the United States Public Health Service Grant NH M-10956.

won't he pick it up and practice?) to urge upon the reader a serious re-examination of the projective tools. I hope to encourage more imaginative directions in the clinical as well as research applications of these fascinating instruments. Our highest allegiance is to psychology which can best be served not by rash rejection of the projective techniques when the literature is replete with fascinating results or on the other hand by a loyal but naïve faith in any given instrument, but by a serious examination of the ways in which a variety of difficult practical and research problems can be solved. An attitude of enlightened curiosity may well lead to experimentation with a host of "projective" or "non-projective" assessment techniques yielding rewards in research knowledge or human welfare.

An Overview of Research Uses of Projective Techniques

If we remember that Rorschach (1942) himself stressed the tentative and experimental nature of his investigations and that Murray (1937) was clearly interested in studying personality generally rather than specifically in devising clinical tests, then we can see that the research history of projective methods is as old as the most popular of the projective methods. Indeed, Rorschach himself performed some crude experiments on empathy and form-color discrimination as an underpinning to his concepts of the roles of movement and color in relation to motor activity. And Murray's (1933) study of the projection of maliciousness by girls frightened by "murder" games at night, however crude by today's "sophisticated" standards, was an early and imaginative effort to use projective methods (pictures from Time Magazine) in examining an intriguing aspect of personality theory.

A sampling of the thousands of references in the psychological and psychiatric literature which involve projective techniques suggests that most studies fall roughly into the following categories:

Research on the projective techniques themselves

1. Reliability studies and other attempts to evaluate the consistency within subjects, within the test or the stability of response patterns under various conditions or across alternate forms.

2. Validity studies including attempts to support a specific underlying premise, to demonstrate comparability of two techniques presumably measuring the same construct (e.g., Rorschach and TAT measures of aggression or imagination), diagnostic accuracy or predictive power and matching of known external characteristics to "blind" personality evaluations.

3. Normative and quasi-parametric studies such as the establishment of response patterns at various age levels, preparation of tables for ade-

quate scoring of certain variables, development of forms for use with special clinical populations, e.g., blind subjects or various racial groups, comparison of various scoring or interpretative systems, etc.

4. Establishment of clinical group patterns on the particular method.

The use of the projective techniques as criteria for evaluation of disturbance or intellectual or personality change

1. Studies of the effects of brain damage, neurological defect, mental retardation, old age or severe emotional disturbance on performance on some projective tool.

2. Studies of the outcome of some particular treatment method on personality, e.g., effects of electroshock or special medication, changes associated with psychotherapy.

3. Studies of the effects of special experimental conditions upon perceptual-motor or fantasy responses, e.g., effects of severe hunger, anoxia, sensory-deprivation or sexual arousal.

Testing of personality or perceptual-motor theories through applications of projective methods

1. Studies of the psychoanalytic hypotheses concerning the motivational or affective structure of a particular clinical group by their response to projective methods.

2. Studies of deductions from a specific theory of perceptual-motor response, e.g., Werner's, through reactions to projective methods.

3. Testing of the effects of a particular theoretically-relevant experimental variable on projective response, e.g., alterations in achievement motivation under different instructions or changes in projective expressions of aggression following certain experimental conditions.

4. Stylistic differences in projective performance predicted from a theory or from some more specific experimental operation, e.g., projective responses associated with perceptual defense, field-dependence, etc.

A detailed examination of the varieties of research falling within the scope of these categories would require a work of several volumes. The reader is referred for specific instances of studies of reliability, validity and research on psychopathology or special technique construction to Chapters 2, 3, 4, 8 and 19 of the present volume, as well as to the separate sections on each technique for relevant studies on a given projective method. The present chapter will touch on some fundamental issues relating to these research applications and then move to some fairly detailed examples of specific problems which have been studied or engendered through the projective methods.

What are some of the special qualities of projective methods as techniques for research? Tentatively lumping these varied procedures under one rubric, we can say that their attractiveness lies in their ambiguity as stimuli, presumably lower susceptibility to conscious or even to unwittingly defensive falsification, disguised purposes, relationship to the types of fantasy or associative material elicited in the course of intensive psychotherapy, presumed ability to tap various "levels" of personality, and capacity to yield evidence on a variety cognitive or personality dimensions simultaneously. Certainly no one ever advocated projective techniques because they were easy to score or obviously reliable! The challenge of projective techniques in the great upsurge of psychological interest in the 1940's lay in the fact that they seemed to provide cross-sectional behavioral samples of cognitive and personality material that were at once moderately well quantified or at least susceptible to some form of organized interpretative scheme and at the same time broad-banded and deep enough to permit personality descriptions that might take a psychiatrist hours to obtain in the course of standard psychotherapy or interviewing. For clinical purposes the possibility of integrating complex material into an ideographic description seemed especially attractive by comparison with the limitations of the paper and pencil personality inventories then available. And, no doubt, there was a certain aesthetic satisfaction in the elucidation of psychological data through quasi-artistic means such as responses to colors and ambiguous forms, story-telling, finger-painting or organization of patterns from mosaic tiles.

From a formal standpoint, however, many critical problems soon emerged. One had to demonstrate, after all, that if responses to inkblots or stories were to be the basic data of a dependent or independent variable then these data should meet certain minimal standards of stability or internal consistency. If one is testing a psychiatric notion that two forms of schizophrenia differ systematically in their affective control or motivational hierarchies then one must be prepared to deal with a negative result. If on separate administrations the projective device doesn't yield comparable results with the same subjects, are negative findings a demonstration of the inadequacy of the original theory or an indication merely that the measuring device is too unstable to permit a suitable test of the theory? For example, Dawo (1952) reported finding a shift from introversion to extratensiveness in the Rorschach Experience-type of women during and prior to menstruation. To evaluate change when two Rorschach tests had to be given a few days apart she used the Behn Inkblots for the second testing. Since there is evidence that the latter series (while grossly suitable as an alternate form) differs specifically from the original series in its elicitation of a greater number of color responses which are used in scoring extratensiveness (Eichler, 1951; Singer, 1952), one can't know whether her positive results reflect an artifact of the techniques employed or an actual psychological change in her subjects.

Without belaboring the many obvious issues concerning the reliability of cumbersome techniques such as the Rorschach, TAT, MAPS, etc., as well as the difficulties in obtaining satisfactory scores from data provided by associations, stories, drawings, etc., it is clear that the serious investigator must take special precautions to make sure that the data to be obtained from projective methods meet some reasonable criteria of objectivity to insure replicability of his investigation. Without attempting coverage of all possibilities, here are some suggestive examples of precautions necessary in research with projective methods—cautions which are designed to insure at least reasonable objectivity of the data without seriously compromising some of the "projective" characteristics of the instruments.

Procedure for obtaining inter-judge agreement in scoring Thematic Apperception Test or related techniques

If one desires to use projective data based on spontaneous productions to measure a recurrent pattern in responses to the TAT, a method such as the following has been successfully employed in research:

1. The investigator decides that it is necessary to obtain a quantitative score for some need or motive or stylistic characteristic from thematic responses. For example, he may want to measure "means-end cognizance" or "achievement motivation" in samples of normals and schizophrenics or middle and lower-class persons, otherwise equated on pertinent variables. He prepares a careful definition of the trait or need in question, specifically relating this definition to the type of material available, i.e., stories told to TAT cards.

2. He delineates appropriate scorable units in the stories obtained, or, if he wishes a more global rating, sets up criteria for evaluating the importance of this variable in each card or for the whole test protocol along some quantitative scale.

3. He prepares a manual of instructions for raters with sample scorings of the variable in question.

4. Two or three raters *unfamiliar with the objectives of the study* are trained in scoring the variable from sample protocols not part of the study itself. When they can pass a test or meet a criterion of agreement satisfactory to the experimenter they are assigned coded protocols which are part of the formal study.

5. Following the blind ratings by the two judges a percentage agreement or reliability coefficient is calculated. If agreement is high (meeting a pre-specified criterion) the two sets of scores may be averaged or a third

rater called in to rate, and the average of the three utilized for those items on which there is disagreement.

A general procedure of this type has proved effective in yielding reliable ratings of TAT data in a number of studies, (e.g., Atkinson 1958; Singer 1954).

Global matching of projective protocols

When it is desired to take into account as much as possible the clinician's skill in integrating various facets of a projective protocol, a matching technique may be more desirable than the type of rating described above. Here the sets of data that are to be compared are set up in coded form and clinicians match the projective test protocol with the data. A simple example is represented by the attempt to ascertain the comparability of the Behn and Rorschach protocols of various persons using clinicians who matched coded records (Singer, 1952). Using techniques based on the original concept of blind matching by Vernon (for use with expressive behavior samples) one can obtain a fairly definitive estimate of judges' agreement and also their accuracy in comparing two projective test protocols or in matching a protocol with a personality description or other relevant data. Cronbach (1949, 1956) has provided a variety of useful suggestions for statistical evaluation of matching techniques. The advantages of matching techniques have most recently been apparent in the recognition that dream reports from various stages of sleep must be subjected to a comparable procedure if we are to move beyond the anecdotal in the objective study of sleep mentation (Monroe, Rechtschaffen, Foulkes, & Jensen, 1965). By careful planning it is also possible to vary the amount of material available to judges for matching and hence, in effect, to "zero in" on the bases for decision in the interpretation of projective data.

Development of specialized scores or new approaches to evaluating projective technique variables

That this area merits a volume in itself is an indication of the many clever and astute research approaches to dealing with the complexities of projective data. Some simple examples will be presented here with the hope that the reader interested in research with projective techniques will be encouraged to explore the relevant literature or to assess carefully the need for such a technique before blindly plunging into a large scale investigation expecting to rely on the traditional scoring methods. The persons who originally devised techniques for evaluating projective protocols were generally insightful clinicians who, however, lacked the statistical sophistication which by today is a regular part of most professionals' repertory.

Consider, for example, Rorschach's notion of the Experience-type, the ratio of Human Movement to Color responses, which is considered one of the most original and fundamental features of the inkblot technique (Singer, 1960). By differentially weighting the color responses so that an FC received one-third the weight of a pure C and by setting up a ratio between color and movement, Rorschach in effect was proposing a quantitative approach to assessing this personality dimension. Yet, in addition to many, by now, obvious limitations of these weightings, e.g., the uneven distributions of color in the cards, it is clear that the ratio is meaningless if one does not take into account the number of responses in a given protocol. Palmer (1955, 1956, 1963) was able to deal with this problem by developing a score for the experience-balance which took into account the response total; he was then able to develop considerable normative data as well as satisfactory statistical comparisons between this Rorschach variable and objective personality scale measures.

Recognizing that there is no intrinsic magic in the original scoring scheme provided by Rorschach, other investigators have moved even further towards developing unique scores for Rorschach data. Fisher's concept of the body-image score (1958) represents one type of revision related to a theoretical construct which has engendered an intriguing series of investigations of correlates of projective test performance. Still another approach has been that developed by Holt, Klein, Lindzey and their collaborators which involved attempts to rescore Rorschach protocols in relation to assumed stylistic dimensions such as tolerance for unreal experiences or primary and secondary process (Gardner, Holzman, Klein, Linton, & Spence, 1959; Holt & Havel, 1960). For example, Eiduson (1959) scored both Rorschach protocols and dream reports using a variant of the "tolerance for unreal experiences" score and was able to show consistency for subjects in these two differing media of experience. Other examples of variants of Rorschach scores will be presented later in this chapter.

Still other approaches to new scorings of the Rorschach blots for specific research uses may be cited briefly. Zubin, Eron and Schumer (1965) have pursued with great care an approach to scoring Rorschach responses along scaled dimensions originally advocated thirty years ago by Zubin. These scales attempt to classify response content such as dominance, mood, definiteness, dehumanization, self references, etc., and have particular advantages in studies comparing normal and pathological groups before and after different types of treatment. Other approaches involving both content and structural scoring are those of Levine and Spivack (1965, discussed below) for measuring "repressive style," or De Vos (1952) and Elizur (1949) for measuring aggressive or hostile manifestations. For research purposes a variety of studies have indicated the decided utility of these last two scoring approaches (Buss, 1961).

While the emphasis so far has been on the Rorschach, comparable indications of the desirability of specialized methods to deal with special problems apply to other types of projective techniques as well. The development of reliable scoring criteria for measuring achievement motivation, affiliation, or other general motives from responses to TAT-type stimuli are amply documented in Atkinson (1958). (See also Chapter 3). Particular mention may be made of the approach of using quasi-multiple choice techniques in obtaining responses from picture story material. Suppose an investigator wishes to test a hypothesis that a certain group of subjects will manifest more indication of maternal attachment than some other group in their reactions to fantasy stimuli. Subjects may be shown pictures varying systematically in their ambiguity in relation to parent-child interaction. The subject (in addition to being asked for a spontaneous response) may be asked to indicate which of a series of statements seems best to apply to the picture in terms of his own imaginative inclination. These statements can be pre-selected on the basis of judge's ratings for maternal dependence on other relevant hypotheses and the subject may be asked to choose one of a group of statements as most relevant or to rank order a series of statements. Quite suitable quantitative data can thus be obtained without seriously interfering with the relative "projective" quality of the subject's reaction (Lane & Singer, 1959).

Specialized modifications of projective techniques for research use

It seems more and more clear that any really serious approach to research study which seeks to take advantage of the relatively disguised or ambiguous quality of projective methods necessitates a careful examination of those characteristics of the method especially *relevant* to the study in question. Thus, Barron (1955), especially interested in examining the imaginative characteristics of groups being assessed on a variety of personality dimensions, developed a series of inkblots which could yield a threshold score for human movement. These blots have been applied with varying success in a number of studies. While it is not clear that the threshold measure itself is satisfactory, the essential notion of pinpointing more specifically the characteristic one wishes to study and eliminating the "noise" produced by a variety of other scores or stimuli has some merit in research.

The Holtzman Inkblots (1961) represent an extension of this notion and a series of parallel forms with special value for research. Holtzman and his collaborators have provided reasonably satisfactory reliability data for the two forms of the test as well as a much more statistically workable instrument. They have also taken advantage of the developments in research in incorporating scoring systems developed for special purposes, such the Fisher Body Image technique or scores for hostility and bizarre verbalization. As a result, research use of the method is decidedly enhanced. A recent example is Lerner's (1966) study which indicated that "dream-deprived" subjects produced more Movement responses than controls. Here Lerner used the Holtzman blots and could employ 22 even- and 22 odd-numbered cards from Form A to provide her with sufficient data to make reasonable comparisons of before and after scores. It is likely that the next decade will witness an increasing reliance on forms such as the Holtzman blots in research studies.

Another example relating to the Thematic Apperception Test has been the increased realization that for picture story material, ambiguity *per se* is not quite as desirable as was thought. If anything, the weight of current evidence in the measurement of motives such as aggression suggests that special pictures depicting some aggression are more useful than the traditional set of cards (Buss, 1961).

It should be clear from the few examples cited above that the trend of evidence and a thoughtful examination of the issues may well lead the reader to anticipate a much more flexible and varied use of projective instruments in future research. Rather than citing a host of specific studies in varieties of fields I shall move now to present some fairly detailed examples, one might almost say, case histories, of the research applications of projective techniques to special problems in the psychology of personality. My hope is to stimulate the reader to examine the research in a variety of fields from a similar point of view before he plunges into a use of traditional projective methods in his own pet research project. Here, then, is an example of how projective methods have been applied to the study of imagination and fantasy processes.

Projective techniques in the study of imagination: their values and limitations

It may seem curious indeed to raise some questions about the use of projective techniques in the study of imagination. After all, the whole exciting development of those colorful and sometimes poetic personality assessment devices we call projective methods grew out of our increasing awareness that man's imagination possessed lawful characteristics related to many layers of his experience and overt behavior. Binet's, and later Whipple's, use of inkblots, Stern's Cloud Pictures, even the composer Scriabin's experimentation with the color-organ, represented early 20th century efforts utilizing loosely structured materials to tap cognitive and affective associations. The important advance from a scientific standpoint came, however, with Hermann Rorschach's recognition that not merely the association to the material but the structure of those associations and their relation to the characteristics of the stimulus material were the link between overt response, imagination and personality style or psychopathology.

Undoubtedly, Rorschach reflected the important influences of Freud, Jung, and Bleuler, all of whom had been especially alert to the necessity of categorizing psychic functioning along structural dimensions that were more related to personality, instinct and social experience than were the more static conceptions of Wundt and his school. Rorschach suggested that by classifying a series of associations to a set of inkblots whose stimulus-evoking characteristics were established through normative data, we could obtain specific sets of scores which reflected corresponding patterns of overt behavior, dispositions towards action, or characteristic cognitive and affective tendencies. More specifically, he indicated that all associations to inkblots were not reflections of the "imagination" of the respondent. Rather, some classifications yielded information concerning emotional reactivity; others, information concerning relative emphasis on concrete or generalized thought; and still others, information on the relative flexibility of imagination. In effect he suggested that imaginativeness was one of a number of dimensions of thought or action tapped by associations. This conception has been extremely influential in the further development of projective methods. Common sense today clearly tells us that *quantity* or *content* of associations to inkblots or ambiguous pictures must reflect some aspects of the ongoing imaginative life of an individual. Still, the information yield from those sources seems far less than that which we get from some system of classification of associations along dimensions that coordinate more precisely with a theoretically consistent classification of man's "psychic structure." In the framework of the Rorschach method the category of scoring that seems closest to tapping man's imagination is the movement response, especially Human Movement. Despite the great proliferation of projective techniques since Rorschach's day (except for some specific approaches used with the Thematic Apperception Test), surprisingly little effort has been made to develop categories within the later techniques to measure the imaginative dimension. Probably most devisers of projective techniques were so impressed with Rorschach's achievement in developing the movement determinant that they looked for other personality dimensions to study and left the field of imagination to Rorschach. Let me therefore summarize some of the work on imagination growing out the inkblot method.

RORSCHACH'S HUMAN MOVEMENT RESPONSE

In experimenting with individual patterns of reaction to various inkblots, Rorschach (1942) made an interesting observation. Persons who tended to respond frequently to inkblots by reporting they might represent human beings in action ("Two men bowing, two girls dancing, a woman with arms upraised doing a Spanish dance," etc.) seemed to show a contradictory pattern in their behavior. They were relatively less active overtly, more controlled in their motility or perhaps somewhat awkward physically. They were also likely to be persons with considerable imagination, much given to inner living or attention to their own thoughts or daydreams. Although much struck by this observation and feeling it was perhaps the single most important outcome of his inkblot studies, Rorschach made no attempt to develop a theoretical formulation about this triadic relationship of Human Movement perception in inkblots, inhibited overt motility, and imaginative tendencies.

Formalized into the M determinant as part of the scoring system for the Rorschach technique, the Human Movement response became an important feature of the interpretation of Rorschach protocols in clinical work. The chief teachers and Rorschach theoreticians, e.g., Beck, Klopfer, Schachtel, Hertz, and Piotrowski in the United States, all were in general agreement that the frequency and quality of M responses were related to overt motility and inhibition and to imagination in much the manner suggested by Rorschach. They differed somewhat in their relative interpretative emphasis on the content of the perceived human movement as a reflection of personality style or role and also on the importance of the relationship of movement to color responses which Rorschach felt was so important.

Despite the general clinical agreement about the inverse relation of M to overt motility, on the one hand, and its direct relation to imagination, on the other, no formal experimental work was carried out to test this observation until well into the 1940's. At that time, the late Heinz Werner, the distinguished investigator in developmental psychology, observed that Rorschach's linkage of perceived motion (in the inkblots) and inhibited overt motion could serve as an exemplification of a perceptual theory which he had developed. Werner (1945) had proposed a sensory-tonic theory of perception, an organismic conception which stressed that the body's tonicity was the dynamic link between muscular activity and perception. He showed in various experiments that alteration in body position altered perceptual response and went on to demonstrate that retarded children who differed characteristically in their overt motility also differed in their perception of motion or in producing movement responses to Rorschach inkblots. The endogenous mentally retarded who were generally more controlled or phlegmatic in motility showed significantly more Rorschach movement responses and lower thresholds for stroboscopic or tachistoscopically presented motion than did the hyperkinetic exogenous mentally retarded.

Meltzoff, Singer, and Korchin (1953) carried this formal experimental approach a step further with a study which demonstrated that persons who were required to inhibit motility by means of a slow-writing task showed a subsequent increase in their perception of Human Movement responses in the Rorschach. Persons who showed numerous M responses also were better able to inhibit writing speed. Singer, Meltzoff, and Goldman (1952) found that Rorschach M responses increased after Ss were required to "freeze in place" for a period of time. Subsequently, a series of studies (Singer, 1960) provided considerable support to the notion that persons who showed more M responses were likely to be able to inhibit motility, showed more deliberation in problem-solving, Porteus Maze performance, and time estimation, were less active during solitary enforced waiting periods, were less likely to use gestures in defining verbs, or, in the case of mental patients, were less likely to be described by nurses or attendants as overactive on the wards.

These findings thus afford considerable support to Rorschach's original observation of the inverse relationship of overt motility and perception of movement on the inkblots. Somewhat less directly they support Werner's sensory-tonic theory, although Werner's formulations apply chiefly to perception and have not been extended to the study of imagination in their more definitive statement (Werner & Wapner, 1952). What of the relationship of the M response to imaginative behavior, daydreaming, or "creative intelligence," as Rorschach also put it?

One approach to measuring imaginative tendencies has been to score stories told to Thematic Apperception Test pictures for degree of creativity or for what Weisskopf termed "transcendance," the ability to include elements in a story that go beyond mere description of the immediate content of the picture. Thus, a story told to Card I of the TAT (a boy gazing at a violin) which merely described in detail the boy's appearance and the shading of the card, would receive a minimal score for transcendance. A story like "This boy is trying to decide whether to practice or not. Outside he hears the other kids playing ball and envies them. Then he thinks of his mother and how much it would mean to her if he could learn to play. He remembers how often she's spoken of how great a violinist his dead father was. He determines he'll play, sets out practicing day after day . . . and at last appears in Lincoln Center before a cheering audience." This story obviously introduces characters, time dimension, and locations not actually represented on the card and seems clearly a more imaginative response (even if it is not, in terms of TAT responses, an unusually original one) than the card-descriptive reaction.

Employing such criteria of imagination, a number of investigators have indeed found considerable support for some degree of relationship between Rorschach's M response and TAT measures of imagination (Singer, 1960). Other studies have shown that persons rated as imaginative or having considerable inner life also show tendencies to produce more M responses (Singer, 1960). King (1960) found that persons with more frequent M responses showed greater interpersonal awareness and sensitivity. Brenner in an unpublished experiment found that persons encouraged to adopt a creative attitude were more likely to give Rorschach M responses, and Bruel, in another unpublished study, found a greater number of M responses in the Rorschach records of students of writing than in those of ballet students. Teltscher (1964) reported that extremely active college athletes gave far fewer Rorschach M responses than did sedentary, literary-minded, but otherwise intellectually comparable, college students. Goldberger and Holt (1961) found that persons in a sensory-deprivation situation who showed the capacity for extended thought devoted to topics other than the immediate experimental situation also gave considerably more Rorschach Movement responses.

More recently some rather striking experimental findings have led to additional intriguing evidence that in a rather general way supports Rorschach's linkage of Movement and imaginative trends and, indeed, dreaming and fantasy inclinations. Loveland and Singer (1959) found that M (taken as a percentage of R) increased significantly in Ss who had incurred 100 hours of sleep deprivation. Palmer (1963), using his measure of experience-balance cited above, found a similar result, a shift towards introversion, in Ss who had been sleep-deprived for 120 hours. An important control involved the fact that Palmer also studied *food*-deprived Ss and found that they *did not* show the increase in the M but rather a shift toward an increase in color responses and extratensiveness. Bendick and Klopfer (1964) were led to a conclusion that M was related to kinesthetic symbolism in their study of sensory deprivation and motoric inhibition. Finally, Lerner (1966), relying on the Holtzman blots as her measure, carried out a careful study of deprivation of the rapid-eye movement phase of sleep (REM) that is generally thought to be most associated with vivid dreaming. Lerner interfered with the normal "dreaming" cycles by administration of a combination of amphetamines and pentobarbitols which tend to minimize occurrence of REM cycles in sleep. Experimental Ss showed a clearly significant increase in production of Movement responses compared with a non-deprived group and also with a group who received placebo drugs and were tested under comparable circumstances. In other words, the interference with normal eye-movement and presumably dreaming cycle of an individual led to an increased projection of Movement on to inkblots shown upon awakening.

Some methodological features ought to be pointed out in keeping with the spirit of this chapter. Lerner assigned weights to responses for evidence of unequivocal human movement as kinesthetically experienced in a special effort to adhere to Rorschach's notion of the empathy in "kinesthesias." She also used several raters to evaluate the increase in total responses as well as her weighted M score and was able to show that the increase in M was the major factor in the change in experimental protocols and not a general increase in responsiveness. A similar significant result although slightly less dramatic was obtained when more conventional Rorschach scoring was used, with Human Movement alone accounting for the major increase in the scores of the experimental Ss rather than animal or abstract movement.

It seems likely therefore that the Rorschach Movement response does indeed relate to tendencies to manifest imaginative or dreamlike responses at least when such activity is apparently interfered with by artificial deprivation techniques. Still another link in the chain of relating M to fantasy processes and daydreaming came in a study by Page (1957). Employing a questionnaire-listing of daydreams quite similar to the type of questionnaire developed somewhat later by Singer and McCraven (1961), Page compared frequency of reported daydreaming to a number of Rorschach variables. Only the number of M responses proved to be significantly associated with daydream frequency. A link between the Rorschach (in this case the Barron Movement threshold score) and *recall* of dreams was found in a study by Schonbar (1965). She studied persons who kept a log of their dreams for several weeks and found that those recalling dreams on more nights during that period were also more likely to show M responses earlier on the Barron series and were likely, too, to do better on the embedded figures test from Witkin's series. An earlier study (Singer & Schonbar, 1961) had already indicated that frequency of reported daydreaming as measured by a scale similar to Page's was also significantly associated with frequency of recall of night dreams. A really critical study linking Rorschach M to perceptual responses, daydreaming, TAT measures, measures of delay and inhibition, still remains to be done, although Singer, Wilensky, and McCraven (1955) in a factor analytic study using schizophrenic patients did take some steps in that direction with positive results.

Pending such a comprehensive study, the evidence linking Rorschach M responses to motor inhibition or delaying capacity and to measures of imaginativeness seems moderately convincing. Is there any systematic theoretical position that bears on this linkage of perception of motion, delaying ability, and imagination or acceptance of inner life? An examination of a number of strains of thought from the period of the turn of the century does indeed suggest that there was a kind of *Zeitgeist* which pervaded the thought of persons otherwise as different as Dewey, Freud, Washburn, and Holt, concerning the inverse relationship between thought and action (Singer, 1955). Perhaps the most elaborated statement of a position came from Freud, however, since it was more clearly an integral part of a general theory of thought and action.

The Psychoanalytic Theory of Thought and Delayed Gratification

Freud's linkage of imagination with deferred gratification and motor control grew out of his attempt to explain the relationship between the illogicality and drive-subordinated thought of the dream with its condensation and displacement and the organized processes of mature thought in which relationships to primitive drives were less obvious or almost absent.

As elaborated by Rapaport (1951), Freud hypothesized that the transition from primary to secondary process thought, or, in effect, from an id-dominated psychic topography to one in which the ego could be differentiated, came through the medium of the hallucinatory imagery of the child. A hungry child, in the absence of immediate gratification or the presence of Mama, automatically hallucinates the image of the bottle or of his mother, since what is wished for occurs at once in primary process thought. The occurrence of the image has a temporarily satisfying value, however, and gradually the child learns that he need not thrash around or spill over into violent crying or fruitless motor activity, but that thinking about the gratification is at least releasing enough so that he can stall until mother's appearance.

In terms of energy concepts, then, Freud postulated that thought and fantasy discharged small quantities of energy and permitted delay and experimental action in this fashion. This partially drive-reducing character of thought decreased the pressure on the child and opened the way for planning, organization of behavior, and the synthetic and defensive capacities which were conceptualized as the ego.

Neither Freud nor Rapaport has dealt in detail with the manner in which the hallucinated image occurs in the first place nor with the way in which the "hallucination" is internalized as daydreaming or fantasy thought. One might speculate that Werner's sensory-tonic theory may serve as a link—the checked motor impulses of the child making him more susceptible to motion in the environment, or lacking that, to the recreation of movement through memory of the previously satisfying movements associated with gratification. Another important link in psychoanalytic theory has been the role of identification with the mother in internalization of thought. Indeed, if the mother is reasonably regular and affectionate in providing gratification, one might guess that in her absence the child might be more likely to attempt to imitate her movements or to reconstruct her image. The implication growing from this notion is that an early experience with a benign, consistent figure, who provides affection or nurturance, is a crucial element in the degree to which the child can internalize fantasy and use it at least to some extent as a means of reducing drive during an enforced delay.

After so long a detour let us return now to the relationship between the psychoanalytic theory and the empirical findings with the M response of the Rorschach. It seems likely that the Freudian conception of an association between delay and thought or imaginative development can serve as a theoretical basis for comprehending the Rorschach findings about motor inhibition, perception of humans in motion, and imagination (Singer, 1955, 1960). Even the notion of the relationship between identification with the mother and fantasy has been supported in relation to Rorschach M responses (Singer & Sugarman, 1955; Singer & Opler, 1956; Shatin, 1953). Sharef (1949) found that young men who report a close, confidante relationship with their mothers are also more inclined towards introspection or imaginative thought. The findings using questionnaire measures on the relationships between maternal identification and frequency of reported daydreaming (Singer & McCraven, 1961, 1962; Singer & Schonbar, 1961) are also in accord with the concept, although they did not specifically involve the M response.

If we examine the relationship of the Rorschach M response and the psychoanalytic theory more closely, however, the connection of theory and empirical results is less clear cut. What the Rorschach results suggest is that some long-term, crystallized cognitive style, linking controlled motility and imagination does appear to exist, but it is less certain that the drive-reducing characteristics of thought or fantasy can be a sufficient explanation for such a crystallized pattern. The increase in M after inhibition of motion, while supportive of Werner's theory, cannot be used to support Freud's concept unless it were shown that after producing the M responses Ss were less inclined towards motility than they were prior to inhibition. Such data have not yet been reported for the Rorschach. In view of the relatively large number of studies supporting the tie between inhibition or delaying capacity, motion perception, and imagination, as well as more positive maternal identification, and the findings of Page that M and reported daydream frequency are positively associated, an intriguing avenue for further study is opened. We need more evidence that M and daydream characteristics are linked; we need to be able to specify whether it is human movement alone or all types of movement responses to the blots that are associated with fantasy, although Lerner's (1966) data emphasize Human Movement. Recall that the Singer and Antrobus (1963) factor analytic study found two poles of a general daydreaming factor at the second order level, one personally oriented, one impersonal. Roe (1952) in her studies of scientists found that physicists, undeniably persons with considerable inner living, also showed more abstract movement responses, while psychologists showed more human movement. This apparent parallel with the Singer and Antrobus results is intriguing but no systematic link has yet been formed. Indeed, Schechter, Schmeidler and Staal (1965) found that art students recalled more dreams and showed more "imaginativeness" in their dreams than did students of science. The possibility exists that other explanations, such as the linkage of verbal habit patterns to motor activity, can more succinctly explain the findings for the Rorschach M than the drive theory of Freud. A great deal clearly remains to be done.

THE THEMATIC APPERCEPTION TEST AND THE STUDY OF IMAGINATION

In the realm of the projective techniques, the TAT is the great companion of the Rorschach in clinical usage. The associations or stories produced to ambiguous pictures or related techniques essentially involving story-telling have proved invaluable tools for clinical practice and, indeed, even more for research, particularly with emphasis upon the motive patterns of the respondent. Our concern here is with what the TAT can tell us about the dimension of imagination. Most of the workers with the TAT have assumed that the stories told to pictures are relatively accurate reflections of the ongoing or unconscious fantasies. TAT's have been scored in three ways that appear relevant to tapping the *degree* or *pattern of imagination* rather than its *content*. Originally, Morgan and Murray indicated that need *introception* could be scored from among the themas of a protocol. A recent use of this has been by Sharef (1961) who related introception to maternal identification in young college men. Tomkins has extended this technique in his clinical scoring scheme by paying careful attention to the frequency and configuration of the characters' resort to thought or action in the respondent's stories.

A third approach to studying the imaginative dimension in TAT productions involves attention to the degree to which the narrator's material transcends the stimulus characteristics of the picture or introduces dramatis personae, emotions, vividness of feeling, novel arrangements and space-time alterations not directly derived from the blots. Some of the work relating these transcendance measures from the TAT to the Rorschach M score has been cited already. It seems clear that techniques of this type, whether relying on specific counts or more global ratings of "imagination in story-telling," such as those used in work with children by Singer (1961) and Singer and Streiner (1966), are useful approaches to obtaining evidence of imagination from the TAT. Indeed, an intriguing study by Pytkowicz (1963) reported evidence that persons revealing considerable predisposition to imagination, on a daydream questionnaire also responded differently to an opportunity for TAT fantasy following insult than did persons low in imagination by these criteria.

In general, however, work with the TAT has been more concerned with the issue of whether material expressed therein is a direct reflection of behavioral predispositions or an alternate channel whose expression on the TAT subsequently precludes direct expression in behavior. This issue, dealt with at length elsewhere (Buss, 1961; Epstein, 1962; Singer, 1966), is not directly related to the study of the imaginative dimension. It does seem clear, however, that to the extent that material describing aggression or antisocial behavior is expressed in unqualified form in TAT content it is likely to be associated with comparable behavioral expression. Where qualification or verbal elaboration and conflict are involved in the fantasy production, the likelihood is that such aggression will not be expressed in direct action. This finding suggests that the more elaborated TAT response pattern represents some aspect of an elaborated imagination or a whole series of differentiated cognitive structures or verbal discriminations, which, in effect, lead to a more subtle analysis of a given situation and hence to less direct "primitive" action.

Work such as that of Epley and Ricks (1963) has carried the relation of Thematic Apperception content to imagination further by delineating important differences in reliance on prospective and retrospective time span. These results open the way for further studies of the distinction between future-oriented rehearsal fantasies, more obviously adaptive, and reveries which recreate past events.

WHAT THE RESULTS OF PROJECTIVES TELL ABOUT IMAGINATION

What do the many clinical and research findings with the Rorschach and TAT tell us about man's imaginative realm? Perhaps most exciting is the recurrent evidence that important stylistic differences do exist in the general tendency to produce varied and flexible imagery and that these differences are also associated with special patterns of overt motor and interpersonal behavior. The fairly sizeable body of data from studies with the M response, for example, suggest that the tendency to report percents of humans in action on inkblots is linked to a number of other measures suggesting imagination, such as greater richness of story-telling, reported acceptance of inner thoughts, adaptation through fantasy under conditions of sensory deprivation, greater interpersonal awareness, planfulness, self-reports of frequent daydreaming, generally greater associational fluency during psychotherapy, and, in the case of schizophrenic adults, emphasis on elaborated paranoid delusion rather than somatic preoccupation in the pattern of symptomatology.

At the opposite pole, ample data from both Rorschach and TAT measures of imagination suggest that absence of elaborated fantasy responses are often associated with tendencies towards impulsive or often antisocial and aggressive action, less capacity to defer gratification, more direct expression of emotion, greater use of motor gesturing or physical movements during adaptive behavior, etc. If we add to the Rorschach M or TAT transcendence score additional data based on scoring systems which are somewhat broader, e.g., Holt and Havel's Primary-Secondary Process Scoring (1960), the genetic scoring scheme based on Werner's work, Klein, Gardner, and Schlesinger's (1962) Tolerance for Unrealistic Experience, Levine and Spivack's (1964) Rorschach Index of Repressive Style, results generally extend the above instances. This is not surprising, since most of these other measures place considerable weight on well-delineated Human Movement responses as components of scoring, or apply criteria to Rorschach blots similar to those used in scoring imagination in TAT stories, e.g., transcendence of the concrete stimulus properties of the blots with the constraint that some control, e.g., "adaptive regression," be involved.

Let us take a closer look at one of these systems and what more it tells us about imagination. Levine and Spivack (1964), in their *Rorschach Index of Repressive Style,* have carefully standardized a system for scoring Rorschach protocols according to the language used. They use Specificity, Elaboration, Impulse Responses, Primary Process Thinking,

Self-References, Movement, and Organization to build up a score which should measure freedom from repressive tendencies. They have obtained satisfactory scorer and retest reliabilities which suggest that they are dealing with a reasonably consistent response-style. The Rorschach M response scored either from the original blots or by the scoring system in the newer Holtzman inkblots was most highly correlated of all scores with RIRS. Levine and Spivack found evidence that Ss in the interesting Holt and Goldberger (1959) sensory-deprivation studies who produced considerable imagery, but were coping adaptively with the situation of deprivation, were those with highest RIRS scores, i.e., least repression. Similarly, greater spontaneous imagery was associated with high RIRS. "The more an S responded to the Rorschach situation with rich and full ideation the more able he was to accept the sensory isolation situation . . ." (Levine & Spivack, 1964, p. 92). Similarly, there were indications that RIRS was somewhat associated with Field Independence in Witkin's experimental situation, with sharpening tendency rather than leveling in the Gardner et al (1959) scoring system. Striking differences in the patterns of fantasy and obsessional rumination also emerged for normal and neurotic individuals who differed in the RIRS, corresponding in general to the difference in degree of elaboration of imagination. The authors write, "The high RIRS [subject] will act but his action is more likely to be a deliberate, a focused and a partial response, rather than a diffuse, impulsive, unthinking reflex-like response. It is more likely that interposed between stimulus and response are a chain of thoughts, or means-end considerations" (Levine & Spivack, 1964, p. 145). Considerable support for this position also emerged in a later study by these authors (Spivack & Levine, 1964) comparing middle class adolescents who differed in the degree of antisocial "acting out" behavior they manifested.

In summary, then, the projective test results suggest that there does indeed exist a dimension of imagination or a capacity or skill in producing spontaneous cognitive responses, images, plans, verbal elaborations or internal monologues. While this may be an adaptive capacity in many instances, it need not be sufficient to avoid pathology, since within pathological individuals this capacity may merely lead to different symptomatology. The evidence from the projectives leads us inescapably to the conclusion that some characteristic such as introversion, in the sense used by Rorschach, is a major feature of the taxonomy of personality. In this respect, therefore, the projective test data are similar to that reported from factor analyses of questionnaire data, except that the behavioral referents of the projective material seem more extensive than those from most questionnaire studies of introversion-extroversion (Carrigan, 1960). Differences in activity preferences along motor and ideational lines (Stein & Craik, 1965) or in patterns of curiosity along personal or interpersonal lines (Singer & Antrobus, 1963; Schonbar, 1965) may also represent comparable manifestations of an important stylistic component of personality related to the type of material elicited from projectives.

BEYOND THE PROJECTIVE TECHNIQUES

A closer scrutiny of the subject of the nature of man's imagination and of individual differences in the realm of fantasy style leaves one wondering what more projective techniques can offer. Some of the questions one can raise about the nature of man's inner stream of thought seem to call for a far more direct approach than what the projectives can provide. I am not going to discuss the limitations of the Rorschach or TAT as psychometric instruments. These are well known, and, for research purposes, newer developments such as the extensive use of well-defined ratings or scales or new standardized blots like Holtzman's make for quite satisfactory data. The issue is rather how many steps of inference are necessary to get at a phenomenon as pervasive but elusive as the stream of thought.

Consider the relation of the human movement response to fantasy. Most people report some degree of daydreaming every day, and since Galton's *Inquiries into the Human Faculty and its Development,* we have been aware of striking individual differences in vividness and modality of imagery. Yet we still know little of the pattern of daydreaming, its relationship to internal or external sources of stimulation, the relationship of types of daydreaming to actual behavioral patterns or the relationships between daydreaming or other spontaneous cognitive processes and affects or the general arousal or activation patterns of the organism. The insight of Rorschach in sensing that M of all the types of associations to inkblots was related to both ideation and motor patterns in a specific way was remarkable. Yet he relied only on human movement. Why should animal movement or abstract movement responses be different from human movement? Does this difference reflect a difference in interest pattern only, as Roe's data (1952) suggest? The limited number of stimuli evoking abstract movement on inkblots may make it impossible to ascertain whether such non-human motion perception does indeed represent an alternative form of "inner living," less personal, and less psychologically oriented, but of as much value for thought and planning along more objective lines. If we rely on the Rorschach or related scores and on responses to inkblots or ambiguous stimuli we are introducing a new set of intermediary steps, the characteristics of the physical stimuli themselves, which may alter the response pattern in unknown ways.

An additional problem is raised by the heavy involvement of language in the production of Rorschach responses. Movement responses generally involve somewhat more elaboration verbally, and Levine and Spivack's work (1965) indicates that the verbal elaboration of all Rorschach responses is more significant than the movement alone. I do not wish to belabor the many technical questions that can be raised about distinctions between human and animal responses versus human and animal *movement,* as well as questions of the form-level, originality, or location of these responses and their relation to the actual ongoing experience.

SOME ALTERNATIVE APPROACHES TO STUDYING THE STREAM OF THOUGHT

A number of possibilities for more direct study of man's ongoing thought stream may be cited briefly. One way is to ask people directly to describe the frequency or vividness or content of their daydreams or other spontaneous cognitive processes. Once one has established a reasonable definition and established a suitable rapport, considerable frank material is obtainable. The use of daydreaming questionnaires has also been very effective, although care must be taken to account for the effects of response styles or acquiescence sets. Page (1957), for example, developed such a questionnaire, a listing of daydreams, with Ss subscribing to their frequency of occurrence. Only M, of all the Rorschach factors, was significantly associated with daydream frequency. A series of studies using similar daydream questionnaires and some structured interviewing (Singer & McCraven, 1961, 1962; Singer & Schonbar, 1961; Singer & Antrobus, 1963) have also been carried out. They open up the possibility of studying personality correlates of daydream frequency, the factorial structure of a series of daydream scales in relation to cognitive variables, and sociocultural variations in content and frequency of daydreaming. I don't mean to suggest that such interview or questionnaire methods are necessarily superior to the projective approach. Questionnaires generate their own problems, despite the greater ease of statistical analysis. The whole literature on response sets begins to develop a superstructure of complex hierarchies of response-significance far removed from the original function that one sought to tap through the questions of the scale.

It would seem desirable, therefore, to view projective and more direct inquiry methods of studying man's ongoing stream of thought as alternative approaches. Future work might include both projective and questionnaire responses, so as to carry out appropriate taxonomic or classifactory analyses (if we can get past the obstacle that questionnaire responses of any type go together better than they do with a behavioral sample of projective measures). One kind of issue that has emerged from the Singer-Antrobus factor analysis is the following: There is evidence that a variety of scales defining a number of daydreaming factors correlate at the second order level in a bipolar fashion. At one pole we have scales or tests suggesting a more "fanciful" pattern of daydreaming, with links to measures of Interpersonal Curiosity. At the other pole, there are measures of controlled, objective thought, philosophical-mindedness and somewhat "masculine" orientation, associated also with Curiosity of an Impersonal Type. These two poles, rather resembling C. P. Snow's distinction between the two humanist-scientific cultures, are both introversive orientations, quite distinct from a rather clearcut extroversion pattern also obtained. We need to replicate this type of finding on different samples and with a variety of types of stimulus materials. What would the Rorschach and the TAT tell us about persons who represent extremes along the dimensions I have described? It seems likely that the capacity for dwelling at length and with some positive satisfaction in an inner realm of experience may take a number of forms, all quite different in content but nevertheless involving a moderately controlled withdrawal of attention from the external stimulus sources which are ordinarily most demanding. Relationships to affective experience, such as Tomkins' distinction of left- and right-wing ideology (Tomkins, 1963), can also be explored, using both affective arousal techniques and questionnaire or TAT-type instruments. The possibilities are exciting. First, I believe we must free ourselves from too rigid a view of the projective methods. If we avoid reifying the given responses, M or C or need introception, but remain constantly aware of their operational properties, we can begin to design better integrative studies using a variety of modalities and stimulus sources.

It may be useful to contrast the approaches via projectives to some recent experimental work which suggest possibilities of more direct approaches to daydreaming and the stream of thought (Antrobus & Singer, 1964; Singer, 1966).

In one experiment, the subject is in a small dark chamber room, monitoring a flickering light. He is detecting signals, pressing a button when a light just a bit brighter than the standard illumination flashes. In one condition, he is required to free associate aloud throughout the course of an hour and a half period of signal detections. White noise fed in by earphones prevents auditory feedback, making the situation more analogous to varied associative thought. A contrasting condition limits S's continuous talk to simple repetitive counting from 1-9 throughout the ninety minute watch. Results from two experiment indicate that varied internal cognitive activity maintains arousal during such a long repetitive task when other external stimulation is eliminated. The subjects under the counting condition tended to fall asleep at the switch. When arousal was maintained by piping in band music periodically, however, the attention to one's varied internal environment occasioned by free association led to a greater number of errors of signal detection than did the routine counting task. What these studies suggest is that a varied stream of internal associations can provide a lively environment for a person and maintain arousal with some cost in attention to a routine. The person with little variety of internal activity may become too dependent on external cares to maintain arousal, and lacking those, may drift off into sleep. Those Ss who reported that they managed to sneak some daydreaming in while counting actually showed greater accuracy in signal detection and greater arousal! Of special interest here is the fact that these Ss did provide a great deal of spontaneous material in their free associations; they kept talking on a whole variety of topics and revealed much about themselves and many personal concerns. While we did not attempt to analyze the tapes of their verbalization for content, such an analysis could be done and would, I suspect, come fairly close to the ordinary interior monologue that many people carry on in themselves when not heavily engaged in social intercourse.

Another approach, somewhat similar to the one above, requires the subject to monitor randomly-presented auditory signals, again in a relatively stimulation-deprived environment. The task is a simple one—pressing a button when a tone is higher-pitched than the one preceding it, or whenever the lower of two experimental tones is presented. By increasing or decreasing the rate of signals or by increasing the demand on S for short-term memory storage, it is possible to vary the demand for attention to external channels. Ss are regularly interrupted and required to report on the degree, vividness, and content of task-irrelevant thought in the preceding brief intervals. These task-irrelevant thoughts are the subject's spontaneous cognitive processes and they range the full spectrum of imagery and fancifulness. By frequent interruptions it has proven possible to get quite reliable evaluations of the degree of daydreaming under various conditions and to study what rate of task demand is necessary before daydream reports disappear almost completely. It turns out that there is a remarkably high degree of such spontaneous cognitive activity, even at very high rates of signal presentation. Interesting individual differences also emerge. For example, a young engineering student showed a pattern of very great control over spontaneous cognitive processes. When being paid only for correct detections, he missed no signals at high rates of presentation and had no spontaneous imagery. When no detections were required, considerable imagery emerged. On being questioned at length, he described a fantasy-life of the impersonal, controlled, objective type we had found in the Factor Analytic Studies. For example, he would plan a weekend date, but if he found himself thinking too much and too warmly about a specific girl, he would stop dating her for a while since he didn't want to get "too involved" until he finished school.

Still a third approach to studying ongoing fantasy involves the study of eye movements and EEG patterns while a person is engaging in spontaneous daydreams or in transitional stages of consciousness. Results from some of these investigations indicate that an extended conscious fantasy is accompanied by relatively little eye-movement, while the attempt at suppressing a fantasy evokes considerable eye-movement. The degree to which consistent patterns of ocular motility, the ability to entertain or suppress vivid fantasies either on demand or spontaneously, and long-standing fantasy tendencies measured either by questionnaire or projective methods are interrelated, also beckons as an avenue for research. These three types of studies are cited not by any means as clinical substitutes for projective techniques, but as indications that considerable opportunity for systematic study of imaginative phenomena exists outside of the realm of the traditional projective techniques. Of special interest is the possibility that by carefully considering the relative contributions of the various approaches, their stimulus evoking character, the degree to which they make demands on internal or external responsiveness, we can begin to tie together some of the loose ends in this field. For example, one would expect that persons chosen because they showed numerous Rorschach M responses and high RIRS scores as well as high transcendence or introception on the TAT should also reveal more extensive imaginative reports in some of the kinds of experimental situations described. We might also test the limits of these individual differences by experimental manipulation, e.g., we might find that high fantasy Ss stay awake longer under conditions of reduced external stimulation during a signal detection task or can, by making a fantasy game of such a task, prolong their stay despite the routine nature of the operations involved. Under conditions of considerable alertness, however, low fantasy individuals might prove more effective in performing the routine signal detections or might report considerably less distraction from their own spontaneous cognitive processes. One might make a beginning at studying conditions condusive to either increasing or suppressing fantasy capacities in persons whose predispositions are strongly indicated by their performance on projective or questionnaire measures of fantasy. And, indeed, we may being to test some of the relationships between Rorschach M, the degree of spontaneous fantasy reports in relaxed conditions, and then, (using EEG measures), the speed of onset of imagery and dream content in the transition to sleep. The point is that we must constantly look for the main chance, rather than reify M or Need Introception or some category peculiar to a specific projective method and assume that these scores *are* imagination. Let us accept the testimony of our phenomenal experience—we do produce spontaneous images and hold internal conversations and engage in a variety of manifestations of an ongoing stream of thought. *That* is what we are out eventually to study—not man's response to inkblots, pictures, or inventory statements, but the spontaneous ongoing experience. Anything we can do to zero in on that target is worth trying. Projective techniques, systematic interviews, questionnaires, and experimental apparatus are all means that we can and ought to use to pin down the elusive "castles in Spain" or "images in our mind's eye," which intrigue us while they bedevil our scientific efforts to study them.

SOME NEW DIRECTIONS IN THE RESEARCH USE OF PROJECTIVE METHODS

It should be clear to the reader from the various examples presented that what is needed is a much more flexible and *problem-centered* approach to the employment of projective techniques in formal research.

Rather than ask, "What will schizophrenics and neurotics do on my new 'Draw-a-Nose test'?" the investigator ought better to consider what underlying psychological process needs measurement and then *choose or devise* his instruments accordingly. Psychologists can lead themselves into an endless morass if they devote themselves only to studying indefinitely the properties of a specific tool. To some extent this has already happened with both the Rorschach as a projective device and the MMPI as an objective test. It seems more important to decide on important human interaction issues that need to be studied and then carefully examine what measuring devices are most applicable.

An example may be drawn from research on acting-out or impulsivity in adolescents. Merely using global projective devices has not proven satisfactory in discriminating these groups. There is, however, ample evidence (Buss, 1961; Spivack & Levine, 1964) that when special instruments specifically geared to tap presumed behavioral or imaginative differences are employed, results can be quite meaningful. Indeed, as we regard the problem in this light, the gross distinction between projective and non-projective techniques begin to blur and we are again confronted with the responsibility of thinking through a research problem in relation to what needs to be studied.

Investigators in the fields of social psychology and children's attitudes and values have shown increasing ingenuity in the development of specialized techniques, many of which could be used quite effectively in clinical situations. A modified combination of thematic technique, doll play, and role-playing was developed by Chein and Evans (1948) for tapping interracial attitudes. Subsequently, Stanton, Back, and Litwak (1958) showed that a similar approach could actually be employed in survey research methods to good effect. In a study of interracial attitudes of Negro and white children attending integrated and segregated schools, Singer (1966) used a modified Bogardus Social Distance Scale and a specially developed quasi-projective technique to elicit attitudes along various dimensions. A picture of a bus with alternate Negro and white children's faces peeping out was presented to 5th grade children. The pictured Negro and white children were given names and the respondents were then presented with a series of statements such as:

.... never likes to study.

.... likes to hit other children at the bus stop.

.... is always quiet and neat.

The respondents had merely to fill in appropriate names from those supplied in the bus picture. It was thus possible in a fairly specific fashion to obtain scores for assignment of various traits or behavioral tendencies to Negro or white, boy or girl, etc. from the children's responses to this simple technique. Yet for younger children the purpose remains moderately disguised and involves the element of choice so often sought in projective techniques.

There is indeed a proliferation of devices of this sort available to the investigator who examines the research literature in a specific field. Obviously one does not wish to abandon the advantages of more complex personality studies. It remains a question, however, as to whether the mere use of measuring techniques whose properties are themselves obscure can deal with the problem of subtlety. An interesting recent development in research studies has been the examination of family interaction patterns. More and more, both clinically and in formal study, the relatedness of family members is of significance. While it is clear that some interesting results have emerged from use of standard projectives with family members (Handel, 1962), it seems increasingly clear that more subtle and specialized techniques may have special advantages in this field. Thus, Strodtbeck's (1954) "revealed difference" technique actually generates an interaction sequence between family members and can lead to a host of intriguing situations, e.g., comparing parents interacting with a normal and then later with a schizophrenic child, or comparing relative degree of maternal or paternal domination in different cultural groups. Techniques such as the "It" test or game choices have also proved to be of considerable value in studies of sex role preferences or sex typing in children (Kagan, 1964) and these, too, open interesting approaches for quasi-projective devices to deal with specific research or clinical problems. Indeed, when one considers how hard clinicians stretch to come up with a notion of sex-role conflict from the few available bits of information usually obtainable from a Rorschach or a TAT, the failure to employ more specific tools of the kind increasingly available in the research literature seems almost like sheer negligence.

The gap between clinical practice and research applications of projective techniques remains wide indeed. To this writer the failure of clinicians to re-examine their tools in the light of increasingly ingenious research developments of specific devices for measuring mood and affect, values, aggression, dependency, achievement, motivation, etc., represents a tragic failure in modern psychology. As society increasingly demands that the psychologist and psychiatrist attend to the largely neglected urban masses, the culturally disadvantaged, the disorganized family, psychology will have to accept the challenge of more ingenious and appropriate measurement techniques for research or practice. Perhaps then the gap will be narrowed, but it would be an embarrassment indeed for the profession if the initiative is not seized by the practitioners and investigators before such an ultimate confrontation. The number of studies employing intriguing tools for special purposes is staggering and perhaps many psychologists are put off by the immensity of the task. But useful aids are available in the form of many helpful summary articles in special areas of child, social and clinical psychology, which point the way to the appropriate segments of the literature. The research application of the projective techniques has been an exciting and fruitful development in psychology—psychologists should not let such ripeness wither on the vine.

REFERENCES

Antrobus, J. S., & Singer, J. L. Visual signal detection as a function of sequential variability of simultaneous speech. *J. experim. Psychol.*, 1964, *68*, 603-610.

Atkinson, J. W. (Ed.), *Motives in Fantasy, Action and Society*. Princeton, N.J.: Van Nostrand, 1958.

Barron, F. Threshold for the perception of human movement in inkblots. *J. consult. Psychol.*, 1955, *19*, 33-38.

Bendick, M. R., & Klopfer, W. G. The effect of sensory-deprivation and motor inhibition on Rorschach movement responses. *J. proj. Tech.*, 1964, *28*, 261-264.

Buss, A. *The Psychology of Aggression*. New York: Wiley, 1961.

Carrigan, P. Extraversion-introversion as a dimension of personality: a reappraisal. *Psychol. Bull.*, 1960, *57*, 329-360.

Chein, I., & Evans, M. The movie study game: a projective test of interracial attitudes for use with Negro and white children. *Amer. Psychol.*, 1948, *3*, 268.

Cronbach, L. J. Statistical methods applied to Rorschach scores. *Psychol. Bull.*, 1949, *46*, 393-429.

Cronbach, L. J. Assessment of individual differences. *Ann. Rev. Psychol.*, 1956, *7*, 173-196.

Dawo, D. Nachweis psychischer Veränderungen gesunder Frauen während de Menstruation mittels des Rorschach Versuches. *Rorschachiana*, 1952, *1*, 238-249.

De Vos, G. A. A quantitative approach to affective symbolism in Rorschach responses. *J. proj. Tech.*, 1952, *16*, 133-150.

Eichler, R. A comparison of the Rorschach and Behn ink-blot tests. *J. consult Psychol.*, 1951, *15*, 186-189.

Eiduson, B. T. Structural analysis of dreams: clues to perceptual style. *J. abn. soc. Psychol.*, 1959, *58*, 335-339.

Elizur, A. Content analysis of the Rorschach with regard to anxiety and hostility. *J. proj. Tech.*, 1949, *13*, 247-284.

Epley, D., & Ricks, D. Foresight and hindsight in TAT. *J. proj. Tech.*, 1963, *27*, 51-69.

Epstein, S. The measurement of drive and conflict in humans: theory and experiment. In M. R. Jones (Ed.). *Nebraska Symposium on Motivation*. Lincoln, Nebraska: University of Nebraska Press, 1962.

Fisher, S., & Cleveland, S. E. *Body Images and Personality*. Princeton, N.J.: Van Nostrand, 1958.

Gardner, R. W., Holzman, P. S., Klein, G. S., Linton, H. B., & Spence, D. P. Cognitive control: a study of individual consistencies in cognitive behavior. *Psychol. Iss.*, 1959, *1*, No. 4.

Goldberger, L., & Holt, R. R. A comparison of isolation effects and their personality correlates in two divergent samples. *WADD Technical Report*, Wright Air Development Division, Wright-Patterson Air Force Base, Ohio, March 1961.

Handel, G. A study of family and personality. Unpublished doctoral dissertation, University of Chicago, 1962.

Holt, R. R., & Goldberger, L. Research on the effects of isolation on cognitive functioning. *WADD Technical Report* 60-260, Wright Air Development Division, Wright-Patterson Air Force Base, Ohio, March 1960.

Holt, R. R., & Havel, J. Primary-secondary process scoring. In M. R. Rickers-Ovsiankina (Ed.). *Rorschach Psychology*. New York: Wiley, 1960.

Holtzman, W., Thorpe, J. S., Swartz, J. D., & Herron, W. *Inkblot Perception and Personality*. Austin, Texas: University of Texas Press, 1961.

Kagan, J. Acquisition and significance of sex-typing and sex role identity. In M. L. Hoffman & L. W. Hoffman (Eds.). *Review of Child Development Research*. New York: Russell Sage Foundation, 1964.

King, G. F. An interpersonal conception of Rorschach human movement and delusional content. *J. proj. Tech.*, 1960, *24*, 161-163.

Klein, G. S., Gardner, R. W., & Schlesinger, H. J. Tolerance for unrealistic experiences: a generality study. *Brit. J. Psychol.*, 1962, *53*, 41-55.

Lane, R., & Singer, J. L. Familial attitudes of paranoid schizophrenics and normals from two socioeconomic classes. *J. abn. soc. Psychol.*, 1959, *58*, 328-339.

Lerner, B. Rorschach movement and dreams. *J. abn. Psychol.*, 1966, *71*, 75-86.

Levine, M., & Spivack, G. *Rorschach Index of Repressive Style*. Springfield, Ill.: Charles C Thomas, 1965.

Loveland, N. T., & Singer, M. T. Projective test assessment of the effects of sleep deprivation. *J. proj. Tech.*, 1959, *23*, 323-354.

Meltzoff, J., Singer, J. L., & Korchin, S. J. Motor inhibition and Rorschach movement responses: a test of sensory-tonic theory. *J. Pers.*, 1953, *21*, 400-410.

Monroe, L. J., Rechtschaffen, A., Foulkes, D., & Jensen, J. Discriminability of REM and NREM reports. *J. pers. soc. Psychol.*, 1965, *2*, 456-460.

Murray, H. A. Techniques for a systematic investigation of fantasy. *J. Psychol.*, 1937, *3*, 115-143.

Page, H. A. Studies in fantasy-daydreaming frequency and Rorschach scoring categories. *J. consult. Psychol.*, 1957, *21*, 111-114.

Palmer, J. O. Rorschach's experience-balance: the concept, general population characteristics, and intellectual correlates. *J. proj. Tech.*, 1955, *19*, 138-145.

Palmer, J. O. Attitudinal correlates of Rorschach's experience-balance. *J. proj. Tech.*, 1956, *20*, 208-211.

Palmer, J. O. Alterations in Rorschach's experience-balance under conditions of food and sleep deprivation. *J. proj. Tech.*, 1963, *27*, 208-213.

Pytkowicz, A. R. An experimental study of the reduction of hostility through phantasy. Unpublished doctoral dissertation, University of Washington, 1963.

Rapaport, D. *Organization and Pathology of Thought*. New York: Columbia University Press, 1951.

Roe, A. *The Making of a Scientist*. New York: Dodd, Mead, 1952.

Rorschach, H. *Psychodiagnostics*. Berne: Hans Huber, 1942.

Schechter, N., Schmeidler, G., & Staal, M. Dream reports and creative tendencies in students of the arts, sciences and engineering. *J. consult. Psychol.*, 1965, *29*, 415-421.

Schonbar, R. Differential dream recall frequency as a component of "life style." *J. consult. Psychol.*, 1965, *29*, 468-474.

Sharef, M. R. An approach to the theory and measurement of introception. Unpublished doctoral dissertation, Harvard University, 1959.

Shatin, L. Rorschach adjustment and the Thematic Apperception Test. *J. proj. Tech.*, 1953, *17*, 92-101.

Siipola, Elsa, & Taylor, Vivian. Reactions to ink blots under free and pressure conditions. *J. Pers.*, 1952, *21*, 22-47.

Singer, D. G. Interracial attitudes of Negro and white fifth grade children in segregated and unsegregated schools. Unpublished doctoral dissertation, Teachers College, Columbia University, 1966.

Singer, J. L. The Behn-Rorschach inkblots: a preliminary comparison with the original Rorschach series. *J. proj. Tech.*, 1952, *16*, 238-245.

Singer, J. L. Projected familial attitudes as a function of socioeconomic status and psychopathology. *J. consult. Psychol.*, 1954, *18*, 325-331.

Singer, J. L. Delayed gratification and ego-development: implications for clinical and experimental research. *J. consult. Psychol.*, 1955, *19*, 259-266.

Singer, J. L. The experience-type: some behavioral correlates and theoretical implications. In M. R. Rickers-Ovsiankina (Ed.). *Rorschach Psychology*. New York: Wiley, 1960.

Singer, J. L. Imagination and waiting ability in young children. *J. Pers.*, 1961, *29*, 396-413.

Singer, J. L. *Daydreaming*. New York: Random House, 1965.

Singer, J. L., & Antrobus, J. S. A factor-analytic study of daydreaming and conceptually-related cognitive and personality variables. *Percept. mot. Skills.* Monograph Supplement 3-17, 1963.

Singer, J. L., & McCraven, V. Some characteristics of adult daydreaming. *J. Psychol.*, 1961, *51*, 151-164.

Singer, J. L., & McCraven, V. Patterns of daydreaming in American subcultural groups. *Internat. J. soc. Psychiat.*, 1962, *8*, 272-282.

Singer, J. L., Meltzoff, J., & Goldman, G. D. Rorschach movement responses following motor inhibition and hyperactivity. *J. consult. Psychol.*, 1952, *16*, 359-364.

Singer, J. L., & Opler, M. K. Contrasting patterns of fantasy and motility in Irish and Italian schizophrenics. *J. abn. soc. Psychol.*, 1956, *53*, 42-47.

Singer, J. L., & Schonbar, R. Correlates of daydreaming: a dimension of self-awareness. *J. consult. Psychol.*, 1961, *25*, 1-6.

Singer, J. L., & Streiner, B. Imaginative content in the dreams and fantasy play of blind and sighted children. *Percept. mot. Skills*, 1966, *22*, 475-482.

Singer, J. L., & Sugarman, D. Some Thematic Apperception Test correlates of Rorschach human movement responses. *J. consult. Psychol.*, 1955, *19*, 117-119.

Singer, J. L., Wilensky, H., & McCraven, V. Delaying capacity, fantasy, and planning ability: a factorial study of some basic ego functions. *J. consult. Psychol.*, 1956, *20*, 375-383.

Spivack, G., & Levine, M, Self-regulation and acting-out in normal adolescents. Progress Report for National Institutes of Mental Health, Grant M-4531. Devon, Penn.: Devereux Foundation, 1964.

Stanton, H., Back, K., & Litwak, E. Role playing in survey research. *Amer. J. Soc.*, 1956, *62*, 172-176.

Stein, K. B., & Craik, K. H. Relationship between motoric and ideational activity preference and time perspective in neurotics and schizophrenics. *J. consult. Psychol.*, 1965, *26*, 460-467.

Strodtbeck, F. L. The family as a three-person group. *Amer. Soc. Rev.*, 1954, *19*, 23-29.

Sundberg, N. D. The practice of psychological testing in clinical services in the United States. *Amer. Psychol.*, 1961, *16*, 79-83.

Teltscher, H. O. A study of the relationship between the perception of movement on the Rorschach and motoric expression. Unpublished doctoral dissertation, Yeshiva University, 1964.

Tomkins, S. S. Left and right: a basic dimension of ideology and personality. In R. W. White (Ed.). *The Study of Lives*. New York: Atherton Press, 1963.

Werner, H. Motion and motion perception: a study on vicarious perception. *J. Psychol.*, 1945, *19*, 317-327.

Werner, H., & Wapner, S. Toward a general theory of perception. *Psychol. Rev.*, 1952, *59*, 324-333.

Zubin, J., Eron, D., & Schumer, F. *An Experimental Approach to Projective Techniques*. New York: Wiley, 1965.

19

Adapting and Devising Projective Methods for Special Purposes

A. I. RABIN

Conventional projective techniques have been, from the start, primarily used as clinical and research instruments for the study of the "total personality." One of the major characteristics which define projective methods, according to some authors, is their multi-dimensionality. Methods such as the Rorschach and TAT attempt a complete and global description of personality and its dynamics. The approach has been primarily idiographic—utilizing Gestalt principles—in which the interrelationships of a multiplicity of personality variables, traits, attitudes, characteristics, sentiments, and motives have been described and delineated with varying degrees of completeness. In clinical situations, diagnostic descriptions and formulations based on these constellations of characteristics have been the final result.

Clinical psychologists and, especially, researchers in the field of personality have often been concerned with more limited objectives than a global description of the total personality, its dynamics or its diagnosis. They have frequently been interested in the investigation of specific personality variables such as aggression, anxiety, the need for achievement, etc. Or, on other occasions, the focus of their concern has been that of prediction to specific behavioral or external criteria, for example, success in psychotherapy, in flight training, in clinical pathology, aggressiveness on a hospital ward, delinquency recidivism and so on. When employing the traditional projective instruments in the contexts just enumerated, the clinician-investigator is often faced with the task of excision. Out of the total personality constellation, or out of the tests that purport to describe it, he has to extirpate certain relevant factors appropriate to the variable to be studied or to the specific prediction to be made. He has to draw inferences from data which have not been intended to be directly relevant to his major concern. It comes, therefore, as no surprise that the Rorschach, TAT and similar procedures have often fallen short of the investigators' expectations. The results have been variable, predictions poor, and the overall findings equivocal at best.

Experience with the global type of projective method, applied to limited variables or specific predictions has motivated researchers to cast about for more effective and appropriate ways of attacking the more circumscribed problems they wished to study. There are two principal procedures which have been employed in the process.

First, investigators attempted to modify, in some specific ways to be elucidated later, the existing projective methods and adapt them to the particular problems with which they were concerned. Second, researchers and clinicians have sought and devised entirely new methods, especially made to order or "tailor-made" for the variables, theories or clinical phenomena they wished to investigate. To be sure, in most instances the new methods did not represent a complete departure from the old ones. The "projective hypothesis" remained fundamental to the new methods, which were often patterned after one of the major conventional techniques.

At this juncture, it may be well to add that not all new projective methods were devised for the reasons enumerated above. Often the novelty of new methods consisted merely in the nature of the stimulus material or the sensory-perceptual modality involved. There was no intent to test any theory of personality or special test variables, but merely to enrich the armamentarium of the "projective clinician" with "still another projective technique." This trend extended the range of possibilities for obtaining projective responses, but did not enrich projective or personality theory. Reliability was ignored, and validity, beyond the demonstration of some group differences, or employment in individual case studies, was similarly neglected. These methods were not devised for specific purposes where the concern was that of testing hypotheses, making specific predictions, or fulfilling a need of special groups (such as the sensory handicapped), but for similar "general purposes" of personality description to which the older methods had already addressed themselves.

Before we embark upon a discussion of the procedures involved in devising new methods for specific purposes and the principles underlying such efforts, we might first summarize the reasons for innovation and modification of available methods. These may be conceptualized as follows:

1. Modification and innovation for the purpose of studying the nature, and testing major underlying hypotheses, of the conventional projective methods themselves.

2. The adaptation of existing and time-honored methods in order to increase their effectiveness in eliciting responses from special populations.

3. Devising new methods, or utilizing new stimulus materials, especially involving non-visual modalities, in order to obtain projective responses in instances where the conventional visual projective methods are unsuitable.

4. Invention of new, or modification of old, techniques in order to maximize accuracy in the prediction of specific behaviors.

5. Devising new methods for the prediction of certain attitudes or personality characteristics underlying actual behavior, i.e., various intervening variables.

6. "Custom-making" of new methods with the aim of testing theories and complexes; interrelationships between constructs hypothesized by the propositions dictated by such theories.

TESTING THE HYPOTHESES OF PROJECTIVE TESTS

The number of investigations which have endeavored to test hypotheses of specific projective methods is legion. In the first place, there are numerous studies in which some aspect of the testing procedure has been altered, or some changes in the characteristics of the stimulus material have been undertaken in order to observe the effects of such alterations upon the responses to the test and upon the variables that are based on such responses. Among the studies that deal with the Rorschach, for example, there are reports of the effects of changes in instructions (Gibby, 1951), in the order of presentation of the cards (Rabin & Sanderson, 1947) and of a structured inquiry (Zax & Stricker, 1960) upon the test responses and scores. In the first instance, the test's alleged independence of "mental sets," was examined; in the second, hypotheses regarding "color shock" and the temporal Gestalt of the Rorschach which occurred by reversing the order of the cards presented were investigated, etc. Similar efforts with the TAT are reviewed and described in some detail by Murstein (1963). Variations in instructions, sequence of card presentation and the degree of structure imposed upon responses (e.g., free vs. multiple choice) were some of the experimental approaches undertaken.

A sizeable number of studies in which the stimulus characteristics of the Rorschach have been modified have appeared during the past 20 years. One of the earliest experiments in this category is the one reported by Lazarus (1949) who was interested in testing some Rorschach hypotheses concerning the meaning of the color response. By eliminating the color from the chromatic cards he was able to compare the responsiveness to the ordinary cards (including the color) with the experimental stimuli (without color) and study the effects brought about by the alterations in the stimulus material. A good deal of work along similar lines was performed by Baughman who also summarized other studies in his review on the "role of the stimulus in Rorschach responses" (Baughman, 1958). Modifications of TAT stimulus cards are not absent. The TAT pictures were tinted in one experiment in order to test the effects of color upon the responses of several groups of subjects (Brackbill, 1951). Early concern with the effects of different degrees of ambiguity of the pictures characterizes still another study (Weiskopf, 1950). Many other types of manipulations of the stimulus material of the TAT, including the ambiguity issue, with which we will concern ourselves later in greater detail, were recently summarized in a fairly comprehensive review (Murstein, 1963).

Secondly, the devising of entirely *new* instruments rather than modifications of the old ones, for the purpose of testing specific hypotheses embedded in projective theory, should receive some mention.

An outstanding example under this rubric is the Levy Movement Blots (Zubin, et al, 1965). This series of blots was especially designed for the purpose of obtaining human movement responses. The directions actually require the seeing of people in action. A test of the Rorschach hypothesis regarding the relationship between movement responses and creativity employed the Levy Movement Blots (Rust, 1948). Also the relationship between the production of movement responses on the Rorschach and on the Levy was reported in another study, by King (1955).

Although not explicitly stated by the authors, the Holtzman Inkblot Technique (1961) which "abandons the basic idea of using only ten inkblots, of permitting the subject as few or as many responses as he cares to give, and of conducting a highly variable inquiry for purposes of illuminating the scoring categories . . ." is an instrument *par excellence* for testing stringently the numerous hypotheses underlying the standard Rorschach method (see Chapter 6).

ADAPTING METHODS FOR SPECIAL POPULATIONS

A global instrument such as the TAT has many advantages—among them are the characteristics of flexibility and adaptability. A major fundamental principle which underlies this method is the assumption that the TAT pictures facilitate the identification of the respondent with a particular figure. This process, in turn, aids substantially in the process of projection on the part of the respondent.

Many clinician-investigators have felt that the figures in the pictures are, possibly, most appropriate for the identification of subjects in Western cultures. The dress, physical and facial characteristics, as well as the surroundings and backgrounds are most suitable for subjects in American and European communities. However, it was felt that when the same pictures are presented to Indians or Eskimos, for example, there is a barrier to adequate identification, which is most effective when there is maximum similarity between the respondent and the physical, facial, and dress characteristics of the portrayed figures and when the characteristic background is consonant wih his culture.

Thus, Henry (1947) devised a special series of pictures used with Indians. Parker (1964) utilized similar adaptations for the study of Eskimos' attitudes towards Westerners. Thompson (1949) modified the standard TAT pictures by making the main characters Negroes in order to facilitate better identification for Negro subjects. There are many other adaptations, too numerous to mention, in which stimulus modification is the main feature and in which the underlying assumption of facilitation of identification, via greater similarity and familiarity of the stimulus to the respondent, is paramount.

Among a number of criteria suggested by Henry for the devising of new sets of pictures, to be discussed below in greater detail, is "the criterion of culture-appropriate symbols. The pictures should be drawn or selected as to employ persons, dress, object, background that are not thought to be inappropriate by the persons being studied . . . they need only be portrayed in a general manner so as to enable the subjects to feel that the persons could be people like them" (1956, p. 51).

In his study of the acculturation of Eskimos, Parker (1964) notes the special import of background and the advantages of varying the backgrounds. Thus, he concludes regarding his Eskimo subjects that ". . . attitudes towards whites differed, depending upon whether the setting in the picture was an Eskimo village or a Western urban community" (p. 337).

In addition to the production of more adequate series of TAT-type stimuli for special groups, there is the procedure of devising new cards to supplement the standard TAT stimuli. The introduction of stimulus cards that deal with work and achievement by McClelland and his co-workers (1953; Atkinson, 1958) is one such instance. Neugarten and associates (1964) also introduced a special card for their purposes. They state that "the standard TAT has no single picture appropriate to the purpose of studying age-sex roles in the integrational family . . . A specially drawn picture was therefore used, one designed specifically to evoke the sentiments and preoccupations of middle-aged respondents in relation to family roles" (p. 46).

Other methods which illustrate the process of adaptation to special populations are the Michigan Picture Story Test (Andrews, et al, 1953) and the Children's Apperception Test (CAT) (Bellack & Bellak, 1961). The MPST consists of a series of TAT-like photographs portraying, for the most part, school-age children, since the aim of this test is to assess the emotional adjustment of this age group. The CAT presents a series of animal figures in various human-like positions and interactions in an attempt to tap problem areas of preschoolers. The substitution of animals for humans was based upon the belief that young children would identify much more readily with animals than with strange adult figures presented in the TAT cards. Detailed discussion of these methods and a critical evaluation of them and their underlying assumptions may be found elsewhere in this book (see Chapter 8).

In summarizing the present section, several points regarding the process of adaptation, with special populations as the target, may be stressed.

1. Instructions to the subjects remain essentially the same as with the standard test.

2. Interpretation of the product obtained, i.e., the responses, remains flexible and depends upon the special needs of the investigators.

3. Paramount is the modification of old stimuli, or creation of new, which are assumed to have greater similarity to the characteristics of, or represent special situations of high potency to, the respondents.

4. In some instances, the justification of the use of special stimuli is supported by pretesting which indicates richness of responses and consistency with responses obtained with the regular TAT cards (Neugarten et al, 1964).

Some of the methods mentioned in this section will again be discussed under a different rubric, below. These methods are not only characterized by modification and adaptation of stimulus materials for special populations, but are designed to make specific predictions with respect to particular personality variables as well.

Still other methods, such as the MAPS (Shneidman, 1949), which have utilized TAT principles to some extent and have sufficiently changed the requirements made upon the respondent *as well* as the stimulus material, are not included in this context.

DEVISING NEW NON-VISUAL METHODS FOR SPECIAL PURPOSES

Traditionally, the pioneering and most popular projective methods involved the presentation of visual stimuli. The degree of structure may have differed, but both the TAT and Rorschach involve visual perception and apperception. As the projective movement developed, the utilization of sense modalities other than visual occurred to a number of investigators. Moreover, there was a practical consideration as well; it had to do with attempts at personality assessment of the blind and visually handicapped for whom the conventional methods are unsuitable.

Thus, auditory and tactile stimuli have joined the visual as proper material for personality projection and projective techniques. Several issues come under consideration in devising such methods. First is the needed characteristics of the stimulus material—ambiguity versus structure. Second is the very practical consideration—richness and variability of responses. And third, of course, is the issue of reliability and validity of such procedures.

Since almost anything a person does or says reveals his unique style and is subject to interpretation as projection, many attempts and descriptions of "new projective techniques" have clogged the professional periodicals. Most are little more than mere suggestions without much demonstration of the theoretical or practical value of these new tests. However, a few deserve some detailed consideration, for a good deal of work and serious effort is involved in their introduction to the psychological public.

Several auditory procedures which have not yet attained the status of "test" were described elsewhere in this volume (see Chapter 8). Essentially two principles have been utilized in devising the stimuli for these techniques—the principles involved in the Rorschach and TAT respectively. In the first instance, garbled (unstructured) auditory stimuli are employed, and the subjects are induced to offer their associations and/or interpretations. Thus, in a sense, an "auditory Rorschach" was attempted.

The second approach, which parallels more closely the TAT, consists of clusters of relatively structured stimuli, i.e., sounds of a bell, of the wind, and snatches of conversation, which the subject is expected to integrate into a story. Unfortunately, as pointed out in Chapter 8, the reliability and validity of these methods are yet to be demonstrated. Also, the advantages of using these methods with sighted subjects need to be investigated; is there something that is obtained in auditory apperception that cannot be gained from data with visual apperceptive techniques?

Tactile stimuli such as "cypress knees" (Kerman, 1959) have been proposed for the blind, but little follow-up and supporting data have been produced. The "Three-Dimensional Personality Test" (Fein, 1960) also described by Neuringer (Chapter 8) involves a combination of kinaesthetic, tactile and visual modalities. Here new stimuli are presented. However, an additional aspect is the gestural nature of the response which presumably facilitates interpretation of non-verbal and mute subjects' responses, for they offer little or no material of a verbal and oral nature, but express themselves kinaesthetically.

DEVISING METHODS FOR MAXIMIZING PREDICTION OF SPECIFIC BEHAVIORS

Under this rubric we may consider some examples of methods especially devised for practical, but rather limited purposes. The aim is to make valid predictions concerning circumscribed behavior, rather than to describe personality or some special constructs on which it may be based.

What is involved in this operation is the creation of new stimuli or selection of certain stimuli from available standard techniques which are *a priori* related to the specific behavior for which predictions are to be made. Of course, the *a priori* step needs to be followed up by pretesting and experimental validation. Moreover, it is of some importance to determine what the ingredients are in the face validity of stimulus materials selected for specific behavioral predictions.

One example which belongs to the category of methods devised for specific behavioral prediction is the Cartoon Situations Test (CST) introduced some years ago (Shapiro, et al, 1957). This method, however, is not a simple empirical tool which is concerned only with prediction to criterion, in this case, teaching behavior. It is also concerned with "assessing aspects of personality pertinent to the teaching process." The "job analysis" performed by the authors dictated the selection of a series of seven cartoons "depicting teachers, children and parents in a variety of situations." The qualities to be tapped are: relation to authority, depth of feeling for child experience, trend toward expression of hostility and punitiveness, etc. *The stimuli of the test portray situations comparable to those in which the criterion behavior occurs . . ."* (italics added). The description of one of the cartoons may give us the flavor of some of the stimulus material.

"II. *A principal's office*: she is sitting at her desk: a teacher—hair awry and sleeve torn—carries in a screaming child; the teacher says, 'Peter is a trifle over-stimulated, Miss Gaffrey—may he visit with you until he calms down?'" (Shapiro, et al, 1957, p. 174).

The responses to these cartoons, written by students in practice teaching, were the basis for ratings on a number of personality characteristics (e.g., quality of expressive tone, orientation to the dilemma, quality of emotional identification with the characters, etc.) deemed to be important in success and effectiveness in the teaching process. The analysis of the S's responses was followed by a systematic comparison with the ratings of their teaching performance. "The findings indicate that responses to the test are reliably related to important aspects of teaching." Thus, the prediction with this instrument was not to a relatively general index such as "success in teaching," but to a more complex set of behavioral elements which might comprise the global evaluation.

Another, less complicated, design involving prediction of a relatively circumscribed realm of behavior may be found in the report by Stotsky and Weinberg (1956) described in an earlier chapter (*cf.* Daston, Chapter 9) of this volume. The sentence completion method is especially flexible and adaptable to specific purposes. In this instance, the authors were interested in the development of an effective tool in the prediction of success or failure of psychiatric patients in institutional work assignments. The stems for the form of the sentence completion technique they employed, excluding some filler items, were directly related to the criterion to which prediction was to be made. For example:

When Dick failed in his new job, he. . . .
Working for yourself. . . .
As the work became more boring. . . .

According to the data presented by these investigators, their method was quite successful in discriminating between the patients who adjusted to the work situation and those who did not.

To be sure, we have glossed over the complexities and details involved

618   PART VII

in objective scoring and classifying responses in the studies just mentioned. Our major goal, however, has been to examine the major principle involved in devising methods for specific prediction purposes. It is quite clear that what is of utmost importance in these and many similar studies is the design of stimulus material which is closely related to the concrete behavioral situation to which prediction is to be made (Rabin, 1961).

DEVISING METHODS FOR THE ASSESSMENT OF
INTERVENING VARIABLES

The approach described in the previous section can be, essentially, strictly empirical and atheoretical. The designers of the new techniques can be primarily concerned with predicting specific behaviors, without hypothesizing any intermediate constructs. Of course, this was not true about the examples cited, especially the first one (Shapiro et al, 1957). The authors postulated certain personality variables important in the teaching process and the test predicted to these variables and was validated by the actual teaching behavior. But, there are some efforts where the design of the stimuli is directed solely to the practical purpose of predicting some specific behavior.

We shall now turn our attention to devices which are designed to predict some specific personality variables and characteristics, but not actual behavior; although, of course, it is hoped that these variables stand in some sort of relationship to overt human action and behavior. Devising methods in this category involves two important differences in comparison to the procedure undertaken in devising methods for specific behavior prediction.

In the first place, whereas prediction of behavior requires that the projective stimulus situation be very close and similar to the criterion situation, prediction to a personality variable or dimension, which is an abstraction, demands that the concrete projective situation be an instance illustrative of the overall construct under consideration. Secondly, construct validation is most appropriate when the prediction intended is with respect to some intervening variable; validation in the methods described in the previous section is via observation or rating of actual behavior, i.e., predictive validity.

An example, illustrative of the principles detailed above, is Allin-smith's (1960) effort concerned with the assessment of severity of guilt in young boys. He devised a series of incomplete stories which were designed to tap the respondents' reactions in situations involving violation of moral taboos (disobedience, theft and wishes). Resistance to temptation, guilt upon violation, and defenses against the guilt were some of the important variables. Care was taken to eliminate possible factors of anxiety (possibility of detection) and to focus primarily on superego anxiety or guilt. The incomplete stories present situations from which the *construct* called "guilt" is abstracted and assessed. In addition to the face validity of the stories themselves, construct validity was achieved by testing the obtained results in the context of certain hypothesized relationships with child-rearing variables which characterized the early experience of the subjects involved. This research, and additional studies which it has stimulated, is discussed in Chapter 10.

The sentence completion technique is especially adaptable to the type of purpose just described. Some of the studies cited in Chapter 7 and the report by Stotsky and Weinberg (1956), mentioned in the previous section, are further illustrations of creating stimulus material which dictates responses directly relevant to some personality variable. In the study last mentioned the investigators were not only concerned with the prediction of behavior, but with such intervening variables as ego strength as well.

CUSTOM-MAKING METHODS IN ORDER TO TEST THEORIES

Finally, there is the creation of special projective methods for the purpose of testing a theory. By that we mean that the new method is designed not only to predict to certain constructs, but the relationship between a number of constructs as well. In such instances the findings concerning the predicted relationship between the several parts of the theory reflect upon the validity of the measuring instrument as well.

The Blacky Pictures (Blum, 1949), described in some detail in Chapter 8 of this book, is an excellent example of this type of technique. In order to test certain theoretical propositions and hypothesized relationships between several variables, dictated by psychoanalytic theory, Blum devised a series of cartoons of a dog named Blacky, in a variety of situations related to specific psychosexual states (e.g., orality, anal eroticism, etc.). Thus, from the subjects' responses to the specific and concrete situation depicted in the cartoons, the investigator generalizes to the relevant construct; so far the process is similar to the one described in the previous section. However, in this instance, the next step, at least in the original investigation, is the interrelationship between the several constructs, dictated by the theory. Blum's report, in fact, offers considerable support to the predictions from psychoanalytic theory. Thus, the instrument devised for the purpose described gains validational strength. To be sure, additional studies, offering construct validation, are desirable. Actually, a number of further investigations by means of the Blacky lend additional support to its validity.

INNOVATIONS IN STIMULUS MATERIAL AND ROLE OF STIMULUS

Hitherto our discussion has concentrated upon the purposes of adaptation of old, and invention of new, projective methods. Modification of old ones were undertaken in order to test some specific hypotheses which underlie the rationale of the conventional tests themselves, to employ with special populations, to improve specific behavioral predictions or to test specific hypotheses regarding isolated variables or personality dimensions and their interrelationship in theoretical systems of personality. To be sure, in some of our illustrations, a combination of purposes is reflected and some overlapping of categories occurs. In all of these instances the adaptation of the stimulus to the purposes of the investigator has been stressed. In passing, some general principles concerning the direction of stimulus adaptation and modification have been briefly mentioned. It would now be proper to examine, in greater detail, the rules governing the invention or custom-making of new projective methods.

Using the Murray TAT pictures as a point of departure, Henry (1956) suggested a number of criteria which may serve as guidelines for the design or selection of special sets of TAT-like stimuli. He lists some of the following:

1. "The criterion of latent stimulus meaning . . . *the emotional issue most usually raised by a given picture is the prime variable.*" (p. 47)
2. "The criterion of basic interpersonal relation . . . a mother-child scene, a father-child scene, a heterosexual scene, a person alone, a group of persons of varying social roles, a scene of two persons of the same sex and age." (p. 48)
3. "The criterion of reality representation. The pictures selected should represent varying degrees of objective reality." (p. 48)
4. The criterion of intensity. Stimulus should intrigue the subject and evoke a solution from him.
5. The criterion of flexibility and ambiguity—ambiguity of persons and emotions and actions to be interpreted.
6. The criterion of culture-appropriate symbols—dress, persons, objects and background not strange or inappropriate to subjects.

In addition, Henry, who is especially interested in cross-cultural research, emphasizes that "events and situations of importance that are characteristic of the specific society under study" should be portrayed in the stimuli that are designed. The study by Parker (1964) mentioned above, illustrates this point.

Murstein (1963) has also suggested some additional principles for constructing new thematic stimuli. His proposals include the scaling of pictures for all personality dimensions, the analysis of responses based on consideration of the stimulus value of the pictures, use of the entire range of a stimulus dimension, etc. These suggestions are in addition to recommendations made by Murray, Crandall and Sherwood, mentioned in his review. However, with the possible exception of Murray's point that "the pictures should contain at least one example where the central figure is of the same sex and relatively the same age as the subject," most of the important points had already been made in Henry's proposals enumerated above.

The foregoing discussion is especially applicable to the devising of new apperceptive techniques, but not so much to techniques that are patterned after other major conventional methods (e.g., Rorschach, sentence completion). Criteria, or rules that govern the invention or adaptation of techniques similar to other methods would have to be spelled out separately and differently from those that involve picture materials. As mentioned earlier, it is the flexibility of the TAT principle that stimulated many emulations. Perhaps the sentence completion method is similarly flexible, but it would require a new set of non-overlapping criteria, although some of the criteria mentioned above may be considered as common denominators. Henry's (1956) criteria of flexibility-ambiguity intensity, basic interpersonal relation and, perhaps, latent stimulus meaning are applicable to the sentence completion as well as to the TAT model.

ADAPTING VS. DEVISING

Some workers in the field may argue, with some cogency, that devising new stimuli is not the sole method available to the investigator. Instead of concentrating on the stimulus, they concentrate on the responses, their selection and relative emphasis. Here the interpretation becomes more central.

The references in this context is to the adaptation of available techniques rather than to the devising of new ones. Either the investigator selects certain responses, obtainable with the global method, which are most relevant to his purposes, or he places certain restrictions on the responses obtained. In the former situation, for example, certain Rorschach content expressive of aggression, hostility, anxiety, primary process, etc. has been selected. In the latter, multiple choice responses to the TAT or Blacky cards may restrict the choice (forced choice) to statements expressive of certain defenses or themes which are of primary import to the investigator. Whether devising new stimuli or adapting conventional ones is the most effective method in personality research and in prediction is still, to a considerable extent, an open question.

SOME PROBLEM AREAS

Devising special projective techniques involves a number of important problems that are basic to these methods and to the "projective hypothesis" in general. Investigators and theorists have proceeded considerably beyond the relatively naive and unsophisticated notions of the early protagonists of the projective movement. We shall attempt to focus briefly upon some of these problem areas, point out the issues, without in the least implying that at this stage of history they have been conclusively or satisfactorily resolved.

Among the criteria needed for devising projective methods, quoted above, ambiguity figures importantly. Murstein (1963) makes the useful distinction between the term "unstructured," referring to the stimulus, and "ambiguity," referring to the aspect of alternative interpretation. Actually, ambiguity is also referable to the stimulus, especially if it is of a thematic apperceptive character. It refers to the lack of structure or definiteness, not in single figures, but in the relationship between the figures, background, emotions and actions. The ambiguity of the portrayal in the stimulus permits a multiplicity of interpretations. It is in the selectiveness of certain interpretations that the individuality of the respondent becomes projected or revealed.

Workers with projective methods have held that the greater the ambiguity of the stimulus, the greater is the relevance of the responses produced to important and, perhaps, covert personality factors in the subject. Conversely, it was felt that the more structured the projective stimulus is, the more is the involvement of objective perceptual and cognitive operations in the responses of the subject and the less personality drives and needs are revealed. Generally, this proposition holds, perhaps, for wide-band techniques, in the clinical situation. However, when the purpose is the investigation of specific personality variables in a relatively non-pathological population, the relationship between ambiguity and response is not quite so simple.

It has been pointed out that researchers have been turning to more highly structured stimuli than to those represented by the standard projective methods (Lesser, 1961). In these instances single variables are considered and the researcher selects stimulus material which is of importance to him and his hypotheses. Lesser's review leads him to point out Kenny's theoretical position that in such instances "the picture stimuli of intermediate ambiguity produce protocols of greater 'personality revealingness.' " In order, however, to determine different degrees of ambiguity, a scaling procedure of the stimulus with respect to the personality dimension under consideration is essential. Moreover, he also points out that it is essential to exclude from the pictures any details which may be distracting and may be irrelevant to the personality variable being studied. This issue of relevance has been mentioned earlier in this chapter and in a previous report (Rabin, 1961). It is essentially related to the problem of ambiguity of the stimulus, for if additional elements besides the variable relevant are permitted to intrude upon the subject's sensory apparatus then various competing responses may interact and often inhibit the relevant one which is of primary interest to the investigator.

One of the series of postulates proposed by Kenny (1964) as a result of his theoretical analysis of "stimulus functions in projective techniques" is particularly relevant in the present context. He states as follows:

1. When only highly structured drive-stimulus material evokes thematic drive content, the individual possesses little or no drive represented by the stimulus material.

2. Where minimal, moderate, and strong cues of the drive material evoke drive content, the individual is neurotically motivated and preoccupied with the goal of the drive.

3. When strong-drive S's are compared with low-drive S's, the magnitude of thematic drive content differences should gradually increase with increasing stimulus relevance to the drive.

4. "As the number of drive cues increase and the drive has anxiety attached to it, anxiety effects should mount" (p. 334).

In another theoretical treatment of the problem of ambiguity of stimuli in projective techniques (Epstein, 1966) the author discusses some of the shortcomings and limitations of both ambiguous and structured stimuli. He points out that "individual differences can reflect random, inconsequential effects as well as significant personality material," that ambiguous stimuli have certain stimulating characteristics of their own and may have potency in arousing specific drives, and may cause a problem of interpretation, for the examiner and subject tend to lose control of the stimulus. The limitations of structured stimuli are seen in the fact that they are narrowband methods (more circumscribed) and "the nature of the stimulus is apt to be as apparent to the subject as to the examiner and can be expected to produce defensiveness." The author advocated combining stimuli at different levels of ambiguity as a means of improvement of the reliability of the assessment measure. Some of the empirical finding cited tend to support this type of procedure in the achievement of positive predictive results as well.

The various attempts of investigators to devise suitable projective measures for testing personality theories and hypotheses based upon them have brought greater focus upon the processes involved in the projective testing and responding process itself. Of major concern is the relationship between the nature of the stimulus and how it interacts with the needs, anxiety and defenses of the respondent. The issues of ambiguity and structure of stimuli in relation to drive arousal via verbal responses is still fraught with controversy. Closely connected with these issues is the problem of levels of awareness tapped by the various methods and the question as to whether responses reflect "momentary dispositions as well as enduring characteristics of personality" (Goldstein, 1961). There is much more work to be done in this fascinating area.

These are not the only theoretical issues involved in projective techniques. Discussion of others will carry us beyond the purpose and confines of the present chapter. Some of the problems involve the relationships of projective techniques to personality theories which are discussed elsewhere in this volume (see Chapter 2).

SUMMARY

The foregoing discussion revolved around recent developments in the field of projective techniques. Adaptation of old and invention of new methods for special clinical populations and for research purposes has been described and some of the procedures involved in such adaptations were discussed. Brief treatment of some theoretical issues underlying these procedures was also included.

It is well to conclude with a statement made by Forer (1961) in opening a symposium on "custom built projective methods." He states: "Diagnostic clinical psychology is no longer the technology of a few instruments of general applicability. It has broadened its scope not only in the direction of adding specific tests to its repertoire, but also toward the establishment of a metapsychology of personality evaluation based upon cognitive cues: perception, thinking, and fantasy. And this metapsychology transcends both specific tests and specific theories of personality" (p. 3).

REFERENCES

Allinsmith, W. The learning of moral standards. In D. R. Miller & G. E. Swanson (Eds.), *Inner Conflict and Defense*. New York: Holt, 1960.

Andrew, Gwen, Hartwell, S. W., Hutt, M. L., & Walton, R. E. *The Michigan Picture Test*. Chicago: Science Research Associates, 1953.

Atkinson, J. W. (Ed.), *Motives in Fantasy, Action and Society*. Princeton, N.J.: Van Nostrand, 1958.

Baughman, E. E. The role of the stimulus in Rorschach responses. *Psychol. Bull.*, 1958, *55*, 121-147.

Bellak, L., & Bellak, Sonya S. *Children's Apperception Test (CAT)*. Larchmont, N.Y.: C.P.S. Co., 1961.

Blum, G. S. A study of the psychoanalytic theory of psychosexual development. *Genet. Psychol. Monogr.*, 1949, *39*, 3-99.

Brackbill, G. A. Some effects of color on thematic fantasy. *J. consult. Psychol.*, 1951, *15*, 412-418.

Engel, Mary. The development and applications of the children's insight test. *J. proj. Tech.*, 1959, *22*, 13-25.

Epstein, E. Some theoretical considerations on the nature and ambiguity and the use of stimulus dimensions in projective techniques. *J. consult. Psychol.*, 1966, *30*, 183-192.

Fein, Leah G. *The Three-Dimensional Personality Test*. New York: International Universities Press, 1960.

Forer, B. R. Custom-built projective methods: a symposium. Introduction. *J. proj. Tech.*, 1961, *25*, 3-5.

Gibby, R. G. The stability of certain Rorschach variables under conditions of experimentally induced sets. 1. The intellectual variables. *J. proj. Tech.*, 1951, *15*, 3-25.

Goldstein, F. J. "Custom-made or store-bought" projective techniques; what do they represent? *J. proj. Tech.*, 1961, *25*, 11-20.

Henry, W. E. *The Analysis of Fantasy.* New York: Wiley, 1950.

Henry, W. E. The TAT in the study of culture-personality relations. *Genet. Psychol. Monogr.*, 1947, *35*, 1-34.

Holtzman, W. H., Thorpe, J. S., Swartz, J. D., & Herron, E. W. *Inkblot Perception and Personality.* Austin: University of Texas Press, 1961.

Kerman, E. F. Cypress knees and the blind. *J. proj. Tech.*, 1959, *23*, 48-56.

King, G. F. Rorschach and Levy movement responses: a research note. *J. clin. Psychol.*, 1955, *11*, 193-195.

Lazarus, R. S. The influence of color on the protocol of the Rorschach Test. *J. abnorm. soc. Psychol.*, 1949, *44*, 505-516.

Lesser, G. S. Custom-making projective tests for research. *J. proj. Tech.*, 1961, *25*, 21-31.

Lindzey, G. *Projective Techniques and Cross-cultural Research.* New York: Appleton-Century-Crofts, 1961.

McClelland, D. C., Atkinson, J. W., Clark, R. A., & Lowell, E. L. *The Achievement Motive.* New York: Appleton-Century-Crofts, 1953.

Murstein, B. I. *Theory and Research in Projective Techniques.* New York: Wiley, 1963.

Neugarten, Bernice L., & associates. *Personality in Middle and Later Life.* New York: Atherton Press, 1964.

Parker, S. Ethnic identity and acculturation in two Eskimo villages. *Am. Anthropol.*, 1964, *66*, 325-340.

Rabin, A. I. Devising projective methods for personality research. *J. proj. Tech.*, 1961, *25*, 6-10.

Rabin, A. I., & Sanderson, M. H. An experimental inquiry into some Rorschach procedures. *J. clin. Psychol.*, 1947, *3*, 216-225.

Rust, R. Some conclates of the movement response. *J. Pers.*, 1948, *16*, 369-401.

Shapiro, Edna, Biber, Barbara, & Minnchin, Patricia. The cartoon situation test: a semi-structured technique for assessing aspects of personality pertinent to the teaching process. *J. proj. Tech.*, 1957, *21*, 172-184.

Shneidman, E. *The Make-A-Picture Story Test.* New York: Psychological Corporation, 1949.

Stotsky, B. A., & Weinberg, H. The prediction of the psychiatric patient's work adjustment. *J. counsel. Psychol.*, 1956, *3*, 193-199.

Thompson, C. E. *Thompson Modification of the Thematic Apperception Test.* Cambridge: Harvard University Press, 1949.

Weiskopf, Edith A. An experimental study of the effect of brightness and ambiguity on projection in the TAT. *J. Psychol.*, 1950, *29*, 407-416.

Zax, M., & Stricker, G. The effect of a structured inquiry on Rorschach scores. *J. consult. Psychol.*, 1960, *24*, 328-332.

Zubin, J., Eron, L. D., & Schumer, Florence. *An Experimental Approach to Projective Techniques.* New York: Wiley, 1965.

Index

INDEX